Readings in Latin American Politics

Readings in Latin American Politics

CHALLENGES TO DEMOCRATIZATION

Peter R. Kingstone

UNIVERSITY OF CONNECTICUT

Houghton Mifflin Company *Boston* *New York*

Publisher: Charles Hartford
Sponsoring Editor: Katherine Meisenheimer
Development Editor: Terri Wise
Editorial Assistant: Kristen Craib
Senior Project Editor: Margaret Park Bridges
Manufacturing Coordinator: Carrie Wagner
Executive Marketing Manager: Nicola Poser
Marketing Assistant: Kathleen Mellon

Cover image: © Keith Dannemiller / CORBIS SABA

Printed in the U.S.A.

Library of Congress Control Number: 2003109918

ISBN: 0-618-37136-2

123456789-FFG-09 08 07 06 05

CONTENTS

4

Traditional and Emerging Actors in the Latin American Polity   111

5

The United States and Latin America   177

PREFACE

Readings in Latin American Politics focuses on challenges to the establishment, maintenance, and deepening of democracy in Latin America. Democracy is not the only issue facing Latin America, but it is central for a variety of reasons. First, the struggle to establish and maintain democracy has been going on in Latin America for more than 100 years, and the evidence from the early twenty-first century is that the struggle is not nearly over. Second, the theme of establishing and maintaining democracy has become a central rhetorical plank of U.S. foreign policy. While we may debate the extent to which rhetoric meets reality in the realm of foreign policy, the rhetorical emphasis has sharpened Americans' attention on the challenges of democracy and the U.S. role in fostering or hindering it. Finally, democracy is a particularly encompassing theme. A central focus on democracy allows one to consider diverse topics from economic development, to the role of the military or women in politics, to political institutions and their impact, or to U.S. foreign policy.

Yet putting together a reader on Latin American politics is a particularly challenging task. Instructors face a wide array of choices when structuring a class on Latin American politics and a wide variety of possible readings. Unlike some fields—notably American politics or international relations—there is no consensus on the crucial topics one must cover, the essential readings associated with each topic, or the order in which they should be covered. Instead, instructors put their own individual stamp on how they organize their Latin American politics courses. Still, teaching Latin American politics pushes every instructor to address at least two basic choices in the design of the course. First, every comparative politics course, regardless of region, faces a fundamental choice over whether to organize the course thematically or by country. Neither option is inherently superior. Instead, each offers distinct advantages and disadvantages. The advantage of a theme-based class is that the instructor can pursue particular themes in depth and explore the nuances and complexities of a particular issue. The downside is that students may not have enough empirical or substantive knowledge to fully appreciate the issue examined. The advantage of a country-based approach is that it allows the students to become more fully acquainted with the history and distinctive problems of specific cases. The downside, of course, is that attention to the specifics of the case may limit the analysis of themes crucial to the whole region.

A second fundamental choice facing teachers of Latin American politics is what kind of readings to assign. The choice is made more difficult by the variety of students in Latin American politics classes, with some having considerable background knowledge of either Latin America or political science, some having both, and some having neither. The field of Latin American politics has yielded a wonderful array of high-quality books and articles on a wide range of themes. Yet most of these works are written for a scholarly audience, and instructors face a choice over what and how to use them. At the same time, a large number of insightful articles appear in a variety of periodicals with broader audiences. These works may offer highly accessible and intelligent discussions of particular issues, but may lack the theoretical base of the more scholarly articles. The two different forms offer different benefits.

APPROACH

The approach in this reader is to bridge the two sides in each of these two fundamental choices. The reader is divided into two parts. The first focuses on important themes in the study of Latin American politics. The second focuses on specific countries. In each country chapter, the articles explore issues related to the themes discussed in the first part. Because this is a reader rather than a textbook, each chapter provides a set of articles that develop the reader's understanding either through historical or background information or through discussions that explore the complexities and nuances of the issue. The readings are drawn from a mix of more academic sources—such as scholarly journals like *Comparative Politics* or *Latin American Politics and Society*—as well as from more accessible sources, such as less theoretically inclined journals like *NACLA Report on the Americas* or *Current History*. This reader incorporates both kinds of articles: scholarly works to provide theoretical grounding on important issues and more accessible works to provide the kind of immediacy and contextual detail that scholarly work often lacks.

THEMES

The tougher challenge is which specific themes and countries to include. A perusal of syllabi on the Web reveals an extraordinary variety of approaches to teaching Latin American politics. The diversity of interests and approaches makes it impossible to make decisions that satisfy every potential user of this reader. Strong, plausible arguments can be made for different themes and different countries. I have chosen four themes and six countries. The four themes are:

- Democracy (definitions and assessments)
- Economic development/neoliberal reform
- Important actors (traditional and emerging)
- U.S. foreign policy

The chapter on democracy (Chapter 2) focuses on defining the concept and providing alternative ways of viewing its health in Latin America. Neoliberal reform is arguably the most controversial and contested area in Latin America today, and economic development/performance is clearly crucial to the establishment and maintenance of democracy. The chapter on actors (Chapter 4) focuses attention on the ways different groups benefit or suffer in Latin American society and how that leads them to press for deepening or undermining democracy. Finally, the chapter on U.S. foreign policy (Chapter 5) explores the United States's decidedly mixed influence on the region. The six countries are Argentina, Brazil, Chile, Colombia, Cuba, and Mexico. Argentina, Brazil, Chile, and Mexico are the most common countries featured in Latin American politics classes and are likely the most "important" in the region by virtually any definition of the word. Colombia, with its turmoil in recent years, and Cuba attract a great deal of interest and are arguably the two central foci of U.S. foreign policy in recent years (or many years in the case of Cuba). The structure of this reader and the reasons for these choices are described in detail in the reader's introduction (Chapter 1).

PEDAGOGICAL FEATURES

Each chapter offers a series of pedagogical tools, to be used at the instructor's discretion.

- Each chapter begins with a brief introduction, giving the background on the issues discussed in the articles—whether thematic or country-specific—and identifying the key themes/debates.
- Each chapter provides a detailed set of data, providing statistical or other relevant data to supplement analytical discussion. For the thematic chapters, the data offers cross-national comparisons on specific issues. For country chapters, the data offer detailed information about issues like the form of government, demographic and basic economic data, and regime histories.

- Each chapter provides suggestions for further reading and listings of useful websites, particularly for readers who may be involved in writing research papers.

ACKNOWLEDGMENTS

The idea of putting together a reader had been suggested to me on a number of occasions in the past, but I never seriously considered it until Katherine Meisenheimer of Houghton Mifflin raised it with me. Since that time, she along with Terri Wise of Houghton Mifflin have been extremely helpful and thoughtful in their guidance of this project. I am also grateful for the very insightful comments from the following reviewers: Howard Handelman, University of Wisconsin–Milwaukee; Roberto M. Garza, Angelo State University; Andrew Mellon, University of Pittsburgh; Leigh Payne, University of Wisconsin–Madison; and Hannah Stewart-Gambino, Lehigh University.

Finally, I am fortunate to be working in a field filled with exceptional scholars and teachers, both in the United States and in Latin America. I am grateful for the insights and understandings I have gained from my colleagues over the years. I hope this reader accurately reflects the benefits of their collective wisdom.

Peter R. Kingstone

CHAPTER 1

Introduction

*I*n the 1970s and 1980s, a movement dubbed "the third wave of democratization"[1] swept through the world bringing on the end of dictatorships and the rise of new democracies. It began in Western European countries like Portugal and reached its most dramatic pinnacle with the breaking of the Berlin Wall and the subsequent breakdown of the Soviet Union at the end of the 1980s and into the 1990s. It was a trend that provoked optimism that the world was moving inexorably toward a universal embrace of democracy and human rights: the "end of history" as one famous observer described it.[2]

The third wave provoked optimism in Latin America as well. By the early 1980s countries like Peru, Bolivia, Argentina, El Salvador, Brazil, and Chile permitted democratic elections that ended dictatorial rule. With few exceptions—notably Mexico (until 2000) and Cuba—the region appeared at the dawn of a new democratic age. By the start of the new millennium, however, the euphoria had worn off and the harder, colder realities of establishing, maintaining, and deepening democracies had

---

[1]The *third wave* refers to the widespread turn to democracy (the third such major trend in modern world history, beginning in the eighteenth century) that began in Portugal in 1973. This wave ultimately saw democracies installed in much of the developing world (including almost all of Latin America) as well as most of Europe. The term comes from Samuel Huntington, *The Third Wave: Democratization in the Late 20th Century* (Norman: University of Oklahoma Press, 1991).

[2]The collapse of the Berlin Wall and the Cold War it symbolized was such a momentous event that one observer, political scientist Francis Fukuyama, labeled it the "end of history." The extraordinary label was meant to evoke the significance of the end of the conflict between the West and the Communist world. Francis Fukuyama, "The End of History?" *The National Interest* 16 (Summer, 1989): 1–18.

revealed themselves. Latin Americans and Latin Americanists recognized that there was much to celebrate in the new democracies of the region, but that many challenges and concerns remained. Democratic governance entails more than simply elections. Instead, democratization rests on changes in culture, values, and behavior as well as on political, social, and economic institutions.

The story of democratization in Latin America over the past twenty years is a mixed one. On the positive side, several Latin American countries are showing signs of greater democratic robustness than at any time in their history. For example, Argentina has managed to preserve constitutional order and to conduct several legal presidential successions despite terrible economic crises in both 1989 and 2001. Mexico held its very first democratic presidential election in 2000, and the party that had ruled continuously since 1929 turned over power peacefully when it lost. Chile and Uruguay have shrugged off extended periods of military dictatorship and returned to the earlier patterns of governance that gave them the reputations of being among the most successful democracies in the region prior to their respective coups. Similarly, Latin American societies have never had such dense civil societies—the complex of voluntary associations of citizens independent of state authority that are crucial for representing diverse interests and protecting against a return to authoritarian rule. Some of those associations are well established, such as labor unions, or associations of better-educated, more elite members of society (e.g., businesspeople or journalists). Yet, the new democratic regimes have also permitted greater organization of groups that have suffered from exclusion and discrimination for centuries—such as women, the poor, and the indigenous populations.[3]

However, the story has a negative side as well. For example, promoting economic growth and reducing the enormous inequality that characterizes most of the region has proved extremely difficult. The turn to democracy was accompanied by a turn toward free market economic orientation, promoted (sometimes coercively) and supported by the United States and international financial institutions, such as the World Bank and the International Monetary Fund. Yet, by the late 1990s, it was clear that this blueprint for producing vigorous growth (often referred to as the "Washington Consensus") made promises well beyond what it could deliver. In fact, this free market or neoliberal[4] agenda arguably produced at best only modest growth in most countries

---

[3]The phrase *indigenous peoples* refers to the original native population. Roughly 90 percent of the indigenous population died with the arrival of European settlers, some due to violence and some due to disease. Nevertheless, many Latin American countries have majority indigenous populations.

[4]While a *liberal* in the context of the United States refers to somebody with a preference for a more active role for government in the economy, in the international arena a *neoliberal* advocates reducing the role of government and increasing the role of markets in the economy. Neoliberal economic policy is discussed further in Chapter 2.

and increased inequality virtually everywhere. As a consequence, many Latin Americans expressed anger, frustration, and disappointment both with the neoliberal model and with democracy itself. Thus, these new democracies have not been as successful as hoped at representing the interests of poor and otherwise disadvantaged citizens and they have done little to address notions of economic and social justice.

In many Latin American societies, democratization also has revealed tensions over the long-standing failure to fully integrate the indigenous populations politically. The 1990s was a decade in which groups of indigenous peoples in places like Bolivia, Ecuador, Guatemala, and Mexico mobilized in ways that challenged elitist political systems dominated by people of European origin. In Bolivia and Ecuador, indigenous mobilizations led to extra-constitutional terminations of presidencies, with a forced resignation in the former and a coup in the latter. The freedom for these groups to organize is in itself a positive sign. But the need to do so points to the persistence of old problems that trace their origins to colonialism and the highly unequal and exclusionary political systems the Spanish and Portuguese created. The same exclusionism led to the mobilization of other marginalized groups in society, such as women and the poor. But, the persistence of these forms of discrimination and exclusion is not the only challenge to new democracies. Indeed, addressing the demands of newly mobilized groups in societies—let alone actually resolving them—challenges the capacity of new democracies to find ways to integrate all of their citizens.

Unfortunately, in many Latin American countries the political institutions necessary to support economic growth, equity-enhancing policies, and integration of new social and political demands are very weak. For example, in many Latin American countries basic institutions, such as the legal system, the courts, political parties, the bureaucracy, and electoral institutions, all function less well than they should ideally. Weak political institutions make corruption and nepotism a more appealing (and *effective*) way of getting things done. But, corruption and nepotism reinforce inequality, undermine the meaning and value of citizenship, and skew representation of interests in favor of the rich, the powerful, and the politically connected.

In short, the Latin American picture at the start of the new millennium is a complex one—neither unambiguously positive, nor unambiguously negative. Different observers—both among Latin Americans and among Latin Americanists—can reasonably look at the evidence and arrive at different conclusions or interpretations. Some observers focus on largely political and procedural issues, such as whether elections are occurring regularly or whether economic reforms that increase the role of markets are proceeding. For many of these observers, the conclusion may be positive. For others, the persistence of gross inequalities in access to health care and education or in the distribution of income points to a much more discouraging conclusion.

The purpose of this reader is to offer a sampling of the evidence of some of the advances, setbacks, and challenges of democracy in Latin America. It does offer a range of interpretations that Latin Americans and Latin Americanists have advanced to explain the issues in the region. In some instances, these views sharply conflict with each other. Few would disagree that Latin America, as a region, faces significant challenges politically and economically. Yet, dispute, at times bitter, abounds over the diagnosis of the problems and the best solutions. It is important to remember that in the social sciences, people can and do disagree both about the facts and about the interpretation of the facts. The articles in this reader are offered not as statements of the truth in Latin America, but as interpretations of the truth in Latin America. Some of the articles take strong positions. Some provide considerable historical background. Some offer considerations of political science theory.

In addition to the articles, each chapter offers some additional features to help understand the range of issues in the region and to assist in further research. These supplements include

- a brief introductory essay, giving background information and identifying the key themes/debates.
- a detailed data page, giving statistical or other relevant data to supplement analytical discussion and further research.
- a further reading list at the end of each chapter and a list of useful websites for students doing further research on the topic.

LATIN AMERICAN DIVERSITY AND DIFFICULT CHOICES

One challenge of trying to present a sampling of such evidence and interpretations is that Latin America is not a monolith: there is a great deal of diversity in the region. It is tempting to portray Latin America as a uniform region with the same economic issues, level of democracy, degree of inequality, racial and ethnic identity, and language. While it is tempting, it would be wrong. Guatemala and Brazil earn a large percentage of their foreign exchange from the export of coffee. Guatemala's other major source of foreign earnings, however, is remissions of earnings from poor Guatemalans who have moved to the United States in search of work. Brazil, by contrast, produces nuclear reactors and sophisticated computer software. Bolivia has suffered terrible political instability; Costa Rica is one of the most stable democracies in the Western World. Some Latin American nations, such as Argentina, are populated predominantly by white Europeans. Argentina, however, is still an ethnic melting pot of Spanish, Italians, English, Germans, and a host of other nationalities. By contrast, Mexico's population is heavily mestizo—a mix of white and indigenous peoples and where issues of identity of the "nation"—that is, of what it means to be Mexican and who is and who isn't Mexican—are still contested. Even the label *indigenous* is misleading, however, as it conceals enormous cultural, religious, political, and linguistic diversity among and within many Latin American countries.

Just as it is impossible to make one definitive statement that describes all of Latin America, it is impossible to choose one set of issues to explore and claim that they cover all of Latin America. This reader focuses on the theme of democracy and democratization, which not only may be the most important issue for Latin Americans and Latin Americanists today but is a broad, inclusive issue that subsumes or at least touches on many other issues of vital concern.

The reader is divided into two parts, the first containing four thematic chapters and the second six country chapters. The thematic chapters explore four themes critical to the understanding of the prospects for democracy in the region. The first thematic chapter offers a definition of democracy and presents a range of views of the challenges facing democracy in the region. The second thematic chapter looks at the problem of economic development and neoliberalism in particular as most studies of democracy and democratization find a close relationship with economic performance. The third thematic chapter takes a different cut at the challenges of democracy by examining the role of four crucial organized groups in modern Latin America: two traditional groups (the Catholic Church and the military) and two relatively recently mobilized segments of society (women and indigenous groups). Finally, the fourth thematic chapter explores the impact of U.S. foreign policy on the region in recognition of the powerful role that the United States has had—sometimes for the better and sometimes for the worse.

The six countries represented in the reader (Argentina, Brazil, Chile, Colombia, Cuba, and Mexico) are among those that draw the most attention in the United States. They also offer some interesting contrasts that highlight the diversity of the region and the challenges of democratization. All six have had authoritarian experiences, but their experiences differ markedly. Chile and Colombia enjoyed long periods of stable democratic rule despite Chile's devastating coup and long dictatorship and Colombia's increasingly chaotic and brutal civil war of the past decade. Argentina and Brazil, by contrast, have histories of alternating between democratic and authoritarian rule. Finally, Mexico enjoyed its first democratic presidential election in 2000 while Cuba is still authoritarian.

In economic terms, Chile has been the poster child for the neoliberal economic agenda, registering the most impressive economic gains in the region over the past two decades. Brazil and Mexico, benefiting from their great size, have the most developed economies of Latin America, but in recent years have had mixed results in their pursuit of economic reforms and economic growth. By contrast, Argentina continues to suffer from its historic pattern of economic volatility, while both Colombia and Cuba have witnessed serious economic erosion over the past decade.

In terms of the important actors, all six have seen an awakening of civil society in recent years, but there are important differences. For example, Argentina's indigenous population was almost completely exterminated in the nineteenth century and barely exists today. To some extent, the same can be said for Chile. By contrast, both Colombia and Mexico have sizable indigenous and mixed populations, and both have important guerrilla movements arising from sentiments of marginalization. Brazil and Cuba have large African and mixed populations, but have managed to limit mobilization around race despite real issues. Another example of the differences lies in the role of the military. In Mexico, civilian, albeit authoritarian, authorities managed to secure control over the military. In Argentina and Brazil, democratic civilian authorities have made considerable progress since the restoration of democracy in the 1980s in the goal of weakening their respective militaries and establishing firmer control over these once very powerful institutions. In Chile, the military left power entirely on its own terms and has resisted civilian control and any encroachment on military jurisdiction and privilege. Finally, in Colombia and Cuba, the persistence of civil war and dictatorship, respectively, has given their militaries an active presence in government.

In foreign policy terms, Mexico and the United States are closely linked: formally through the North American Free Trade Agreement (NAFTA) as well as informally through ties of immigration. Colombia and Cuba are two of the primary foci of U.S. foreign policy as well. By contrast, Argentina, Chile, and Brazil are more removed from U.S. policy, but that does not mean that the United States has not had an influence on them. The United States was implicated in coups in all three countries (especially in Chile), and the United States today has an important economic relationship with all three (again especially with Chile, which in 2003 signed a free trade agreement with the United States). Yet, U.S. foreign policy is much less a factor in the internal politics of these three countries than it is in Mexico, Colombia, and Cuba.

The thematic chapters do not address all of the most pressing issues in Latin America, and they do not offer an exhaustive treatment of the issues they do cover. One could organize an entirely different reader focused on issues like the environment, race relations, poverty, the judiciary, or electoral and party systems. In each of the thematic chapters, one could easily pursue a more intense debate of the theme. In the same vein, one could also choose six other countries or study each individual country in greater depth. The purpose of this reader is to give a taste of the issues that Latin Americans and Latin Americanists care about and to focus on one or two key issues in each of the six countries. Hopefully, that taste will lead to a desire to learn more about the region. The following section presents the chapter themes and the specific focus of the articles.

STRUCTURE OF THE READER

Chapter 2: Democracy

The central concern of the reader is democracy. More than any other possible theme, this one is arguably the most important issue facing Latin America at the turn of the century. Latin American nations have been working to establish stable democracies for most of the twentieth century, with many countries experiencing an unfortunate history of regime instability and brutal dictatorships. This chapter centers on the theme of democracy in Latin America and presents a variety of interpretations of the extent to which Latin America has overcome its authoritarian legacy.

Chapter 3: Economic Development/Neoliberal Reform

There are probably few issues as controversial in Latin America today as the pros and cons of neoliberal economic reform. As of the mid-1990s, neoliberalism appeared to be the uncontested model for growth in the region. Yet, by 2003, a number of countries had paused rather than continue on that path, and many—both masses and leaders—expressed a preference for reversing the process. This chapter provides background information on neoliberal reform as well as the import-substitution-industrialization model that dominated the region prior to the emergence of the Washington Consensus. In addition, several articles lay out alternative and conflicting assessments of the neoliberal program and its underlying diagnosis of the region's economic problems.

Chapter 4: Important Actors—Emerging and Traditional

Latin American societies have grown increasingly complex and diverse in the last two to three decades. As they have, the influence of older actors has changed, while new ones have attained prominence. This chapter focuses on two traditional actors and the changes they are experiencing—the Catholic Church and the military—and provides an overview of two new sets of actors— indigenous movements and women's movements and their role in modern Latin America. For much of the twentieth century, one could say with some confidence that there were only three well-organized and well-institutionalized actors in most Latin American societies: labor, the Church, and the military (although they differed considerably in how much power they wielded).[5] The

---

[5]Domestic business groups were also influential throughout this period, although their influence was typically through informal channels rather than well-defined, representative organizations.

nature of politics was profoundly shaped by the roles that each of these actors played in their respective societies. As of the twenty-first century, however, at least two of these groups, the Church and labor, have lost some of their status (especially labor), while many militaries have retained influence, but are less capable of threatening civilian politics. Among new actors, the mobilization of indigenous groups in Latin America is one of the striking and surprising changes in recent years. Whether it is their role in provoking Ecuador's recent coup or in Mexico's Zapatista rebellion, indigenous movements are making themselves felt in important ways. In the same period of time, women's roles have altered dramatically as well. Women have become increasingly organized and influential politically although many traditional constraints remain. The mobilization of both indigenous people and women reflects a larger trend of new social movements that provide channels for political expression in ways that formal political institutions have failed to do.

Chapter 5: The Role of the United States

The United States has been an active neighbor for Latin America throughout the post-colonial history. The role of the United States has been controversial and attitudes in Latin America toward the United States have varied over time and across countries. This chapter provides some of the history of the role of the United States in the region and offers differing perspectives on the negative and positive aspects of that role.

Chapter 6: Argentina

Argentina is included in the reader because it is one of the largest countries in Latin America, and in certain respects offers one of the most complex puzzles. In 1920, Argentina was one of the richest nations in the world. Among Latin American countries, Argentina is among the most racially homogenous countries, with among the highest levels of educational opportunity, and lowest levels of economic inequality. All three conditions are highly conducive to a stable democracy and strong economic development. Instead, the country has suffered from a long history of economic volatility and political instability. The most recent example of this pattern unfolded over the opening years of the new millennium. Thus, the central theme for this chapter is, how has the country fallen apart so quickly and what does that say about the state of Argentine democracy? For many observers, the ability of the Argentine political system to recover from the crisis and re-establish legitimate political order is one of the more promising signs in Latin America.

Chapter 7: Brazil

Brazil is included because it is the largest country in the region and has the largest economy. Brazil also poses one of the critical puzzles in Latin America today. It is a complex country fragmented by regional, ethnic, and racial differences and burdened with one of the most unequal distributions of income in the world. Academic analysts frequently argue that Brazil's political institutions—its party and electoral systems in particular—are among the most poorly designed and least effective in the region. Thus, it is little surprise that the country has a history of military rule and poorly performing democracies. Yet, the democratic regime established in 1985 has managed to function and ultimately elected a genuine working-class hero as president in the 2002 presidential elections, a process characterized by its smoothness and the easy acceptance of the results by all Brazilians. This chapter offers an assessment of the significance of this election, as well as a sampling of evidence of positive and negative aspects of the new democracy.

Chapter 8: Chile

Chile experienced one of the most brutal dictatorial regimes in the Western world. The 1973 coup led by General Augusto Pinochet was shocking both for the regime it established as well as for the disruption of what had been, until that point, considered one of the most effective democratic regimes in the region. Since the return of democratic rule in 1989, Chile has again assumed a place of honor as one of the most effective democratic regimes in the region. In addition, Chile has become the model of successful neoliberal economic reform. On the surface, it is hard to argue with the evidence. Yet, for many observers there is a dark side of this success story. The chapter offers varying perspectives on the legacy of authoritarian rule in Chile and the limits that legacy places on the deepening of what is otherwise a political and economic success story.

Chapter 9: Colombia

Colombia presents a tragic story of regime breakdown and a case study of the controversial role that the United States can and has played in the region. For decades, two political parties governed Colombia, alternating power in a stable system of party competition. On the surface, the country was one of the region's most successful democracies, while economically the country's performance was less volatile than many of its neighbors. Yet, significant problems of exclusion and inequality persisted, while a small, relatively ineffectual guerrilla movement challenged the legitimacy of the government. The situation changed through the 1980s and into the 1990s, as narcotics helped transform small guerrilla movements and right-wing paramilitaries into increasingly well-armed and profoundly threatening ones. Over the course of the 1990s, the Colombian regime steadily disintegrated as the country descended into deeper and deeper violence. This chapter offers alternative assessments of the crisis of the Colombian state as well as a perspective on the expanding role of the United States in the crisis.

Chapter 10: Cuba

Cuba is a unique case in the Latin American context and another critical case study of the role of the United States in the region. Cuba's 1959 revolution put the country on a path of socialist development that persisted even as the rest of the region began its turn to neoliberal reform. It has remained a dictatorship despite the growing international norm of democratic rule and protection of human rights. Also against regional trends, Cuba successfully resolved virtually all of the issues of social and economic injustice that characterize most of the rest of the region, although these policy successes started to unravel in the 1990s. Finally, the country also stands out for the intensity of U.S. hostility to the Fidel Castro regime. This chapter offers varying interpretations of two key puzzles of Castro's Cuba. Two articles offer different views of the complexity of Cuba's dictatorship, while the third offers an overview of the history and underlying causes of U.S. policy to the island.

Chapter 11: Mexico

One party, the Institutional Revolutionary Party (PRI), ruled Mexico continuously from 1929 until 2000 in one of the world's most impressively enduring dictatorships. The party largely avoided obvious coercion, but it still produced considerable anger, frustration, and charges of exclusion. Thus, Mexico's authoritarian experience under the PRI generated numerous predictions of collapse. Instead, the PRI's control of Mexican politics outlasted the much more overtly coercive dictatorship of the Soviet Union. Yet, the 2000 presidential elections in Mexico produced a genuine transition to the conservative, Catholic party, the PAN (National Action Party), a party in conflict with many of the values enshrined in the country's 1917 Revolutionary Constitution. This chapter offers views on the emergence of this dramatic electoral transition to democracy and an assessment of the performance of the new Mexican president, Vicente Fox, and his contribution to democracy.

PART I

CHAPTER 2

The Challenges of Democratization

*L*atin America has experimented with democracy almost continuously since the late nineteenth century. Independence came to most Latin American countries in the years between 1810 and 1830 in a turbulent process that pitted Latin American liberating armies against their Spanish colonial leaders, but also divided Latin Americans amongst themselves. The various wars for independence in the early 1800s left the region physically and economically devastated and politically unstable. By the late nineteenth century, however, politics in the region stabilized as most Latin American nations established regimes that were often referred to as "liberal republics." Despite the label, these regimes were neither very liberal, nor very democratic.[1] Nevertheless, some of the basic elements of democratic governance started to emerge. For example, political parties began to form to contest elections (which were often marred by fraud and coercion and always with substantial limits on voting rights). Society became more complex as the middle and working classes grew larger and more insistent on expanding their political and economic rights. These emerging classes tested democratic principles, such as freedom of association and freedom of speech, in their efforts to open political space for their participation. Unfortunately, the essentially corrupt, elitist republics ultimately failed to find a political solution to the demands of non-elites for inclusion in the political process. The additional pressure of the Great Depression, which began in 1929, led virtually all Latin American republics to collapse, ushering in a new period of authoritarianism in most of the region. Since that time, the democracy experiment in Latin America has advanced in fits and starts, varying over time and across the different countries of the region. Most Latin American nations have had one or more, frequently short-lived, experiences of democracy, typically alternating with periods of military rule. In the 1970s and 1980s, the region experienced a wave of democratization (the so-called third wave of democratization) that ended particularly brutal dictatorships in many countries. These new democracies, however, continue to confront tremendous challenges with varying degrees of success.

Scholars have offered a variety of reasons for Latin America's difficulties with establishing stable democracies. For some, Latin America struggles with

---

[1]Liberal in the classic definition used throughout the world, rather than the U.S. definition. In the United States, a *liberal* is typically somebody who favors use of government intervention to support redistribution of wealth or promotion of the poor through a variety of government programs—thus *a tax and spend liberal*. By contrast, *liberal* in the classic sense of the word refers to one who supports limits to the size and role of the government in the economy and liberty and equality of opportunity in the political realm. By the classic definition, the United States is a distinctly liberal society in the political sense while U.S. conservatives are the economic liberals in the country.

an Iberian tradition of Catholicism and corporatism[2] that lend themselves to more hierarchical, authoritarian forms of government. Other scholars reject the idea that Latin Americans are somehow culturally undemocratic, and instead point to colonialism (and in particular Spanish and Portuguese colonialism) as the culprit. In this view, Spain and Portugal reproduced feudal society in the new world, with unrepresentative political institutions and a politically dominant landed elite (typically referred to as the *oligarchy* in Latin America) controlling a rural peasant population and resisting movements that make politics more democratic or egalitarian. For others, Latin America's dependent economic situation weakened the classes with a preference for democracy (particularly the middle class and the working class) and limited the government's power to pass policies that mitigated the extraordinary poverty and inequality that has characterized the region since colonial times. There is no consensus among scholars as to the answer, but there is no doubting that Latin America's past includes a host of factors that challenge the stability of democracy. These challenges include poverty and inequality, elite groups opposed to or at least uninterested in democracy, weak political institutions, poor integration of indigenous populations, and limits to economic development.

Nevertheless, these new third wave democracies appear to be more durable than earlier democratic regimes in Latin America. Civil society—the range of organizations and associations formed by private citizens—has become denser and more complex in virtually all Latin American societies. These associations—ranging from neighborhood associations to womens' organizations to professional associations, such as of journalists or of lawyers—have a much greater vested interest in maintaining democracy and therefore provide a stronger defense against authoritarianism than that which existed in the past. Furthermore, many Latin Americans have been scarred by the experience of brutal dictatorships that prevailed in so many countries in the 1960s, 1970s, and 1980s. The legacy of those regimes is a greater concern for protecting democratic rule and deepening the quality of democracy. Yet, it is too soon to declare victory over authoritarian rule. As the articles in this chapter show, threats to democracy persist throughout the region, and therefore, the struggles to secure Latin American democracy are not yet over.

---

[2]*Corporatism* refers to a way of organizing society in which the state structures interest group representation into compulsory, state-sanctioned, monopolistic interest associations. This is in sharp contrast to the pluralist model found in the United States in which any group can form an association and in which no group can claim a monopoly on representation. Corporatist organization can be found in Europe, where it has been a democratic form of interest organization, and in Latin America, where it has more authoritarian characteristics. A crucial study of the emergence of corporatist organization in Latin America is Ruth Berins Collier and David Collier's *Shaping the Political Arena* (Princeton, N.J.: Princeton University Press, 1991).

How one evaluates the success of Latin America's experiment with democracy depends on how one defines democracy. As it turns out, defining democracy is not a simple task. Democracy is an essentially contested concept—that is, a concept for which there is no agreed upon definition and therefore is always open to dispute. The word *democracy* is a loaded term because we invest in it our own normative beliefs and preferences. So, arguing about the definition of democracy inherently involves arguing about values and moral beliefs. Because we have different normative beliefs about what a democracy is and what it should be, we cannot resolve our disagreements through logical debate alone.

In fact, Robert Dahl, a distinguished political scientist, coined the term, *polyarchy* to escape the difficulties of defining democracy. Regimes can vary on various dimensions that most of us believe are related to democracy. For example, they can vary on the extent to which there is political competition; they can vary on the extent of citizen participation; they can vary with regard to the extent of civil liberties; they can vary with regard to the degree of equality, and so on. Dahl's notion of polyarchy focuses particularly on the rules and procedures that promote and protect political competition, such as freedom of the press or the selection of leaders through elections. Thus, polyarchy is sometimes also called "procedural democracy." While it is very difficult to agree on one standard definition of democracy, this procedural definition is arguably the most widely used standard both among political scientists and among American policy-makers.

But, defining democracy by rules such as regular elections, freedom to form political parties, or freedom of the press, dissatisfies many scholars as it leaves many issues outside of the definition of democracy. For example, some critics of procedural emphases point out that gross, socioeconomic inequality, which is not considered under the procedural definition, violates democratic norms and undermines the meaningfulness of democratic procedures. Others may point to failings in a country's legal system that allow widespread corruption to persist and that typically have terrible consequences for the poor. There is a wide array of issues that fall outside of the consideration of the procedural definition on which individuals may evaluate regimes and ways in which regimes may be considered undemocratic or limited democracies. In fact, no regime in the world is totally immune from being criticized as undemocratic on one dimension or another. Ultimately, how one defines and evaluates democracies depends largely on one's point of emphasis.

The articles in this chapter illustrate some of the different ways of thinking about democracy in Latin America and democracy in general. In the first essay, Philippe Schmitter and Terry Karl provide a detailed definition of democracy, essentially drawing on Dahl's conception of polyarchy. Schmitter and Karl list and discuss several elements critical to establishing and protecting open and fair political competition in a system in which leaders are chosen by the people, and through regular elections are held accountable by the people. That requires a system where political parties can form freely and citizens can stand for election freely. The elections must be free from interference and citizens' need to have unrestricted access to information. Given Latin America's volatile history, Schmitter and Karl also specifically discuss the role of the military and the need to narrowly circumscribe the military's privileges and role in politics. Schmitter and Karl also point out what, in their view, democracy is not. In their view, democracy has no connection to social equality, wealth, economic growth, or effective government.

Forrest Colburn provides a review of the state of democracy, drawing on the conception described by Schmitter and Karl. In his view, democracy is in a fragile condition at the start of the new millennium. Colburn notes that the region has become particularly vulnerable to foreign capital and "financial shocks" and wonders how well these fragile democracies can weather them. For Colburn, the most telling gap in Latin America is the absence of well-established, legitimate political parties. The absence of parties that reliably mobilize and organize citizens helps produce a polity of highly skeptical voters who are deeply dissatisfied with the state of affairs and have unrealistic expectations about what their politicians can and cannot do. Unfortunately, the weakness of parties also helps discourage participation by talented individuals and managers, leaving politics instead to the professional politicians.

Paulo Sergio Pinheiro, a distinguished Brazilian scholar and activist in the area of urban violence and human rights, highlights a critical issue that the procedural definition discussed by Schmitter and Karl does not fully address. For Pinheiro, one of the great failings of Latin American society is the failure of the rule of law and the appearance of impunity for law breakers—especially in elite segments of society. This "(un)rule of law" sustains a gross unfairness in the political system, but it also exposes citizens—mostly poor citizens—to physical insecurity. The police are not able to control crime and violent attacks on the poor, but in turn the police themselves represent a physical threat.

The failures of Latin American democracy to solve problems of poverty, inequality, physical security, corruption, and fairness of the law (among others) are very important sources of discontent among Latin Americans and the fragility of democracy discussed by Colburn. How do these factors affect the attitudes of average Latin Americans? Perhaps it is not surprising that Marta Lagos (director of Latinobarómetro, the most comprehensive source of Latin American public opinion) finds that support for democracy is not terribly robust, although it varies considerably by country. Overall, Latin Americans express support for democratic rule, but it is a support that is qualified by deep discontent and mitigated by low levels of trust in key institutions and in each other ("interpersonal trust"). It is always important to be careful how one interprets public opinion, especially in poorer countries where cultural, logistical, and political barriers may weaken the reliability of the data. Nevertheless, the general attitudes reported by Lagos are consistent with the understandings and impressions of many scholars of the region.

Some of the issues raised in the articles are mirrored in the data section at the end of the chapter. Freedom House, a U.S. government supported agency, provides annual rankings of democracy for every country in the world (Table 2.1). The ranking system provides two scores: one for political liberties (e.g., restrictions on voting rights or the ability of political parties to campaign openly) and civil liberties (e.g., restrictions on rights like freedom of speech or assembly, or protection from arbitrary arrest). The scores range from 1 to 7, with lower scores better. Tracking the changes over time, it is clear that some countries are becoming more democratic, like Chile or the Dominican Republic. But in others, such as Argentina and Brazil, democratic governance is less secure. The problem in Latin America also shows up in the corruption ratings by Transparency International (TI), an international NGO (non-governmental organization) dedicated to honesty and transparency in government worldwide (Table 2.2). TI conducts surveys with business executives and academics about the transparency and honesty in government and generates ratings for most of the countries in the world, with lower scores better. Unfortunately, most Latin American countries have high scores, with many of them clustered among the most corrupt countries in the world. The economic and social data reported in Chapter 3 reveal more about the problems of poverty and inequality in Latin America. But the human development profile table in this chapter points to low levels of wealth per person [Gross Domestic Product (GDP) per capita] and low levels of enrollment in schools, although it is also important to recognize the diversity of the region (Table 2.3). For example, Argentina has a per capita GDP of over $12,000 (in comparison to GDP per capita in the United States, which is roughly $20,000). Argentina also has a student enrollment percentage of 83 percent. By contrast, Guatemala has a GDP per capita of $3,800 and a student enrollment percentage of only 49 percent. Argentina's human development profile is well below that of the United States, but Guatemala is clearly much poorer and much more unequal. All of these issues contribute to the fragility of democracy in the region.

DATA TABLES

Table 2.1
Freedom House Rankings of Democracy,
Selected Latin American Examples, 1988–2002
(F = Free; PF = Partially Free; NF = Not Free)

Country	Freedom Scores		
	1988–1989	**1995–1996**	**2001–2002**
Argentina	1,2 F	2,3 F	3,3 PF
Belize	1,2 F	1,1 F	1,1 F
Bolivia	2,3 F	2,4 PF	1,3 F
Brazil	2,2 F	2,4 PF	3,3 PF
Chile	4,3 PF	2,2 F	2,2 F
Colombia	2,3 F	4,4 PF	4,4 PF
Costa Rica	1,1 F	1,2 F	1,2 F
Cuba	7,6 NF	7,7 NF	7,7 NF
Dominican Republic	1,3 F	4,3 PF	1,1 F
Ecuador	2,2 F	2,3 F	3,3 PF
El Salvador	3,3 PF	3,3 PF	2,3 F
Guatemala	3,3 PF	4,5 PF	3,4 PF
Honduras	2,3 F	3,3 PF	3,3 PF
Mexico	3,4 PF	4,4 PF	2,3 F
Nicaragua	5,4 PF	4,5 PF	3,3 PF
Panama	6,5 NF	2,3 F	1,2 F
Paraguay	4,3 PF	4,3 PF	4,3 PF
Peru	2,4 PF	5,4 PF	1,3 F
Uruguay	2,2 F	2,2 F	1,1 F
Venezuela	1,2 F	3,3 PF	3,5 PF

Source: Freedom House, available at www.freedomhouse.org

Notes: Scores refer to rankings from 1 to 7 on political liberties and from 1 to 7 on civil liberties, with high scores indicating less freedom. All countries are scored on the two dimensions. Full details of the scoring criteria and methods are available on Freedom House's website.

Table 2.2
Transparency International Corruption Rankings, 2002

Rank	Country	CPI 2002 Score	Surveys Used	Standard Deviation	High-Low Range
1	Finland	9.7	8	0.4	8.9–10.0
16	USA	7.7	12	0.8	5.5–8.7
17	**Chile**	7.5	10	0.9	5.6–8.8
18	Germany	7.3	10	1.0	5.0–8.1
	Israel	7.3	9	0.9	5.2–8.0
	Portugal	6.3	9	1.0	5.5–8.0
32	**Uruguay**	5.1	5	0.7	4.2–6.1

(*cont.*)

Table 2.2

Transparency International Corruption Rankings, 2002 (*cont.*)

Rank	Country	CPI 2002 Score	Surveys Used	Standard Deviation	High-Low Range
40	**Costa Rica**	4.5	6	0.9	3.6–5.9
	Jordan	4.5	5	0.7	3.6–5.2
	Mauritius	4.5	6	0.8	3.5–5.5
	South Korea	4.5	12	1.3	2.1–7.1
45	**Brazil**	4.0	10	0.4	3.4–4.8
	Bulgaria	4.0	7	0.9	3.3–5.7
	Jamaica	4.0	3	0.4	3.6–4.3
	Peru	4.0	7	0.6	3.2–5.0
	Poland	4.0	11	1.1	2.6–5.5
57	**Colombia**	3.6	10	0.7	2.6–4.6
	Mexico	3.6	10	0.6	2.5–4.9
59	China	3.5	11	1.0	2.0–5.6
	Dominican Republic	3.5	4	0.4	3.0–3.9
	Ethiopia	3.5	3	0.5	3.0–4.0
62	Egypt	3.4	7	1.3	1.7–5.3
	El Salvador	3.4	6	0.8	2.0–4.2
67	**Panama**	3.0	5	0.8	1.7–3.6
70	**Argentina**	2.8	10	0.6	1.7–3.8
71	Côte d'Ivoire	2.7	4	0.8	2.0–3.4
	Honduras	2.7	5	0.6	2.0–3.4
	India	2.7	12	0.4	2.4–3.6
	Russia	2.7	12	1.0	1.5–5.0
	Tanzania	2.7	4	0.7	2.0–3.4
	Zimbabwe	2.7	6	0.5	2.0–3.3
81	Albania	2.5	3	0.8	1.7–3.3
	Guatemala	2.5	6	0.6	1.7–3.5
	Nicaragua	2.5	5	0.7	1.7–3.4
	Venezuela	2.5	10	0.5	1.5–3.2
89	**Bolivia**	2.2	6	0.4	1.7–2.9
	Cameroon	2.2	4	0.7	1.7–3.2
	Ecuador	2.2	7	0.3	1.7–2.6
	Haiti	2.2	3	1.7	0.8–4.0
	Madagascar	1.7	3	0.7	1.3–2.5
	Paraguay	1.7	3	0.2	1.5–2.0
102	Bangladesh	1.2	5	0.7	0.3–2.0

Source: Transparency International, available at www.transparency.org/cpi/2002.

Notes: *CPI 2002 score* relates to perceptions of the degree of corruption as seen by business people, academics, and risk analysts, and ranges between 10 (highly clean) and 0 (highly corrupt).

Surveys Used refers to the number of surveys that assessed a country's performance. A total of fifteen surveys were used from nine independent institutions, and at least three surveys were required for a country to be included in the CPI.

Standard Deviation indicates differences in the values of the sources: the greater the standard deviation, the greater the differences of perceptions of a country among the sources.

High-Low Range provides the highest and lowest values of the different sources.

Full details of the CPI 2002 methodology is available at www.transparency.org/cpi/index.html#cpi.

Table 2.3

Profile of Human Development, 2000

Country	GDP per Capita (purchasing power parity)	Life Expectancy at Birth	Adult Literacy Rate	Gross School Enrollment Ratio
Argentina	12,377	73.4	96.8	83
Belize	5,606	74	93.2	73
Bolivia	2,424	62.4	85.5	70
Brazil	7,625	67.7	85.2	80
Chile	9,417	75.3	95.8	78
Colombia	6,248	71.2	91.7	73
Costa Rica	8,650	76.4	95.6	67
Cuba	—	76	96.7	76
Dominican Republic	6,033	67.1	83.6	72
Ecuador	3,203	70	91.6	77
El Salvador	4,497	69.7	78.7	63
Guatemala	3,821	64.8	68.6	49
Honduras	2,453	65.7	74.6	61
Mexico	9,023	72.6	91.4	71
Nicaragua	2,366	68.4	66.5	63
Panama	6,000	74	91.9	74
Paraguay	4,426	70.1	93.3	64
Peru	4,799	68.8	89.9	80
Uruguay	9,035	74.4	97.7	79
Venezuela	5,794	72.9	92.6	65

Source: Data from *Latin America and the Caribbean: Selected Economic and Social Data, 2001/2002.* Washington, D.C.: United States Agency for International Development, May 2003.

2.1 What Democracy Is . . . and Is Not (1991)

PHILIPPE C. SCHMITTER AND TERRY LYNN KARL

For some time the word democracy has been circulating as a debased currency in the political marketplace. Politicians with a wide range of convictions and practices strove to appropriate the label and attach it to their actions. Scholars, conversely, hesitated to use it—without adding qualifying adjectives—because of the ambiguity that surrounds it. The distinguished American political theorist Robert Dahl even tried to introduce a new term. "polyarchy," in its stead in the (vain) hope of gaining a greater measure of conceptual precision. But for better or worse, we are "stuck" with democracy as the catchword of contemporary political discourse. It is the word that resonates in people's minds and springs from their lips as they struggle for freedom and a better way of life; it is the word whose meaning we must discern if it is to be of any use in guiding political analysis and practice.

The wave of transitions away from autocratic rule that began with Portugal's "Revolution of the Carnations" in 1974 and seems to have crested with the collapse of communist regimes across Eastern Europe in 1989 has produced a welcome convergence towards a common definition of democracy. Everywhere there has been a silent abandonment of dubious adjectives like "popular," "guided," "bourgeois," and "formal" to modify "democracy." At the same time, a remarkable consensus has emerged concerning the minimal conditions that polities must meet in order to merit the prestigious appellation of "democratic." Moreover, a number of international organizations now monitor how well these standards are met; indeed, some countries even consider them when formulating foreign policy.

WHAT DEMOCRACY IS

Let us begin by broadly defining democracy and the generic *concepts* that distinguish it as a unique system for organizing relations between rulers and the ruled. We will then briefly review *procedures*, the rules and arrangements that are needed if democracy is to endure. Finally, we will discuss two operative *principles* that make democracy work. They are not expressly included among the generic concepts or formal procedures, but the prospect for democracy is grim if their underlying conditioning effects are not present.

Philippe C. Schmitter and Terry Lynn Karl, "What Democracy Is . . . and Is Not." *Journal of Democracy* 2, no. 5 (1991): 75–88. © The Johns Hopkins University Press and National Endowment for Democracy. Reprinted with permission of The Johns Hopkins University Press.

One of the major themes of this essay is that democracy does not consist of a single unique set of institutions. There are many types of democracy, and their diverse practices produce a similarly varied set of effects. The specific form democracy takes is contingent upon a country's socioeconomic conditions as well as its entrenched state structures and policy practices.

Modern political democracy is a system of governance in which rulers are held accountable for the actions in the public realm by citizens, acting indirectly through the competition and cooperation of the elected representatives.

A *regime or system of governance* is an ensemble of patterns that determines the methods of access to the principal public offices; the characteristics of the actors admitted to or excluded from such access; the strategies that actors may use to gain access; and the rules that are followed in the making of publicly binding decisions. To work properly, the ensemble must be institutionalized—that is to say, the various patterns must be habitually known, practiced, and accepted by most, if not all, actors. Increasingly, the preferred mechanism of institutionalization is a written body of laws undergirded by a written constitution, though many enduring political norms can have an informal, prudential, or traditional basis.

For the sake of economy and comparison, these forms, characteristics, and rules are usually bundled together and given a generic label. Democratic is one; others are autocratic, authoritarian, despotic, dictatorial, tyrannical, totalitarian, absolutist, traditional, monarchic, oligarchic, plutocratic, aristocratic, and sultanistic. Each of these regime forms may in turn be broken down into subtypes.

Like all regimes, democracies depend upon the presence of *rulers*, persons who occupy specialized authority roles and can give legitimate commands to others. What distinguishes democratic rulers from nondemocratic ones are the norms that condition how the former come to power and the practices that hold them accountable for their actions.

The *public realm* encompasses the making of collective norms and choices that are binding on the society and backed by state coercion. Its content can vary a great deal across democracies, depending upon preexisting distinctions between the public and the private, state and society, legitimate coercion and voluntary exchange, and collective needs and individual preferences. The liberal conception of democracy advocates circumscribing the public realm as narrowly as possible, while the socialist or social-democratic approach would extend that realm through regulation, subsidization, and, in some cases, collective ownership of property. Neither is intrinsically more democratic than the other—just *differently* democratic. This implies that measures aimed at "developing the private sector" are no more democratic than those aimed at "developing the public sector." Both, if carried to extremes, could undermine the practice of democracy, the former by destroying the basis for satisfying collective needs and exercising legitimate authority; the latter by destroying the basis for satisfying individual preferences and controlling illegitimate government actions. Differences of opinion over the optimal mix of the two provide much of the substantive content of political conflict within established democracies.

Citizens are the most distinctive element in democracies. All regimes have rulers and a public realm, but only to the extent that they are democratic do they have citizens. Historically, severe restrictions on citizenship were imposed in most emerging or partial democracies according to criteria of age, gender, class, race, literacy, property ownership, tax-paying status, and so on. Only a small part of the total population was eligible to vote or run for office. Only restricted social categories were allowed to form, join, or support political associations. After protracted struggle—in some cases involving violent domestic upheaval or international war—most of these restrictions were lifted. Today, the criteria for inclusion are fairly standard. All native-born adults are eligible, although somewhat higher age limits may still be imposed upon candidates for certain offices. Unlike the early American and European democracies of the nineteenth century, none of the recent democracies in southern Europe, Latin America, Asia, or Eastern Europe has even attempted to impose formal restrictions on the franchise or eligibility to office. When it comes to informal restrictions on the effective exercise of citizenship rights, however, the story can be quite different. This explains the central importance (discussed below) of procedures.

Competition has not always been considered an essential defining condition of democracy. "Classic" democracies presumed decision making based on direct participation leading to consensus. The assembled citizenry was expected to agree on a common course of action after listening to the alternatives and weighing their respective merits and demerits. A tradition of hostility to "faction," and "particular interests" persists in democratic thought, but at least since *The Federalist Papers* it has become widely accepted that competition among factions is a necessary evil in democracies that operate on a more-than-local scale. Since, as James Madison argued, "the latent causes of faction are sown into the nature of man," and the possible remedies for "the mischief of faction" are worse than the disease, the best course is to recognize them and to attempt to control their effects. Yet while democrats may agree on the inevitability of factions, they tend to disagree about the best forms and rules for governing factional competition. Indeed, differences over the preferred modes and boundaries of competition contribute most to distinguishing one subtype of democracy from another.

The most popular definition of democracy equates it with regular *elections,* fairly conducted and honestly counted. Some even consider the mere fact of elections—even ones from which specific parties or candidates are excluded, or in which substantial portions of the population cannot freely participate—as a sufficient condition for the existence of democracy. This fallacy has been called "electoralism" or "the faith that merely holding elections will channel political action into peaceful contests among elites and accord public legitimacy to the winners"—no matter how they are conducted or what else constrains those who win them. However central to democracy, elections occur intermittently and only allow citizens to choose between the highly aggregated alternatives offered by political parties, which can, especially in the early stages of a democratic transition, proliferate in a bewildering variety. During the intervals between elections, citizens can seek to influence public policy through a wide variety of other intermediaries: interest associations, social movements, locality groupings, clientelistic arrangements, and so forth. *Modern democracy, in other words, offers a variety of competitive processes and channels for the expression of interests and values—associational as well as partisan, functional as well as territorial, collective as well as individual. All are integral to its practice.*

Another commonly accepted image of democracy identifies it with *majority rule.* Any governing body that makes decisions by combining the votes of more than half of those eligible and present is said to be democratic, whether that majority emerges within an electorate, a parliament, a committee, a city council, or a party caucus. For exceptional purposes (e.g., amending the constitution or expelling a member), "qualified majorities" of more than 50 percent may be required, but few would deny that democracy must involve some means of aggregating the equal preferences of individuals.

A problem arises, however, when *numbers* meet *intensities.* What happens when a properly assembled majority (especially a stable, self-perpetuating one) regularly makes decisions that harm some minority (especially a threatened cultural or ethnic group)? In these circumstances, successful democracies tend to qualify the central principle of majority rule in order to protect minority rights. Such qualifications can take the form of constitutional provisions that place certain matters beyond the reach of majorities (bills of rights); requirements for concurrent majorities in several different constituencies (confederalism); guarantees securing the autonomy of local or regional governments against the demands of the central authority (federalism); grand coalition governments that incorporate all parties (consociationalism); or the negotiation of social pacts between major social groups like business and labor (neocorporatism). The most common and effective way of protecting minorities, however, lies in the everyday operation of interest associations and social movements. These reflect (some would say, amplify) the different intensities of preference that exist in the population and bring them to bear on democratically elected decision makers. Another way of putting this intrinsic tension between numbers and intensities would be to say that "in modern democracies, votes may be counted, but influences alone are weighted."

Cooperation has always been a central feature of democracy. Actors must voluntarily make collective decisions binding on the polity as a whole. They must cooperate in order to compete. They must be capable of acting collectively through parties, associations, and movements in order to select candidates, articulate preferences, petition authorities, and influence policies.

But democracy's freedoms should also encourage citizens to deliberate among themselves, to discover their common needs, and to resolve their differences without relying on some supreme central authority. Classical democracy emphasized these qualities, and they are by no means extinct, despite repeated efforts by contemporary theorists to stress the analogy with behavior in the economic marketplace and to reduce all of democracy's operations to competitive interest maximization. Alexis de Tocqueville best described the importance of independent groups for democracy in his *Democracy in America,* a work which remains a major source of inspiration for all those who persist in viewing democracy as something more than a struggle for election and re-election among competing candidates.

In contemporary political discourse, this phenomenon of cooperation and deliberation via autonomous group activity goes under the rubric of "civil society." The diverse units of social identity and interest, by remaining independent of the state (and perhaps even of parties), not only can restrain the arbitrary actions of rulers, but can also contribute to forming better citizens who are more aware of the preferences of others, more self-confident in their actions, and more civic-minded in their willingness to sacrifice for the common good. At its best, civil society provides an intermediate layer of governance between the individual and the state that is capable of resolving conflicts and controlling the behavior of members without public coercion. Rather than overloading decision makers with increased demands and making the system ungovernable, a viable civil society can mitigate conflicts and improve the quality of citizenship—without relying exclusively on the privatism of the marketplace.

Representatives—whether directly or indirectly elected—do most of the real work in modern democracies. Most are professional politicians who orient their careers around the desire to fill key offices. It is doubtful that any democracy could survive without such people. The central question, therefore, is not whether or not there will be a political elite or even a professional political class, but how these representatives are chosen and then held accountable for their actions.

As noted above there are many channels of representation in modern democracy. The electoral one, based on territorial constituencies, is the most visible and public. It culminates in a parliament or a presidency that is periodically accountable to the citizenry as a whole. Yet the sheer growth of government (in large part as a byproduct of popular demand) has increased the number, variety, and power of agencies charged with making public decisions and not subject to elections. Around these agencies there has developed a vast apparatus of specialized representation based largely on functional interests, not territorial constituencies. These interest associations, and not political parties, have become the primary expression of civil society in most stable democracies, supplemented by the more sporadic interventions of social movements.

The new and fragile democracies that have sprung up since 1974 must live in "compressed time." They will not resemble the European democracies of the nineteenth and early twentieth centuries, and they cannot expect to acquire the multiple channels of representation in gradual historical progression as did most of their predecessors. A bewildering array of parties, interests, and movements will all simultaneously seek political influence in them, creating challenges to the polity that did not exist in earlier processes of democratization.

PROCEDURES THAT MAKE DEMOCRACY POSSIBLE

The defining components of democracy are necessarily abstract, and may give rise to a considerable variety of institutions and subtypes of democracy. For democracy to thrive, however, specific procedural norms must be followed and civic rights must be respected. Any polity that fails to impose such restrictions upon itself, that fails to follow the "rule of law" with regard to its own procedures, should not be considered democratic. These procedures alone do not define democracy, but their presence is indispensable to its persistence. In essence, they are necessary but not sufficient conditions for its existence.

Robert Dahl has offered the most generally accepted listing of what he terms the "procedural minimal" conditions that must be present for modern political democracy (or as he puts it, "polyarchy") to exist:

1. Control over government decisions about policy is constitutionally vested in elected officials.
2. Elected officials are chosen in frequent and fairly conducted elections in which coercion is comparatively uncommon.
3. Practically all adults have the right to vote in the election of officials.
4. Practically all adults have the right to run for elective offices in the government. . . .
5. Citizens have a right to express themselves without the danger of severe punishment on political matters broadly defined. . . .
6. Citizens have a right to seek out alternative sources of information. Moreover, alternative sources of information exist and are protected by law.
7. . . . Citizens also have the right to form relatively independent associations or organizations, including independent political parties and interest groups.

These seven conditions seem to capture the essence of procedural democracy for many theorists, but we propose to add two others. The first might be thought of as a further refinement of item (1), while the second might be called an implicit prior condition to all seven of the above.

8. Popularly elected officials must be able to exercise their constitutional powers without being subjected to overriding (albeit informal) opposition from unelected officials. Democracy is in jeopardy if military officers, entrenched civil servants, or state managers retain the capacity to act independently of elected civilians or even veto decisions made by the people's representatives. Without this additional caveat, the militarized polities of contemporary Central America, where civilian control over the military does not exist, might be classified by many scholars as democracies, just as they have been (with the exception of Sandinista Nicaragua) by U.S. policy makers. The caveat thus guards against what we earlier called "electoralism"—the tendency to focus on the holding of elections while ignoring other political realities.

9. The polity must be self-governing: it must be able to act independently of constraints imposed by some other overarching political system. Dahl and other contemporary democratic theorists probably took this condition for granted since they referred to formally sovereign nation-states. However, with the development of blocs, alliances, spheres of influence, and a variety of "neocolonial" arrangements, the question of autonomy has been a salient one. Is a system really democratic if its elected officials are unable to make binding decisions without the approval of actors outside their territorial domain? This is significant even if the outsiders are themselves democratically constituted and if the insiders are relatively free to alter or even end the encompassing arrangement (as in Puerto Rico), but it becomes especially critical if neither condition obtains (as in the Baltic states).

PRINCIPLES THAT MAKE DEMOCRACY FEASIBLE

Lists of component processes and procedural norms help us to specify what democracy is, but they do not tell us much about how it actually functions. The simplest answer is "by the consent of the people"; the more complex one is "by the contingent consent of politicians acting under conditions of bounded uncertainty."

In a democracy, representatives must at least informally agree that those who win greater electoral support or influence over policy will not use their temporary superiority to bar the losers from taking office or exerting influence in the future, and that in exchange for this opportunity to keep competing for power and place, momentary losers will respect the winners' right to make binding decisions. Citizens are expected to obey the decisions ensuing from such a process of competition, provided its outcome remains contingent upon their collective preferences as expressed through fair and regular elections or open and repeated negotiations.

The challenge is not so much to find a set of goals that command widespread consensus as to find a set of rules that embody contingent consent. The precise shape of this "democratic bargain," to use Dahl's expression, can vary a good deal from society to society. It depends on social cleavages and such subjective factors as mutual trust, the standard of fairness, and the willingness to compromise. It may even be compatible with a great deal of dissensus on substantive policy issues.

All democracies involve a degree of uncertainty about who will be elected and what policies they will pursue. Even in those polities where one party persists in winning elections or one policy is consistently implemented, the possibility of change through independent collective action still exists, as in Italy, Japan, and the Scandinavian social democracies. If it does not, the system is not democratic, as in Mexico, Senegal, or Indonesia.

But the uncertainty embedded in the core of all democracies is bounded. Not just any actor can get into the competition and raise any issue he or she pleases—there are previously established rules that must be respected. Not just any policy can be adopted—there are conditions that must be met. Democracy institutionalizes "normal," limited political uncertainty. These boundaries vary from country to country. Constitutional guarantees of property, privacy, expression, and other rights are a part of this, but the most effective boundaries are generated by competition among interest groups and cooperation within civil society. Whatever the rhetoric (and some polities appear to offer their citizens more dramatic alternatives than others), once the rules of contingent consent have been agreed upon, the actual variation is likely to stay within a predictable and generally accepted range.

This emphasis on operative guidelines contrasts with a highly persistent, but misleading theme in recent literature on democracy—namely, the emphasis upon "civic culture." The principles we have suggested here rest on rules of prudence, not on deeply ingrained habits of tolerance, moderation, mutual respect, fair play, readiness to compromise, or trust in public authorities. Waiting for such habits to sink deep and lasting roots implies a very slow process of regime consolidation—one that takes generations—and it would probably condemn most contemporary experiences *ex hypothesi* to failure. Our assertion is that contingent consent and bounded uncertainty can emerge from the interaction between antagonistic and mutually suspicious actors and that the far more benevolent and ingrained norms of a civic culture are better thought of as a *product* and not a producer of democracy.

HOW DEMOCRACIES DIFFER

Several concepts have been deliberately excluded from our generic definition of democracy, despite the fact that they have been frequently associated with it in both everyday practice and scholarly work. They are, nevertheless, especially important when it comes to distinguishing subtypes of democracy. Since no single set of actual institutions, practices, or values embodies democracy, polities moving away from authoritarian rule can mix different components to produce different democracies. It is important to recognize that these do not define points along a single continuum of improving performance, but a matrix of potential combinations that are *differently* democratic.

1. *Consensus:* All citizens may not agree on the substantive goals of political action or on the role of the state (although if they did, it would certainly make governing democracies much easier).
2. *Participation:* All citizens may not take an active and equal part in politics, although it must be legally possible for them to do so.
3. *Access:* Rulers may not weigh equally the preferences of all who come before them, although citizenship implies that individuals and groups should have an equal opportunity to express their preferences if they choose to do so.
4. *Responsiveness:* Rulers may not always follow the course of action preferred by the citizenry. But when they deviate from such a policy, say on grounds of "reason of state" or "overriding national interest," they must ultimately be held accountable for their actions through regular and fair processes.
5. *Majority rule:* Positions may not be allocated or rules may not be decided solely on the basis of assembling the most votes, although deviations from this principle usually must be explicitly defended and previously approved.
6. *Parliamentary sovereignty:* The legislature may not be the only body that can make rules or even the one with final authority in deciding which laws are binding, although where executive, judicial, or other public bodies make that ultimate choice, they too must be accountable for their actions.
7. *Party government:* Rulers may not be nominated, promoted, and disciplined in their activities by well-organized and programmatically coherent political parties, although where they are not, it may prove more difficult to form an effective government.
8. *Pluralism:* The political process may not be based on a multiplicity of overlapping, voluntaristic, and autonomous private groups. However, where there are monopolies of representation, hierarchies of association, and obligatory memberships, it is likely that the interests involved will

be more closely linked to the state and the separation between the public and private spheres of action will be much less distinct.

9. *Federalism:* The territorial division of authority may not involve multiple levels and local autonomies, least of all ones enshrined in a constitutional document, although some dispersal of power across territorial and/or functional units is characteristic of all democracies.

10. *Presidentialism:* The chief executive officer may not be a single person and he or she may not be directly elected by the citizenry as a whole, although some concentration of authority is present in all democracies, even if it is exercised collectively and only held indirectly accountable to the electorate.

11. *Checks and Balances:* It is not necessary that the different branches of government be systematically pitted against one another, although governments by assembly, by executive concentration, by judicial command, or even by dictatorial fiat (as in time of war) must be ultimately accountable to the citizenry as a whole.

While each of the above has been named as an essential component of democracy, they should instead be seen either as indicators of this or that type of democracy, or else as useful standards for evaluating the performance of particular regimes. To include them as part of the genetic definition of democracy itself would be to mistake the American polity for the universal model of democratic governance. Indeed, the parliamentary, consociational, unitary, corporatist, and concentrated arrangements of continental Europe may have some unique virtues for guiding polities through the uncertain transition from autocratic to democratic rule.

WHAT DEMOCRACY IS NOT

We have attempted to convey the general meaning of modern democracy without identifying it with some particular set of rules and institutions or restricting it to some specific culture or level of development. We have also argued that it cannot be reduced to the regular holding of elections or equated with a particular notion of the role of the state, but we have not said much more about what democracy is not or about what democracy may not be capable of producing.

There is an understandable temptation to load too many expectations on this concept and to imagine that by attaining democracy, a society will have resolved all of its political, social, economic, administrative, and cultural problems. Unfortunately, "all good things do not necessarily go together."

First, democracies are not necessarily more efficient economically than other forms of government. Their rates of aggregate growth, savings, and investment may be no better than those of nondemocracies. This is especially likely during the transition, when propertied groups and administrative elites may respond to real or imagined threats to the "rights" they enjoyed under authoritarian rule by initiating capital flight, disinvestment, or sabotage. In time, depending upon the type of democracy, benevolent long-term effects upon income distribution, aggregate demand, education, productivity, and creativity may eventually combine to improve economic and social performance, but it is certainly too much to expect that these improvements will occur immediately—much less that they will be defining characteristics of democratization.

Second, democracies are not necessarily more efficient administratively. Their capacity to make decisions may even be slower than that of the regimes they replace, if only because more actors must be consulted. The costs of getting things done may be higher, if only because "payoffs" have to be made to a wider and more resourceful set of clients (although one should never underestimate the degree of corruption to be found within autocracies). Popular satisfaction with the new democratic government's performance may not even seem greater, if only because necessary compromises often please no one completely, and because the losers are free to complain.

Third, democracies are not likely to appear more orderly, consensual, stable, or governable than the autocracies they replace. This is partly a byproduct of democratic freedom of expression, but it is also a reflection of the likelihood of continuing disagreement over new rules and institutions. These products of imposition or compromise are often initially quite ambiguous in nature and uncertain in effect until actors have learned how to use them. What is more, they come in the aftermath of serious struggles motivated by high ideals. Groups and individuals with recently acquired autonomy will test certain rules, protest against the actions of certain institutions, and insist on renegotiating their part of the bargain. Thus the presence of antisystem parties should be neither surprising nor seen as a failure of democratic consolidation. What counts is whether such parties are willing, however reluctantly, to play by the general rules of bounded uncertainty and contingent consent.

Governability is a challenge for all regimes, not just democratic ones. Given the political exhaustion and loss of legitimacy that have befallen autocracies from sultanistic Paraguay to totalitarian Albania, it may seem that only democracies can now be expected to govern effectively and legitimately. Experience has shown, however, that democracies too can lose the ability to govern. Mass publics can become disenchanted with their performance. Even more threatening is the temptation for leaders to fiddle with procedures and ultimately undermine the principles of contingent consent and bounded uncertainty. Perhaps the most critical moment comes once the politicians begin to settle into the more predictable roles and relations of a consolidated democracy. Many will find their expectations frustrated; some will discover that the new rules of competition put them at a disadvantage; a few may even feel that their vital-interests are threatened by popular majorities.

Finally, democracies will have more open societies and polities than the autocracies they replace, but not necessarily more open economies. Many of today's most successful and well-established democracies have historically resorted to protectionism and closed borders, and have relied extensively upon public institutions to promote economic development. While the long-term compatibility between democracy and capitalism does not seem to be in doubt, despite their continuous tension, it is not clear whether the promotion of such liberal economic goals as the right of individuals to own property and retain profits, the clearing function of markets, the private settlement of disputes, the freedom to produce without government regulation, or the privatization of state-owned enterprises necessarily furthers the consolidation of democracy. After all, democracies do need to levy taxes and regulate certain transactions, especially where private monopolies and oligopolies exist. Citizens or their representatives may decide that it is desirable to protect the rights of collectivities from encroachment by individuals, especially propertied ones, and they may choose to set aside certain forms of property for public or cooperative ownership. In short, notions of economic liberty that are currently put forward in neoliberal economic models are not synonymous with political freedom—and may even impede it.

Democratization will not necessarily bring in its wake economic growth, social peace, administrative efficiency, political harmony, free markets, or "the end of ideology." Least of all will it bring about "the end of history." No doubt some of these qualities could make the consolidation of democracy easier, but they are neither prerequisites for it nor immediate products of it. Instead, what we should be hoping for is the emergence of political institutions that can peacefully compete to form governments and influence public policy, that can channel social and economic conflicts through regular procedures, and that have sufficient linkages to civil society to represent their constituencies and commit them to collective courses of action. Some types of democracies, especially in developing countries, have been unable to fulfill this promise, perhaps due to the circumstances of their transition from authoritarian rule. The democratic wager is that such a regime, once established, will not only persist by reproducing itself within its initial confining conditions, but will eventually expand beyond them. Unlike authoritarian regimes, democracies have the capacity to modify their rules and institutions consensually in response to changing circumstances. They may not immediately produce all the goods mentioned above, but they stand a better chance of eventually doing so than do autocracies.

2.2 Fragile Democracies (2002)

FORREST COLBURN

I asked a young Brazilian in Rio de Janeiro how President Fernando Henrique Cardoso was doing. "Oh, he is doing fine." A pause. "It is the rest of us who are not doing so well." This beguiling response can serve as a leitmotiv for how many Latin Americans view their new democratic regimes. It has just been a few years since authoritarian regimes—most military led—were replaced with popularly elected civilian governments throughout the region. These new regimes have survived. But the fanfare and enthusiasm that marked the transition have given way to a more guarded view of democratic governance in the region, and, indeed, to increasing cynicism and apathy.

The first Latin American country to restore democratic institutions was Ecuador, in 1979. It was followed by its neighbor Peru in 1980, and then Argentina in 1983 and Uruguay in 1984. In Central America, the militaries returned to the barracks in El Salvador in 1984 and in Guatemala in 1986. In 1989 Brazil finally broke free from a military regime that had begun in 1964. Dating the transition in Bolivia and in Honduras is more difficult, but in both countries 1985 seems to have been a pivotal year. Two of the last countries to join the fashionable embracing of democracy, Chile and Nicaragua in 1990, did so after experiencing "socialism." Paraguay closed the cycle with its open and competitive elections in 1993 (some Paraguayans date their transition to the elections of 1989 even though the victor was a general who had a few months earlier overthrown the dictator Alfredo Stroessner). These new democracies joined the three countries where democratic processes had been established earlier: Costa Rica (1948), Colombia (1958), and Venezuela (1958).

As can be expected with such a diverse group of countries, there are many degrees of "success" with democracy. Countries that appear more successful include Chile, Uruguay, Bolivia, Argentina, El Salvador, and Costa Rica. On the other end of the continuum are Peru, Ecuador, Venezuela, Brazil, Honduras, and Nicaragua. Differing outcomes are not easy to explain. There is no correlation between those countries that embraced democracy "early" or "late" and the initial set of outcomes of that transition. Peru, for example, was one of the first countries to return to civilian rule, and its governance remains most problematic. Brazil was one of the last countries to embark on democratic rule, and it, too, is problematic. Similarly, there is no easy correlation between the depth of earlier political conflict and present stability. Bolivia has a history of extreme political instability—characterized by military coups d'état—yet today it seems stable. Venezuela has a history of constitutional rule, but it is floundering. Surprisingly, there are no socioeconomic indicators, such as per capita income, that predict political outcomes.

Certain generalizations, however, can be made for Latin America as a whole.

1. A number of indicators suggest that both new and old democratic regimes are under stress, their legitimacy is being questioned, and their public support is increasingly fragile.

Public opinion polls in individual countries, and for the region as a whole, demonstrate declining public confidence in democracy. A comprehensive survey of attitudes on government and politics in 17 Latin American countries undertaken in 1996 by a private polling organization based in Chile, Barómetro Latinoamericano, showed only a minority of those polled expressing satisfaction with the performance of their country's democracy. The same frustration—or disappointment—was registered in polls conducted in 1997 and 1998. Support for the performance of democratic regimes is highest in Uruguay and Costa Rica, and lowest in such countries as Brazil, Paraguay, Ecuador, and Honduras. The sweeping conclusion from the 1998 polling was that only 35 percent of Latin Americans are satisfied with the performance of their democracy. Public opinion polls also suggest widespread disappointment with the institutions of democracy, in particular with legislatures and political parties.

Also indicative of the fragility of democracy in Latin America is the declining voter turnout in elections. In Brazil, for example, voting is obligatory, yet in the 1998 presidential elections, 36 percent of the 106 million Brazilians eligible to vote stayed home or cast blank or invalid votes. Fernando Henrique Cardoso was reelected president by only 34 percent of the total voting population. In Colombia, abstention has climbed to over 50 percent. In Guatemala's 1996 presidential elections, in the departments of Huehuetenango and Quiché, where the population is overwhelmingly indigenous, 74 percent of eligible voters stayed home. In the country's 1999 national referendum, the abstention rate was 81 percent.

Another disturbing indicator is the lack of support offered to candidates of traditional political parties. In some countries, such as Peru and Venezuela, important parties have all but collapsed. Alternatively, candidates with no political experience have won elections. Alberto Fujimori in Peru is the best-known case. There also appears to be an increasing tendency—accepted by the public—to concentrate power in the executive, who rules by decrees instead of by laws. Finally, many in the media and the academic community openly express doubts about the desirability of democracy.

They talk of the "Pinochet model," a "democracy of low intensity," and of a "façade of democracy."

What is happening? Why the declining support for democracy so soon after the scandals of "dirty wars," "*los desaparecidos*," and incompetent economic management by befuddled generals?

2. Public dissatisfaction is not directed at the economic model of the day, unfettered markets.

Public disenchantment is instead focused on corruption and ineptitude in governing. A regionwide survey of public attitudes by the Spanish magazine *Cambio 16* revealed that for the overwhelming majority the most serious problem in their countries is corruption. In impoverished Bolivia, most Bolivians say that corruption is a greater problem than unemployment. Election results also do not demonstrate public rejection of the liberal economic model. Wealthy businessmen with programs of economic liberalization win elections, such as Juan Carlos Wasmosy in Paraguay. In the 1993 Chilean election, 90 percent of the votes went to candidates who accepted the reigning economic model. Even the 1998 election in Venezuela of Hugo Chávez—a former army colonel and coup plotter—can be interpreted not as a vote against liberalism, but instead a vote against corruption in the country's traditional political parties. The dominant attitude in the region is best captured by a Mexican intellectual who said he no longer cared about governments of the right or the left; he would settle for any honest government.

3. The public has sweeping (and perhaps unfair) criteria for granting political legitimacy.

Intellectuals may separate regime type from everyday public administration, but the public makes no such distinction. Legitimacy is accorded governors not on the basis of how they acquired power, but what they do with it. The abrupt transition from authoritarianism to democracy in the 1980s was not accompanied by a wholesale remaking of the bureaucracies that provide (or do not provide) important services to a needy public. In too many instances, the state remains inefficient, unresponsive, and corrupt. Costa Rica has been a democracy since 1948, but a bumper sticker suggests the challenge facing winners of elections in Latin America: "Every time I hit a pothole, I think of the president." In neighboring Nicaragua, a congressional leader told me that a survey of Nicaraguans revealed that the expectation of members of Congress is that they help secure jobs and visas to the United States. Throughout Latin America, there is a need not just to improve the machinery of government, but also to explain what are reasonable expectations of government—and democratic government in particular. The Uruguayan statesman Julio María Sanguinetti goes further, suggesting that democracy demands a supportive political culture. As he puts it, in the most telling of phraseology, "Consumers need to be citizens too."

4. Political parties are the weakest link in Latin America's democracies.

In contemporary democratic theory, political parties are the essential building blocks. They have responsibility for aggregating public preferences, formulating plans for governing, and fielding candidates. With only limited exceptions, political parties in Latin America are not institutionalized, they are not stable, they do not have roots in society, they are not independent of ambitious leaders, and they are not democratic in their internal organization. In the aftermath of military rule in Ecuador, the country has seemingly made a habit of electing a president from a different political party. Between 14 and 17 parties routinely compete in legislative elections, with at least 10 of them winning seats. The strongest party in Congress at any one time has never represented anything close to a majority of voters, polling between 15 and 30 percent of the vote, and usually about 20 percent.

None of Ecuador's political parties has deep roots in society. Indeed, even politicians have shallow roots in their own political parties. One of the features of Ecuador's politics is what is called *cambio de camiseta* (change of shirt): candidates for positions in Congress run for office under a party banner, but once elected they commonly change parties, or just proclaim themselves independents. At times, more than a fourth of the members of Congress claim no party affiliation. Party affiliation is shed so as to enhance the bargaining power of individual members of Congress. I asked an Ecuadorian congressman, in the privacy of his office, how much a congressional vote was worth. "If it is not a vote of great importance, something like two jobs in the customs authority."

Other countries, notably Brazil, also suffer from political fragmentation. Brazil has 20 political parties, so everything depends on "coalitions." And the stability of coalitions is continually undermined by members of Congress changing parties at will. Even in regimes that are essentially two-party systems, such as Honduras, there are no strong connections between society and party. Electoral competition has not been sufficient to end cronyism, indifference, and corruption. In Honduras, public sentiment toward the country's two political parties is captured by the quip, "They eat from the same plate." In the Dominican Republic there is an even more disturbing maxim about the country's political elite: "They are white and they understand one another."

5. The reform of political parties is stymied by a lack of political involvement on the part of many of the middle class, and the managers and professionals whose skills are sorely needed.

Throughout Latin America, there is a common fatalism about politics, as if all outcomes are foreordained. Political parties are left to *politicos*. As a Guatemalan manager put it, "*Los buenos no se meten*" (Decent people do not get involved). This lack of political participation in the management of political parties, and in politics in general, is at odds with common ideas about the economy, which is held to need constant scrutiny and calibration. A similar attitude toward politics is lacking.

6.   Political participation is retarded in part by the lack of ideas, of conflicting paradigms on how best to organize state and society.

As a member of Venezuela's Congress put it, "There is no debate because there are no alternatives." A Peruvian journalist, Raúl Wiener, has argued that Peruvian politics has suffered from a "general crisis of intellectual production." It is telling—and depressing, too—that no one reads anymore. Before, those on the left were the most studious, the most inclined to read political theory. But now they do not read: not Marx or Lenin, and not any substitutes. A former guerrilla in El Salvador, now a member of the Democratic Party, told me: "There is nothing to read; there are no reference points." For her and her colleagues, one learns only from the experience of governing.

The silence of intellectuals and politicians is striking. They both are terribly short of ideals that can mobilize people. In particular, there is little evidence of energy and creativity in searching for ways in which state and society can ameliorate inequality and poverty. Innovation in public administration is largely confined to public finance, where the guiding aspiration is inevitably to rein in government spending (and so avoid inflation-spawning deficits). Private initiatives are few. The poor are seen as an inevitable part of the social landscape.

Even Latin America's last guerrillas, those of Colombia, are seemingly bereft of ideas. Guerrillas operate in nearly half of Colombia and control a sizable part of the country. They are fought by the military and by paramilitary forces. The fighting is savage and has generated a major social crisis. But what is the fighting about? The largest rebel group is the Revolutionary Armed Forces of Colombia (FARC). What, if anything, does it advocate? It has not articulated an ideology or a set of proposals, leaving it open to charges that it fights for the spoils of the trade in narcotics and the gains from such crimes as kidnapping. The FARC has not contributed to political debate in Colombia, let alone elsewhere in Latin America.

7.   In the absence of ideas—and passions—there are only interests.

These, of course, have always existed. But perhaps they are more transparent now. Latin America has always been characterized as being both more culturally homogeneous and more radically inegalitarian than other parts of the world. In fact, inequality is real enough, homogeneity less so. The ethnic schism between indigenous people and those referred to as *ladinos* is pronounced. Indigenous populations are better organized and more independent today, especially in countries where they constitute a substantial part of the population. Afro-Brazilians—who represent perhaps 40 percent of the population of Brazil—are also increasingly able to make demands for a redress in their subordinate status.

There are now more pronounced—and growing—divisions, not based on ethnicity, but rather between the capital and the rest of the country (the "interior" as it is still sometimes called in Havana). The economic and cultural disparities between the capital and the remainder of the country introduce an odd disjunct into the politics of representation. In Guatemala, for example, it can be argued that the winner of the 1996 presidential election was the candidate of Guatemala City; the loser was the candidate of the rest of the country. Increasingly, the route to the presidency in Latin America includes serving as mayor of the capital.

In some countries regional disparities are pronounced. The wealthiest state in Mexico, Nueva Leon (located in the north), has a per capita income 10 times that of the poorest Mexican state, Chiapas (located in the south). In a number of countries, including Colombia, Ecuador, Peru, and Bolivia, there is a rivalry between the sierra and the lowlands. (Ecuadorians from the *sierra* call their brethren on the coast "monkeys.") It remains to be seen how ethnic, regional, and urban-rural divisions will play themselves out, but the basic political fault lines are becoming decidedly less ideological.

8. In the fragile democracies of Latin America, the political risk is not, as in decades past, a return to military rule.

The military realizes that the international context has changed and that the pressures on anyone seeking to usurp power would be overwhelming. In any case, the soldiers have no inclination to govern. There are no visible dangers to the nation or their own prerogatives. Like so many others today in Latin America, ranking military officers are interested in making money. Many officers throughout the region have business interests on the side. And the military as an institution often owns and operates businesses, sometimes of an ominous kind, such as the cemetery run by the armed forces in Honduras.

Instead, the greater political danger to democracy in Latin America comes from a growing number of voters who either abstain from voting altogether or vote for antidemocratic candidates who offer "simple solutions" to complex problems. "Simple solutions" are a populist mantra. Populism in Latin America is an elastic concept, but it is most commonly associated with redistributive economic policies, usually financed in an unsustainable manner. Populism has a less well-understood political dimension, however: the "politics of antipolitics." Populists who come to power through democratic elections govern in an authoritarian style justified by continual attacks on traditional political elites and established institutions.

Today, economic populism is not the threat it was in earlier decades. There has been considerable "economic learning" by elites, including those of the private sector and governmental bureaucracies, and the international financial community is always on guard. A political leader bent on pursuing populist economic policies would quickly confront opposition from a daunting coalition of institutionalized actors who can put unbearable pressure on any maverick leader.

Much more likely are forms of political populism á la Alberto Fujimori—antiparty politics. Alberto Fujimori, the son of Japanese immigrants, assumed the presidency of Peru in 1990 after winning a competitive election. But he augmented his power in 1992 by what is now known throughout Latin America as a *"fujimorazo"*—dissolving Congress under the pretext that legislators were corrupt and inept. Democracy's "checks and balances" were dismantled with the argument that public faith in Peru's traditional political parties had declined. Fujimori offered "administration," not "politics." Surely all Peruvians recognized that this gambit was antidemocratic. Nonetheless, in Peru—and elsewhere in Latin America—voters can become so frustrated with the traditional parties that they opt for exciting if dangerous leaders. Even elites, fearful of economic populism, may acquiesce in a political leadership that is determined to govern. But this kind of heady and combative government inevitably contributes to the further weakening of democratic institutions, including political parties, legislatures, and the judiciary.

9. The democracies of Latin America are hostage to economic trends and are vulnerable to economic shocks.

There is statistical evidence that the percentage of poor people in Chile has declined because of robust economic growth, up to an enviable 6 to 8 percent per year. In Costa Rica, the successful promotion of exports and the development of tourism have resulted in a low unemployment rate. In many other countries, though, the "new" economic strategy has brought painful dislocations, such as the surge in unemployment in Argentina and the political crisis that has gripped the country since December. And there is scattered but persuasive evidence that economic liberalization and the development of new export commodities are exacerbating inequality. These unequal gains—or losses, as the case may be—translate into political tensions. For example, in El Salvador, the National Republican Alliance is threatened with fragmentation because of divisions between the agro-export elite, who founded the party but are not faring so well, and the financial-sector elite, who increasingly dominate the party. Shifts in economic policies bring sharp and sudden shifts in economic fortunes. Resilient democracies can cope, but can fragile democracies?

Another, more nettlesome question: How dependent has Latin America become on a healthy world economy, and, in particular, on capital inflows? For a number of years Latin America has had a very large capital inflow, billions of dollars annually. This investment, along with healthy markets for many of the region's exports, has caused a spurt of economic growth and patched over many problems—including increased inequality. What happens if capital dries up, or if world trade contracts? The economic difficulties in Latin America during the 1980s were exacerbated by indebtedness. Latin American countries continue to have considerable foreign debt, which is constraining and which makes the region especially vulnerable to a contraction in the world economy. There is an expression in financial circles: When the United States sneezes, Europe gets a cold. Perhaps the corollary is, and Latin America gets pneumonia.

10. Mexico may be a bellwether rather than an exception.

In Latin America there is an expression, "*Como México no hay dos*" (There is no place like Mexico). Mexico is sui generis. Before the wave of democracy in Latin America, Mexico did not look so bad: the military was nowhere to be seen, there were elections, and there was a periodic change of presidents. After the "transitions" elsewhere, though, Mexico looked like what the Peruvian writer Mario Vargas Llosa labeled it: "the perfect dictatorship." Elections and a new president every six years no longer masked the fact that the country was essentially a one-party state, the kingdom of the Institutional Revolutionary Party (PRI), founded in 1929. The party mixed paternalistic populism with electoral skulduggery to become the longest-ruling political party in the world.

The PRI provided a façade of legitimacy for cronyism, clientelism, and corruption. The 1982 economic crisis in Mexico stimulated some effort at political reform, as did—again—the 1994 crisis. Although the leadership of the PRI sometimes gave the impression that its attitude was "things have to change so that nothing changes," a variety of circumstances and some statesmanship led to elections in 2000 that were free and competitive. And the PRI lost.

The candidate of the National Action Party (PAN), Vicente Fox, won the election. His campaign appearances included his stomping a plastic dinosaur, representing the PRI, with his cowboy boots. In Fox's December 2000 inauguration address to Congress, he promised there would be, after 71 years of continuity, a "new political future," with a "reform of the state, breaking paradigms." But is a new "paradigm" for governing truly in the offing?

Mexicans voted for an alternative to the PRI only when it was safe to do so, when there was an end to ideological differences that might reverberate throughout state and society. Conflict is being averted, but so is the possibility of profound change. A Mexican president who is not from the PRI is now a threat only to the cronyism of the PRI. Mexico is different, in so many ways, from the rest of Latin America; yet politically Mexico enters the twenty-first century with the same absence of ideological—and thus programmatic—contestation that is lacking elsewhere.

In sum, Latin America's democracies are not in danger of collapse at this time. But there are many real problems—and not many indications—that these problems are being addressed with imagination and determination. It is not clear how tired and cynical voters will react if further deterioration takes place, or if the region is subjected to economic shocks. True, the region's democracies have brought peace and greater protection of basic human rights. Democratic governments have brought a welcome sense of "normalcy," too. What is notable, though, is not just that the democracies are "rickety," hardly prepared to tackle difficult economic and social problems, but that the populace is not prepared to engage in deep discussions about state and society, about needs and aspirations, and about how these needs and aspirations could be met. The considerable promises of democracy have yet to be fulfilled in Latin America.

2.3 Democracies Without Citizenship: Injustice for All: Crime and Impunity in Latin America (1996)

PAULO SERGIO PINHEIRO

Official violence continues unabated in many of Latin America's new democracies. While under military rule, the targets were political dissidents, today's victims are the continent's "undesirables"—the poor, the homeless, minority groups, homosexuals, landless peasants.

In the middle of Rio Branco Avenue in downtown Rio de Janeiro, three men robbed a bank. As they were making their getaway, private security guards assaulted them, stealing their spoils and killing one of the thieves in the ensuing struggle. The bank robbers, whose weapons were rented, decided to file a complaint at the police station to try to recoup their stolen weapons at least—which they did after the police apprehended the private guards. Six other bank robberies occurred on that same day in Rio de Janeiro, but in only one case did the banks file charges with the police. The inversion of justice has reached the point that criminals seem to trust the police more than established businesses do.

In Brazil, as in many Latin American countries, there is a dramatic gap between the letter of the law and the brutal reality of law enforcement. Brazil's new Constitution, promulgated in 1988, incorporated broad provisions for the protection of individual rights, which were systematically violated during two decades of military rule. The document explicitly rec-

Paulo Sergio Pinheiro, "Democracies Without Citizenship," *NACLA Report of the Americas*, September–October 1996, Vol. 30, no. 2, pp. 17–23. Reprinted by permission.

ognizes the rights to life, liberty and personal integrity, and torture and racial discrimination are now considered crimes. But despite these constitutional protections, official violence continues unabated.

This gap between the law and reality is rooted in the failure of Latin American democracies to consolidate one of the most basic cornerstones of democratic governance: the state's monopoly over the means of coercion. This failure has resulted in the persistence of endemic violence throughout the region. On the one hand, violence is exercised by elites to maintain "social order." In countries like Brazil, deadly force, torture and arbitrary detention continue to characterize police behavior because this official violence enjoys widespread impunity. On the other hand, violent crime and delinquency have also increased in Latin American societies, particularly in the 1980s and 1990s. Crimes against life and physical integrity—homicide, assault, rape—have risen sharply, and murders account for a growing percentage of unnatural deaths. In Sao Paulo, for example, the homicide rate jumped from 41.6 per 100,000 inhabitants in 1988 to 50.2 in 1993. Crimes against property—theft, robbery, fraud—are also on the rise. So is organized crime, especially drag trafficking and money laundering.

This endemic violence—embedded in a context of broad economic inequalities and a system of profoundly assymetric social relations—is hardly a new phenomenon in the region. It has worsened over the past two decades, at least in part because neoliberal economic policies have widened the gap between rich and poor and doomed millions of Latin Americans to lives of poverty and social exclusion. But violence also stems from the continuation of a long tradition of authoritarian practices by elites against "non-elites"—practices that are often reproduced in social relations among poor people themselves. The return to democratic constitutionalism did little to eradicate the authoritarian practices embedded in the state and in society.

While the most egregious forms of human rights violations committed by the region's military regimes have been eliminated under civilian role, the long-awaited democracies have not fulfilled their role as guardians of public order and protectors of the fundamental rights of all citizens. Consequently, the role of law remains precarious in many Latin American countries. In Brazil as elsewhere, the difference is that the victims are no longer political activists, many of them educated members of the middle class, whose opposition to the military regimes got them killed or brutally tortured. Today, the principal targets of arbitrary police behavior are the most defenseless and vulnerable groups in Brazilian society: rural workers, trade-union activists, minority groups and destitute children and adolescents, many of whom live in the streets. Arbitrary detention and torturing suspects are still common police practices. Extrajudicial killings are also shockingly common, including the assassination of street kids by off-duty police and the repression of rural workers struggling for land and labor rights in the Northeast. Much of this violence is fueled by ingrained discrimination against poor people and racial minorities, who constitute a high percentage of all homicide victims. The common denominator in all these cases is impunity. The failure to enforce the law not only makes a mockery of the principle of the equality of citizens before the law, but also makes it more difficult for governments to strengthen their legitimacy. It feeds the circle of officially sanctioned violence.

Brazil, like other Latin American countries, is a society based on exclusion—a democracy without citizenship. The impact of globalization, coupled with the crises resulting from economic adjustment programs, separates the rich and poor as never before—"as if," says Hector Castillo Berthier, "they were oil and water." Countries with greater inequality—high rates of income concentration in upper-income groups—tend to have higher crime rates as well as higher levels of human rights violations. Brazil is a shocking example in this regard. A country with one of the most appallingly uneven distributions of income on the planet—in 1992, the richest 20% earned 32 times more than the poorest 20%—Brazil also has correspondingly high rates of crime and official violence. For example, worldwide, residents of Rio de Janeiro—along with Buenos Aires, Kampala and Pretoria—run the highest risk of having their homes broken into. And Brazil's militarized police forces, which come under the authority of state governments, are among the most deadly in the world. In 1992, for example, military police killed a record 1,470 civilians in Sao Paulo alone (compared to 27 police killings in New York City that year).

Those who are most affected by unemployment and most marginalized from the education system are also the most likely victims of both arbitrary police repression and common crime. In Brazil, for example, those most frequently victimized by violent crime live below the poverty line. The perpetrators of violent crimes, such as homicide, are usually from the same social strata as the victims. These crimes usually occur in poor neighborhoods and shanty-towns. In fact, in most of Latin America's huge metropoli, there is a correlation between poor neighborhoods and death from violent causes, and a clear link exists between living conditions, violence and mortality rates.

This is the case in the shantytowns that dominate the landscape of almost all Latin American cities—favelas in Rio de Janeiro and Sao Paulo, ranchos in Caracas, barriadas in Lima, campamentos in Santiago, ciudades perdidas in Mexico City, villas miserias in Buenos Aires. In these "geographic and social pre-cities," says Ignacy Sachs, "the majority do not possess the minimum conditions of what could be called urban life." They lack adequate housing, have little access to work and income, and have difficulty obtaining basic services. Moreover, the state, particularly those institutions charged with maintaining peace and order, is rarely present in these "pre-cities," leaving the socially excluded to fend for themselves. In such a milieu, violence often becomes the mediator of daily social relations. Whenever the state's monopoly on legitimate violence is relaxed, survival may depend on an individual's ability to maintain his or her reputation by displaying a "credible threat of violence." "A seemingly minor affront is not merely a 'stimulus' to action, isolated in time and space," according to one study of violent behavior among poor classes in the United States. "It must be understood within a larger social context of reputations, face, relative social status and enduring relationships." The offended party may feel the need to use violence to defend his or her status. In this sense, violence is, to a large extent, performance.

This kind of inner-city violence may be the result of a "loss of structure in society." In other words, where social restraints have been loosened, violence is considered a legitimate means of resolving conflict and may actually be encouraged. But violence may also simply be a reaction by normal people to oppressive circumstances—be it poverty, the humiliation of unemployment, the pressure of organized crime or the arbitrary power of the police.

Young people are increasingly the victims of violent crime in large cities across Latin America. In Sao Paulo, an average of 102 youths between 15 and 24 years of age are murdered for every 100,000 inhabitants in that age range. In some poor neighborhoods, the figures for this age group reach epidemic proportions of up to 222 homicides per 100,000—more than ten times the national average. The degree to which young people are either victims or perpetrators of crime reveals the clear link between poverty and violence. This is not to say that there is a direct or mechanistic relationship between poverty and violent crime, but it is imperative to consider how inequality factors into the problem of growing crime in Latin America. As a result of economic-adjustment policies, many young people are unable to find jobs or pay university tuition fees. To compensate for their sense of marginality, many youths join street gangs, while others become involved in drug trafficking. Crime becomes a quick, easy means to climb the social ladder in a society in which legal and "respectable" channels for such mobility are largely cut off.

Most analyses of crime, however, rarely make these distinctions. Even though most victims of crime are poor, the middle and upper classes perceive crime as a problem that only affects them. They see crime, moreover, as a constant threat from the lower classes—the "dangerous classes"—that must be held in check, whatever the cost. The police tend to act as border guards protecting the rich from the poor, and police violence remains cloaked in impunity because it is largely directed against these "dangerous classes" and rarely affects the lives of the well-to-do. Crime-prevention policies—especially those proposed during election time—are aimed less at controlling crime and delinquency than diminishing the fear and the insecurity of the ruling classes. Elite perceptions of the poor as part of the "dangerous classes" are fueled by a judicial system that prosecutes and convicts crimes committed by poor people, while the crimes of the elites go unchallenged. Middle-class crime—including corruption, financial scams, tax evasion and the exploitation of child or slave labor—are not perceived as threats to the status quo. The same is largely true for organized crime, including drug trafficking, money laundering and contraband, and even the very profitable arms trade, none of which are targets of consistent enforcement policies.

Even if the state no longer engages in systematic coercion against political dissidents, as it did during the dictatorships, it remains accountable for the repressive illegal practices of the police and the military which have survived the transitions to democracy. The state needs to work towards eradicating the impunity for official crimes to the same extent it tries to punish violent crimes committed by common criminals. In much of Latin America, the state has shown itself incapable—or, more likely, unwilling—to punish the criminal practices of state agents.

The problem, of course, is that the election of civilian governments does not necessarily mean that state institutions will operate democratically. Guillermo O'Donnell referred to this as passing from the "first transition"—away from authoritarian rule toward elected civilian government—to the "second transition"—institutionalizing democratic practices at all levels of the state. In many postdictatorship countries that lack a strong democratic tradition, the "second transition" has been immobilized by innumerable negative legacies of the authoritarian past.

This continuity suggests that, notwithstanding the political transitions to elected rule, the authoritarian regimes of the past and the new civilian democratic governments are barely differentiated expressions of the same system of domination by the same elites. Political democratization does not attack "socially rooted authoritarianism." This authoritarianism also persists in what could be called the "microdespotisms" of daily life, manifested as racism, sexism and elitism. The combination of a lack of democratic controls over the ruling classes and the denial of rights to the poor reinforces historical social hierarchies. Civil rights and the rule of law are little more than smokescreens for domination. As a consequence, only the middle and upper classes actually benefit from the effective control that democracy exercises over the means of violence in the social interactions of daily life. For the poor and destitute majority of the population, unchecked power continues to be the most visible face of the state.

State institutions charged with providing law and order are widely perceived as dysfunctional. A large percentage of Latin American citizens do not believe that their civilian governments have implemented—or have attempted to implement—the rule of law with equality and impartiality for all citizens. Formal guarantees enshrined in the Constitution and the legal code are systematically violated, largely because of the glaring gap between what the law says and the way the institutions charged with protecting and implementing the law—i.e., the police and the judiciary — function in practice.

In almost all Latin American countries, the poor see the law as an instrument of oppression at the service of the wealthy and powerful. The judicial system has been widely discredited for its venality, inefficiency and lack of autonomy. It is deficient in every respect: material resources are scarce; judicial procedures are excessively formalistic; judges are insufficiently trained; and too few judges oversee too many cases. Many judges, moreover, have been impotent to prosecute cases of organized crime, and some have even been linked to drug trafficking. In most countries of the region, the investigative capacity of the police is very limited, and a low percentage of investigated cases make it to the courts. Almost half of the nearly 5,000 homicides that occurred in Sao Paulo in 1995, for example, remain unsolved.

In most countries, the way the courts function is intimately linked to the hierarchical and discriminatory practices that mark social relationships. In Brazil, for example, the criminal-justice system has failed to investigate and prosecute numerous cases of rural violence against the poor. According to Brazil's Pastoral Land Commission, of the 1,730 killings of peasants, rural workers, trade union leaders, religious workers and lawyers committed between 1964 and 1992, only 30 had been brought to trial by 1992. Of those, only 18 resulted in convictions. In Chile, not a single assassin of the 1,542 trade unionists killed since 1986 has been successfully convicted. Throughout the continent, impunity is virtually assured for those who commit offenses against victims considered "undesirable" or "subhuman." As a result, those responsible for serious human rights violations go unpunished. And undeterred, they continue to commit other violations.

As a result of the failure of Latin America's democracies to rein in the police by imposing greater civilian controls, abusive practices against suspects and prisoners have become entrenched. The police in many countries have been criticized for the unjustified use of deadly force. In Chile, for example, the UN criticized the police for their policy of "shoot first, ask questions later." In Brazil and elsewhere, torture is still practiced in the majority of police inquiries. Accusations of torture are rarely investigated; when they are, those responsible are even more rarely punished.

Military police throughout Brazil continue to practice summary executions of suspects and criminals. In Sao Paulo, there are 18 killings by police a month, and in Rio de Janeiro, the monthly average is 24. Most of these deaths take place in the poor neighborhoods, and the victims are usually from the most vulnerable groups—the poor, the homeless and African Brazilians. The military police see the rule of law as an obstacle rather than an effective guarantee of social control; they believe their role is to protect society from "marginal elements" by any means available. Such killings enjoy broad support from elites as well as the poor—who are, after all, the largest category of victims of violent crime. In each of Brazil's 26 states, crimes committed by the police and military are tried in military-police courts. Made up of military officials and based on shoddy criminal investigations, these courts often sanction the impunity of acts like police killings and other violent crimes.

Police massacres—like the summary executions of 19 landless peasants in the northern state of Para in April—are all too frequent. In areas where rural conflict, largely over control of the land, is widespread, the police often act in collusion with large landowners and local politicians. On August 9, 1995 in Corumbiara, in the state of Rondonia, for example, ten squatters were killed when 200 military-police officers stormed a camp of 1,200 rural workers and their families who hoped to farm the land. Deadly force has also been frequently used to suppress prison riots. After a riot of more than 7,000 inmates at the House of Detention in Sao Paulo in February, 1992, the military police killed 111 detainees.

This series of killings and massacres in the countryside and in the city are the legacy of a militarized approach to public security. This approach was carried to its logical extreme in December, 1994 when the army occupied the city's slums in the hills of Rio de Janeiro. The government said the army occupation was necessary in order to regain control of these areas from the drug mafias. While some have referred to these areas as a "parallel state" because the police often refuse to enter them, these are not "occupied territories" that need to be "liberated" by the armed forces. In fact, the current situation of disrespect for the law continues in these areas largely because of the extensive association between organized crime, public officials, business people and state agents. Organized crime flourishes in these neighborhoods because public officials tolerate—and sometimes finance—these illicit activities, and because consumers among the elites assure a regular market, which is protected by the police. On the other hand, the populations of Rio's slums have been abandoned by public officials. Their main experience of state authority is extortion and illegal police repression. It is not surprising, then, that traffickers in the slums—usually adolescents acting as intermediaries for the real traffickers that live in the city—are venerated as benefactors when they distribute some crumbs from the enormous profits of their patrons in the form of jobs and protection. The army occupation of the favelas failed to put even a small dent in drug trafficking or in the criminal gangs that continue to terrorize the residents of these poor neighborhoods. Military strategies to fight crime—an approach that is increasingly common in many new democracies—are doomed to failure. Crime prevention requires more complex and subtle forms of intervention.

The massive delegitimization of the police and the criminal-justice system has led to a wave of vigilantism in poor neighborhoods throughout Latin America. Local groups carry out "justice" on their own and criminals caught en flagrante delicto are spontaneously lynched. Lynchings have become commonplace in Brazil, Peru and Venezuela. In a recent study, sociologist José de Souza Martins counted 515 lynchings in Brazil between 1970 to 1994, which resulted in a total of 366 deaths. In Brazil's largest cities, justicieros, or gunmen, are charged with maintaining order in poor neighbor-hoods. Merchants, and at times local neighborhood associations, often support these private "enforcers" of public order. The abundance of lynchings and justicieros indicates the ineffectiveness of state institutions charged with controlling violence and crime, and the degree to which the state has abdicated its role as provider of order and security to all citizens. These private acts of "justice" thus consolidate the cycle of illegality and violence.

Across the continent, an important network of human rights organizations has developed since the dictatorships. These organizations, in coordination with professional associations, environmentalists and indigenous-rights groups, have been organizing campaigns to deal with the problems of crime, impunity and human rights abuses. The organization Viva Rio, created in 1993 in the state of Rio de Janeiro, is an example of how groups in civil society have tried to build networks to confront the problem. Viva Rio includes religious activists, popular movements, business people, private foundations, churches and the media. In 1995, protesting crime and ongoing official impunity in Rio, the group organized a huge "walk for peace" along the central avenues of the city—the first large public demonstration in Brazil since the campaign for direct elections decades before. Bringing together grassroots groups, businesses and government, the organization is trying to tackle the problem of urban violence and how to integrate the city's slums into the larger metropolis.

While groups like Viva Rio face serious disadvantages in terms of resources and influence—and in some countries they are still subject to death threats and other forms of intimidation—their efforts represent remarkable attempts to defend vulnerable groups in society. At the same time, however, their work has been more difficult to define in the postdictatorship period. Under the dictatorships, human rights victims were predominantly small groups of political dissidents. It is harder to define the new victims, because they do not constitute a homogeneous and immediately identifiable group, and their numbers are infinitely greater. An additional obstacle is that poor people are often not aware of their rights. In addition, the illegal practices of state agents are widely viewed as acceptable by the population at large.

Despite the general failure of Latin American democracies to address the problem of official violence and impunity, there have been a handful of government attempts to tackle some of these problems. At the UN World Conference on Human Rights, which took place in Vienna in 1993, several countries championed the idea of trying to ensure human rights protection through special laws and government-assistance programs. The Australian and the Fallopian governments were the first to unveil their national plans, followed by Brazil's promise to implement a national human rights charter. The human rights charter includes 168 proposals, ranging from guidelines for police training to directives for a witness-protection program and assistance to the victims of violent crime. The reforms proposed by the current government of Fernando Henrique Cardoso, such as federally mandated investigations into human rights crimes, would radically change the status quo of arbitrary police violence and impunity. The Congress has already approved one of those reforms—transferring cases of intentional homicide committed by the military police from military to civilian courts.

Yet despite these positive developments, Brazil and other new democracies in Latin America are still far from being capable of assuring liberty and justice for all. In this context, governments that attempt to promote reforms to address the multifaceted problems of crime and impunity often find themselves in a no-win situation. The failure of the new democracies to respect their own laws, as well as their international obligations, has seriously compromised their legitimacy. As a result, these governments are likely to have difficulty garnering popular support for their reform efforts.

The current international conjuncture is not the most propitious for implementing redistributive policies that would reduce social polarization and for instituting principles of social justice. Globalization pushes Latin American countries toward greater integration into the world economy, but the only countries that are likely to accrue any benefits from this integration are those that have laid the requisite foundations for industrialization and development—by investing in human resources and physical infrastructure, raising productivity in the agricultural sector and promoting technological and managerial capacities at the microlevel. Since most Latin American countries have not laid these foundations, globalization will likely have disastrous consequences. "The countries which have not created these preconditions could end up globalizing prices without globalizing incomes," says economist Deepak Nayar. "In the process, a narrow segment of their population may be integrated with the world economy, in terms of consumption patterns or living styles, but a large proportion may be marginalized even further."

This is exactly what has happened in Latin America during the "lost decade" of the 1980s and beyond. In addition to traditional unemployment, in which many are simply "left behind" even as the economy grows, Latin American democracies must grapple with the problem of the "new poor" generated by technological competition and increasing globalization. Such economic and social imbalances—which lie at the root of inequality and victimization—cannot be corrected by the market alone. The state—as defender and promoter of human rights—has a critical role to play if these societies are to tackle the growing problem of poverty and the associated problems of crime and impunity. Only the state can provide consistent national programs to promote health and education—the preconditions for a social order, based not on the silence of official abuse and impunity, but on democracy and development.

2.4 How People View Democracy: Between Stability and Crisis in Latin America (2001)

MARTA LAGOS

Two decades after Latin America began returning from authoritarian rule to democracy, public opinion in the region remains conflicted and ambivalent. Three countries—Costa Rica, Uruguay, and, to some extent, Argentina—manifest levels of support for democracy, satisfaction with democratic functioning, and institutional trust comparable to those in the stable democracies of Western Europe. At the same time, the other 14 countries that have been regularly surveyed by the Latinobarémetro since 1995 show much more tentative patterns of democratic commitment, and a few may even be said to suffer at present from a crisis in public attitudes toward democracy. In most of Latin America, majorities of the public accept democracy as the best form of government, but in many countries there are also sizeable pockets of authoritarian sentiment. Most Latin American publics are also skeptical—if not actively cynical—about key institutions of democracy, and Latin Americans manifest some of the lowest levels of interpersonal trust observed anywhere in the world.

The picture that emerges from the latest survey of the Latinobarómetro, conducted during January–March 2000, is thus a mixed one. The initial euphoria evoked by democratic change has long since disappeared. There was, no doubt, too much enthusiasm on the part of analysts at the beginning of this wave of democratic change in Latin America. The difficulties in the way of democratic consolidation were not sufficiently conceptualized and appreciated. A few countries have made progress toward consolidation, but others have regressed.

What is most striking, perhaps, is the relative stability of public attitudes and values over the past five years in Latin America. Many countries in the region are far from showing sufficient changes in their political and social culture to indicate movement toward consolidation. In a few countries, such as Brazil, Paraguay, Venezuela, and Colombia, the most recent public-opinion data indicate that democracy is in serious difficulty. In most of the rest of the region, democracy is suspended somewhere between stability and crisis. It is neither consolidated nor in imminent danger. For these countries, the problem is not so much the threat of renewed authoritarianism but the existence of distinct, and in some ways diminished, forms of democracy.

Marta Lagos, "Between Stability and Crisis in Latin America," *Journal of Democracy*, Vol. 12, no. 1 (2001): 137–145. © National Endowment for Democracy and The Johns Hopkins University Press. Reprinted with permission of The Johns Hopkins University Press.

SUPPORT FOR DEMOCRACY

Political legitimacy constitutes the most important element of public opinion in a democracy. To what extent do Latin Americans believe that democracy is the best form of government for their country? To assess public opinion on this issue, the Latinobarómetro asks respondents to choose among the following three statements (also employed by the Eurobarometer): "Democracy is preferable to any other kind of government"; "In certain situations, an authoritarian government can be preferable to democracy"; or "It doesn't matter to people like me whether we have a democratic or nondemocratic government."

In the aggregate, across all the Latin American countries surveyed, support for democracy has been remarkably stable over the last few years, as has been support for the authoritarian option (see Table 1). Yet the stable regional average of 60 percent support for democracy masks some important trends within and distinctions among particular countries. Most striking is the sharp decline in support for democracy in Brazil, Paraguay, and Colombia. Since 1996, support for democracy has declined from 50 percent to 39 percent in Brazil, from 59 to 48 percent in Paraguay, and from 60 to 50 percent in Colombia. At the same time, openness to authoritarian rule has increased from 26 to 39 percent in Paraguay, while remaining stable at 24 percent in Brazil (the same as in Venezuela today) and increasing from 20 to 23 percent in Colombia. (Support for democracy in Mexico has also declined, from 53 to 45 percent, while the preference for authoritarian rule has increased from 23 to 34 percent. This change, however, was measured well in advance of the July 2000 presidential election of opposition candidate Vicente Fox, and any judgments about the current state of public opinion toward democracy in Mexico would best be made with data gathered subsequent to this historic democratic breakthrough.)

To put these numbers into perspective, Uruguay and Costa Rica manifest levels of support for democracy (84 and 83 percent, respectively) and authoritarianism (9 and 6 percent, respectively) comparable to those in the most democratic European countries. In the last several years, Argentina's support for democracy has also consistently topped 70 percent (with about 15 percent favoring authoritarian rule). In no other Latin American country today do two-thirds of the public express support for democracy (64 percent do so in Peru, Honduras, and Nicaragua). It is important to examine variation on this measure by social stratum as well as by country. It is striking that the better-educated are not necessarily more supportive of democracy. Our recent survey data also challenge the assumption that a new democratic cohort is being socialized throughout Latin America in the postauthoritarian era. Far from having absorbed a new democratic culture, younger people with medium to high levels of education tend to be indifferent to the type of political regime. The younger cohort does not seem to be ushering in the cultural orientations

Table 1
Support for Democracy

	1996		1998		2000	
	Democracy	Authoritarian	Democracy	Authoritarian	Democracy	Authoritarian
South America and Mexico						
Argentina	71	15	73	16	71	16
Bolivia	64	17	55	22	62	13
Brazil	50	24	48	18	39	24
Colombia	60	20	55	17	50	23
Chile	54	19	53	16	57	19
Ecuador	52	18	57	19	54	12
Mexico	53	23	51	28	45	34
Paraguay	59	26	51	36	48	39
Peru	63	13	63	12	64	13
Uruguay	80	9	80	9	84	9
Venezuela	62	19	60	25	61	24
AVERAGE	61	18	59	19	58	20
Central America						
Costa Rica	80	7	69	21	83	6
El Salvador	56	12	79	10	63	10
Guatemala	51	21	54	29	45	21
Honduras	42	14	57	9	64	15
Nicaragua	59	14	72	9	64	6
Panama	75	10	71	8	62	18
AVERAGE	61	13	67	15	64	13
Overall Latin American avg.	**61**	**17**	**62**	**17**	**60**	**17**

Survey questions: Which of the following statements do you agree with most? 1) Democracy is preferable to any other kind of government; 2) In certain situations, an authoritarian government can be preferable to democracy; 3) It doesn't matter to people like me whether we have a democratic or nondemocratic government.
Source: Latinobarómetro.

that would deepen and consolidate democracy in the region, nor do rising levels of education ensure stronger support for democracy.

A more balanced perspective on attitudes toward democracy can be gained from responses to two additional questions posed in the 1997 survey and repeated in 2000. Respondents were asked whether they thought that "without a national congress there can be no democracy," or rather, that "democracy can work without a national congress." The same question was asked with regard to political parties. On these two questions, we observe not stability but some signs of erosion in support for the institutions of representative democracy. In 1997, some 63 percent of Latin Americans surveyed believed that there could be no democracy without a national congress; in 2000, only 57 percent believe so. Similarly, the percentage of Latin Americans viewing political parties as essential to democracy declined from 62 percent in 1997 to 57 percent in 2000.

Again, the country data are revealing. From 1997 to 2000, the percentage of Venezuelans who could imagine democracy without a national congress increased from 38 to 57 percent. While 61 percent of Venezuelans say that democracy is the best form of government, it may increasingly be a populist, plebiscitarian democracy that they have in mind, responding to the model being constructed by President Hugo Chávez. In one of Latin America's most troubled democracies, Ecuador, where 54 percent of the people say that "democracy is best," the percentage believing that democracy is possible without a parliament increased from 47 to 62 percent. In no other Latin American country among the 17 surveyed does a majority of the population consider democracy possible without a national legislature. But the proportions believing so are also high in Paraguay (34 percent), Brazil (37 percent), Colombia (45 percent), and Panama (47 percent). The increase in Colombia (from 38 percent in 1997), and the parallel rise in the number of Colombians who believe that there can be democracy without parties (from 38 to 46 percent), provide additional evidence of the growing disillusionment with established democratic institutions.

In general, the responses by country to the question of parties are similar to those with respect to the congress. Together, they reinforce the standing of Uruguay, Costa Rica, and Argentina as the three countries that are most strongly democratic in attitudes and values, with 70 percent or more of the public in each viewing the congress and political parties as essential to democracy. Interestingly, El Salvador and Nicaragua also show strong democratic orientations on these twin measures (at or near the 70 percent mark), as they do on the question of preference for democracy, while in Chile, despite its long tradition of democratic parties, a third of the public says that democracy can work without political parties.

The erosion of support for democracy, particularly in its representative form, is no doubt being driven by the travails of democracy in the region. In Colombia and Venezuela, as well as in Ecuador, democracy's poor performance in recent years appears to have contributed to the decline of popular democratic commitment. Economic difficulties in these countries, as well as in Brazil and elsewhere in Latin America, are also a contributing factor. Statistical analysis shows that the assessment that respondents give of the current economic situation is a significant predictor of their support for democracy. The more positively they assess the current situation, the more likely they are to support democracy.

SATISFACTION WITH DEMOCRACY

We know from extensive survey data on the established European democracies that satisfaction with the way democracy works varies much more extensively over time than does support for democracy. Moreover, satisfaction with democracy is particularly sensitive to swings in economic conditions; it is also systematically lower than support for democracy. Support for democracy can coexist with relatively low levels of democratic satisfaction. But in a context where democratic legitimacy is only partially established and where citizens may exhibit low levels of trust in institutions and in one another, low levels of satisfaction can be another sign of future democratic difficulty or instability.

The question we employ (a 4-point scale of how satisfied respondents are with the way that democracy works in their country) has been used repeatedly in opinion barometers worldwide. It is a good measure of perceptions concerning the effectiveness of democracy in dealing with economic, social, and political problems (as opposed to more deep-seated and enduring feelings about the legitimacy of democracy). Yet when dissatisfaction persists over a long period of time, it may indicate democracy's inability to solve the problems that the people had hoped it would address, and this prolonged performance gap can erode popular support for the democratic regime.

The numbers are sobering. For example, only in Uruguay (69 percent), Costa Rica (61 percent) and Venezuela (55 percent)—in its current populist infatuation with Chávez as a leader—are majorities of the public satisfied with the way that democracy works (that is, they report that they are "very" or "fairly" satisfied with the way that democracy works, as opposed to "not very" satisfied or "not at all" satisfied). In Argentina and Panama, half the public expressed satisfaction in 2000. In most of the other countries surveyed, no more than a third of the public is satisfied, and in Brazil, Peru, Bolivia, Ecuador, Paraguay, and Nicaragua, the proportion is less than a quarter.

In Latin America on the whole, only 37 percent of the public are satisfied with the way that democracy works. Since 1996, the regional figure has never exceeded 41 percent (see Table 2). This compares with recent averages of 57 percent for the Southern European democracies and 53 percent for the EU countries, and an average of 48 percent for Ghana, Zambia, and South

Table 2
Satisfaction with Democracy in Latin America

	1996	1997	1998	2000
Very satisfied or fairly satisfied	27	41	37	37
Not very satisfied or not at all satisfied	65	56	59	60
Don't know or no answer	8	3	3	3

Africa (all surveyed in 1997). In Central America, satisfaction has declined from 57 percent in 1996 to 49 percent in 1997 and 39 percent in 2000. In South America and Mexico combined, satisfaction has hovered around 34 and 36 percent between 1997 and 2000 (up from 27 percent in 1996).

TRUST

The extent of dissatisfaction, even disenchantment, with democratic politics in Latin America becomes more sharply apparent when we examine the levels of public confidence, or trust, in various types of institutions. As can be seen in Table 3, most Latin Americans have at least some confidence in the Church (indeed, in most Latin American countries, a majority expresses "a lot" of confidence in the church). Television is trusted by almost half the public in Latin America, and the armed forces by half of the South American public (but only by a quarter in Central America, where the memories of civil war and human rights abuses are generally more recent). Political institutions command much less confidence among Latin Americans, however. Overall in Latin America, the courts are trusted by only 34 percent of the public, parliament by 28 percent, and parties by only 20 percent. Yet, as we shall see below, people in the region have more trust even in political parties (the institution with the lowest level of trust) than they do in one another. Central and South Americans exhibit virtually identical attitudes toward these political institutions. These levels of institutional trust, with the exception of trust in the Church, are not really any higher than the low levels recorded by Richard Rose and his colleagues in their study of postcommunist Europe, when one allows for the fact that the latter survey afforded the respondents a neutral position on the scale of institutional trust and distrust.

Writing in this journal [*Journal of Democracy*] four years ago, I suggested that low levels of trust in other people constitute a defining feature of Latin American political culture. Correlated with these low levels of interpersonal trust are very high levels of skepticism about the honesty and law-abidingness of fellow citizens. These low levels of confidence in other people, taken together with the generally low levels of institutional confidence indicated above, derive from and confirm "a common regional heritage of distrust." Underlying this culture are certain continuing social

Table 3

Trust in Institutions

Institution	1996	1997	1998	2000	CEU 1997–98
Church	76	74	78	77	46
Armed forces	42	42	38	43	49
Judiciary	33	36	32	34	29
President	n/a	39	38	39	44
Police	30	36	32	36	30
National congress	27	36	27	28	22
Political parties	20	28	21	20	13
Television	50	46	45	42	37

Note: Percentages are those expressing "a lot" or "some" (in contrast to "a little" or "no") confidence in various institutions. CEU indicates Central and Eastern Europe. This data is drawn from Richard Rose and Christian Haerpfer, "New Democracies Barometer V: A 12-Nation Survey, *Studies in Public Policy* 306 (Glasgow: University of Strathclyde, 1999).

patterns, including the hierarchical structure of authority at many levels and the passivity of citizens toward the patron, the local boss, and now the state. People are still accustomed to hoping that "someone" will solve their problems—in the past they turned to the patron, and more recently they have turned to the state. Now they look to democracy to solve all problems. It is even possible to interpret the data as saying that Latin Americans want democracy because they see it as a new type of patron. This interpretation suggests a people who want the rights but not the obligations of citizenship. In fact, 53 percent of Latin Americans consider themselves very demanding with respect to their rights, while only 36 percent say they are very conscious of their obligations and duties.

The 2000 Latinobarómetro reveals an even further decline in the overall level of interpersonal trust in the region, from 20 percent in 1996 to 16 percent in 2000 who say that "you can trust most people" (rather than that "you can never be too careful when dealing with others"). Altogether, institutions are trusted more than people. Even where support for democracy is strongest, as in Uruguay and Costa Rica, interpersonal trust is low and has declined sharply in the past two years (from 34 to 23 percent in Uruguay and from 34 to 13 percent in Costa Rica). In Argentina, trust fell from 23 to 12 percent in these two years. In Colombia, with its endemic political violence, trust has fallen from 32 percent in 1997 to 16 percent in 2000. In Brazil, which has one of the highest crime rates in the world, trust has practically disappeared, plummeting from 11 percent in 1996 to 4 percent today. Mexico remains the only one of our 17 countries in which more than a quarter of the population is trusting of others, and even there, trust has fallen from 43 percent in 1997 to 34 percent today.

These levels of social trust are low not only historically, but relative to other regions of the world. Data from the Eurobarometer and the 1995 World Values Survey indicate that in highly advanced societies the average level of interpersonal trust is about 60 percent. (It is, for example, 68 percent in Sweden and 50 percent in the United States.) The low levels of trust in Latin America derive from deeply rooted historical, social, and institutional factors, but the recent decline in trust is driven at least in part by social change. The social networks of family, friends, and work that sustained society in the past have been disbanded with the liberalization of markets and economic modernization of the last few years. These disappearing networks, however, have not been replaced by new support systems like those that exist in the United States, with its dense array of voluntary associations. Latin America thus consists of lonely populations who have a hard time finding support in an increasingly competitive world.

Latin America has never had formal support networks; its trust has always resided within the great field of *jus sanguinis* ("the right of blood"). Everything here runs on the basis of blood ties; where you come from determines to a great extent where you go. This is the time cycle that Gabriel García Márquez describes in *One Hundred Years of Solitude*. Our survey data provide little support for the possibility that Latin Americans will begin to look for support networks beyond *jus sanguinis*, in unknown third parties, because they have no trust in people whom they do not know.

Our data testify powerfully to the strength of traditional mores and the limited impact of new elements in the civic culture. In contrast, economic modernization and its consequences, generated by the strong economic growth in some countries of the region, produce the other well-known effects of development, like the substantial incorporation of women into the labor force, a decrease in fertility rates, the declining strength of families, an increase in divorce, and so on. These social factors, along with increasing disparities in income, heighten distrust, diminishing the possibilities for citizens to associate themselves with unknown third parties.

Low and declining levels of interpersonal trust thus constitute an important barrier to the accumulation of social capital and the development of a civil society that could provide crucial foundations for the stabilization, deepening, and consolidation of troubled, dissatisfied, cynical democracies. Interpersonal trust lies at the heart of attitudes toward institutions, democracy, politics, and the economy. Trust is a prerequisite for the development of effective political participation and for the operation of the rules of the democratic game. People who do not trust their peers will have difficulty trusting the leaders and institutions that represent them. This is the stubborn dilemma that Latin America confronts more than a decade after the return to civilian, democratic rule. Even where democracy appears to enjoy substantial popular legitimacy and to confront no immediate threat, it rests on shallow social foundations. The most fundamental challenge for Latin American democracy in the years ahead is how, amid the fragmenting pressures of globalization and economic liberalization, to generate social trust and to widen and reconstruct networks of social capital.

SUGGESTIONS FOR FURTHER READING

Agüero, Felipe, and Jeffrey Stark, eds. *Fault Lines of Democracy in Post-Transition Latin America.* Miami: North-South Center Press, 1998.

Beezley, William H., and Judith Ewell, eds. *The Human Tradition in Latin America.* Wilmington, Del.: Scholarly Resources, 1997.

Chalmers, Douglas, Carlos Vilas, Katherine Hite, Scott Martin, Kerianne Piester, and Monique Segarra, eds. *The New Politics of Inequality in Latin America: Rethinking Participation and Representation.* New York: Oxford University Press, 1997.

Cleary, Edward L. *The Struggle for Human Rights in Latin America.* Westport, Conn.: Praeger, 1997.

Colburn, Forrest D. *Latin America at the End of Politics.* Princeton, N.J.: Princeton University Press, 2002.

Dahl, Robert A. "Polyarchy," in *Participation and Opposition.* New Haven, Conn.: Yale University Press, 1971, 1–16, 33–47.

Diamond, Larry, Jonathan Hartlyn, Juan J. Linz, and Seymour Martin Lipset, eds. *Democracy in Developing Countries: Latin America,* 2nd ed. Boulder, Colo.: Lynne Rienner, 1999.

Garretón, Manuel Antonio, and Edward Newman, eds. *Democracy in Latin America (Re)Constructing Political Society.* Tokyo: United Nations University Press, 2001.

Mainwaring, Scott. *Rethinking Party Systems in the Third Wave of Democratization.* Pala Alto, Calif.: Stanford University Press, 1999.

O'Donnell, Guillermo. "Delegative Democracy," in *Counterpoints: Selected Essays on Authoritarianism and Democratization,* ed. Guillermo O'Donnell. Notre Dame, Ind.: University of Notre Dame Press, 1999.

O'Donnell, Guillermo, and Philippe C. Schmitter. "Tentative Conclusions about Uncertain Democracies," in *Transitions from Authoritarian Rule: Prospects for Democracy,* ed. Guillermo O'Donnell, Philippe C. Schmitter, and Laurence Whitehead. Baltimore: Johns Hopkins University Press, 1986, pp. 3–8, 15–47.

Peeler, John. *Building Democracy in Latin America.* Boulder, Colo.: Lynne Rienner, 1998.

Skidmore, Thomas E., and Peter H. Smith, eds. *Modern Latin America,* 5th ed. New York: Oxford University Press, 2001.

Stepan, Alfred. "Political Leadership and Regime Breakdown: Brazil," in *The Breakdown of Democratic Regimes: Latin America,* ed. Juan J. Linz and Alfred Stepan. Baltimore: Johns Hopkins University Press, 1978.

USEFUL WEBSITES

Freedom House: Provides a ranking of countries on political and civil liberties.
www.freedomhouse.org

Latin American Network Information Center: Comprehensive site housed at the University of Texas with extensive Latin American links on a wide array of topics.
http://Lanic.utexas.edu

Political Database of the Americas: Provides reference materials on a number of topics, such as civil society and political parties.
www.georgetown.edu/pdba/

Transparency International: International, private agency that uses surveys to produce corruption reports and rankings.
www.transparency.org

USAID: Democracy and Governance: Offers official U.S. perspective on issues of democracy throughout the world.
www.usaid.gov

World Movement for Democracy: Offers a comprehensive list of organizations in Latin American countries that are working for democracy.
www.wmd.org

CHAPTER 3

Neoliberal Economic Reform

READINGS IN THIS CHAPTER

*E*conomic policy in Latin America is arguably the most controversial issue in the region today and has been for the past two decades. Since the 1980s, almost all Latin American countries have been engaged in an economic reform project, typically referred to as "neoliberalism." The overall aim of neoliberal economic reform is to limit the state's involvement in the economy and to increase the role of markets. Government involvement in the economy can take the form of basic policies, such as tax and monetary policy, but it can also include trade policy, protection and/or promotion of domestic industries, regulation of businesses and labor markets, and even welfare policies. Governments typically make decisions about the economy for political reasons. Even when they have the best intentions—and that's not always the case—governments are prone to making errors about how to allocate their society's resources because they cannot accurately measure what consumers really need and want. Those errors lead to inefficiencies and imbalances in the economy that market mechanisms eliminate because they are much more adept at measuring the real level of demand for goods and services. For neoliberals, the key to economic prosperity is to "get prices right," that is, eliminate the distortions produced by government interference and allow the market mechanism and reliable price information to shape how individuals use their resources. Such an economy is more dynamic and more efficient and, therefore, can produce more wealth. For critics, neoliberalism makes the wealthy wealthier and has terrible social costs for the poor and even the middle class. Furthermore, the critics argue, the neoliberal program does not even generate the economic growth it promised in the 1980s when neoliberal economic philosophy was being refined. The debate over neoliberalism is particularly intense because, as we explain later in this introduction, in the past two decades Latin American governments have had little choice but to follow neoliberal prescriptions.

Latin American economic development has varied across the different countries, but a general pattern effectively characterizes the process in many, if not most, countries. From the late nineteenth century until roughly the start of the Great Depression, Latin American governments pursued a policy of economic liberalism (i.e., minimal government involvement) based on export of commodities, such as minerals or agricultural products, and import of manufactured goods. Governments derived their revenues from taxes on trade and were content to limit their role in the economy. They made no effort, for example, to promote industrialization. The emergence of labor unions forced these governments to get more involved in regulating labor markets and employer-employee relations, which happened largely through physical or legal coercion. The Great Depression changed the situation. The collapse of global trade deprived Latin Americans of the manufactured goods they depended on and adversely affected Latin American elites, who for the most part either individually controlled the commodity trade or did so in conjunction with foreign corporations. With elites economically weakened, Latin American governments devised a new economic policy that promoted domestic industry in order to produce the needed manufactured goods. The new policy eventually acquired the label "import-substitution industrialization" (ISI) and a theoretical justification developed by Raúl Prebisch of the United Nations Economic Commission for Latin America and the Caribbean. The new program used protectionism and government subsidies to promote domestic industries that could substitute local production for the hard to obtain imported goods. The policy had a rapid economic effect as it generated significant growth and helped foster large increases in the size of the middle and working classes. It turned out to be appealing politically as well because in its initial stages it facilitated the construction of new political coalitions that joined industry, the middle class, and the working class together in support of the economic program.

The initially positive results of the new policy did not last, however. Import-substitution industrialization quickly revealed itself to be a flawed economic program. ISI tended to stoke high rates of inflation, created or exacerbated balance of payments problems (having sufficient foreign currency, such as dollars, to engage in trade and pay foreign debts), and ultimately even stopped generating growth. By the late 1950s and early 1960s, ISI appeared exhausted as an economic strategy and many Latin American governments turned back to foreign corporations to help renew growth. In many instances, the change in ISI to greater reliance on foreign corporations led to or intensified political conflicts between workers and owners and between domestic and international capitalists. In many countries, democracy broke down in a context of weakened economic performance and intensified political struggle.

Economic strategy shifted again in the 1970s after the 1973 oil shock. The Arab oil embargo drove oil prices up sharply with harsh consequences for all oil-importing nations. It also produced a new source of financing for developing countries. The oil revenues from the Arab oil exporters circulated back into the Western banking system. Banks, in turn, sought new borrowers. Latin American governments wrestling with the effects of the oil shock were eager borrowers, often on risky terms, such as floating interest rates. When the second oil shock of 1979 hit, many Latin American nations, especially Argentina, Brazil, and Mexico were heavily indebted, which started a process that led to Latin America's debt crisis. In 1982 Mexico defaulted on its debt. As a consequence of Mexico's default, further bank lending to Latin America virtually dried up, leaving governments throughout the region facing serious recessions and brutal debt obligations without the resources to address them. It was an untenable situation and it effectively put an end to ISI as an economic program. Thus, as Latin America entered the 1980s—a period referred to as the "lost decade"— governments throughout the region were imposing harsh policies to squeeze any available resources out of society in order to meet the obligations of the debt.

It was in that context that neoliberalism emerged as a policy solution for Latin America. Champions of the new economic policy appeared in both domestic and international agencies and institutions. Many of the ideas of this so-called new liberalism were connected to the economics program at the University of Chicago and were brought to Latin America by Latin American graduates of the program. In fact, neoliberal ideas were first put to the test in Chile after 1973 by the government of General Augusto Pinochet. His economic team consisted of a group of PhDs in economics from the University of Chicago—frequently referred to as the "Chicago Boys." The economic team vigorously applied neoliberal policy well before it reached any other Latin American nation. Many adherents of neoliberalism in many Latin American nations were content to take advantage of the crisis to advance their beliefs about policy. These individuals and groups allied with international creditors and agencies and pressured governments to adopt the economic policy reforms. Agencies such as the International Monetary Fund, the World Bank, and the United States Treasury Department required Latin American governments to implement neoliberal reforms in order to secure new loans or roll over existing ones. The outside pressure led many to refer to the set of reforms as the "Washington Consensus." In some instances, outside pressure *was* the driving force behind reform. In others, domestic reformers played an important role. In any event, some ten to fifteen years after the start of the process, the results remain uncertain and the prescription for Latin America's economic future remains the subject of intense disagreement.

Duncan Green provides a basic account of import-substitution industrialization and traces its transition to neoliberal economic reform in the chapter's first reading, "State versus Market: The Rise and Fall of Import Substitution." Green shows how failings in the international marketplace in the context of the Great Depression and World War II led domestic policy-makers to move toward substituting local production of manufactured goods for imported ones. He also shows, however, how ISI failed to generate efficient production of quality goods. The narrative then traces the fall of ISI through the debt crisis and the way advocates of neoliberal reform triumphed politically and in the realm of ideas.

In "What Washington Means by Policy Reform," John Williamson, one of the leading intellectual voices for neoliberal reform, details the precise list of ten reforms that constitute the Washington Consensus. These reforms all involve diminishing the role of the state, eliminating state policies that affect prices, and increasing the market's role in determining how and why individuals make decisions about how to use their resources.

In the third reading, James Mahon offers a current assessment of the Washington Consensus and finds that the state of the Consensus is not very healthy. After more than a decade of neoliberal reforms, Latin American nations have progressed considerably on most reform dimensions, but the results have not been uniformly positive. While the reforms brought some gains, there have been several negative trends, especially in the last years of the 1990s and into the new millennium. In particular, the region has been suffering from growing scarcity of investment funds, primarily due to changes in the domestic markets of rich countries. Unfortunately, Latin American nations are tightly constrained by their need for external financing from these countries. The result is that they have little flexibility in how they respond to the downside of neoliberal reforms. This financial straightjacket has not led to a reversal of the reform process yet, but it threatens to undermine its continued political support in the future.

Finally, Carlos Vilas offers one last critical argument about neoliberal reform. In Vilas's view, the emphasis on "getting prices right" forces states to cut their spending. But the only places they are able to cut spending are in discretionary areas, typically programs for health, education, housing, and other public welfare programs that affect the poor the most. For Vilas, cutting back these protections in societies already characterized by high levels of poverty and inequality amounts to a "dismantling of citizenship."

The data tables presented in this chapter illustrate the consequences of neoliberal economic reform and highlight some of the enduring challenges in the region. On the positive side, the data show that neoliberal economic reform has had some success in promoting modest economic growth, renewing foreign investment flows to the region, and, perhaps most strikingly, taming inflation. On the negative side, however, growth has not been as robust as the proponents of neoliberalism hoped, while unemployment levels have remained high and real wages have stagnated. Thus, neoliberalism has produced less than promised while inflicting more pain on populations already suffering from high levels of poverty and inequality—the twin economic dilemmas that have plagued Latin America continuously since before independence.

DATA TABLES

Table 3.1
Economic Data, Average Performance, 1987–1998

Country	Investment/ GDP	Foreign Direct Investment/GDP	GDP Growth	Fiscal Deficit	CPI (inflation)	Real Wages	Interest/ Exports
Argentina	21	1.3	3.3	-1.7	553	-3.6	29.7
Barbados	15	0.5	1.2	-2.2	3.9	-1.5	2.5
Bolivia	15	2.4	3.8	-4.5	12.7	4.0	26.0
Brazil	22	0.8	2.0	-3.0	1,048.0	-1.5	24.1
Chile	28	3.1	2.0	3.0	14.6	3.5	13.6
Colombia	28	2.6	4.1	-0.5	24.5	1.9	16.3
Costa Rica	27	3.7	3.9	-1.8	18.3	1.5	12.1
Dominican Republic	29	3.1	4.3	0.91	23.3	1.47	9.1
Ecuador	20	2.1	2.8	-2.5	42.3	-0.1	25.6
El Salvador	17	0.3	4.3	-2.0	15.0	-3.0	9.1
Honduras	28	1.7	3.8	-4.3	17.2	0.98	16.6
Jamaica	28	2.3	2.3	0.56	26.4	—	14.5
Mexico	23	2.2	2.6	-3.0	39.8	1.2	17.6
Nicaragua	27	3.5	0.19	-8.1	2,382.0	2.1	80.5
Paraguay	22	1.8	3.6	0.57	19.8	0.9	7.3
Peru	25	2.3	1.9	-2.8	1,106.0	-5.9	33.2
Trinidad and Tobago	13	5.2	0.44	-1.7	7.6	-5.6	10.2
Uruguay	14	0.6	3.5	-0.96	57.9	0.52	13.5
Venezuela	17	1.2	2.72	-2.7	50.6	-5.8	13.8

Source: Inter-American Development Bank, Annual Report, Washington, D.C., 2001.

Table 3.2

Poverty Index, Unemployment Rate, and Economic Freedom Score

Country	Gini Coefficient (survey year)	Average Unemployment Rate (%), 2001	Economic Freedom Score, 2002
Argentina	—	17.4*	2.5
Belize	—	—	2.7
Bolivia	44.7 (1999)	8.5*	2.7
Brazil	60.7 (1998)	6.2*	3.1
Chile	56.7 (1998)	9.1	1.9
Colombia	57.1 (1996)	18.2*	2.9
Costa Rica	45.9 (1997)	5.8*	2.7
Cuba	—	4.1	4.8
Dominican Republic	47.4 (1998)	15.6	3.0
Ecuador	43.7 (1995)	10.4*	3.5
El Salvador	52.2 (1998)	7.0	2.1
Guatemala	55.8 (1998)	3.8 (1998)	2.8
Honduras	56.3 (1998)	6.3*	3.2
Mexico	53.1 (1998)	2.5*	2.9
Nicaragua	60.3 (1998)	10.7	3.2
Panama	48.5 (1997)	16.9*	2.7
Paraguay	57.7 (1998)	10.8*	3.1
Peru	46.2 (1996)	9.3*	2.8
Uruguay	42.3 (1989)	15.3*	2.6
Venezuela	49.5 (1998)	13.4	3.7

Source: Data from *Latin America and the Caribbean: Selected Economic and Social Data, 2001/2002.* Washington, D.C.: United States Agency for International Development, May 2003.

Notes: *Gini coefficient* is a number from 1 to 100 that measures the inequality of the distribution of income in society. The higher the number the more unequal the society.

Economic Freedom Score is a measure of the economic freedom that exists in a country: 1 = most free; 5 = least free. The Heritage Foundation defines *economic freedom* as the absence of government control or coercion of the production, distribution, and consumption of goods and services.

*Unemployment rates in major urban areas only.

3.1 State versus Market: The Rise and Fall of Import Substitution (1995)

DUNCAN GREEN

Anybody who has ever used a Brazilian disposable nappy (diaper) will probably have first-hand experience of how import substitution failed the consumer. They didn't work. Until recently, Brazil's nappies were treacherous things, liable to leak or spring open with disastrous consequences for your carpet. The tale of the Brazilian disposable is a microcosm of what went wrong with much of Brazil's industry, stemming from the flawed model for economic development adopted in Latin America after the 1930s.

The offending items were made by Brazilian workers in a Brazilian factory. They were protected by import taxes against competition from better-quality foreign varieties. The taxes were originally designed to encourage the development of a Brazilian nappy industry, thereby reducing the economy's reliance on manufactured imports. However, protection also absolved the manufacturer from having to worry about quality or keeping prices down.

This is particularly true because the market is so small in Brazil. Only one Brazilian baby in forty wears disposables—the poor majority can't afford them, and many of the rich prefer to pay the poor to wash their babies' cloth nappies rather than buy disposables. Consequently, there was little room in the market for more than a few producers, who could fix prices between themselves to prevent competition. The consumer was the loser.

Like many of the beneficiaries of Brazilian protectionism, the producer was a transnational company, Johnson & Johnson. It had built a factory in Brazil in 1975, 'tariff hopping' to take advantage of the protected market, where it had an effective monopoly. It could undoubtedly have invested to upgrade the quality, but in the absence of competition, why bother? When the Brazilian government tried to open up the economy to imports, Johnson & Johnson did their utmost to prevent it:

> The Argentine nappies on sale in Mappins, one of the country's largest store chains, at half the price of Brazilian ones, required a long battle. When Mappins began the imports, trucks were held up on the border while Johnson & Johnson, which monopolises the Brazilian nappy market, found a helpful bureaucrat with an ancient regulation classifying nappies as pharmaceutical products which could be imported only if accompanied by a qualified pharmacist, transported and kept in cold storage.

Faced with a small local market, Johnson & Johnson might have tried to cut costs by exporting to other countries. This would allow them to increase output, bringing economies of scale which would lower the unit cost. But who would buy an over-priced, substandard Brazilian nappy? The problem recurs throughout Brazilian industry. A 1990 study of the performance of 220 São Paulo companies showed them to be "generally dozens or hundreds of times worse than that necessary to compete on world markets."

Yet even in Brazil, routinely branded by the financial press as the laggard of the silent revolution, times are changing. The imports from Argentina eventually got past the bureaucratic hurdles and broke Johnson & Johnson's monopoly. In the years that followed, a number of competitors got in on the act, both importing and producing locally. By late 1993 prices were down to about a third of their former levels and Johnson & Johnson had been driven into third place in the nappy market, behind brands such as Procter & Gamble's Pampers. The quality of life (and carpet) of a small number of disposable-dependent foreigners and wealthy Brazilians undoubtedly improved, lending further support to the arguments in favour of the switch from import substitution to the free market.

Brazil was something of a late convert to the merits of the market. In the rest of Latin America the state-versus-market pendulum, which had swung so completely to the side of the state in the 1950s, reached the opposite extreme in the early 1980s, in the first days of the debt crisis. Free marketeers in the US and Latin America hailed the demise of import substitution as proof that the state should stay out of running the economy. Governments were inherently bureaucratic, inefficient and corrupt and always put short-term political advantage before long-term economic prosperity, they argued. The only way forward was the standard IMF recipe of deregulation, privatization and free trade, which would free the region from the dead hand of statism and let Adam Smith's "invisible hand" of the market lead it to a golden dawn of prosperity and growth.

One of the strongest cards in neo-liberalism's hand is its self-belief. Its diagnosis and cure are presented as common sense: the market is obviously more efficient than the state; free trade has to be better for growth than protectionism; the state should not spend more than it earns. As one US critic complained, "So completely do the free market ideas of neoliberalism dominate the current Latin American debate that opposing ideas are increasingly treated with the bemused condescension usually reserved for astrological charts and flat-earth manifestos." At a seminar in London's Institute of Latin American Studies, Paul Luke of Morgan Grenfell Debt Arbitrage and Trading (a man introduced as "the leading City analyst on Latin America") caused barely a stir when he informed his audience in urbane tones of absolute certainty that "protectionism is obviously bad for growth" (Japan? Taiwan?) and that in Latin America only those of "low IQ" (among whom he included the recently elected Venezuelan president Rafael Caldera) dissented from the basic neo-liberal recipe. Like Mrs. Thatcher's grocer's shop analogy of the British economy, the arguments convince because they are simple and endlessly repeated. But are they right? Furthermore, if they are so obvious, why did Latin America (or the US or Europe) ever opt for anything else?

Since independence in the early nineteenth century, debt crises have scourged Latin America at roughly 50-year intervals—the 1820s, 1870s, 1930s and 1980s. Each crisis has swept away the previous economic model and laid the basis for the next 50-year experiment. Each birth has been painful and each model has entailed more losers than winners in Latin America's historic search for the road to long-term development. After the crisis of the 1820s, Latin America chose an export-led model based on selling raw materials (commodities) to North America and Europe. After the second crisis in the 1870s, the larger republics began some modern manufacturing. The disastrous world depression of the 1930s set Latin America on the path of vigorous import substitution which duly came unstuck in the "lost decade" of the 1980s. At the beginning of each change of direction, successive generations of economists and politicians were just as convinced as Juan Carlos Aguilar in his office in La Paz that their way was the only way; it was just "common sense."

Up until the 1930s Latin America's economy depended on exporting raw materials to the industrialized world in order to earn hard currency with which to buy manufactured products. Following the Wall Street Crash of 1929 and the ensuing depression in Europe and North America, this classic free-trade model fell apart. World coffee prices fell by two-thirds, cutting Brazil's exports from $446m in 1929 to just $181m by 1932. In El Salvador the coffee slump drove impoverished workers to rebel in 1932, ending in an army massacre of 30,000 peasants which virtually wiped out the country's Indian population. Most of Latin America in the 1930s experienced growing poverty, social unrest, repression, economic recession and defaults on the foreign debt. Latin America's export markets disappeared, and economies starved of hard currency had drastically to curtail imports.

IMPORT SUBSTITUTION

What began as emergency measures to produce goods which could no longer be bought abroad eventually grew into the fully-fledged model of import substitution, which became the unchallenged economic gospel in Latin America after the Second World War. Import substitution's theoretical foundations were mainly laid by the UN's Economic Commission for Latin America and the Caribbean (known by its Spanish acronym, CEPAL). Free trade had failed the region, and "common sense" dictated that the state should intervene to encourage national industry and protect its citizens from the cold winds of the world market.

Import substitution built on the ideas of John Maynard Keynes, whose arguments for state management of the economy had inspired New Deal economics in the US and the creation of the welfare state in Britain. At its height, import substitution's brand of state-led development was the unquestioned orthodoxy of the age. "In the 1960s the economics department taught you Keynes and *Cepalismo*," says Humberto Vega, Chile's donnish chief of the Treasury. "Classical economics was only taught in economic history! The role of the state was obvious, no one argued with it, not even the right, which was very protectionist." Soviet industrialization and the heavily state-led revival of the European economy after the Second World War had further established the centrality of the state in successful economic planning.

The state stepped in with a "big push" to redirect the economy away from its dependence on primary exports and kickstart it into producing manufactured goods for the domestic market. To achieve this, it:

- invested heavily in the kind of infrastructure required by industry, such as new roads, water and electricity supplies;
- kept labour costs down in urban areas by subsidizing basic foods and imposing price controls;
- protected local industries against foreign competition by imposing import taxes and "non-tariff barriers" such as import quotas;
- nationalized key industries such as oil, utilities and iron and steel, and established new ones. This produced a large state sector, intended to play a leading role in developing the economy;
- supported an overvalued exchange rate, making Latin America's exports expensive and imports cheap. This hurt exports, but helped industry by reducing the price of imported machinery and inputs, while tariff and non-tariff barriers ensured that the relative cheapness of imports did not undercut their products. An overvalued exchange rate also kept inflation down by ensuring cheaper imports.

The new economic model went hand in hand with the political phenomenon known as populism. Charismatic leaders such as Juan Domingo Perón (Argentina), Lázaro Cárdenas (Mexico) or Getulio Vargas (Brazil) preached a message of nationalist development and became the darlings of the new urban masses. Such men made brilliant leaders, but poor economists. They avoided politically divisive decisions over how to distribute wealth, preferring to print enough money to keep everyone happy in the short term. They bequeathed an inflationary legacy with which the region is still grappling.

Although now widely derided by the new generation of liberal economists, import substitution transformed the region's economy. By the early 1960s, domestic industry supplied 95 per cent of Mexico's and 98 per cent of Brazil's consumer goods. From 1950 to 1980 Latin America's industrial output went up six times, keeping well ahead of population growth. Infant mortality fell from 107 per 1,000 live births in 1960 to 69 per 1,000 in 1980; life expectancy rose from 52 to 64 years. In the mid-1950s, Latin America's economies were growing faster than those of the industrialized West.

Industrialization transformed the continent's economy. In what had previously been a predominantly rural, peasant society, great cities sprang up in an unplanned sprawl of cheap concrete tower blocks, dirty factories, flyovers and congestion. Rich, smart central districts with luxury shopping malls and mirror-glass skyscrapers were dwarfed by the vast shanty towns of the poor which ring all the major cities, epitomizing the sharp inequalities of wealth in the region. Convinced by their own boom-time, we-can-do-anything rhetoric, the Brazilian military embarked on huge road and dam-building sprees. In 1968 and 1970 Mexico City hosted the Olympics and the World Cup to announce its arrival as an international capital. The state played the pivotal role in achieving this transformation.

Import substitution also changed the political face of the continent, as leaders like Perón and Vargas built their support on the burgeoning urban working class. Especially in its earlier phase (before the Brazilian military coup of 1964), this broadened political participation to new areas of society, building up a strong trade union movement (albeit often with an unhealthily close relationship with the state) and greatly strengthening democratic politics.

Brazil and Mexico were the success stories of import substitution. Between 1960 and 1979 they increased their share of Latin America's industrial output from 50 per cent to over 60 per cent and attracted over 70 per cent of foreign direct investment over the same period. Brazil, whose industrial output per person went up over fourfold between 1950 and 1970, became Latin America's economic giant, producing a third of the regional GDP by 1981, making it the seventh largest industrial producer in the world.

Yet the cracks were already beginning to show by the late 1950s. Industrialization was capital-intensive, and failed to generate the expected number of new jobs for the region's unemployed masses. Transnational companies proved particularly ineffective in creating new jobs. The result was a two-tier labour force, a small "aristocracy of labour" employed in the modern industrial sector of the economy, and a mass of un- or under-employed workers elsewhere.

Sheltered by tariff barriers, industries became inefficient, producing shoddy and expensive goods for consumers who had no choice. In 1969 the Chilean domestic prices of electric sewing machines, bicycles and home refrigerators were respectively three, five and six times higher than international prices. The small domestic markets for such goods were usually dominated by a few companies, who established "oligopolies," fixing prices between themselves and thereby avoiding the pressures of competition which might have forced them to invest more and produce better quality goods. "Before it was easy to be a businessman in Argentina, with subsidies, speculation and protection," says the country's president and leading neo-liberal crusader, Carlos Menem. "This was a country of rich businessmen and poor companies." Local middle classes soon came to equate local manufacture with low standards. When Argentina liberalized imports in the late 1970s, the shops of Buenos Aires would plaster their windows with signs saying *todo importado,* "everything imported," to attract customers.

Although import substitution successfully ended the need to import some goods, especially consumer durables like cars and TVs, it merely replaced that dependence with a new kind, stemming from industry's reliance on imported capital goods such as heavy machinery, turbines and cranes. This meant that Latin America did not solve its trade deficit. The overvalued exchange rates and priority given by government to producing for the domestic market made matters worse, as neglected and uncompetitive exports failed to keep up with booming imports.

Countries undergoing import substitution were dogged by the economic consequences of inequality, which the model further exacerbated. Only a small proportion of the people in most Latin American republics actually functioned as consumers for the new industries—the great majority were too poor to buy anything. In all but the largest countries, such as Brazil and Mexico, the domestic market was therefore too small for fledgling industries to achieve the necessary economies of scale. Foreign companies were particularly reluctant to invest outside the big economies for this reason. Few governments were willing to undertake the kind of fundamental redistribution of wealth required to create a sizeable domestic market. Instead, they opted for regional free trade agreements, hoping that by grouping the middle classes of, for example, all the Central American countries, they could reach the market size required for industrial take-off. In practice, these agreements soon foundered, as they worked to the benefit of the stronger economies, and the weaker ones quickly pulled out.

Knowing that the government would always bail them out in the end, many (though not all) state industries proved inefficient producers, saddling the treasury with large operating losses. The widespread subsidies and increased state spending on social services as well as state investment further contributed to chronic government spending deficits. When governments covered these by printing money, inflation started to gather pace.

Import substitution was particularly disastrous for the countryside, which was starved of public investment and social services as the government gave priority to urban areas. Peasants selling their harvests suffered when price controls were imposed on their crops, while import substitution's overvalued exchange rates also encouraged a flood of cheap food imports which undercut local farmers. The deepening misery in the countryside, coupled with the industrial boom in the cities, provoked a massive spate of migration. Between 1950 and 1980, 27 million people left their farms and villages and joined the great exodus to the cities.

Other aspects of government policy benefited rural areas, however. In the wake of the Cuban revolution, the US promoted land reform throughout the region via President Kennedy's Alliance for Progress. Limited amounts of land were distributed, and credit provided for small farmers through the state banking system in countries such as Chile, Colombia and Venezuela.

The neglect of the countryside, where most of Latin America's poorest people live, along with the failure to generate jobs, meant that import substitution had a negative effect on income distribution. The region became increasingly polarized between rich and poor, the worst offender being Brazil, where from 1960 to 1970 every social class increased its income, but the bulk of the increase went to the rich. The richest 10 per cent of Brazilians increased their share of total income from 28 per cent to 48 per cent. Today, according to admittedly patchy UN figures, Brazil is the second most unequal country in the world (after Botswana); the richest fifth of the population earns 32 times more than the poorest fifth. Modern Brazil is a country of extraordinary contrasts, from the blighted rural north-east, where conditions are as bad as many of the poorest parts of Africa, to the high-rise opulence of downtown Rio or São Paulo.

Import substitution also deepened Latin America's love-hate relationship with transnational companies. Although nationalists objected to the transnationals' repatriation of profits and the limited benefits they brought to the rest of the economy, Latin America's leaders saw them as a vital source of technology and capital, both in short supply in the region. Especially from the 1960s, transnationals extended their grip on the most dynamic sectors of the economy, leaving the more sluggish industries to local capital. The stranglehold exerted by the transnationals allowed the state to neglect spending on research and development (R&D), leading to a growing technology gap between Latin America and the North. This gap made it even more difficult for Latin American–owned companies to break into the fastest growing areas of world trade, such as electronics and pharmaceuticals, which are also the areas of most rapidly developing technology.

As the flaws in the model became apparent, governments modified their policies. From the late 1960s onwards, countries such as Brazil and Mexico gave increased priority to manufactured exports to try and fill their growing trade gaps. Although Mexico's sudden oil bonanza in the late 1970s meant it temporarily lost interest in industrial exports, Brazil achieved some extraordinary results. Following the military coup of 1964, a combination of devaluation (to increase exports' competitivity) and the army's ruthless suppression of labour to bring down wages, led to the "economic miracle" of 1967–73; manufacturing exports tripled in the three years to 1973. Having already built factories in Latin America to produce for the protected local markets, transnational companies were best placed to turn their attention to exports, and dominated the export boom in Mexico and Brazil. In the region as a whole, manufactured exports increased forty-fold from 1967 to 1980, but even then they represented only a fifth of industrial output, which remained predominantly directed at the local market, and the continued reliance on imported capital goods meant that the trade gap in manufactures continued to grow.

THE DEBT CRISIS

The final decline of import substitution began with the sudden rise in world oil prices in 1973. The billions of "petrodollars" which OPEC countries recycled onto the world's financial markets had to go somewhere, and western banks fell over themselves to lend to Third World governments. The banks fell into the trap of believing, in the words of Citicorp chairman Walter Wriston, that "a country does not go bankrupt" as a private company could. Understandably, the Latin American governments flocked to borrow at the low or even negative real interest rates being offered by the banks. They believed such rates would be permanent, enabling them both to grow their way out of poverty and pay off their debts. Almost everyone had a good reason to borrow: Brazil was faced with an acute foreign exchange crisis and as its oil import bill soared, it chose to borrow abroad to keep importing the oil, machinery and inputs it needed for its industrial growth. The economy kept on growing, but so did Brazil's foreign debt. By 1978 its debt service took up 64 per cent of its export income.

> [From 1978–82] Brazil borrowed $63.4bn, well over half of its total gross foreign debt, in a frenzied, and eventually useless attempt to avoid default. Almost all of this money did not even enter Brazil, but stayed with the foreign banks ($60.9bn) . . . [Brazil was forced to] contract a huge paper debt that it would later be forced to honour through the export of real goods. It was a financial con trick on an unprecedented scale.

In other oil-importing countries such as Chile and Argentina, the neoliberals made their first appearance on the scene following bloody military coups in 1973 and 1976 respectively. The military governments chose not to try and grow their way out of trouble, opting instead for an end to import substitution and the sudden removal of import barriers. The results were catastrophic, as both countries went through a swift deindustrialization involving a spate of bankruptcies and job losses. The Argentine military opted for a particularly spectacular form of industrial suicide by removing import controls and tariffs at the same time as leaving the peso massively overvalued; the result was a flood of artificially cheap imports. Argentina's consumer goods imports increased over five times between 1975 and 1981, while local industrial output fell by 3 per cent a year over the same period. Since the import boom had to be paid for with foreign borrowing, the Argentine and Chilean debts rose just like the Brazilian one, but without the benefit of industrialization.

In Mexico, the advent of the OPEC price rise just as massive new oil finds came on stream ought to have been good news. But the government borrowed massively to build up the oil industry. Pemex, the state oil giant, ran up a company debt of $15bn by the early 1980s.

Although some of the proceeds from aid and oil exports went into building up heavy and export industries, far more was spirited out of the country into US banks as capital flight. As loans poured in, dollars also poured out, as government officials or business leaders siphoned as much as possible into US bank accounts. In many cases this involved corruption, such as taking kickbacks on government contracts, but in Venezuela and Mexico, for example, it was quite legal to export dollars into a US account. Estimates of the extent of capital flight vary wildly, but according to one World Bank report: "Between 1979–82, $19.2bn left Argentina, $26.5bn left Mexico and $22bn left Venezuela: 64 per cent, 48 per cent and a staggering 137 per cent respectively of the gross capital inflows to those countries." The Bank concluded, "Much of the money being borrowed from abroad was funnelled straight out again." Even in 1986, at the height of austerity, one banker confessed that his bank regularly "sends a guy with two empty suitcases" to Mexico City to pick up dollar deposits.

The "dance of the millions," as the influx of petrodollars became known, also coincided with a period of military rule in Latin America; from 1972–82 arms imports grew at an annual rate of 13 per cent. In 1986, the Peruvian Foreign Minister estimated that Latin America's total defence spending over the previous 10 years came to over $114bn, roughly half the region's entire foreign debt.

It seemed that whatever a Latin American government's policies, the temptation of cheap foreign capital seduced it into running up huge debts in the 1970s. One of the few exceptions was Colombia, which refused to be sucked into the borrowing frenzy and consequently, in economic terms at least, was an island of growth and falling poverty and inequality throughout the 1980s. Even Chile's first attempt at neo-liberal reform under Pinochet foundered under the weight of debt—Chile's economy was actually worse hit than any other by the initial shock of the debt crisis. Brazil, Mexico and Argentina became the Third World's top three debtors. The flood of foreign borrowing allowed Latin America to stave off the collapse of import substitution for a few more years, but the delay proved expensive in both financial and human terms.

Outside the region, the world economy and political thinking had changed radically since the days of Keynesian consensus in the 1950s. In the late 1960s, the unprecedented global economic boom of the post-war years began to run into trouble, and both Keynesianism and import substitution came under academic siege from a new generation of economic liberals. The resurgent free marketeers argued for a sharp cut in the state's role in the economy, and took over the commanding heights of the world economy with the elections of Margaret Thatcher (1979) and Ronald Reagan (1980). The monetarist obsession with reducing inflation supplanted Keynesian concerns with full employment and the welfare state. In just twenty years, the roles had been reversed: neo-liberalism had become the common sense of the day, and statism consigned to the junkyard of history.

For Latin America the problems began with the second big oil price rise of 1979. A new generation of First World conservative leaders reacted to rising global inflation by raising interest rates. The move prompted a deep recession in their own economies, which formed the main markets for Latin American exports. Latin America had to pay higher interest rates just as its exports began to fall; the sums no longer added up. In August 1982, the crash finally came when Mexico announced it was unable to meet its debt repayment obligations. Latin America's "lost decade" had begun.

The debt crisis which broke over the continent in August 1982 brought in its wake recession and hardship for millions of Latin Americans. But for Sir William Ryrie, a top World Bank official, it was "a blessing in disguise." The debt crisis forced Latin America into a constant round of debt negotiations, providing the Reagan government, along with the IMF and the other international financial institutions with all the leverage they needed to overhaul the region's economy, in alliance with northern commercial creditor banks and the region's home-grown free-marketeers. Latin America was ripe for a free-market revolution.

WINNING THE ARGUMENT

Ideas are powerful, as Keynes observed:

> The ideas of economists and political philosophers, both when they are right and when they are wrong, are more powerful than is commonly understood . . . I am sure that the power of vested interests is vastly exaggerated compared with the gradual encroachment of ideas . . . Soon or late, it is ideas, not vested interests, which are dangerous, for good or evil.

Critics of neo-liberalism often talk as if Washington, the IMF and the World Bank have single-handedly imposed neo-liberalism on a uniformly reluctant continent. While the Fund has undoubtedly played an important role, it would never have been possible without the support of local economists and politicians, the pre-existing crisis in import substitution and the perceived lack of alternatives. A sizeable élite in Latin America, perhaps 20 to 30 per cent of the population, have stood to gain from access to First World consumer goods, jobs with international companies and the opportunities brought by deregulation and increased trade. As one veteran Central American intellectual observed, "Neo-liberalism has united the élites of the South with those of the North and created the biggest convergence of financial, technological and military power in history." By the time the debt crisis swept away the remnants of import substitution in the early 1980s, neo-liberalism enjoyed an unstoppable coalition of influential supporters and potential beneficiaries both inside and outside the region, and had the intellectual high ground to itself.

Ideological shifts are partly generational. The young men and (occasionally) women who end up as policy-makers grow up, go to school and usually university, read the newspapers, argue and debate the new ideas of the time, and often go on to post-graduate studies. By the time they leave university for their first job, their mental frameworks are well established and do not easily change in later years, barring the occasional road-to-Damascus style conversion. For the academic generals grooming new generations of ideological warriors for the fray, the message is, get them young.

Fresh from university, the eager, young, would-be policy-makers join up for the war of ideas, where the battalions from the university economics departments, private think tanks, government ministries, banks and international institutions meet and argue their case in a global merry-go-round of conferences and seminars. To the winners, the spoils: jobs in universities, government departments, international agencies and eventually, perhaps, Minister of Finance or one of the other key posts in the economic cabinet. With them, the chance to change the nature of the economy and influence the fate of millions of citizens, followed by a well-paid directorship or two after leaving office. For the losers, unless they switch sides, years in the intellectual wilderness, trying to build up a critique and an alternative model that will eventually drive the pendulum back in their direction. In this world, the big institutions like the World Bank and IMF command enormous influence; when it comes to the broad issue of "development," their huge research budgets decide what is researched and by whom, both by their own staff and an army of thousands of consultants. The arrangement has been described by one scholar as an "intellectual-financial complex," enabling the Bretton Woods institutions to set the parameters, and to some extent conclusions of the debate on world development.

Chile provides a good example of the connections between academic research, institutional power and the harsh realities of politics. There, the first steps in the neo-liberal counter-attack against the state took place almost 20 years before General Pinochet seized power. In the mid-1950s the Economics Faculty in the far-off University of Chicago was nurturing the flame of liberalism at a time when Keynes's thinking was the orthodoxy of the age. In their academic redoubt, the high priests of Chicago, Friedrich von Hayek, Milton Friedman and Arnold Harberger, laid the intellectual foundations for the liberal crusade which swept the world in the 1970s.

Friedman and Harberger were the economists, specializing in fierce critiques of state intervention and laying the theoretical basis of monetarism. Von Hayek was the philosopher, expanding liberal ideas to include the social and political arguments for "taking the politics out of politics": using an authoritarian state to prevent pressure groups such as trade unions and political parties from interfering with a government's ability to make decisions free from immediate political pressures. Such interference, they argued, could only inhibit the efficiency-maximizing role of the market and hinder growth. The combination of reducing the state's role in the economy, while greatly strengthening its powers to undermine trade unions and other potential opponents became the hallmark of neo-liberal rulers from General Pinochet to Mrs. Thatcher.

Taking note of CEPAL's growing influence, Chicago decided to launch a counter-attack on its doorstep. In 1955 Professor Theodore W. Shultz, President of the Department of Economics, visited the Catholic University of Chile to set up a scholarship system for a select group of Chilean post-graduate students. Between 1956 and 1961 at least 150 promising Chilean students received US government-sponsored fellowships to study economics at Chicago. It was money well spent. Many of the students went back to academic posts in the Catholic University, which became the intellectual powerhouse for neo-liberal ideas as Chile's statist experiment ended in spectacular economic collapse (helped by Washington's destabilization programme and other forms of sabotage) during the years of Salvador Allende.

In 1973 General Augusto Pinochet overthrew Allende in a military coup. Within three months, the army had killed at least 1,500 people in a savage assault on trade unionists and political activists. Whatever their feelings about the massacre, the coup was a golden opportunity for the neo-liberals. The inexperienced technocrats faced initial scepticism from both the military and Chile's business community until March 1975, when they flew in Milton Friedman and Arnold Harberger for a high-profile lobbying effort. A month later Pinochet ditched his initially cautious economic team and put the "Chicago Boys" in charge. Chile has never been the same since.

Ever since the Chicago Boys arrived, the running of the Chilean economy has remained firmly in the hands of the technocrats. After 1973, a mirror image of the rise of the Chicago Boys got under way as a new generation of anti-Pinochet technocrats began to assemble in the wings. Many were driven into exile and had little option but to enrol in post-graduate studies in order to earn a living. In Chile, intellectual opponents of Pinochet set up private think tanks, often with funding from international aid agencies. By 1985 there were 30 private research institutes in Chile working in the social sciences, employing 543 researchers. Of these, 30 per cent held MA or PhD degrees from foreign universities. Academic rigour in their work was essential to fend off accusations that the new think tanks were mere front organizations for proscribed left-wing political parties, and as a result their analyses and opinions won widespread respect.

In the libraries and cafes of exile, and later back in Chile after the early 1980s, Chile's intellectuals endlessly argued over the reasons for the collapse of the Allende government, the world's first elected Marxist government. The failure of Allende's economic programme could not wholly be

blamed on the saboteurs, and a radical rethink gathered pace, further fu-
elled after 1985 by the swift growth of the Chilean economy under Pinochet
and the startling collapse of statist systems in Eastern Europe.

By the time General Pinochet left power in 1990, the opposition had accepted many of the Chicago Boys' ideas: the state should be kept out of economic management where possible; foreign investment and economic
stability, including low inflation, are essential for growth; the government
should not spend its way into a deficit. However, the "CIEPLAN monks" as
they became known (named after one of the leading think tanks) took a
more pragmatic approach to economic planning, and believed the benefits
of growth had to be more fairly distributed than during the Pinochet years
which had seen a sharp increase in inequality within Chile. This also involved a real commitment to democratic government.

As the soldiers retired to their barracks, a new generation of technocrats
moved smoothly from think tanks to ministries and Chile's economy continued to grow with scarcely a blip. They were still almost all post-graduates
from US and European universities, but fewer of them came from Chicago.
Within weeks of their defeat, General Pinochet's leading economists were
busily setting up a new series of think tanks in which to lick their wounds
before mounting an eventual counter-offensive.

ON ECONOMICS AND ECONOMISTS

The rise of Latin America's technocrats is part of a world-wide phenomenon
in recent decades, the exaltation of economists as the natural leaders of the
world order.

Since the days of Newton, physics has been a role model for other disciplines because of its elegance, simplicity and above all, its ability to predict
events in the real world. Physics moves from hypothesis to prediction using
mathematics, then checks the prediction against reality. Other sciences, such
as biology, concentrate on description, emphasizing change and empirical
observation rather than theoretical abstraction.

Unfortunately, economics wants to be like physics. Over the years, what
started off as a fairly empirical discipline has been drawn towards the se-
ductive certainties of mathematics. Some pure (if politically suspect) mathe-
maticians pour scorn on the whole idea:

> Just as primitive peoples adopt the Western mode of denationalised clothing
> and of parliamentarism out of a vague feeling that these magic rites and vest-
> ments will at once put them abreast of modern culture and technique, so the
> economists have developed the habit of dressing up their rather imprecise
> ideas in the language of calculus . . . Any pretence of applying precise formu-
> lae is a sham and a waste of time.

Academic prestige (including the lion's share of Nobel laureates) within the economics establishment increasingly stems from mathematical wizardry, not from engaging with real world events or people. As one economist admitted, "I must confess to an instinctive conviction that what cannot be measured may not exist." So much for human happiness, job satisfaction, anxiety and stress at the workplace.

To enable mathematics to be applied, a series of assumptions must be made to simplify the real world into a model fit for the computer. Wassily Leontieff, a Nobel prize-winning mathematical economist, poured scorn on the whole idea:

> Page after page of professional economic journals are filled with mathematical formulas leading the reader from sets of more or less plausible, but entirely arbitrary assumptions to precisely stated but irrelevant theoretical conclusions.

At the cutting edge, neo-liberal practitioners like the World Bank's Lawrence Summers prefer to be seen as engineers rather than physicists. In a speech to delegates at the joint IMF–World Bank meeting in Bangkok in 1991, Summers revealed the origins of his self-belief:

> The laws of economics, it's often forgotten, are like the laws of engineering. There's only one set of laws and they work everywhere.

At that time Summers was the Bank's Chief Economist and Vice-President for Development Economics. In 1993 he became President Clinton's Under-Secretary to the Treasury.

The most basic assumption of all is Homo Economicus, an abstraction of the human being. Homo Economicus has no friends, family, community nor any other non-economic links. S/he has an insatiable urge to acquire goods and his/her happiness is directly proportional to consumption. A person with ten cars is ten times happier than a person with one. S/he acts purely on the basis of short-term self-interest. With assumptions like these, it is small wonder that the end result—neo-classical economics — leads to a society that is strong on materialism and fails miserably on issues like justice, inequality or quality of life. Small wonder that Thomas Carlyle famously labelled the discipline "that Dismal Science."

The variables used by economists to describe the world around them are themselves open to question. Most governments and commentators measure a country's economic performance in terms of Gross Domestic Product (GDP), the sum of all the goods and services produced by a country. Yet as an indicator of well-being or misery, GDP leaves out almost as much as it describes:

- it excludes important areas of activity that lie outside the money economy, such as unpaid domestic labour, thereby ignoring a large part of women's contribution to the economy. If women are forced out to work and end up paying for their childcare, GDP goes up for both the job, and the paid childcare, distorting the picture as well as ignoring the impact of a "double day" on women's lives;

- it excludes issues of wealth or income distribution within a country (although other standard, if rarely used, indicators can fill in the gap);
- GDP assumes nature is infinitely bountiful, and excludes the exhaustion of natural resources. "Costa Rica between 1970 and 1990 lost natural capital (such as soils and forests) amounting to more than 6 per cent of its total GDP in that period. Yet the national accounts were silent on this continuing haemorrhage." GDP also fails to allow for depletion of natural capital caused by using nature as a "sink" for dumping waste. In fact, waste disposal is classed as a productive activity and therefore contributes positively to growth.
- GDP compares different countries by converting at the official exchange rate, even though this can be massively over- or undervalued. This weakness is now widely recognized, and the United Nations Development Program produces annual estimates of per capita GDP at "purchasing power parity" which attempt to compensate for exchange rate distortions. To date, however, the World Bank has largely insisted on using conventional measures of GDP.

Unfortunately, no one has yet come up with a better alternative. For the time being, whatever its flaws, GDP growth will continue to be used as the yardstick of economic success and this book will be forced to talk in terms of free markets, free trade and GDP, despite serious reservations as to their value as objective and useful concepts.

A further myth arising from the mathematical pretensions of the discipline is that of objectivity. Many economists genuinely believe that theirs is an impartial, scientific trade. As one of Pinochet's economic aides recalled, "I never dealt with politics; I was only perfecting economic laws. President Pinochet created compartments: the cavalry, the artillery, the economists." In fact, economists are highly political animals, and their assumptions are usually a pretty clear guide to their personal beliefs. Take Deepak Lal, for instance, World Bank analyst and one of the fathers of neo-liberalism, writing about the special interest groups created under import substitution: "A courageous, ruthless and perhaps undemocratic government is required to ride roughshod over these newly-created special interest groups."

A political choice is implicit in any technical debate over the rival merits of state and market. States are, to some degree, accountable and representative. Markets are not. Whatever the flaws of the Latin American state, many grassroots organizations and other pressure groups have spent decades learning how to pressure it into listening to their needs and demands. Replacing the state with the market disenfranchises them, unless they are to acquire genuine influence over the decisions of transnational corporations, large local companies and others, an implausible scenario which the technocrats seek to avoid at all costs in the name of economic efficiency. Some critics believe that the central purpose of neo-liberalism is political rather than economic:

> The aim of the last generation of free market thinkers, notably Hayek and his followers, was less to build a robust view of what actually happens in a market economy than a model that could compete with Marxism. The aim was ideological and required all kinds of contortions to produce the desired result. As a source of inspiration in a battle of ideas which the West needed to win, it worked; as a source of policy recommendations, millions have reason to curse the theory for the avoidable suffering exacted in its name.

The division of the academic world into disciplines has driven economics ever further into abstraction, creating an aloof élite who frequently dismiss the views of non-economists. As Paul Samuelson (another Nobel prize-winner) said in a presidential address to the American Economic Association, "In the long run, the economic scholar works for the only coin worth having—our own applause."

Such matters would be of little concern if the rise of the technocracy had not given economists such enormous (and growing) influence over the way governments decide policy. Things can go disastrously wrong when academics are invited to take theories developed in the closed world of the economics faculty and apply them remorselessly to millions of their fellow citizens. In extreme cases, as in Pinochet's Chile, the economic cabinet can end up resembling Aztec high priests, sacrificing thousands of lives on the altars of the unfathomable gods of monetarism or structural adjustment.

3.2 What Washington Means by Policy Reform (1990)

JOHN WILLIAMSON

No statement about how to deal with the debt crisis in Latin America would be complete without a call for the debtors to fulfill their part of the proposed bargain by "setting their houses in order," "undertaking policy reforms," or "submitting to strong conditionality." The question posed in this paper is what such phrases mean, and especially what they are generally interpreted as meaning in Washington. Thus the paper aims to set out what would be regarded in Washington as constituting a desirable set of economic policy reforms. An important purpose in doing this is to establish a baseline against which to measure the extent to which various countries have implemented the reforms being urged on them.

The paper identifies and discusses 10 policy instruments about whose proper deployment Washington can muster a reasonable degree of consensus. In each case an attempt is made to suggest the breadth of the consensus, and in some cases I suggest ways in which I would wish to see the consensus view modified. The Washington of this paper is both the political Washington of Congress and senior members of the administration and the technocratic Washington of the international financial institutions, the economic agencies of the US government, the Federal Reserve Board, and the think tanks.

The 10 topics around which the paper is organized deal with *policy instruments* rather than objectives or outcomes. They are economic policy instruments that I perceive "Washington" to think important, as well as on which some consensus exists. It is generally assumed, at least in technocratic Washington, that the standard economic objectives of growth, low inflation, a viable balance of payments, and an equitable income distribution should determine the disposition of such policy instruments.

FISCAL DEFICITS

There is very broad agreement in Washington that large and sustained fiscal deficits are a primary source of macroeconomic dislocation in the forms of inflation, payments deficits, and capital flight. They result not from any rational calculation of expected economic benefits, but from a lack of the political courage or honesty to match public expenditures and the resources available to finance them. Unless the excess is being used to finance productive infrastructure investment, an operational budget deficit in excess of around 1 to 2 percent of GNP is *prima facie* evidence of policy failure.

PUBLIC EXPENDITURE PRIORITIES

When a fiscal deficit needs to be cut, there are three major expenditure categories on which views are strongly held: subsidies, education and health, and public investment.

Subsidies, especially indiscriminate subsidies (including subsidies to cover the losses of state enterprises) are regarded as prime candidates for reduction or preferably elimination. Everyone has horror stories about countries where subsidized gasoline is cheaper than drinking water, or where subsidized bread is so cheap that it is fed to pigs, or where telephone calls cost a cent or so because someone forgot (or lacked the courage) to raise prices to keep pace with inflation, or where subsidized "agricultural credit" is designed to buy the support of powerful landowners, who promptly recycle the funds to buy government paper. The result is not just a drain on the budget but also much waste and resource misallocation, with little reason to expect any offset from systematically favorable effects on income distribution, at least where indiscriminate subsidies are concerned.

Education and health, in contrast, are regarded as quintessentially proper objects of government expenditure. They have the character of investment (in human capital) as well as consumption. Moreover, they tend to help the disadvantaged. Just how much help expenditures on education and health in fact provide to the disadvantaged depends on their composition as well as their level. Primary education is vastly more relevant than university education, and primary health care (especially preventive treatment) more beneficial to the poor than hospitals in the capital city stuffed with all the latest high-tech medical gadgets. This is not to say that there is no need for universities or state-of-the-art hospitals; developing countries need to train and retain an educated elite as well as to raise the standards of the masses and the poorest. But it is to assert that many in Washington believe that expenditures need to be redirected toward education and health in general, and most especially in a way that will benefit the disadvantaged.

The other area of public expenditure that Washington regards as productive is public infrastructure investment. There is of course a view that the public sector tends to be too large (see the section on privatization below). However, that view coexists with the view that spending on infrastructure that is properly within the public sector needs to be large (and also that an industry should not be starved of investment just because it is, however inadvisedly, within the public sector).

Policy reform with regard to public expenditure is thus perceived to consist of switching expenditure from subsidies toward education and health (especially to benefit the disadvantaged) and infrastructure investment.

TAX REFORM

Increased tax revenues are the alternative to decreased public expenditures as a remedy for a fiscal deficit. Most of political Washington regards them as an inferior alternative. Much of technocratic Washington (with the exception of the right-wing think tanks) finds political Washington's aversion to tax increases irresponsible and incomprehensible.

Despite this contrast in attitudes toward the merits of increasing tax revenue, there is a very wide consensus about the most desirable method of raising whatever level of tax revenue is judged to be needed. The principle is that the tax base should be broad and marginal tax rates should be moderate.

INTEREST RATES

Two general principles about the level of interest rates would seem to command considerable support in Washington. One is that interest rates should be market-determined. The objective of this is to avoid the resource misallocation that results from bureaucrats rationing credit according to arbitrary criteria. The other principle is that real interest rates should be positive, so as to discourage capital flight and, according to some, increase savings.

The question obviously arises as to whether these two principles are mutually consistent. Under noncrisis conditions, I see little reason to anticipate a contradiction; one expects market-determined interest rates to be positive but moderate in real terms, although high international interest rates may make it difficult to hold rates quite as moderate as might be desired. Under the sort of crisis conditions that much of Latin America has experienced for most of the 1980s, however, it is all too easy to believe that market-determined interest rates may be extremely high. It is then of interest to examine whether either principle has been followed or what sort of compromise between the two may have been achieved.

THE EXCHANGE RATE

Like interest rates, exchange rates may be determined by market forces, or their appropriateness may be judged on the basis of whether their level seems consistent with macroeconomic objectives. Although there is some support in Washington for regarding the former principle as the more important (a view held in particular by those who deny the possibility of estimating equilibrium exchange rates), the dominant view is that achieving a "competitive" exchange rate is more important than how the rate is determined. In particular, there is relatively little support for the notion that liberalization of international capital flows is a priority objective for a country that should be a capital importer and ought to be retaining its own savings for domestic investment.

The test of whether an exchange rate is appropriate is whether it is consistent in the medium run with macroeconomic objectives. In the case of a developing country, the real exchange rate needs to be sufficiently competitive to promote a rate of export growth that will allow the economy to grow at the maximum rate permitted by its supply-side potential, while keeping the current account deficit to a size that can be financed on a sustainable basis. The exchange rate should not be more competitive than that, because that would produce unnecessary inflationary pressures and also limit the resources available for domestic investment, and hence curb the growth of supply-side potential. A competitive real exchange rate is the first essential element of an "outward-oriented" economic policy.

TRADE POLICY

The second element of an outward-oriented economic policy is import liberalization. A policy of protecting domestic industries against foreign competition is viewed as creating costly distortions that end up penalizing exports and impoverishing the domestic economy.

The worst form of protection is considered to be import licensing, with its massive potential for creating opportunities for corruption. To the extent that there has to be protection, let it be provided by tariffs, so that at least the public purse gets the rents. And keep distortions to a minimum by limiting tariff dispersion and exempting from tariffs imports of intermediate goods needed to produce exports.

The free trade ideal is generally (although perhaps not universally) conceded to be subject to two qualifications. The first concerns infant industries, which may merit substantial but strictly temporary protection. Furthermore, a moderate general tariff (in the range of 10 percent to 20 percent, with little dispersion) might be accepted as a mechanism to provide a bias toward diversifying the industrial base without threatening serious costs. The second qualification concerns timing. A highly protected economy is not expected to dismantle all protection overnight.

FOREIGN DIRECT INVESTMENT

As noted above, liberalization of foreign financial flows is not regarded as a high priority. In contrast, a restrictive attitude limiting the entry of foreign direct investment (FDI) is regarded as foolish. Such investment can bring needed capital, skills, and know-how, either producing goods needed for the domestic market or contributing new exports. The main motivation for restricting FDI is economic nationalism, which Washington disapproves of, at least when practiced by countries other than the United States.

PRIVATIZATION

Privatization may help relieve the pressure on the government budget, both in the short run by the revenue produced by the sale of the enterprise and in the longer run inasmuch as investment need no longer be financed by the government.

However, the main rationale for privatization is the belief that private industry is managed more efficiently than state enterprises, because of the more direct incentives faced by a manager who either has a direct personal stake in the profits of an enterprise or else is accountable to those who do. At the very least, the threat of bankruptcy places a floor under the inefficiency of private enterprises, whereas many state enterprises seem to have unlimited access to subsidies. This belief in the superior efficiency of the private sector has long been an article of faith in Washington (though perhaps not held quite as fervently as in the rest of the United States), but it was only with the enunciation of the Baker Plan in 1985 that it became official US policy to promote foreign privatization. The IMF and the World Bank have duly encouraged privatization in Latin America and elsewhere since.

DEREGULATION

Another way of promoting competition is by deregulation. This was initiated within the United States by the Carter administration and carried forward by the Reagan administration. It is generally judged to have been successful within the United States, and it is generally assumed that it could bring similar benefits to other countries.

The potential payoff from deregulation would seem to be much greater in Latin America, to judge from the assessment of Balassa:

> Most of the larger Latin American countries are among the world's most regulated market economies, at least on paper. Among the most important economic regulatory mechanisms are controls on the establishment of firms and on new investments, restrictions on inflows of foreign investment and outflows of profit remittance, price controls, import barriers, discriminatory credit allocation, high corporate income tax rates combined with discretionary tax-reduction mechanisms, as well as limits on firing of employees. . . . In a number of Latin American countries, the web of regulation is administered by underpaid administrators. The potential for corruption is therefore great.
>
> Productive activity may be regulated by legislation, by government decrees, and case-by-case decision making. This latter practice is widespread and pernicious in Latin America as it creates considerable uncertainty and provides opportunities for corruption. It also discriminates against small and medium-sized businesses which, although important creators of employment, seldom have access to the higher reaches of the bureaucracy.

PROPERTY RIGHTS

In the United States property rights are so well entrenched that their fundamental importance for the satisfactory operation of the capitalist system is easily overlooked. I suspect, however, that when Washington brings itself to think about the subject, there is general acceptance that property rights do indeed matter. There is also a general perception that property rights are highly insecure in Latin America.

CONCLUDING REMARKS

The economic policies that Washington urges on the rest of the world may be summarized as prudent macroeconomic policies, outward orientation, and free-market capitalism. A striking fact about the list of policies on which Washington does have a collective view is that they all stem from classical mainstream economic theory, at least if one is allowed to count Keynes as a classic by now. None of the ideas spawned by the development literature—such as the big push balanced or unbalanced growth, surplus labor, or even the two-gap model—plays any essential role in motivating the Washington consensus. This raises the question as to whether Washington is correct in its implicit dismissal of the development literature as a diversion from the harsh realities of the dismal science. Or is the Washington consensus, or my interpretation of it, missing something?

■

3.3 Good-Bye to the Washington Consensus? (2003)

JAMES E. MAHON JR.

A certain gloominess has spread across Latin America. Argentina has fallen into the deepest economic slump in its modern history, with a poverty rate now surpassing 50 percent and an overwhelming popular repudiation of the country's political class. Venezuela seems to be slipping into civil war. The moment prompts dire observations. In *The New York Times*, columnist Nicholas Kristof asks if South America is the next Africa; "our neighborhood," he says, "risks falling apart." For United Press International's Ian Campbell, Latin America's "torment is not over and may get worse." Ricardo Infante, an analyst in the South American division of the International Labor Organization, describes a "social time bomb" in the region. Many observers, pointing to President Hugo Chávez in Venezuela, the recent election of Lucio Gutiérrez in Ecuador, the halted privatizations in Peru and Bolivia, and the presidential triumph in Brazil, after three failed attempts, of Luiz Inácio Lula da Silva, have pronounced that Latin America is moving to the left—or ought to do so soon.

The problem with this assessment is that it has been made before: repeatedly, and wrongly. Looking at South America in 1983, in the middle of the

James E. Mahon Jr., "Good-Bye to the Washington Consensus?" Reprinted with permission from *Current History*, February 2003. © 2003 Current History, Inc.

debt crisis, it was easy to predict a rise in organized class conflict and maybe the arrival of a few more pro-Cuban regimes. Instead we saw the spread of electoral democracy. After the elections between 1988 and 1990 of Carlos Andrés Pérez in Venezuela, Carlos Saúl Menem in Argentina, and Alberto Fujimori in Peru, all of whom ran populist campaigns, a new outbreak of economic heterodoxy was predicted. Instead, all three spun to the right and joined the parade of market-oriented economic reform. Today, Chile's socialist president, Ricardo Lagos, has concluded a free-trade agreement with the United States; in Ecuador, Gutiérrez, who as an army colonel in January 2000 had joined arms with leaders of the country's largest indigenous organization in a coup (while excoriating greedy bankers), wants a new agreement with the International Monetary Fund; and Lula himself, having taken office amid financial turmoil, has calmed the markets with reassuring words, economically orthodox cabinet appointments, and an investor-friendly trip to the United States.

What, if anything, makes this moment different? First, external trends have turned negative. World economic conditions have become more uncertain, credit flows to Latin America have slowed to a trickle, and we have seen an apparent rise in protectionism by the North. Second, many of Latin America's social and economic problems are worse. Crime, unemployment, and inequality, which had already risen in the 1980s, have brought increasing popular frustration with ineffective governments. Latin Americans might have expected, after following the free-market economic policies of the "Washington consensus" for a dozen years, that the region would have begun to savor the fruits of openness. But with some exceptions—notably Chile, Costa Rica, and much of Mexico—the fruit has turned out to be bitter, as economic openness appears to have accelerated social disintegration.

THE SKITTISH INVESTOR

One lesson from the great twentieth-century shifts in Latin America's economic orientation is that external forces matter considerably. Import-substituting industrialization—based on the erection of high trade barriers to protect domestic industries—began as a necessity, prompted by the Great Depression and World War II, and only later became a deliberate strategy. Except in Chile, the neoliberalism of the Washington consensus was born of the regional debt crisis. Only after they failed to form a debtors' cartel, discovered that nationalizing banks or printing money did not work, and received a strong push from the United States and the international financial institutions, did Latin American governments embrace market-friendly policies with apparent conviction. The next watershed is likely to look similar.

The embrace of neoliberalism has not brought economic disaster to Latin America, but the full picture is mixed and recent trends are mostly negative.

Economic growth was faster in the 1990s than in the 1980s (which is not saying much), but it slowed abruptly in 1995 and 1998 and has decelerated
steadily since late 1999. According to figures from the UN Economic Commission for Latin America and the Caribbean (ECLAC), real wages in 2001
stood above 1990 levels in 12 of 14 major countries, and above those of 1980
in nine of them. During the 1990s, urban unemployment fell in five countries and rose in ten (most alarmingly in Argentina and Colombia). Income
distribution grew worse in most countries (although by one measure—the
participation of the poorest 40 percent of urban households in total income—it had improved in the majority of countries as of 2000). But these
figures predate Argentina's financial collapse and the deepening of recession in Venezuela. Preliminary World Bank figures for 2002 show a drop of
1.1 percent in Latin America's GDP. In per capita terms this equals a 2.6 percent fall, the second successive year of decline and the worst year since the
debt crisis in the 1980s.

Over the past ten years, every economic slump in Latin America could be
easily connected to a financial crisis in some "emerging market." In the
1990s the entire region suffered the "tequila" effect from Mexico's peso devaluation (1994–1995) and later a panic induced by Russia's bond default
(1998–1999). Following this pattern, most observers have ascribed the contraction of 2001 and 2002 to Argentina's default on its foreign debt and to investors' worries about Brazil's Lula.

But a closer look at the data suggests that the last two events are part of a
longer-term pattern: a reversal of net capital flows. Data from the Institute
for International Finance show that the sum of net portfolio flows (equity
and bonds) and net commercial bank lending to Latin America was negative
in 1999, 2001, and 2002. Strong direct investment flows kept the net amount
of private external financing positive, but decreasingly so—from $71 billion
in 1999 to an estimated $29 billion in 2002. If we consider ECLAC figures
that look more broadly at the capital accounts of Latin American countries,
we find that the region has generally had a net outward transfer of resources from 1999 onward. By this measure, the net outflow was $39 billion
in 2002, driven by capital flight from Argentina, Brazil, and Venezuela.

Insofar as the reversal of net capital flows was due to systemic problems,
these were mostly to be found outside Latin America. The region's burden
of foreign debt, at least in the aggregate, has not suddenly become unsustainable. Since 1990 external debt has remained relatively stable as a proportion of GDP, while generally declining as a proportion of exports (a trend
that was interrupted only in 1998). The borrowers have also become less
public and more private: according to the World Bank, public debt fell from
93 percent of all long-term foreign debt in 1990 to 63 percent in 2001. It grew
17 percent over those 11 years, while private debt grew 872 percent.

Granted, the aggregate figures miss important individual variations.
They do not count Brazil's massive internal obligations, a sign of its financial

The Washington Consensus

The policy, in rough order of "consensus":

1. Limit fiscal deficits to what can be financed (voluntarily) in bond markets.
2. Maintain an independent central bank and market-determined interest rates.
3. Welcome foreign direct investment.
4. Liberalize trade.
5. Develop local bond and stock markets.
6. Privatize state companies, especially those losing money.
7. Reform taxation, making the value-added tax the main source of revenue.
8. Let markets set the exchange rate (floating) or dollarize (the Argentine collapse has reinforced the perception that policies between these two extremes are not feasible).
9. Liberalize capital movements.

J.M.

strength (few emerging markets sell as much domestically) as well as fragility (average bond maturity is still less than two years). And Argentina's foreign-debt-to-export ratio climbed well above twice the regional average before its default. On the positive side, Chile and now Mexico issue sovereign bonds that are rated investment grade.

As this suggests, the recent crisis has also seen less of the mindless financial contagion that was visible in 1994–1995 and 1998. The Argentine collapse was so clearly foreseen that it barely affected the markets in other Latin American bonds. Jitters about Brazil in mid-2002 did have a moderate effect on the rest of the region. But instead of undiscriminating financial markets, the most important vectors of contagion have been trade (Paraguay, Uruguay, and Bolivia), return migration and falling labor remittances (Paraguay and Bolivia), and bank runs (Uruguay).

The central problem is that falling United States and European stock markets have left rich-country investors more risk-averse. They discriminate more strongly among countries just as they discriminate more strongly (with larger interest-rate spreads) between riskier corporate bonds and treasury bonds in rich-country markets. According to JP Morgan, if we remove Argentina and Brazil, risk premia on Latin American bonds have followed the rising trends of United States corporate junk bonds, with Mexico and Chile paying less. Thus, while the midyear financial contagion was only moderate (and affected other regions not at all), combined with the new risk

Table 1

Latin America and the Caribbean: Net Resource Transfers
(millions of dollars)

Country	1993	1994	1995	1996	1997	1998	1999	2000	2001*
Argentina	9,349	8,107	354	5,072	9,138	10,449	5,767	1,829	-13,099
Bolivia	200	46	251	459	433	648	324	199	43
Brazil	-1,633	-723	19,951	19,743	6,242	7,497	-1,273	4,490	7,965
Chile	1,071	2,004	-625	1,952	4,176	29	-2,551	-1,181	-1,895
Colombia	784	2,369	3,028	4,408	3,767	2,055	-2,158	-2,013	-340
Costa Rica	464	273	355	27	301	-100	-645	-656	79
Dominican Republic	-9	-785	-455	-528	-593	-455	-352	-84	965
Ecuador	-89	116	-685	-1,185	-375	231	-2,713	-2,263	-567
El Salvador	118	36	338	243	179	321	165	103	107
Guatemala	704	599	210	356	716	1,101	709	1,355	1,206
Haiti	54	-15	168	-14	114	-35	1	7	87
Honduras	-4	151	50	110	260	64	509	178	225
Mexico	18,427	-1,748	-2,065	-9,336	5,174	4,599	1,661	6,496	10,048
Nicaragua	359	511	426	598	835	597	1,051	702	453
Panama	-97	-132	81	282	802	517	749	212	-422
Paraguay	84	735	262	423	-75	85	220	144	13
Peru	1,343	3,827	3,236	3,916	3,540	1,141	-502	-140	76
Uruguay	231	293	203	185	485	798	391	627	514
Venezuela	134	-5,610	-5848	-4,076	-2,797	-2,377	-4,484	-9,001	-8,850
Latin America	**31,490**	**10,054**	**19,235**	**22,635**	**32,322**	**27,165**	**-3,131**	**1,003**	**-3,393**

Source: UN Economic Commission for Latin America and the Caribbean (ECLAC), on the basis of information supplied by the International Monetary Fund and by national institutions.

Notes: Negative figures indicate outward transfers of resources. Net resource transfers are equal to net capital inflows less the balance of income (net payments of profits and interest).

*Preliminary estimates.

aversion, the contagion blocked borrowing by countries that did not enjoy an investment-grade bond rating, even if they were not suffering a crisis.

Moreover, as a recent IMF report observes, foreign direct investment "has in the past been correlated with [rich countries'] equity market performance." And with fewer privatization projects to carry out and political opposition to them rising, inflows of foreign direct investment might never again reach the record levels of 1999. Barring a sudden decision to privatize state-owned energy companies in Mexico or Venezuela, inflows will likely respond to political stability, economic recovery, and (as they did in 1999 in Brazil) the massive currency depreciation that makes assets look cheap to foreign buyers.

Most disturbing is that the new scarcity of external financing coincides with a greater need for it. Commodity prices fell steeply from November 1997 through mid-1999, and have stayed in a low range since. As the World Bank has noted, many products exported by Latin America (sugar, bananas, arabica coffee, aluminum) saw further price declines in 2002. Along with the Argentine catastrophe, this further depressed economic growth in the region. Declining output, in turn, led to falling fiscal revenues and helped push the region's estimated budget deficits to 2.6 percent of GDP, up from 1.8 percent in 2000 and 2001. This is not to exonerate the poor fiscal management in many countries. It is to point out that at a moment when Latin American governments need external financing to fight recession, the same recession has aggravated fiscal problems—and, it is reasonable to expect, political uncertainty—that could further discourage risk-averse foreign investors.

THE FALLOUT: SOCIAL DISINTEGRATION

We have not yet seen a popular rejection of neoliberalism. Voters still reward leaders who keep inflation low, so it is now the rare president who pays for fiscal deficits by printing money. Most governments still actively welcome foreign investment and trade. But according to Latinobarómetro's 2002 poll, across the region only 35 percent of the people (compared with 51 percent in 1998) said that the state should leave economic activity to the private sector. Most respondents also opposed privatizations. Still, their shift seems to bespeak anxiety rather than rebellion: in terms of the average respondent's self-described politics, the same poll showed that 11 countries moved right and only 2 (Argentina and Peru) moved left between 1996 and 2002.

Behind the anxiety lies social disintegration. The homicide rate in Latin America is now the highest of any region in the world. Although figures vary widely across countries (with Colombia, Guatemala, El Salvador, and Brazil setting the grim pace), the rate increased from about 8 per 100,000 in the 1970s to about 13 in the 1990s, according to the Interamerican Develop-

Table 2

Latin America and the Caribbean: Total Disbursed External Debt (millions of dollars)

Country	1990	1993	1994	1995	1996	1997	1998	2000	2001*
Argentina	62,233	72,209	85,656	98,547	109,756	124,696	140,489	146,200	142,300
Bolivia[1]	3,768	3,777	4,216	4,523	4,366	4,234	4,655	4,461	4,465
Brazil	123,439	145,726	148,295	159,256	179,935	199,998	241,644	236,157	226,820
Chile	18,576	19,665	21,768	22,026	22,979	26,701	31,691	36,849	37,060
Colombia	17,848	18,908	21,855	24,928	29,513	32,036	35,696	35,851	38,170
Costa Rica	3,924	4,011	3,818	3,889	3,376	3,290	3,500	4,050	4,225
Cuba	—	8,785	9,083	10,504	10,465	10,146	11,200	11,100	11,100
Dominican Republic	4,499	4,563	3,946	3,999	3,807	3,572	3,537	3,676	3,800
Ecuador	12,222	13,631	14,589	13,934	14,586	15,099	16,400	13,564	13,440
El Salvador[2]	2,076	1,976	2,056	2,168	2,517	2,689	2,631	2,795	3,425
Guatemala	2,487	2,323	2,644	2,936	3,033	3,210	3,619	3,929	3,900
Guyana	1,812	2,062	2,004	2,058	1,537	1,514	1,500	1,250	1,250
Haiti[1]	841	866	875	902	914	1,025	1,100	1,170	1,190
Honduras	3,588	3,850	4,040	4,242	4,121	4,062	4,404	4,685	4,650
Jamaica	4,152	3,687	3,652	3,452	3,232	3,278	3,300	3,200	3,200
Mexico[2]	101,900	130,524	139,818	165,600	157,200	149,000	161,300	149,300	146,100
Nicaragua[1]	10,616	11,987	11,695	10,248	6,094	6,001	6,287	6,660	6,340
Panama[2]	3,795	3,494	3,663	3,938	5,069	5,051	5,180	5,604	6,330
Paraguay	1,670	1,254	1,271	1,439	1,434	1,473	1,599	2,491	2,450
Peru	19,996	27,489	30,392	33,515	33,805	28,508	29,477	28,353	28,240
Trinidad and Tobago	2,520	2,102	2,064	1,905	1,876	1,541	1,430	1,550	1,550
Uruguay	4,472	3,578	4,251	4,426	4,682	4,754	5,195	5,492	5,800
Venezuela	36,615	40,836	41,179	38,484	34,222	31,212	29,526	31,545	30,000
Latin America	**443,049**	**527,303**	**562,830**	**616,919**	**638,519**	**663,090**	**745,360**	**739,930**	**725,805**

Source: UN Economic Commission for Latin America and the Caribbean (ECLAC), on the basis of information supplied by the International Monetary Fund and by national institutions.

Note: Includes public- and private-sector external debt. Also includes International Monetary Fund loans.

*Preliminary figures.
[1]Public external debt.
[2]Public debt does not include investments made in government securities by nonresidents.

ment Bank. (The United States rate was 5.6 in 2001.) Meanwhile, the young and educated are leaving. Emigration has risen most distressingly in Argentina, Colombia, and Venezuela, and is increasing across most of the region. Although spurred by crime and civil conflict in some places, the basic motivation has been economic—specifically, the mismatch between education systems that turn out large numbers of aspiring professionals and the economies that cannot employ them. As a result, many of the same kind of people who once hoped to prosper in market-friendly economies at home are now entering the market elsewhere.

The old party systems are also decomposing. As democracy spread in the 1980s and traditional political parties reentered the arena, most followed their old reflexes, building support through forms of patronage. In addition to the familiar dispensation of state jobs to party regulars, they had also granted favored status to party-linked labor unions and, in some countries, peasant organizations. After 1980, however, economic crises, neoliberal reform, and urbanization greatly weakened the last two and narrowed the scope of the first. Also, once-loyal partisan voters grew disenchanted when, under the pressure of financial circumstances, leaders elected as populists governed as neoliberals. As "schools" for politics, unions and parties have increasingly given way to neighborhood associations, evangelical Protestant churches, and television.

As Latin American societies have changed, so have the region's dominant political issues. Depending on the estimate and the country, between 33 and 60 percent of all economically active Latin Americans work in the urban informal sector at such jobs as street vendors, day laborers, and maids. Not tied to the fraying networks of patronage, they tend to distrust or resent political parties. Their key political concerns revolve around the home and the street rather than the workplace. While they deeply resent the privatizations and bank bailouts that have favored the rich and well connected at the expense of the rest, they look to the state first for public security, functioning schools, monetary stability, and affordable prices for the utilities that allow a decent urban life.

Into this void have stepped new plebiscitarian antiparty movements, often headed by former military men. Consider the similarities of Venezuela's Chávez, Ecuador's Gutiérrez, and Lino Oviedo (Paraguay's most popular politician, now in exile in Brazil). Each led an unsuccessful coup attempt and later ran for office as a civilian. Their supporters see coup making not as a disqualification but as a testament to their "manly" transcendence of shady partisanship. Each man rose to power at a time when his country's political parties, although still powerful in the legislature, had public approval ratings among the lowest in the region. (According to Latinobarómetro's measure of those registering "a lot" and "some" confidence in parties, Venezuela in 1996 scored 11 percent; Ecuador in 2002, 7 percent; and Paraguay in 2002, 7 percent.) Also compared to others in the region, these parties were known for their unusual devotion to patronage. And all three movements had similar social contexts. According to ECLAC figures, by the end of the 1990s over half the urban population in these three countries was employed in the informal sector, proportions that were among the highest in the region (exceeded only by Peru, Bolivia, and Nicaragua). In Venezuela's case, this sector grew more rapidly in the decade (from 39.2 percent in 1990 to 53.7 percent in 1999) than it did in any other country.

As more Latin Americans struggle in the most unforgiving realms of market society, more also feel alienated from the existing institutions of democracy. They are poor and have seen a few others grow rich—often, they believe, through graft, fraud, or drug trafficking. They fear disorder and, since most now reside in sprawling cities, they care most immediately about the kind of public housekeeping issues that typically land on the desks of big-city mayors. (Examples of effective and popular municipal government—Bogotá, Curitiba, Mexico City—have been a source of hope.) They are ready to welcome earnest, once-uniformed leaders who promise to take partisanship out of administration and to punish the corrupt.

This does not amount to a rebellion against neoliberalism. Yet when parties weaken and large electoral movements coalesce quickly around charismatic heroes, politics becomes even more unpredictable. While this worries foreign investors in Latin America, global trends might continue to discourage them more.

THE SELF-CORRECTING WASHINGTON CONSENSUS?

Can Washington turn these trends around? The first challenge is trade. As capital flows to Latin America diminish and fiscal austerity weighs on domestic markets, the region will have to export more. In theory, this prospect ought to generate sincere Latin enthusiasm for the proposed Free Trade Area of the Americas. But the Bush administration must overcome its own lack of credibility when it comes to freeing trade and ending subsidies in areas Latin Americans care about, such as steel or agriculture. The European Union has behaved no better. And if the United States and Europe fall back into recession, trade liberalization is likely to slip off the agenda.

Finance is equally sticky and of more immediate importance. In mid-2002, as economic jitters spread north and east from Argentina, the international financial institutions, led by the IMF, stepped in with major countercyclical packages for Brazil and Uruguay. But the story has been different in Argentina. There the fund, already highly exposed from previous loans and still smarting from its manipulation by then Economy Minister Domingo Cavallo in August 2001, has acted more like a commercial creditor. For the Peronists' undeniable sins—above all, making insolvent many local affiliates of international banks by converting their loans and deposits to pesos at different rates—it has imposed a heavy penance: the IMF has required Eduardo Duhalde's government to demonstrate credibility in its fiscal austerity efforts while in the midst of a devastating economic depression.

One important difference between today and 1990 is that nothing like a Brady Plan is in the wings (the United States–initiated Brady Plan promised a negotiated debt-service reduction in exchange for liberalization and privatization). Why not? First, most of the liberalization is done and, as was noted, fewer economic activities are left to privatize. Second, since much of the debt now takes the form of bonds (issued to a wide variety of private companies as well as governments), and existing bond contracts generally require unanimous assent of the bondholders to any changes, a consensual restructuring cannot take place as easily as bank debt renegotiation. Argentina's debt default, for example, involved some 82 contracts.

. . . Reform proposals [as of 2003] suffer from weak support, limited coverage, and bad timing. The IMF favors a kind of international bankruptcy court (the Sovereign Debt Restructuring Mechanism) to handle government bonds, yet the proposal has generated strenuous opposition from private financiers, including a former managing director of the fund itself. The reform most likely to pass—the incorporation of collective-action clauses in bond contracts that would allow a supermajority to approve restructuring— would apply only to newly issued debt. To ease the reduction of debt service, old bonds would have to be swapped in the market for new. But debtors (especially those enjoying an investment-grade rating) fear that the clauses would mean worse borrowing terms, which would raise their debt-service costs in the short run. Financiers claim that the entire discussion is spooking the markets at the wrong time. Apparently, the absence of rampant contagion like that seen in 1995 makes systemic reform less likely.

This suggests that major relief is not in the cards for 2003. In the late 1980s, during discussions on the Brady Plan, persuading commercial banks of the virtues of a 35 percent reduction of loan principal was relatively easy because they were selling many of their Latin American loans in the secondary market at a discount twice that size. Regionwide bond-market declines of a similar magnitude today would be devastating, in part because Latin American economies are now more tightly integrated with international finance. The problem is how to engage in orderly debt restructurings without provoking a deeper crisis.

FAITH, HOPE, AND CREDIT

Despite the recovery of Brazil's financial markets in the months after Lula's victory, it can be said that capital punished the country heavily for electing a leftist. In the middle of the storm, a few United States commentators darkly warned of Lula's friendship with Fidel Castro and Venezuela's Chávez as evidence of a crumbling southern front in the war on terrorism. Yet this "enemy" proceeded to calm the markets by agreeing to a large fiscal surplus in 2003, impressing bankers with his cooperativeness. Had Lula not done so, investor wariness would have turned into a true panic, leading to a self-fulfilling financial explosion. But it was bad enough. By year's end [2002], stock market and bond country-risk indices for Brazil had returned to June levels (leaving the latter still almost twice as high as it was in March), and the rise in interest rates over the interim put an added debt burden on the new government, while depressing the rest of the economy.

As Lula now tries to manage financial fragility, many details of his strategy should sound familiar to Latin American presidents who have had to deal with financial stress. First, obtain credit from the IMF, contingent on promises of fiscal austerity, and thereby calm the bond markets further so that the federal government can handle a daunting schedule of domestic debt rollovers in the middle months of 2003. This will reduce interest rates, which should keep economic activity from falling more than a percentage point or two for the year. Next, before the honeymoon ends, use the crisis atmosphere to reform taxes and a pension system that bleeds red ink as it rewards the well connected. Perhaps by the second full year, having displayed fiscal rectitude and maybe enjoying a revived economy, turn to the task of adjusting federal spending priorities to more closely accord with those of the party.

All this sounds like a fiscally sound route to social democracy. And Lula might even navigate it successfully—if the legislature cooperates, the public-sector pension beneficiaries go quietly, the public remains patient, and the markets rebound. But he also has to worry that, in tacking to the center, he could end up viewed as yet another faithless Latin American politician who sacrificed his ideals on the altar of the bond market.

What else might the affected governments do to help end the slump? As in Brazil, fiscal decisions will take center stage. Governments will have to tax more effectively, cracking down on evasion (especially by the richest), but without putting a brake on economic growth. They will need to resist the temptation to privatize in the sole pursuit of revenue, as many did in the early 1990s. Because this entailed granting weakly regulated private monopolies (so as to maximize the purchase price), it made such sales unpopular. In the long run, governments should recognize that the Washington consensus works better as a guide to macroeconomic management than as a development strategy. In the short run, they might begin to negotiate debt restructuring.

But why can they not just quietly default? At this time, most Latin American leaders would lose much more from defaulting on their bonds than they would gain. Even if partial and nonconflictual, a default would push interest rates to punishing levels while making trade finance more expensive. True, it would free up government spending, but in countries where the fiscal deficit exceeds interest payments, it would not eliminate the need to borrow. Thus, the damage would be immediate and severe, while the benefit would come later, its size and shape determined by the government. But if commodity prices stay low, if rich countries continue to close important markets, and above all, if the financial flows continue to remain weak, Latin American governments will reevaluate their choices. Obviously, the argument that they must repay promptly and fully to preserve their access to international capital markets will become less persuasive if, for these borrowers at least, the markets have no capital.

When Lula traveled to Washington on December 10 [2002], he had three priorities: "credit, credit, and credit." We all ought to hope that he gets it. If he does not, and if the financial drought persists another year, the consequences are likely to displease Washington.

3.4 Neoliberal Social Policy: Managing Poverty (Somehow) (1997)

CARLOS M. VILAS

The debt crisis of the early 1980s and the macroeconomic adjustment and neoliberal reforms that the region's governments implemented to deal with it resulted in a dramatic increase in the number of people living in poverty. In 1980, 118 million Latin Americans—about a third of the region's total population—were poor. By 1990, that number had increased to 196 million, or nearly half the total population. Eighty percent of these 78 million "new poor" live in cities, which helps explain the congestion and deterioration of many Latin American capitals. This 42% growth rate of the "new poor" between 1980 and 1990 was almost double the 22% population growth rate in the region during the same period.

This veritable process of poverty production contrasts sharply with socioeconomic trends of the preceding decades. The proportion of poor people within the overall population in Latin America fell from 51% in 1960 to 33% in 1980. During this 20-year period, the number of poor people increased by 9 million, or 8%, while the total population grew by 145 million, or 67%. This drop in the percentage of poor people was obtained without programs designed to "combat poverty." It was, rather, the result of the overall functioning of the economy, which integrated large segments of the population

Carlos Vilas, "Neoliberal Social Policy: Managing Poverty (Somehow)," *NACLA Report on the Americas,* July–August 1997, Vol. 37, no. 1, pp. 57–65. Reprinted by permission.

by creating new jobs, and helped to progressively distribute income through business-labor negotiations regulated by the state.

Latin America's economy began to rebound from the economic recession in the mid-1980s. Gross domestic product (GDP) grew 9.5% between 1986 and 1990, and another 15% between 1991 and 1995. As poverty levels remained constant or increased despite economic growth, it became clear that structural adjustment does not by itself reduce poverty and macroeconomic recovery does not translate into significant social improvement. This provoked alarm among Latin American governments, and the multilateral lending institutions like the World Bank and the Inter-American Development Bank (IDB) that were advising them on how to implement the adjustment measures. This burgeoning poverty was seen as a source of political instability, and as fertile terrain for demagogues and populists that might threaten the neoliberal restructuring process. As a result, these multilateral agencies began to emphasize the need to create programs to combat poverty.

In this way, social policy entered into the neoliberal reform agenda as a question of poverty and, in fact, was reduced to that. Neoliberalism considers the growth of poverty to be a pathology, not a consequence of the economic system. Hence it isolates poverty from the process of capital accumulation and economic development, and reduces the solution to designing specific social policies.

Any social policy performs two essential functions. First, it supports the process of capital accumulation through the social reproduction of the labor force. Second, it legitimizes the overall political order by offering social services that help create consensus among the population that benefits from them. The way in which these two functions are performed depends on the political and social dynamics of each country. Social policy is an arena of social and political conflict among social groups, whose outcome is expressed in government decisions.

Over the past decade, the passage from a Keynesian-Fordist model of economic development to a neoliberal one has had significant repercussions on the nature of social policy in Latin America. In the Keynesian-Fordist model, the state regulated economic activity and intervened in specific sectors, including the establishment of state-owned enterprises. Increases in economic productivity led to salary increases and expanded employment, which benefited the population as a whole.

Social policy in this model reinforced the process of capital accumulation to the degree that it created externalities for private enterprises. For example, public investment in education, health care, worker training, and low-income housing represented a savings for the private sector, which would otherwise have had to invest in these areas. Meanwhile, employment, wage and pricing policies improved the purchasing power of individual workers and the domestic market as a whole. Social policy was seen as an element of investment, not an expense. Both economic and social policies in the Keynesian-Fordist model facilitated the incorporation of broad sectors of the poor, especially the urban poor, into the political and economic system.

Latin America during this period was characterized by widespread social mobility, stimulated—within certain limits—by the state. Together these varied elements helped constitute what was known as the "national-popular state," or the "national-developmentalist state"— the Latin American proxy of the western European "welfare state." Social policies contributed to capitalist development, were reformist by nature, and fed social mobility. As a result, they gave broad legitimacy to the political system. Citizen rights were thus imbued with socioeconomic rights. Citizen rights were also expanded into the political realm, as women and indigenous people were granted the right to vote. The implicit paradigm of social policy—and of state policies in general—was integration.

With variations from country to country, the Keynesian-Fordist model peaked between the 1930s and 1970s. It entered into crisis because of changes in the international system since the 1950s, increasing divergence between business interests and labor demands, and recurring fiscal crises. Military dictatorships, authoritarianism, and later, the debt crisis that detonated in 1982, led to the exhaustion of this model of development and its corresponding social policies.

Recognizing the limitations and inefficiencies of the Keynesian-Fordist model should not lead us to minimize its successes. The integrating dynamic of this model reduced poverty by moving labor from low-productivity activities to modern ones, improving employment levels and the quality of jobs, and increasing disposable income through wage hikes and price subsidies for urban workers as well as redistributive state social policies.

The crisis of the 1980s created the conditions for the application of the neoliberal model. This model is characterized by the deregulation of the economy, trade liberalization, the dismantling of the public sector, and the predominance of the financial sector of the economy over production and commerce. The state has abandoned its role as an agent of social development and integration. Instead, it helps define winners and losers in the marketplace by setting the exchange rate, interest rates and tax policy, all of which pump income toward the financial sector.

Social policy is reduced to a limited series of measures intended to compensate the initial negative effects of structural adjustment among certain sectors of the population. These negative effects, neoliberal policy makers purport, are rooted in the irrationality of the previous system's distribution of resources. Social policy is considered transitory: after an initial painful phase, structural adjustment will reestablish basic macroeconomic equilibrium and promote economic growth without inflation. New jobs will be created within the modern sector of the economy—the "trickle-down" effect—which will raise incomes and leave only a small proportion of the population in need of public attention.

As a matter of principle, neoliberal economics does not concern itself with social policy. A strong economy, it is argued, will make permanent social policies unnecessary. Social issues are considered a government expense, not an investment; the concept of social development gives way to that of social compensation. With the drastic cuts in social spending, however, only minimal compensatory mechanisms can be sustained. As a result, social policy has contracted, and its two traditional functions—accumulation and legitimization—have experienced severe adaptations.

Neoliberal social policy helps promote capital accumulation through financial maneuvers. For example, the privatization of the retirement and pension systems in many Latin American countries has handed over huge financial resources to the private capital market. For their part, social-investment funds promote capital accumulation by supporting small-business activities like repair shops and industrial homework enterprises.

For the rest, neoliberal social policy operates like a charity, directing aid toward the extremely poor. Rather than improving the working and living conditions of low-income groups, social policy tries to assist the many victims of structural adjustment, and to prevent further deterioration in the living standards of the population already below the poverty line. Neoliberal social policy doesn't help these people get out of the hole of poverty; it simply tries to prevent them from sinking further into it.

These characteristics of neoliberal social policy severely limit its capacity to fulfill a legitimizing function for the political system. In fact, social policy is essentially reduced to putting out fires so that situations of extreme social tension do not become larger political problems. Neoliberals fear that such problems would create a climate of instability that might negatively affect the inflows of foreign capital, putting the whole economic model at risk. In this sense, social policy becomes closely linked to the politics of the moment. On the eve of the 1994 presidential elections in Mexico, for example, the government of Carlos Salinas poured huge sums of money into "Procampo," a new program to provide temporary relief to the rural poor. The implicit objective of the Mexican social-investment fund Pronasol was to reduce the level of political conflict in those parts of the country where the opposition might gain ground.

Central America's health-sector reform dramatically illustrates the internal tensions and contradictions of neoliberal social policies in poverty-stricken countries. Although Central American governments began discussing the need to reform the health sector in the late 1980s, the recent health-care reform was prompted by loans offered by the World Bank and the IDB. These loans were granted only on the condition that governments implement broader public-sector reforms. The development banks' concern with health reform reflects their wider interest in macroeconomic adjustment and state deregulation. The scope and content of reform in the health sector are tailored to the overall goals of neoliberalism.

Since macroeconomic reform usually involves sharp cuts in already meager public spending on infrastructure and social services, the impact of health reform has been ambivalent and even contradictory. In Nicaragua, for example, public spending on health dropped from 5% of GDP in 1990 to 4.4% in 1994. Today [1996] the government spends an average of $19 per person a year on health services, or $1.50 per person per month. The figures for Guatemala are even worse. Public health expenditures dropped from 1.5% of GDP in 1980 to 0.9% in 1990, climbing to just over 1.3% in 1993. Costa Rica, on the other hand, spent 7.5% of its GDP on public health in 1993, an average of $60 per person. Efficiency, cost-cutting, and better managerial skills—all of which are urgently needed in Central America—are emphasized. Yet, efficiency is undermined by budget cuts that reduce the impact of policies and actions. Cost-cutting is urged upon countries that already devote meager resources to health and other social services. The emphasis on management skills and techniques is abstract, and frequently bears little relation to the specific character and needs of the health sector.

Most health ministries in Central America face increasing shortages in infrastructure, equipment and personnel—shortages that cannot be offset by the "self-management" of civil society in countries in which the overwhelming majority of the population is poor. In recent years, greater emphasis has been placed on improved training for health-care specialists, but low salaries and poor working conditions jeopardize efforts to recruit and retain skilled personnel. Since health is not—despite the rhetoric—a priority for most Central American governments, high turnover of personnel in top-level positions in health ministries reinforces the lack of continuity and the loose commitment to healthcare reform.

Within this general framework, differences exist among countries. In Costa Rica, decision-making regarding health-care reform is more independent from the multilateral lending agencies. Even as reform takes the shape that these agencies favor, the notion of health as a social service has been preserved. By contrast, in the health-reform program designed by the IDB in Guatemala, the Ministry of Health must get explicit IDB approval for 43 out of 63 components of the program in order to move to the next step and have funds disbursed.

Neoliberal social policy has three basic characteristics, which are tightly interwoven: privatization, targeting, and decentralization. Privatizing social services is considered a way to alleviate the fiscal crisis, to make service delivery more efficient, and to avoid the micro- and macroeconomic distortions that arise from free public services. Users' fees have been imposed or increased, and new operating principles based on the criteria of business and commercial profit have been introduced. These have had significant repercussions on the quality and breadth of coverage. Users' fees, it is argued, are a way of reducing the financial burden assumed by lending agencies. They are also supposedly a way of ensuring that public services will be used only by those who really need them, avoiding the waste of resources.

Privatization implies the abandonment of the notion of public service, and its replacement with that of a business out to make a profit. Access to social services is no longer considered one's right as a citizen, but is based on one's ability to pay. The privatization of social services generates new social inequalities because only wealthier groups can now afford them. This explains the resistance to privatization from broad sectors of the lower and middle classes who believe that they have a right to health care and education. In Argentina, for example, low-income salaried workers lost access to medical attention when the social security system was privatized. As a result, these workers are forced to rely on the public health system, which is already overwhelmed. In a domino effect, the poorest of the poor have ended up excluded from public hospitals. Making matters worse, after problems in his economic program became apparent [in 1995], President Carlos Menem and his minister of economics, Domingo Cavallo, ordered further cuts in social spending. As a result, several public hospitals in Buenos Aires have been forced to close, leaving thousands of people completely without access to basic medical care.

Privatization also entails the loss or reduction of state financing for projects once run by the government as a function of its role as representative of the public interest. In El Salvador, for example, the government delegated to the Business Foundation for Educational Development (FEPADE), a business-oriented think tank, several important worker-training programs for ex-combatants from the Farabundo Marti National Liberation Front (FMLN) and demobilized members of the armed forces. The program was designed by FEPADE, and financed with foreign funds.

The efficiency of the privatization process usually depends on the state's regulatory capacity. In Latin America today, however, the state has abdicated this function, paving the way for the formation or consolidation of oligopolies in the health, education, and social-security markets. As a result, social policy becomes shaped in ways amenable to particular groups and special interests that can exert the most pressure. In the case of the health sector, for example, medical laboratories, large private clinics, and professional organizations have gained significant influence. In housing policy, construction companies and banks have become major players.

With privatization, health and education are no longer rights. They are luxuries or, at least, pieces of merchandise to be bought and sold in the marketplace. If you cannot afford the merchandise, don't buy it. In other words, if you can't afford medical care, die. If you can't pay for education, stay illiterate and sell chewing gum on the street corner. The privatization of pensions in Bolivia illustrates this logic with particular cruelty: the government set the age to begin to "enjoy" retirement benefits almost ten years higher than the life expectancy of the average Bolivian.

The second principal tenet of neoliberal social policy is targeting. Given the contraction of funds assigned to social policy, targeting is promoted as a way to guarantee that resources effectively reach those to whom they are directed. The arguments in favor of targeting echo the criticisms of the Keynesian-Fordist model. That model was based on the principle of universal, free social services. Neoliberals argue that the model benefited workers in the urban wage-labor force and the middle classes, but did not reach the poorest of the poor—the rural poor and the informal sector. Targeted social programs, specifically designed to reach the neediest, impose new management practices and efficiency criteria on state social policy. Clearly, however, targeting responds less to the supposed inefficiencies of the Keynesian-Fordist social-security model, than to the need to respond to mounting social problems with scarce resources.

In theory, targeting aims to fulfill a basic requirement of any public policy: reaching the intended constituency, and optimizing the use of resources. The first obstacle is defining the beneficiary group given the magnitude of needs. This process normally involves much more than a technical breakdown of the population according to particular statistical indicators. Who benefits from these special programs is the outcome of a complex interplay of pressures and competition among potential beneficiary groups. In this sense, targeting is highly sensitive to struggles over income redistribution, which grow more acute as the economic crisis deepens and resources become scarcer. These programs are also used as patronage tools to create and maintain clientelistic relationships. In the same way, targeting is open to bureaucratic or political manipulation for electoral purposes.

Experience shows that it is extremely difficult to redirect resources that used to go to the middle class toward the poorest. In general, the poor exert little pressure, either because of their lack of experience or their sheer vulnerability. Moreover, it is usually middle-class professionals, not the poor, who design the projects. In Bolivia, for example, the Social Emergency Fund (FSE) did not reach the poorest Bolivians. The majority of the projects were carded out in the wealthier or relatively less-impoverished areas, since there was little demand for funding from groups in the poorest regions of the country. Targeting may in fact aggravate inequality, since targeted programs can improve the situation of one particular community while others languish in poverty. In the end, the desire to keep people who are not poor from receiving benefits often results in the exclusion of many of the poor.

Targeting frequently puts a heavy burden on women. In particular, community-based programs such as food supplements rely on the direct involvement of women. Women can gain important organizing experience by participating in these programs, which have the potential to become the basis for a truly participatory social policy. At the same time, however, they make women's workload heavier. As unpaid female labor grows, gender inequality is reinforced.

But above all, the neoliberal approach to fighting poverty has proven incapable of answering a fundamental question: What does the notion of target groups mean when 60 to 80% of the population lives below the poverty line, either because of the impact of structural reform or for pre-existing or other reasons?

The final basic tenet of neoliberal social policy is decentralization. Neoliberals criticize the Keynesian-Fordist model for being too centralized. They argue that decisions concerning social policy should be assumed by lower echelons of government such as provinces or municipalities, and eventually by the local organizations of the affected population and other NGOs.

Decentralization can give people a sense of the importance of working together to directly confront their problems. It encourages the development of local leadership and gives poor people training in management practices. The Orcamento Participativo—the participatory budget — under the municipal administrations controlled by the Workers' Party in Brazil is an example of a genuine decentralization of social policy. Citizens participate directly in the decision-making process both in terms of defining government policies and determining how money is spent. This experience, however, belongs to a specific political project that is completely at odds with neoliberalism.

Up to now, decentralization in the neoliberal context has focused on program implementation, not program design. This amounts to functional decentralization—also referred to as "deconcentration"—but not political decentralization. This lack of political decentralization lends credence to the hypothesis that the objective of decentralization is not the democratization of social programs and policies, but rather achieving greater efficiency from scarce resources.

Making the transition from a highly centralized system to a decentralized one is complex and takes time. This is particularly true when the centralized structures have been around for more than a century and have become part of the mindset of the actors. One of the problems facing the decentralization process—including the operative kind—is the inability of actors at the local level to assume the tasks delegated to them. Virtually overnight, for example, municipalities have found themselves responsible for providing a gamut of social services without the necessary financial, human, administrative, and material resources. This often translates into inefficiency—at least initially—in service delivery, deterioration in the quality of services, and the emergence of multiple entities that perform functions that used to be the responsibility of a single institution.

While it is true that grassroots participation in social-policy implementation is greater in local structures than in the centralized entities that were usually far away and bureaucratic, not all sectors of society get involved. Participation is the result of an array of factors that are normally absent, or exist to a lesser degree, in the neediest social groups: organizing capacity, a sense of efficacy, and basic education. Without the presence of a central state with the political will to correct inequalities, decentralization ends up leaving out the weakest social groups.

Criticism of the inefficiencies of the Keynesian-Fordist social policy points to its limitations and uneven reach, but doesn't improve the results of neoliberal social policy. Even if we evaluate neoliberal social policy only in the limited sense of combating poverty, the results after a decade of neoliberalism are meager. The majority of the poverty-alleviation programs represent a new form of relating with the poor, but this hasn't translated into a significant reduction in overall poverty.

Until now [1996], neoliberal social programs have demonstrated their capacity only to reduce the number of people living in extreme poverty. Emergency employment programs, food subsidies and the like can effectively attend to extreme needs. Rising out of poverty, however, is a much more complicated process that depends on a diverse set of economic, financial, political and institutional factors that go far beyond social policies.

All models of capital accumulation assume a given portion of "surplus population"—in other words, people who look for work, but don't find it. Since neoliberalism privileges the financial sector of the economy over the productive one, it presumes a much larger portion of surplus population than the Keynesian-Fordist model of the past. In this context, one can expect little of neoliberal social policy, regardless of its technical merits.

Simply put, neoliberalism marginalizes and expels people at a greater rate than these programs can compensate. The case of Mexico is especially illustrative of the tension between the technical efficiency of a particular sectoral policy and the logic driving the overall economic model. While Pronasol, Salinas' poverty-alleviation program, succeeded in reducing the number of extremely poor Mexicans by 1.3 million between 1989 and 1992, the very same number of people lost jobs in the industrial sector of the economy between 1988 and 1992.

This kind of juxtaposition highlights the inability of targeting to have any significant impact given the profound social inequalities that the economic system generates. In Chile in 1970, for example, only 17% of households were poor; in 1989, after almost two decades of neoliberalism and dictatorship, poor households represented 38.1%. In 1995, the richest 20% of Chilean households earned 18 times the income of the poorest 20%. Chile, praised as a neoliberal success story, now has the fifth worst income distribution in the region.

Overall neoliberal economic restructuring defines the possibilities and limitations of the new social policy much more than the technical limitations of the programs themselves or the "errors of the past." For example, this year [1996] Mexico will have to make more than $32 billion in payments on its debt to foreign creditors, which equals 35–40% of the total value of its exports. In such circumstances, there isn't much money left over to fight poverty or to promote social development.

The neoliberal hypothesis that economic growth ultimately generates increased employment and lessens poverty doesn't hold up against the facts.

The passage from economic crisis to economic recovery in much of Latin America has not produced substantial social improvements. The increase in productivity and economic output have not generated corresponding increases in employment levels and better working conditions. Employment, when it expands, does not keep pace with population growth. Real wages remain depressed as well. The biggest surge in employment is taking place in the informal sector, which offers work that is precarious and low-paying. Of the 15.7 million jobs created in all of Latin America over the [early 1990s], 13.6 million of those came from the informal sector.

Faced with the rigidities of the free market and the bias of government policies, there is little that neoliberal social policy can accomplish with respect to legitimation of the social order either. Job insecurity, violence, urban congestion, rising common crime, and growing social inequality are products of the crisis of the 1980s and the social and economic policies adopted to confront that crisis. The economic recovery that followed the initial period of structural adjustment has left a trail of victims among small and medium-sized business owners and employees, urban wage earners, women, rural communities, and children.

Costa Rica represents an example of the positive results that can be obtained in a public welfare system when equity is genuinely valued. Direct public subsidies through health programs, education, housing, food, social security, and water and sewage infrastructure have reduced total poverty by two-thirds over the course of the 1980s. Thanks to its heterodox, balanced and creative approach, Costa Rica is one of the two countries in Latin America which in that traumatic decade succeeded in reducing poverty levels, even in the countryside. The other country is Cuba.

SUGGESTIONS FOR FURTHER READING

Cardoso, Eliana, and Ann Helwege. "Import Substitution Industrialization," in *Modern Political Economy and Latin America: Theory and Policy,* ed. Jeffry Frieden, Manuel Pastor, and Michael Tomz. Boulder, Colo.: Westview, 2000, 155–164.

Cardoso, Fernando Henrique, and Enzo Faletto. *Dependency and Development in Latin America.* Berkeley: University of California Press, 1979.

Dornbusch, Rudiger. "The Case for Trade Liberalization in Developing Countries," in *Modern Political Economy and Latin America: Theory and Policy,* ed. Jeffry Frieden, Manuel Pastor, and Michael Tomz. Boulder, Colo.: Westview, 2000.

Gereffi, Gary. "Paths of Industrialization," in *Manufacturing Miracles: Paths of Industrialization in Latin America and East Asia,* ed. Gary Gereffi and Donald L. Wyman. Princeton, N.J.: Princeton University Press, 1990, 3–23.

Krauze, Enrique. "Old Paradigms & New Openings in Latin America." *Journal of Democracy* 3, no. 1 (January 1992).

Smith, William C., and Patricio Korzeniewicz, eds. *Politics, Social Change, and Economic Restructuring in Latin America.* Miami: University of Miami, North-South Center Press, 1997.

Thorp, Rosemary. *Progress, Poverty and Exclusion: An Economic History of Latin America in the 20th Century.* Baltimore: Johns Hopkins University Press, 1998, Chapter 7.

Veltmeyer, Henry, James Petras, and Steve Vieux. *Neoliberalism and Class Conflict in Latin America: A Comparative Perspective on the Political Economy of Structural Adjustment.* New York: St. Martin's Press, 1997, Chapters 3, 4.

USEFUL WEBSITES

The Association for Womens' Rights in Development: Clearing-house for information and network for mobilizing on women's rights in development.
www.awid.org

The Heritage Foundation: Free market–oriented organization that provides annual rankings of economic freedom in all countries in the world.
www.heritage.org

Interamerican Development Bank: Key U.S. agency providing development assistance.
www.iadb.org

International Monetary Fund: International financial watchdog and lending institution of last resort.
www.imf.org

World Bank: Main international financial institution—albeit controversial—supporting development finance.
www.worldbank.org

CHAPTER 4

Traditional and Emerging Actors in the Latin American Polity

*D*emocratization scholars argue that civil society is a critical defense against authoritarianism. Civil society is the collection of *private* organizations and institutions that mobilize citizens and mediate their relationship with the state. Civil society constitutes a defense against authoritarianism because it is a space separate from state power where private individuals can organize, mobilize, communicate, and ultimately even form political coalitions and alliances. One of the paradoxes of Latin America in the twenty-first century is that the region is filled with fragile democracies even though it also has the densest civil society in its history. Latin American countries have all manner of professional associations—from lawyers to doctors to journalists—as well as neighborhood associations, environmental associations, womens' groups, human rights groups, a variety of religious associations, and indigenous movements. In many respects, the social and political landscape of the region has become much more complicated and much more democratic than it was in the past.

For centuries, most of Latin America had a social structure in which a tiny white, European elite dominated an indigenous population. In some instances, a new mixed race (mestizo) population came to predominate, as in Mexico. In others, the two populations remained much more visibly separated with the small European elite continuing to dominate, while the indigenous population remained only weakly integrated politically and economically into the country. This is the case in Guatemala, for example, and in some of the Andean countries, like Ecuador or Bolivia. In some countries, the indigenous population was either small or largely supplanted by a large, imported slave population. Such was the case in Brazil. Finally, in a very small number of countries, such as Argentina, Chile, and Uruguay, the indigenous population was largely destroyed, leaving behind a population that was relatively homogeneous racially. This racial separation with a dominant white population was maintained in many countries with the help of two other key institutions in society: the military and the Catholic Church, which remained a politically conservative force in most countries well into the twentieth century. Latin American militaries became increasingly focused on internal order starting in the late nineteenth century, when European military advisors were sought to help professionalize their Latin American counterparts.

As mentioned in Chapter 1, however, Latin American societies began to change at the end of the nineteenth century and into the beginning of the twentieth century. An emergent urban middle class began to make demands for political inclusion and organize into groups, such as student associations. In addition, labor unions, inspired by European (and occasionally American) counterparts, grew in number and influence. The growth of industry under import-substitution industrialization increased workers' economic importance. The growth of the working class as a voting bloc enhanced their political influence. In response, local business groups became increasingly organized as well, although in most countries the business community remained fragmented into multiple associations based on different areas of production that often competed with each other. In most cases, individual businesses, business groups, and businesspeople exercised significant influence on the government without needing support from a business association. Thus, by the mid-twentieth century, the military, the Church, business, and the unions were probably the most influential and significant political actors in the region, but new organizations, associations, and political parties were becoming more significant over time.

By the end of the twentieth century, some of the traditional actors had begun losing their influence and emerging actors were growing in importance. The military has remained an important actor in many Latin American countries, but with some limits on the scope of its influence. Latin American militaries were threats to democratic society in the past because—in sharp contrast to Western Europe or the United States—they defined internal order and security as one of their central missions. Thus, militaries in Latin America were by design inclined to intervene for political or moral reasons. Today, such intervention has been discredited in many Latin American countries. For the most part, Latin American militaries have not performed well while ruling, and many have committed serious human rights abuses. For many middle class and even elite Latin Americans, military solutions to political, social, and economic problems do not appear tenable. Yet, militaries in many countries continue to exert considerable influence and maintain their importance because of issues like combating narcotrafficking and confronting rising rates of violent crime. Moreover, in countries such as Colombia, Ecuador, or Venezuela, civil war and other violent expressions of polarized politics keep the military deeply involved in politics.

The same cannot be said for the Church or for labor unions. In both cases, changes over time have weakened their influence. For the Church, the rise of Pentecostal Protestant movements has seriously eroded the Church's near monopoly status in religion over the past several centuries. Estimates vary, but it is probably safe to say that various Protestant denominations today represent up to one-quarter of the population of the region. For labor unions, the shift to neoliberal economic development strategies over the past twenty years have undermined the centrality and power of organized labor. The large concentrations of unionized workers that typified state-owned enterprises also guaranteed them political influence. Yet, privatization of state-owned enterprises has led to a loss of political power as new private owners have frequently laid off large numbers of employees to increase efficiency and profits. As a result, neither traditionally important political actor has the same influence over politics today as it did in the past. Business remains influential—and some would argue even more influential in the context of neoliberal reform—but business influence continues to be fragmented and divided by internal competition in many countries. In some, however, the business community's political power represents an important check on government behavior. For example, in Chile, the threat of business hostility and ties between the military and an unusually well-organized business community limits government options in economic and social policy and constitutes a limit to the extent of democratization.

While many of the traditional actors have lost influence, new movements have risen, challenging the political and social landscape and the continuing influence of elite members of society. The development of these movements has benefited from the protection of democratic rule. At the same time, the purpose of many of these movements is to challenge the status quo and to focus on ways in which existing democracies continue to marginalize and exclude traditionally politically weak segments of society. In the case of indigenous movements, some of those challenges have threatened the survival of democracy itself. For example, indigenous mobilization helped produce an impeachment and a coup in Ecuador, a forced resignation of the president in Bolivia, and a virtual collapse of public support for the government of Peru. The mobilization of indigenous groups in Latin America is one of the striking and surprising changes in recent years. Whether it is the role of indigenous mobilization in the Andes, or Mexico's Zapatista rebellion, indigenous movements are making themselves felt in important ways. In the same period of time, women's roles have altered dramatically as well. Women have become increasingly organized and influential politically although many traditional constraints remain. In addition, women have played a disproportionate role in shouldering the burdens of economic reforms.

The articles in this chapter provide an overview of the situation for some of these traditional and emerging actors in Latin America today. In "The New Military Autonomy in Latin America," Consuelo Cruz and Rut Diamint warn against complacency about the military's role in Latin America. The authors note that the tendency in the past two decades has been for a return of the military to the barracks. But that does not mean that civilian governments have developed the kind of control over the military that civilian governments in the advanced industrial democracies exercise. Instead, the military in Latin America enjoys an autonomy that has facilitated the emergence of new roles for the military and its officers and has allowed them to creep into civic and political functions. For example, the inability of most Latin American governments to provide basic security for their citizens has led to a growing practice of military members hiring out for security services to private customers. In general, the essentially unregulated movement of the military into areas they designate "national security" has dangerous implications for the deepening and strengthening of democracy in the region.

While the military has remained an influential and potentially dangerous actor in Latin America, the labor movement faces much more difficult challenges. The labor movement was a part of the democratization story in Latin America in the early twentieth century and an even more critical part of the resistance to authoritarianism in the 1970s and 1980s. Yet, as M. Victoria Murillo argues in "Latin American Labor," the context in the 1990s and into the twenty-first century is much less favorable for unions and workers. Murillo points to two significant challenges for labor. On the economic front, the shift from inward-looking import-substitution industrialization to neoliberalism has had a significant impact on workers. Unemployment has risen while union membership has declined. Furthermore, open trade has made it harder for workers to obtain higher wages. Instead, concerns about competitiveness have led to pressure to keep wages low. As a result, workers are facing harder circumstances and unions are less effective at protecting their members. On the political front, democracy leads workers to focus their political attention and mobilization on the electoral arena. Unions have been slow to respond to this shift in workers' priorities and have therefore lost influence on the course of politics and policy.

Women, traditionally an underrepresented, poorly organized segment of Latin American society, have long suffered economically and socially in proportion to their political marginalization. In recent times, that has changed, as Mala Htun documents in "Women in Latin America: Unequal Progress Toward Equality." The opportunities available to women, politically and economically, have opened up with the re-establishment of democracy in much of the region. Women are better represented in political parties and in legislatures. Women have better access to education and health resources than in the past and more women are finding employment outside of the home. A number of Latin American countries have responded to women politicians and women's political organizations to change old laws and enact new laws to increase protection of women from abuse and assault, particularly in domestic cases. Nevertheless, Htun warns that the progress is uneven, laws and policies are unevenly enforced, and women remain a politically underrepresented group in society.

Deborah J. Yashar documents the rise of another critical, underrepresented group in Latin American societies. Indigenous populations are very large in a number of Latin American countries, particularly Mexico, Peru, Ecuador, Guatemala, and Bolivia. Historically, the approach of most Latin American governments was a combination of violent repression and hoped for (frequently forced) assimilation. For decades, indigenous populations existed at the margins of political life, neither assimilated nor integrated into national politics. Yet, as Yashar notes, the combination of democracy, with its attendant opening of political space, and neoliberal economic reform, with its attendant painful costs, have led to a wave of mobilizations of newly organized indigenous groups. The goals of these groups have not been revolutionary for the most part, but their aspirations pose crucial challenges for the new democracies nonetheless.

DATA TABLES

Table 4.1
Gender and Development in Latin America

			Indicator		
Country	Life Expectancy at Birth	Receiving Prenatal Care (%), 1998	Labor Force Parity Index, 2000	Maternity Leave Benefits—Percentage of Salary Paid During Covered Period	Women in Ministerial Positions (%), 1998
Argentina	77	—	0.9	100	14
Bolivia	64	52	0.6	70	6
Brazil	72	74	0.6	100	4
Chile	79	91	0.5	100	13
Colombia	75	83	0.6	100	18
Costa Rica	80	95	0.5	100	15
Cuba	78	100	0.7	100	5
Dominican Republic	70	97	0.4	100	10
Ecuador	71	71	0.4	100	20
El Salvador	73	69	0.5	75	6
Guatemala	68	53	0.4	100	0
Honduras	69	73	0.5	100	11
Mexico	76	71	0.5	100	5
Nicaragua	71	71	0.6	60	5
Panama	77	72	0.4	100	6
Paraguay	73	83	0.5	50	7
Peru	72	64	0.5	100	10
Uruguay	78	80	0.7	100	7
Venezuela	76	74	0.5	100	3

Source: World Bank. World Development Indicators, 2002. Available at www.worldbank.org.

Note: *Labor Force Parity Index* measures the percentage of women in the workplace in comparison to men in the workplace.

Table 4.2

Estimates of Indigenous Peoples in America, 1979–1991

	Estimated Population	**Total Population (%)**
Argentina	477,000	1.5
Belize	15,000	9.1
Bolivia	4,985,000	71.2
Brazil	325,000	0.2
Canada	892,000	0.8
Chile	767,000	5.9
Colombia	708,000	2.2
Costa Rica	19,000	0.6
Ecuador	3,753,000	37.5
El Salvador	500,000	10.0
French Guyana	1,000	1.2
Guatemala	5,423,000	60.3
Guyana	29,000	3.9
Honduras	168,000	3.4
Mexico	10,537,000	12.4
Nicaragua	66,000	1.7
Panama	194,000	8.0
Paraguay	101,000	2.5
Peru	8,097,000	38.6
Surinam	11,000	2.9
United States	1,959,000	0.8
Uruguay	0	0
Venezuela	290,000	1.5

Source: Deborah J. Yashar, "Indigenous Protest and Democracy in Latin America," in Jorge Dominguez and Abraham Lowenthal, eds., *Constructing Democratic Governance: Latin America in the 1990s—Themes and Issues.* Baltimore: Johns Hopkins University Press, 1996, 92.

Table 4.3
Military Spending in Latin America

	Defense Expenditures (millions of U.S. dollars)		Defense Expenditures per Capita (U.S. dollars)		Defense Expenditures as a Percentage of GDP	
	1985	1998	1985	1998	1985	1998
Argentina	5,157	5,157	169	147	3.8	1.8
Bolivia	181	147	28	17	2	1.8
Brazil	5,515	18.053	41	108	1.8	3.2
Chile	2,287	2.952	189	200	10.6	3.7
Colombia	604	2,542	21	68	1.6	3.2
Ecuador	405	692	43	42	1.8	2.6
Paraguay	85	128	23	24	1.3	2.4
Peru	913	970	49	39	4.5	1.6
Venezuela	1,174	1,281	68	55	2.1	1.5
Guatemala	167	153	21	13	1.8	1.2
Honduras	103	95	23	15	2.1	2
Mexico	1,768	3,755	22	39	.7	1
Nicaragua	314	29	96	6	17.4	1.1

Source: Rut Diamint, "The Military," in *Constructing Democratic Governance in Latin America,* ed. Jorge Dominguez and Michael Shifter. Baltimore: Johns Hopkins University Press, 2003, 66.

Table 4.4
Unionization as a Percentage of the Formal Sector Wage Earners

	Year	Union Density (%)
Argentina	1995	65.5
Bolivia	1994	59.7
Brazil	1991	66.0
Chile	1993	33.0
Colombia	1995	17.0
Costa Rica	1995	27.3
Ecuador	1995	22.4
El Salvador	1995	10.7
Guatemala	1994	7.7
Honduras	1994	20.8
Mexico	1991	72.9
Nicaragua	1995	48.2
Panama	1991	29.0
Paraguay	1995	50.1
Peru	1991	13.3
Uruguay	1993	20.2
Venezuela	1995	32.6
United States	1995	14.2

Source: M. Victoria Murillo, "Latin American Labor," in Jorge Dominguez and Michael Shifter, eds. *Constricting Democratic Governance in Latin America.* Baltimore: Johns Hopkins University Press 2003, 107.

TRADITIONAL ACTORS

4.1 The New Military Autonomy in Latin America (1998)

CONSUELO CRUZ AND RUT DIAMINT

Latin America was once called a "living museum" because archaic elites never quite disappeared from the scene. Instead, they became part of an "exhibit" which, far from being inert, actually ran the place. Now, on the eve of the twenty-first century, Latin America is more politically diverse and dynamic. The tanks that not too long ago roamed the streets have vanished from sight, military uniforms seem passé and coups obsolete, and the era of the generals appears finally to have been consigned to the archives.

Most observers and practitioners seem to agree that Latin American military governments are a thing of the past, and that the future will probably look like the present. The autonomy of the armed forces, according to this vision, will likely remain limited by the defeat or discrediting of the military. But a degree of autonomy will also remain guaranteed—by transition pacts in Chile and Uruguay; by a high degree of homogeneity among military and governing elites in Brazil; by the sheer debility of democratic control mechanisms, as in Paraguay and Nicaragua; and by historical settlements that long ago simultaneously imposed a low profile on the army and secured its place among state institutions, as in Mexico and Ecuador.

This conventional view is neither particularly optimistic nor pessimistic, neither a best-case scenario (deep institutionalization of civilian-democratic supremacy) nor the worst alternative (military insubordination). But it may not be realistic, either. For the ways and means of military autonomy are changing. Everywhere in the region, officers are metamorphosing into a combination of armed seigneurs (in increasingly unsafe societies) and soldiers-cum-entrepreneurs (in restructuring economies). They are crafting institutional and individual strategies to meet an expanded definition of "threats to national security," even as they take advantage of new opportunities to pursue profits. And the new democracies condone these trends in different ways, some more obvious than others, all pernicious in the end.

Consuelo Cruz and Rut Diamint, "The New Military Autonomy in Latin America." *Journal of Democracy* 9, no. 4 (1998): 115–126. © National Endowment for Democracy and The Johns Hopkins University Press. Reprinted with permission of The Johns Hopkins University Press.

So disarming is the notion of the obsolescence of military rule that for the last decade it has led the region's political elites and civil society activists to neglect the balance between civilian-democratic authority and military autonomy. Domestic political actors repeat the old mistake of accommodating—with varying degrees of comfort—the military's self-insulation. Elected officials, in the main, favor streamlining military establishments; but after making resource allocations, they leave the armed forces to their own devices. Politicians tend to avoid the military question. And while civic associations multiply rapidly, they pursue particularistic agendas, which in any case are often shaped or reshaped by those same elected officials and politicians whose involvement in military matters, to say nothing of their leverage over the armed forces, is quite limited.

FEUDAL AUTONOMY AND MILITARY ENTREPRENEURS

Democratic states, like all others, depend on organized coercive power. Hence the unavoidable need for armed forces endowed with sufficient institutional autonomy to perform their duties well. At the same time, democracies are democracies in part because their armed forces remain both functionally integrated with the state and subordinated to legitimate authority. Put another way, civilian authorities bar soldiers from making independent forays into civil and political society, or even into the international arena, and subject the military to the state's internal rules of accountability.

This bundle of prohibitions and allowances is at the core of "dedicated autonomy"— our term for the kind of autonomy that allows the military discretionary decision-making authority and reserved zones of expertise and action, but harnesses its institutional prerogatives to the service of a higher order that it does not determine. The 1960s and 1970s were dark times for Latin America precisely because militaries freed themselves from the prohibitions and controls imposed by civilians and enjoyed unbounded autonomy. But the end of the *unbounded* autonomy characteristic of military dictatorships does not necessarily mean that we can take for granted the establishment of the dedicated autonomy so essential for a democratic order. The 1980s and 1990s may well turn out, instead, to be a prelude to the era of a new kind of civil-military relationship: *feudal* autonomy.

Latin American governments can claim some significant institutional accomplishments in the direction of reining in military autonomy. In the context of post-statist economic restructuring and postauthoritarian politics, reductions in military personnel and cuts in defense budgets serve to help rationalize public finances and to realign the balance between legitimate authority and organized coercive power. The Latin American democracies may be counted among the rationalizers and realigners of the late twentieth century. This is an unambiguously positive development. So too is the ideological and partisan neutrality proclaimed by military elites, not to mention the institutionalization of electoral politics. At the close of the millennium, most Latin American societies remain free of the armed Leviathan that stifled them not so long ago, and this is all to the good.

These gains notwithstanding, a close inspection of Latin American civil-military relations reveals disconcerting signs. Alfred Stepan has identified three areas of potential conflict between the armed forces and democratic governments. One area has to do with accountability for past human rights abuses. The other two areas, more germane to this essay, have to do with the policy-making processes whereby democratic political actors: 1) exert control over the military; and 2) establish criteria for the structuring of defense budgets and their post-allocation supervision. We suggest that it is precisely in these last two areas that a process of "feudalization" may be under way among the armed forces of several Latin American countries.

Like medieval lords, the armed forces are becoming, all at once, guardians of their own limited autonomy, protectors for hire, and de facto guarantors of domestic order. Some of the conditions underlying this "retro-novelty" have deep roots in the region—most notably the corrupt police forces and weak judicial systems that handicap the democratic state. Others are of more recent origin. Over the last decade-and-a-half, economic stabilization and structural adjustment have been the democratic state's most urgent priority. Selected macroeconomic indicators suggest that the region's democracies have, in the main, met their goal. But widespread criminality and the persistence of organized violence also suggest that these democracies have inadequately managed the socioeconomic dislocations that follow from economic crisis and adjustment.

Indeed, the mutually reinforcing effects of institutional weaknesses and socioeconomic dislocations have gradually led to a crisis of democratic governability, one that had already become evident in the early 1990s. In Peru, to take a striking illustration, the Shining Path [guerrilla movement] had by then become an informal provider of "social order" and "justice" in the *barriadas* [poor neighborhoods] of Lima. In Brazil, meanwhile, the majority of citizens expressed the belief that the state had not attempted and would never attempt "to enforce laws on all citizens equally and impartially."

The democratic state's continued incapacity has not been lost on private economic groups and even public managers, who now routinely make their own security arrangements by contracting miniature armies from the "professionals," which is to say the armed forces themselves. In Argentina, private and semi-private demand for protection has resulted in the proliferation of security firms that are privately owned and operated by military officers. Similarly, Colombian petroleum companies routinely avail themselves of security services provided—formally and informally—by the ministry of defense.

If in Argentina and Colombia the military is now an entrepreneurial class with business interests of its own, the cases of Ecuador, Paraguay, Venezuela, Guatemala, Honduras, and Nicaragua are more blatant still. In Ecuador, the armed forces have set out to create a parallel "developmental" state that high-ranking officers claim will remedy national deficiencies in key economic sectors like banking, telecommunications, and transportation. In Paraguay, Venezuela, and Honduras, officers are deeply involved in commercial ventures. In Guatemala, they are shareholders in important industries. In Nicaragua, they are major agricultural producers and highly competitive building contractors.

This kind of military entrepreneurship is a novelty even in Central America, in that it is much more unabashed and formal than the parasitic business deals often associated with the unscrupulous armed forces of yore. In the age of economic liberalism, an officer's self-interested incursions into the market no longer seem an affront to the armed forces' professional code of conduct. In the age of budget-cutting, moreover, the military's institutional integrity, previously deemed incompatible with entrepreneurial activity, is now seen as dependent on it. Although direct control of government is considered off limits to the armed forces, not much else seems to be disallowed.

This enhancement of the military's sphere of action has both paradoxical and plainly deleterious consequences for political-economic reform. In the realm of the market itself, military entrepreneurship fosters unfair competition in two ways. First, military entrepreneurs are better positioned than their private-sector counterparts to influence official decision makers and, thereby, to extract information, concessions, and patronage from the state. Second, because military entrepreneurs control the infrastructure of the armed forces, they can reduce their own businesses' costs by making informal use of everything from military transport vehicles and telephone lines to clerical personnel.

In the political sphere, meanwhile, military entrepreneurship further weakens the democratic state. At the most obvious level, it enables officers to procure independent revenue sources for themselves as individuals and for the military as an institution, thus reducing their dependence on the civilian government. At a more profound level, it expands the range of opportunistic strategies for the military—strategies that can culminate in destructive competition within the state itself. The armed forces of Argentina, Brazil, Chile, and even Bolivia were initially reluctant to get involved in the war against drug trafficking. But in the face of budget cuts, they have done a *volte face,* on the (reasonable) expectation that involvement in this "war" will afford them greater access to foreign aid. The military's bid, in turn, has provoked a defensive reaction from police and security forces—traditionally embroiled in turf rivalries of their own. In Bolivia, the result has been an internal maze of obstructionist moves and countermoves, as police, security, and military forces set out to enhance their respective domains by under-mining one another's efficacy.

The public image of the democratic state cannot afford further erosion. But the search for greater state efficacy can have potentially dangerous con-sequences, as in Brazil, where the armed forces, the police, and the security forces have undergone a process of formal and informal institutional blend-ing. This process, which simultaneously strengthens the three bodies and gives the military additional leverage vis-à-vis both elected governments and civil society, has recently reached a new peak with the creation of the Agencia Brasileira de Inteligéncia (ABIN). The principal task of ABIN, es-tablished under General Alberto Cardozo's leadership, is telling: to keep an eye on "potentially dangerous" popular organizations and prevent their "political manipulation."

THE FAILURE OF DEMOCRATIC ACCOUNTABILITY

If the democratic state's public image continues to erode, so too will its abil-ity to command the loyalty of social groups. But these allegiances will not remain unclaimed for long. Already, the armed forces—and no other single institution—appears capable of responding to society's clamor for public order and the protection of life and property.

That the military enjoys a favorable image should not surprise us. The armed forces in countries like Argentina, Brazil, and Colombia have become the main purveyors of security for important clients, who are then left be-holden to their protectors. In addition, because democratic governments are plagued by weak law-enforcement, those same governments must rely on the military to manage social crises. Hence the view expressed by former Bolivian president Gonzalo Sánchez de Losada that "any president in Peru or Bolivia has to have a very close relationship with the armed forces."

But a "very close relationship" between elected officials and the armed forces can take many forms, depending on the broader context. In most Latin American democracies, this context is partly set by political institu-tions and civil societies that lack both the capability and the will to impose strict control over their military establishments. Take an obvious starting point: the ministries of defense. Brazil has no defense minister. Nicaragua appointed one only in 1997. And in Mexico, Ecuador, Venezuela, Guatemala, El Salvador, and Honduras, either active or retired military officers occupy the post.

More importantly, while defense ministries play a formal role in decision-making processes related to military budget allocations, ministerial monitor-ing is reduced to little more than a fiction once disbursements have been made. This is true even in countries where civilians serve as defense ministers. In

Argentina and Chile, for instance, they exercise limited influence in shaping either the patterns of military expenditure and investment, or the profile of military appointments and promotions.

Other institutional factors hinder democratic control over the military. Most notably, legislative oversight is virtually nonexistent. Like the ministries of defense, legislatures have a say in assigning resources, but they are routinely left in the dark about their subsequent application.

Civil society also remains inattentive to matters having to do with the military's prerogatives. Societal actors, to be sure, have discovered the merits of civic association. In Mexico, for example, there has been an explosion of nongovernmental organizations (NGOs). But there, as elsewhere in Latin America, NGOs understandably define their tasks in discrete terms—women's rights, environmental protection, indigenous concerns. And as elsewhere in the region, NGOs have become dependent for visibility and leverage on political parties and congressional actors.

In South America, this dependency hooks NGOs to legislatures and organized parties that lack both the investigative machinery and the political will required for effective oversight of the military. In Mexico, where the impartiality of military tribunals is highly questionable, oversight becomes all the more problematic (witness the longstanding, symbiotic arrangements between high-ranking officers and the drug cartels). In addition, although the Mexican Supreme Court has opened up the possibility for individual citizens to seek protection from military abuse by appealing to the civil judicial system, the fact remains that ministerial officials charged with the task of investigating such appeals prefer to turn a blind eye. We might call the ultimate result "layered impunity": The abuse of citizens' rights is compounded by officials' tacit disregard of court mandates, which in turn is capped by the court's inability to enforce its own rulings.

These institutional problems find expression in a lack of political will. Politicians across the board show a marked disinclination to press the armed forces for greater accountability, with the result that political parties have no working teams specifically assigned to develop positions on security and defense issues. Nor is there any noticeable executive-legislative cooperation aimed at a serious rethinking of the relationship among public safety, national security, and defense in the radically altered context of a democratic state.

CIVIC ACTORS IN UNIFORM

These institutional, political, and civic weaknesses stand in sharp contrast to the effectiveness of the armed forces' own "civic action" projects, which not only enhance the military's outreach capacity, but also allow it to build and develop clientelistic bases of support. The Peruvian army is simultaneously involved in a new social "mission"— the fight against poverty—and in the creation of mass political organizations. Similarly, the Mexican military's participation in literacy campaigns gives it both a high civic profile and the opportunity to establish informal ties with local *políticos,* party bosses, and even community leaders. In Brazil, where the armed forces have traditionally been depicted as the nation's "civilizers," soldiers provide on-site health services. In Ecuador and Peru, personnel stationed in frontier communities are able to develop patron-client linkages.

Accompanying these civic action projects by the armed forces is a troubling public discourse that recasts socioeconomic and collective action problems—poverty, migration waves, displaced workers, and ecological degradation—as "threats to national security." This free-ranging national security discourse overextends the national defense agenda. Potential enemies of the nation now range from guerrillas and paramilitary organizations to drug traffickers and foreign economic competitors in a globalized market.

Reasserting the classical distinction between public safety and national security might serve as something of a corrective to this overextension. Indeed, in an age of presumed globalization, this distinction only becomes more relevant. To retain some influence over the shape of their institutional roles and the boundaries separating their spheres of action, domestic political actors must have a clear sense of their core responsibilities and prerogatives.

Insisting on a distinction between public safety and national security is only a start, but we believe that it is a good one. The reason is as straightforward as it is old. The concept of national security remains at its core a matter of "us vs. them." Nations traditionally deploy this outward-looking concept when facing other nations as potential foes. Public safety, in contrast, is inward-looking. It aims, ideally, at the establishment and preservation of legitimate order in the internal commons. In Latin American countries, reordering the internal commons would entail professionalizing the police and security forces, shoring up judicial systems, and reforming local government institutions, particularly at the municipal level. It also would require careful government regulation of joint police-military operations when responding to such transnational threats as drug trafficking.

Meeting these challenges presumes the capacity to shift resource allocation in favor of institution-building and away from the kinds of expenditures on sophisticated weaponry we discuss below. It also presupposes a recognition that public "threats" are rooted in problematic social conditions best addressed through well-rounded public policy. After all, displaced workers, migrant flows, drug trafficking, and guerrilla and paramilitary challenges to state authority are interrelated problems, ones that are exacerbated by the dislocations that attend political and economic restructuring.

These daunting problems begin to appear less daunting the moment we draw a sharp distinction between public safety and national security. For it is precisely this distinction that opens up the possibility for joint intervention by governments and civil society groups, even when elected representatives are (unduly) excluded from national security decisions. Witness the theme of Cuauhtémoc Cárdenas' successful campaign for the mayoralty of Mexico's Federal District—*ciudadanización*, an almost untranslatable term that elicited citizens' interest in joining with elected officials to fight institutionalized graft, common criminality, and urban degradation.

THE "TOYS-R-US" SCHOOL OF MODERNIZATION

The possibility of mobilizing cooperation between government and civil society—and it is only a possibility—may well prove illusory. But reasserting the distinction between public safety and national security also serves another useful purpose: It calls attention to the risks of blurring the line between the two. Thinly spread among so many "security" fronts, the armed forces may appear sapped of their capability to provide for national defense. This perception, in turn, is used by the armed forces to justify high-end weapons purchases that would otherwise be precluded.

We believe, for reasons spelled out below, that this perception of weakness is detrimental to democratic development partly because of the expenditures it justifies. This claim goes against two prevailing views of military expenditures. One view has it that expensive arms acquisitions merely indicate that the region's armed forces are trying to protect their comparatively small (and diminishing) shares of the Gross Domestic Product. Another common view hinges on the notion that by letting the military have its "toys," civilian governments can keep the generals out of politics.

The first—call it the "resource protection" view—is both inaccurate and simplistic. The region's armed forces, no doubt, do try to protect their resource allocations (in this their behavior is no different from, say, their U.S. counterparts' hesitant adjustment to the end of the Cold War). But judging from the last decade's trends in military expenditures, most of the region's militaries have managed to avoid a significant and/or secular decline in their shares of GDP. As Table 1 shows, a clear and sustained decrease is observable only in Argentina. (Having gorged on resources even more than the armed forces of Chile and Brazil during the years of dictatorship, the Argentine military was particularly vulnerable to budget cutting.) Colombia, unsurprisingly, actually registered clear increases in military expenditures as a percent of GDP. The trends elsewhere, as can be gleaned from the table, are markedly uneven.

The "resource protection" view, moreover, fails to capture the complex motivations behind the military's bid for greater shares. The armed forces are also driven to acquire sophisticated weapons by a genuine fear that one country's arms purchases can unsettle the regional strategic balance to the

Table 1

Military Expenditures as a Percentage of GDP (period averages)

	1988–90	1991–95	1996–97
Argentina	2.0	1.5	1.2
Brazil	1.4	1.2	1.3
Chile	3.3	3.3	2.9
Colombia	1.7	2.0	3.0
Ecuador	1.9*	2.1	2.1
Uruguay	1.5	1.8	1.4
Paraguay	1.1	1.4	1.3

Source: The Western Hemisphere Macroeconomic Information System, February 18, 1998.

*This figure is a two-year average for 1989–90.

detriment of the rest. In the mid-1990s, Chile's acquisition of Scorpene submarines and Leopard-1 combat vehicles from West European suppliers, as well as Peru's rush (after its 1995 border war with Ecuador) to acquire equipment from Ukraine alarmed the Argentine Ministry of Defense. Soon a call went out for a "spiritual retreat"— a closed meeting of high-ranking defense officials and military officers. The overriding concern at this meeting was the impact of possible shifts in the region's "strategic balance" on their country's national security.

If such reciprocal fears are commonplace in the politics of nations, they also can be destabilizing—especially to new democracies in a region plagued by old rivalries. Argentina and Brazil, for instance, share a long history of hostility. MERCOSUR (the Southern Cone Common Market) may well turn out to be the alchemist that, through the logic of mutual economic gains, transforms this hostility into cooperation. But this transformation is not likely to extend to other regional players, especially Chile and Peru. Declarations by high-ranking military officers in both countries hint instead at a potential revival of old animosities in the face of regional economic integration. In Chile, Brigadier General Hugo Jaque has publicly favored the creation of an "Economic Security Division" within the armed forces in order to deal with conflicts that might arise as a direct consequence of MERCOSUR. In Peru, General Walter Ledesma has speculated that "problems on the economic front may unleash conflict"— noting tersely that Chile's Armed Forces are already "prepared," and warning that it is not inconceivable that "the enemy is coming."

With regard to the acquisition of arms, both transparency and trust are sorely lacking in the region. Age-old suspicions among neighboring countries are still there, in places deeply entrenched. These suspicions may push professional strategists to propose, and nationalist publics to support, unreasonable increases in military spending, especially on high-end material.

This brings us to the the "Toys-R-Us" argument, which says: "Let the generals have their weapons and they will stay out of domestic politics."

This line of reasoning is flawed on several counts. First, it justifies institutionalized intrastate extortion—not a prudent move from the perspective of democratic development. Second, the argument is reminiscent of the modernization hopes nourished in the 1950s and 1960s, which were dashed in the 1970s precisely because the armed forces graduated from playing with weapons to playing with countries. Third, elemental notions of fairness, not to mention political prudence, dictate that, barring a foreign threat to the nation, even the military must share in the sacrifices of restructuring. Fourth, even if we set aside prudence, justice, and the lessons of history, this argument is still flawed because it assumes that the region's militaries have "modernized" their worldview and therefore will be satisfied with "adequate" resource allocations.

Adequacy can be an extremely subjective concept. How much is enough? Should we, in addition, overlook the disturbing adaptive strategies used by the region's armed forces to cope with the past decade's budget cuts? Nothing in these strategies suggests that a process of military professionalization, as normally understood, is under way. Quite the contrary. Private security firms owned and managed by members of the military hardly fit the notion of a professional corps. Blurred institutional boundaries among police, security, and military forces, and the latter's hegemony, are also at odds with the broader ideal of modernization. Equally incongruous with the image of professional armed forces is their involvement in the "war" against drug trafficking for purposes of revenue enhancement and turf-building. Nor does the military's cultivation of clientelistic support or its effective exemption from democratic rules of accountability suggest that modernization has occurred.

REQUIREMENTS FOR PEACE
AND DEMOCRACY

Democratic transformation in Latin America's formal political arrangements is at once real and mesmerizing, and is thus neither to be derided nor to be taken entirely at face value. Close scrutiny of informal practices and structures is warranted. In the area of civil-military relations, these already give pause on a number of counts. To recapitulate briefly: Civil societies are resurgent, but they are also segmented and dependent on elected officials, who in turn are embedded in political structures too weak to control the creeping autonomy of the armed forces. Militaries have transgressed the boundaries that previously barred them from both entrepreneurial action and civic action, in pursuit of an expanded definition of "national security." The armed forces may well cross the increasingly blurry line between limited autonomy and a kind of feudal sovereignty.

This is no overstatement. The news is bad indeed when military expenditures as a percentage of GDP become an unreliable indicator of the armed forces' influence, because the figures tell us virtually nothing about officers' business profits and the military's institutional control of assets that are not monitored by the national *contralorías.* The news is even worse when the shocking becomes an accepted fact of life. The armed forces' profit-making and asset-accumulation are one example. The increasingly dense patron-client linkages directly connecting the military to an array of social groups are another. The list goes on, and as it grows longer, the military continues to enhance its autonomy.

Neither the established democracies of the West nor the citizens of Latin America's democracies can afford to ignore these new forms of military autonomy. The stability of regional peace and the quality of the region's democracies are simultaneously at stake. To support both peace and democracy, three requirements must be met. First, resurgent civil societies must take an active interest in things military. Second, democratic political actors must develop and exercise ministerial, legislative, and party-based oversight capabilities vis-à-vis the military. And third, major established democracies, particularly the United States, must prove willing and able to implement policies conducive to achieving the first two goals. It is not clear that any of these requirements is being met. If anything, we detect trends in the opposite direction. In the midst of political and economic restructuring, it may seem too much to ask for greater and more responsible involvement in issues of civil-military relations by all parties concerned. The alternative, however, is to risk losing a great deal of what has been accomplished in the last two decades by democracy-builders in Latin America.

4.2 Latin American Labor (2003)

M. VICTORIA MURILLO

At the beginning of the twentieth century, Latin American workers in early industrializing nations organized in a hostile political environment, while in other countries, labor unions were almost absent or incipient. At the end of the twentieth century, labor unions enjoyed more freedom to organize in new democracies, albeit challenged by capital mobility, economic liberalization, and state retrenchment. This chapter analyzes the new challenges faced by organized labor in Latin America at the turn of the century, with special attention to South America and Mexico. In doing so, it emphasizes the previous development of labor political strategies in closed economies

Maria Victoria Murillo, "Latin American Labor" from Jorge I. Dominguez and Michael Shifter, eds., *Constructing Democratic Governance in Latin America.* pp. 100–117. © 2003 The Johns Hopkins University Press. Reprinted with permission of The Johns Hopkins University Press.

with highly interventionist states. These strategies become less effective in open economies with shrinking public sectors. However, at the time of economic liberalization and institutional transformation, the political influence of labor unions still serves to affect the design, implementation, and schedule of market reforms. At the same time, partisan loyalties between unions and labor-based political parties shape the interaction between organized labor and the government. Partisan loyalties generate trust and increase the willingness of labor unions to bear some of the costs of reforms. Additionally, competition for leadership within the union movement explains labor militancy against market reforms, whereas union fragmentation influences labor effectiveness in shaping policy implementation during the period of economic liberalization.

The temporal coincidence between democratization and economic liberalization imposed further challenges for organized labor. Whereas labor unions had usually been at the forefront of political liberalization protests, democratization reduces the influence of labor mobilization once elections became the principal means of expressing citizen preferences. In the context of this dual transition, labor unions try to deliver better wages and more secure employment to their members, but they encounter new challenges, such as increasing economic volatility. Even when they realize the need for innovative strategies to deal with new issues, strategic innovation develops slowly. It can take one of three forms: new alliances, organizational autonomy, or industrial participation. In the first case, labor unions break with old allies and seek new partners, including political parties and other sectors of the population also hurt by economic liberalization. In the case of organizational autonomy, they concentrate on the survival of the organization through the acquisition of new resources created by the opening of the economy, such as the provision of new services in competitive markets or the acquisition of privatized property. Industrial participation involves labor unions adopting a more proactive role in the implementation of new technologies to increase labor productivity in a competitive economy. Strategic innovation is important because the traditional strategies of labor unions have become less effective. The article concludes by arguing that institutional reform and leadership competition can accelerate the slow pace of strategic innovation while providing a new role for labor unions in new democracies.

FROM THE LABOR MARKET TO THE POLITICAL MARKET

In the twentieth century, labor organized first in mutualist associations and later through unions. It started earlier where foreign investment in extractive activities and the association of employers prompted labor organization as well as in the urban centers of early industrializing nations. Immigration waves, which contributed to the supply of labor, imported labor organizers and provided new ideologies, such as anarchism and socialism. These imports contributed to the organization of labor unions. For the most part, governments and employers resisted and repressed labor organization, fearing distortions in labor markets, attacks on private property, and the threat of large-scale social conflicts. State repression curtailed workers' bargaining power on the shop floor while the limitations to universal suffrage restricted their citizenship rights in many countries. Thus, workers fought to organize for collective bargaining in the labor market, but did not pursue political strategies.

During the first half of the twentieth century, political liberalization changed workers' options. The expansion of suffrage made workers an electoral constituency for political parties. Elites' concern with the "social question" brought even non-labor-based governments toward the institutionalization of industrial relations. Moreover, in countries experiencing high political volatility, organized labor could become an important ally for aspiring political elites. The partnerships between politicians and labor unions provided the latter with channels to reach the state and the former with political constituencies. The value of labor political strategies became apparent once labor partisan allies gained power.

In Mexico, the House of the International Workers of the World organized Red Battalions during the Mexican Revolution. In return for their military support, the 1917 constitution included labor rights. By 1919, the Mexican Regional Workers' Confederation (CROM) had chosen a political strategy to compensate for its industrial weakness and organized the Mexican Labor Party (PLM) to support the candidacies of Presidents Álvaro Obregón and Plutarco Ellías Calles. In exchange, Calles appointed CROM labor leader Luis Morones as the minister of industry, trade, and labor. Morones was explicit in the use of a political strategy as an alternative to industrial action under the label of "tactical flexibility" (*acción múltiple*). This strategy was followed by subsequent union leaders after the establishment of the Mexican Workers' Confederation (CTM) during the administration of pro-labor President Lázaro Cárdenas (1934–40).

A decade later, in Argentina, Colonel Juan Perón used his position as secretary of labor to build a political support base in an alliance with labor leaders tired of dealing with hostile governments. Many Argentine labor leaders dropped previous political identities, from syndicalism to socialism, to embrace a strategy that, as in Mexico, was labeled "tactical flexibility." This strategy included the compensation of industrial weakness with political influence and the provision of services that workers were not receiving from employers.

Despite the predominance of labor political strategies, there was variation in their effectiveness. Political strategies did not guarantee success. These strategies were most effective when labor unions were strong enough to define favorable terms of exchange with their allies and when these allies gained power. The partisan relationship with organized labor, politicians' need for workers' support, and the strength of organized labor defined the degrees of "inducements" and "constraints" for labor organization in the labor code. Strong labor movements were able to obtain better terms in their political exchange with politicians building up their support coalitions. Allies in power often facilitated unionization, and sometimes made it compulsory, as in the Argentine and Mexican public administrations. If allies were in the opposition, the state could curtail unionization or limit it to the company level, as in Chile and Peru.

Labor market regulations further reinforced the value of political strategies because they provided the benefits that were not achieved through collective bargaining. As a result, even when allies had not yet reached power, the promise of access to the state made political strategies more appealing. Hence, organized labor followed political strategies even when allies were not in power. During the 1920s, labor unions were affiliated with APRA and the Socialist Party in Peru, the Communist and Socialist parties in Chile, and the Communist Party in Brazil. Political strategies brought further repression when labor allies were in the opposition. In Peru, the Peruvian General Workers' Confederation (CGTP) was dissolved by President Luis Sánchez Cerro after a failed Aprista insurrection in 1932. Nonetheless, Aprista labor leaders would increase their influence at the expense of communist leaders during the administration of José Luis Bustamante (1945–48). In Brazil, President Getúlio Vargas also repressed communist labor leaders after a failed series of attempted insurrections in 1935. However, he would later move to control labor unions, co-opt labor leaders, and enact a labor code favorable to urban workers in 1943. In Chile, the labor-based parties were allowed to be elected to Congress first and to the executive later as part of the Chilean Popular Front in the 1930s. However, communist leaders were persecuted from the end of World War II until the late 1950s.

During the Great Depression, Latin American governments began to adopt trade protectionism and currency-appreciating exchange rate policies, building the conditions that would facilitate domestic industrialization even before import substitution industrialization and state intervention became public policies. In a context characterized by closed economies and state intervention, organized labor's use of political strategies became more effective. Protectionism reduced the pressure on labor costs while state expansion facilitated unionization because public managers with soft budget constraints were more concerned with labor peace than with productivity. Moreover, state-owned companies were large and involved sectors with relatively skilled labor, which facilitated unionization. Additionally, the weak bargaining power of labor unions in small and medium-size private companies further increased their support for state intervention into labor markets. Finally, in addition to the economic context and employers' resistance to workers' organization, state-driven ideologies of social change further contributed to labor preferences for political strategies.

Concerns about labor unrest and a simultaneous search for labor constituencies prompted Latin American governments to regulate labor markets even in the absence of explicit alliances. The movement toward labor market regulation increased labor's attention to political developments. Once regulations were in place, labor unions found that state intervention in industrial relations made the appeal to labor peace or electoral support more effective with politicians than with private employers. This situation resulted in politicized labor movements trying to achieve by regulations what they could not reach through collective bargaining. As described by Silvia Sigal and Juan Carlos Torre,

> Except in some particular cases of unions whose productive location made them strategic, industrial unionism was, in general, too weak to follow an economic strategy centered at the company level. Due to this weakness and the scope of state intervention, labor relations issues, such as work time, vacations, job mobility, and minimum salary have been subject to regulation rather than to collective bargaining between unions and employers (author's translation).

Not even the wave of authoritarianism that spread through the region in the second part of the twentieth century eroded labor preference for political strategies. Instead, when military rulers and repressive regimes hindered political strategies, labor unions politicized industrial action to counteract political repression. Because democratization became, in many cases, a precondition for workers' organization and collective bargaining, labor unions used strikes and mobilizations to resist military regimes. Their mobilization contributed to create a climate of social unrest during the process of political liberalization that preceded democratic transitions.

There were early instances of anti-authoritarian mobilization. Venezuelan labor unions mobilized against the dictatorship of Marcos Pérez Jiménez, and in support of political liberalization, leading to the Punto Fijo pact and the inauguration of democracy in 1958. Twenty years later, Brazilian military rulers faced a "new unionism" (*novo sindicalismo*), which became an important democratizing force through the formation of the Workers' Party (PT). In Chile, Uruguay, and Argentina, organized labor also appealed to general strikes to protest against military rulers in the wake of the 1982 debt crisis.

In sum, political volatility, economic protectionism, and state intervention favored the politicization of Latin American labor unions. In turn, governmental elites perceived labor unions as one of the few organized groups in weak civil societies. Their reactions ranged from co-optation of political constituencies to repression of challengers to the established order. In either case, state reactions confirmed the importance of political strategies for labor unions, demonstrating that they could not ignore politics even if all they wanted was to bargain collectively in the industrial arena. Therefore, union politicization was not provoked solely by left-wing ideologies or partisan co-optation. It was the response to a context that made political strategies more useful than industrial action. However, at the end of the twentieth century, economic liberalization and increasing capital mobility challenged the political strategies of Latin American labor.

ECONOMIC LIBERALIZATION: TRANSFORMATION AND CHALLENGES

The Latin American debt crisis and the recession of the 1980s triggered a process of economic liberalization in the region that challenged both labor political strategies and their industrial bargaining power. In an effort to cope with the crisis, most Latin American countries began opening their economies and retrenching their states through privatization, deregulation, and decentralization of the provision of services. Additionally, capital mobility increased at a much faster rate than labor mobility around the world. This situation increased labor insecurity even in countries with scarce capital due to growing financial volatility and competition for attracting mobile capital with cheaper labor costs. These processes challenged labor unions' emphasis on states and national public policies. Meanwhile, union members suffered the costs of the transitions toward open and competitive economies as well as the dramatic changes in the organization of work provoked by the crisis of Fordism.

At the turn of the century, economic and industrial transformations were weakening the power of traditional labor unions. Economic liberalization and state reform particularly affected formal-sector workers, that is, the natural constituencies of labor unions. Trade liberalization sharpened differences among workers, in particular between those in tradable and non-tradable sectors and more and less competitive firms. This heterogeneity made it harder to organize workers based on horizontal solidarity. International competition and privatization also provoked labor restructuring and layoffs in sectors that had been among the most highly unionized in the past, thus reducing the relative influence of unions. Despite cross-national differences, higher unemployment, starting during the recession of the 1980s, further hurt labor bargaining power by increasing job insecurity for workers, as shown in Table 1. Even as the region emerged from the recession in the 1990s, unemployment continued to be high in Argentina, Colombia, Panama, Peru, Uruguay, and Venezuela. Indeed, even Chile, which had experienced a dramatic reduction in unemployment after the end of the 1980s recession, had an unemployment rate of more than 10 percent by 2000. The effect of unemployment is dual because it erodes the ranks of unions while increas-

Table 1

Open Unemployment (annual averages)

	1985	1990	1995	1997	1998
Argentina	6.1	7.5	17.5	14.9	13
Bolivia	5.7	7.2	3.6	4.4	—
Brazil	5.3	4.3	4.6	5.7	7.7
Chile	17	7.4	6.6	5.3	6.2
Colombia	13.8	10.5	8.8	12.4	15.1
Costa Rica	7.2	5.4	5.7	5.9	5.4
Ecuador	10.4	6.1	6.9	9.3	8.1
El Salvador	—	10	7	7.5	7.6
Honduras	11.7	6.9	6.6	5.2	5.8
Mexico	4.4	2.8	6.2	3.7	3.2
Panama	15.7	20	16.4	15.4	15.5
Paraguay	5.1	6.6	5.5	6.4	13.9
Peru	10.1	8.3	7.9	8.4	8.2
Uruguay	13.1	9.2	10.8	11.6	10.1
Venezuela	14.3	11	10.3	11.4	11.3

Source: International Labour Organization, *OIT Informa: Panorama Laboral* (Lima: International Labour Organization, Statistical Annex, 1998).

ing the competition between those employed and those searching for a job. This hinders the bargaining position of unionized formal workers as a result of the absence or insufficiency of unemployment insurance systems.

Perhaps more important, market reforms made workers more uncertain about their future labor market position, particularly in the protected and public sectors, which were the most unionized. Formal- and public-sector employment with the highest degree of unionization experienced the sharpest decline during the period of market reforms. During the 1990s, the informal sector grew by more than 3 percent as a percentage of urban employment. Argentina, Colombia, Ecuador, Honduras, Mexico, and Peru, however, have informal sectors that are larger than the average. Additionally, the public sector shrank by almost 3 percent in the region (Table 2). The reduction of the public sector was more dramatic in Argentina, Costa Rica, Ecuador, Honduras, and Panama, whereas Chile had already a slim state because the shrinkage had taken place before 1990. These variations are important for understanding that, despite common traits, the region's union experiences are very different.

The variation in union experiences can also be perceived in the diversity of unionization of formal-sector wage earners in the region. Table 3 confirms the diversity in unionization across countries. However, it is important to note that figures on union density can be deceptive because they tend to be self-reported and Ministries of Labor only compute membership when they register unions. Moreover, they are taken as a percentage of

Table 2

Changes in Urban Employment

	Informal Sector (percent urban employment)		Public Sector		Other Formal Urban Employment	
	1990	1998	1990	1998	1990	1998
Latin America	44.4	47.9	15.8	13	40.1	39.1
Argentina	52	49.3	19.3	12.7	28.7	38
Brazil	40.6	46.7	11	9.3	48.4	44
Chile	37.9	37.5	7	7.2	55.1	55.3
Colombia	45.7	49	9.6	8.2	44.7	42.8
Costa Rica	41.2	45.4	22	17	36.8	37.6
Ecuador	55.6	58.6	18.7	14.8	25.7	26.6
Honduras	57.6	57.9	14.9	10.3	27.5	31.8
Mexico	47.5	49.6	25	21.7	27.5	28.7
Panama	36	38.5	32	21.8	32	39.7
Peru	52.7	53.7	11.6	7.2	35.7	39.1
Uruguay	39.1	41.2	20.1	16.8	40.8	42
Venezuela	38.6	43	22.3	19	39.1	38

Source: International Labour Organization, *OIT Informa: Panorama Laboral* (Lima: International Labour Organization, Statistical Annex, 1998).

formal workers, yet the informal sector grew substantially, as shown in the previous table.

In summary, market reforms created new challenges for Latin American labor. Open economies made labor costs salient because they could not be transferred to consumers, thereby heightening productivity concerns for international competition. Latin American labor unions (and employers) have relatively little experience in dealing with productivity and training to make workers more competitive in order to keep their jobs in an open economy. State retrenchment increases the number of private employers relative to public managers or state bureaucrats dealing with labor unions. Strict budget constraints and production costs became more important than social unrest and political support. Thus, political influence lost relevance vis-à-vis labor market strength after the economic transition. Labor unions have to learn to deal with these new conditions while their members are suffering the cost of economic transition. Labor political strategies need to be reassessed in light of the new economic conditions, where collective bargaining may be more useful than pressure on a retrenching state.

However, because there is a difference between open and opening economies, political strategies and access to government can still be effective during the period of institutional reform commonly associated with trade liberalization and state reform. Governments wanted to implement the changes as quickly and smoothly as possible to make their economies at-

Table 3

Unionization as a Percentage of the Formal Sector Wage Earners

	Year	Union Density (in percents)
Argentina	1995	65.5
Bolivia	1994	59.7
Brazil	1991	66
Chile	1993	33
Colombia	1995	17
Costa Rica	1995	27.3
Ecuador	1995	22.4
El Salvador	1995	10.7
Guatemala	1994	7.7
Honduras	1994	20.8
Mexico	1991	72.9
Nicaragua	1995	48.2
Panama	1991	29
Paraguay	1995	50.1
Peru	1991	13.3
Uruguay	1993	20.2
Venezuela	1995	32.6
USA	1995	14.2

Source: International Labour Organization, *World Labour Report* (Geneva: International Labour Organization, 1998), 237.

tractive for capital. In this context, organized labor can demand input in institutional reforms or compensation for the costs of the transition. Hence, although in an already open and privatized economy unions' political influence loses effectiveness, organized labor could use its political clout during the process of institutional change. For this reason, partisan loyalties between labor unions and governments implementing market reforms were able to provide labor unions with policy input and compensations even as economic liberalization and deregulation reduced the influence of politics on economic activities and industrial relations.

PARTISAN LOYALTIES AND LABOR COMPETITION

The legacy of previous political strategies and alliances influenced the response of organized labor to economic liberalization. Previous interactions between labor unions and political parties created mutual expectation, which, in turn, shaped their interactions at the time of stabilization and market reforms. Labor unions trusted their allies when they claimed the need to implement these policies despite their costs to their constituencies. Hence, when partisan allies were in government, organized labor usually cooperated. Most labor unions accepted market reforms in Mexico under PRI President Carlos Salinas (1988–94), in Argentina under Peronist President Carlos Menem (1989–99), and in Chile during the administration of Concertación President Patricio Aylwin (1990–95). In contrast, when partisan allies were in the opposition, organized labor distrusted the government's goals with the new policies and usually rejected market reforms. The Brazilian Single Workers' Confederation (CUT), associated with the opposing PT, boycotted the stabilization attempts of President José Sarney (1985–90) and tried to sabotage the privatization efforts of Presidents Fernando Collor (1990–92) and Fernando H. Cardoso (1995–2002). The Bolivian Workers' Confederation (COB), controlled by left-wing groups, resisted market reforms under Víctor Paz Estenssoro (1985–89) and Gonzalo Sánchez de Lozada (1993–97), following a long history of hostility with the National Revolutionary Movement (MRN). In Uruguay, the Inter-Union Workers' Plenary—National Workers' Convention (PIT-CNT) associated with the FA also resisted adjustment efforts under Colorado President Julio María Sanguinetti (1985–90) and market reforms attempts under Blanco President Luis Alberto Lacalle (1990–95).

Although market reforms created similar challenges for organized labor in different countries, partisan loyalty or hostility to the governing party provoked different reactions to these policies. Partisan loyalties influenced the interaction between labor unions and governments implementing market reforms. The trust placed in labor allies or the distrust of long-term adversaries shaped labor perceptions of the trade-offs associated with market reforms and the unions' disposition for negotiating with the government. Labor unions were predisposed to collaborate with labor-based parties implementing market reforms although these policies created uncertainty and distress for their membership. They trusted the long-term benefits of these policies based on previous interactions with the governing party when political influence effectively compensated for industrial weakness to the benefit of union constituencies. Partisan loyalties also provided communication channels to inform labor leaders about the constraints faced by governing politicians. Labor-based parties, therefore, had a comparative advantage in implementing market reforms because they were less likely to face labor opposition. Because labor-based parties wanted to keep this comparative advantage, they tried to avoid reforms that could facilitate the replacement of their labor allies from leadership positions within the unions. For that reason, they were less likely to reform the institutions that regulate collective bargaining and labor organization.

In Mexico, during the administrations of Presidents Carlos Salinas (1988–94) and Ernesto Zedillo (1994–2000), and in Argentina, under President Menem (1989–99), several discussions and proposals sought to reform the regulations on labor organization and collective bargaining. In Mexico, a single labor code regulated individual and collective labor law and labor organization. Both the Salinas and Zedillo administrations left the labor code untouched. In Argentina, different laws regulated individual labor contracts, collective bargaining, and labor organization. This separation allowed the government to modify individual labor law regarding temporary contracts without touching the laws on collective bargaining and labor organization until 1998. That same year, Menem passed a reform that strengthened the power of national unions by centralizing collective bargaining, opposing demands of decentralization made by businesses and international financial institutions. Despite the zeal with which these administrations implemented market reforms and the fact that opposition political parties and private businesses also demanded changes in those regulations, reform of collective labor rights and regulations of labor organization did not occur. In these cases, labor-based administrations used their links with unions to facilitate economic liberalization and state retrenchment. Hence, they did not want to face the risk of breaking with labor allies that had supported the process of market reform.

Conversely, governments hostile to labor or competing with labor-based parties had more incentives to reform labor legislations. In Chile, military ruler Augusto Pinochet pioneered economic liberalization and state withdrawal from economic activities after he ousted Socialist President Salvador Allende in a 1973 coup. Pinochet banned a large number of unions and suspended collective bargaining and the right to strike. In 1979, under international pressure, he reformed the labor code to permit worker organization only at the company level as well as collective bargaining without unions. Although the law authorized unionization, it introduced important limitations in the activities and scope of unions. For instance, the 1979 law imposed restrictions on the organization of the public sector and temporary workers as well as banning confederations and any form of collective bargaining beyond the company level. In 1994, after the democratic transition, the Center-Left coalition Concertación, which controlled the Chilean Unified Workers' Confederation (CUT), reformed labor regulations. This reform facilitated collective bargaining and labor organization in an effort to reward labor allies that restrained their militancy and supported further economic liberalization and privatization. The 1994 law authorized unions within the public sector and abolished the prohibition on intercompany collective bargaining. It also protected union leaders from dismissal and facilitated union financing by demanding that workers who benefited from collective bargaining contribute 75 percent of union fees to avoid free riding.

The influence of partisan loyalties in generating trust and facilitating collaboration between labor unions and governing parties was more apparent for the cases where labor allies were in the opposition. The lack of trust and communication between governments and labor unions usually resulted in labor resistance to market reforms. In Brazil, labor union resistance hindered the stabilization efforts of President José Sarney and boycotted market reforms under his successors. The mutual distrust of labor unions and non-labor-based administrations often resulted in repression of the former in order to implement market reforms. In Bolivia, President Paz Estenssoro resorted to a state of siege in order to impose structural adjustment on the bellicose COB. In Peru, President Alberto Fujimori (1990–2000) undertook market reforms against the resistance of left-wing and Aprista unions. Furthermore, to counteract labor hostility, Fujimori passed labor reforms targeted at liberalizing the labor market and weakening labor unions. Therefore, partisan loyalties and trust influenced the interaction between organized labor and governments during the process of economic liberalization and state retrenchment.

In addition to partisan loyalties, leadership and interunion competition also shaped union-government interactions. Leadership competition within the unions weakened their tendency to collaborate with their partisan allies in the government during the period of economic opening. If opposition to market reforms attracts the electorate and union members, it may result in the growing influence of militant union activists who threaten to replace allied labor leaders. In this case, leadership competition could make allied labor unions more militant against market reforms. This was the case of the Venezuelan Workers' Confederation (CTV). Although a proportional representation electoral system allowed other parties in the executive committee, AD union leaders who had supported President Perez in the party primaries controlled the CTV. However, after Perez's announcement of market reforms provoked urban riots showing popular discontent, AD union leaders ceded to the pressures of left-wing activists in the CTV and called a general strike less than six months into his administration. Additionally, the growing influence of union challengers, associated with the left-wing Causa R, which opposed market reforms, continued to induce the militancy of AD union leaders later into Perez's administration. In contrast to the experience of Argentina's Menem and Mexico's Salinas, who were able to sustain labor support for the process, the opposition of the CTV contributed to the demise of Perez's market reforms.

Interunion competition or organizational fragmentation weakened labor bargaining power, and thus the capacity to achieve concessions of economic liberalization. Coordination problems made collective action of rival organizations more difficult and weakened their bargaining power. For instance, the Mexican labor movement was divided into several national confederations, all associated with the PRI, but competing for members outside the public administration (where the Federation of Public Services' Unions, or FSTSE, had a monopoly of representation). During the Salinas administration, government officials manipulated the competition among these rival confederations for scarce resources. Interunion competition allowed the government to make fewer concessions in return for labor quiescence, support in social pacts, and campaigning for the North American Free Trade Agreement (NAFTA).

Union monopoly, in contrast, strengthened labor bargaining power at the time of institutional reforms because it reduced coordination problems in the exchange of labor support for concessions. In the case of Argentina, the General Labor Confederation (CGT) faced no interunion competition since its unification in 1992. Whereas before its unification, Peronist President Carlos Menem was able to play one faction against the other, after unification union monopoly strengthened CGT bargaining power and policy input. Organized labor succeeded in changing several laws, creating union pension funds, and modifying social security reform in order to restrict private providers from competing with union-run health funds. Additionally, privatizations included a provision for employee ownership with union administration that facilitated union purchase of companies in their sectors. Likewise, the reform of individual labor regulations introduced clauses that required union agreement for the use of short-term temporary contracts.

Therefore, partisan loyalties, partisan leadership competition, and interunion competition are important variables in understanding the interaction between unions and governments during a period of economic liberalization. We cannot assume a uniform labor reaction to the common challenges created by market reforms without considering these variables and their effect on labor influence in the process of economic liberalization.

DEMOCRATIZATION AND LEADERSHIP COMPETITION

The simultaneous development of market reforms and democratization had important political consequences for the region's citizens, who gained access to government during the 1980s recession. The economic downturn and later the costs of the transition toward open economies frustrated citizens in new democracies and made democratic consolidation a more difficult task. Organized labor not only faced the costs of economic liberalization but also discovered the erosion of its political strategies, which had been hidden during the democratic transitions, when politics became legal again.

The mobilization of labor unions and other organized groups (such as social movements) had more visibility during political liberalization undertaken in the final phase of authoritarian regimes. Labor unions organized strikes and mobilized workers in public demonstrations against authoritarian rulers, pushing for the acceleration of transitions toward democracy. After democratic transition, elections rather than mobilization became the primary means of expressing citizens' preferences in new democracies. Labor protests were redirected toward policy implementation, but democratic elections focused on counting numbers rather than measuring the intensity of preferences. Moreover, economic liberalization made the number of workers in the most "unionizable" sectors shrink while business concerns and "free market" ideologies became predominant. Thus, aspiring politicians sought to gain the votes of a growing unorganized informal sector rather than those of a shrinking formal working class that had already established partisan loyalties. Weak democratic institutions further reinforced this process by facilitating the emergence of "new populisms" whose political support base was the informal sector as opposed to the traditional populist link with organized labor.

Political liberalization also affected the internal dynamics of labor unions by providing more options for electoral allies and by creating an environment more favorable to the democratization of unions themselves. The experience of the *novo sindicalismo* in displacing the *Varguista* leadership in the Brazilian labor movement was linked to the process of political liberalization. In fact, in those countries where labor political strategies had been more effective, "incorporating" governments had regulated leadership competition to make the replacement of their loyal allies more difficult, thus controlling labor unrest. In those cases, the process of internal leadership competition was restricted and required legal changes. In Mexico, where labor unions had been associated with the seventy-year governing party, unions feared that democratization would reduce their access to the state and facilitate their replacement. Mexican union leaders thus resisted democratization because this process challenged the efficiency of their political strategies by increasing the risk of having the PRI lose power while prompting internal leadership competition within their unions.

In short, dual transitions toward open politics and economies created conditions that made the traditional political strategies of labor less effective. Economic liberalization reduced the bargaining power of organized labor whereas democratic politics reduced their political influence due to the emergence of new constituencies, shrinking ranks, and increasing independence of voters. Therefore, it was not only harder, but also less meaningful, to gain access to the state. Hence, the influence of organized labor declined in electoral politics and its access to the state became less effective in shaping work conditions.

LABOR PROSPECTS IN THE NEW MILLENNIUM

Labor mobilization and political influence were able to affect the pace of economic and political transitions, but elections and industrial relations became more important once the transitions were over. However, because labor unions used political strategies during periods of political and economic liberalization, they were slow in adapting their behavior to open politics and economies. In fact, numerous unions resisted economic liberalization while refusing to change their strategies and discourses even in a context of dramatic institutional transformation and political decay. In cases where change in strategies occurred, they took one of three non-exclusive forms: (1) new political and social alliances, (2) organizational autonomy, (3) industrial participation. The change in the environment and leadership competition create incentives for strategic innovation, albeit if at a slow pace.

The first strategy involved the formation of new political and social alliances. These alliances broke old partisan loyalties and resulted in workers participating in the creation of new political parties, extending their alliances to other popular sectors, particularly in the informal sector. These new labor groups rejected corporatist mediations and state control of labor unions. Subordination to state regulations offered less rewards than at the time of the original "incorporation." Moreover, these labor activist ranks were challenging incumbent labor leaders who had maintained their control of labor movements helped by state regulations on union governance. In fact, due to the existence of such regulations, these new labor leaders had to break formally with the unions recognized by the state and claimed "autonomy" from the state. In Venezuela and Brazil, they called themselves "new unionism" and refused to join the national confederations associated with corporatism. In Argentina, they broke with the Peronist CGT and founded the Congress of Argentine Workers (CTA). In Mexico, the National Workers Union (UNT) joined union leaders with a long tradition of "independence" from the PRI with others who just had broken with PRI corporatism.

These new labor unions defined alliances with sectors of the population previously excluded by unions and with emerging political parties. They made efforts to reach out to the growing informal sector, the landless peasants, and the unemployed. They joined their efforts in popular protests against the uneven distribution of the costs created by adjustment and economic liberalization. Their relationship with political parties, though, was more diverse. Brazilian union leaders in the *novo sindicalismo* were at the core of the founding group of PT and their Venezuelan counterparts followed their example when organizing Causa R. The Argentine CTA union leaders participated in the creation of FREPASO and Mexican "independent" union leaders, for the most part, joined the Mexican PRD when it emerged. However, because the latter two were not labor-based parties as the PT and Causa R, labor played a minor role in defining the internal dynamic of these parties. Moreover, although these new parties enjoyed reasonable electoral success, they were unable to match the labor-based parties founded in the 1930s and 1940s. During the 1990s, the PT always came in second in presidential elections. In its best nationwide performance, Causa R won a fourth of the votes for the 1993 presidential election. The PRD has remained the third party in Mexico, and although the FREPASO won the

1999 presidential elections, it did so in alliance with the traditionally middle-class-based Radical Civic Union (UCR).

A second strategy was organizational autonomy. It did not require breaking partisan loyalties or building new ones, but rather concentrating on useful resources for the survival of the labor union organization after state retrenchment and economic opening. Unions offered services previously provided by the state to their members. To cover these services, they took advantage of their influence at the time of market reforms. Unions in privatized sectors that were most challenged by the economic transition have adopted this strategy in Argentina and Mexico. Some Argentine unions, for example, have participated in the privatization of state enterprises in their sectors. In Argentina, the oil workers' union owns the oil fleet of the former state-oil company Yacimientos Petrolíficos Fiscales (YPF). The electricity workers' union bought various public utilities and electricity transmission companies and received the concession of a coal mine while the railroad workers' union was granted the concession of a railroad. Along with other unions, they have created their own pension funds after the government enacted a pension reform, and have also reorganized their health care funds to improve competition. These new union-run "business" activities emerged from the market reforms implemented by President Menem and provided unions with resources to compensate for declining union dues while serving their members. In Mexico, too, the teachers' union and the telephone workers' union abandoned their dependence on state-regulated social security. Instead, after breaking their official links with the PRI, they developed their own provision of services for members, including credit unions and other social benefits.

The third strategy, industrial participation, involves adopting new ways of implementing productivity and competitiveness with the involvement of labor unions and workers' input. The Union of Telephone Workers of Mexico (STRM) participated with management in the training of workers and the measurement of productivity while joining quality circles. Causa R unions have introduced member voting on collective contracts. In Brazil, the automobile unions of the *novo sindicalismo* led a process of mid-level corporatism with automakers', autoparts', and autodealers' organizations around long-term restructuring programs that included union participation. Despite these examples, most unions were either slow or failed to participate in the productive process with the aim of increasing productivity to keep their members' jobs. The reasons are twofold. First, market reforms lacked institutional incentives, such as worker councils, to foster such participation while employers were reluctant to share company information or decisions with labor unions. Second, labor unions accustomed to mechanisms of mobilization and political influence were slow to build the professional expertise necessary to sustain this third strategy. Furthermore, the costs of the economic transition made this strategy very difficult to follow in those areas where increases in productivity involved more layoffs than training.

Strategic innovation evolves only at a slow pace even though labor unions have become aware of the limitations created by traditional strategies. Even traditional unions are starting to distance themselves from their allied parties and strikes can still result in labor gains, particularly in the public sector. In Mexico, after the PRI lost the 2000 presidential elections, public-sector employees went on strike for the first time and were successful in obtaining a special bonus from the lame-duck administration of President Ernesto Zedillo. In Venezuela, despite the dramatic decline of AD and President Chávez's continuous attempts to co-opt unions, AD union leaders still controlled the labor movement and organized a successful strike in the oil sector, taking advantage of high oil prices in early 2000. However, these were exceptions rather than the rule. For workers producing tradable products and in the private sector increasing international exposure curtailed the effectiveness of strikes. What are the elements that can facilitate strategic innovation in this context?

Leadership competition in open economies can accelerate innovation while increasing the voice of workers as citizens of new democracies, thus potentially reducing the political distress that increasing economic exposure creates. Liberalizing governments attempted to increase competitiveness by deregulating labor markets and reducing labor costs (e.g., by curtailing payroll taxes). However, there has been little institutional innovation to foster labor unions' involvement in increasing the productivity of the company (e.g., through work councils). Additionally, labor market deregulation, for the most part, did not target the rules related to leadership competition within unions. Reducing the cost of leadership competition within trade unions to deal with Michels' "iron's law of oligarchy" would foster competition on what leaders can offer members in open economies, thus leading to innovation. However, governments seem to fear that militancy against economic liberalization would be the new "offer" provided by leadership competition to union constituencies.

Leadership competition and rotation imply a trade-off regarding labor strategic innovation. Labor involvement in productivity and training or in the development of organizational autonomy requires specialization, which often creates an asymmetry of information. Asymmetries of information usually empower incumbent leaders and make leadership competition more costly. However, the fear of replacement can make leaders responsive to workers who should be involved in new work technologies associated with increasing productivity and worker involvement in production (e.g., flexible specialization, quality circles). Moreover, at a time when workers face growing insecurity due to increasing exposure to international shocks in opening economies, union democracy offers workers the possibility to voice their concerns and have them expressed by their leaders. That is, union democracy improves the quality of leaders (and probably provides checks on corruption) while giving voice to workers as part of an organized civil society. In new democracies that are undergoing enormous institutional change and have weak civil societies, the inclusion of organized groups such as labor unions in the public debate could help to avoid disillusionment with the political process and provide more time for democratic consolidation.

CONCLUSION

Latin American organized labor adopted political strategies at a time when these were more effective than industrial action. Political strategies were still somewhat effective during economic and political liberalization because labor unions could obtain concessions in return for facilitating the development of these processes. After the dual transition, these strategies lost effectiveness because labor costs became more important than labor peace for policy makers. At the same time, citizens' votes (including those of the unorganized poor) became more necessary to win elections than the mobilization of organized labor, further weakening labor unions' bargaining power vis-à-vis politicians.

Despite the decline in the effectiveness of their traditional political strategies, labor unions were slow to adapt to new circumstances. The reasons for the delay can be found in the institutional inertia of labor organizations after so many years of operating in a context where political strategies were useful. Additionally, labor leaders were concerned with maintaining leadership positions that risked being challenged by experimentation and innovation. At the same time, policy makers did not provide institutional incentives because their agenda sought to neutralize labor opposition rather than promote union innovation. In this context, the promotion of leadership competition could serve as an instrument for fostering innovation. However, government officials fear its effect on increasing militancy and managers worry about efficiency losses derived from the ensuing specialization. Nevertheless, because the challenges for Latin America in the early twenty-first century include democratic consolidation and competitive economies, the risk implied in leadership competition may be worth taking. Although the role of labor as umpires of some political systems has declined, responsive labor unions can give workers a voice in the workplace and in a strong civil society needed for democratic consolidation. Thus, dual transitions toward democracy and markets in the region may gain from similar changes in labor unions. Workers are being exposed to increasing economic competition. Political competition can strengthen their voice in the workplace and in the policy discussion of new democracies.

EMERGING ACTORS

4.3 Women in Latin America: Unequal Progress Toward Equality (1999)

MALA HTUN

[At the end of the twentieth century], the basic elements of democracy, such as free elections and the rule of law, have been consolidated in virtually every Latin American country. But the extension of democratic rights and liberties to all citizens remains an unfinished task. Improving the rights of women, who make up just more than half the region's population, represents a fundamental and immediate challenge.

Women form one-third of Latin America's labor force, constitute more than half of university students in many countries, and hold 16 percent of the seats in national legislatures. Governments have created state agencies on women, changed discriminatory laws, and introduced new public policies designed to improve women's lives. Yet, many new laws and policies are poorly implemented and funded, or target only small groups of women. Women's status varies greatly between and within countries according to socioeconomic status, regional origin, and skin color. In short, progress toward gender equality in Latin America is uneven.

A NEW TREND IN POLITICS . . .

Women's political representation in Latin America has increased gradually since the 1970s, but it is still low relative to women's share of the electorate and their participation as active party members. Historically, women tended to rise to power at the margins. Their opportunities to participate in decision making were greater at lower levels of the organizational hierarchy, in less prestigious government ministries, and outside major cities. Many women leaders gained power as the wives, daughters, or sisters of prominent men.

The 1990s brought some changes to these traditional patterns. Women in Argentina, Costa Rica, and Guatemala headed political party lists in national elections. A woman was named president of Peru's Congress, and there are women at the helm of powerful ministries, such as justice in Chile and foreign affairs in Mexico.

Governments are taking dramatic steps to boost women's presence in decision making. Under pressure from women politicians and women's movements, Argentina, Bolivia, Brazil, Costa Rica, the Dominican Republic, Ecuador, Peru, and Venezuela have adopted national laws requiring political parties to reserve 20 to 40 percent of candidacies for women.

Whether quotas actually improve women's presence in power depends on each country's political parties and its electoral system. Quotas work best in a closed-list electoral system under which voters cast ballots for a party list, not for individual candidates, and the party leadership controls the placement of candidates on the list. In this system candidates have an incentive to cooperate to maximize votes for their party. In Argentina, where a closed-list system is in place and a quota law was passed in 1991, women occupy 28 percent of the seats in Congress, the highest percentage in the region.

There must also be effective enforcement mechanisms to ensure that political parties comply with the quota. In Argentina in 1993, when male party leaders failed to apply the women's quota to the placement of candidates on party lists, women challenged the lists in court, where they were declared invalid.

In Brazil, applying the women's quota has proved more problematic because of the country's open-list electoral system and undisciplined parties. In the national elections of October 1998, Brazilian parties uniformly failed to comply with the 25 percent women's quota. Brazil's open-list electoral system provokes competition for votes among candidates from the same party. Because they are relative newcomers, women lose out to their male colleagues in the struggle for money and resources. Thus, despite the quota, the number of women in the Brazilian Congress actually decreased following the October election.

Women legislators have also been able to exercise power more effectively by uniting into broad, multipartisan alliances. Organized around specific women's issues, political alliances have secured the approval of new laws on domestic violence, sex crimes, and workplace discrimination in Argentina, the Dominican Republic, Mexico, and Peru.

. . . BUT AN UNCHANGED LEGAL CULTURE

Latin American countries have adopted major reforms to grant women equal rights in family and constitutional law, to recognize domestic violence as a crime, and to outlaw sex discrimination. In the region's labor codes, women have long enjoyed mandatory maternity leave and they cannot be dismissed from their jobs for becoming pregnant. All Latin American countries have ratified the United Nations Convention on the Elimination of All

Forms of Discrimination against Women, and most have ratified the Inter-American Convention to Prevent, Punish, and Eradicate Violence against Women.

However, in many countries laws remain in force that are antithetical to gender equality. Women in all countries except Chile, Cuba, Mexico, and Venezuela are prohibited from certain types of employment, including working at night, holding dangerous or unhealthy jobs, lifting heavy objects, working in mines, and distilling or manufacturing alcohol.

In many countries, rape is considered a crime against custom, not against a person. This means that the goal of the law is to protect good customs, not the person who is raped. In some countries rape and other sex crimes can only be committed against "honest women."

With the exception of Cuba, abortion is considered a crime in all Latin American countries. Many permit "therapeutic abortion," or abortions performed to save the life of the mother, and some countries also permit abortions if the pregnancy results from rape. However, legal abortions are rarely performed in public health facilities. Middle- and upper-class women who can afford private doctors and clinics have safe access to legal abortions, but poor women do not.

Although few women are prosecuted for having abortions, criminalization pushes the practice underground. The millions of women who undergo abortion every year in Latin America must do so in unregulated and often dangerous circumstances. Clandestine abortions put women at risk of infection, hemorrhage, damage to the uterus or cervix, and adverse reactions to drugs. Botched abortions account for a high proportion of maternal mortality in the region today.

Even where laws reflect principles of gender equality, discriminatory practices persist. The central problem with women's legal rights in Latin America is not the lack of legislation and regulation, but the inconsistent application of the law. Women's movements today are focusing on increasing a woman's knowledge of her rights and training lawyers and judges to be sensitive to gender prejudice. A promising trend is the growing number of women with legal training and the entrance of more women into the legal profession; in many countries almost half the students enrolled in law school are women. Women now make up 45 percent of trial court judges in the region as a whole but merely 20 percent of appeals court and almost no supreme court judges.

Fifteen Latin American countries have human rights ombudsman offices, and six of these (Colombia, Costa Rica, El Salvador, Guatemala, Mexico, and Peru) have a specific institution charged with working with women. These "women's rights ombudsman" agencies receive complaints about human rights violations, investigate cases, work to train and sensitize judges and law enforcement personnel, and have challenged the constitutionality of discriminatory laws in court. Improving women's legal rights in the region requires not only changing old laws but also transforming the legal culture.

ATTACKING VIOLENCE AGAINST WOMEN

Domestic or intra-family violence against women is widespread in Latin America. Surveys show that approximately 50 percent of all Latin American women have suffered violence at the hands of their husbands or partners. The problem is compounded by women's unequal economic and social positions. Since women have fewer opportunities than men in the labor market, receive lower wages, and are subject to family and social pressures, leaving an abusive relationship appears unviable, both to women victims and to their male abusers. A 1997 study conducted by the Inter-American Development Bank in Nicaragua found that 41 percent of non-wage-earning women are victims of violence, compared with 10 percent of women holding salaried jobs outside the home.

By 1997, 12 Latin American countries had adopted new laws to define the crime of domestic violence, map out policy measures, and offer judges and prosecutors greater power to issue protective orders. Following models created by feminist non-governmental organizations (NGOs), governments have established shelters, launched educational campaigns, and set up centers to counsel women who have been victims of violence and to offer legal advice. Inadequate resources have, however, led to poor enforcement of new laws and incomplete implementation of preventive and treatment programs. Moreover, most efforts have focused on urban areas, leaving rural women with little recourse.

The most important policy change has been the establishment of women's police stations. First created in Brazil in 1985, the stations are staffed by women police officers trained to handle cases of domestic violence and rape. Today hundreds of women's police stations can be found throughout Latin America.

Women's police stations have helped communities recognize domestic violence as criminal behavior that constitutes a violation of human rights. And with the establishment of the stations, the reporting of domestic violence and rape has grown. However, the rates at which violent offenders are investigated, prosecuted, and sentenced remain low.

Studies from Brazil show that only about one-third of the complaints received by women's police stations lead to an investigation, and far fewer than this to prosecution. In Chile, only one in five domestic violence suits ends in a judgment, and only one in twenty of these results in conviction of the offender. In Ecuador in the early 1990s, the state prosecuted 10 percent of those arrested for sexual violence, with little more than half of these convicted. Although victims of violence feel increasingly empowered to seek help, perpetrators continue to enjoy impunity.

A major problem is securing medical evidence acceptable to law enforcement authorities. Many victims find it difficult to obtain medical examinations because of the scarcity of officially recognized facilities, few female personnel at those facilities, and demeaning treatment. Women's police stations, unfortunately, are often inadequately funded and poorly organized; working at these stations is also considered to be a low-prestige position within the police force.

NEGLECTED HEALTH ISSUES

Latin American women's basic health has improved from a generation ago: female average life expectancy was 54 years in the 1950s, 64 years in the 1970s, and is now 71 years. Still, there are major gaps in the area of reproductive and sexual health, and in some countries there have been alarming increases in rates of breast and cervical cancer, heart disease, and AIDS.

The 1994 United Nations Conference on Population and Development in Cairo urged governments to approach women's health in an integral manner. The integral approach represents a major advance over past policies, which tended to treat women exclusively in their roles as mothers and reproducers.

Brazil has been a pioneer in the integral approach. In 1984 the government introduced a Program for Integral Assistance to Women's Health that had been designed according to the recommendations of experts and activists from the women's movement. However, the program remains unimplemented in the vast majority of cities and states around the country. The Brazilian example reveals that women's health programs often lack sufficient funding and the political will to seriously implement them.

Women's access to prenatal care and obstetric services has increased in most countries, leading to lower rates of maternal mortality since the 1970s, although the variation among countries is substantial. In general, the coverage and quality of health care remain inadequate, a situation reflected in the low frequency of screening for cervical cancer. In most of the region, cervical cancer is the most common form of cancer death in women. Cervical cancer is preventable by regular pap smears and effective laboratory analysis, but few women have access to prevention and treatment options. In Mexico, for example, a 1997 survey of 4,000 women found that 42 percent were unaware of the purpose of a pap smear, and that 97 percent had never had one. In Peru, one study in 1997 estimated that merely 7 percent of Peruvian women had had a pap smear taken.

Limited access to health care is also reflected in high unmet demand for modern contraceptives. Government-run family planning programs frequently have limited coverage, so many women have no access to safe and reliable contraception, or they self-medicate, without good information and at some risk. As a result, illegal abortions are frequent and many poor women suffer complications because of dangerous and unsanitary conditions. In many countries, women's NGOs, such as Sì Mujer in Nicaragua and

SOS Corpo in Brazil, have begun to fill the gap left by inadequate state action in family planning and women's health.

Sterilization is among the most widely used methods of family planning in Latin America, except in countries such as Argentina and Chile, where it is illegal or access is restricted. High rates of sterilization are common in most developing countries: the percentage of contraceptive users who are sterilized is two times higher in developing countries than in developed countries (22 versus 11 percent). Latin America is not an exception. In 1990, the percentage of women contraceptive users who were sterilized was 38 percent in Mexico, 44 percent in Brazil, and 69 percent in El Salvador. Data from Brazil show that there is a high correlation between low levels of economic development and the frequency of sterilization: in 1991 there was a much higher proportion of sterilized female contraceptive users in the poorer northeast (63 percent) than in the wealthier city of São Paulo (36 percent). Sterilization is seen as the cheapest option for women who have little money to buy other methods or who lack information about their options and proper usage.

Many women are sterilized without receiving prior information about the procedure or without giving their consent. A recent study from Mexico found that one-quarter of women who had been sterilized were not informed beforehand that the procedure is irreversible. Nationwide family planning targets in Peru have created incentives for public health officials to pressure women into sterilization, leading to widespread abuses that have been documented by women's organizations, members of the Peruvian Congress, and the Roman Catholic Church.

In Argentina and Chile, improved economic conditions have led to improvements in women's general health. But the governments of these two countries continue to neglect reproductive health, which contributes to high abortion rates. Although the procedure is considered a crime, in 1990 there were an estimated 4.5 abortions per 100 women aged 15 to 49 in Chile, compared with 2.7 in the United States, 2.3 in Mexico, and 1.2 in Canada. Abortion rates are high in Chile because of a lack of information about contraceptive methods. In Mexico, Colombia, and Brazil, state activity in family planning has lowered the abortion rate. Many Latin American governments do little concerning reproductive health and sexuality because they are reluctant to confront the Roman Catholic Church. The consequences of this inaction are grave for women's health.

WOMEN'S WORK?

One of the most salient trends in Latin America over the past several decades has been the increasing participation of women in the economy. Women make up one-third of the region's labor force, but they continue to participate on unequal terms with men.

Women are generally clustered into lower-status and lower-paying jobs from which promotions are rare. In Brazil, for example, 50 percent of women work in occupations that employ only 5 percent of the male labor force; conversely, 50 percent of men work in areas where only 5 percent of the female labor force is employed. More than 80 percent of tailors, primary school teachers, secretaries, telephone or telegraph operators, nurses, and receptionists are women.

As a result, women earn less than men. Women's average wages were between 20 and 40 percent lower than men's in 1992 (a gap comparable to that found in Western Europe and North America). Since the 1970s, however, income differentials between men and women have generally decreased, particularly in urban areas. And the gap is smaller for younger women than for older women. In 9 out of 12 countries surveyed by the United Nations Economic Commission on Latin America and the Caribbean, women 25 to 34 years of age earned between 80 and 90 percent of men's income in 1992.

The problem of pregnancy discrimination is widespread in the region. In theory, laws in Latin America demand that employers protect the rights of pregnant women and new mothers to care for their babies and retain their jobs. Labor laws designed to protect women include mandatory maternity leave, protection from being fired for becoming pregnant, prohibitions in some countries against the administration of pregnancy tests, and requirements that businesses with a certain number of women workers provide day-care services on the premises and allow women to take breaks to nurse their babies. Many countries forbid companies from firing workers during their maternity leave, and others protect new mothers from dismissal for an established period of time following their return to work. Women are often allowed to take a paid leave to care for young children who are sick.

In practice, however, employers, in order to cut costs, go to great lengths to avoid situations where the law is applied. Some companies are reluctant to employ women full time and resort to strategies such as subcontracting, part-time employment, and paying for piecework done at home. Others deliberately pay women less than men to compensate for the perceived higher costs of employing women.

Even when child-care facilities do exist, many women find that commuting to work with children in tow is time-consuming and unpleasant for the child, and prefer instead to use child care that is close to home. Most mothers working outside the home rely on family members or domestic employees to care for their children.

Some businesses require a pregnancy test or a sterilization certificate as a condition of employment, or fire women workers once they become pregnant. Pregnancy tests are widespread in the maquiladoras and factories in the export processing zones of Mexico, Central America, and the Dominican Republic, even though national laws prohibit them.

EDUCATION: NOT SEPARATE, BUT NOT EQUAL

Women's enrollment in schools and in institutions of higher education has advanced in the region, but there are substantial variations among countries in women's access to the educational system, women's levels of educational attainment, and women's choices in school. Although Latin Americans have become steadily more literate since the 1970s, female illiteracy tends to be higher than men's; women's illiteracy is most acute in rural areas and among older populations.

In 1995, 48 percent of primary level students and 52 percent of secondary level students in Latin America were female. Yet there is tremendous variation among countries. In Guatemala, primary school education is obligatory, but only 45 percent of school-age girls are enrolled.

The percentage of women enrolled in universities in the region has climbed steadily: in 1970, women made up 35 percent of enrolled university students; in 1980, 43 percent; and in 1995, 49 percent. In terms of gender equity, enrollment rates offer some encouragement, but need to be carefully examined among other trends. Women are enrolled at higher rates than men in several countries, and women tend to repeat fewer grades than men. However, because of labor-market discrimination, women are in practice required to have higher levels of education than men—in one case four more years of schooling—in order to compete in the workforce on equal terms.

School dropout rates are highly correlated with poverty and maternity. Families who take children out of school generally cite the lack of economic resources as the reason. Forced to pick between keeping a son or a daughter in school, families generally choose the son on the assumption that he will be a more profitable investment for the family's future. Adolescent pregnancies also keep women from completing their education.

Certain areas of study remain predominantly masculine or feminine. Women are underrepresented in fields related to science and technology, but overrepresented in lower-paying occupations such as education, nursing, and library science. However, women's presence in schools of business administration and, as noted, law is growing steadily.

School textbooks and curriculum content tend to reproduce gender stereotypes. Women appear less frequently than men in images and references in textbooks. When they do appear, they are frequently depicted in stereotypical roles, cooking or cleaning in the home.

Women's studies programs are becoming more numerous, and have consolidated into a reputable field of study and research. Brazil was one of the first countries in the region to develop women's studies programs and [at the start of the twenty-first century] there are more than 20 university centers around the country dedicated to the field. However, few courses about women are offered to undergraduates, even though this is a crucial mechanism for teaching future generations about women's rights and equal opportunities.

THE BALANCE SHEET

The status of women in Latin America is generally improving. Women's basic opportunities have increased from a few decades ago, which can be seen in better health, higher levels of educational attainment, and greater access to economic resources. International conventions and agreements related to women's rights have proliferated in the 1990s, intensifying the pressure on local governments to take steps to improve women's status. Most have responded at least symbolically to this pressure by formulating national plans concerning women, announcing new public policies, and creating special mechanisms to represent women's interests in public decision making. When pressured by women's movements and women politicians, some governments have made major advances in the areas of legal reform, violence against women, and education. Still, many new laws and policies are not enforced or implemented, leaving an immense variation in women's status between and within countries.

Relative to their numbers and potential, women are an underorganized social constituency and political force. Women's movements have become more numerous and diverse since the 1970s but lack the national political presence of other interest- and identity-based organizations such as labor movements and church groups. The socioeconomic, political, and ideological differences that exist among women often serve as barriers to women's organization. But when women find ways to mobilize despite their differences, they are able to push local governments and civil societies to take more action to promote gender equality.

■

4.4 Indigenous Protest and Democracy in Latin America (1996)

DEBORAH J. YASHAR

On New Year's Day 1994 the Chiapas rebellion captivated Mexico and the rest of the Americas. Shocked by the well-planned and executed military maneuvers, analysts were left wondering where this movement had come from, whom it represented, and what it wanted. Yet, from a comparative perspective, the Chiapas uprising represents perhaps only the most dramatic and internationally followed example of organizing within indigenous communities. Indeed, in the 1980s and 1990s, there has been a rise in

Deborah J. Yashar, "Indigenous Protest and Democracy in Latin America." In Jorge I. Dominguez and Abraham F. Lowenthal, *Constructing Democratic Governance: Latin America and the Caribbean in the 1990s*. pp. 87–105. © 1996 The Johns Hopkins University Press. Reprinted with permission of The Johns Hopkins University Press.

indigenous organizing and mobilizing in Latin America, including international campaigns for the five hundred years of resistance and the 1993 Year of Indigenous People, the emergence of Indian organizations in Ecuador, Bolivia, Colombia, and Guatemala, the rise of autonomy movements in Panama and Nicaragua, the 1993 election of Víctor Hugo Cárdenas, a prominent indigenous leader, as vice-president of Bolivia, and the awarding of the 1992 Nobel Peace Prize to Rigoberta Menchú, a Mayan Indian leader from Guatemala.

The codevelopment of the increasing organization of indigenous communities and the hemispheric embrace of political democracy in the 1980s and 1990s present the opportunity and responsibility to reevaluate the relationship between ethnic cleavages and democracy in Latin America. Why have indigenous communities become increasingly politicized along ethnic lines in recent years? What are the conditions under which strong ethnic identities are compatible with, and even supportive of, democracy?

This chapter argues that these movements are primarily a response to the twin emergence of delegative democracies and neoliberal reforms. Democratization in the 1980s provided greater space for the *public* articulation of ethnic identities, demands, and conflicts. Nonetheless, indigenous communities have experienced a new stage of political disenfranchisement as states fail to uphold the individual rights associated with liberal democracy just as neoliberal reforms dismantle state institutions that had previously extended legal corporate class rights, representation, and social welfare. Building on social networks left in place by prior rounds of political and religious organizing, indigenous groups have mobilized across communities to demand rights and resources denied them as Indians.

Confronted with the lost momentum of traditional leftist parties and popular movements that have yet to define a political vision that resonates in indigenous communities, newly mobilized indigenous communities have organized and gained a new domestic and international presence. Yet, in contrast to the examples of the former Yugoslavia, Sri Lanka, Rwanda, and Burundi, indigenous mobilization in Latin America has rarely been a prelude to civil war struggles to capture the state; Sendero Luminoso, the guerilla movement in Peru, is the obvious exception, although even here the combatants do not see their struggle as part of an ethnic conflict. Rather, Latin America's indigenous movements have largely demanded greater democracy, including greater political representation in and access to national political institutions as well as greater local autonomy.

This chapter constitutes, therefore, a springboard for preliminary ruminations and discussions about a topic that has received scant attention within the Latin American context. It is sure to overgeneralize and misrepresent, particularly given the multiple meanings associated with ethnicity and democracy. These are problems associated with delineating ethnic identities, boundaries, and relations in the different Latin American countries, and an-

alyzing the intersection of ethnic and democratic politics from a macrocom-
parative perspective when very little work to date has explored these issues
in a systematic, reliable, and crossnational framework. Yet, against the history of exclusion, denial, and repression of Latin American indigenous peoples coupled with the knowledge that the failure to address ethnic cleavages
elsewhere has unleashed a politics of xenophobia and a xenophobia of violence, it is important to begin addressing the future of democracy in pluri-
ethnic states in Latin America. I begin with two descriptive overviews of the
ways in which Latin American states have interpreted ethnic relations, followed by a discussion of the recent mobilizations within and by indigenous
communities. The final two sections explain why these movements have
emerged and how to bridge ethnic cleavages in a way consonant with
greater indigenous representation and the deepening of democracy.

THE "INDIAN QUESTION" IN LATIN AMERICA

The history of ethnic relations in Latin America has been one of violence,
subordination, denial, and assimilation. With the arrival of Columbus and
the ensuing conquest by Spanish and Portuguese settlers, indigenous communities were subsequently subordinated to the political authority of newly
created Latin American states and the spiritual authority of the Catholic
Church. Military expeditions against the indigenous population were particularly brutal in Uruguay, Argentina, Chile, and to a lesser degree in
Brazil. These same countries, like many others in Latin America, enacted
legislation to attract European immigration, arguing that this would improve the racial composition and therefore the economic and political
prospects of the new states. Latin American states treated indigenous peoples as heathens, a threat to security, an impediment to economic development, and a source of cheap, if not free, labor. The various states enacted
corresponding, if at times internally contradictory, policies to address these
fears, perceptions, and goals. They killed those perceived as a threat to an
emerging nation-state, isolated or denied the existence of those in remote
areas, coerced populations for their labor, and promoted a policy of assimilation.

Indeed, in the twentieth century, goals of assimilation informed educational programs and state policies designed to construct a homogeneous nation. Most politicians and scholars assumed that the existing state was
legitimate but that the construction and identification of primary identities,
be they around the mestizo nation or class, needed fixing. To this end, Latin
American governments created Indian institutes to study indigenous populations—much as one would analyze national folklore—and to create the
mechanisms to assimilate them into the national (read modern mestizo)

population. While Brazil formed an Indian office in 1910, other Latin American countries founded these offices in the 1930s and 1940s. Moreover, in 1940, the first Interamerican Indigenista Congress was held and led to the founding of the Interamerican Indigenista Institute. This policy was designed in places like Mexico, Guatemala, Peru, and Bolivia to incorporate people perceived as backward into the ranks of a new, presumably more civilized nation. States encouraged indigenous men and women to discard any public display of indigenous identity, encouraged the adoption of a mestizo identity, and thus publicly encouraged miscegenation to "whiten" the population.

Latin American states, therefore, promoted ethnic assimilation (and often miscegenation) to arrive at a mestizo national identity where population reflected ideology. According to positions articulated by state officials and intellectuals, mestizaje allowed for social mobility as one's ethnic status changed from indigenous (other) to mestizo (us); this process presumably depoliticized ethnic cleavages. Yet, if ideologically, ethnic identity became fluid, states and landlords often continued to repress these same communities (particularly when rebellious in the face of state colonization, development plans, and repressive rural labor relations) according to a rigid understanding of the appropriate ethnic and class rights of the assimilated population. Consequently, economic mobility of the newly assimilated rarely advanced beyond a relatively low ceiling.

The dominant paradigms in the social sciences after World War II tended to reinforce nineteenth-century liberal discourse in Latin America regarding the primordial, transitory, and atavistic nature of indigenous groups. The social sciences, in general, tended to devalue the salience and contemporary character of ethnicity in Latin America and elsewhere. While anthropologists conducted invaluable ethnographic work in the region, much of this work drew from paradigms that assumed that ethnic identities, particularly among indigenous groups, were an expression of a past world. Whether informed by traditions as diverse as modernization or Marxist theory, scholars tended to reduce ethnic identity to primordialism. They often assumed that, with economic development and the further integration of ethnic groups into an industrializing capitalist economy, presumed atavistic identities would and should subside. One anthropologist, writing in the early 1970s, stated that "Ecuador is not a country inhabited by white folk, for as an ethnic minority they only add up to scarcely one-tenth of the total population. Neither is it a country of Indians, for in that case its history would be one of regression, or else, of stratification . . . the nation is Mestizo. . . . Once the Indians enter civilized life . . . the Mestizo part of the population will be more homogeneous."

Modernization theorists posited that, with economic growth, the proliferation of technology, and social mobilization, individuals would transcend ethnic ties and become, among other things, more individuated, secular, and eventually more committed to the nation-state. Marxists, however, tended to argue that, with the increasing impoverishment associated with capitalism and the increasing integration of ethnic groups into the labor market, primary ethnic identities would subside as economically exploited individuals realized that the more salient and liberating corporate identity would revolve around class. In short, the expression of ethnic identities was seen as a problem. In practice and ideology, states and intellectuals identified ethnicity and the ethnic problem as coterminous with the indigenous and the indigenous problem. From this perspective, getting rid of Indians (through assimilation or repression) was necessary to arrive at and sustain modernity on the basis of a mestizo nation.

THE RISE IN INDIGENOUS ORGANIZING AND THE ARTICULATION OF NEW AGENDAS

Against this backdrop, indigenous men and women seem to disappear, responding passively to the incursion of new states, markets, and clerics whose very purpose to undermine the political structures, economies, and cosmologies of indigenous groups remains unchallenged. Yet these assumptions regarding the passivity and obsolescence of indigenous peoples have been repeatedly challenged, particularly in the 1980s and 1990s. First, while economic development has often occurred at the expense of indigenous communities, and while many indigenous men and women outwardly assimilated into mestizo culture—severing or weakening ties with their local communities and practices—self-identified indigenous communities have survived, albeit as with all communities, they have changed over time.

While current, reliable, crossnational data is hard to find, it is commonly stated that approximately four hundred ethnic groups live in Latin America, composing 35–40 million people, 6–10 percent of the total Latin American population, and an estimated 10 percent of the world's more than 300 million indigenous peoples. The Andean region and Mesoamerica claim 90 percent of Latin America's indigenous peoples. These populations, which have been largely agricultural and sedentary, are the ones that the colonists made the greatest effort to incorporate and dominate in Latin America. By contrast, the other 10 percent of indigenous peoples are located in Orinoguia, Amazonia, Mato Grosso, Gran Chaco, Araucania, and Patagonia. Their economies have historically revolved largely around hunting, gathering, fishing, and occasionally small-scale agriculture. This great diversity of regions and economies coincides with great cultural and numerical differences between indigenous communities within and across regions.

It is commonly argued that indigenous peoples constitute the majority of the population in Bolivia and Guatemala, followed by substantially large populations in Ecuador, Mexico, and Peru. In absolute terms, the largest numbers of Indians reside in Mexico, followed by Peru, Guatemala, Bolivia, and Ecuador (see Table 1). The estimated, though not terribly reliable, figures in Table 1 do not reveal the ways in which indigenous communities have changed with respect to the meaning, content, scope, and form of identities, practices, or goals of indigenous peoples. Nor do these figures intend to stipulate a shared identity among indigenous peoples. Indeed, the very idea of an "indigenous people" is predicated on the arrival of "settlers" against whom indigenous peoples identify themselves and are identified. Hence there is a dual image that needs to be kept in mind. While indigenous peoples differ substantially among themselves with respect to primary identities, practices, and so on, often leading to conflict or competition, they have often shared common opposition to those who have tried to dominate them as a people.

By the mid-1980s, indigenous organizations had emerged in almost every country and had begun developing nationally and internationally recognized personas. Particularly important examples of these first organizations included the Shuar Federation of Ecuador, the Regional Council of Cauca in Colombia, and the Kataristas in Bolivia. From the outside looking in, the most striking pattern seemed to be the increasingly public and vocal position articulated by indigenous leaders and the increasing scope of indigenous networks and mobilization outside of state- or party-initiated mobilization. Indeed, the organizations of largely indigenous communities were new insofar as the emerging movements generally emerged from within and across indigenous communities; publicly articulated demands in opposition to state-defined national (assimilationist) and development goals (that seemed to be taking place at the material and cultural expense of the communities); and began challenging the failure of class-based parties or peasant movements and coalitions to address the demands, practices, and identities of indigenous members.

From the inside looking out, however, the emergent organizations are quite diverse with respect to goals, strategies, representativeness, and scope of networks. These differences are played out within and between indigenous organizations over the primacy of material versus cultural orientation of the organization and its demands, alliances with popular movements and political parties, and tactics for change.

Despite the diversity within coalitions of indigenous peoples, one can discern an emerging agenda. In what follows, I discuss four interrelated demands: land rights, human and civil rights, spaces for greater political participation, and rights to political and cultural autonomy. It is important to reiterate that not all indigenous groups work toward each of these goals addressed here, nor are all indigenous groups working in coalition. Indeed, as with any political organization, there are internal debates over goals, allies, strategies, tactics, and related conflicts. Rather, in what follows, I paint a

Table 1

Estimates of Indigenous Peoples in the Americas, 1979–1991

	Estimated Population	% of Total Population
Argentina	477,000	1.5
Belize	15,000	9.1
Bolivia	4,985,000	71.2
Brazil	325,000	0.2
Canada	892,000	0.8
Chile	767,000	5.9
Colombia	708,000	2.2
Costa Rica	19,000	0.6
Ecuador	3,753,000	37.5
El Salvador	500,000	10.0
French Guyana	1,000	1.2
Guatemala	5,423,000	60.3
Guyana	29,000	3.9
Honduras	168,000	3.4
Mexico	10,537,000	12.4
Nicaragua	66,000	1.7
Panama	194,000	8.0
Paraguay	101,000	2.5
Peru	8,097,000	38.6
Surinam	11,000	2.9
United States	1,959,000	0.8
Uruguay	0	0.0
Venezuela	290,000	1.5

Source: Stefano Varese, "Think Locally, Act Globally," in North American Congress on Latin America, *Report on the Americas: The First Nations, 1492–1992* 25, no. 3 (1991): 16; computed from Enrique Mayer and Elio Masferrer, "La población indígena en América en 1978," *América Indígena* 39, no. 2 (1979), World Bank, *Informe sobre el desarrollo mundial 1991,* and United States and Canada census. A slightly different set of numbers is provided in James W. Wilkie, Carlos Alberto Contreras, and Christof Anders Weber, eds., *Statistical Abstract of Latin America,* vol. 30, pt. 1 (Los Angeles: UCLA Latin American Center Publications, 1993), table 662, 150; data also derived from Mayer and Masferrer, "La población indígena," quoted in *Intercom, International Population News Magazine of the Population Reference Bureau* 9, no. 6 (1981).

canvas in broad brush strokes to highlight issues that have emerged in one form or another in various parts of the region.

One of the most pressing and pervasive issues articulated by indigenous groups has revolved around land or property rights. Demands have included agrarian reform, land titling, and territorial demarcation. In Mexico, Guatemala, and Peru, for example, a number of indigenous groups have mobilized for agrarian reform. Associated demands also include access to credit, technology, and other agricultural resources. In each of these three countries, the state alienated land from the indigenous population and coerced indigenous communities into providing labor for plantations, mining, and so on. Subsequent land reforms did not have a lasting effect on these communities. In Guatemala the 1952 land reform was largely reversed with the 1954 counterreform. In Mexico the land reform of the 1930s seems to have had the least effect in regions with the largest indigenous populations, amply documented in the discussions of the Chiapas rebellion. In Peru the 1960s land reform was not implemented evenly in all regions.

Land reform in these cases has historically been articulated and understood largely as a class issue—to redistribute land to peasants or small farmers—even if "objectively" the beneficiaries have included a large number or even a majority of indigenous men and women. Moreover, traditional land reform projects have looked at land reform as a way to distribute private property to individuals rather than to indigenous corporate communities. More contemporary indigenous movements, however, have demanded land on the basis of ethnic, community, and class-based identities.

Indigenous movements in Argentina, Chile, Costa Rica, and Panama, which are considerably smaller in both absolute and relative terms to those in Mexico, Guatemala, and Peru, have largely demanded land titling. For example, in April 1993 approximately 7,000 Kuna and 15,000 Embera Indians in Panama organized to protest the slow deliberations of a land titling bill by blockading the highway and briefly taking hostage the governor of the province of Panama. While the Kuna and Embera are each demanding around 180,000 hectares of land, the Guaymí and Bugle are demanding title to around 11 million square kilometers.

Land reform and titling defer to the state to arbitrate and regulate property rights. However, other demands for land rights have emerged which challenge the state's right either to influence all political relations within a certain territory or to assume property rights to natural resources. Demands for territorial demarcation, as in Brazil, Colombia, and Panama, and for rights to natural resources within a given territory, ultimately refer to issues of political and cultural autonomy in addition to material well-being. With these ideas in mind, the 1991 Colombian Constitution referred to indigenous lands as "territorial entities" in article 286; according to this article, existing political authority structures assume governing capacity, including criminal and civil jurisdiction, in these territories; moreover, the territories are responsible for determining their own development strategy and for administering public resources as if they were municipalities. At the time of this writing, complaints have emerged within the Colombian indigenous community that the actual distribution of these territories remains undecided and that the regulation of disputes between the national government and the future territorial entities remains unclear.

These demands for a clearly demarcated territory and for control over the resources contained within those boundaries have become particularly salient as developers, ranchers, settlers, poachers, and the like increasingly penetrate areas that previously had been the de facto home of indigenous communities, as in the Amazon. In Ecuador and in Chiapas, Mexico, indigenous groups have protested the acquisition of titles over land and resources acquired by foreign oil companies. This increasing encroachment on Indian lands has not only resulted in the decline in indigenous-held territories but also in the decline of populations as violence, environmental destruction, and new diseases threaten indigenous people residing in these areas. The human rights commission of the American Anthropological Association, referring to the Awa-Guaja Indians in Amazonia, forecasts that they face extinction.

In addition to land-related demands, a second set of demands implores the existing government to uphold and protect human and civil rights. In Mexico, Guatemala, and Peru, the governments have often orchestrated or turned their back on human rights abuses targeting indigenous peoples. Human rights groups have documented nationwide abuse of indigenous communities in Guatemala and Peru. In these two countries, military and paramilitary practice have tended to suspect indigenous communities as sympathetic to, if not members of, the guerrillas. In Mexico, human rights abuses occur in regions with large indigenous populations, as in Chiapas and Oaxaca. Stavenhagen notes that while the constitutions of many Latin American countries have stipulated the juridical equality of its citizens, that in fact indigenous men and women do not experience a continual respect for human rights. These human rights abuses obviously mock the rights constitutive of democracy.

A third set of demands addresses issues of political representation in national politics. The constitutions of Latin America, in fact, do not directly discriminate against Indians as individuals (although they have been discriminated against historically through literacy requirements for suffrage). However, legislation has often treated Indians as wards of the state. For example, despite comparatively liberal Brazilian legislation, indigenous men and women are often discussed in statutes referring to legal minors and the juridically handicapped. Pedro Balcúmez, a Mayan Indian leader with the Consejo de Organizaciones Maya stated: "We do not want protection but effective participation in society and the economy."

In the 1990s there have been scattered albeit important advances in indigenous participation in national positions. Indigenous leaders have assumed prominent national positions including the 1993 election of Bolivian vice-president Víctor Hugo Cárdenas; the Guatemalan minister of education, Celestino Tay Coyoy, as the first Mayan cabinet appointment in that country; and indigenous representation in Colombia's Constituent and Legislative Assembly. The inclusion of indigenous representatives has been a significant advance over the near, if not total, exclusion in the past of indigenous participation at the national level. However, electoral participation has served to highlight the diversity of ethnic groups (in countries such as Ecuador and Bolivia) and the salience of often conflicting agendas. Indeed, in the significant example of the Bolivian vice-president, he was able to win office by forming an electoral alliance with the MNR (National Revolutionary

Movement), leaving some to question the integrity and endurance of the vice-president's party.

Finally, indigenous communities have called for autonomy and self-determination, widely used concepts that in fact mask a diversity of demands from cultural to political to developmental. Calls for cultural autonomy and self-determination are reacting against the assimilationist policies discussed earlier. They are reacting against the image projected abroad by tourist offices of quaint Indians marketing ethnic artifacts. Against pressures to assimilate and folkloric images presented by tourist offices, many indigenous leaders have begun to define their own culture, both for themselves and others. Hence, in Guatemala, for example, a number of indigenous groups have emerged to promote cultural autonomy, integrity, and respect that the state has traditionally denied them. Mayan priests have come forth to announce and to celebrate Mayan cosmology and history, as illustrated by the 1990 gathering at Iximché, projects promote indigenous language study; women who had stopped wearing indigenous clothing have begin to wear *traje* [traditional clothing]. These demands and actions highlight the changing boundaries of identity that are transcending localized communities to embrace a broader Mayan identity. Hence women who have chosen to wear *huipiles* again now often do so irrespective of the community from which their families originate. This seems to be the case particularly for women who now live in the city.

Demands for political autonomy present, along with demands for territory, the most dramatic challenge to Latin American states as some communities want indigenous jurisdiction over a given territory, as in the Nicaraguan case of the Miskito and the Colombian case of territorial entities. Finally, calls for increased autonomy over and input into development projects have taken place through international and national forums. Throughout the region, indigenous communities have applied for and some have received funding from international nongovernmental organizations committed to local development projects. Moreover, indigenous communities have called for increased access to participation in state development agencies.

In Chile, for example, indigenous communities have attempted to increase access to state programs and funding for the increased economic, political, and cultural autonomy of the Mapuche (160,000), Aymara (170,000), and Easter Islanders (3,000). According to the *Latin American Weekly Report* (February 11, 1993), Chilean Indians acquired "a national development corporation of their own, a fund for land and water, and a fund for 'ethno-development,' to help them preserve their language and their culture. Already one Mapuche organization is pressing for more official recognition that they are a 'people,' not just another sector of society."

Demands for recognition as a people have raised legal eyebrows, for fear that recognition as a people is the first step toward secession or a threat to the power of the national state. This might be the case among a few groups, but it appears to be uncommon. Miguel Sucuquí, a Mayan organizer in the governing board of the Council of the Ethnic Communities "We Are All Equal" (CERJ), a largely indigenous human rights organization, for example, said:

> So our most immediate task is organization and unification, and this must be done on the basis of our culture and our traditions. With that unification, we Mayans would have an enormous capacity to build our own life within the Guatemalan state. We are not forming a state within another state—we want that to be well understood. But were there freedom of organization, of expression, of religion, the Mayan people could unite, strengthen ourselves, and create the proper institutional expressions for sustaining our lives as a people.

This set of demands around land, human and civic rights, political representation, and political autonomy has been articulated at the national as well as international level. Indigenous groups have gained access to international forums where they have influenced political agendas. The United Nations, for example, created in 1983 a working group on indigenous peoples that has included representation from member states and indigenous organizations to draft a declaration of indigenous rights; this working group declared 1993 the Year of Indigenous People. Indigenous peoples have formed transnational organizations such as the South American Indian Council, the International Indian Treaty Council, and most dramatically for the Campaign for Five Hundred Years of Indigenous, Black, and Popular Resistance that culminated in 1992. And they have gained a presence in international environmental movements, displayed with fanfare at the 1992 Earth Summit in Rio de Janeiro, Brazil. Indigenous communities have also found an institutional space within transnational environmental groups, which have worked in coalition to promote equitable and sustainable development.

WHY THE INCREASE IN INDIGENOUS MOBILIZATION?

Why have indigenous communities mobilized in increasing numbers and scope in the past decade? Given the widely divergent types of groups that we have discussed and the as yet limited comparative information available on ethnic relations in Latin America, the following comments are initial observations that form part of an ongoing research project.

Ethnic and Class Conflict
It is a given in Latin America that indigenous populations experience ethnic discrimination, marginalization, material deprivation, and economic exploitation. "World Bank and other development agencies indicate that Indians remain the poorest and most destitute of the region's population, with

the highest rate of infant mortality and childhood malnutrition and the lowest rates of literacy and schooling." Carlos Fuentes, speaking of the inextricable fusion of ethnic and class identities among the Mayas in Chiapas, said: "What has an extremely long lifespan is the sequence of poverty, injustice, plunder and violation in which, since the sixteenth century, live the Indians who are peasants and the peasants who are Indians."

These structural conditions have disadvantaged indigenous communities for centuries and constitute a constant source of conflict and object of change. Resistance has assumed multiple forms from sporadic rebellions to everyday forms of resistance embedded in dances, stories, and rituals that are an integral part of indigenous communities. The dance of the conquest, for example, has been amply studied by anthropologists who have highlighted the ways in which the dance is a vivid reminder of an ongoing process of colonization, anger toward the landlord, and expression of resistance. Similarly, the Popul Vuj weaves many complex tapestries of meaning, one of which is the oft-repeated phrase: "May we all rise up, may no one be left behind." Violent resistance and everyday forms of resistance against these conditions will continue so long as sharp discrepancies between ethnic and class communities continue to be delineated so sharply.

Yet, looking at these structures alone cannot explain why in recent years there has been a continentwide rise in indigenous organizing along ethnic-based demands. Indeed, if we want to explain the recent increase in indigenous organizing, we need to look beyond these constant causes to the new conditions that have led these dominated groups to resort to what Albert O. Hirschman has called voice (in its legal and violent forms), as opposed to exit or loyalty.

Democratic and Neoliberal Reforms: The Changing Role of the State

The recent round of democratization has created the legal space for the expression of new identities as the resort to repression has become more problematic, although certainly not altogether absent. Indigenous groups have occupied these legally sanctioned spaces, which are not always respected by the militaries of the different countries. Indigenous groups have assumed this space particularly in the wake of popular movements and leftist political parties, many of which had played an important role in anti-authoritarian struggles but rarely succeeded in proposing viable political and economic alternatives.

Yet, if indigenous communities have largely applauded the recent wave of democratization and efforts at demilitarization, they have remained wary of other efforts to dismantle the state in response to neoliberal reforms. Indeed, the 1980s and 1990s have witnessed a change in state-society relations in ways that have affected indigenous communities in contradictory and often adverse ways. As Latin American states dismantle many of the social programs, they take away corporate benefits and representation that had previously defined state relations with indigenous communities. The move toward privatization, for example, has affected de jure and de facto indigenous lands. In Mexico the state's decision to withdraw protection of *ejidos* has generated anxiety, and rightfully so, over indigenous communities' loss of previously communal lands to large agribusiness. In Brazil the opening up to foreign direct investment has resulted in an increased number of developers (and illegal poachers) who have encroached on Amazonian lands that had (often by default) effectively been the domain of indigenous communities. In Ecuador, austerity measures, agrarian development laws, and oil exploration threaten indigenous land tenure and the environmental standards of the region.

Many indigenous leaders, alongside others in the popular movement, therefore, interpret the consequences of neoliberal reforms as an assault on physical, material, and cultural well-being. For example, efforts by Ecuadorian president Sixto Durán-Ballén to pass an agricultural development law prompted widespread protests by the National Confederation of Indigenous Nationalities of Ecuador (CONAIE), which opposed the law on the grounds that it would break up communally owned land and that it sold water rights. The threat of nationwide protests led the government to amend the law to limit the sale of land by communities and to allow for the expropriation of private property if carried out for a social reason, among other things. CONAIE has also participated in coalitions with workers in general strikes to protest neoliberal reforms and the granting of further oil exploration licenses. They have called for study of the environmental impact of any future oil exploration and for research into alternative development strategies.

With the implementation of neoliberal reforms, the corporate basis of state-society relations is being renegotiated. Rather than finding economic interests articulated through corporate laws and through more populist parties, indigenous peasants (and workers alike) are facing a situation in which social welfare issues are not being addressed by the state or through political parties. This has weakened representation for indigenous communities that had previously articulated demands (however feebly) with the state as peasants, as in Mexico and Bolivia.

Finally, the neoliberal concern for the individual in theory has not always translated into concern for the individual in practice. O'Donnell has analyzed this phenomenon in his discussions of the uneven ways in which democracy is experienced in Latin America. This is in large part because efforts to downsize an overbearing and inefficient state have often neglected to strengthen those parts of the state that are necessary for the effective functioning of democracy. Indeed, the uneven practices of judicial and bureaucratic branches of the state have been particularly disadvantageous to indigenous peoples who often remain subject to the political power of local and regional elites.

In the absence of state reforms, individuals cannot necessarily practice their theoretically state-sanctioned civil and political rights that the new democratic regimes claim to uphold; unsurprisingly, the excluded tend to include the indigenous, the impoverished, and women. In this sense, the dismantling of corporate forms of representation and protection, without establishing more effective forms of individual representation and mediation, has left many indigenous communities and individuals without effective access to state resources and with an unreliable judicial and bureaucratic state apparatus. This has proven particularly disadvantageous for the poor, indigenous, and women.

Building Upon Existing Organizational Networks

Indigenous organizations appear to have mobilized against changes in state and social relations by building upon and drawing strength from existing institutional networks left by groups that had previously organized in rural areas. The Catholic Church, followed by peasant union and leftist parties, has left a particularly significant institutional legacy. The church, alongside the military, has traditionally been seen as one of two institutions that most successfully penetrated rural areas and historically attempted to control indigenous areas. As is now well known, following Vatican II and inspired by liberation theology, representatives of the church promoted new forms of organization within and across urban and rural communities.

Indigenous lay leaders, drawing on consciousness raising, community networks, strategizing, and the legitimacy and resources of the church, emerged to promote community organizations. These originally revolved around material struggles within a Christian framework and were often subsumed within class-based popular movements and leftist parties. They also provided a forum for subsequently strengthening indigenous networks and developing a generation of indigenous leaders with authority often within and beyond traditional community-based authority structures. This was clearly the case in Guatemala and Mexico and likely played a role in other countries inspired by liberation theology or with previously strong leftist movements or parties. I suggest that indigenous communities particularly capitalized on these institutional legacies with the recent wave of democratization and neoliberal reforms.

The New International Moment

While international communication among organized indigenous groups began in the early 1970s, it accelerated in the late 1980s with the approach of 1992 and with the increased concern of transnational organizations and lending agencies for equitable and sustainable development, environmental protection, and human rights. On the one hand, the struggles to redefine 1992 as five hundred years of resistance rather than five hundred years of celebration sparked continentwide conferences that grew in size and scope with each meeting. The meetings provided the forum for indigenous leaders to gather together and in the process appears to have both heightened and deepened awareness of an "Indian" identity *shared* by indigenous groups throughout the Americas. Moreover, it increased networks between and within indigenous communities. In response to a question as to whether Mayan rites had become more widespread or more public in recent years, Miguel Sucuquí of the CERJ said:

> Actually, it is both. . . . But when Spain and the Latinamerican countries started to make a lot of noise about celebrating the Columbus Quincentenial [*sic*], this caused a restlessness, a curiosity, in our people, and an investigation of the Mayan religion began, and more people began to consult with priests and elders about what had happened. The message of these leaders has been received by the people with great interests, and our Mayan religious practices are being revived publicly, and are being accepted by our people.

On the other hand, international organizations and lending agencies have become more receptive to and supportive of indigenous groups and their demands. Indigenous people have gained an increased presence within the United Nations and its working groups. International coalitions with nongovernmental organizations and advocacy groups have significantly increased access to material resources, information, and the media. Moreover, international lending agencies have created and strengthened new programs that have increased funding possibilities for indigenous groups. Lending programs that include environmental and democratic conditionalities have also created new political opportunities for indigenous groups to pressure their respective governments. Alison Brysk notes, however, the very severe limitations for promoting domestic citizenship when work is focused on the international arena. Local- and national-level organizing continues to be an essential component in indigenous struggles for more equitable citizenship rights.

DEEPENING DEMOCRACY AS PART OF BRIDGING ETHNIC CLEAVAGES

Increased indigenous mobilization coincided with the hemispheric transition from authoritarian rule. However, by the end of the 1980s and the beginning of the 1990s, many of the countries that had ethnically heterogeneous societies experienced political closure. Witness, for example, the successful coup attempts in Peru and Haiti and failed ones in Guatemala and Venezuela. Yet it would be foolhardy to conclude that ethnically heterogeneous societies and political democracy are incompatible. Indeed, if we assume that a strong civil society is important to democracy, then we should embrace many of these mobilizations while thinking about the creation of institutional arenas for expressing dissent and conflict as well as consent and compromise.

To return to the final question raised at the beginning of this chapter, what are the conditions under which this increased articulation of indigenous communities is compatible with, and even supportive of, democratic practices and consolidation? The following suggests ways in which we need to reconceptualize citizenship in Latin America while looking at institutional mechanisms for creating more participatory, representative, and durable political democracies in ethnically heterogeneous societies.

Reconceptualizing the Nation

First, at an ideological level, Latin American states need to begin by reconceptualizing the very idea of a homogeneous mestizo nation. As Stefano Varese has noted, the emergence of indigenous movements and their denunciation of assimilationist policies challenge the conception in Latin America that a mestizo nation does or should correspond to the existing states. Indeed, the very process of nation building in the late nineteenth and most of the twentieth century is being fundamentally questioned as people begin to talk about difference and equality. The challenge becomes to articulate a way in which democracy can emerge and endure in multi-ethnic states.

Rustow, in his pathbreaking essay, argued that one needs a sense of national unity to achieve democracy: it provides the sense of loyalty that glues the pieces together in the face of societal conflict. Yet it is questionable if one needs "national" loyalty or loyalty to a "state" to achieve and sustain democracy. If Latin American indigenous communities are to develop or sustain commitment to democratic regimes, then multi-ethnic states need to revise the ideology of a mestizo nation to account for the more diverse composition of a given country's citizenry. This is particularly the case given that citizenship rights in practice are often derivative of whether one is conceived of as part of the nation. In some countries, such as Colombia, Paraguay, Mexico, and momentarily in Peru, constitutional changes have been made. These are important steps.

Rethinking the Institutions of Political Representation

A discursive and constitutional recognition of a pluri-ethnic population is an important beginning. However, without institutional changes, it remains a symbolic advance. Indeed, the new Latin American governments need to redesign political institutions in creative ways to allow for greater and more effective political representation. In this spirit, I tentatively highlight issues of institutional design that merit additional research and analysis.

How does one provide for democratic representation and governance in ethnically divided societies in which ethnic cleavages seem increasingly politicized? This is largely a question of who is to be represented and how. In the case of indigenous communities, this question encompasses the dilemma of how to balance respect for individual and corporate representation.

A first and older set of arguments originally called for consociationalism. The simplified argument was that elite representation of the major ethnic groups needed to be institutionally guaranteed; the ensuing "cartel of elites" would defuse conflict over who controls the state while increasing the spaces for discussion and compromise over issues that had been particularly contentious. In recent years, this approach has been criticized on the following grounds. First, this political arrangement assumes the primordial nature of ethnic identity and institutionalizes these very differences. Second, a political cartel of elites can and does lead to antidemocratic behavior; in turn, it inhibits democratic participation by groups whose identities and interests are assumed rather than expressed. The cases of Venezuela and Colombia, which implemented consociational-like solutions (although ones that revolved around partisan rather than ethnic identities), have highlighted the limits of this kind of institutional approach, as has Lebanon. Finally, it assumes that ethnic conflicts are vertically organized with varying ethnic groups vying for state power. Yet in Latin America, as we have seen, ethnic groups overwhelmingly remain horizontally organized and geographically concentrated, often seeking input or power over more local or regional politics rather than control over national politics.

A different set of arguments has highlighted the need to redesign district boundaries to increase indigenous electoral representation. The mechanisms for doing so vary according to the district magnitude of electoral regions, whether and how these regions coincide with ethnic groups, and the methods for calculating representation (proportional representation versus plurality voting). Redesigning electoral boundaries to coincide with indigenous territories or majority indigenous populations should compel politicians, be they indigenous or not, to begin to respond to varied demands as they are articulated by communities in a given district.

An alternative way of envisioning increased representation and participation within ethnically heterogeneous societies, therefore, is to decentralize political control. Decentralization can accommodate calls for more localized control and cultural autonomy while maintaining centralized decision making over issues that affect the country as a whole. While this boundary between local and national issues is clearly a source of tension itself, a more decentralized system at least allows for a more heterogeneous and changing vision of identity, provides more control over regional political economies, and might increase local participation. This type of system would require tax reform to protect against the increasing economic disparity between regions and to ensure relatively comparable provision of social services. However, for this system to function differently than it already does, say in Mexico, we need to look at reforming clientelist control over regional politics that occurs through corrupt party systems, privatized power holdings, and inefficacious state apparatuses.

Reforming the State

In many of the countries, reforming the military institution to prevent human rights abuses, particularly in the countryside, is a necessary measure for consolidating democracy and bridging ethnic cleavages. On the one hand, human rights abuses are clearly inimical to democracy. On the other hand, military repression itself often compels groups to resort to violence as they find limited legal spaces for organizing and confront democratic practices subverted by the military's presence and practices in the countryside.

Moreover, the issue of state capacity has to be further problematized in Latin America. At the very moment that Latin American regimes are negotiating the retreat of the state from the economy, fairly little is being done to increase the transparency, efficiency, and legal practices of such central state institutions as the courts, the bureaucracy, and the police—all essential to the rule of law and one's rights as a citizen. The absence of more pervasive and functional courts and bureaucracies has particularly affected indigenous sectors as they are located in areas in which political power is often exercised independently of and often in disregard for the law. As O'Donnell and Lehmann have both indicated, constitutional political equality is symbolically meaningful but substantively meaningless without the state capacity to make it a reality for sectors that have been marginalized along class, ethnic, and gender lines.

Indeed, in the absence of the functioning of the rule of law, responsive bureaucracies, and military and police forms subordinated to democratically elected civilian rule, it is difficult to practice the rights of political citizenship. From this perspective, political order is not just a question of the organization and representation of social groups but also about creating states with the capacity to carry out their respective functions in the presence of competing private power centers. In the absence of effective reform, participation remains what O'Donnell has called low-intensity citizenship, contributing, I contend, to the increasing politicization of ethnic cleavages in cases such as Guatemala, Mexico, and Peru.

Material Conditions and Citizenship

T. H. Marshall, echoing a refrain from Tocqueville, argued three decades ago that the political equality associated with liberal democracy was at odds with the social and economic inequalities associated with class/capitalism. The welfare state was the response. In Europe and parts of Latin America, political coalitions sought to alleviate the poverty and conflict produced by capitalism and articulated an ideology in which the state was responsible for ensuring that its citizens sustained a certain standard of living.

With the move toward market-oriented macroeconomic reforms, and fiscal and political limits of social welfare spending, many countries have cut back on social programs originally intended to alleviate poverty. While these reform programs are associated with macroeconomic growth in some countries, they have also coincided with increasing impoverishment among the poor, a pattern that has particularly affected indigenous communities. In each of these states, this dramatic retreat of the state has compounded already serious problems related to property relations and living standards within indigenous communities.

If this increasing impoverishment continues (particularly if government measures are seen as a threat to land access or sustainable development) *and* indigenous communities conclude that they are left without legally assured and functioning state channels to influence policy and access resources, more indigenous communities will be left with little option but to take to the streets in protest, as in Ecuador and Guatemala, or turn to violence as in Mexico. From this angle, it is essential to address those "constant causes" mentioned earlier and to redress conditions of poverty and political marginalization as part of a respect for and pillar of democratic citizenship (as opposed to an explanation of rising mobilization, per se).

Here, of course, the issue of land—its distribution, titling, and political jurisdiction—reemerges as the central issue and dilemma. Where indigenous groups demand land, traditional elites are sure to bristle, and in the past this bristling has never been good for the maintenance of democracy. At a minimum, therefore, countries with strong elites need to find creative fora to address these issues directly, involving both indigenous communities and elites in the process of developing political solutions. Moreover, more integrated development strategies are needed that allow not only for local participation in their design, but that promote economic sustainability, credit, investment, training, and infrastructure. With this thought in mind, we return to the Chiapas uprising. As the Indigenous Revolutionary Clandestine Committee of the Zapatista General Command stated in a January 6, 1994, communiqué, its central goal after all is "making known to the Mexican people and the rest of the world the miserable conditions in which millions of Mexicans, especially we indigenous people, live and die." At a minimum, governments need to democratize politics and promote an idea of citizenship in which the provision for basic economic needs is seen as a right and not a privilege.

■───

SUGGESTIONS FOR FURTHER READING

Military

Fitch, Samuel. *The Armed Forces and Democracy in Latin America.* Baltimore: Johns Hopkins University Press, 1998.

Loveman, Brian. *For la Patria: Politics and the Armed Forces in Latin America.* Wilmington, Del.: SR Books, 1999.

O'Donnell, Guillermo. *Modernization and Bureaucratic-Authoritarianism.* Berkeley: University of California Press, 1998.

Remmer, Karen. *Military Rule in Latin America.* Boulder, Colo.: Westview, 1991.

Stepan, Alfred. *Rethinking Military Politics: Brazil and the Southern Cone.* Princeton, N.J.: Princeton University Press, 1988.

The Catholic Church and Religion

Dodson, Michael. "Pentecostals, Politics, and Public Space in Latin America," in *Power, Politics and Pentecostals in Latin America,* ed. Edward L. Cleary and Hannah W. Stewart-Gambino. Boulder, Colo.: Westview, 1997.

Levine, Daniel H., and David Stoll. "Bridging the Gap Between Empowerment and Power in Latin America," in *Transnational Religion and Fading States,* ed. Susanne Hoeber Rudolph and James Piscatori. Boulder, Colo: Westview, 1997.

Labor

Bergquist, Charles. *Labor in Latin America: Comparative Essays on Chile, Argentina, Venezuela, and Colombia.* Stanford, Calif.: Stanford University Press, 1986.

Buchanan, Paul G. *State, Labor, Capital: Democratizing Class Relations in the Southern Cone.* Pittsburgh: University of Pittsburgh Press, 1995, 65–112, 167–208.

Collier, Ruth, and James Mahoney. "Adding Collective Actors to Collective Outcomes: Labor and Recent Democratization in South America and Southern Europe." *Comparative Politics* 29, no. 3 (April 1997): 285–301.

Murrillo, M. Victoria. "From Populism to Neoliberalism: Labor Unions and Market Reform in Latin America." *World Politics* 52, no. 2 (January 2000): 135–174.

Roberts, Kenneth. "Neoliberalism and the Transformation of Populism in Latin America: the Peruvian Case." *World Politics* 48, no. 1 (October 1995): 82–116.

Indigenous Peoples

Kearney, Michael, and Stefano Varese. "Latin America's Indigenous Peoples: Changing Identities and Forms of Resistance," in *Capital, Power, and Inequality in Latin America,* ed. Sandor Halebsky and Richard L. Harris. Boulder, Colo.: Westview, 1995, 207–232.

Van Cott, Donna Lee, ed. *Indigenous Peoples and Democracy in Latin America.* New York: St. Martin's Press in association with the Inter-American Dialogue, 1994.

Yashar, Deborah. "Contesting Citizenship: Indigenous Movements and Democracy in Latin America." *Comparative Politics* 31, no. 1 (October 1998): 23–42.

Women and Gender

Alvarez, Sonia E. *Engendering Democracy in Brazil.* Princeton, N.J.: Princeton University Press, 1990.

Icken Safa, Helen. "Women's Social Movements in Latin America," in *Women in the Latin American Development Process,* ed. Christine E. Bose and Edna Acosta-Belén. Philadelphia: Temple University Press, 1995, 227–241.

Jaquette, Jane, ed. *The Women's Movement in Latin America: Participation and Democracy,* 2nd ed. Boulder, Colo.: Westview, 1994.

Jaquette, Jane S., and Sharon L. Wolchik. *Women and Democracy: Latin America and Central and Eastern Europe.* Baltimore: Johns Hopkins University Press, 1998.

Navarro, Marysa. "The Personal Is Political: Las Madres de Plaza de Mayo," in *Power and Popular Protest: Latin American Social Movements,* ed. Susan Eckstein. Berkeley: University of California Press, 1989, 241–258.

Stephen, Lynn. *Women and Social Movements in Latin America: Power from Below.* Austin: University of Texas Press, 1997.

Yeager, G. M., ed. *Confronting Change, Challenging Tradition: Women in Latin American History.* Wilmington, Del.: SR Books, 1994.

Social Movements

Alder Hellman, Judith. "The Riddle of New Social Movements: Who They Are and What They Do," in *Capital, Power and Inequality in Latin America,* ed. Saddol Halebsky and Richard L. Harris. Boulder, Colo.: Westview Press, 1995, 165–184.

Domínguez, Jorge I., ed. *Social Movements in Latin America: The Experience of Peasants, Workers, Women, the Urban Poor, and the Middle Sectors.* New York: Garland, 1994.

Oxhorn, Philip. *Organizing Civil Society: The Popular Sector and the Struggle for Democracy in Chile.* University Park: Pennsylvania State University Press, 1995.

USEFUL WEBSITES

The Inter-American Commission of Women: Organization of American States commission to promote and protect women's rights.
www.oas.org/cim

The Pan-American Health Organization: World Health Organization website with special attention to issues of women's health and issues pertaining to domestic abuse.
www.paho.org

United Nations Development Program Inter-Agency Campaign on Women's Human Rights in Latin America
www.undp.org/rblac/gender/

Woman in Development: Inter-American Development Bank website dedicated to issues pertaining to women and sustainable development.
www.iadb.org/sds/wid/index_wid_e.htm

There are a very large number of websites dedicated to indigenous peoples in specific Latin American countries as well as websites specific to particular indigenous peoples. The Latin American Information Network (LANIC) at the University of Texas, Austin, provides links to many. Below is a small sample of more general links.

Indian Law Center: An organization dedicated to the promotion and protection of indigenous peoples' legal rights.
www.indianlaw.org/default.htm

Indigenous Knowledge: Webpage dedicated to the collection and dissemination of indigenous knowledge.
www.nuffic.nl/ik-pages/

Indigenous People's and Community Development: Inter-American Development Bank website dedicated to issues pertaining to indigenous peoples and sustainable development.
www.iadb.org/sds/IND/index_ind_e.htm

International Labour Organization: The ILO is the branch of the United Nations dedicated to labor rights globally.
www.ilo.org/

Jane's Information Group: One of the leading military research organizations in the world.
www.janes.com/

Latin American Military: An independent website that gathers and disseminates public information about Latin American militaries.
www.lamilitary.com/

Native Web: An international organization dedicated to disseminating information about native peoples.
www.nativeweb.org/

Resource Center of the Americas: An organization that promotes human rights and disseminates information supporting resistance to globalization.
www.americas.org/

Stockholm International Peace Research Institute: An internationally known center that collects information on conflict and militaries globally.
www.sipri.org/

CHAPTER 5

The United States and Latin America

READINGS IN THIS CHAPTER

*I*t is virtually impossible to overstate the influence the United States has had on Latin America over the past century. The U.S. role in the region has run from invasions and/or support for coups to leading (and often dominating) trade and finance discussions, to support for a wide array of democratization initiatives and social policy programs. In turn, the large-scale migration of Latin Americans to the United States, particularly since the 1960s, has changed U.S. society profoundly as Latinos have grown in number to become the largest minority group in the country. Thus, the United States and Latin America are inextricably bound together and have significant impact on each other.

Perhaps the most obvious impact of the United States on Latin America is through the many interventions in the region's politics. U.S. intervention in Latin America has passed through a number of stages. Initially (in the mid-1800s), the U.S. position was defined by the vision of Manifest Destiny and the Monroe Doctrine. Manifest Destiny was a vision of U.S. greatness and expansionism based on beliefs about the country's unique and superior character. The Monroe Doctrine was a defining statement about the right of the United States to intervene anywhere in what it considered to be its sphere of influence. The U.S. sphere of influence included virtually all of the Western Atlantic region and thus constituted a justifiable (in the U.S. context) claim for intervening in the affairs of virtually any Latin American country. In the twentieth century, the Monroe Doctrine and Manifest Destiny gave way to the more pro-democracy and pro-economic development policies of Franklin Delano Roosevelt's Good Neighbor Policy and John F. Kennedy's Alliance for Progress. At the same time, these more supportive policies clashed with Cold War considerations and U.S. efforts to contain communist and other left-wing movements in the region. In the 1980s and 1990s, policy shifted again, focusing on democracy, human rights, free-market oriented economic development, as well as counternarcotics and in the wake of 9/11, counterterrorism.

Regardless of the label and the actual orientation of policy, the United States has consistently and actively intervened—with or without an invitation from the specific national government—throughout the past century. U.S. forces occupied part of Mexico during the Mexican revolution of 1910–1917 (after conquering roughly half the country in the 1850s). The United States helped to create and support Panama, as well as set up and support regimes in Cuba and Haiti. In 1954, U.S. forces helped oust one of the very few democratically elected leaders in Guatemala's history. U.S. diplomatic and intelligence officials were supporters and facilitators of military coups in Argentina, Brazil, and, most notoriously, Chile. Brutal regimes in El Salvador, Guatemala, and Nicaragua fought civil wars while committing monstrous human rights abuses with U.S. support. U.S. officials justified this support in terms of the Cold War: the insurgents in all three cases were left-wing movements with varying levels of contact with Communist nations or movements.

The most obvious one was the Sandinista movement in Nicaragua that developed strong ties to Fidel Castro and Cuba, while in the Guatemala case it is hard to make the claim that Cold War logic had any relevance. In the 1980s and 1990s, with the Cold War over, U.S. policy and rhetoric shifted to a greater emphasis on democracy and development. Yet even in this new context, U.S. forces invaded Panama and Haiti, removing dictatorships in both instances, and the U.S. military is involved in a civil war in Colombia, focused primarily on support for counternarcotics operations. In short, Latin America's past has been marked and changed considerably by the presence of the United States in the region.

The U.S. presence has also been felt economically. In roughly the past twenty years, the U.S. policy has been to support economic liberalization (neoliberalism), focusing specifically on easing restrictions on the flows of finances and eliminating barriers to trade. In fact, in the early years of the new millennium, the United States has been leading an effort to negotiate a regional free trade agreement, the so-called Free Trade Area of the Americas (FTAA). This initiative builds on the existing free trade agreement (NAFTA) among Mexico, the United States, and Canada. Some, but not all, Latin American governments welcome the U.S. position. Chile, for example, was the region's first neoliberal reformer and aggressively sought a free trade agreement in advance of the FTAA. Alternatively, some Latin American governments and a great many Latin Americans believe that the neoliberal model has been imposed on the region, with poor, heavily indebted governments unable to resist U.S. demands for policy change. Successive Brazilian governments have been among the most resistant to the FTAA, and Brazil has been without question the most capable of challenging the United States' position in the region.

The United States however, has not always been the champion of open markets. From the 1940s to the 1980s, Latin American governments overwhelmingly followed economic development models that were focused on the internal market, with tight restrictions on the flow of finance and trade. For decades, the U.S. government and U.S. policy helped to sustain that inward-oriented development program. U.S. aid was an important source of financing and technical assistance for Latin American governments. Financial support came through direct aid as well as loans, while U.S. technical advisors supported Latin American governments in a wide range of economic activities, from setting up steel plants to developing infrastructure. Even the International Monetary Fund and the World Bank, key international financial institutions in which the United States has considerable influence, were supportive of Latin America's development model. In fact, it was only with the onset of the debt crisis in the late 1970s and the start of the 1980s that the approach of the United States and international financial institutions shifted.

Finally, the United States has also played a role in support of democracy, albeit inconsistently and frequently in conflict with the overarching security concerns. U.S. support for democracy has come through promotion and support for democratic elections, such as in El Salvador in the 1980s. U.S. emphasis on human rights has also played an important role at various times in Latin American history. For example, the U.S. government bolstered human rights and pro-democracy groups in Guatemala by refusing to grant a visa to General Efraín Rios Montt, the former dictator whose slash-and-burn tactics in the 1980s led to tens of thousands of deaths of noncombatants. The United States also supports democracy through financial support for a wide array of social policies. For example, poor countries like Bolivia finance much of their social policy through foreign donations (as well as foreign non-governmental organizations). In short, the U.S. presence in Latin America is and historically has been strong. It is, however, a complex mix of both supportive and constructive as well as coercive and domineering approaches. This chapter explores some of the complexities of the U.S. role.

The articles in this chapter capture the range of influences the United States has had on Latin America. Peter Hakim presents an overview of the issues that have affected United States–Latin American relations through the 1990s and into the new millennium. In "The Uneasy Americas," Hakim observes that in many respects the relationship is a solid one. Latin American countries have made a considerable move toward democracy and open markets. In doing so, they have moved closer to the U.S. model of democratic capitalism and consequently look more to the United States as a leader while also depending on the United States to support their efforts to consolidate these trends. Hakim shows that in a number of important ways, the United States has lived up to the responsibility. But in other areas, Hakim argues that the U.S. government is not listening as closely to Latin American concerns as it should be and that failure is heightening tensions that make the relationship more volatile than it appears on the surface.

J. Patrice McSherry agrees with Hakim only to the extent that the U.S. government and Latin American governments are in accordance on the economic program for the region and that the United States is not supporting military coups. Otherwise, McSherry's view of the relationship is darker and emphasize's the ongoing involvement of the United States with the militaries of various Latin American governments. McSherry reviews the U.S. commitment to support for Latin American militaries in areas of counternarcotics, counterterrorism, and "foreign internal defense" missions that ultimately bear a great deal of resemblance to the Cold War–era policies that tolerated, facilitated, and even promoted military dictatorships.

DATA TABLES

Table 5.1
Select List of U.S. Interventions in Latin America

1846	War with Mexico. U.S. ends up annexing large portions of Mexican Territory.
1850s	Multiple interventions in Nicaragua.
1856	First U.S. interventions in Panama to protect the Atlantic-Pacific railroad from Panamanian nationalists.
1898	U.S. war with Spain. Leads to occupation of Cuba and Puerto Rico.
1903	U.S. support for Panamanian separation from Colombia. Panama Canal Treaty.
1904	Intervention in Dominican Republic over debt payment.
1905	U.S. intervention in Honduras. First of several interventions over border and commercial disputes.
1906	U.S. occupation of Cuba.
1910	U.S. occupation of Nicaragua in support of pro-U.S. regime.
1914	U.S. occupies Vera Cruz, Mexico, in response to growing revolutionary violence and threats to U.S. interests.
1915	U.S. occupies Haiti.
1916–1924	U.S. occupation of Dominican Republic.
1926–1933	U.S. occupies and operates in Nicaragua.
1933	FDR announces Good Neighbor Policy.
1954	Jacobo Arbenz Guzmán elected president of Guatemala, deposed by CIA-led coup.
1961	Bay of Pigs (failed). U.S. backed anti-Castro invasion by Cuban expatriates.
1961	CIA supports coup in Ecuador.
1963	CIA backs coup in the Dominican Republic.
1964	CIA and U.S. embassy support coup in Brazil. João Goulart of Brazil proposes agrarian reform, nationalization of oil. Ousted by U.S.-supported military coup.
1973	U.S. supports coup in Chile that removes elected socialist president Salvador Allende.
1976	Election of Jimmy Carter leads to new emphasis on human rights in U.S. foreign policy.
1979	Panama Canal Treaty pledging return of control to Panama in 1999.
1980s	U.S. policy simultaneously supports the move to democratic elections in El Salvador and Honduras, while supporting dictatorship in Guatemala and actively seeking to overthrow Nicaragua's revolutionary government.
1983	U.S. invasion of Grenada.
1984	U.S. mines Nicaraguan harbors; loses World Court case to Nicaragua, but refuses to recognize Court's jurisdiction.
1989	U.S. invades Panama.

Table 5.2
United States–Latin America Trade and Investment

	Exports, Growth Rate (%),	Imports, Growth Rate (%),	Direct U.S. Investment (millions of U.S. dollars)		Investment Income (millions of U.S. dollars)	
	1991–2001	1991–2001	1995	2001	1995	2001
Argentina	6.7	9.0	7,660	14,234	836	−433
Bolivia	1.4	−2.1	300	332	33	−37
Brazil	10.0	7.9	25,002	36,317	3,759	756
Chile	5.5	10.2	6,216	11,674	1,038	598
Colombia	6.4	7.5	3,506	4,844	498	280
Costa Rica	9.2	9.8	921	1,614	343	20
Ecuador	4.1	4.1	889	417	101	4
El Salvador	12.7	20.1	150	657	36	59
Guatemala	7.0	11.2	233	477	47	19
Honduras	14.5	18.9	68	49	26	19
Mexico	11.8	15.7	19,351	52,168	1,585	14
Nicaragua	11.7	26.1	88	206	2	40
Panama	3.1	1.6	15,123	25,296	1,421	452
Paraguay	0.6	−2.8	83	415	15	33
Peru	6.4	9.6	1,335	3,591	362	74
Uruguay	6.7	−0.5	345	734	76	103
Venezuela	2.0	6.2	3,634	10,680	631	1,543

Source: Data from *Latin America and the Caribbean: Selected Economic and Social Data, 2001/2002.* Washington, D.C.: United States Agency for International Development, May 2003.

5.1   The Uneasy Americas (2001)

PETER HAKIM

KEEPING IT TOGETHER

This April [2001], President George W. Bush will travel to Québec City for a summit meeting of the western hemisphere's heads of state. Thirty-three other leaders will attend the conference, the third such gathering since 1994, and each will come eager to hear the new U.S. president's plans for dealing with the region. The summit will be an ideal place for Bush to try out his ideas before an attentive foreign audience. But if he really wants to improve hemispheric ties, Bush must come prepared to do some serious listening, to get to know his Latin American colleagues, and to hear firsthand their priorities and concerns.

Should he make such an effort, Bush will learn that the United States' relations with Latin America are fundamentally sound. Most American governments are happy to cooperate with Washington, and they expect it to take the initiative on many crucial matters.

Probing a bit more deeply, however, Bush and his advisers will discover a number of serious problems under the deceptively smooth surface. Hemispheric affairs are far more troubled today than they were only a few years ago. Many of Latin America's leaders face serious political and economic troubles at home, and many are disappointed with current U.S. policies—particularly with Washington's expanding intervention in Colombia and its lagging efforts to pursue economic cooperation and hemispheric free trade.

Bush should heed the warnings. If Latin America loses confidence in Washington—which has seemed indifferent at some points and headstrong and inflexible at others—the opportunities for American leadership in the hemisphere will diminish, along with hopes for an effective U.S.–Latin American partnership.

COOPERATION AND CONVERGENCE

For the last 12 years—roughly since the start of the first Bush administration and the end of the Cold War—relations between the United States and Latin America have been more cordial and cooperative than at any other time in memory. With almost every Latin American nation scrambling for U.S.

investment and trade preferences, the once familiar cry of "Yankee go home" is no longer heard anywhere in the hemisphere, and "gringo" has ceased to be a term of opprobrium. Even Brazil, which has frequently clashed with the United States over specific issues and initiatives, now boasts that its relationship with Washington has never been better.

Many factors contributed to this improvement in the texture and tone of U.S.–Latin American links. The dramatic turn toward democratic politics and market economics in Central and South America was a powerful element; in 12 years, nearly every nation in the region came to share the same basic political and economic ideals. Another factor was the passing of the Cold War. With it, U.S. policy toward Latin America became more relaxed, and security concerns no longer trumped everything else.

A number of constructive U.S. policy initiatives also contributed to the growing goodwill. Within weeks of taking office in 1989, the first President Bush put forth the kind of debt relief plan that Latin America had long sought to resolve its decade-long economic crisis. The Bush administration also contributed to the peaceful settlements of Central America's festering civil wars, negotiated the North American Free Trade Agreement (NAFTA) with Mexico and Canada, and announced a plan to forge free trade ties with every other country in the Americas.

When its turn came, the Clinton administration carried these initiatives forward without missing a beat. Within a year of taking office, Bill Clinton got Congress to approve NAFTA. Shortly thereafter, in 1994, he convened in Miami the first hemispheric summit meeting since 1967. And at that conference, the assembled leaders agreed to complete an all-Americas free trade pact by 2005. Under Clinton's leadership, Washington also orchestrated generous financial rescue packages for Mexico and Brazil, which stemmed the deepening economic crises in those countries.

THE HONEYMOON ENDS

Despite these many accomplishments, however, relations are starting to sour once more, and in the near future, U.S.–Latin American ties are likely to become far more contentious. Indeed, there are already clear signs that the goodwill and cooperation that characterized most of the past decade are evaporating.

To begin with, most Latin American countries are worse off today than they were just a few years ago. The early 1990s were years of heady optimism throughout the region. Democracy took hold in country after country, promising greater justice and enhanced security. The magic of economic reform produced an upswing in growth and a sharp drop in inflation. These developments were expected, in turn, to translate into higher wages, lower unemployment, declining poverty, and improved public services. The United States, the region's most important trading partner and its largest source of capital, promised more secure access to U.S. markets and investment capital for Latin American producers. These promises were widely seen as a sure-fire means to anchor and accelerate the region's economic and political growth.

Things did not work out that way, however. Two debilitating financial crises, in 1995 and 1998, interrupted Latin America's economic progress and revealed its continuing vulnerability. As economic growth rates dropped by 40 percent between the first and second halves of the decade, unemployment soared and the region's halting social advances came to a standstill. These reversals sapped Latin America's confidence in its ability to compete successfully in the globalized economy. Although no American country has yet retreated from market economic policies as a result, doubts have multiplied about the benefits of free trade and about the pace and breadth of the economic reforms long advocated by Washington.

The setbacks to democracy throughout the region have been even more serious. They are not, as some U.S. officials have portrayed them, mere bumps in the road. To be sure, Latin American democracy has scored some recent triumphs—none more stunning than last year's presidential race in Mexico, in which an opposition candidate, Vicente Fox, triumphed in the country's first truly free elections. But in most other countries, the news has been more distressing, and nowhere more so than in South America's Andean region. In Peru, the government of Alberto Fujimori grew increasingly autocratic and corrupt until it finally imploded last year. With Fujimori now in exile in Japan, Peru confronts the enormously difficult task of rebuilding its institutions. Meanwhile, Colombia's elected government is losing control while democratic institutions are being battered by a relentless guerrilla war, horrendous human rights abuses, and pervasive criminal violence. Last year, Ecuador suffered South America's first successful military coup in 24 years, and in Venezuela, political power is being concentrated in the hands of President Hugo Chávez, who scorns representative democracy. Such governance problems are not confined to the Andes, either. Democracy is also under assault to varying degrees in many other countries—Haiti, Nicaragua, Guatemala, and Paraguay, to mention a few.

Meanwhile, although democracy still prevails in most of Latin America, political institutions—including parties, legislatures, and courts—perform dismally. Contrary to expectations, the demise of Latin America's military rulers has not led to the steady consolidation of democracy and the rule of law, which remain weak and vulnerable in many countries. Even in the sturdiest regional democracies, citizens are deeply unhappy with their governments. In the past year, the approval ratings of more than half of South America's leaders fell below 20 percent.

Most Latin Americans do not blame the United States for their problems. Even those countries suffering the worst political and economic turmoil have not cast Washington as the villain. Indeed, the United States is still often seen as critical to solving many national problems. When their economies teetered on the brink of disaster, both Mexico City and Brasília turned to Washington for help. From the day it took office, Andrés Pastrana's government in Colombia has sought massive U.S. support for its struggle against guerrillas and drug criminals. In Peru, the opposition looked to Washington for assistance in the battle against Fujimori's authoritarian ways. And two countries—Ecuador and El Salvador—have adopted the U.S. dollar as their national currencies to ward off economic crises.

Still, throughout Latin America, the United States is closely identified with the widely implemented reform programs (known as the "Washington consensus") that have yielded such disappointing economic and social results in so many countries. The reforms, although essential for economic success, are popularly associated with austerity, insecurity, and high unemployment. For many Latin Americans, closer relations with the United States simply mean more of the same. Opposition to these reforms could therefore easily turn into opposition to U.S. leadership in general—and into antagonism toward the International Monetary Fund and the World Bank, both of which are seen as U.S.-dominated institutions.

The timing of events, moreover, has not helped perceptions. Even while most of Latin America has remained caught in economic doldrums, the United States has enjoyed its longest economic boom ever. In this light, it is hardly surprising that many in the region have come to think that the global economy is stacked in favor of the United States and other wealthy nations—and that new rules, different from those long advocated by Washington, are needed if Latin America and other developing areas are ever to compete successfully.

FREE TRADE FREEZE

Trade and investment dominate the agendas of nearly every Latin American country in their relations with the United States. Nothing is considered more important to the region's economic future than expanded access to U.S. markets and investment capital. And nothing has raised more doubts about Washington's commitment to regional cooperation than its foot-dragging on hemispheric trade—particularly during a time of such prosperity in the United States.

It was only last December, in the eleventh hour, that the Clinton administration finally took steps to fulfill two pledges it made during the 1994 summit in Miami—to incorporate Chile into NAFTA and to provide Central America and the Caribbean with enhanced access to U.S. markets. For six years, the U.S. Congress, pressed hard by a handful of domestic textile manufacturers, had regularly rejected such preferences, which were finally approved in May 2000 as part of a larger trade package for Africa. Although this step was welcomed as the first expansion of NAFTA since 1994, Latin Americans hardly considered it a strong signal of U.S. commitment to regional trade.

Chile's experience has also been disheartening. For the past decade, there has been broad support in the United States for a free trade arrangement with Chile, the region's outstanding economic performer. But disputes within the White House kept negotiations on ice. Then, with only a month left in his presidency, Clinton announced that Chile talks would finally begin. Having suddenly initiated such negotiations with Singapore, it had become too embarrassing for the White House to put off Chile any longer. Now it is up to the Bush administration to conclude an agreement with Chile and gain congressional approval for it. Bush's success or failure will be widely viewed as an indicator of his future stance on hemispheric trade policy. [The agreement was approved in July of 2003.]

Even more damaging to Washington's credibility on Latin American trade was Clinton's failure, over a six-year period, to get Congress to renew fast-track negotiating authority. Fast-track authority, which expired in 1993, basically waives Congress' right to amend trade agreements by forcing it to vote either yes or no on a trade bill without making any changes. Because it was discussed so often and promised for so long, fast track became emblematic of the United States' commitment (or lack thereof) to hemispheric free trade—and to broader economic and political cooperation with Latin America. With Congress' ongoing refusal to renew fast track, Latin Americans became increasingly skeptical of U.S. support for the so-called Free Trade Area of the Americas (FTAA) and other U.S. pledges to the region. Should President Bush now fail to move quickly to recover fast-track power, he will send the message that hemispheric trade relations are not a high priority for his administration.

Fortunately, Bush's campaign rhetoric suggests that he understands just how important the free trade agenda is to Latin America and its relations with the United States. In a speech in Miami last August, Bush stated that he intended to achieve "free trade agreements with all the nations" of the region and later insisted that "fast-track trade authority is on the way."

But no matter how sincere were these pledges, the new administration's good intentions will hardly guarantee the passage of fast track. Even with a full-court press by the White House, the outcome remains in doubt. To succeed, President Bush may have to compromise with Democratic lawmakers on the sensitive issues of workers' rights and environmental protection, backing away from the standard Republican position that these issues have no place in trade negotiations. It was just such a compromise that allowed for NAFTA's approval in 1993, when labor and environmental standards were incorporated into special side clauses. But many congressional Democrats, union officials, and environmental activists are convinced that the 1993 measures have proven toothless, so achieving a compromise agreement today will be much harder. Still, such an agreement is probably the only way the White House will obtain fast track any time soon.

Such a compromise may create another problem, however. The inclusion of labor or environmental standards in the FTAA is vehemently opposed by the great majority of Latin American governments. These governments fear that such standards will raise new and unfair barriers to their exports and end up as just another U.S. restriction on foreign trade. Latin Americans are especially hostile to the idea of using trade sanctions to enforce labor and environmental standards—an approach that President Clinton seemed to endorse at last year's World Trade Organization meeting in Seattle. Given the importance of U.S. markets to their economic prospects, Latin American countries may end up swallowing such demands. But this will not resolve their underlying opposition or quell their resentment; it will only postpone conflict until the implementation stage.

Assuming that the Bush administration does manage to secure fast track relatively soon, there is still no guarantee that FTAA negotiations will proceed smoothly, even aside from labor and environment conditions. The final round of FTAA talks, which begins in 2003, is scheduled to be chaired jointly by the United States and Brazil and may prove particularly difficult. The two countries publicly disagree on a number of core issues that will not be easy to resolve. And President Fernando Henrique Cardoso's government has already made it clear that it is in no hurry to negotiate on the FTAA, which it views as a second-order priority, or to conclude matters by the agreed-upon 2005 deadline. This position reflects the strong opposition that exists to the FTAA, not only in Brazil's labor movement, but also among many in its powerful business community who doubt that Brazil can compete with U.S. suppliers. [As of 2004, there has been no agreement.]

Complicating matters further is Brazil's growing assertiveness and influence in regional and global affairs. The country seems bent on establishing a second pole of power in the western hemisphere. This was most evident in August of last year, when Cardoso convened in Brasília the very first summit meeting of South American heads of state. And it is not only on trade matters that Brazil's independent policy has put it at odds with the United States. This past year, the Brazilian government opposed U.S. efforts to challenge Fujimori's rigging of the Peruvian elections. And having made plain its aversion to U.S. policy in Colombia, Brazil succeeded in excluding any mention of the U.S.-supported Plan Colombia from the final communiqué of the South American summit. As it negotiates toward hemispheric free trade, then, Washington cannot avoid taking account of its broader relationship with Brazil, a nation that can affect the success or failure of U.S. policy on a broad array of issues.

A QUAGMIRE IN THE ANDES?

Nothing, however, is more likely to produce an open clash between the United States and Latin America than Washington's growing military assistance to Colombia. That assistance is part of Plan Colombia, Bogotá's multibillion-dollar, multiyear strategy to retake control of the country from left-wing guerrillas, right-wing vigilantes, and drug criminals. Every Latin American government recognizes the depth of Colombia's problems and its need for outside support. Yet U.S. aid, which will reach $1.6 billion over the next two years, has provoked wide opposition in the region.

The first concern is that U.S. funds, most of which are meant for the purchase of military hardware to battle drug traffickers, will escalate Colombia's wars and end hopes for a negotiated settlement with the country's guerrillas. This would be an unwelcome outcome, for negotiation remains the solution favored by every Latin American government, despite the continuing failure of peace talks. Colombia's neighbors also fear that a widening war will spill over the country's borders, spreading the violence and criminality that have plagued Colombia for so long.

Latin American countries also recall earlier U.S. interventions in the region, particularly in Central America in the 1980s, and worry about the impact of a U.S. military presence in South America—where the United States has never sent its soldiers. These countries lack confidence that Washington will be able to keep its intervention limited and avoid becoming more deeply engaged and reliant on military force, leading to a Vietnam-style quagmire.

Opposition to the U.S. role in Colombia also goes beyond Latin America. Many in the U.S. Congress, as well as a large number of American nongovernmental organizations (NGOs), have criticized U.S. military assistance to Bogotá—and the Bush administration is likely to face growing objections as U.S. involvement increases in the coming months. European governments have already made clear their distaste for the U.S. approach, and their financial contributions to Plan Colombia have fallen far short of what was anticipated—leaving Washington as the only major stakeholder (apart from Bogotá itself) in a substantially underfunded effort.

The critics of the plan make a number of compelling arguments that reflect more than mere knee-jerk anti-Americanism. Even a joint task force of the Inter-American Dialogue and the Council on Foreign Relations, chaired by two supporters of U.S. aid to Colombia—former National Security Adviser Brent Scowcroft and Senator Bob Graham (D-Fla.)—recently criticized Washington's Colombia policy as too narrowly focused on counternarcotics programs. It called for broader efforts to bolster government authority in Colombia and to underpin peace negotiations. The task force also argued that only with the firm backing of Latin American and European nations could U.S. policy hope to succeed.

Although President Bush has strongly endorsed U.S. assistance to Colombia in general, he has not said much about how he plans to confront the key policy questions, including whether to sustain (or even increase) the level of resources devoted to the program, whether to remain focused on antidrug efforts or move more toward a counterinsurgency strategy, and whether to continue emphasizing military assistance or initiate a more comprehensive aid program.

Whatever choices Bush makes, his most difficult challenges will be, first, to maintain the support of Congress and the American people for a large-scale, multiyear commitment (making Colombia the third largest recipient of U.S. security aid after Israel and Egypt) and, second, to secure the needed political and financial cooperation from Latin America and Europe. The United States cannot count on the support of other countries unless it starts consulting them far more systematically than it has done to date.

HURRICANE HUGO

Venezuela's firebrand president, Hugo Chávez, has further complicated the Colombia situation. The most vociferous opponent of Washington's assistance to Bogotá, Chávez has warned that U.S. actions could "generate a medium-intensity conflict in the whole of northern South America." Chávez has frequently and loudly disparaged the Colombian government as well and maintains regular communication with the guerrilla armies, which have been invited to speak before the Venezuelan Congress. So far, no evidence has emerged to implicate Chávez in providing material support to these guerrillas, but there have been credible allegations that he has aided opposition groups in Ecuador and Bolivia.

Ever since Chávez took office two years ago [in 1999], U.S.-Venezuela relations have become increasingly strained. Chávez has already defied the United States on an array of issues and is fast becoming a leader of anti-American sentiment in the hemisphere. Venezuela has refused U.S. planes permission to fly over its territory for counternarcotics activities. Among OPEC members, it has most strongly resisted U.S. appeals to increase oil production to ease pressure on prices. In August, Chávez became the first head of state since the Persian Gulf War to disregard U.N. sanctions by visiting Saddam Hussein. And Chávez has consistently flaunted his friendship with Fidel Castro, recently agreeing to subsidize petroleum exports to Cuba. A direct clash with the United States may be brewing, particularly if the Venezuelan leader suffers political reversals at home and starts looking for scapegoats. Washington is already apprehensive about the lack of institutional checks on Chávez's power and the risks it poses for the future of democracy in the region.

Cuba, Haiti, Nicaragua, and a few other countries are also likely to present challenges to the new Bush administration—as they have to most previous U.S. governments. Several of these problems may be costly and difficult to resolve. Haiti, for example, could at any moment produce another massive flood of boat people headed to the United States. Bitter partisan squabbles in Washington, however, continue to impede the framing of a sustained and coherent policy toward the impoverished country.

Fortunately, developments in Haiti or in others of these small, troubled nations are unlikely to have much impact on the broader sweep of U.S.–

Latin American relations, since the problems are relatively self-contained. Cuba, however, could be the exception, because its leadership is so unpredictable, because the United States often overreacts to Cuba's actions, and because Cuba has such a high international profile. Nearly every Latin American government has strong misgivings about U.S. policy toward Cuba, which they consider exaggerated, anachronistic, and at times reckless. Aside from Venezuela, however, Cuba has virtually no allies or supporters in the region. But while one can imagine scenarios in which the United States forcibly intervenes in Cuba and provokes an uproar in the rest of Latin America, none of these seems very likely today. Washington is clearly softening its policy toward Havana. Notwithstanding Bush's tough campaign rhetoric and the debt he owes Cuban Americans for their overwhelming electoral support, that trend is likely to continue. Past votes make it clear that a majority in Congress is now ready to lift most U.S. restrictions on Cuba.

THINGS GO BETTER WITH FOX

Critical as all these issues are, the United States' most important relationship in Latin America is with Mexico. No other country in the world affects the lives of Americans as much, and no country is more intensely affected by U.S. policies. Against the backdrop of an often bitter history, U.S.-Mexican relations have taken a constructive turn in recent years. Economic ties have flourished, and Mexico is now the United States' second largest trading partner after Canada—outdistancing Japan, the United Kingdom, and Germany. In the past ten years, U.S. exports to Mexico have tripled to some $100 billion a year. Approximately 350,000 Mexicans head north each year, reshaping U.S. society in multiple ways. The Mexican economy, in turn, is highly dependent on U.S. markets. Mexico sends more than 80 percent of its exports northward, while capital flows from the United States, as well as remittances from Mexican workers, have fueled Mexico's stunning economic performance in the past several years. Tensions over trade and other economic issues have by no means been eliminated, but NAFTA now provides the institutional mechanisms for addressing trade disputes. Other institutional arrangements are also in place to manage troublesome issues such as migration, drug trafficking, environmental contamination, and water rights.

There is every reason, therefore, to expect that U.S.-Mexican relations will get even better in the coming years. Mexico has become Latin America's star performer. Hitched to the flourishing U.S. economy, for two years now [from 1999 to 2001] Mexico has enjoyed its highest rates of growth in two decades and has kept inflation well in check. Even more impressive has been Mexico's decisive break from its authoritarian past—marked by the election of an opposition leader as president for the first time in the nation's history. These two developments augur stronger and more productive U.S.-Mexico ties. Mexico's giant step toward democracy should make cooperation easier across the board and far more appealing to a U.S. public and a Congress that were leery in the past of their undemocratic neighbor. President Fox—a business leader and former governor from northern Mexico who ran the national Coca-Cola company and speaks fluent English—should be a compatible partner for Bush. Fox has already expressed a commitment to enhancing U.S.-Mexican ties in many areas and has offered a series of far-reaching proposals on trade, immigration, and drugs. For his part, Bush takes pride in his connections to Mexico. He and many of his advisers have made it clear that Mexico will be a foreign policy priority. During his campaign, Bush declared, "I have a vision for our two countries. The United States is destined to have a special relationship with Mexico, as clear and strong as we have had with Canada and Great Britain."

Of course, expectations may have been driven too high—and if progress stalls, bitterness and frustration could quickly replace the optimism on both sides of the border. Another concern is that impatient U.S. policymakers may find it difficult to deal with the resulting diffusion of power and increased uncertainty that democracy will bring to Mexico. Decision-making there will probably grow slower and less tidy. Fox will also have to face unaccustomed scrutiny from a divided Mexican Congress and an increasingly assertive press.

Conflicts in U.S.-Mexican relations are likely to arise over the traditionally contentious issues of illegal immigration, narcotics trafficking, and economic relations. Many of the economic conflicts swirl around NAFTA. Each side complains that the other is not faithfully implementing the treaty. But although it would surely be better for both countries if these differences could be resolved, they are not likely to cause any wider conflicts—or to put the trade relationship at risk. NAFTA has produced too many valuable benefits for either side to jeopardize it. Even an economic downturn in the United States, which would quickly translate into a Mexican slump, would not cause bitterness in Mexico. Mexicans of all economic strata support close economic ties with the United States.

On drugs and immigration, however, the two countries deeply distrust one another. From the Federal Bureau of Investigation and the Drug Enforcement Agency to local police, U.S. law enforcement authorities have little faith in Mexico's ability or willingness to reduce the flow of cocaine and other drugs into the United States. Along with many influential members of Congress, they believe Mexico is too corrupt and indifferent to be a trustworthy partner in the drug war—and this message is regularly (if not always intentionally) communicated to understandably resentful Mexican officials.

For their part, Mexicans believe that U.S. demand has created their drug problem, that the United States is lackadaisical in fighting drugs on its side of the border, and that U.S. politicians and government agencies are intent on shifting the blame and political costs to Mexico. The U.S. certification process, through which Washington passes judgment each year on the antidrug efforts of other countries, is especially humiliating to Mexicans. Fox has made it clear that the United States and Mexico will never enjoy productive cooperation on drugs until the unilateral certification process is replaced by a more equitable and multilateral formula. Bush has not publicly commented on certification yet, but he will have to do so soon, before the White House offers its judgments. [The Bush and Fox administrations have made a number of advances that have eased the tension on the certification issue.]

Immigration poses an even more difficult problem. On drugs, the United States and Mexico can at least claim compatible objectives. Both governments ostensibly want to reduce the drug flow and the crime associated with it. But on immigration issues, Mexico and the United States have very different perspectives. Mexico wants the relatively free movement of people across the border, parallel to the free movement of capital and goods enshrined in NAFTA. The United States seeks to selectively restrict entry by maintaining a closed and monitored border. The discord has been somewhat muted over the past several years because a prospering U.S. economy has created an enormous demand for low-wage labor, and Americans— with an all-time low unemployment rate—have been less troubled than usual by the influx of Mexican workers. A prolonged dip in the U.S. economy and rising joblessness, however, will revive political pressure to slow migration. Tensions with Mexico will again emerge.

Still, so far the signs are encouraging. Soon after his election last July [2000], President Fox proposed that Washington join him in exploring the eventual establishment of an open border between the two countries. Although it gained enormous media coverage, the suggestion fell on deaf ears among U.S. officials and has not been resuscitated. Unfortunately, it may have also overshadowed Fox's most important statement—his offer to work with the United States to monitor and regularize the flow of migrants. This is an offer that no other president of Mexico has ever made. And it provides, for the first time ever, a strong basis on which to build cooperative migration policies that are acceptable to both countries.

FIRST THINGS FIRST

By the time he travels to Québec in April [2001], President Bush will have discovered that, with the prominent exception of Mexico, U.S. ties to Latin America have become increasingly tense. His administration confronts some very difficult policy choices at a time when many Latin Americans are losing confidence in U.S. leadership and questioning the reliability of Washington as a partner.

With many countries facing hard economic times and with democracy eroding in some places, Latin Americans are also losing faith in their own leaders and institutions. Of course, these are problems that Latin American nations have to resolve themselves. If they cannot, they will never make very attractive partners for their powerful neighbor to the north.

Indeed, there is not much that the Bush administration can do to prevent the souring of Latin America's economic and political climate. The White House can, however, show that it stands ready to establish enduring partnerships with Latin American nations that are ready to do the same. President Bush must promptly move ahead on hemispheric trade matters, therefore, by taking quick steps—ideally before the summit in Québec—to gain Congress' approval of fast-track negotiating authority. Early and significant attention to Colombia would also be helpful. Latin American governments would welcome a signal from the Bush administration that it plans to thoroughly review the current U.S. aid package and, in the process, consult extensively with other countries in the region and beyond. The Bush administration, in addition, has a historic opportunity to break new ground in U.S.-Mexican relations by seriously engaging the issues that President Fox has already put forth. Washington may have misgivings about Fox's specific proposals, but the Mexican president has clearly identified the right subjects for debate and discussion. By seizing these opportunities, President Bush can make up for the lost momentum in U.S.–Latin American relations, begin to alleviate some of Latin America's concerns, and blunt the region's growing criticism of the United States.

5.2 Preserving Hegemony: National Security Doctrine in the Post–Cold War Era (2001)

J. PATRICE McSHERRY

The U.S. government is no longer supporting military subversion, coups and dictatorships in the name of anti-Communism in Latin America. But it continues to strengthen military and security forces to buttress the neoliberal order.

Has U.S. foreign policy dramatically changed with the end of the Cold War? Clearly, the collapse of the Soviet bloc transformed the international system. There is no longer a rival superpower that challenges the United States ideologically, militarily and economically. U.S. security doctrine today is primarily designed to secure and advance the global economic and

J. Patrice McSherry, "Preserving Hegemony: National Security Doctrine in the Post–Cold War Era," *NACLA Report on the Americas,* November–December 2001, Vol. 35, no. 3, pp. 14–23. Reprinted by permission.

political predominance of the United States, the main beneficiary of the "new world order" of corporate-driven globalization. In effect, Washington has assumed the role of hegemonic stabilizer of the system. The Pentagon sees as its current tasks "to encourage all nations to recognize and address domestic problems that have transnational security implications"— a sort of tutelary function—and "to shape the strategic environment to prevent conflict and promote regional stability." Instability is seemingly defined as challenges to U.S. leadership or to the seamless functioning of globalized market capitalism. But along with affluence for a few, globalization has generated massive social dislocations, increased inequality, and sharpened social tensions in Latin America and elsewhere. "Stability" is not a neutral concept in this context. It means preserving a global system in which the assets of the world's three richest individuals are larger than the combined national income of 48 less-developed countries.

In Latin America, the U.S. government is no longer encouraging or supporting military subversion, coups and dictatorships in the name of anti-Communism. This change in Cold War policy—a policy that led to terror, suffering, torture and death for millions of Latin Americans—should not be minimized or dismissed. Essentially, Washington now accepts pluralist, if narrow, democracies. The new U.S. attitude has deterred potential coups and provided an environment in which democratic movements and governments—with all their limitations and weaknesses—have opened new political spaces in the region. President Bill Clinton opposed military coups in Guatemala in 1993, when President Jorge Serrano attempted to stage one, and in Venezuela in 1992, Paraguay in 1996 and Peru today. Clinton proclaimed a policy of supporting human rights, peace processes, and "market democracy" (free elections and free trade). He apologized for the U.S. role in Guatemala (to the outrage of former Reagan officials), and Secretary of State Madeleine Albright made a similar statement about the U.S. role in the Southern Cone. The President ordered government departments and agencies to declassify all documents on the violence in Chile and the role of the U.S. government during the 1970s. It is hard to imagine these steps occurring under a right-wing Republican administration.

Yet it is equally important to note the continuities in U.S. policy since the Cold War and before. Washington continues to interpret events in Latin America in light of its own geopolitical and economic interests and still assumes the right to monitor the region, supervise its development, and intervene in serious cases of instability (as in Colombia [in 2000]). Now that the region's governments have embraced market capitalism, opened their economies to foreign investment, and generally acquiesced to other demands of the United States and global capital, there is little need for direct or indirect U.S. military intervention. But Washington continues to work closely with military forces in the region and to train them in counterdrug and counterterrorism operations and in "foreign internal defense," missions virtually indistinguishable from Cold War counterinsurgency operations that targeted domestic opposition. The core Cold War military missions of "containment of Communism" and counterinsurgency have been superseded by a new security paradigm that gives military-security forces a leading role in confronting diffuse "non-state threats" in a globalized world: drug trafficking, terrorism, illegal immigration, social unrest, threats to democracy and others. Meanwhile, Washington continues to tolerate autocrats and protect notorious human rights abusers (notably Alberto Fujimori and Vladimiro Montesinos in Peru) and to bolster military, security, and intelligence forces, to secure their loyalty and to guarantee U.S. interests. The U.S. government's promotion of expansive roles for Latin American military, security and intelligence forces contradicts its stated commitments to democracy and human rights and reveals its enduring objective: to decisively influence or control outcomes in the region. Moreover, in the 1990s, U.S. strategic and business interests outweighed concerns for democracy and human rights in several cases, reproducing Cold War patterns.

Essentially, Washington continues to pursue hegemony in Latin America, but through use of different instruments and strategies. The preferred U.S. model [in 2000] is procedural democracy, with some civil and political rights (but limited economic and social rights for the majority), tightly bound by the restraints of the global market economy and monitored by military-security forces still ready to combat the "threat from below." The elite-based democracies in place in Latin America facilitate neoliberal restructuring and global economic integration because popular participation is limited, political opposition is weak, and constitutional institutions are often ineffective.

Despite the homage paid by U.S. officials to "market democracy," neoliberal economic models imposed on much of the region have undermined democratic struggles by citizens to make their voices heard and fight for their rights. Civilian governments have used authoritarian means to enforce austerity and to meet the demands of the international markets and financial institutions, leaving citizens impoverished, frustrated and desperate. While Latin Americans can now vote, many analysts note that political and civil rights in these systems are tenuous. Elites with government connections have been the primary beneficiaries of the sweeping economic transformations carried out by fiat, while millions of people have become marginalized and social unrest has erupted through the region.

In this context, U.S. Special Forces deployments in Latin America have actually increased from 147 in 1995 to some 200 [in 2000]. The expansive new security paradigm, forcefully promoted by U.S. Southern Command (SOUTHCOM) in the region, emphasizes domestic intelligence and internal security capabilities for the militaries, functions that strengthen their most anti-democratic sectors. But the new paradigm reconstitutes the role of the military forces that wielded state power during the Cold War. The new doctrine inserts the military within strategic areas of state and society and enlarges its role in civilian institutions and functions, enhancing military capacities for guardianship and social control—but within the framework of electoral democracy. The "war on drugs" has replaced the war against Communism as the primary U.S. military mission and policy priority in Latin America. But as one U.S. officer noted, "There's not much difference between counterdrug and counterinsurgency. We just don't use the [latter] word anymore because it is politically too sensitive." In practice, the new paradigm strengthens the military, security and intelligence forces that have been the greatest danger to democracy for decades, and weakens civilian and democratic institutions.

To better understand the continuities between today's security doctrine and that of the Cold War, a brief discussion of the earlier period is helpful. Significant expansion of U.S. economic interests and military presence throughout the world occurred during World War II, contributing to a redefinition (and globalization) of U.S. security doctrine. The anti-Communist crusade became the primary strategic mission, and it combined military, economic, and political interests. National Security Council Paper No. 68 (NSC-68) of 1950 presented a vivid statement of U.S. Cold War policy. It frankly portrayed U.S. rivalry with the Soviet Union as a battle for world hegemony, and stated that "our overall policy at the present time may be described as one designed to foster a world environment in which the American system can survive and flourish" and to develop "a successfully functioning political and economic system" in the non-Communist world, which required "an adequate military shield" under which it could develop. While the Soviet Union has disappeared, this statement continues to be a fair summary of U.S. foreign policy goals.

In 1961, following the 1959 Cuban revolution, the Kennedy Administration introduced a new mission for the U.S. Armed Forces in the anti-Communist struggle: counterinsurgency. U.S. strategists sought to develop counterinsurgency forces in Latin America and worldwide to monitor restive populations and "dissuade" political or social opposition—an approach that led to repression. U.S. security was seen as inextricably linked to promotion of the private enterprise system and to unobstructed U.S. access to Third World economies and raw materials, goals that predated the Cold War. In effect, Washington sought to secure its informal economic empire and its sphere of influence. A secret State Department document of September 1962 entitled "United States Overseas Internal Defense Policy" made clear these economic-security linkages:

The broad U.S. interests in the underdeveloped world are as follows:
    1) A political and ideological interest in assuring that developing nations evolve in a way that affords a congenial world environment for international cooperation and the growth of free institutions.

2) A military interest in assuring that strategic areas and the manpower and natural resources of developing nations do not fall under communist control . . .

3) An economic interest in assuring that the resources and markets of the less developed world remain available to us and to other Free World countries. . . .

This document called for the creation of counterinsurgency forces even if there were no insurgents:

Where subversive insurgency is virtually non-existent or incipient (PHASE I), the objective is to support the development of an adequate counterinsurgency capability in indigenous military forces through the Military Assistance Program, and to complement the nation-building programs of AID [the U.S. Agency for International Development] with military civic action. The same means, in collaboration with AID and CIA, will be employed to develop a similar capability in indigenous paramilitary forces.

Clear from this document was the U.S. strategy to build up military-security forces as a proactive measure, to control populations, secure allegiance to U.S. objectives, and prevent outcomes seen as inimical to U.S. interests. Washington consolidated a sort of political trusteeship over Latin America by bolstering counterinsurgency militaries. Direct U.S. intervention—as in the Dominican Republic in 1965, Grenada in 1983 and Panama in 1989—was a last resort, considered too costly both economically and politically. Key elements of U.S. counterinsurgency doctrine were military civic action programs, aimed to capture the "hearts and minds" of the people (and develop infrastructure useful for military operations, such as roads and bridges). The doctrine also included special operations capabilities such as internal defense, intelligence, psychological operations (PSYOPS), and unconventional warfare.

The transformation of the Latin American military mission from national defense to internal security had fateful consequences in the 1960s and 1970s. As a series of popular struggles for political and socioeconomic change swept the region, the militaries targeted large sectors of their populations as subversive enemies. The coups of that era left nearly the entire Latin American region under military dictatorship.

The collapse of the Communist bloc afforded vast new opportunities for U.S. investment and political domination worldwide. The current form of globalization was not inevitable, however; it rests on ideology, institutions and military force. Ideologically, the Clinton Administration posited that U.S.-style laissez-faire capitalism and electoral democracy were inevitable and universally beneficial. The system rested institutionally upon the powerful supranational lending organizations, transnational corporations and banks, and governmental and non-governmental bodies that administered and perpetuated the system, with little or no democratic input. Finally, Washington continued to strengthen military and security forces in Latin

America and worldwide: "The military shield" was still an inseparable component of the emerging neoliberal order.

In 1994, the Clinton Administration's first national security strategy document called for defending U.S. strategic objectives by "protecting, consolidating, and enlarging the community of free-market democracies" through active, if selective, U.S. engagement worldwide. In 1995, the complementary military strategy was outlined in "A Strategy of Flexible and Selective Engagement." It described engagement as including military-to-military contacts, security assistance, and counterdrug and counterterrorism operations. Despite the change in emphasis and terminology, long-standing geopolitical and economic interests underlay the new doctrine. As General Alfred M. Gray, commandant of the Marines, wrote in 1991, the U.S. needed "unimpeded access" to "established and developing economic markets throughout the world," implying that opening foreign markets to U.S. penetration was still a military mission.

Similarly, the former commander of SOUTHCOM and later Drug Czar General Barry McCaffrey said in 1994 that SOUTHCOM's headquarters "looks NorthSouth . . . where it can pay attention to what I would suggest are permanent and increasingly important economic, military, and security interests in Latin America." The CIA's Deputy Director for Intelligence argued in 1996 that Latin America remained a central focus for the agency because U.S. exports to the region nearly equalled exports to Europe, and drugs were a new threat to U.S. stability.

Other significant elements of U.S. Cold War doctrine persist in the new security paradigm: the use of "civil-military operations," the concept of "dissuasion" of unrest, the targeting of "terrorism" or "instability," and the build-up of intelligence capabilities. The 1997 U.S. Army Command and General Staff College Field Manual 100–20 stated, for example: "Civil-military operations (CMO) include all military efforts to support host nation development, co-opt insurgent issues, gain support for the national government, and attain national objectives without combat. . . . They also help prepare the area of operations for combat forces, if they are required." "Dissuasion" implies an intrusive military strategy to block "instability" before it begins. This function has disturbing implications in countries where, not long ago, ruthless military forces presided over repressive dictatorships. Explaining his concept of dissuasion, Argentine General—and second in command of the army—Anibal Laino wrote in 1996 that:

> [A]ny potentially critical situation . . . might require military action to prevent, dissuade, or confront threats to the vital interests of the nation. [These] are any psychological-cultural, political, religious, economic, and military situation that may affect . . . a nation-state. . . . [They] must be continually monitored. The difficulty of defining the operational environment in which action might be necessary makes necessary a Military Instrument designed with the capability to

dissuade any threat to the vital interests of the Nation and not in regard to any particular enemy.

This expansive vision of the military role reflected concepts of Cold War national security doctrine and suggested that the Argentine military, despite its denials, still conducted political intelligence and targeted internal enemies—an unsettling thought, given the thousands of people who were disappeared by Argentine security forces in the 1970s.

The U.S. Army School of the Americas (SOA) was a key Cold War-era center where Latin American militaries were trained in counterinsurgency techniques. Today the SOA survives, despite repeated efforts to close it by a broad citizen movement and by members of Congress. The school's Command Brief of August 1998 stated that its curriculum had "evolved" in line with the new post-Cold War paradigm, with the elimination of some tactical courses and the addition of others such as "Civil Military Operations," "Peace Operations," "Counterdrug Operations," and "Democratic Sustainment." Meanwhile, military force was frequently used by the Clinton Administration for "operations other than war," and in some areas of the world, U.S. military officers became the de facto political agents of U.S. foreign policy, eclipsing civilian diplomats. Analyst Andrew J. Bacevich argues that Clinton routinely used bombing raids, cruise missiles, and other bellicose acts "to convey disapproval, change attitudes, and dictate behavior."

Political scientist Kenneth Waltz also notes the irony that in the post-Cold War era, Washington has further militarized international affairs: "To an increasing extent, American foreign policy relies on military means. America continues to garrison much of the world and to look for ways of keeping troops in foreign countries. . . ." He cites the 1992 draft of the Pentagon's Defense Planning Guidance, which described U.S. policy as "discouraging the advanced industrialized nations from . . . even aspiring to a larger global or regional role." Such presumptions of permanent global economic and military domination have a marked imperial quality. U.S. policy has subtly shifted from defense of the "free world" to domination of it.

The rationale for that domination is no longer couched in terms of the Communist threat in the hemisphere, but by official warnings of "narcosubversion" and terrorism, warnings used to justify large budgets and a newly expanded military role. In 1987—before the end of the Cold War—U.S. officers pressured their counterparts in the Conference of American Armies to make "narcosubversion" a key military mission, and in 1991, the Conference confirmed it as a primary mission for all the region's armies. In the 1995 Conference, officers added other major challenges for nation-states and their armies: poverty and lack of social development, massive migration flows, environment, structural inequalities within states, narcotrafficking, terrorism, subversion, tensions caused by economic competition, and territorial disputes. In short, the new paradigm created a central role for the military in combating major national social, economic and security problems, at the expense of civilian control and preeminence in new democracies.

The expansive new missions were seen with alarm by Latin American democracy advocates struggling to narrow the powerful military role and strengthen civilian institutions. Important steps have been taken in some countries to increase civilian control. But most of the region's militaries retain significant political and coercive power. Structures, ideologies, and personnel from the days of the military dictatorships remain entrenched in military, security and intelligence forces, and many officers remain unrepentant about the human rights violations of the recent past. In some countries, armed and security forces have used dirty war methods and repression to control insurgencies, popular unrest and political opposition. Military units in Guatemala, Mexico, Peru and Colombia carried out summary executions, disappearances and torture in the 1990s. In Argentina, Bolivia, Venezuela, Chile, Paraguay and Brazil, military and security forces used force to quell social discontent and political movements protesting the wrenching consequences of free-market restructuring.

Like the national security doctrine of the Cold War, the new paradigm blurs the line between internal security and national defense. Counterdrug and counterterror operations draw on Cold War counterinsurgency doctrine and are a form of low-intensity warfare (a type of unconventional warfare that blends political, psychological, social and economic strategies of coercion). The language of counterterrorism and "instability" is not new in Latin America. It was used by previous military dictatorships to justify repression of unions, journalists, opposition party leaders, social organizations and dissidents, and the dismembering of the constitutional apparatus of democratic government. The new mission also provides a means for continued U.S. involvement in military and political institutions throughout Latin America.

Since the end of the Cold War, U.S. unconventional forces have again begun working with every army in the hemisphere but Cuba's (and with those of 110 countries worldwide), conducting specialized training exercises called Joint Combined Exchange Training, or JCET, without significant civilian oversight. JCETs are officially justified as training missions for U.S. Special Operations Forces, but their main function in practice is to train other militaries in foreign internal defense. A 1991 law exempted U.S. Special Operations Forces from many executive and legislative restrictions, including human rights criteria, freeing them to train brutal foreign militaries in counterdrug and counterterror operations, urban warfare, intelligence, and lethal tactics. In some cases, the units trained by U.S. forces were committing human rights atrocities, as in Colombia and Indonesia. Nevertheless, U.S. training continued, recalling Cold War practices. U.S. Special Forces have sometimes worked at cross purposes to stated U.S. foreign policy. In Colombia, for example, JCETs continued even after Clinton decertified the country for military assistance in 1996 and 1997 because of the country's alleged failure to cooperate in the U.S. drug war. Only after media coverage spotlighted the role of JCETs did Congress stipulate human rights criteria in Defense Department appropriations legislation.

The U.S. Special Operations Command, created in 1987 to consolidate all the Special Operations Forces such as the Navy Seals, Army Green Berets, and the covert Delta Force, increased in size while the rest of the military downsized (in 1998 Special Operations had 47,000 personnel). Along with training militaries in foreign internal defense, a key mission of the Command is to combat "instability." One U.S. officer told Washington Post reporter Dana Priest, "We are setting the conditions for stability by insuring security. The threat of instability, that is the major threat." Field Manual 31-20 of 1990 defined "foreign internal defense" exercises as training military forces to combat "subversion, lawlessness, and insurgency." Priest noted that even "where armed domestic opposition is negligible or nonexistent (as in Argentina), U.S. forces are teaching armies how to track down opponents, surprise them in helicopter attacks, kill them with more proficiency or, in some cases, how to lead house-to-house raids in 'close quarters combat' designed for cities." The combined impact of U.S. security training and funding throughout the region has been to augment the guardian capabilities of military-security forces.

Under Clinton, U.S. military assistance, as well as equipment and training for Latin America more than tripled from FY 1996 to 1997. In 1997, the Administration lifted its ban on sales of advanced weaponry and heavy arms to Latin America, in a clear case of complementary military and economic interests. Lockheed Martin and McDonnell Douglas had lobbied heavily for lifting the ban. Most U.S. arms sales to Latin America in the 1990s were used for counterdrug operations and paid for with counterdrug-related military aid. The State Department's International Narcotics Control program (which channels most of the military aid to Latin America) rose from $180 million in 1998 to $430 million in 1999. According to one report, some 10,000 military men and police were trained by U.S. forces in 1998, and over half of all training was in counterdrug operations.

The Latin American militaries are not simple instruments of neoliberal power or of the United States, however. Internal factions with populist or nationalist tendencies exist, and military leaderships have their own national security and strategic interests. Many resent the U.S. drug certification process. Hugo Chavez rode to the Venezuelan presidency by defying neoliberal economics and U.S. dictates. But most of the military commands seemingly have calculated that their interests lie in support of the new paradigm and an alliance with the United States, with its attendant U.S. aid, training and weapons sales.

Two examples demonstrate the U.S. interests in preserving stability and securing the uninterrupted functioning of capital flows and market economics in Latin America. The volatile Andean region, which includes a major

U.S. source of oil (Venezuela), provides stark evidence that in crisis situations, U.S. economic and security interests still outrank promotion of democracy and human rights.

In Colombia, U.S. aid to the military was terminated in 1994 when human rights organizations and government studies indicated that money earmarked for counterdrug operations was actually used by the armed forces for counterinsurgency, marked by human rights violations. Savage paramilitary forces linked to the military continue to commit widely reported massacres of civilians. In 1998 Human Rights Watch noted that more murders of human rights advocates took place in Colombia than in any other country in the hemisphere. Yet Washington began sharing high-tech intelligence directly with the Colombian armed forces in March 1999 and built radar and electronic surveillance stations in Colombia, staffed by U.S. personnel. U.S. Special Forces trained a new army counternarcotics battalion of 1,500 elite Colombian soldiers and is now training a second, supported logistically and technologically by specialized U.S. units. Additionally, the Pentagon has reportedly attempted to create a multinational intervention force for Colombia, though U.S. officials deny this. Clearly, Washington's overriding priorities are to halt the insurgency in Colombia while securing access to the region's oil fields and other strategic resources.

Clinton escalated U.S. involvement in Colombia's civil war this past July [1998] when he waived human rights conditions as he approved Congress' massive $1.3 billion aid package mainly aimed at strengthening the Colombian military. Conservative members of Congress called openly for U.S. counterdrug equipment and funds to be used against the insurgency. The Pentagon named an army general with a background in counterinsurgency—a former advisor in El Salvador—to oversee Plan Colombia.

In Peru, U.S. officials looked the other way as President Fujimori incrementally eliminated key civil and political rights during the 1990s. Because he defeated an insurgent threat, promoted foreign investment and cooperated with U.S. counterdrug operations, Washington tolerated Fujimori's dismantling of constitutional democracy, again recalling Cold War priorities. Stability was the ultimate goal of U.S. policy in Peru. During a visit there in August 1999, McCaffrey eulogized Fujimori's counterdrug efforts as "an example for other countries to follow," and made a point of visiting Vladimiro Montesinos—the shadowy intelligence chief who was the CIA's main liaison, and who directed Peru's National Intelligence Service (SIN), the base of operations for death squads that carried out torture and murder in the early 1990s, and later covert operations to crush dissent. After the meeting, McCaffrey said he wanted to "state my public admiration for the work developed by the intelligence service." Washington did little when Fujimori claimed an illegal third term, putting continued counterdrug cooperation with his militarized regime above commitment to democratic principles. When Montesinos finally lost CIA support in September (he was apparently involved in gun-running to the Colombian guerrillas), Washington helped arrange his passage to Panama and heavily pressured the Panamanian government to give him safe haven. In short, Cold War mentalities endured.

Meanwhile, the U.S. government extended its network of bases in the region, justified by the war on drugs, and established new "Forward Operating Locations" in Ecuador, Honduras, the Dutch Antilles and Puerto Rico. In Manta, Ecuador, protesters denounced the stationing of U.S. forces at the air base there in mid-summer, and the Confederation of Indigenous Nationalities collected one million signatures to demand a national referendum on the U.S. presence as well as the neoliberal restructuring of the economy.

In the post-Cold War era, Washington's earlier practices of promoting coups, contra-style forces or dictatorships were at last left behind. But U.S. strategic, political and economic interests in Latin America endured, and the U.S. government's commitment to democracy seemed dangerously thin. Hegemonic presumptions and power politics continued to characterize U.S. security policy in the region, at times reproducing Cold War patterns.

The United States has assumed the post-Cold War role of hegemonic stabilizer of the "new world order." While reaping the economic benefits of the globalized stage of free-market capitalism, Washington continues to pursue stability, order and social control in Latin America, through its bases and intelligence networks and through the local military-security forces it trains and finances. The new security paradigm sponsored by the Pentagon inserts the Latin American militaries in strategic roles in state and society and bolsters their guardian capabilities.

There is growing popular resistance to the neoliberal world order and to U.S. dictates, as evidenced, for example, by the refusal of Latin American presidents to subscribe to Plan Colombia at their August 2000 summit. New organizations and broad social groups throughout the region are demanding greater social, political and economic rights, and an end to militarization. The question is whether the military-security forces, backed by U.S. power, will again block the ascendancy of new social forces and opposition political organizations struggling for social justice, participation and political independence.

SUGGESTIONS FOR FURTHER READING

Cleary, Edward L. *The Struggle for Human Rights in Latin America.* Westport, Conn.: Praeger, 1997.

Falcoff, Mark. *A Culture of Its Own: Taking Latin America Seriously.* New Brunswick, N.J.: Transaction, 1998.

Harrison, Lawrence E. *The Pan-American Dream: Do Latin America's Cultural Values Discourage True Partnership with the United States and Canada?* Boulder, Colo.: Westview, 1997, Chapter 1.

Jelin, Elizabeth, and Eric Herschberg, eds. *Constructing Democracy: Human Rights, Citizenship, and Society in Latin America.* Boulder, Colo.: Westview, 1996.

McClintock, Michael. *The American Connection.* 2 vols. London: Zed Books, 1985.

Pastor, Robert. *Exiting the Whirlpool: U.S. Foreign Policy Toward Latin America and the Caribbean.* Boulder, Colo.: Westview, 2001.

Schoultz, Lars. *Beneath the United States: A History of US Policy Toward Latin America.* Cambridge, Mass.: Harvard University Press, 1998.

United States Senate Select Committee on Intelligence. *Covert Action in Chile, 1963–1973.* Staff Report. Washington, D.C.: U.S. Government Printing Office, 1975.

USEFUL WEBSITES

Brookings Foreign Policy Studies: Brookings' website allows searches of its publications on U.S. foreign policy.
www.brook.edu/fp/fp_hp.htm

Center for International Policy: Online research and news-oriented webpage emphasizing U.S. defense and security assistance to Latin America.
www.ciponline.org/

Inter-American Development Bank: Leading United States lending agency to Latin America.
www.iadb.org

PART II

CHAPTER **6**

Political Instability and Argentina's Boom and Bust and Boom Again Cycles

READINGS IN THIS CHAPTER

6.1 Argentina: Crisis and Democratic Consolidation (2002)
HECTOR E. SCHAMIS

6.2 Argentina: Anatomy of a Crisis Foretold (2003)
PAMELA K. STARR

6.3 The Nature of the New Argentine Democracy:
The Delegative Democracy Argument Revisited (2001)
ENRIQUE PERUZZOTTI

*I*n December 2001, growing street protests coupled with a rapidly escalating economic crisis led Argentine president Fernando de la Rúa to resign. The decision may have satisfied public anger at the embattled president, but it did little to actually resolve the crisis. Over the next two weeks, four more individuals would wear the presidential sash, only to resign in favor of the next victim of the crisis. The situation finally stabilized only when Eduardo Duhalde, the governor of Buenos Aires province, assumed the presidency and began the slow, painful process of moving the country back to some semblance of normalcy. The country took one more step toward normalcy in May 2003 when Duhalde handed the presidency to fellow Justicialist Party (PJ) member Néstor Kirchner. The election of a new president with greater public legitimacy helped the process of recovery, but the Argentina that Kirchner presided over remained in a fragile state—more stable, but hardly healthy. The country continued to be plagued by disastrously high levels of poverty, debt, unemployment, and bankruptcy as well as street crime and uncertainty about the future.

This shocking situation in Argentina is in some ways surprising and in other ways not. In many respects, Argentina should be the most prosperous and stable country in Latin America. Although it was remote, underpopulated, and underdeveloped in the colonial period, the country attracted large-scale immigration and grew dramatically in the last part of the nineteenth century. By the turn of the century, Argentina enjoyed a number of advantages. Its population was relatively homogeneous, ethnically and racially, and economic inequality was less pronounced than in most of Latin America. By the early twentieth century, some of Latin America's most enduring political parties had formed and were contesting elections, benefiting from the introduction of the secret ballot in 1912. In addition, Argentina's fertile pampas supported a rich agricultural yield, especially in cattle and grain. The success of Argentine agriculture made the country one of the richest in the world in the early twentieth century. All of these conditions tend to make democracies easier to establish and maintain.

Yet, neither democracy nor economic development flourished. Argentine elites, backed by the military, did not easily accede to the rise of middle class and working class demands for political rights. However, repeated efforts to repress working class organization came to an end with the arrival on the political stage of Juan Perón, supported by his charismatic wife Eva. Together, they united working class organizations into one General Confederation of Workers (CGT) and further mobilized support behind a new political party, the Justicialist Party (often referred to simply as the "Peronist Party"). Argentine politics became deeply divided between Peronist supporters and anti-Peronists, including wealthy landed elites (cattle ranchers), the military, and the middleclass–based Radical Party. The heated, and often even violent, political competition between the two sides undermined Argentina's economic development potential and produced considerable regime instability, with frequent military intrusions into politics. Ultimately, economic and political stability culminated in a coup in 1976 that ushered in the darkest period of Argentine history.

In the 1970s, to rid the country of left-wing insurgents and to restore economic order in a period of severe economic instability, the military embarked on a so-called dirty war. In the course of their campaign, thousands and thousands of Argentines were killed, tortured, and jailed. Perhaps the most traumatizing legacy of military rule was that thousands of Argentines simply disappeared without a trace—kidnapped by soldiers in the course of the dirty war. Many of these insurgents and their sympathizers were college students and other members of Argentina's large middle class who had been dragged into the military's widening war. As of 2004, their whereabouts are still unknown. The military government also introduced neoliberal economic reforms with devastating consequences. The military's dismal record left them without any societal support and they returned to the barracks in 1983, disgraced by their disastrous record.

This history of instability and turmoil seemed to have come to an end in the 1990s as Argentina emerged as one of Latin America's real success stories. In 1990, Argentina was a country struggling with both economic and political challenges. On the economic side, Argentina was one of the countries most profoundly affected by the debt crisis of the 1980s. Over the course of that decade, the government struggled to control the rate of inflation as it spiraled higher and higher. By 1989, inflation appeared to be out of control and the country's financial system was on the verge of collapse as citizens lost confidence in the nation's currency as well as in the government. Politically, Argentina was still dealing with the legacy of its brutal military dictatorship (1976–1983). President Raúl Alfonsín (Radical Party, 1983–1989) had been elected on a pledge to prosecute members of the military for human rights abuses. But, by 1989, his efforts to do so had been stymied by repeated military rebellions by junior officers (*carapintadas*). Ultimately, Alfonsín was forced to abandon his efforts to prosecute members of the military and instead was intimidated into passing laws granting amnesty to soldiers and officers. The combination of economic and political failures left Alfonsín utterly disgraced in the public mind. In recognition of his inability to continue governing, Alfonsín resigned ahead of schedule to allow President-Elect Carlos Saul Menem (PJ, 1989–1999) to assume the presidency.

Despite an inauspicious start to his tenure, Menem soon proved himself an effective leader. As the obscure governor of a small, very poor state, it was not clear that Menem would be capable of governing the country or controlling his powerful party, the PJ, built by Juan Peron in the 1940s. However, Menem effectively gained control over both the party and the powerful labor unions allied with the party. He then surprised all observers by introducing neoliberal economic reforms to Argentina, including liberalization of trade and privatization. After thirteen failed anti-inflation plans, he introduced a controversial solution that ended inflation by linking the Argentine peso to the U.S. dollar. By guaranteeing that anybody could always exchange one Argentine peso for one

U.S. dollar, Menem effectively restored public confidence in the national currency and in the financial system. Inflation virtually disappeared and Argentina became one of the economic success stories of Latin America. Menem's successes, however, concealed serious problems lying under the surface.

The theme of this chapter is the breakdown of Argentina's successes in the 1990s and the apparent return of Argentina's volatile past. Hector Schamis focuses on the political aspect of Argentina's breakdown. For Schamis, the situation presents both good and bad news. On the bad side, the crisis of 2001 stemmed from an unfortunate, but probably avoidable, set of political errors and miscalculations by the successor to Carlos Menem, Fernando de la Rúa of the Radical Party. De la Rúa's ruling style cut him off from his own party and his congressional allies, as well as from society at large. As a result, he did not have the political base to confront the growing economic crisis over the late 1990s. Nevertheless, his resignation—along with the reign and resignation of three more interim presidents over the next couple of weeks—revealed something positive and important. Argentina managed a severe political crisis without violating the constitution and the law. In that respect, the handling of the crisis raises confidence that Argentine democracy is much more consolidated than the situation might have suggested.

Pamela Starr examines the economic crisis that hit Argentina and reveals it to be a highly predictable event. Under Carlos Menem and his finance minister, Domingo Cavallo, inflation stabilized and the economy began to grow. As noted earlier, this came about as a direct result of the so-called Convertibility Plan that linked the Argentine peso to the U.S. dollar. But, as Starr details, this linkage had negative consequences that began to appear within a few short years of the onset of the plan. Most importantly, linking the Argentine economy to the U.S. dollar undermined the competitiveness of Argentine industrial production. The rigidity of the plan, however, limited the government's options in response. Ultimately, Starr shows how a combination of political obstacles and bad timing in international financial markets turned Argentina's problems into a major crisis.

In "The Nature of the New Argentine Democracy: The Delegative Democracy Argument Revisited," Enrique Peruzzotti offers an intriguing argument as to why Argentine democracy survived the severe crisis of 2001–2002. In the article, Peruzzotti engages Guillermo O'Donnell, one of the leading scholars of Latin American democracy, on one of O'Donnell's most important arguments about the nature of the new Latin American democracies. In O'Donnell's argument, Latin America is characterized by "delegative democracies," in which citizens, for cultural and historical reasons, delegate authority to their elected presidents and expect little accountability or transparency from them. Peruzzotti looks at the emergence of civil society and a "rights-based" politics among Argentines that suggests a much greater desire for the development of constitutional checks on executive power. Thus, in Peruzzotti's view, Argentine democracy since 1983 is qualitatively different than older "populist" models of democracy in the country.

DATA TABLES

Table 6.1
Argentina Fact and Data Sheet

Population (July 2003, estimated):	38,740,807
Ethnic Groups:	White (mostly Spanish and Italian) 97%; mestizo, Amerindian or other nonwhite groups 3%
Religions:	Roman Catholic 92% (less than 20% practicing), Protestant 2%, Jewish 2%, other 4%
Government Type:	Republic
Capital:	Buenos Aires
Administrative Divisions:	23 provinces and 1 autonomous city
Date of Independence:	Revolution Day, May 25, 1810
Constitution:	May 1, 1853; revised August 1994
Executive Branch:	President Néstor Kirchner, elected May 25, 2003; president and vice president elected on the same ticket by popular election to a 4-year term.
Legislature:	Bicameral National Congress
	• Senate has 72 seats. Elected by direct vote to a 6-year term. Distribution of seats as of 2003: PJ, 40 seats; UCR, 24 seats; Provincial Parties, 6 seats; Frepaso, 1 seat; ARI, 1 seat.
	• Chamber of Deputies has 257 seats. Elected by direct vote to a 4-year term. Distribution of seats as of 2003: PJ, 113 seats; UCR, 74 seats; Provincial Parties, 27 seats; Frepaso, 17 seats; ARI, 17 seats; AR, 9 seats.
Main Political Parties:	Action for the Republic (AR), Alternative for a Republic of Equals (ARI), Front for a Country in Solidarity (Frepaso), Justicialist Party (PJ), Radical Civic Union (UCR), several provincial political parties.
Military Spending (FY1999):	U.S. $4.3 billion
Military Spending, Percentage of GDP (FY2000):	1.3
GDP (2002, estimated):	PPP $391 billion
GDP Composition by Sector (2002, estimated):	Agriculture: 5% Industry: 28% Services: 67%
Main Industries:	Food processing, motor vehicles, consumer durables, textiles, chemicals and petrochemicals, printing, metallurgy, steel
Main Agricultural Products:	Sunflower seeds, lemons, soybeans, grapes, corn, tobacco, peanuts, tea, wheat, livestock
Export Partners (2000):	Brazil, 26.5%; United States, 11.8%; Chile, 10.6%; Spain, 3.5%
Import Partners (2000):	Brazil, 25.1%; United States, 18.7%; Germany, 5%; China, 4.6%
External Debt (2001, estimated):	U.S. $155 billion

Table 6.2
Presidents of Argentina

Tenure	President
1826–1827	Bernardino Rivadavia
1827	Vicente López y Planes
1854–1860	Justo José de Urquiza
1860–1861	Santiago Derqui
1862–1868	Bartolomé Mitre
1868–1874	Domingo F. Sarmiento
1874–1880	Nicolás Avellaneda
1880–1886	Julio Argentino Roca
1886–1890	Miguel Juárez Celman
1890–1892	Carlos Pellegrini
1892–1895	Luis Sáenz Peña
1895–1898	José Evaristo Uriburu
1898–1904	Julio Argentino Roca
1904–1906	Manuel Quintana
1906–1910	José Figueroa Alcorta
1910–1914	Roque Sáenz Peña
1914–1916	Victorino de la Plaza
1916–1922	Hipólito Yrigoyen
1922–1928	Marcelo T. de Alvear
1928–1930	Hipólito Yrigoyen[1]
1930–1932	José Félix Uriburu[2]
1932–1938	Agustín Pedro Justo
1938–1942	Roberto María Ortiz
1942–1943	Ramón Castillo[2]
1943–1944	Pedro Pablo Ramírez (acting)[2]
1944–1946	Edelmiro Julián Farrel (acting)[2]
1946–1955	Juan Domingo Perón[1]
1955	Eduardo Lonardi (acting)[2]
1955–1958	Pedro Eugenio Aramburu (acting)[2]
1958–1962	Arturo Frondizi[1]
1962–1963	José María Guido (acting)
1963–1966	Arturo Umberto Illia[1]
1966–1970	Juan Carlos Onganía[2]
1970–1971	Roberto M. Levingston (acting)[2]
1971–1973	Alejandro A. Lanusse (acting)[2]
1973	Héctor José Cámpora
1973	Raúl Alberto Lastiri
1973–1974	Juan Domingo Perón (2nd time)
1974–1976	Isabel Perón[1]
1976	Junta Militar (acting)[2]
1976–1981	Jorge Rafael Videla (acting)[2]
1981	Roberto Eduardo Viola (acting)[2]

(*cont.*)

Table 6.2 (cont.)

Presidents of Argentina

Tenure	President
1981–1982	Leopoldo Galtieri (acting)[2]
1982–1983	Reynaldo Bignone (acting)
1983–1989	Raúl Alfonsín[3]
1989–1999	Carlos Saul Menem
1999–2001	Fernando de la Rúa[3]
2001	Ramón Puerta (interim)
2001–2002	Adolfo Rodríguez Saá (interim)
2002	Eduardo Camaño (interim)
2002–2003	Eduardo Duhalde (interim)
2003–present	Néstor Kirchner

[1]Removed by coup.

[2]Military.

[3]Resigned.

6.1 Argentina: Crisis and Democratic Consolidation (2002)

HECTOR E. SCHAMIS

Throughout the end of 2001 and the beginning of 2002, Argentina made news around the world. A rapidly deteriorating economic situation weakened the indecisive government of President Fernando de la Rúa of the Radical Civic Union (UCR) past the point of no return. Unrest broke out in the streets, as crowds in the poorer suburbs looted supermarkets while middle-class groups in the capital city of Buenos Aires marched on the Casa Rosada (the seat of the executive branch) beating pots and pans. As a result, and after 30 people had lost their lives in the disturbances throughout the country, first Economy Minister Domingo Cavallo, then the rest of the cabinet, and finally the president himself all resigned on December 20–21.

Economic difficulties had been long brewing, but the social explosion of late December and the subsequent collapse of the De la Rúa government took most observers by surprise. Equally unexpected were the serial handovers of executive power—including three different interim presidents—that ensued until a special session of Congress on 1 January 2002 chose leading Peronist senator Eduardo Duhalde to take office for two years. Typically, accounts of the Argentine economic crisis blame the exchange-rate and monetary regime—the currency board that pegged the peso one-to-one to the dollar for more than a decade—or the propensity of politicians to spend and borrow too much. Each of these characterizations contains some truth, but each tells only part of the story. In fact, the intricacies of the currency board and the swelling of Argentina's foreign-debt burden must be examined in the context of unfavorable and volatile international conditions, particularly toward the end of the 1990s, and a complicated domestic political process, especially since the second presidential term of Carlos Saúl Menem (1995–99).

Another widely heard account looks to economic decline as the main reason for the De la Rúa administration's collapse. Indeed, the negative effects of a four-year recession with 20 percent unemployment can hardly be exaggerated, and the decision of the government "to pay the debt under all circumstances" greatly increased popular discontent. But those were merely precipitants. As we will see, a closer look at the peculiarities of the coalition that brought De la Rúa to office, as well as an examination of previous crises—including the October 2000 resignation of Vice-President Carlos Alvarez—would show that the

Hector E. Schamis, "Argentina: Crisis and Democratic Consolidation." *Journal of Democracy* 13, no. 2 (2002): 81–93. © National Endowment for Democracy and The Johns Hopkins University Press. Reprinted with permission of The Johns Hopkins University Press.

events of mid-December followed patterns seen in earlier crises, and that the process leading to De la Rúa's resignation was inherently political.

To understand both the recent past and the road that lies ahead for Argentina, we must go beyond the immediate economic factors that triggered the crisis of late 2001 and consider the longer-term dynamics that have been and are at play. Moreover, most analysts, focusing on the gravity of the debt default, the drama of the riots, the police repression that cost 30 lives, the resignation of the president, and the initial difficulties in finding a formula for succession, have failed to see that the crisis has in fact also opened up certain opportunities. For by acting under difficult circumstances to choose a new government through congressional bargaining and accommodation, Argentina took a firm step toward democratic consolidation. Careful examination of the quasi-parliamentary institutional mechanisms and behaviors that produced the political solution of New Year's 2002 bears out this tentatively hopeful conclusion. Despite the host of problems that Argentina still faces, the resilience and resourcefulness shown by its democratic politicians and institutions during the hot and uncertain days of this past southern summer should be a source not of despair but of cautious optimism.

ECONOMIC EMERGENCY: NOT JUST THE CURRENCY BOARD

While society's response was unexpected and De la Rúa's fall surprised most analysts, the build-up of the crisis was hardly news. A prolonged recession had eroded the country's fiscal base, weakening its ability to service its large foreign debt. In the context of the currency board, the government could not intervene with stimulative policies. As the recession dragged on, the country's fiscal position got weaker still. Throughout 2001, this dynamic steadily pushed up Argentina's debt-repayment "risk index" (as documented by analysts at the firm of J.P. Morgan), which translated into exorbitant interest-rate increases and even worse debt-repayment problems. After a cycle best captured by the notion of self-fulfilling prophecies, the dam broke in mid-December 2001 when, determined to continue making debt payments, the government tapped previously sacrosanct central-bank reserves and rolled over obligations with the private pension funds to do so. The former step flew in the face of the logic behind the currency board, while the latter constituted an expropriation of private property in the form of people's life savings. The rules that had governed the economy since Menem's first term back in 1991 were broken, irrespective of the fact that the exchange-rate level remained stable. As if to prove this beyond any possibility of doubt, the government froze bank deposits—imposing another loss of wealth on millions of citizens—to prevent a massive flight to the dollar and with it the collapse of the banking system.

To understand why and how the country got to that point requires us to consider the decision to introduce the currency board in 1991. In March of that year, after three bouts of hyperinflation reaching as high as 3,000 percent, President Menem turned to Domingo Cavallo, naming him economy minister. Cavallo submitted to Congress a new approach to stabilization under the "convertibility law." The program pegged the peso to the dollar one-to-one, and determined that monetary and exchange-rate policy were to be based on a currency board. Thus, the law directed the central bank to maintain liquid international reserves to cover 100 percent of the monetary base. As a result, the authorities could increase monetary aggregates only when international reserves expanded, that is, through trade surpluses or net capital inflows.

Cavallo's strategy soon paid off: Inflation dropped to a single-digit rate after just three months. Price and exchange-rate stability also helped to speed up Menem's privatization program, which had stalled because of the persistent inflation. The commitment to rules, rather than discretion, was necessary given growing private-sector demand for credit in both domestic and international capital markets. After the "lost decade" of the 1980s, foreign investment in Argentina began to rise again. In 1992, the country obtained debt relief under the plan sponsored by U.S. treasury secretary Nicholas Brady, and the terms of trade—which had collapsed in the late 1980s—became favorable once more.

By 1992, therefore, the economy had entered a phase of growth and stability, but major problems lingered. One was the central government's weak fiscal position. While one-time receipts from the sale of nationalized assets let the government nearly erase its deficit by 1993, no lasting means of controlling deficits were put in place. This omission was at least partly deliberate, and resulted from Menem's strategy for constitutional reform and reelection. While exchange-rate stability was meant to attract the urban middle classes, keeping the federal-spending tap open for the provinces was necessary to obtain their votes in the constitutional reform process. Sooner or later Menem's maneuvering was bound to impinge on the macroeconomic fundamentals—as it did when world economic conditions became less propitious in the mid-1990s.

Another difficulty had to do with the dynamics of exchange-rate-based stabilization itself: cycles of boom and bust associated with a fixed exchange rate in the context of an open capital account. As a wealth of scholarly research has shown, under this type of policy mix, real exchange-rate appreciation and the oversupply of foreign credit finance a consumption boom and with it growing current-accounts deficits. In the medium term, difficulties financing those deficits tend to lead to inconsistent fiscal policies, affecting the credibility of the peg. At that point, attacks on the currency may become widespread, with important losses in foreign-exchange reserves, followed by devaluation, inflation, and recession. Various experiments with exchange-rate stabilization in the region had provided evidence for the regularity of this type of cycle, but those who by 1993 began to urge a gradual exit from the currency board found no hearers among the holders of political power.

The problem was not just that Menem was building his reelection drive around constant but unexamined invocations of the need for "stability." It was also that by the 1990s, after decades of high and at times out-of-control inflation as well as an ongoing "dollarization from below," Argentine voters were demanding such stability, and meting out rewards and punishments at the ballot box based on politicians' ability to deliver it. Moreover, the electorate's preferences as between full employment and low inflation began to shift decidedly in favor of the latter, bespeaking a higher tolerance for recession.

Thus by the mid-1990s the currency board appeared to be in place to stay, just as conditions beyond Argentina's control began to go bad. The first signs of trouble came in the banking sector. The convertibility law mandated backing the monetary base with international reserves, but it entailed only narrow definitions of the money supply. That loophole allowed the authorities to expand "bank money" by cutting reserve requirements—the equivalent of a monetary stimulus. This plus continued strong capital inflows spelled easy credit and increased the exposure of the banking system. When Mexico devalued the peso in December 1994, Argentina experienced its first major bout of financial turbulence since the inception of the currency board. Although financial restructuring was clearly needed at the time, Menem was loath to act during the run-up to the May 1995 presidential election. Delay became the order of the day, compounding the fragility of the banking sector later on. Additional financial volatility in emerging markets toward the end of the 1990s, the strong U.S. dollar, the Brazilian continuous devaluation, and drops in commodity prices did not help either. Argentina approached the turn of the century deep in recession, with a weak fiscal base and serious debt exposure.

The question of the debt merits three more comments. First—and despite complaints about profligate spending—the two main items in the new debt contracted during the 1990s corresponded to structural reforms: the financing of social-security privatization (during which the public system lost contributors but kept beneficiaries) and the bank restructuring of 1996–97 (demanded by the Spanish banks then negotiating to buy them). Both reforms won the support of international financial institutions and the U.S. Treasury Department. At the time, both Cavallo and the free-spending Menem were darlings of the International Monetary Fund (IMF). In fact, when they were in office during the 1990s Argentina rarely received anything like the tough treatment that the IMF doled out during 2001–02.

Second, in addition to the recession, international creditors, worried by falling solvency indicators, began hiking interest rates in autumn of 2000. This, of course, only made the fiscal bleeding worse. By spring 2001 Argentina was paying as much as 12 percent interest on a big chunk of its debt, even though as late as summer 2001 its ratio of debt to Gross Domestic

Product and exports was no worse than Brazil's. Exchange-rate and fiscal policies more tightly focused on fostering economic activity might have averted the crisis. But little could be done when, as early as the spring of 2001, U.S. officials began declaring categorically that there would be no bailout if Argentina got in over its head.

With signals like this coming from Washington, default became inevitable. U.S. treasury secretary Paul O'Neill said repeatedly that the decision to terminate emergency aid to Argentina was made because it was "ridiculous for America's plumbers and carpenters to pay for someone else's bad decisions." But as one Argentine policy maker observed to me, the step that O'Neill rejected may have been "less ridiculous than the unemployed and the poor in Argentina subsidizing American bond-holders with interest rates four to five times market levels."

POLITICAL CRISIS:
NOT JUST THE ECONOMY

On the afternoon of 20 December 2001, just after his cabinet resigned, President De la Rúa called leaders of the Peronists (the Justicialist Party, or PJ) to invite them to form a government of national unity. They said no, and De la Rúa resigned. Alarmed by what was looking like a case of what Juan Linz might call "semi-loyal opposition," I spoke that night with a PJ official of the Buenos Aires province. By refusing to join the government, I asked, were the Peronists not flirting openly with behavior that could destabilize the whole system? In the past, I pointed out, mutual backstabbing between the Peronists and their Radical Civic Union rivals had arguably helped to pave the way for the breakdown of democracy. To this my interlocutor calmly replied that when De la Rúa made his offer, the PJ congressional leaders took it to their Radical peers for discussion, only to hear the stunning news that the congressional wing of the president's own party was withdrawing its support for him, and would not take part in any government he might head. Soon thereafter, newspapers carried comments by UCR chief Angel Rozas criticizing De la Rúa and saying that "the ex-president" owed the whole country "a major apology."

This anecdote paints a telling picture of the crisis. Fernando de la Rúa fell in precisely the same way he had governed: cut off from the larger political society, at odds with his own party, and surrounded by a clique of unelected, nonpartisan advisors, several of whom had no previous political experience of any kind.

How had things come to such a pass? De la Rúa had won the 1999 election at the head of a coalition—known as the Alianza—between his own UCR and a center-left group of breakaway Peronists and others called the Front for a Country in Solidarity (Frepaso). Frepaso had begun to take shape in the early 1990s when a small group of Peronist congressmen (later called the Eight) became unhappy with the direction that the Menem administration was taking, and sought a way to "challenge Menemism from outside." Over the years they managed to incorporate wider constituencies, including a number of socialists, Christian Democrats, and important leaders of human rights organizations.

By 1994, in fact, Frepaso was gaining support not only from Peronists and leftists, but from Radicals too. Much of the anger among the last group was directed at the decision of their party leader and ex-president Raúl Alfonsín (sealed in the so-called Olivos Pact) to support Menem's push for a new Constitution, which he secured in July 1994. With the old provision limiting presidents to one term now gone, Menem could at last officially declare himself a candidate for reelection. As the dissenter in a process that both major parties had supported, Frepaso could now present itself as the lonely voice of principle crying out against "the attempt of any politician to perpetuate himself or herself in office." Frepaso's standing rose accordingly. When the votes were counted in May 1995, its presidential candidate, PJ senator José Octavio Bordón, had finished second behind Menem with 30 percent. The Radicals, who had come to be seen by many of their own voters as sellouts who were helping Menem, struggled in his shadow and turned in their worst showing ever with less than 17 percent.

At first glance the results looked good for Frepaso, but appearances were misleading. To win nearly a third of the vote in its maiden presidential campaign might seem like a great achievement for any party, but it would soon become clear that for Frepaso this figure was not a floor but a ceiling. Its support came lopsidedly from middle-class urbanites, and across vast swaths of the interior it practically did not exist. The urban voters, moreover, were not really converts but UCR-leaning citizens who were punishing their own party for the Olivos Pact. To those capable of looking beyond the gaudy but flukish numbers of 1995—a group that included Frepaso's top leaders—it was apparent that the project of creating a strong and lasting third party was not going to work. Bordón himself returned to the Justicialist fold to fight Menemism from within. Most of the other leaders stayed nominally in Frepaso, but began exploring prospects for a partnership with the still bruised and reeling UCR. The Alianza was the result.

Formed in 1996, the Alianza came out on top in its first contest, the 1997 congressional elections. Then its leaders began to prepare for a run at the presidency in 1999. One of the two obvious frontrunners for the nomination was De la Rúa, a former Radical senator then serving as mayor of Buenos Aires. The other was Graciela Fernández Meijide, a senator and a veteran leader of human rights organizations. It was unclear which would head the ticket, or how the question would be settled, but the Alianza eventually decided to hold an open presidential primary. Frepaso did not have the infrastructure of an established party capable of mobilizing constituencies. The

Radicals had been watching their own support plummet for years—first because of the 1989 hyperinflation and later because of the Olivos Pact—but they did boast a sophisticated electoral machine and an organized presence in every district in Argentina. Thus the choice of an open presidential primary essentially sealed De la Rúa's victory. Backed by the Radical Party's nationwide organization, he won by a comfortable margin and took his place at the top of the ticket. Fernández Meijide declined to be part of the ticket, and Carlos Alvarez, the original leader of the Eight and Bordón's 1995 Frepaso running mate, took her place. This created resentment among Frepaso leaders, who felt that, as one told me at the time, "we [had] resuscitated the Radicals, [only to become] . . . their casualty."

This metaphor would prove prescient, for the Radicals would soon join Frepaso as a statistic in the political body count. Seemingly forgetting that he had just been carried into the presidency by a coalition, De la Rúa first pushed Frepaso into the background, giving it just two second-tier cabinet posts. Then—and still more ominously—he turned his back on his own party, surrounding himself with "friends and family" and shutting top Radicals out of his inner circle. With these democratically suspect and politically foolish first steps, the De la Rúa administration's slide toward self-destruction was under way in earnest. The October 2000 resignation of Vice-President Alvarez, followed by that of Graciela Fernández Meijide (at the time social-welfare minister) in March 2001, made it painfully clear that just one year after De la Rúa had taken office a severe—in retrospect irresolvable—political crisis had hit the executive branch.

It is worth noting that following the vice-president's resignation, Argentina's crucial country-risk number began to climb. The resultant skyrocketing interest rates meant that the increasingly precarious economic situation and the brewing political crisis were about to meet and reinforce each other. As 2001 began, De la Rúa was facing complex problems posed by Frepaso's departure from his government, the disaffection of his own party, and the worsening of the economic situation. His response was to look for more support on the center-right and to tackle the economic problems with resolve. He brought back Domingo Cavallo, once Menem's economic czar, and named him economy minister, hoping thereby to gather political support from economic and financial elites as well as to put in place a man whom he could trust to attack the deficit aggressively, foster growth, and service the debt.

As we have seen, trying to accomplish these three economic goals while maintaining the currency board was an incoherent strategy that was probably doomed from the outset. Yet the political harm that Cavallo caused in his nine months in office was no less serious than the economic damage. Appointed as a "savior," the technocratic Cavallo demanded vast discretionary powers over economic policy, just as he had done under Menem. This only exacerbated the ill will caused by Cavallo's autocratic style (he typically refused to distinguish between the governing party and the opposition, for instance), reinforced a policy-making process already heavily dependent on executive decrees, marginalized Congress, and devalued the overall process of representation. Ironically, all these had been central features of the Menem legacy that De la Rúa, in theory at least, had come to office to eradicate.

The rest of the story is well known. By October 2001 it was obvious to most analysts that Argentina would have to default on its debt, but Cavallo—some said with an eye on his ties to Wall Street—stubbornly refused to admit it. Instead, he made the most irrational decisions imaginable while the president, unwilling or unable to grasp the gravity of the situation that he had delegated to his economy minister, stood back and did nothing. In the end, they both lost touch with the realities of the country they were supposed to be governing. While the alleged fiscal irresponsibility of the country's political elite is and will continue to be debatable, the political irresponsibility of the top leaders of the Alianza government is clear beyond cavil.

QUASI-PARLIAMENTARISM TO THE RESCUE

Seasoned observers of Argentine politics have recognized that in the past it would have taken a lot less than the events of December 2001 for the military to intervene and break the constitutional order. Does this mean that Argentina's democracy has become "consolidated"? The short answer is yes. In part, this is because the military is weaker than it used to be, while political society has become much stronger. But perhaps more important even than this shift in the balance of influence is the way in which, at the critical moment, institutional incentives and behavioral patterns swung into play and saved the system. In earlier times the eruption of a major political crisis would have been a signal for members of Congress to stay home, either to prepare for exile or to start calling military officers to discuss coup plans. This time, however, legislators stayed at their desks and met in special session to fill the power vacuum left by De la Rúa and reach a settlement of the crisis. Nothing like this had ever happened in Argentina before, and it may well have made all the difference.

Before getting into an examination of the process and mechanisms that explain this behavior, a brief digression about consolidation is in order. Consolidation is a widely used concept in political science, and definitions abound. The term was popularized by the early academic literature on transitions, which sketched the process as a sequence, a kind of conceptual railroad train running from liberalization and "opening" right on through, ultimately, to a terminus called consolidation. Presumably, therefore, consolidation is that final stage of development where democracy becomes stable, immune to authoritarian reversal, and self-reinforcing.

Seen in this teleological way, however, the term has problems. First, it is prone to conceptual stretching, as characteristics we generally attribute to "unconsolidated" democracy are often found in securely "consolidated" democracies as well. Consider, for example, Italy's recurring "musical chairs" government crises or Margaret Thatcher's ample use of executive discretion. Second, the notion may be historically misleading, for mature democracies have collapsed, and in not insignificant numbers. In Latin America alone, take the examples of Chile and Uruguay in 1973. And third, since the most compelling evidence of a democracy's lack of consolidation is its actual collapse, the concept has little or no predictive power. Consider how the widespread characterization of Venezuelan democracy as "consolidated" in the 1980s prevented analysts from looking for signs of erosion prior to its virtual breakdown in the early 1990s.

It is perhaps because of these flaws that the most common reference to consolidation in current debates is to Adam Przeworski's notion that democracy is consolidated "when it becomes the only game in town." But this is a metaphor rather than a definition, and not a particularly helpful metaphor at that. In fact, it is difficult to imagine a relatively complex polity like a modern democracy in which only a single game is being played. Crises, political and economic, increase the incentives to play other games. In Argentina during the recession of the last four years and the recent crisis, there have been many games in town besides democracy: rent seeking, plotting, shirking, conspiring, and the exercise of various "exit" options such as capital flight, emigration, and disaffection, to name a few. Democracy has been only one game among others, yet it has survived. In other words, it appears to have consolidated itself. The key question then becomes: Under what conditions will the game of democracy prevail despite the presence of other games that might threaten to undermine and break up the democratic game? Or to phrase the question retrospectively (now that Argentina seems to have weathered the most acute phase of the crisis): What made 2001 different and kept the other games from disrupting the rules of democracy?

The first key difference is the new Constitution, especially the quasi-parliamentary innovations that have now proven their effectiveness in relaxing the country's rigid presidentialism. Under the old Constitution of 1853, the order of succession was fixed, extending downward from the president through the vice-president, the head of the Senate, the leader of the Chamber of Deputies, and finally the chief justice of the Supreme Court. The electoral calendar was fixed as well, and political parties had no say in the process. Of course, under this type of formula, each step down the ladder would entail a legitimacy loss, perhaps to the point of political unsustainability. The new Constitution, by contrast, allows Congress to deal with the incumbent president's resignation by calling an election or naming a new chief executive. Congress thus has a role that it never had in the past. What is even more significant is that, in the context of a serious political crisis, the new Constitution immediately devolves power to Congress, thereby reinforcing its role as a locus of popular sovereignty. In terms of the history of democracy in Argentina, this is almost revolutionary. To entertain a counterfactual for a moment, could this crisis have been resolved peacefully and within the very halls of Congress—the country's leading democratic institution—under the strongly presidentialist Constitution of 1853? Probably not, and the adoption of new succession rules has to be seen as a positive, if unintended consequence of the Olivos Pact. To the extent that Menem's goal was just his reelection, he had no problem deferring to the parliamentarist leanings of his partner in the pact, former president Raúl Alfonsín.

In sum, Argentina has resolved a serious political crisis without violating the laws, procedures, and institutions of the democratic process. When tested, the game of democracy managed to subordinate the other games and prevented a rupture. That should count as evidence of consolidation. Institutions may hold the key to this process, but only insofar as they lead crucial players to choose certain types of behaviors over others. In the Argentine case, some of the quasi-parliamentary actions that solved the crisis took place under the influence of new institutional incentives. But institutions were only part of the answer. The other part had to do with socialization, political learning, and a pervasive growth of democratic sentiment across large segments of civil and political society. A few observers continue to speculate about the possibility of an Argentine equivalent of Venezuela's Hugo Chávez or Peru's Alberto Fujimori somehow stepping in to seize power, but such concerns seem exaggerated. Moreover, they do not adequately consider that Argentina today, unlike Peru and Venezuela in the 1990s, has a robust party system which not only failed to collapse under the strain of recent events, but indeed may have even become stronger.

A few examples illustrate the point, starting with the process of presidential succession. Since the PJ holds majorities in both houses of Congress, a result of the mid-term election of October 2001, it was clear as soon as De la Rúa quit that his successor would be a Peronist. But from which wing of this divided party would the new president come? Would it be the group based in and around Buenos Aires—a city and province that together are home to about two out of every five Argentines—or would it be a governor of one of the major provinces? Congress initially chose Adolfo Rodríguez Saá, the Peronist governor of San Luis, a relatively small province located deep in the Pampas country. Rodríguez Saá presented himself as the best broker among contending groups and across the two preeminent issues of 1) whether to devalue the peso, and 2) whether the new government would complete the remaining two years of De la Rúa's term or step down as soon as a special election could be held. Rodríguez Saá initially opposed devaluation and stated that he would call for an election within two months. Within days, however, it became clear both that devaluation would be unavoidable and that an early election would fragment the PJ. Leaders from the UCR and all the main Peronist factions agreed that the currency peg would have to go and that the still-jittery country needed time before it should be asked to face another electoral campaign. They further agreed that no arrangement would be stable unless all the camps within the Peronist party came together to support it. At that point, it came to seem obvious that only Eduardo Duhalde could devalue the peso, serve as interim president not for weeks but for two years, and rally the Justicialist Party.

The head-turning spectacle of five presidents in little more than a week raised eyebrows and made headlines around the world, of course, but the situation was not as grave as it might have seemed to casual outside observers, nor as serious as it would have been in a more purely presidential system. In essence, what happened was a week of high-level bargaining of the kind that is typical of parliamentary systems after an election has been held or a government has collapsed. President De la Rúa's resignation, and Rodríguez Saá's immediately thereafter, resembled that of a prime minister who steps down after a vote of no confidence. Parliamentary negotiations followed his departure, and the legislators chose a new leader whom they deemed best suited to accomplish the agreed-upon goals. The joint session of Congress that concluded the process wound up on New Year's Day 2002, with many members wearing T-shirts and sneakers (the combination of marathon sessions and the holiday season exerted a downward pull on dress codes). Informal attire or no, it was a historic occasion that concluded after midnight with President-designate Duhalde's sobering acceptance speech, in which he reminded his erstwhile colleagues that "we have nothing to celebrate, and much to worry about." The entire session was televised, moreover, which made it a sort of educational event. It is not yet clear whether, in their current anger at just about everyone who holds elective office, Argentines realize that their democracy has never been stronger. As Martín Balza, the former commanding general of the army, put it in an interview, "the crisis of democratic values is resolved with more democracy."

THE ROAD AHEAD

Are the "quasi-parliamentary" arrangements that produced the Duhalde presidency here to stay? The president himself seems to have reinforced a trend toward multiparty accommodation by drawing three key cabinet members from opposition parties. A total of six new ministers come from Congress, which means that people who are used to responding to constituencies are holding executive power—a comparative novelty in Argentine politics. In February 2002, as part of discussions concerning a larger political agreement, Duhalde pointed to the need to consider the adoption of a full-fledged parliamentary regime. There are many more issues that his administration needs to take on, and it has just two years to do so. In fact, even a cautious optimist such as myself must admit that the challenge ahead is monumental. On the economic front, Argentina needs external support for a program aimed at growth and stability. The IMF (and hence the U.S. Treasury) has already made support conditional on Argentina's willingness to adopt policies that trim public spending, particularly the federal remittances which account for such a big chunk of the deficit.

Spending discipline will in turn require a broader political agreement with the provinces. But here is where Duhalde's Achilles' heel is to be found, whatever the magnitude of the economic crisis. As of this writing, in early March 2002, there are still more questions than answers. One is how to tame the governors, who continue to demand elections right away, and avoid tensions that could badly split the ruling Peronist party. Another is how to produce a formula—a new federal pact, someone has called it—that both the center and the provinces can accept. Still another is how the president, who must continue to be a figure of national unity, can maintain the support of the other parties even as they fill their proper and vital democratic role as a loyal opposition.

Whether the Duhalde government will be able to cope with all these challenges remains to be seen. One condition, however, appears necessary: Duhalde must keep the promise he made in his inaugural address and refuse any thought of running for election to a full term in 2003. In a country (and a region) where politicians always try to stay in office no matter what, only this would give him the authority necessary to put the country's economic and political life back on track. Only by being an institution builder rather than a power seeker can he garner the legitimacy he needs to attack the massive challenges facing his country. If, as he has promised, Duhalde succeeds in transferring power to an elected president in December 2003, he will merit being remembered as not merely a chief of state but a guarantor of his country's democratic future. On that day, Argentine democracy may at last have become fully "consolidated."

—7 March 2002

6.2 Argentina: Anatomy of a Crisis Foretold (2003)

PAMELA K. STARR

The trajectory of the Argentine economy during the past 13 years has zigzagged from hyperinflation and economic stagnation to rapid growth with low inflation to the deepest depression in Argentine history. All this has been overshadowed by the effective disappearance of the middle class in a country whose national identity has long been associated with being a middle-class country. What happened? How did Argentina go from

Pamela K. Starr, "Argentina: Anatomy of a Crisis Foretold." Reprinted with permission from *Current History*, February 2003. © 2003, Current History, Inc.

economic basket case during the late 1980s to "poster child" for economic reform and a favorite of international investment bankers during the mid-1990s back to basket case in the first years of the twenty-first century?

Some analysts and politicians argue that the crisis was caused by neoliberal economic reforms, especially Argentina's experiment with a currency board that oversaw the exchange rate of the peso and its subsequent overvaluation. Others insist that the failure of Argentine politicians to place the national interest above their individual needs caused the crisis. Still others blame the policies of the International Monetary Fund. But the Argentine crisis was the result of a combination of forces: a restrictive economic model, poor implementation of that model, bad luck in the form of unexpected shifts in international financial and goods markets, and only secondarily, the policies of the IMF. The interplay among these factors between 1991 and 2001 drove the Argentine economy first into recession and then into depression, default, and financial collapse.

CURRENCY CHEMOTHERAPY

After taking office in July 1989, the administration of President Carlos Saúl Menem struggled for 18 months with four-digit inflation and a shrinking economy. Desperate for tangible signs of success in advance of the 1991 midterm elections, the Menem administration took an extreme measure—it adopted a currency board monetary system.

Under a scheme not unlike the gold standard of the nineteenth century, Argentina's currency board fixed the peso's exchange rate with the United States dollar and required the Central Bank to maintain foreign reserves to cover the value of 80 percent of all pesos in circulation. The effect was to take monetary policy away from the Argentine government and to sharply constrain its use of fiscal policy (which meant that the Central Bank could no longer print pesos to finance the government's fiscal deficits). In return for this huge policy concession, the currency board would prohibit inflationary increases in the money supply.

The currency board rapidly reduced and ultimately pulverized inflation (from 2,300 percent in 1990 to 4 percent in 1994 and 1 percent from 1996 to 1998). The "convertibility plan" won broad public support for the government. Further, this stunning success seemed to come largely free of costs during the first years of the board's operation. Declining inflation produced a real increase in fiscal revenues; confidence that inflation had finally been defeated led to renewed capital inflows, increased investment, and growth. At the same time, growing international reserves permitted a rapid expansion in the money supply. It was the best of all possible economic worlds.

No monetary order is cost free, and beginning in 1994 Argentina began to pay the price inherent to a currency board. An increasingly overvalued peso had begun to undermine the competitiveness of the Argentine economy, leading to a growing deficit in the current account (that is, foreign trade in goods, services, and income). Capital inflows easily financed this deficit through 1994, but in the wake of the shaken foreign-investor confidence that followed the Mexican financial crisis in 1994 and 1995, capital flows evaporated. Lacking capital inflows, Argentina was forced to dig into its foreign reserves to cover its current account deficit. As reserves fell, the currency board restricted the money supply and sent the economy into recession. The recession then drove down tax revenues, and without easy access to capital markets to cover the resulting fiscal deficit, the Argentine government was forced to cut spending sharply and thereby reinforce the recessionary effect of a diminishing money supply.

This sort of imported recession and the government's inability to cushion the domestic economy from international economic disequilibria are inevitable consequences of a currency board. A currency board further demands that a country preserve the international competitiveness of its national firms to ensure a healthy balance of payments, a stable supply of international reserves, and a resulting stability in the domestic money supply. It does this by reducing its domestic costs of production (since devaluation is prohibited). These economic policy constraints are often difficult to sustain, especially in the presence of open international capital markets and democratic politics. Democratic polities are rarely forgiving of a government that leads the country into recession and is too inept to revive the economy or to relieve the ensuing social costs. Unfortunately, Argentina's democratic political structures were poorly suited to dealing with the policy demands of a currency board.

THE COSTS OF NOT CHOOSING

Argentina's decision to adopt a currency board to combat inflation left the country with two options: either implement the policies demanded by the board, or transition out of it. The country did neither, creating an enormous vulnerability to sudden shifts in international capital markets.

The overvalued currency created by the currency board was the first challenge facing the Argentine economy. It undermined the competitiveness of Argentine firms, especially those producing for the domestic market and now forced to compete with less expensive imported goods. Many of these firms laid off workers in an effort to reduce costs and were forced into bankruptcy; almost none reemployed workers displaced by privatization in the state sector. The overvalued currency thus contributed to rising unemployment and a rapidly expanding trade deficit as Argentines substituted imported goods for domestic products.

The competitive pressure produced by an overvalued currency can be a positive force if firms can respond by modernizing and becoming more efficient. In the Argentine case, the overvaluation was large and developed rapidly, making adjustment much more difficult. Further, privatization in Argentina created monopolies under terms extremely favorable to the new owners. This led to high prices for a variety of services on which firms depend—phones, water, electricity, transport, and banking—thereby increasing their costs of production and further undercutting competitiveness. Competitiveness also suffered from a bit of bad luck. Throughout most of the decade in which Argentina used a currency board, the value of the United States dollar rose relative to other currencies. Since the Argentine peso was pegged to the dollar, the value of the peso rose along with that of the dollar, further undermining the competitiveness of Argentine products relative to European and Asian goods.

Argentina's highly competitive beef and grain industries managed to make the adjustment to an overvalued currency, as did some of the country's largest companies, since they were able to access international credit to finance modernization. But other agricultural sectors and other industries, especially the small- and medium-sized enterprises responsible for the bulk of employment in the Argentine economy, found it much more difficult to compete. Although the government tried to help these firms by cutting their taxes, many simply ceased making their tax payments. Argentine productivity (and hence competitiveness) declined throughout the 1990s. The competitiveness problem and the efforts of Argentine firms to adapt thus reinforced high unemployment rates, a large current account deficit, a persistent fiscal deficit, and Argentina's growing dependence on imported capital to finance these twin deficits.

A temporary solution to Argentina's competitiveness problem emerged in the mid-1990s in the form of Mercosur, the Southern Cone Common Market established by Argentina, Uruguay, Paraguay, and Brazil that created preferential trading arrangements among the member nations. The combination of Mercosur's common external tariff and Brazil's overvalued currency (also pegged to the United States dollar) created an environment in which Argentine producers were competitive. The cost of this "solution" to Argentina's competitiveness problem, however, was high: it deepened Argentina's economic dependence on the Brazilian market and its overvalued currency.

More permanent solutions to the competitiveness problem and to the persistence of Argentina's twin deficits would have benefited from reform of the labor laws that imposed high costs on the hiring and firing of workers (and thereby contributed both to unemployment and competitiveness problems) and from fiscal reform. The structure of Argentine politics ensured that both were beyond political reach.

Argentine political institutions place enormous power in the hands of provincial governors, and Argentine provinces enjoy a great deal of political autonomy, including the right to determine how and when provincial elections will be held and who the candidates for provincial and national office will be. Provincial autonomy enables the governors (or party leaders when a party is out of office) to control the levers of the parties' electoral machinery. Control over this structure gives the governors considerable influence in the direct election of the national president; it is also the central means by which governors control their provincial representatives in the national Congress. Support of the governors is essential both for election to the presidency and the ability to govern once elected.

Argentina's fiscal structure made the power of the governors particularly problematic with the introduction of the currency board. Over time, the governors exploited their political power to create a system of guaranteed transfers of federal fiscal resources to the provinces that cannot be modified without the unanimous consent of the governors. Given the size of these transfers (nearly 1 billion pesos per month in 1999) and the number of taxes involved, real reform of the Argentine tax system was not possible without the governors' unanimous consent to reform this tax-sharing system.

Unfortunately for the effective operation of the Argentine currency board, the governors had no interest in reducing the transfer of federal revenues to their provinces (even though the 1994 constitution required a new tax-sharing law before 1996). Although a promise to reform the tax-sharing program was included in two letters of intent to the International Monetary Fund, President Menem could never implement tax reform. To the contrary, each time the issue was brought before Congress, it led to an increased transfer of funds to the provinces. Argentina's fiscal accounts thus remained in deficit throughout the Menem presidency even in boom times, regardless of huge inflows of privatization revenues and despite significant off-budget expenditures and provincial deficits that were not included in the publicly touted primary budget balance.

The structure of Argentine politics, and more specifically of Peronist Party politics, was equally efficient at blocking labor reform during the Menem administration. Although union power declined dramatically in the 1980s and early 1990s, unions retained two important sources of influence. They still possessed the power to organize general strikes (which they did three times during the second half of 1996), and they occupied a strategic position within the Peronist Party. As the economy turned sour during 1995, Peronist politicians who had always been uncomfortable with Menem's economic reforms began to raise their voices. Most prominent among them was Eduardo Duhalde, the governor of Buenos Aires province and a presidential hopeful. To differentiate himself from Menem and position himself within the party for a presidential run, Duhalde sided with the unions in their struggle against "radical" neoliberal reforms. In control of Buenos Aires's decisive bloc of 37 votes in the lower house of Congress, Duhalde was able to bar labor reform throughout the second Menem presidency.

In the absence of both fiscal and labor reforms, the Argentine economy became more dependent on the Brazilian market and capital inflows. Access to the Brazilian market, made possible by Mercosur and the overvaluation of the Brazilian real, helped ease the costs of declining competitiveness in the Argentine economy. But it also increased Argentine vulnerability to a devaluation of the real. The combined fiscal and current account deficits, meanwhile, produced an explosion of government debt during the Menem years (from 29.5 percent of GDP in 1993 to 50.3 percent of GDP in 1999) that fueled the fiscal problem as debt payments grew. This made the Argentine economy hugely vulnerable to any sudden negative shift in international capital markets. Argentina's twin deficits also made it impossible for Argentina to regain some economic policy flexibility by exiting from the currency board.

SETTING THE STAGE

The beginning of the end for Argentina's currency board dates to the outbreak of the Asian financial crisis in July 1997. Although Argentina suffered little direct financial impact from the Asian crisis, it had an important indirect effect on the Argentine economy. With the financial crisis driving many Asian economies into recession, their demand for Argentine raw material and food exports declined, as did the prices of these goods on international markets. Although Argentina managed to redirect much of its lost grain sales to the Brazilian market, export earnings and hence its trade balance suffered under the weight of collapsing world prices.

The Asian crisis also affected the Argentine economy by way of its impact on Russia. Highly indebted and dependent on petroleum exports to meet its debt payments, Russia was devastated by the drop in petroleum prices caused by the Asian crisis. As export earnings fell, Russia was faced with the need to cut essential imports to meet its international debt payments. Russia chose to avoid this politically costly option and took the dramatic decision to devalue its currency and become the first country in the post–cold war international financial order to default on its international debt. This unexpected decision produced billions of dollars in losses for international investors and confusion, uncertainty, and instability in financial markets. It also created an incentive to avoid similar losses and thus retreat from other markets where the same kind of payment difficulties could produce another devaluation and default. Argentina was not yet such a market, but Brazil was.

Throughout fall 1998, capital streamed out of Brazil as doubts grew about the country's ability to sustain the real's fixed and overvalued rate of exchange. On January 15, 1999 the Brazilian government surrendered to market pressure and unpegged the real from the dollar and allowed its value to float; this led to a 30 percent depreciation by the end of the month and a 45 percent depreciation by the end of the year. For Argentina the Brazilian devaluation was catastrophic. An economy that was already cooling rapidly during the second half of 1998 suddenly found itself a third less competitive with its main trading partner. In a fortnight, Brazilian imports were 30 percent cheaper and Argentine exports were 30 percent more expensive. Foreign direct investment in highly integrated sectors such as automobiles and auto parts was quickly directed away from Argentina and toward Brazil, and many established investments in these sectors began to move eastward into Brazil. The inevitable consequence for Argentina was a deepening recession, rising unemployment, and a sharp increase in its fiscal deficit.

These circumstances should have produced a quick and decisive policy response to minimize the inevitable increase in Argentina's fiscal deficit and its borrowing needs. Instead, the Argentine government attempted to divert the attention of financial markets as it dithered. Rather than implement the needed fiscal adjustment, the Menem government announced a proposal to "dollarize" the economy. In an attempt to convince investors that Argentina would never follow Brazil's lead and devalue its currency, the government indicated that if pressure on the peso were to become too great, Argentina would abandon it and adopt the dollar as its national currency rather than devalue. But the spending cuts needed to narrow Argentina's borrowing requirements and thereby sustain the fixed exchange rate were not announced until three months later as part of a revised loan agreement with the IMF. From mid-January to early April, the Argentine government continued to spend at predevaluation rates in a conscious attempt to pump-prime the economy to limit the depth and duration of recession during a presidential election year.

When the government, under pressure from the IMF finally announced plans to cut spending by $1 billion, negotiations in Congress over how to implement the cuts quickly bogged down. A combination of provincial opposition to proposed reductions in federal tax-sharing, popular opposition to cuts in education spending, a near civil war between Duhalde and Menem over control of the party and hence the Peronist presidential nomination, and Menem's official passage into lame-duck status in early May were lethal to fiscal responsibility. Congress not only blocked the vast majority of the proposed cuts but increased budgeted spending for the year. Ultimately the Menem government was able to limit the increase in primary spending during the year, but this was insufficient in the face of declining tax revenues, rising debt payments, and significant off-budget spending. Despite privatization income that largely compensated for the falloff in tax revenues, the fiscal deficit exploded.

THE RUN-UP TO CRISIS, ROUND TWO

Public discontent with a declining economy and endemic political corruption, along with sharp divisions within the Peronist Party, combined to secure an opposition victory in the October 1999 presidential elections. The euphoria surrounding victory was tempered by the extremely difficult fiscal situation Carlos Menem bequeathed to the new administration of Fernando de la Rúa.

The fiscal deficit was large and the recovery expected during 2000 would put upward pressure on the trade deficit; should growth not materialize, the government's reduced borrowing needs stemming from a smaller trade deficit would be replaced by deeper fiscal problems. Further, the new administration faced $12.3 billion in maturing debt during the year, which made some refinancing both inevitable and essential. This inherited financial straitjacket meant that sustaining investor confidence and thereby capital inflows was the key to everything economic during 2000. Without capital inflows there would be no recovery, and without recovery there would be no increase in jobs and social spending—as the new president had promised during his campaign.

The government moved quickly to retain investor confidence. On taking office in December 1999 it announced far-reaching austerity measures designed to lower the fiscal deficit and reduce Argentina's borrowing needs. When tax receipts did not recover as hoped during the first quarter of the year, the government enacted a second round of spending cuts to demonstrate its fiscal resolve. And in May, de la Rúa won congressional approval of long-promised and long-postponed labor reform.

As impressive as these efforts seemed, they ultimately proved insufficient to the task for four reasons. First, investors and businesspersons continued to harbor doubts about de la Rúa's economy minister, Jose Luis Machinea, who had been Central Bank president during the hyperinflationary late 1980s. Although most of the private sector was publicly willing to give Machinea the benefit of the doubt, its behavior belied the official "wait and see" attitude. This view of the economic team was reinforced at home and abroad by the nature of the political alliance that brought de la Rúa to power. The alliance between the Radical Party and Frepaso had been shaky since its formation in 1997. (Frepaso is a coalition of leftist parties and Peronist defectors formed in the early 1990s to oppose the economic policies and corruption of the Menem administration.) After nearly splitting in 1998, Frepaso managed to regroup to defeat a common enemy—Carlos Menem and the Peronist Party. But the brief and tumultuous history of the alliance did not engender confidence about its ability to remain united in government.

Further, to govern effectively the new administration needed to preserve unity within its governing alliance and cooperate with the defeated and divided Peronists, who continued to control the Senate, the majority of the provinces, the Supreme Court, and the main labor confederation. Yet this implied a serious contradiction. While de la Rúas Frepaso allies insisted on uncovering and punishing corruption in the Menem government, any anti-corruption campaign that targeted Peronists could have produced legislative and judicial gridlock as well as labor instability. Last, the new president did not inspire confidence. De la Rúa was a plodder, a competent manager who took his time reaching decisions. His was not the sort of personality that could inspire his supporters, assure alliance unity, and lead the nation by force of will.

With international investors and all of Argentina watching to see how he would perform, de la Rúa stumbled badly. His initial austerity measures had the effect of cutting off an incipient recovery in the Argentine economy that had been stimulated by deficit spending during 1999. The second round of austerity produced the first defections from the alliance, followed by the president's acquiescence to alliance pressures to avoid further austerity measures. But the worst of de la Rúa's troubles were yet to come.

A corruption scandal surrounding the passage of labor reform and de la Rúa's mismanagement of the resulting political crisis undermined the government. Rumors emerged in September that Peronist senators received bribes for their votes approving the reform package. Despite credible evidence implicating the labor minister and the chief of intelligence in this scandal, de la Rúa stood by his colleagues, attempting to use the affair as an opportunity to reshuffle his cabinet and thereby strengthen his hand at the expense of his Frepaso allies. But the president made a fatal mistake. Although Frepaso had been willing to set aside its traditional opposition to austerity measures to support its alliance partner in the first months of the de la Rúa presidency, it would not countenance corruption in "its" administration coupled with an apparent purge. Vice President Carlos Álvarez resigned in protest, leaving the alliance in tatters. The leader of de la Rúa's own Radical Party also began to criticize the government's economic policies as confidence in the government plunged—from 70 percent in early 2000 to just 23 percent in October.

With the economy mired in recession and the government's credibility severely eroded, investors began to leave. Two multibillion-dollar bailouts organized by the IMF, in November 2000 and in August 2001, and a costly debt restructuring initiated in June 2001 merely postponed the inevitable. By the end of 2000 Argentina clearly was politically and economically unable to meet its debt obligations. Matters worsened in March 2001 when a rotating door in the Economy Ministry (in a period of two weeks, three different individuals led the ministry), disarray within the alliance, and growing opposition to de la Rúa from within the Radical Party created the image of a government on the verge of collapse. Out of desperation, de la Rúa turned to former Economy Minister Domingo Cavallo.

As the architect of Menem's economic policies, Cavallo was strongly disliked in Frepaso and by the more liberal faction of the Radical Party. His appointment thus carried significant political risk for de la Rúa. Once in office, Cavallo proposed modifying the Argentine peso's peg to the dollar alone to a combination of the dollar and the euro once the euro reached parity with the dollar. Given that parity between the dollar and the euro was considered to be a long way off in May 2001 and that Cavallo must have known that suggesting a change in the currency board at this time would weaken investor confidence in the value of the peso, investors were puzzled and suspicious about the real purpose behind Cavallo's announcement. Within weeks Cavallo's proposal to modify the currency board undercut what little confidence his appointment had managed to reestablish in the government.

THE "CRISIS FORETOLD" STRIKES

By mid-2001 Argentina was headed inextricably for default and financial crisis. The interplay between the currency board, political constraints on its implementation, and bad luck had brought Argentina to the precipice. Precisely when the crisis would explode depended on when investors' fear of risk finally outweighed their love of high returns. This occurred in November 2001 and led to a rapid outflow of capital from the Argentine banking system, threatening it with collapse. How the crisis played out was then determined by IMF policy, the reaction of Argentine society to the government's emergency measures, and the political importance of the provincial governors.

After years of unwavering support for Argentina and its currency board, the IMF reversed course in late 2001. The new Bush administration in the United States publicly questioned the wisdom of IMF "bailouts" for wayward regimes and the use of United States taxpayer money to rescue "Wall Street bankers." This criticism of the IMF was not only expounded forcefully by Treasury Secretary Paul O'Neill but also took root in the IMF through the administration's choice for the fund's first deputy managing director, Anne Krueger. Although the IMF did approve one last loan for Argentina during 2001, its new mindset solidified into a firm policy toward Argentina as it watched these funds drained from the Argentine financial system in November. It was time to stop throwing good money after bad. In early December the Argentine government requested a waiver on its fiscal targets to enable the disbursal of $1.2 billion from one last loan in August 2001. The IMF refused Argentina's request. Without the IMF funds Argentina would not be able to make debt payments due later in the month. Since Argentine banks held huge quantities of Argentine government debt, a default by the government would inevitably threaten the solvency of the country's banking system. Under these circumstances, the run on the banks turned into a stampede, placing the domestic banking system at risk of collapse. The Argentine government took an extreme measure: freezing all funds in the system.

This was the last straw for a population that had suffered greatly during the previous decade. Although inflation had been brought under control, unemployment had grown from 7.7 percent in 1991 at the establishment of the currency board to 15 percent in 2000 (and to 18.3 percent in October 2001). Poverty rates exploded as inequality in the distribution of income widened, leading to the gradual disappearance of the Argentine middle class, a cornerstone of Argentine national identity and pride. Yet Argentines did not blame the currency board for this calamity. They instead held their government responsible, especially the endemic corruption among government officials that the de la Rúa administration had promised to end.

Now Argentines were being asked to accept a freeze on virtually all their funds in the banking system. The middle class saw this as a robbery perpetrated by inept or corrupt politicians. For those working in the cash-dependent informal sector, which encompassed about half the economy, the impact was devastating—earnings were cut nearly in half during the first month of the freeze. Argentines took to the streets in protest, some banging pots in spontaneous expressions of discontent, some sacking grocery stores in search of food, and some in organized rioting.

As the country teetered on the brink of social and economic chaos, de la Rúa had but one hope for political survival: a national unity coalition with the opposition. But when he approached the Peronist governors with the idea, he was rebuffed. Lacking both popular and legislative support, de la Rúa was forced to resign the presidency. Argentina then passed through a mind-boggling period of five sitting presidents in less than two weeks (one of whom formally defaulted on Argentina's debt in December), in large measure because Peronist governors could not agree on how to replace de la Rúa. By the end of the month, the governor of Buenos Aires province, Eduardo Duhalde, was able to cobble together an anti–currency board coalition that enabled him to finally rise to the presidency. On this foundation, Duhalde followed up the December default with a devaluation and de-dollarization of the economy, measures that did little to help rebuild investor confidence. He then turned to the IMF.

The cohesion of Duhalde's anti–currency board coalition, however, was tenuous at best. Soon the Buenos Aires faction of the Radical Party defected, arguing that it had supported Duhalde only to end the currency board, not to implement the austerity measures required to obtain funding from the IMF. More troubling, Peronist governors, including several allied with Duhalde's political nemesis, Carlos Menem, openly expressed their opposition to Duhalde's leadership. Lacking the political support to implement the demands of the IMF, the government was cornered. Without an IMF accord, there would be no capital inflows. Without capital inflows, the freeze on bank accounts could not be lifted. Without money circulating in the economy, economic activity contracted rapidly. And as the economy shrank, so did what remained of President Duhalde's support and his capacity to govern. The resulting downward political-economic spiral decimated Argentina during 2002.

As 2002 came to an end, the Argentine economy seemed to have touched bottom after contracting more than 10 percent. But a robust recovery during 2003 will be blocked by many of the same forces that helped create Argentina's economic catastrophe: the hard-line stance of the IMF, the muddle that is Argentine politics, and a dispirited and politically disaffected populace.

Argentina began the new year without an agreement with the IMF, even though an accord had appeared to be on the verge of completion during 2002, only to slip from Argentina's grasp. Making matters worse, Argentina was also on the verge of a formal default on its debt to international financial institutions such as the World Bank. Should this default actually occur in early 2003, the process of reaching a final accord with the IMF and resolving the new Argentine debt crisis will be delayed significantly.

On the political front, 2002 ended much as it began. After a year in the presidency, Eduardo Duhalde continued to battle governors over needed austerity measures, national legislators over essential economic reforms, and the Supreme Court over the constitutionality of freezing funds in the banking system. As ingovernability reigned, the IMF correctly questioned the ability of the Argentine government to implement any agreement with the fund.

In an effort to reestablish the legitimacy of the presidency and thereby governability in the country, Duhalde announced his resignation effective in late May and called early presidential elections. Unfortunately, this decision is unlikely to resolve Argentina's political crisis. With the announcement of new elections, Duhalde created a new front in his never-ending civil war with Carlos Menem. Menem is actively pursuing the presidential nomination of the Peronist Party, and Duhalde has dedicated himself to doing anything and everything required to stop his nemesis. History suggests that in this political war, rational economic policymaking will be sacrificed. Equally important, whoever wins the April 2003 election will find his or her ability to govern hampered by the provincial governors, a hold-over legislature lacking leadership and concerned about reelection later in the year, and a populace that is likely to abstain en masse, undermining the new president's legitimacy. Argentina will face another difficult year.

6.3 The Nature of the New Argentine Democracy: The Delegative Democracy Argument Revisited (2001)

ENRIQUE PERUZZOTTI

Guillermo O'Donnell's diagnosis about the delegative nature of the new democracies has won wide acceptance in current debates on the obstacles and challenges at institutional consolidation in Latin America. Latin American democracies, it is frequently argued, have displayed a poor institutionalising performance. Terms such as "delegative" "fragile," "unstable" are commonly used to characterise the unconsolidated status of most of the region's democratic regimes. This commentary challenges the "delegative-

Enrique Peruzzotti, "The Nature of the New Argentine Democracy: The Delegative Democracy Argument Revisited," *Journal of Latin American Studies,* February 2001, Vol. 33, no. 1, pp. 135–155. Reprinted with the permission of Cambridge University Press.

ness" diagnosis, arguing that it rests on a one-sided interpretation of current political developments and that it turns a blind eye to the truly innovative processes that have taken place within many of Latin American societies and that make this democratising wave distinctive.

THE NATURE OF THE EMERGING LATIN AMERICAN POLITICAL REGIMES: THE DELEGATIVE DEMOCRACY ARGUMENT

What is the institutionalising record of the postdictatorial period? Are Latin American democracies moving toward institutional consolidation? If the latter is the case, which type of democracy is being consolidated? The challenges posed by the current democratising wave have produced an extensive corpus of studies aimed at determining the nature and prospects of the emerging Latin American democracies. "Transitology" has gradually been displaced by "consolidology," i.e. the analysis of the dynamics of regime breakdowns has been replaced by the study of the conditions for institutional reconstruction. Such a major analytical shift has been followed by a mood swing: the initial optimism of the literature on democratisation concerning the outcome of current transitions has given way to a more sombre diagnosis about the prospects of democratic consolidation.

Democratisation literature's disenchantment with recent political processes does not originate, as in the past, from fear of regression to authoritarianism. Analysts are bewildered by the exceptional endurance exhibited by most democratic administrations. At least in this aspect, the current democratising wave deviates from previous continental transitions. The pendulum movement between democracy and authoritarianism characteristic of contemporary Latin American history has apparently come to a halt. Latin American societies seem to have reached a democratic plateau. No sustained authoritarian regression can be seen to loom on the political horizon of most societies. When confronted with serious military, political or economic crises, democratic administrations have displayed unusual manoeuvring skills. Yet, the stopping of the pendulum has not resulted in the solving of the chronic institutional deficit of those societies. The literature on democratic consolidation has called attention to the poor institutionalising performance of these new democracies. As far as democratisation theory is concerned, underinstitutionalisation remains a major problem of Latin American societies.

Guillermo O'Donnell characterised such a peculiar version of a noninstitutionalised (but enduring) regime as "delegative" democracy. The model of delegative democracy resurrects Huntington's argument about the low level of institutionalisation of Latin American polities. Huntington considered institutional underdevelopment to be the most distinctive developmental pathology of Latin American societies. In most of Latin America, he argued, the development of political institutions lags behind social and economic change, leading to the emergence of crisis-ridden praetorian polities. Huntington postulated a direct correlation between underinstitutionalisation and political ungovernability. Recent developments seem to challenge Huntington's equation. At present, underinstitutionalisation has not led to a praetorian scenario but has given birth to a distinctive form of democracy that relies for its integration more on the skills of specific personalities than on formal institutional mechanisms. The glue that holds those democracies together, O'Donnell argues, is charisma, not legality. A discretionary executive is the cornerstone of this distinctive democratic model where presidents rule free of mechanisms of horizontal or vertical accountability, except from post facto electoral verdicts.

The notion of delegative democracy draws attention to a twilight zone between authoritarianism and democracy that does not correspond to any of the scenarios delineated by the literature on democratic transitions. Democratisation literature assumed that the transitions from bureaucratic authoritarianism were going to lead either to the establishment of representative democracies or to regression to autocracy. The other considered options, democraduras or dictablandas, did not embody alternative regimes but a distinctive interregnum of the transitional period. Democraduras and dictablandas represented partially liberalised or democratised forms of authoritarianism that were far from fulfilling the procedural criteria of polyarchies. The actual outcome of the transitions, delegative democracy, does not conform to any of the predicted scenarios: it points to an unanticipated outcome in which the successful completion of the transition led neither to representative democracy nor to autocracy but to some sui generis form of unconsolidated democracy. If successful at installing democracy, the transition stopped short at consolidating it. O'Donnell argues for the need at a "second transition," the latter entailing the movement from a democratically elected government to consolidated democracy.

How to account for such an unexpected outcome? For O'Donnell, the theoretical tools of transition literature seem ill equipped to provide a satisfying explanation. He argues for a need to move away from the shortsighted focus on strategic elite interactions to introduce historical and structural variables into the analysis of political democratisation. The delegative democracy argument rightly calls attention to long-term variables that might be affecting the outcome of current democratising processes. O'Donnell's model is built upon two distinctive sets of arguments: the first one focuses on the type of political culture that sustains such a form of democracy, the second one, on the structural environment in which those regimes emerged. Let us briefly review each of his arguments.

O'Donnell's analysis focuses on the problematic cultural heritage of populism. Although they are referred to as a "new species that has yet to be theorised," his overview of the most salient features of the political culture that supports delegative democracies seems to imply that the breakdown of bureaucratic-authoritarianism has allowed for the resurrection of past populist styles and identities. See for example the following description:

> Delegative democracies rest on the premise that whoever wins election to the presidency is thereby entitled to govern as he or she sees fit . . . The president is taken to be the embodiment of the nation and the main custodian and definer of its interests . . . Since this paternal figure is supposed to take care of the whole nation, his political base must be a movement . . . In this view, other institutions—courts and legislatures, for instances—are nuisances that come attached to the domestic and international advantages of being a democratically elected president . . . Delegative democracy is strongly majoritarian. It consists in constituting, through clean elections, a majority that empowers someone to become, for a given number of years, the embodiment and interpreter of the high interests of the nation . . .

There is nothing specifically original in the above characterisation of the political culture of delegative democracies. Movementism, radical majoritarianism, nationalism, and paternalism are all ingrained features of populist forms of self-understanding. Rather than indicating the existence of processes of cultural renewal, O'Donnell's argument seems to indicate that Latin American populist traditions are still alive and in good health in most of the region. In fact, delegative democracy emerges only in those countries with populist heritage, like Argentina, Brazil or Peru. In societies where liberal-democratic traditions have been stronger, like Chile and Uruguay, the outcome of the transition has been significantly different, leading to a type of democracy that is closer to the representative ideal.

If in cultural terms delegative democracy seems to be an aggiornamento of populist traditions, what is then the source of its distinctiveness? According to O'Donnell, what distinguishes delegative from past versions of democracy is the structural context of its emergence. The argument correctly concentrates on the chronic problem of underinstitutionalisation exhibited by those societies in which delegative democracy emerges. Delegative democracies are found in countries affected by serious economic and political crises. On the one hand, there is a profound crisis of the state that translates into a legitimacy and effectiveness deficit. The state is unable to establish its authority over society since the former is perceived by most actors not as a public institution but as an arena to be colonised by private interests. On the other hand, there is an economic crisis of dramatic dimensions that only exacerbates the crisis of state institutions. Recurrent and escalating inflationary (and hyperinflationary) outbursts are followed by unsuccessful attempts by state authorities to control inflation and reform the economy. Every governmental effort at economic stabilisation is easily challenged by a plurality of unruly corporatist interests.

Repeated failures to achieve economic stabilisation contribute to a perverse process of collective learning: actors assume that every new governmental effort at taming inflation will have the same fate as previous attempts, and therefore bet against the success of the economic policies. Praetorian societies became trapped in a dramatic and spiralling zero-sum game. In each new round, the stakes and the level of praetorianism increases, as does economic and social deterioration. The result is a general crisis of state and society: O'Donnell talks of an "evaporation of the public dimension of the state" and the "pulverisation" of society into a myriad of opportunistic actors. Such a scenario only reinforces the delegative tendencies present in those societies that, in turn, undermine any efforts at institutional reconstruction. As a result, O'Donnell argues,

> . . . Very little, if any, progress is made toward achieving institutions of representation and accountability. On the contrary, connecting with historical roots which are deep in these countries, the atomisation of society and state, the spread of brown areas and their peculiar ways of pushing their interests, and the enormous urgency and complexity of the problems to be faced feed the delegative propensities of these democracies.

These societies are consequently entangled in a colossal prisoner's dilemma that not only perpetuates but also escalates a praetorian game that is inimical to democratic consolidation. "The prisoner's dilemma—O'Donnell concludes—has a powerful dynamic": Delegative democracy seems to be part of the foreseeable future of many Latin American polities.

O'Donnell's model focuses on some problematic traits of the new Latin American democracies such as the negative implications for democratic institutionalisation of excessive executive discretionality. Presidential delegativeness, he argues, hampers the institutional development of the judicial and legislative branches, depriving democracy of an effective system of horizontal accountability. Decretismo [governing through executive decrees] also impoverishes the policy-making process. According to O'Donnell, the apparent gain in "effectiveness" that results from insulating decision-makers from societal pressures is deceptive: a more incremental and consensual process of policy-making might prevent the "gross mistakes" that could derive from executive arbitrariness, while increasing the likelihood of its implementation. It might also reduce the uncertainty that wild swings in policymaking and in presidential popularity create among the population. Lastly, the argument links the analysis of democratisation to chronic problems of Latin American societies: underinstitutionalisation and political and economic praetorianism. For all these reasons, O'Donnell's observations about delegative democracy should be considered a refreshing departure from the excessive myopia displayed by most of transition literature toward the cultural, institutional and economic environment of democratisation processes. Yet, is the delegative democracy argument the model that best characterises the nature of the recent democratising transitions?

This commentary will argue that the delegative democracy argument fails to acknowledge the innovative features of the current democratising process. While the model rightly highlights cultural and structural variables that conspire against democratic consolidation, it fails to recognise those dynamics that might be leading those societies away from praetorianism and authoritarianism. Through the analysis of the Argentine case, it challenges two basic assumptions of O'Donnell's model: first, the existence of a populist or neopopulist "delegative" political culture that feeds a vicious cycle of praetorianism and underinstitutionalisation (parts II and III), second, the assertion that the so called delegative democracies operate in an institutional vacuum (part IV).

POLITICAL CULTURE I: CULTURAL INNOVATION OR RETURN TO POPULIST TRADITIONS?

Centring exclusively on the political practices and styles of the executive branch, the delegative democracy argument overlooks the dramatic changes that have operated within society at large, and that makes this last democratising wave distinctive. The various arguments about the delegativeness of actual Latin American democracies turn a blind eye to processes of cultural change that are crucially relevant to the analysis of institutional consolidation. The real novelty in the Latin American scenario is not the delegative behaviour of political elites, but civil society's consciousness about it.

Political culture does represent a key variable for understanding processes of institutional reconstruction. A fundamental aspect of the institutionalising dynamic is the anchoring of the validity principles of an order in a specific political culture. Comprising the social realm where collective identities originate, the analysis of political developments within civil society emerges as a crucial variable of the process of democratic consolidation. The role of social movements, associations and independent publics in reshaping political identities is decisive for determining the chances of success of current institutionalising processes, particularly in societies where democratic identities and practices have been notably absent.

Far from displaying cultural continuity, there are two innovative features that suggest a profound metamorphosis of Argentine political culture. First, there has been a considerable erosion of past populist/antipopulist allegiances which allowed for the emergence of an autonomous "public opinion." Second, a new form of rights-oriented politicisation has developed that has contributed to the constitutionalisation of state-society relations.

1. The erosion of populist traditions created conditions conducive to the emergence of autonomous publics. In the past, populist identities inhibited the formation of a genuine public opinion. Populism's democratic ideals were opposed to a discursive formation of a public will from below, resting instead

on an acclamative model of democratic will formation. In this form of self-understanding, there is no institutional space for the formation of a democratic will outside the state. The leader and the movement monopolised public representation: those who opposed them were considered pariahs that did not belong to the demos. The polarisation and over-politicisation that resulted from such form of self-understanding made the formation of publics with certain degree of autonomy from political society impossible, leading instead to the fragmentation of society into two irreconcilable camps.

The electoral defeat of Peronism in 1983 was the first sign of the breakdown of past allegiances, a tendency that was confirmed in following elections. The dissolution of "captive electorates" has given way to fluid and unpredictable electoral behaviour. Many electoral analysts have emphasised the weakening of the percentage of captive or loyal voters on both parties, and the existence of considerable transference of votes from election to election. The significant growth of independent voters suggest a healthy process of depoliticisation of civil society, i.e., it indicates a process of autonomisation of civil with respect to political society. This phenomenon should not be unilaterally interpreted as indicating a worrisome trend toward societal depoliticisation and demobilisation. The demise of a type of politicisation linked to populist forms of self-understanding is the precondition for the emergence of more productive forms of politicisation, like the politics of rights and of influence described below.

2. I have argued elsewhere that the politics of human rights acted as a catalyst for cultural change, triggering a profound renovation of the country's democratic traditions. The democratic ideal defended by the human rights movement differed drastically from previous forms of populist self-understanding. The discourse on rights reunites two elements that populist political culture has kept apart: democracy and the rule of law. The human rights movement inaugurated a new form of rights oriented politics that openly challenges the principles of populist state-corporatism. The politics of rights developed by the human rights movement implies a redefinition of corporatist forms of articulation between state and society in favour of a liberal model. If populist corporatism contributed to the institutional dedifferentiation between state and society, the politics of rights aims instead at drawing clear legal boundaries between those institutional spheres. It also represents a self-limiting form of politicisation that contrasts sharply with the "movementist" identity of past democratising movements.

The emergence of a rights-oriented politics greatly contributed both to the "authorisation" and effectiveness of rights as institutions and, consequently, to the juridification of state-society relations. A major heritage of the politics of human rights was the establishment of a permanent associative network for the supervision of state authorities. Human rights groups, legal aid associations, movements and organisations against police and military violence, etc., have played a crucial watchdog role in the defence of societal autonomy and have led to a wide variety of actions aimed at making political authorities accountable. This form of politicisation is not circumscribed to the human rights movement, but has been continued by a second generation of movements and associations. In the last decade, the Argentine political landscape has been shaken by the emergence of multiple social movements, civic associations and to a more inquisitive type of journalism organised around demands for accountability. Social mobilisations, the monitoring of the public authorities by civic organisations, and press denunciations have resulted in a series of widely publicised "cases" (the most notorious being the Carrasco, the Maria Soledad and the Cabezas cases) and of numerous media scandals (such as Swiftgate, IBMgate, Yomagate, Armsgate, etc.) that exerted a considerable toll in the Menem administration.

Cultural innovation has restored the authority of constitutionalism and rights as institutions, which allowed for the legal stabilisation of the realm of the social as civil society. The struggle for rights initiated by the human rights movement is aimed at drawing clear institutional boundaries between state and civil society. Such forms of politicisation have been continued and deepened by a second generation of civic associations and movements that adopted a more offensive stand: their actions were not simply aimed at protecting society but also at holding public authorities accountable. This phenomenon, which has largely been overlooked by the democratisation literature, distinguishes the last democratising wave from previous transitions to democracy. The real novelty then is not delegativeness but societal efforts at making state authorities accountable: alongside "horizontal" mechanisms of accountability there has evolved innovative forms of making authorities accountable that rely on "vertical"—yet non-electoral—mechanisms.

POLITICAL CULTURE II: ECONOMIC EMERGENCY AND DELEGATIVE CRISIS MANAGEMENT

It has been argued that the erosion of populist political traditions has been due to the emergence of a new form of democratic self-understanding that has re-legitimised a constitutional form of democracy. However, the irruption of a delegative presidential figure like Menem into the national political scene casts some doubts on the argument about the erosion of populist political culture. Who epitomises the unrestrained presidentialism of delegative democracy argument better than Menem? At first sight, the phenomenon of Menemism seems to confirm O'Donnell's hypothesis. Before jumping to hurried conclusions, it is necessary to put Menemism into context.

Concerning Menem's delegativeness, two questions should be raised: (1) what determined his delegative behaviour?, (2) what was the reason for his steady electoral success? It is argued here that neither Menem's behaviour nor the popular support to his figure were the product of a reawakening of populist majoritarian ideals. Movementism, nationalism, majoritarianism are not central features of Menem's legitimating discourse. The current phenomenon of delegativeness is not rooted in an authoritarian form of (populist or neopopulist) political culture. The irruption of delegative executive leadership is intimately associated with the breakdown of systemic integration at the economic level. Furthermore, it is argued that this delegative phenomenon at the political level is related to a demand for economic governability that indicates a noteworthy effort at collective self-limitation at the economic level. This effort complements the culture of political self-limitation that the politics of rights reflects at the political level.

1. Menem's delegative behaviour can be understood as a dramatic attempt to restore the steering capacities of a state overburdened by economic praetorianism. Menem took power in the midst of the worst hyperinflationary crisis of Argentine history, a crisis that forced an impotent Alfonsin to hand power to the recently elected administration six months ahead of time. In an environment where all institutional channels of interest intermediation had long been overwhelmed by unruly socio-economic powers, only decisive state action could restore acceptable levels of governability. As Juan Carlos Torre argues,

> When prices increase at a daily rate it is almost impossible to negotiate a social truce . . . in such a conjuncture the basis for co-operative action is missing . . . Once a certain inflationary threshold is reached, the intervention of an agent that can assure a quick and effective economic stabilisation becomes imperative . . . there are not many candidates to fulfil that role apart from the executive.

In the absence of effective "filtering" institutions, the enhancing of the state's steering capabilities appears as the only way out of the crisis. The latter requires the insulation of the administrative system from both the praetorian societal environment and from "colonised" state institutions. Concentrating executive power and administrative technocracy (represented respectively by the figures of Menem and finance minister Cavallo) contributed to restore the steering capacities of the administration—by insulating the state from the praetorian struggle. Through centralised executive authority, the Menem administration could restore a minimum of regulatory power that in turn would increase the efficiency of democratic institutions. The effective insulation of the process of economic policy-making circumvented earlier policy stalemates generated by defiant corporate interests. The combination of decisive executive authority with a strong electoral mandate successfully faced down the coalition of interests that had so effectively blocked previous attempts at economic stabilisation and reform.

At this point it is important to make a digression about the issue of accountability. The problem of accountability highlighted by O'Donnell and others refers to the embeddedness of the executive's decisions horizontally (in other state institutions) and vertically (in the electorate and on the autonomous associations of civil society). O'Donnell advocates horizontal accountability across state institutions, although he acknowledges—within the praetorian context of Argentina, Brazil and Peru—the permeability of the state to the influence of powerful corporate interests capable of blocking state initiatives. As he himself puts it, in a praetorian context the government "dances at the rhythm of the crisis, its capacity to formulate policies is very limited, and very often their implementation is cancelled or captured by the disaggregated strategies just described." The colonised state is victim of a perverse form of accountability that destroys the public dimension of institutions. When discussing accountability and delegativeness it is important to keep in mind the praetorian context in which the processes of economic stabilisation described above took place. To initiate any effective process of institutional reconstruction in a praetorian situation, it is first imperative to insulate institutions from colonising particularistic powers. In other words, before making state institutions accountable, it is necessary to restore state sovereignty. The fundamental challenge of the next stage is to make state institutions accountable while avoiding the reemergence of rent-seeking "bureaucratic rings."

Seymour M. Lipset has long argued that legitimacy and effectiveness are both indispensable attributes of any democratic regime. Democracies need to perform both functions simultaneously and consequently a point of equilibrium between institutional legitimacy and the material outcomes of governmental policies must be reached. For decades, the Argentine polity suffered a double crisis of legitimacy and efficiency that translated into political and economic praetorianism. The process of collective learning described in the previous section restored the legitimacy of democratic institutions. Yet, throughout the Alfonsin administration, democratic institutions showed a troublesome economic performance. Democracy successfully confronted authoritarian challenges to its legitimacy, yet the Alfonsin administration finally fell due to its inability to maintain minimum levels of economic governability. After that, any further crisis of governmental performance such as the one suffered throughout that administration would have greatly diminished the prospects at democratic consolidation. Economic praetorianism is incompatible with political institutionalisation. Menem's contribution to democratic consolidation was to restore efficiency to the policy-making process, thus solving the effectiveness crisis that had strained Argentine democracy.

2. After highlighting the historical obstacles to political and economic institutionalisation in societies characterised by a chronic institutional deficit and a high propensity to praetorianism, O'Donnell asks himself whether there is any way out of those downward spirals. Such perverse dynamics can be broken, he argues, only when most actors perceive the costs of the game

as intolerable. Such "ceiling consensus" is likely to emerge in societies where the crisis has reached its culmination. I have previously argued that in Argentina the dramatic experience of state terrorism triggered a process of collective learning that put an end to political praetorianism. Is the electoral support to the policies of economic stabilisation and reform a signal of a similar process of collective learning at the economic level? If this were the case, the delegative phenomenon would have a much more ambiguous meaning than the one attributed by recent debates on unconsolidated democracies.

This commentary argues that the phenomenon of delegativeness is intimately associated to processes of collective learning triggered by the experience of successive hyperinflationary crises that culminated in the dramatic events of 1989. In 1989, Argentine society, borrowing O'Donnell's expression, "reached bottom." Hyperinflation left a deep cultural imprint on Argentine society, only comparable to the one previously left by state terrorism. Both events represent turning points in Argentine history: if state terrorism contributed to the emergence of a culture of political self-limitation, the 1989 hyperinflationary crisis ushered a similar consciousness of self-limitation at the economic level. Both forms of self-limitation denote a conscious collective effort at avoiding a reversion into praetorianism. The episodes of state terrorism and of hyperinflation acted as catalysts of crucial learning processes that, by relegitimating the media of power and money, greatly contributed to the establishment of a cultural environment conducive to political and economic institutionalisation.

The economic emergency drastically altered the political agenda of Argentine society: demands for constitutionalisation and political accountability were postponed in the face of a more immediate need at reestablishing normal economic conditions. Monetary stabilisation became the unifying cry of a society torn by economic ungovernability. Such a delegative mandate should not be misinterpreted as the resurrection of majoritarian democratic ideals or of authoritarian validity claims. On the contrary, this delegative mandate pinpoints to an element of collective learning that should not go unnoticed. The demand for accountability and constitutionalism is still present in society, though in a latent state. It first re-emerged on the constituent elections of 10 April 1994. The latter represented a rare occasion for "pure" political voting (designation of candidates to the constituent assembly) in which the issue of economic stability was not at stake. The impressive (and unexpected) electoral strength shown by the improvised coalition organised around the Frente Grande, which emerged as a credible third alternative to Peronism and Radicalism, suggests far-reaching changes in the political culture. Throughout the campaign the Frente criticised the authoritarianism of the Menem's administration and demanded greater transparency in the political system.

The demands for accountability intensified after the removal of Finance minister Cavallo from his post. The latter represented a tacit acknowledgement by the administration that the economic emergency (which had gained renewed urgency after the Tequila crisis) was finally over. In subsequent months the administration has been bombarded by denunciations of corruption and by media scandals. The unexpected public impact of the murder of the journalist Cabezas is a clear case of the unfreezing of juridifying demands in the post-economic emergency period. Albeit a parenthesis on the demand on constitutionalisation, the support to the process of economic reform represents a noteworthy collective effort at economic self-limitation that helped to restore the efficiency of state institutions.

INSTITUTIONAL DIFFERENTIATION: THE "CONSTITUTIONALISING" RECORD OF ARGENTINE DEMOCRACY

It has been argued that a delegative facade has prevented us from seeing fundamental processes of change in the political and economic culture of Argentine society. However, changes in the political culture do not guarantee political institutionalisation. Normative learning can affect the democratising path only if the institutional context can be redefined. Transposing normative learning into specific institutional changes is perhaps the fundamental problem of the present period of democratic consolidation. Broadening the perspective to include the analysis of political and institutional dynamics to evaluate the success of current processes of political institutionalisation is necessary. What is the institutionalising record of the process of democratic consolidation? To determine the index of "constitutionalisation" of the Argentine democratic regime, it is necessary to distinguish two different dimensions of the concept of constitutionalism:

(a) the institutional differentiation between state and society and their legal stabilisation through the establishment of an effective rights complex and,
(b) the institutional differentiation of the state in the direction of a separation of powers.

The emergence of rights-oriented politics, it was argued above, expressed a juridifying process from below aimed at establishing clear institutional boundaries between state and civil society. Cultural and institutional change within civil society restored the authority of rights as institutions, after they had been badly damaged by the corporatist and movementist practices of populist movements. This favoured the constitutionalisation of state/civil society relations.

However, it is the second dimension of the process of constitutionalisation, which is at the centre of O'Donnell's critique of current democracies, and which is perhaps more problematic. It refers to the processes of institutional differentiation within the state in the direction of a separation of powers. The constitutionalisation of state authority is crucial for ensuring societal autonomy, for the very possibility of a rights complex depends on the existence of an effective separation of executive, legislative and judicial powers. Has democratisation been followed by the constitutionalisation of the Argentine State? The delegative hypothesis gives a clear negative answer to the question. However, as a more detailed analysis of the institutional dynamics will show, the institutionalising record of the democratic period has been more mixed and ambiguous than that suggested by the delegative democracy argument.

It would be unfair to catalogue Alfonsin's administration as delegative. Both in its rhetoric and political practices, the Radical government disconfirmed the delegativeness argument. Under Alfonsin's administration, the executive power made a conscious effort at political self-limitation, particularly in relation to the judicial power. The strategy of self-limitation followed by the executive under Alfonsin's tenure broke with a well-entrenched tradition of judicial subordination to the executive branch. The strengthening of judicial autonomy was attained at a considerable cost to the administration. Indeed, this contributed to the failure of the government's human rights strategy. Judicial autonomy translated into continuous challenges to presidential resolutions. The legal logic of the judiciary clashed with the political goal of the executive power: namely, to exert limited and exemplary punishment for human rights violations committed under military rule.

Judicial authorities constantly challenged the official human rights policy. These challenges came from ordinary judges right up to the Supreme Court. The administration made many attempts at bringing the juridical procedures to a close. The ruling by the Federal Court concerning the sentence passed on the military junta, far from closing the chapter on human rights violations as was the government's aspiration, left legal channels open for the initiation of new trials. The subsequent attempt by the Ministry of Interior to limit prosecutions encountered the open opposition of Federal Courts. The executive tried to settle the controversy by appealing to the Supreme Court but the latter supported the position of the federal courts. The sanctioning of the "Punto Final" law backfired on the administration due to a new challenge from the judiciary, which suspended its summer recess and speeded the indictment of hundreds of cases involving human rights violations that would otherwise have been prescribed because of that law.

The combination of (a) a politics of rights within civil society that relied on the judiciary as its main interlocutor, (b) the redefinition of the judiciary's own self-understanding and (c) a politics of self-limitation in the executive, contributed to a successful process of institutional differentiation in the direction of a separation of powers. The judiciary moved from its traditional subordinated role to the forefront of political developments. The national and international impact of the trial of the military leaders redefined the historical position of the Argentine judicial power and marks its entrance into the national landscape as an autonomous and legitimate branch of the state, with institutional weight of its own. Since then, the judiciary has established itself as a central actor within the institutional landscape, to the extent that some analysts are talking about a judicialisation of political conflicts that place the judiciary at the very centre of political development.

This redefinition of the institutional role of the judiciary was a significant accomplishment in the direction of a constitutionalisation of state power to contradict the delegativeness argument. However, such an auspicious trend has unfortunately suffered a major reversal with the packing of the Supreme Court by the Menem administration. Taking advantage of the majority that he enjoyed in both houses of congress, Menem began his first term by raising the number of Supreme Court justices from six to nine, filling the three new seats with judges beholden to the government. The government also demanded the resignation of the Public Prosecutor and of the Attorney General. Undoubtedly, the administration's actions represented a serious setback to judicial autonomy. However, the demands for justice and the tendency toward the judicialisation of conflicts remain an established feature of post-dictatorial politics. The judiciary as an actor has far from vanished from the public scene.

As for the role of the legislative power in the new democracy, the results are also far from being conclusive. A close look at executive legislative relations shows a much more complex picture than the one delineated by O'Donnell. Different analyses of executive-legislative dynamics show a legislative power that has refused to play a subordinated role in relation to the executive. The independence displayed by the legislative power under the Radical administration led to a drastic curtailment of presidential ambitions. Alfonsin was forced to share power with a legislative power divided between a Radical controlled house of deputies and a Peronist controlled Senate. Such parity of forces at the legislative level did not lead, however, to the paralysis of congress as a legislative body. Radicals and Peronists found modalities of cooperation. A sign of cooperation was the high proportion of laws sanctioned by a bipartisan majority of votes. Even in very controversial issues, such as the budget or fiscal reform, cooperation prevailed over confrontation. The emergence of a culture of compromise should not be misinterpreted as an abdication of the role of congress as a comptroller of executive ambitions. Although compromise was reached on issues that prevented the paralysis of the administration (such as the approval of the budget), Congress did not abstain from blocking many presidential initiatives.

With Menem in the presidency, a pattern of government by decree was established that profoundly affected the equilibrium between executive and legislative powers. During his first presidential tenure, Menem enacted 308 decrees (figures are for the 1989–1993 period). The figure is even more impressive if contrasted with the number of decrees enacted from the establishment of the 1853 constitution to 1989: 35 in total, ten of which were enacted under the Alfonsin administration. The repeated resort to the so-called decrees of "urgency and need" represent a clear invasion of legislative prerogatives by the executive. While traditionally, decrees had a "political content," such as the irregular declaration of a state of siege or of a federal intervention, most of the decrees enacted since 1983 entailed an arrogation of legislative prerogatives by the executive. Of the 305 decrees enacted by Menem, 159 fit this latter category.

Decretismo has been further complemented by the repeated use of the veto prerogatives by the executive. Both under Alfonsin and Menem, the number of presidential vetoes to congressional initiatives increased way above the historical median. Alfonsin vetoed 8 per cent of the total of legislative initiatives (49 vetoes) while Menem vetoed 3 per cent of them (109 vetoes). Moreover, the Menem administration has resorted to the device of enacting part of the bill it had just vetoed. The dramatic increase in legislation by decrees and presidential vetoes indicates the existence of worrisome de facto presidential practices that openly contradict the spirit of the constitutional principle of separation of powers. As Ana Maria Mustapic rightly argues, those practices contributed to the crystallisation of institutional mechanisms not contemplated by the constitution.

At first sight, the review of presidential practices seems to corroborate O'Donnell's hypothesis. Indeed, a considerable amount of literature supports his diagnosis. Yet, the presence of hegemonic presidential practices should not lead to overhasty conclusions. Delegative executive behaviour does not necessarily imply the existence of an institutional vacuum at the legislative and judicial levels. In fact, they might well be indicating the opposite: that the executive is bypassing congress due to the latter's refusal to act as a mere rubber stamp. Viewed from this perspective, the repeated resort to emergency decrees and presidential vetoes by the executive could reveal the existence of an important degree of institutional conflict between legislative and executive powers; conflict that might indicate a clash between autonomous institutional clusters due to institutional differentiation. These presidential practices suggest a conflict of powers due to the refusal of congress to adopt a subordinate position toward the executive. It is congressional autonomy that has been forcing the executive to bypass normal legislative procedures. The analysis of Mariana Llanos of the privatisation process seems to corroborate this hypothesis. In her view, the whole privatisation process was carried out not in an institutional vacuum but within an institutional frame. She distinguishes a delegative, a cooperative and a conflictive phase in the relationship between legislature and the presidency throughout the privatisation process:

(a) The delegative phase corresponds to the launching of the process of structural reform and economic stabilisation and is characterised by an uneven relation between legislative power and the presidency due to the express delegation of legislative powers to the president by congress.

(b) The cooperative phase is characterised by an attempt by congress to regain some of the institutional power it had delegated at the initial stage. This translated in a slower rate of the reform and in the introduction of congressional modifications to the projects submitted by the executive. The Congress did not refuse to collaborate in Menem's policy of reform, but it demanded participation in the process of legislation. In this period, we witness a tendency of the executive to resort to the veto in order to preserve some of the initiative it had on the previous stage.

(c) The conflictive phase indicates a situation of relative institutional equilibrium between the executive and the legislative that led to a series of confrontations due to the refusal of the latter to endorse some of the initiatives of the former. Due to the lack of congressional support, many of the laws were passed by executive decree. As Llanos rightly indicates, in such conditions the resort to decree measures is a sign of the weakening of presidential leadership even within the ruling party.

The fact that many of the vetoes were directed against a Peronist-dominated congress further contradicts the delegativeness argument. The conflict not only reflects a clash between powers but also disagreements between the administration and the official party. The latter is clearly at deviance with the hypothesis of a rebirth of movementism, instead it indicates processes of institutional differentiation operating at two different levels: on the one hand, a trend toward a constitutional separation of powers within the state and, on the other hand, a process of differentiation between state and political society. Both types of conflicts would have been unthinkable under the classical Peronist regime, where a vertically integrated movement and a submissive congressional majority followed the populist leader's directives. This fusion of administration and movement that characterised previous populist democratic experiments are clearly absent under Menemism.

Overall, the current balance seems detrimental to the legislative; although it should be noted that congress has registered important victories over the Menem administration. In any case, the picture is far from indicating a situation of institutional vacuum. Far from endorsing all presidential initiatives, congress modified or blocked many presidential initiatives. The cases of the social security and labour reforms were two notorious examples. The packing of the Court and of key hierarchical positions in the judiciary by Menem have not prevented the existence of many independent initiatives by lower rank magistrates and, occasionally, by the Court itself.

Finally, it should be added that delegativeness exerts its toll on the presidency. Menem's tampering with the court and judicial designations

triggered national and international criticism. His attack on judicial autonomy only contributed to heighten public consciousness of the need for an
independent judiciary. Decretismo is also not free of cost: policies unilaterally implemented by the executive, sometimes in open opposition to congressional will, are often less effective at generating trust in the prospects of
the reforms than policies that are consensually reached. While discretionary
executive authority may have been crucial for overcoming the stalemate of
praetorianism and stabilising the economy, the consolidation of reform required the reduction of discretionality and the establishment of calculable
institutional arrangements. If the process of economic reform is perceived as
resting exclusively on a strong willed president, then the prospect of an
electoral defeat can be highly discouraging to prospective investors, since
they may justly believe that a future administration could reverse many unilaterally imposed policies. The discretional path toward economic reform is
self-defeating for it fails at establishing the long-term frame that only legal
institutions can provide. The success of any long-term project at economic
restructuring requires some important degree of congressional collaboration
and of juridical calculability. Decisionism can backfire on the administration, hurting the very prospects of the reforms.

EVALUATING POST-POPULIST DEMOCRACIES: TOWARD A JURIDIFICATION OF POLITICS?

Does the concept of delegative democracy do justice to current processes of
democratisation? Is delegativeness the most distinctive feature of the new
democracies? This commentary has argued that the "delegativeness" diagnosis overlooks the innovative processes taking place in many Latin American societies that clearly differentiates this democratising wave from
previous populist processes of democratisation. Through the analysis of the
Argentine case, it has shown that, both in cultural and institutional terms,
the new democracy greatly differs from the populist democratic model that
for decades provided the hegemonic form of democracy in the region. Cultural learning, it has been argued, has eroded populist identities, leading to
the emergence of a political culture supportive of a constitutional form of
democracy. This has resulted in the emergence of a new type of politics organised around demands for transparency and accountability. Such societal
efforts at making public authorities accountable represent a major push toward the constitutionalisation of the state and of the political system.

The form of politicisation described above, as well as the type of interaction that exist within political society, differ greatly from the unrestricted
majoritarianism of past populist movements. The politics of civil society has
contributed to the re-legitimation of rights and constitutionalism as institu-

tions while the dynamics of political society have permitted the stabilisation of a competitive party system. Finally, at the institutional level, the analysis shows that far from operating in an institutional vacuum, the Argentine democratic system has made significant progress towards constitutionalism, both in the direction of a legal stabilisation of state-society relations and of a separation of powers.

A great contribution of O'Donnell's model was to broaden the perspective of democratisation analysis by bringing into the picture long term cultural and institutional variables that might have historically hindered the development of stable democracies. His argument called attention into the praetorian and populist heritage of many of those societies. It is precisely from such a historical comparative standpoint that this commentary has argued that Argentine society has entered a post-praetorian and post-populist political stage.

SUGGESTIONS FOR FURTHER READING

Acuña, Carlos H. "Politics and Economics in the Argentina of the Nineties (Or, Why the Future No Longer Is What It Used to Be)," in *Democracy, Markets, and Structural Reform in Latin America. Argentina, Bolivia, Brazil, Chile, and Mexico,* ed. William C. Smith, Carlos H. Acuña, and Eduardo A. Gamarra. New Brunswick, N.J.: Transaction Publishers, 1994, 265–295.

Bouvard, Marguerite Guzman. *Revolutionizing Motherhood: The Mothers of the Plaza de Mayo.* Wilmington, Del.: Scholarly Resources, 1994.

Brody, Reed, and Felipe González. "Nunca Más: An Analysis of International Instruments on 'Disappearances.'" *Human Rights Quarterly* 19, no. 2 (1997): 365–405.

Brysk, Alison. *The Politics of Human Rights in Argentina: Protest, Change, and Democratization.* Stanford, Calif.: Stanford University Press, 1994.

Corrales, Javier. "Why Argentines Followed Cavallo," in *Technopols,* ed. Jorge Domínguez. University Park: Pennsylvania State University Press, 1997, 49–93.

Feitlowitz, Marguerite. *A Lexicon of Terror: Argentina and the Legacies of Torture.* New York: Oxford University Press, 1998.

Levitsky, Steven. "The 'Normalization' of Argentine Politics." *Journal of Democracy* 10, no. 2 (April 2000): 56–69.

Lewis, Paul. *The Crisis of Argentine Capitalism.* Durham: University of North Carolina Press, 1990.

Murillo, Victoria. "Union Politics, Market-Oriented Reforms, and the Reshaping of Argentine Corporatism," in *The New Politics of Inequality in Latin America,* ed. Douglas A. Chalmers, Carlos M. Vilas, Katherine Hite, Scott B. Martin, Kerianne Piester, and Monique Segarra. New York: Oxford University Press, 1992.

Navarro, Marysa. "Evita's Charismatic Leadership," in *Latin American Populism in Comparative Perspective,* ed. Michael L. Conniff. Albuquerque: University of New Mexico Press, 1982, 47–66.

Peruzzotti, Enrique. "The Nature of the New Argentine Democracy." *Journal of Latin American Studies* 33 (February 2001): 133–155.

Powers, Nancy. *Grassroots Expectations of Democracy and Economy.* Pittsburgh: University of Pittsburgh Press, 2001.

Rock, David. *Argentina, 1516–1987: From Spanish Colonization to the Falklands War and Alfonsin,* rev. ed. Berkeley: University of California Press, 1987.

Smith, William C. *Authoritarianism and the Crisis of the Argentine Political Economy.* Stanford, Calif.: Stanford University Press, 1989.

Wynia, Gary W. *Argentina: Illusions and Realities,* 2nd ed. New York: Holmes and Meier, 1992, 37–59.

USEFUL WEBSITES

Newspapers
Buenos Aires Herald: English language paper
   www.buenosairesherald.com.ar

Clarín
   www.clarin.com.ar

La Nación
   www.lanacion.com.ar

Página 12
   www.pagina12.com.ar

Government
Chamber of Deputies
   www.diputados.gov.ar

Congress
   www.congreso.gov.ar

Ministry of the Economy (English version available)
   www.mecon.gov.ar

President's Office
   www.presidencia.gov.ar

Senate
   www.senado.gov.ar

General
CIA World Fact Book: Resource for general information on Argentina.
   www.odci.gov/cia/publications/factbook/geos/ar.html

Latin American Network Information Center: Comprehensive website housed at the University of Texas with extensive Latin American links on a wide array of topics.
   http://Lanic.utexas.edu

The Vanished Gallery: Website that features documents and photos chronicling victims of the dirty war. (in English and Spanish)
   www.yendor.com/vanished/index.html

CHAPTER **7**

Brazil: The Democratizing Giant

*I*n October 2002, Brazilians went to the polls to elect their president for the fourth time since the restoration of democracy in 1985. The election featured on the losing end, José Serra, a Cornell-educated economics Ph.D. with a distinguished resume as both a politician and an academic. Serra would find that running to be successor of the unpopular incumbent president, Fernando Henrique Cardoso, put him in a difficult position. Cardoso governed Brazil from 1994 to 2002, achieving important successes in the realms of economic and social policy. Under Cardoso, Brazil tamed inflation and became one of the favorite destinations for foreign investment. Yet, by 2002, the president's popularity had declined substantially in part because of a series of corruption scandals, but even more so because neoliberalism had done little to resolve Brazil's deep problems with poverty, inequality, urban violence, and unemployment. Serra, a cabinet minister in the Cardoso government and a critic of neoliberal policy, was left with the difficult task of campaigning against the Cardoso government's neoliberal orientation while simultaneously defending the Cardoso administration. Not surprisingly, it was not a viable campaign strategy.

The winner of the election, Luíz Inácio Lula da Silva, was the exact opposite of his opponent. Da Silva, referred to simply as "Lula," was a veritable working class hero who played a key role in challenging military rule in the 1970s and 1980s and had the distinction of being the losing candidate in the three previous presidential elections of Brazil's young democracy. In contrast to his opponent, Lula, an immigrant from the very poor Northeast to the mega-city São Paulo, had only an eighth-grade education. His formal education ended with the divorce of his parents and the need for Lula to begin selling nuts in the streets as a way to supplement the family income. Ultimately, Lula worked in the economically vital metalworking factories of the city of São Paulo, rising to leadership in the metalworkers' union and subsequently to leadership of the political party he helped found, the Workers' Party (PT). Lula's campaign challenge was also a stark contrast to Serra's political challenge. The PT had been unambiguously opposed to neoliberal economic reform throughout its existence. The PT was openly hostile to global markets, multinational corporations and other forms of foreign investment, freer trade, and American economic policies for the region. These positions emerged out of internal party debates and votes among the organized grassroots base of the PT—the only political party in Brazil with so much internal democracy. Yet, as electoral victory became a more possible scenario over the course of the 1990s, Lula moderated his positions more and more, bringing his party—not entirely willingly—with him as he moved to the political center. By 2002, Lula's campaign had to walk—successfully as it turned out—the fine line between criticizing the government and its neoliberal policies while simultaneously convincing Wall Street, U.S. government officials, and international financial institutions such as the IMF that he would be a fiscally responsible president.

The election was a watershed moment and of interest to observers throughout Latin America as well as in Washington. There are interesting aspects to the election, but this introduction points to two in particular. On one hand, the election was an important indicator of the state of Brazilian democracy. Brazil's history with democracy has been discouraging. After independence in 1821, Brazil retained a monarch—descendants from the Portuguese crown—through 1889. The period thereafter was dubbed "The Republic of Milk and Coffee" after the states (Rio Grande do Sul—milk—and São Paulo—coffee) that dominated the presidency in an essentially corrupt arrangement among elites. In the century following the establishment of this republic, Brazil suffered from repeated military interventions, small-scale revolts, and ultimately a coup, which brought military rule to the country from 1964 to 1985.

The restoration of democracy in 1985 did not, however, put to rest concerns about Brazil's unstable history. The early years of this so-called New Republic did not augur well for the future. The political party system splintered into multiple parties as political freedom allowed politicians to openly campaign and compete. By the first direct presidential election in 1989, thirty-six parties competed for power, with nineteen succeeding in gaining representation in the Congress. Furthermore, most of these parties were loosely organized, relatively incoherent vehicles for gaining access to government patronage resources as opposed to standing for some clear programmatic or ideological goal. Policy deliberations in Congress and negotiations between the executive and the legislature were held hostage to demands for patronage made by members of Congress. The result was a state of general ungovernability and, more specifically, an inability to address the severe economic problems plaguing the country. The situation appeared to worsen when in 1992 the Congress impeached President Fernando Collor de Mello—the first directly elected president since 1960—on corruption charges. Opinion polls showed that Brazilians were highly dissatisfied with democracy and many firmly believed that the country would be better off with the military ruling.

The election of Fernando Henrique Cardoso in 1993 helped to restore some semblance of stability and normalcy to Brazilian politics. Cardoso, an internationally renowned sociologist with a distinguished record as a senator, brought a much-needed dose of integrity, dignity, and technical competence. Over the course of his presidency (1994–1998 and [reelected] 1998–2002), the government enacted a series of significant reforms in the areas of economic and social policy. Brazil became the leading destination for foreign investment in the developing world and poverty declined for a short period into the later 1990s. Nevertheless, Cardoso had to work within Brazil's political system and with the existing political parties. As a result, the government was able to do much less than it had hoped (and promised) and corruption scandals continued to plague important allies of the president. In 1999, Brazil suffered a financial shock similar but less severe than the one that hit Argentina in 2001 (discussed in Chapter 6). In the aftermath, many of the economic gains the country enjoyed in Cardoso's first term weakened and even reversed. The various setbacks and scandals, combined with the government's own political errors eroded Cardoso's political support and helped turn the 2002 presidential election into an explicit referendum on his government's neoliberal orientation.

The striking thing about that election, however, was the extent to which it demonstrated the resilience of Brazilian democracy despite the problems of corruption, crime, poverty, inequality, and regional disparities. Lula, once a figure openly despised and condemned by Brazilian elites, had successfully become an accepted mainstream figure. Some domestic business leaders openly backed his election bid. Even those that didn't went out of their way to openly declare that a Lula victory was not a threat to Brazilian democracy or its economy. Similarly, the image of the Workers' Party had changed as well. In the early 1990s, many voters were concerned that the PT's embrace of socialist and nationalist ideas were unrealistic and that as a result the party lacked the qualities necessary to govern effectively. Over the course of the 1990s, however, the PT won a number of important gubernatorial and mayoral elections and acquired real, practical lessons in governance. By this last election, the PT had gained an acceptance as a legitimate governing party. Thus, the 2002 election stands as a critical testament to the remarkable gains Brazil has made in establishing and maintaining democratic rule.

The election was critical and widely observed for another reason as well—namely that it was an important referendum on the neoliberal reform program. Brazil was the last large Latin American country to implement neoliberal reforms. As the largest economy by far, Brazil was able to maintain the nationalist, state-led, import-substitution industrialization strategy (as discussed in Chapter 3) for a longer time than any other country in the region. Brazil's ISI policies helped foster an enormous (by developing world standards) middle class and domestic industrial community. The growth of these classes was supported by a Brazilian ideology of *grandeza,* or greatness, that envisioned a powerful industrialized Brazil built on a partnership of the state, domestic industry, and multinational corporations. The result was that both Brazilian industrialists and policy-makers resisted neoliberalism as it swept through Latin America.

By the late 1980s, however, neither policy-makers nor industrialists could avoid the conclusion that neoliberal policies were necessary to address chronic, severe economic problems plaguing the country. In particular, inflation was spiraling out of control by the 1989 election, defying repeated dramatic and invasive government plans to tame it. Neoliberal reform finally began in Brazil with the election of Fernando Collor, who campaigned on a pledge to modernize Brazil and kill inflation with a single bullet. He failed in the latter task, but by the time of his impeachment in 1992 he had effectively broken the back of the nationalist, ISI orientation and started Brazil on a gradual and somewhat chaotic road toward neoliberal reform. The chaotic character of the reform process reflected the extraordinary difficulties of negotiating with legislators in Brazil's fragmented party system. With the election of Cardoso in 1993, the erratic pace of reform continued, but building on the base of Collor's reforms, Cardoso was able to advance the reform agenda substantially and, perhaps most importantly, tame inflation. Cardoso's successes secured Brazil's reputation in the international financial community and foreign investment flowed into the country.

But neoliberal reform and praise from international financial institutions were not enough. Perhaps foremost among the limitations of the reform process was that it did not do nearly enough to alleviate the deep, persistent poverty and inequality of Brazilian society. Brazil is one of the most unequal societies in the world—a place where modern wealth comparable to that found in rich democracies stands side by side with crippling, desperate poverty. As much as Cardoso did accomplish, it was not nearly enough to overcome this situation. In addition, Brazil also could not protect itself from the volatility of international investment capital. In 1999, investors lost confidence that the Cardoso government could maintain control over its debts and budget deficits and money poured out of the country rapidly and suddenly. The financial shock undermined many of the accomplishments of the Cardoso administration, weakened his political support, and inflicted significant economic hardship on much of the population. Thus, the 2002 election was also important in highlighting the limitations—economically and politically—of neoliberal reform. To some extent, this election was the most important plebiscite on neoliberalism in Latin America of the past twenty years.

The issues presented in this discussion make up the theme of this chapter. In "Brazil's New Direction," Wendy Hunter examines the future of Brazil under Lula and the PT after their electoral victory. Hunter notes that Brazil seems to be enjoying an impressive degree of democratic stability despite serious problems that include relatively low levels of societal support for democracy, deep poverty, persistent inequality, and perverse political institutional rules.

Bolívar Lamounier addresses one of the fundamental dilemmas noted by Hunter: the way the political system impedes effective and efficient decision making. Lamounier details the functioning of the party system and the electoral system. In both instances, the rules foster the fragmentation of the party system and the weakness of the resulting parties. Party weakness refers to both weakness of party leaders vis-à-vis their members, as well as weakness of the parties in relation to their bases in society. This cluster of traits produces a perverse political situation where the legislature is constantly engaged in a flurry of reform efforts while simultaneously stymied by its own internal logic: thus "hyperactive paralysis."

Finally, Timothy Power and Timmons Roberts offer a distinct perspective on democracy in Brazil. Power and Roberts examine the Brazil of the 1990s, comparing it to the Brazil of the 1960s, and find crucial changes. This "new Brazil" is far likelier to remain committed to democracy because of crucial changes in the structure of society, although important tensions and concerns remain. The authors discuss trends such as the shift from being a largely rural society to a primarily urban one and the rise of television and other means of mass communications. In both of these cases, the change makes citizens more informed and more demanding of political rights and participation. By contrast, steep increases in urban crime make people more tolerant of police and military force to contain it. Thus, even though the tendency is toward a more durable democracy, opponents of authoritarian rule must remain vigilant.

DATA TABLES

Table 7.1
Brazil Fact and Data Sheet

Population (July 2003, estimated):	182,032,604
Ethnic Groups:	White (includes Portuguese, German, Italian, Spanish, and Polish) 55%, mixed white and black 38%, black 6%, other (includes Japanese, Arab, and Amerindian) 1%
Religions:	Roman Catholic 80%
Government Type:	Republic
Capital:	Brasília
Administrative Divisions:	26 states and 1 federal district
Date of Independence:	September 7, 1822
Constitution:	October 5, 1988
Executive Branch:	President Luíz Inácio Lula da Silva, elected October 27, 2002; president and vice president elected on the same ticket by popular election to a 4-year term.
Legislature:	Bicameral National Congress

- Senate has 81 seats. Elected by direct vote to an 8-year term. Distribution of seats as of 2003: PMDB, 19 seats; PFL, 19 seats; PT, 14 seats; PSDB, 11 seats; PDT, 5 seats; PSB, 4 seats; PL, 3 seats; PTB, 3 seats; PPS, 1 seat; PSD, 1 seat; PPB, 1 seat.
- Chamber of Deputies has 513 seats. Elected by proportional representation to a 4-year term. Distribution of seats as of 2003: PT, 91 seats; PFL, 84 seats; PMDB, 74 seats; PSDB, 71 seats; PPB, 49 seats; PL, 26 seats; PTB, 26 seats; PSB, 22 seats; PDT, 21 seats; PPS, 15 seats; PCdoB, 12 seats; PRONA, 6 seats; PV, 5 seats; other parties, 11 seats.

Main Political Parties:	Brazilian Democratic Movement Party (PMDB), Brazilian Labor Party (PTB), Brazilian Social Democracy Party (PSDB), Brazilian Socialist Party (PSB), Brazilian Progressive Party (PPB), Communist Party of Brazil (PCdoB), Democratic Labor Party (PDT), Green Party (PV), Liberal Front Party (PFL), Liberal Party (PL), National Order Reconstruction Party (PRONA), Popular Socialist Party (PPS), Social Democratic Party (PSD), Workers' Party (PT)
Military Spending (FY1999):	U.S. $13.408 billion
Military Spending, Percentage of GDP (FY1999):	1.9

(*cont.*)

Table 7.1 (cont.)
Brazil Fact and Data Sheet

GDP (2002, estimated):	PPP $1.34 trillion
GDP Composition by Sector (2001, estimated):	Agriculture: 8% Industry: 36% Services: 56%
Main Industries:	Textiles, shoes, chemicals, cement, lumber, iron ore, tin, steel, aircraft, motor vehicles and parts, other machinery and equipment
Main Agricultural Products:	Coffee, soybeans, wheat, rice, corn, sugarcane, cocoa, citrus, beef
Export Partners (2001):	Brazil, 26.5%; United States, 24.2%; Argentina, 11.6%; Germany, 5.4%; Netherlands, 4.4%
Import Partners (2001):	United States, 27.4%; Argentina, 13.5%; Germany, 8.9%; Japan, 5%
External Debt (2002):	U.S. $222.4 billion

Table 7.2

Presidents of Brazil

Tenure	President
1889–1891	Deodoro da Fonseca
1891–1894	Floriano Peixoto
1894–1898	Prudente de Moraes
1898–1902	Campos Sales
1902–1906	Rodrigues Alves
1906–1909	Afonso Pena
1909–1910	Nilo Peçanha
1910–1914	Hermes da Fonseca
1914–1918	Venceslau Brás
1918	Rodrigues Alves (died before assuming)
1918–1919	Delfim Moreira
1919–1922	Epitácio Pessoa
1922–1926	Artur Bernardes
1926–1930	Washington Luís[1]
1930–1934	Getúlio Dorneles Vargas—Temporary Government
1934–1937	Getúlio Dorneles Vargas—Constitutional Government
1937–1945	Getúlio Dorneles Vargas—Dictatorship
1945–1946	José Linhares
1946–1951	Eurico Gaspar Dutra
1951–1954	Getúlio Dorneles Vargas[1]
1954–1956	Café Filho, Carlos Luz, Nereu Ramos
1956–1961	Juscelino Kubitschek
1961	Jânio Quadros[2]
1961–1964	João Goulart[1]
1964–1967	Humberto Castelo Branco[3]
1967–1969	Arthur da Costa e Silva[3]
1969–1974	Emilio Garrastazu Médici[3]
1974–1979	Ernesto Geisel[3]
1979–1985	João Baptista de Oliveira Figueiredo[3]
1985	Tancredo Neves (died before assuming)
1985–1990	José Sarney
1990–1992	Fernando Collor de Mello[4]
1992–1995	Itamar Franco
1995–2003	Fernando Henrique Cardoso
2003–present	Luíz Inácio Lula da Silva

[1]Removed by coup.

[2]Resigned.

[3]Military.

[4]Impeached.

7.1   Brazil's New Direction (2003)

WENDY HUNTER

On 27 October 2002, the voters of Brazil chose Luiz Inácio Lula da Silva of the Workers' Party (PT) to be their next president, giving him a wide margin of victory with 61.3 percent in a two-candidate runoff against José Serra of the Social Democratic Party (PDSB). Does the election—on his fourth try—of this lathe operator turned trade union leader and the ascendance of his leftist party signal a historic shift in Brazilian politics? What are the implications of a Lula presidency for democracy in Brazil, and what is the larger situation of that democracy now?

Should 2002 be seen as marking a new era in Brazilian politics? Is it the start of a period in which a programmatic leftist party that has championed popular participation, accountability, and redistributive change supplants the political clientelism, social elitism, and technocratic policy making for which Brazil is known? Or is it wiser to focus on the pragmatic adjustments that the PT has made, the continuing sway of conservative forces, and the multitude of constraints—political and economic, domestic and international—that will hem in efforts to make major changes?

On the one hand, the election of a candidate who is a true outsider is a dramatic break with the pattern of Brazilian politics since the postauthoritarian period began in 1985. President José Sarney (1985–90), who inaugurated the civilian regime, had been a leading member of the official government party under the military regime that ruled from 1964 to 1985. His successor, the disgraced Fernando Collor de Mello (1990–92), had similar political origins. After serving as an opposition Brazilian Democratic Movement (MDB) senator during the military period, Fernando Henrique Cardoso played a leading role in brokering Brazil's transition to democracy, forging an array of compromises with outgoing actors and solidifying his establishment credentials, albeit as a moderate social democrat affiliated initially with the PMDB and then the PDSB.

Sarney, Collor, and Cardoso all came from elite backgrounds in a society where class origins still mean a great deal. While the former two hailed from oligarchic families in the Northeast, Cardoso was the son and grandson of army generals and was a distinguished academic who had spent part of his career teaching social sciences at Stanford and Cambridge universities. Lula

Wendy Hunter, "Brazil's New Direction." *Journal of Democracy* 14, no. 2 (2003): 151–161. © National Endowment for Democracy and The Johns Hopkins University Press. Reprinted with permission of The Johns Hopkins University Press.

is the son of hardscrabble tenant farmers from the poverty-stricken Northeast. With his election, the exclusive club of Brazilian presidents has broadened its membership.

The PT now holds 91 of the 513 Chamber of Deputies seats and 14 of the 81 Senate seats, making it the single largest party in Congress. In 1986, it controlled 16 of 487 lower-house seats and had no Senate seats. The story behind the increase is one of steady growth in every election, not merely in the large industrial cities of the country but also in less-developed regions such as the Northeast, an oligarchic bastion. Although it is not without internal factions, the PT is the most ideologically coherent and disciplined party in a field dotted with parties whose politicians possess few principled commitments and have been known to switch allegiances in order to get ahead.

LEAVING THE LEFT BEHIND?

While rejecting the patronage-based politics and social elitism associated with the right, the PT has also tried to distance itself from some of the orthodoxies of the old left, including populism, corporatist labor ideology, and excessive centralization. The party's hallmark is its embrace of participation, accountability, and transparency, as exemplified in the participatory-budgeting programs for which PT-run municipal governments have become well known. Core PT supporters include members of the largest labor confederation, the Central Unica dos Trabalhadores; middle-class intellectuals; elements of the Catholic Church; and new social movements such as the one that defends the cause of Brazil's landless agricultural workers.

The relative tranquility of the 2002 campaign is noteworthy as well. In 1989, when the PT ran a strong race (it nearly beat Collor), there was severe left-right polarization and a spate of antidemocratic machinations as traditional contenders—the military, big business, and large landowners—warned that chaos would follow a PT victory. While the most recent election stimulated financial circles to express concern about the economic impact of a Lula presidency, the public conduct of other elites suggested a basic acceptance of the outcome that eventually transpired. That their respect for the electoral process was strong enough to override their (presumed) substantive preferences suggests a significant maturing of Brazilian democracy.

All this notwithstanding, other signs suggest that the 2002 election results should be interpreted neither as a massive rejection of the Cardoso administration's market-oriented approach to development nor as a resounding endorsement of the PT's program, an impression made all the stronger when one considers that all the other PT candidates combined drew barely half the number of votes that Lula himself received.

The PT's dominant faction, known as the Articulação, has turned ever more pragmatic. While party moderates began to distance themselves from socialist rhetoric and symbolism even before Lula's third bid for the presidency in 1998, further edging away from radicalism took place as the 2002 race loomed. Throughout the campaign, beyond making superficial changes toward a "lighter" image, Lula strove to project moderation. He pledged to work within the political principles enshrined in the 1988 Constitution, and to be mindful of the needs of markets both at home and abroad. He expressed his commitment to fiscal responsibility, debt repayment, low inflation, and most notably the International Monetary Fund. He also promised to pursue new policies to boost employment, wages, and exports while fighting poverty and inequality. He condemned the violent tactics of the Movement of Landless Rural Laborers (MST) while acknowledging that the problem of landlessness desperately needed to be addressed. He broke with the party's previously restrictive coalition policy and forged a crucial link to the rightist Liberal Party (PL), whose leader is a business entrepreneur and whose ranks include voters from Brazil's conservative-leaning evangelical Christian churches. The words "socialist" and "socialism" were absent from the PT's official 2002 platform. In short, the Lula who ran in 2002 was not the Lula who had run in 1989, 1994, or 1998. It was this moderation—combined with an electorate exasperated by the lost promise of Cardoso's economic policies—that enabled Lula to shatter his customary 30 percent ceiling and take 46.4 percent in the first round, thereby setting up his landslide victory over Serra in the runoff.

The exigencies of electoral politics and economic globalization, coupled with the self-examination that PT leaders undertook after losing the 1998 presidential election, induced a move to the middle. At the time of this writing in late February 2003, the new government seems to be holding its course. The appointment of an economic team headed by figures such as Finance Minister Antônio Palocci and Central Bank president Henrique Meirelles, is perhaps the clearest evidence of this. Both intend to guarantee fiscal and monetary stability. Meirelles is a former director of the Bank of Boston and ex-federal deputy elected on the center-left PSDB ticket.

ANATOMY OF A VICTORY

A key point in Lula's favor and a big problem for Serra was simply that the latter—a man with more administrative experience and arguably more technical competence than Lula—was Cardoso's handpicked successor. The outgoing president had become widely popular after taming inflation with the 1994 Real Plan, but fell from grace in the wake of the 1999 currency devaluation and a recession that hurt real wages as well as employment. The public perception was that Cardoso preferred price stability and the approval of foreign lenders to growth and jobs for Brazilians. By 2002, sizeable shares of people polled before the runoff said that they were planning to vote for Lula as a protest against Cardoso. Besides losing the presidency, the PSDB and its allies had to endure substantial losses in both houses of Congress as well. Voters did not want to risk the economic stability that Cardoso's policies had achieved, nor did they want to reject the market model altogether, yet they did want change.

A splintering of the political center and right contributed crucially to the PT's success as well. In 1989, centrist and right-leaning forces had managed to close ranks before facing Lula in a runoff, but they could not repeat the feat in 2002. Moreover, no single candidate had sufficient personal appeal to prevail among the voters of the newly fragmented coalition.

Recognition of the continuing strength of conservative forces in the political system provides further perspective on the PT's recent advances. The Liberal Front Party (PFL) and the Party of the Brazilian Democratic Movement (PMDB) continue to have substantial weight in the Chamber of Deputies and Senate. Among their ranks (especially in the PFL) are scores of politicians known for their strongly conservative views and their control over patronage networks. For the most part, the political elite remains narrow in social terms as well. Embodying this image is former Brazilian president José Sarney (PMDB), the new president of the Senate. Cardoso resorted to using state resources to "buy" the legislative support of the political class on a number of key occasions. It is less certain that Lula will rely on such a strategy to get things done. As of this writing, he can count on 250 votes in the Chamber and 30 in the Senate, too little to guarantee the passage of ordinary legislation, much less constitutional amendments, which require 257 and 308 votes, respectively. Further weakening the PT's grip on the political system is its thin representation among Brazil's influential governors: Only 3 states out of 27 have PT chief executives, while the opposition PSDB and PMDB have a total of 12 governorships. The opposition parties' control over state governments will give these parties significant leverage when it comes to various federal reform efforts and policies. Ironically, the party that in many ways would seem most ideologically open to Lula's platform, Cardoso and Serra's PSDB, is in the opposition. While PSDB politicians claim they will not be as obstructionist as the PT was when it was in opposition, it is too early to tell whether they mean those words. Legislators from the PMDB could play a significant swing role as well. Lula will need to cultivate ideologically sympathetic members of the PSDB and PMDB in order both to broaden his coalition and to provide a counterweight to the most conservative elements within his own camp. For now it appears certain that Lula will have to work with narrower congressional support than Cardoso enjoyed throughout most of his term, with all that this implies regarding the maneuvering room available to the new president.

THE QUESTION OF POLITICAL STABILITY

Could a PT-led government—especially if the economy deteriorates or the polity becomes polarized—present a threat to the stability of democracy? Brazilian democracy has survived a number of serious crises since the 1985 return to civilian rule. These include President Collor's 1992 impeachment on corruption charges and subsequent resignation; the failure of no fewer than seven economic-reform packages between 1985 and 1993; political turmoil during the interim presidency of Itamar Franco (1993–94) that threatened to result in a Fujimori-style self-coup; and the 1999 currency devaluation, which threatened the country's hard-won economic stability and undermined the broad support that Cardoso had previously enjoyed. Over the same period, political changes occurred that might have presaged unrest. Civilians eventually challenged the armed forces over numerous political prerogatives that senior military officers had inherited from the authoritarian period and had used to exercise tutelage over the new democracy in its initial years. The Collor government reduced the military's once-dominant presence in the intelligence and national-security agencies. President Cardoso abolished separate ministries for the army, navy, and air force and transferred many of their functions to a civilian-run defense ministry. Taken together, the presidents since 1985 represent a movement from right to left across the ideological spectrum. Whereas Sarney and Collor had been loyalists under the military regime, Cardoso came home from exile to spearhead the institutionalized opposition as Senate leader of the MDB. As president, he moved to the center but retained some social democratic inclinations Lula, an "authentic" member of the working class and former leader of the "new unionism," is identified with a party of a far more radical tradition and vision than Cardoso's MDB or more recent PSDB.

In the midst of these and related developments, Brazilian democracy has proven remarkably resilient and sustainable. Even in the worst of times, capitalists have continued to invest in the Brazilian economy, social tensions have rarely resulted in debilitating mass protests, and the military has kept its saber-rattling within limits. Relative to the previous democratic era, elite groups have been quiescent, never threatening to topple governments, much less the democratic regime itself. Brazil's third-wave democracy is more stable than its second-wave democracy (1945–64), and has shown surprising increases in adaptability since its inception in 1985.

At first glance, this resiliency is surprising. Brazil is well known for social conditions—deep poverty, sharp inequalities, teeming urban slums, and weak social safety nets—that are not usually associated with democratic durability. The polity, moreover, features both strong presidentialism and a highly fragmented party system—a one-two punch that should, in theory, undermine coherent policy making and render conflicts tougher to solve. Moreover, opinion polls suggest that citizens feel a less than wholehearted commitment to democracy. In the 2002 Latinobarómetro survey, only 37 percent of Brazilian respondents agreed with the statement, "Democracy is preferable to any other kind of government." This is 20 percentage points below the average for Latin America—a region with a tenuous relationship to democratic government. Moreover, it represents a steep decline from the 50 percent who expressed support for democracy in 1996 and 1997, and stands as one of the sharpest drops on this measure in Latin America.

What then accounts for Brazil's impressive democratic stability since 1985? To begin with, the sheer complexity and heterogeneity of Brazilian society make it hard to organize for any massive change. Stark barriers divide the urban and rural poor, formal and informal workers. The growth of different branches of industry and of the service sector has created further divisions, preventing even organized workers from advancing their demands in a united fashion. Ideological fragmentation and varying degrees of militancy further limit the labor movement's potential to challenge and transform the status quo. Instead, as in the corporatist system that President Getúlio Vargas established in the 1930s (albeit to a lesser degree), workers advance their narrow interests, often to the detriment of the working class more collectively.

The persistence of conservative forces and the ongoing reliance on patronage networks, especially in poor rural and urban areas, act like an anchor, steadying democracy but also limiting it. Powerful elites including landowners, business interests, and politicians of the right continue to have substantial representation in Congress. One estimate holds that landed elites controlled about 30 percent of the seats in the Chamber of Deputies during the Cardoso administration. Family-based oligarchies persist in states such as Maranhão, Rio Grande do Norte, and Santa Catarina. Central to the national-level influence of these oligarchies and other conservative forces is the overrepresentation of rural areas in the heavily malapportioned Chamber of Deputies. The politics of clientelism—sometimes with a modern twist—is still alive and well in some parts of Brazil.

While Brazil's political system safeguards elite interests, it also offers channels of influence to new forces that might otherwise take an "antisystem" stand. An electoral system based on open-list proportional representation with a relatively large number of members elected, on average, from each district keeps entry barriers low and gives space to new outside forces such as parties advocating popular interests and inclusionary practices. That a party like the PT was able to integrate activists and make steady electoral headway throughout the 1980s and 1990s no doubt helped to legitimate democracy in the eyes of core PT members. Innovation and success in government—most notably at the municipal level—helped the PT to widen its coalition, which in turn gave the moderate leadership within the party a boost and eased fears about the PT's advance.

The marked prodemocratic shift in post–Cold War international norms has also shielded Brazilian democracy. The country's commitment to a market-oriented transnational economic order raises the costs of a break-down in democratic rules and procedures. Should domestic factors be insufficient to secure democratic stability, external forces such as pressure from other democracies could serve as final safeguards. Indeed, they may already have done so: In late 1993, when democracy's prospects were arguably at their lowest ebb of the entire post-1985 period, persons close to President Itamar Franco began sounding out elite support for a Fujimori-style executive coup. They got few takers, in part perhaps because there were fresh memories of how U.S. condemnation had helped to scotch an attempted presidential putsch in Guatemala earlier that same year.

MALIGN RULES AND PRACTICES

While Brazil's "third wave" democracy has proven remarkably adaptive and stable, it has been less impressive in other ways, bearing out the observation that democratization is a complex process in which change unfolds unevenly. Informal practices and patterns as well as formal rules diminish the quality of Brazilian democracy.

The persistence of extreme poverty bars legions of Brazil's citizens from meaningful participation in the democratic system. Absolute levels of deprivation are stark, with about 50 out of 175 million deemed poor, an incidence that is above average for a middle-income country (estimated per-capita GDP in 2000 was US$7,400 in purchasing-power–parity terms). The population as a whole is poorly educated, especially in relation to Brazil's overall level of development. In cities and the countryside alike, poverty renders voters vulnerable to the machinations of patronage-wielding politicians who buy votes with handouts. This perverts the participatory ideal of democracy. It also diminishes the potential for formal democratic participation to generate policies meant to advance human welfare in more systematic ways. While electoral rights were broadened in 1985 to include illiterates, this segment of the population (estimated at 15 percent by the World Bank) is among the most likely to be manipulated by politicians who rely on patronage networks and are indifferent or even opposed to institutionalized policies aimed at poverty reduction.

Pronounced social inequality poses its own challenges to democratic ideals. Levels of income inequality in Brazil are among the highest in the world. Roughly 63 percent of total income goes to the wealthiest 20 percent of the population, while the poorest 20 percent gets a mere 2.5 percent. Government policy on taxes and public benefits favors the most affluent as well. As a case in point, the World Bank estimates that "less than one percent of social security spending reaches the poorest ten percent of Brazilians, while about fifty percent is cornered by the wealthiest ten percent," This reflects a pension system that evolved by incorporating privileged categories of public servants and private-sector employees over time, leaving most of those in the informal sector to fend for themselves. The most outrageous example of corporatist privilege is the system of lifetime pensions paid to unmarried adult daughters of deceased military officers, numbering presently some 58,000 women, many of whom have been all but legally married for decades. The Cardoso government gave new attention and resources to the social area, but did little to narrow stark differences in people's civil status and public entitlements. Inequality on this scale effectively means that Brazilians enjoy widely varied rights as citizens.

Unequal treatment is sharply manifest in the legal sphere as well. Poor people are frequent targets of arbitrary police violence and have little recourse when they are victimized. The law often goes unenforced against private thugs or paramilitaries when they assault rural unionists and their followers. Corruption is widespread among politicians and public officials. In a recent 91-country ranking of corruption (from best to worst), Transparency International placed Brazil 46th, far below Chile, Costa Rica, and members of the OECD. While public authorities launch many more investigations than they did before 1985, and guilty officials sometimes lose their posts, the prospect of convicted offenders going to jail is almost nil. While the double standards of the legal system are not necessarily codified, a uniform system of rights and obligations among Brazilians does not exist in practice. As a consequence, the institutions of law and justice lack legitimacy and the realization of democratic citizenship remains limited.

Of the formal rules that dilute the quality of democracy, the most salient concern the electoral system. As noted above, representation in the Chamber of Deputies is lopsidedly rural due to longstanding malapportionment. There is a huge gap between the share of legislative seats allocated to urban electoral districts and the share of the population that actually lives in them. It is generally accepted that in federal systems the upper house of the national legislature will represent geographic units of varying population more or less equally. Yet Brazil has *lower-house* malapportionment that exceeds the Latin American average and greatly exacerbates the skewing effects that already stem from the way the Senate is apportioned. The city of São Paulo alone, for instance, is more than 50 seats short of its proportional share in the Chamber of Deputies.

Even those not committed to the one person, one vote ethic should recognize on practical grounds that such a situation can hamper governability. By creating a rural bias, malapportionment generally strengthens the patronage-wielders and weakens more progressive forces. It invites chronic conflict between a conservative-leaning, malapportioned legislature and a president chosen by something that closely resembles a national plebiscite. Relatedly, as Richard Snyder and David Samuels point out, malapportionment can contribute to the "proliferation of subnational authoritarian enclaves." That Brazil's Congress acts as a megaphone amplifying the voices of conservatives almost certainly contributes to stability, but it is just as clear that this exacts a price in terms of coherent governance.

Brazil's unique system of open-list proportional representation and districts of high average magnitude is similarly double-edged. While the openness and flexibility of this electoral system facilitate the entry of small parties, thus giving voters more options and bolstering stability, weighing against these advantages is the negative effect on governability. Volumes have been dedicated to analyzing and dilating upon these consequences. Suffice it to say here that current electoral arrangements have encouraged the proliferation of weak and undisciplined patronage-oriented parties, reinforced personalistic leadership, and obstructed the legislative process. Brazil's electoral rules also diminish accountability, raising the chances of poor legislative performance and even corruption and other forms of malfeasance. Since one top vote-getter can lay claim to additional legislative seats for his or her party, even politicians who as individuals lack the confidence of voters may end up holding office.

The deepening of democracy in Brazil therefore demands reforms in various spheres. If the poor are to become full citizens and not merely the objects of demagogues and patronage handouts, the country will have to find ways of raising levels of education and material wealth. Socioeconomic inequality and distinctions in social privileges must narrow until there is a modicum of common ground among citizens. The civil component of citizenship must also be extended. Brazilians need to be able to count on state institutions to secure their civil rights, either as protections or immunities. All individuals—regardless of social status—must be equally subject to the rule of law. Finally, toward the greater goal of enhancing governability, political reforms must be undertaken to strengthen parties, enhance accountability, and correct for distortions in representation.

Addressing these and related issues will pose a series of formidable challenges for the new government. In light of the political system's capacity to absorb change, there is little doubt that it would take a crisis of unprecedented proportions to derail Brazilian democracy altogether. The big question is whether the multiple constraints at hand and Lula's commitment to pursuing a pragmatic political course will ultimately allow his government to carry out even the most basic of reforms in these areas.

CAN LULA COME THROUGH?

What prospects exist for a PT-led government to deepen democracy along these lines? Alleviating extreme poverty and enhancing social equity are top priorities. The government sent a strong public message to this effect in showcasing its Zero Hunger program, a PT-designed policy innovation aimed at eradicating malnutrition among 23 million Brazilians. It has also pledged to reform social security in equity- and efficiency-enhancing ways—a goal that eluded even the politically skillful Cardoso—although doing so risks alienating core PT supporters who benefit from the current system, especially unionized public-sector workers, schoolteachers, and university professors. As has happened time and time again, however, measures to strengthen the rule of law and reform political institutions will likely be postponed for the sake of attending to urgent economic and social demands. The political capital it would require to take on these formidable problem areas, coupled with the lack of immediately obvious benefits to voters from even successful reform efforts, render them low priorities.

At center stage are the economy and the social sphere. Lula has promised a new economic model that will raise exports, employment, wages, and government expenditures to alleviate poverty, improve social services, and enhance public security. He will need to walk a tightrope between making good on social commitments and respecting Brazil's very tight economic constraints, which include debt repayment and budgetary austerity. In advancing his progressive social agenda he will have to keep conservative antagonists at bay. In addressing the country's severe economic problems, he will need to keep critics on the left in check, including trade unions, the landless movement, and perhaps most of all, the radical elements within his own party, who have already begun to demand greater decision-making influence over the government.

Expectations run high—especially in relation to employment, wages, and poverty alleviation—and failure to fulfill core promises could result in bitter disappointment. Approximately 70 percent of respondents in one recent poll expressed confidence that the government would reduce poverty and unemployment. Nearly three-quarters said that they thought Lula would make a good-to-excellent president. This compares with 66 percent for Cardoso at a similar point in his administration.

Such high hopes mean that Lula will have to produce results quickly in order to govern effectively. Present circumstances test Lula's leadership talents like never before. So far, he has shown imagination and creativity in this regard. The flagship Zero Hunger program, for instance, is politically unassailable since it speaks to such a basic need and can be accomplished within reasonable financial limits. It has quickly become the darling of major institutions such as the World Bank and the UN Food and Agriculture Organization. It aims to generate the kind of immediate concrete results that will be crucial to sustaining the popularity required to implement much-needed structural reforms in the economy. Will the extraordinary talent and fortitude that it took for Lula to rise from poverty to the presidency of a major country like Brazil help him defy the odds at a broader national level? Only time will tell, and yet one thing is already clear: The very fact that he is president speaks volumes about how far Brazilian democracy has come.

7.2 Brazil: An Assessment of the Cardoso Administration (2003)

BOLÍVAR LAMOUNIER

Early in his first term President Fernando Henrique Cardoso told an Italian newspaper that "Brazil [is] an easy country to govern." At first glance, one is tempted to think he was right. Setbacks there certainly were, but the achievements of the Cardoso administration are quite impressive. First and foremost, the Brazilian government managed to keep inflation under control (in itself a major feat, given Brazil's long record of currency instability), despite the three severe blows that originated in Mexico in 1994, in Asia in 1997, and in Russia in 1998. Despite some initial confusion due to the precipitous devaluation of January 1999, the country successfully moved from its traditionally rigid to a floating exchange rate system. Reform of the banking system—including privatization of banks owned by the member-states and opening up the market for foreign banks—was another important achievement of the Cardoso administration, one that partly explains why Brazil was quickly able to overcome the devaluation crisis of 1999. In fact, progress in privatization includes sectors such as telecoms and the mining giant, Companhia Vale do Rio Doce (CVRD), once regarded as nearly sacred public monopolies. Fiscal performance also improved markedly in terms of both government attitude and legal framework, the latter including the adoption in 1998 of an ambitious Fiscal Responsibility Law. Substantial progress was also made in social policy, notably in land reform and in the quality of government spending in education. In order to achieve his policy goals, Cardoso managed to get the country's notoriously cumbersome legislature to approve a remarkable number of bills and constitutional amendments.

But clearly, Cardoso's record and his remark about how easy it is to govern Brazil are rather like that glass that may be half-empty or half-full, depending on how we look at it. Economic growth rates for the six-year period considered above were quite modest in view of the country's needs, reflecting persistent constraints due to inadequate infrastructure, fiscal imbalances (notably in the financing of social security), and external vulnerabilities (with mediocre export performance, despite the substantial devaluation of early 1999). Rather than promoting tax reform, the administration chose to increase tax collection on the basis of the existing flawed taxation framework and specifically on "cascading" taxes that seriously hinder the economy's efficiency and external competitiveness. Last but not least, the administration took a lot of blame for the energy crisis of 2001, interpreted by most Brazilians as a result of under-investment combined with poor short-term management.

On a broader historical canvas, not limited to Cardoso's presidency, the fact is that from 1986 to 1993 Brazilians witnessed the dramatic failure of five successive attempts to stabilize their economy, chronic super-inflation aggravating the country's steep social inequalities, the impeachment of the first elected president in twenty-nine years, numerous corruption scandals and serious clashes between the branches and levels of government. This al-ternative picture suggests that Brazil is anything but "easy to govern." More than anything else, Cardoso's success may reflect the high caliber of his per-sonal leadership and the inevitability of much of his reform agenda; indeed, plausible as that evaluation may have sounded at the beginning, Cardoso would later publicly admit that that was not a felicitous statement.

Cardoso's administration may well turn out to be seen as one of the most effective in Brazilian history, but the extent to which it will leave irreversible improvements in Brazil's governance patterns is a moot point. The perfor-mance of individual presidents will of course vary over time, but the quality and effectiveness of the Brazilian political system as such remain open to question. The key point seems to be that it is a system structurally geared to-ward dispersing and diluting political power, constantly eroding the strength and cohesion of any majority. Not by chance, this description strongly evokes Arend Lijphart's consensus model of democracy, which he opposes to the majoritarian or Westminster one. In his study of thirty-six countries, Lijphart claims that Westminster democracies do not perform bet-ter than consensus democracies in terms of macroeconomic management. Important as his study is, the policy process under the majoritarian model tends to be more effective and intelligible to the common citizen than under the consensus model. This is because the need to include and obtain the consent of many actors and veto players to make relevant decisions is more manageable under the majoritarian system. The consensus model, Lijphart argues, is more adequate for some types of societies:

> In the most deeply divided societies, like Northern Ireland, majority rule spells majority dictatorship and civil strife rather than democracy. What such societies need is a democratic regime that emphasizes consensus instead of op-position, that includes rather than excludes, and that tries to maximize the size of the ruling majority instead of being satisfied with a bare majority. . . . The consensus model is obviously appropriate for less divided but still heteroge-neous countries, and it is a reasonable alternative to the Westminster model even in fairly homogeneous countries.

Is Brazil a "deeply divided" society in this sense—and hence one in need of a consensus democracy? Let us first look at the cleavages structuring polit-ical conflict in the country. Political conflict in Brazil is clearly unidimen-sional, centered on the distribution of wealth and income among social classes and regions, the latter pitting the richer regions of the South and Southeast against the poorer of the North, Northeast, and Center-West. There are marked differentials by race in a variety of social indicators associated with upward social mobility, but few analysts would include race among the main determinants of political behavior and open political conflict. Social inequality is obviously steep, but ethnic and religious (not to speak of linguistic and cultural) cleavages are mild in comparison with other large countries. It is a heterogeneous society, but one with a much simpler cleavage structure than India, South Africa or Indonesia, or even the United States, to name but a few of the world's big countries. In short, it is not a divided society in the sense emphasized by Lijphart. I would wholeheartedly grant that Brazil's heterogeneity justifies some measure of "consensus" democracy, but not the extremely "consociational" (to use Lijphart's original terminology) character of the country's existing political arrangements. In this sense, President Cardoso got it right by saying it wrong. What he probably meant to say was that, given its comparatively simpler cleavage structure, Brazil should be easier to govern than it has been during the whole of the twentieth century.

This [article] begins with an evaluation of Brazil's political system—a combination of presidentialism and consociationalism, which ultimately hinders democratic governance. A highly fragmented political party system with loose party discipline, as well as a cumbersome judiciary and an extremely federative structure, further complicate governability. The [article] analyzes the implications of "provisional measures" for democratic governance—a policy instrument utilized by the Brazilian executive to bypass the legislature. The second part of the [article] explores the effects of plebiscitarian democratic regimes on Brazil's political system, with a special emphasis on Cardoso's ability to improve the presidentialist/consociationalist system through a broad-based legislative coalition. In particular, it delineates Cardoso's strategies for navigating Brazil's multiple economic and political challenges, showing how Cardoso's patient and skillful political management style (as well as changes in the global political and economic context) helped to facilitate effective policymaking. Finally, the [article] analyzes the development of Brazil's political system during the Cardoso presidency and the challenges that lie ahead for future administrations.

BRAZIL'S POLITICAL STRUCTURE: MUCH ADO ABOUT LITTLE

Consociationalism cum Presidentialism

The dispersion of political power in Brazil is generated by the combination of multipartyism, coalition governments, strong bicameralism, robust federalism, judicial review, and an extensive and detailed constitution protected by supermajority amendment rules. It would take us far afield to inquire into why the 1987–88 Constitutional Assembly chose to greatly reinforce the consociational character of the political system—but the fact is that it did. When the constitution-makers set about to reorganize the country's political institutions after twenty-one years of military rule, they came close to turning the country into a full-fledged consensus democracy. But perhaps aware that they were going too far, they chose at the same time to keep a key anti-consociational feature: the pure presidential system of government established in the early days of the Republic, at the end of the nineteenth century. I have elsewhere argued that this combination of consensus institutions with presidentialism is at the root of Brazil's institutional difficulties. In the case of Brazil, as in much of Latin America, presidentialism *cum* consociationalism further weakens already fragile institutions because, as soon as presidents begin to face the complexities of faltering party and legislative support, they tend to bypass the legislature and appeal directly to "the people." Populism, or plebiscitarianism, as I prefer to call it, is a constant temptation in systems characterized by a low level of institutional consolidation and where the executive must somehow overcome the hurdles posed by consociationalism. To this structural feature some historians often add the "Iberian authoritarian legacy," an argument which I prefer not to take up here. My point is simply that, in the institutional context just described, the executive seeks to outflank the legislative and the judicial branches (notably by abusing the prerogative of issuing decree-laws), while these and the whole myriad of "consociational" institutional agents react, attempting to rein in the executive using the give-and-take of legislative and party politics, porkbarrel, and power-sharing, or else by attempting altogether to undermine and delegitimize presidential power.

Plebiscitarianism is obviously not a Latin American invention. Even in the United States and Europe presidents and party leaders occasionally resort to plebiscitarian appeals. But in Brazil and in Latin America, the formal institutions of government, the party system, and the civil society organizations that together should temper and countervail such appeals are far weaker. Conflicts thus tend to occur more frequently and to be sharper and more dangerous. Under such conditions, presidentialism *cum* consociationalism does not seem conducive to democratic stability and effectiveness.

Political Parties and the Party System

Political parties played a key role in Brazil's transition to democracy by mobilizing popular opposition to the military regime (1964–85). This task, however, was facilitated by the structure of the party system imposed by the military in 1965, which allowed the existence of only two parties, one to support and the other to oppose the government. In 1979 an electoral reform enacted by the government of General João Figueiredo, the last military president, and designed to divide the opposition, made room for the emergence of new parties. Table 1 shows that five parties obtained lower chamber seats after the 1982 elections. Yet communist parties were still legally banned. With the formal return to civilian rule in 1985, all restrictions

Table 1

Seat Shares per Party in the Chamber of Deputies After Five Elections, 1983–1999 (in percents)

Party	1983	1987	1991	1995	1999
PDS/PPR/PPB	49.1	6.8	8.3	10.1	11.7
PMDB	41.8	53.4	21.5	20.9	16
PDT	4.8	4.9	9.1	6.6	4.9
PTB	2.7	3.5	6.8	6	6
PT	1.7	3.3	7	9.6	11.3
PFL		24.2	16.5	17.3	20.7
PDC		1	4.4		
PSB		0.2	2.2	2.9	3.7
PC do B		0.6	1	1.9	1.4
PCB/PPS		0.6	0.6	0.4	0.6
PL		1.2	3	2.5	2.3
PSC		0.2	1	0.6	0.4
PSDB			7.4	12.1	19.3
PRN			8.2	0.2	
PMN			0.2	0.8	0.4
PRP			0.2	0.2	
PTR			1		
PSD			0.2	0.6	0.6
PRS			0.8		
PRT			0.2		
PST			0.4		0.2
PP*				7	
PRONA					0.2
PV				0.2	0.2
PSL					0.2
Total (= 100%)	479	487	503	513	513

Source: Jairo Marconi Nicolau, *Multipartidarismo e Democracia* (Rio de Janeiro: Fundação Getúlio Vargas, 1996), 78; and Brazil—Tribunal Superior Eleitoral, available at www.tse.gov.br.

*The PP merged with the PPR to form the PPB.

to the formation of parties were lifted. This resulted in the proliferation of many new parties, which contested the 1986 election for Congress, which would become a Constitutional Congress in 1987–88. Seven new parties entered the Brazilian Congress, although six of them held one percent or less of lower chamber seats, and the largest party, the Brazilian Democratic Movement Party (PMDB), commanded a majority of seats (53.4 percent).

At this juncture, Brazil's party system seemed more manageable. However, during the workings of the Constitutional Congress, the PMDB would prove to be a fissiparous party, and would suffer a major breakaway (today's Brazilian Social Democracy Party [PSDB]) in 1988. The decline of the PMDB, the standard-bearer of the opposition to the military, coupled with the defeat of all major parties by the outsider Fernando Collor de Mello in the 1989 presidential race, constituted a turning point in the evolution of Brazil's post-authoritarian party system, which became highly fragmented and volatile. As shown in Table 1, twenty-one parties entered the Congress after the 1990 elections, eighteen of them obtaining legislative seats in the 1994 and 1998 general elections, thus greatly increasing the dispersion of legislative power.

The nominal number of parties, however, is not the best indicator of legislative fragmentation because it overstates the weight of tiny labels. The best measure available of legislative fragmentation is Marku Laakso and Rein Taagepera's effective number of parties (N). By squaring parties' seat shares, N assigns more weight to larger parties, thus providing a politically more valid indicator than a simple count. Amorim Neto calculated N for every year from 1985 to 1999. The reason for this year-by-year count is that party switching (*troca-troca*, in Brazilian political parlance) has become rampant in Brazil, particularly from 1985 on. Brazilian deputies change parties either to go to older labels or to form new ones. By doing so, they alter the party membership of the Congress many times within a single legislature. (Table 2 provides the values of N for Brazil in 1985–99.)

The 1988–90 period marks the transition from a moderately fragmented party system to a highly fragmented one. In 1992 Brazil was certainly one of the most fragmented democracies in the world. From this year on fragmentation declined a bit, but Brazil's party system remained highly fragmented throughout the 1990s.

In addition to legislative fragmentation, Brazil's largest parties (PSDB, PMDB, Liberal Front Party [PFL], Brazilian Progressive Party [PPB], and Brazilian Labor Party [PTB]), especially those making up Cardoso's governing alliance, are loosely disciplined in contrast with the left-wing opposition, which is fairly disciplined. Although some authors contend that Brazil's larger governing parties are actually disciplined and that their behavior is predictable rather than chaotic, the fact that there is within them approximately a 10 to 15 percent minority consistently voting against the majority on key roll call votes further aggravates the problems inherent in high legislative fragmentation. This is particularly true if we consider that in Brazil harnessing legislative majorities requires complex coalition arrangements. A significant defection in any of the largest parties creates a high risk of defeat for an executive-initiated bill. On December 2, 1998, for example, an executive-initiated proposal (indeed, a decree-law!) on social security reform was unexpectedly voted down, producing a major scare among investors and accelerating the exchange rate crisis. Supported by large but loosely disciplined parties, presidents have no alternative but to assemble fiscally costly, oversized multiparty coalitions.

Legislative fragmentation *cum* loose party discipline also creates serious problems for the electorate. The Brazilian voter is clearly faced with too

Table 2
Effective Number of Legislative Parties, 1985–1999

1985	1986	1987*	1988	1989	1990	1991*	1992	1993	1994	1995*	1996	1997	1998	1999
3.2	3.3	2.8	4.1	5.5	7.1	8.7	9.4	8.5	8.2	8.1	7.1	6.9	6.8	7.1

Source: Adapted from Octavio Amorim Neto, "Gabinetes Presidenciais, Ciclos Eleitorais e Disciplina Legislativa no Brasil," *Dados* 43, no. 3 (2000): 491.

*First year of a new legislature elected in the last quarter of the previous year.

many options, due to the fact that there are too many parties and not even the larger ones behave consistently, whether in the electoral or in the legislative arena. By raising voters' information costs, legislative fragmentation *cum* loose party discipline also blurs the accountability lines between voters and Congress. The high and increasing number of blank and null votes cast in congressional elections in the transition period from a moderately fragmented party system to a highly fragmented one may well have been due to such faulty accountability lines. In the 1986 elections 28.6 percent of the votes for congressional seats were either blank or null. In 1990 those figures jumped to 43.7 percent, and stayed close to that level in 1994 (41.2 percent). Interestingly, in the 1998 race the percent of blank and null votes went down to 20 percent. However, turnout rates have consistently been declining since 1986. In this election year 95 percent of registered voters went to the polls. In 1990 this figure was 85.8 percent, going down to 82.3 percent in 1994 and to its lowest point in 1998, 78.5 percent.

A Cumbersome Judiciary
The difficulties stemming from Brazil's consociational model are compounded by some specific features of the country's federation and judiciary. By Third World standards, the Brazilian judiciary and federation are both deeply rooted and important institutions. Developments since the 1988 constitution have on the whole been quite positive for democracy, with the justice system becoming more independent and the federation more decentralized. Combined with the sharply consociational nature of the political system, both can and do, however, give rise to additional problems, as we shall now briefly indicate.

At the federal level, Brazilian courts are generally respected for their independence vis-à-vis the executive and legislative branches of government; but the whole system and especially the state courts have been sharply scrutinized in recent years in view of their many organizational flaws, including corruption and nepotism. These problems are partly explained by the fact that the supply of material and human resources, particularly new judges, has not kept pace with demands created by the 1988 constitution, which greatly broadened access to the justice system. Broadened access, as Sadek points out, does not necessarily mean democratic access, but rather the multiplication of points of pressure for a few, still leaving out many who never take their grievances to court. But the most significant part of the problem seems to derive from some basic institutional features. Castelar Pinheiro claims that judicial malfunctioning—especially slowness and unpredictability (high probability of different outcomes in similar cases)—significantly affects economic performance, raising transaction costs and discouraging investment. The freedom that individual judges, even those at the lowest level, have to reach very different decisions on similar cases and the power granted to them to paralyze government policies have encouraged society to seek in the judiciary the solution to its social and political conflicts. This has led to the twin evils referred to in public debate as the "judicialization of politics" and the "politicization of the judiciary," which overload the courts and compromise their ability to remain impartial. The demands on the judiciary have also increased as a result of market-oriented reforms, which brought complex new issues to the courts. In this environment, the important increase in public resources allocated to the judiciary has not been sufficient to allow the adequate management of the numerous cases that are initiated each year.

Perhaps even more important in an institutional perspective, as pointed out by Rogério Arantes, and Arantes and Fábio Kerche Nunes, the Brazilian judicial review mechanism is a complex hybrid, combining features of both the U.S. and the European systems. It is neither a pure diffuse system, as the American one, in which the (un)constitutionality of laws can be declared by any judge or lower court anywhere in the country, nor a centralized system, as the European one, in which unconstitutionality can only be declared by constitutional courts, at the top of a judicial hierarchy. "In fact," Arantes and Kerche Nunes write, "the 1987–88 Constituent found itself faced with a dilemma: on the one hand, as an important part in the liberalization process, it was necessary to restore the judiciary's independence and autonomy. In this sense, reaffirming the diffuse principle—allowing every judge to exercise judicial review—was one of the most important points. On the other hand, the experience had demonstrated that the increasing centralization of the judicial review in a special body, although associated with authoritarianism, was more conducive to efficiency and stability of the political system." The consequence, they go on to say, is that today the Brazilian system is not diffuse, as the Supreme Federal Court (SFC) can directly declare unconstitutionality with *erga omnes* (against all) effect; from this point of view, the SFC is a quasi-constitutional court. On the other hand, the system is not centralized, because the SFC does not hold a monopoly: it shares the prerogative of declaring (un)constitutionality with lower courts and judges throughout the country. From this perspective, when the SFC receives appeals from the lower courts regarding constitutional issues, it will manifest itself only as the judiciary's highest body: contrary to the U.S. case, its decisions are not binding on the lower courts. This hybrid judicial review system is extremely permeable to demands and non-uniform in its responses. Moreover, the scope of judicial review is such that the courts are inevitably brought into the political arena. The judiciary can control the constitutionality not only of ordinary and organic laws passed by the legislatures and of extraordinary measures enacted by the executive through *provisional measures* (i.e., decree-laws), but even of *constitutional* amendments, given its power to question any of these with regard to substantive merit or to the deliberation method through which they come into being.

An Unbalanced Federation

The federative nature of the Brazilian republic also contributes decisively to the complexity of the country's political system. In the late nineteenth century, the highly centralized monarchy inherited from Portuguese colonization gradually gave way to an unstable federation in which state governors often challenged presidential authority. The federative ideal as such was seldom questioned, but the extent and form of decentralization were matters of contention until recently. Authoritarian arguments demanding concentration of power at the federal level remained strong until the transition from military to civilian rule in 1985, and at least one governor (Itamar Franco, of Minas Gerais) gestured defiantly against the president as late as 1999, when he defaulted on his state's foreign debts, adding momentum to the exchange crisis that took place early that year.

Federal arrangements are inherently consociational, and a strong case can of course be made for them in a country of continental size. But at least two features deserve particular attention with regard to the Brazilian case. One is that the 1988 constitution reacted against the centralization carried out by the military dictatorship in a radically decentralizing way. In addition to transferring a substantial part of tax revenues to the lower levels, it gave full political and administrative autonomy to the municipalities, not only to the states, thus turning Brazil into a full-fledged, three-layer federation. From the political and electoral point of view, then, Brazil is a composite of one national, twenty-seven state, and some 5,500 local constituencies. Healthy as this arrangement may be in abstract democratic terms, the sad truth is that some states and about half of the local governments lack revenues to sustain themselves adequately. One consequence of this discrepancy between local political autonomy and actual financial dependency is of course that the quality of local democracy is often not as high as one would desire.

While it is undeniable that federal arrangements are inherently consociational, in some federations the consociational argument is further invoked to justify the under-representation of electoral majorities, through the over-representation of the less populated states. In Brazil this has long been a matter of contention, especially in view of the sharp under-representation of the largest state, São Paulo, and the over-representation of the sparsely populated states of the Center-West and North-West regions. Alfred Stepan refers to this feature somewhat awkwardly as "demos-constraining," but provides important comparative evidence of the extent to which this majority-constraining effect takes place in the Brazilian federation:

> Brazil is the most *demos*-constraining federation in the world. . . . In Brazil, the overrepresentation is even more extreme [than in the United States]. One vote cast for senator in Roraima has 144 times as much weight as a vote for senator in São Paulo. Moreover, Brazil and Argentina are the only democratic federations in the world that replicate a version of this overrepresentation in the lower house. With perfect proportional representation, São Paulo should have 114 seats. It actually has 70. With perfect representation, Roraima should have one seat. It actually has eight. The Brazilian Constitution, inspired by the ideology of territorial representation, specifies that no state can have more than 70 seats in the lower house (thereby partially disenfranchising São Paulo) and that no state can have fewer than eight.

Provisional Measures: A Doubtful Democratic Instrument

In a nutshell, Brazil has a political system geared more to blocking than to making decisions. Healthy as this may sound in terms of abstract democratic theories concerned with the limits of government, the cost in terms of democratic effectiveness is undoubtedly high. Insofar as executive-legislative relations are concerned, the chief means by which the near-impasse embedded in the country's institutional structure has been managed is the sweeping presidential prerogative of issuing "provisional measures"—a rose that smells very much like the old "decree-laws" of the military regime. Once adopted by the 1987–88 Constitutional Congress, this legislative instrument quickly became an overwhelming source of power to which the executive resorts in order to overcome the obstacles posed by the country's weak and fractionalized party and legislative systems. It is important to remember that, from 1988 on, every conceivable obstacle to economic stabilization and reform became entrenched in the new constitution, which could only be amended with the approval of 60 percent of the total membership of each house of Congress, twice and separately. Considering that the largest parties hardly get 20 percent of the seats each, this means that during this period the executive was at the mercy of Congress in the numerous matters that demanded constitutional change. Operating in the opposite direction, the prerogative of legislating by very broadly defined emergency decrees (the above-mentioned "provisional measures") place the executive in a paramount position with regard to ordinary legislation. Viewed from this angle, it is not far-fetched to say that the pattern of executive-legislative relations in Brazil is one in which Congress is hostage to the executive in matters subject to ordinary legislation (i.e., decree-law regulation), while the president is hostage to the Congress in matters demanding constitutional reform. Since both are quite elastic realms, due to sweeping decree-law prerogatives given to the president and the detailed nature of the constitution, this perverse mutual dependence is clearly a matter for serious concern.

Some authors contend that the issuance of decree-laws does not necessarily mean that the executive has usurped congressional powers, but the fact remains that the civilian presidents since the late 1980s have resorted all too often to this arguable form of legislative initiative. As established by the 1988 constitution, "provisional measures" (MPs) go immediately into effect with force of law, and can be issued to regulate an enormous variety of subjects—as long as they fulfill the conditions of being "urgent and relevant" matters. Here, of course, is where the difficulty lies. From 1988 up to now, presidents have overstepped these loosely defined bounds of constitutional authority, legislating by decree in areas that seemed neither appropriate nor urgent enough for this kind of legislative decision making. From fishery in the Amazon River to sweeping economic measures (the "Real Plan" of 1994 itself being a case in point), an impressive spectrum of policymaking has been dealt with by means of decree-laws. But this is not all. Already in early 1989, a Supreme Court ruling allowed the executive to reissue MPs not voted upon in due time by Congress. Presidents swiftly took advantage of this opportunity, to the point even of reissuing decree-laws with changes in the original content.

Table 3 reports original decree-laws, decree-laws reissued with changes in the original text, and decree-laws reissued without changes. It is clear that the total number of decree-laws per year has increased sharply since the 1988 constitution was adopted. It was only in August 2001 that the Brazilian Congress finally passed a constitutional amendment tightening the criteria for the issuance of decree-laws.

Cardoso ranks first among post-1988 presidents in terms of the total number of decree-laws they signed. Of the 5,764 decree-laws issued in 1988–2000, he signed no less than 4,951, that is, 86 percent of the total. However, if we look only at original decree-laws issued per year, he no longer holds the first position. In 1989, 1990, 1993, and 1994, the incumbent president(s) issued more original decree-laws than in any year of Cardoso's six years in office. Yet, as regards the reissuance of decree-laws without changes in the text of the original decree, every year of Cardoso's first term constituted a new record.

Cardoso is also the winner in terms of decree-laws reissued with changes in the original text. Amorim Neto and Tafner argue that the high number of reissued decrees is not evidence of congressional passivity. As the Brazilian Congress lacks staff, information, and expertise to assess policy decision in a timely fashion, it lets the executive reissue decree-laws so it can have more time to ponder their effects on the different constituencies. In case the latter are eventually hurt by a decree, legislators press the executive to reissue it with changes so as to redress their constituencies' demands. According to this view, decree politics involves a lot of inter-branch bargaining, not just unilateral decision making.

Table 3

Decree-Laws (DLs) per Year, 1998–2000

Year	Incumbent President(s)	Original DLs	DLs Reissued with Changes	DLs Reissued Without Changes	Total Number of Reissued DLs	Total
1988*	Sarney	6	2	7	9	15
1989	Sarney	92	0	11	11	103
1990	Collor/Sarney	88	20	55	75	163
1991	Collor	9	0	2	2	11
1992	Collor/Franco	7	1	2	3	10
1993	Franco	57	1	48	49	106
1994	Franco	92	36	277	313	405
1995	Cardoso	29	90	318	408	437
1996	Cardoso	38	89	521	610	648
1997	Cardoso	35	142	543	685	720
1998	Cardoso	56	132	615	747	803
1999	Cardoso	45	108	973	1,081	1,126
2000**	Cardoso	25	114	1,078	1,192	1,217
Total		579	735	4,450	5,185	5,764

Source: Brazil—Senado Federal. *Levantamento e Reedições de Medidas Provisórias: Dados Atualizados em 28 de Fevereiro de 1999* (Brasília: Senado Federal–Subsecretaria de Informações and www.planalto.gov.br, 1999).

*Presidents were constitutionally granted the right to issue decree-laws in October 1988. Thus, this row covers only the last three months of the year.

**Updated to December 17, 2000.

It is also noteworthy that in the final two years of the aborted Collor presidency the issuance of decree-laws witnessed its lowest rates (1988 cannot be compared to the other years because only from October on President Sarney could start signing decree-laws): nine and seven original decree-laws in 1991 and 1992, respectively. This is evidence that without stable majority legislative support, no president can implement his or her policy agenda via decree for a long period of time. As Collor was never able or willing to form a legislative majority, his decree-based policymaking strategy was tolerated by Congress as long as the "honeymoon" phase of his presidency lasted. In the second year of his term Congress threatened to pass a law restricting resort to decree power, thus sending him a clear sign that it was no longer willing to be outflanked. No wonder, in 1991 and 1992 Collor issued far fewer decrees.

The Cardoso presidency is the reverse image of Collor's. Cardoso has been able to keep using decrees throughout his two terms precisely because he counts on majority legislative support. Such support allows him to initiate policy safely by standard legislative procedures such as bills and constitutional amendments, all requiring congressional approval. This is why the number of original decree-laws he issued per year is lower than that of Presidents Sarney,

Collor, and Franco, all three politically weaker than him. And the high number of decree-laws reissued by Cardoso, as mentioned above, should be seen as a mechanism chosen by the executive and the legislative majority to accommodate the former's need for timely policymaking and the latter's concern with the effects of decrees on their constituencies.

Even granting that resort to decree-laws does not ipso facto imply emasculation of Congress, as some authors claim, the over-abundance of MPs is a serious distortion in the democratic legislative process, which can only be understood and accepted as a means to bypass some deeper flaws in the Brazilian institutional structure. It would take us too far afield to assess how much instability the abuse of this legislative instrument has brought to Brazil's legal order. The fact that legal codes regulating key aspects of social life can be changed overnight by executive fiat and *ex post* legislative consent is undoubtedly a threat to individual rights and the predictability required by the normal operation of a complex economy.

THE PLEBISCITARIAN PSEUDO-SOLUTION TO A FLAWED INSTITUTIONAL STRUCTURE

In the late 1980s and early 1990s, legislative fragmentation, loose party discipline, and steep inflation eroding popular support of the presidency had the effect of rendering the Brazilian political system unable to aggregate issues for negotiation and decision. Caught in the vicious circle of political disarray and monetary instability, Brazil seemed doomed to lag behind the rest of Latin America in the path to structural economic reform. During the 1980s and early 1990s, Brazil's nightmarish legislative fragmentation problem was compounded by two other factors: the resilience of the statist economic ideological legacy (much of which had been entrenched in the 1988 constitutional text) and weak presidential leadership under the last military and the initial three civilian presidents (João B. de Oliveira Figueiredo [1979–85], José Sarney [1985–90], Fernando Collor [1990–92], and Itamar Franco [1992–94]).

Contrary to what happened in Argentina or Chile, in Brazil the state-centered industrialization model continued to be perceived by many as successful until the early 1990s, causing the Brazilian business and technocratic elites to send Congress contradictory signals as to which route it should take. This is why the Constitutional Congress of 1987–88 paid little attention to the deep fiscal crisis underlying Brazil's chronic super-inflation and wrote much of the economic model inherited from the Vargas era (1930–54) into the new constitution. To make things worse, the executive leadership provided by the three first post-transition presidents was weak and not always wise with regard to economic stabilization. President Sarney, who unexpectedly ascended to the presidency when president-elect Tancredo Neves died before his inauguration in 1985, never fully understood the need to control inflation and promote comprehensive reforms in the public sector. Fernando Collor did understand that, but saw the popular support he initially enjoyed vanish as his stabilization plan quickly failed, and ended up impeached on charges of corruption in September 1992. Itamar Franco, the ill-tempered vice-president who took office after Collor's impeachment, zigzagged quite a bit in both policy orientation and cabinet appointments at the beginning, but was wise enough to recognize his own weakness in 1993, when he appointed Fernando Henrique Cardoso to a key ministerial position.

Collor epitomizes the difficulties inherent in Brazil's pattern of executive-legislative relations and the risks involved in the attempt to overcome them by means of direct plebiscitarian appeals to "the people." Although he faced a highly fragmented Congress, and his party, the Party of National Reconstruction (PRN), commanded only about 5 percent of lower chamber seats, Collor thought he could govern without a coalition agreement with the largest parties, which would imply a measure of "parliamentarization" of the political process, so he could count on stable legislative support. His strategy was, on the one hand, to try to stabilize the currency by means of a major heterodox shock, blocking some 70 percent of the country's financial liquidity by decree-law, and, on the other, resorting to wildly theatrical appeals to the citizenry as a way of compensating his weakness in the legislative arena. Except for the final chapter—the congressional impeachment vote against him on grounds of corruption—the results of Collor's strategy were quite predictable: three months after his attempt to stabilize the economy by means of an heterodox shock, inflation was already making a robust comeback and support for him in public opinion began to plummet.

President Franco (1992–94) also began his caretaker administration trying to keep political parties at arms' length, but to a lesser extent than Collor. The problem was again popular dissatisfaction due to high inflation and the widely disseminated perception among the elites that he was ideologically and psychologically unprepared to take up the urgent tasks of stabilization and economic reform. After six months of populist gesturing, he had managed to fire three finance ministers and Brazil's economic prospects once again seemed somber. It was at this juncture, in May 1993, that Franco took the country by surprise, appointing his then foreign relations minister, Fernando Henrique Cardoso, as finance minister. This step was key in reducing the dangers inherent in Brazil's combination of extreme plebiscitarianism and extreme consociationalism: as an experienced senator, Cardoso fully understood that broad congressional support was essential to pass the legislation the country badly needed and to withstand the difficulties likely to arise when popular support falls sharply.

Cardoso's Rise to Center Stage
From the very beginning after Fernando Henrique Cardoso's appointment to the Finance Ministry, President Itamar Franco placed him in the role of a

de facto prime minister, thus turning his administration into an informal parliamentary government. From this point on, executive-legislative relations improved markedly. Cardoso's ambitious objectives as finance minister were also helped by a corruption scandal involving the lower chamber budget committee, which further reduced whatever intent Congress might have harbored to resist the fiscal measures required prior to the launching of a new stabilization plan. Brazil's protracted vicious circle of economic and political disorganization—or what I have elsewhere dubbed as the country's "hyper-active paralysis syndrome"—thus began to be broken from the economic end. On July 1, 1994, the Real Plan came fully into effect and monthly inflation rates came down from something like 50 percent to 3 percent. Within four weeks, Cardoso, as the presidential candidate of a large coalition, had overtaken the front-runner, Lula (of the Workers' Party), and emerged clearly as Franco's successor, winning the election already in the first round.

Despite the institutional shortcomings analyzed in previous sections, there can be little doubt that Cardoso will go on the record as one of the most effective presidents in Brazilian history. Triggered, as indicated above, by the "parliamentarist" twist that consciously or unconsciously President Itamar Franco gave to the Brazilian political system, this positive turn was extended in time by a conjunction of several favorable factors. Prominent among them was undoubtedly the end of the Cold War, which reduced ideological distances and the range of economic policy choices, thus helping Cardoso to put together an unprecedentedly large electoral and governing party coalition. Another significant factor was that Brazilian society, still plagued by high inflation after the failure of five successive heterodox stabilization plans, was ready to support a credible new effort. Fourth, this new effort was now embodied in a political leader endowed with substantial credibility, strong academic credentials, a known ability to form and work with first-rate technical teams, and of course significant political experience. Cardoso's affable personality and strong analytical skills surely go a long way toward explaining his conscious choice of an oversized legislative coalition model as an alternative to the country's ill-starred tradition of plebiscitarian executives in a minority position and at loggerheads with fragmented legislatures. In a nutshell, Brazil's crisis-prone blend of presidentialism *cum* consociationalism started to work better under Cardoso, from 1995 on. This was made possible, on the one hand, by the less polarized atmosphere brought about by the end of the Cold War and the new worldwide agenda, and, on the other, by the rise to the presidency of a skilled consensus-builder with a firm sense of priorities regarding inflation and economic reform.

Cumbersome and contradictory as it certainly was (is), Cardoso's large legislative coalition cannot be said to have been (be) "consociational," if by this term we understand a skew toward blocking rather than toward facilitating the task of legislative decision making. This was signaled from the be-ginning of Cardoso's first term (1995–98), as Deputy Luís Eduardo Magal-hães, the speaker of the lower house, firmly led the government majority in an effort to pass a series of important constitutional amendments quickly.

An evidence of Cardoso's penchant for consensus-building is that, when appointing his inauguration cabinet, he drafted not only politicians from the parties that had joined his electoral coalition (PSDB, PFL, and PTB) but also from the PMDB, Brazil's largest party at that moment, which had endorsed the candidacy of São Paulo's former governor, Orestes Quércia, an adver-sary of Cardoso's in that state. This step was decisive in providing the new administration with the 3/5 majority required to enact constitutional re-forms, which were at the top of Cardoso's legislative agenda. In April 1996 Cardoso would include politicians from the PPB, a medium-size rightist party, in his cabinet, thus adding one more bloc of seats to his legislative majority.

Brazil's combination of pure presidentialism with consociationalism was historically aggravated by short terms of office and a rigid ban on reelection for executive offices. In early 1997, the Congress lifted that ban, passing a constitutional amendment that allowed Cardoso to become the first Brazil-ian president to run for a consecutive term. In October 1998, having Lula again as his main opponent, Cardoso would again win in the first round, scoring 53.1 percent against Lula's 31.7 percent. In January 1999, Cardoso began his second term, backed by the same multiparty coalition that had supported him in the previous four years.

Backed by an oversized legislative coalition cemented by key cabinet and subcabinet appointments, Cardoso's relations with Congress throughout his first term were on the surface smooth. If an approval rate of executive-initiated bills is used to measure Cardoso's legislative performance, we come to the conclusion that he was very successful indeed. Moreover, a very high share of the bills enacted by the Brazilian Congress were sponsored by the executive. Pereira shows that of the 805 bills passed by the Congress between 1995 and 1997, 80.5 percent were sponsored by the executive. But useful as aggregate measures of legislative performance may be, they do not tell the whole story of executive-legislative relations under Cardoso. Persistent fiscal pressure and an overvalued exchange rate (dubbed by some critics as ex-change rate populism) were among the risks incurred by Cardoso as he strove to hold his multiparty coalition together. Another significant cost was the watering down or the sheer abandonment of important executive pro-posals, as well as a few devastating setbacks. Prominent among these was the defeat of three executive-sponsored proposals to reform the social secu-rity system, which seriously compromised the administration's efforts to place the country's fiscal accounts on a firmer long-term footing. As already mentioned, one of these votes in which the majority helped defeat an execu-tive-sponsored bill took place in December 1998, severely affecting the country's credibility vis-à-vis foreign investors and mightily compounding the exchange rate crisis that led to the precipitous devaluation of January 1999.

Indeed, by the time of Cardoso's reelection (October 1998), Brazil already faced a mounting exchange rate crisis. In mid-January 1999, only two weeks after Cardoso's reinauguration, the government was forced to devalue the *Real* to stem a massive outflow of resources. As one should expect, the devaluation severely undermined the president's popularity. Cardoso's reelection bid had been strongly staked on the promise to keep the *Real*'s domestic and foreign exchange value. The sudden collapse of the *Real* brought back a sense of frustration, distrust, and pessimism that Brazilians apparently thought they had exorcised forever. In the wake of the devaluation, key opinion leaders and economic pundits began to voice doomsday forecasts predicting that the Brazilian economy would dramatically recede, inflation would soar, and unemployment would skyrocket, therefore bringing about social unrest and political instability. But the devaluation's actual impact was much more moderate: the GDP growth rate in 1999 was low, but still slightly above zero; the inflation rate stood at 8.3 percent and unemployment at 7.6 percent (as compared to 8.4 percent in 1998!).

As pointed out, Cardoso's popularity did plummet in the wake of the exchange crisis, and particularly after the January 1999 devaluation, dropping again a few months later as a consequence of popular discontent with public utility and fuel price hikes. Without underestimating Cardoso's qualities as a political leader, it is worth noting that he was also quite lucky in 1998: if the Russian crisis of August had taken place a few months earlier, the exchange rate crisis and its negative impact on Cardoso's popularity might well have occurred before the October presidential election. But between January and March 1999, market confidence began to be restored as Congress swiftly approved an array of emergency measures demanded by Brazil's agreement with the IMF. Already by mid-March the exchange rate began to appreciate and the business climate started to improve. But as often happens in Brazilian party politics, something strange then began to take place. Instead of going along with improving economic prospects, the political picture quickly worsened. As soon as the situation of financial emergency that had prompted Congress to come to the aid of the executive was over, key party leaders engaged in a fierce struggle in the Senate, thus engendering an atmosphere of political crisis that proved quite detrimental to short-term economic recovery.

From March through September 1999, a great deal of prudence and tolerance was required from Cardoso and his ministers to prevent the development of a fairly artificial political crisis—artificial in the sense that it derived from gross miscalculation on the part of key party leaders, who apparently began to take it for granted that Cardoso would quickly become a lame duck, and also in the sense that those leaders' bleak prospects ran counter to the very plausible indications that Brazil would not take too long to recover from the devaluation.

To make sense of the negative political scenario that prevailed in Brazil in 1999, it should first be noted that the executive, for the first time since Cardoso's inauguration in 1995, had temporarily lost its tight grip on the country's political agenda. Constrained by the IMF agreement and with his political authority undermined by the loss of popularity, Cardoso was drawn into a defensive position vis-à-vis public opinion and Congress. Having given passage to the IMF emergency package, the legislature was left with an empty agenda. Also, new governors had just taken office, one of them Itamar Franco, the governor of Minas Gerais who defaulted on his state's foreign debts on January 4, 1999, speeding up the exchange rate crisis. It was in the wake of these events that several political leaders, some of them key figures of the governing alliance itself, badly miscalculated and started behaving as if Cardoso's second term had a high probability of collapsing. Worth recalling in this respect is that Senators Antonio Carlos Magalhães (the strong man of the PFL and then chair of the Senate) and Jader Barbalho (Senate leader of the PMDB) then started a fierce struggle for political space. This was typically a position-taking battle, each attempting to out-maneuver the other in search of media exposure; a banal episode, one might say, were it not for the fact that it prolonged the crisis atmosphere from which the country had begun to reemerge. Given the fact of Cardoso's loss of popularity, this position-taking struggle between the two senators was part and parcel of a movement to distance their respective parties from what they seem mistakenly to have perceived as an irreversible decline in presidential power. In their outbidding tactical maneuvers, Magalhães and Barbalho led their parties to establish investigative committees on corruption in the judiciary and on the financial system, respectively. Needless to say, the hearings captured public attention, and thus made it more difficult for the executive to keep Congress and the media focused on its priorities—social security and public administration reforms, both related to the administration's intent to improve the country's fiscal picture.

This pattern of unrestrained position-taking and competition among Cardoso's key coalition partners put the administration under increasing pressure, forcing Cardoso to display extra initiative and authority at a time when he lacked the means (notably public opinion support) to do so. This created the impression that the governing coalition would not support additional fiscal measures, and might even fall apart. This chain of events and misperceptions was among the reasons why the economic optimism emerging around March 1999 submerged again and did not reappear until mid-2000.

By early 2001, halfway down the road in his second term, Cardoso's popularity had begun slowly to recover from the very low point it reached after the January 1999 devaluation crisis. Not only this, he had undoubtedly recovered much of his strength vis-à-vis the political elite and the media; instead of a lame duck, he had again begun to be regarded as an important potential influence shaping the game of his own succession in the presidency. On the economic side, adoption of the floating exchange rate and effective management of monetary policy by the central bank were the initial stepping stones toward Brazil's comparatively quick recovery. On the political side, an important factor was Cardoso's patience and skill in diluting the then prevailing self-fulfilling prophecy of a mounting crisis. With hind-sight, there can be no question that he adequately handled challenges from allies such as Senators Magalhães and Barbalho and from determined opponents such as former president Itamar Franco, now governor of Minas Gerais, as well as from a myriad of protest movements, notably the Landless Workers Movement (MST), inclined to see Cardoso as a precocious lame duck and his second term as an opportunity to stage major and ever more aggressive demonstrations.

Restocking the legislative agenda, empty after the more urgent part of the IMF package was approved in early 1999, was also an important step. Given the bargain and collective action problems faced by Brazil's fragmented Congress, vigorous presidential leadership is key to providing the country with a measure of effectiveness in policymaking. In April 1999, the executive sent Congress an ambitious Fiscal Responsibility Bill, which would be finally approved in 2000, and which thus became the framework for managing public finances at federal, state, and municipal levels of government. The budget proposal and a Pluriannual Investment Plan (PPA) were also shuttled to Congress in August, along with other matters relevant for fiscal adjustment, including a new proposal through which the administration succeeded in indirectly introducing a minimum age requirement into the social security system. With improved political coordination and a substantial legislative agenda, the executive was thus able, contrary to the doomsday forecasts of the previous year, to gradually sterilize a long series of disruptive initiatives and pass relevant fiscal policy measures. The energy shortage of 2001 again hurt Cardoso's popularity quite badly, but fortunately enough for him, not too late for him to recover and still play a relevant role in the nomination process toward the 2002 presidential race.

CONCLUSION

The shortcomings of Brazil's extreme consociational model and particularly of its pathetically weak party system have long been prompting calls for institutional reform. The key issue in institutional reform debates has been the perceived need to make Brazil's multiparty presidentialism more wieldy by reducing the number of parties, strengthening party discipline, creating more efficient mechanisms to coordinate executive-legislative relations, and establishing stronger accountability lines between voters and their representatives. Yet, despite widespread discontent with the functioning of political institutions, attempts at political reform have always failed. Even under Cardoso—who, together with his party, had previously advocated profound changes in the political system—political reform has stalled. The one important exception to this statement was the approval of the constitutional amendment allowing presidents to run for a consecutive term.

Paradoxical as it may sound, failure of political reform during the 1990s was caused by two remarkable success stories: the orderly impeachment of President Collor and Cardoso's record in economic stabilization and public-sector reform. Successful management of the Collor crisis led many to think that the country's political institutions were not that flawed after all, and Cardoso's rise to center stage added further "proof" that this new diagnosis should be right. As pointed out earlier, the launching of the Real Plan in 1994 began to break Brazil's long-drawn vicious circle of economic and political debilitation from the economic end. As the Cardoso administration draws to a close, there is also plenty of room for the hypothesis that, although political reform has not taken place, the functioning of the political system has been changed indirectly and in practice, as a consequence of economic and public-sector reform. Privatization of state banks and the recently approved Fiscal Responsibility Law are important illustrations of this new reasoning, as both have come to be regarded as severe blows to Brazil's deep-rooted practices of clientelism and corruption. According to this hypothesis, political reform *strictu sensu* has not taken place, but the conditions under which parties and politicians must act have changed. Not much has been done toward reforming formal political institutions, but a great deal has been accomplished that may become permanent and thus change their functioning over the medium term.

The apparently irreversible impact of Cardoso's reforms and the fact that he was able to launch them despite the manifest dysfunctionality of the political system will of course require much scholarly analysis in years to come. But the starting point of such analysis will undoubtedly be the new world-wide agenda, with the end of the Cold War, globalization, the narrower range of viable economic policy choices, widespread acceptance of market-oriented reforms, and, in the case of Latin America, the high priority given to inflation control by governments as well as citizens. Cardoso's caliber as a political leader is one side of the coin, but the other was the previous ripening of this mighty public agenda, which gave the unprecedented chance of launching a whole range of important initiatives in the legislative as well as in the executive arenas.

Whether and to what extent Cardoso's achievements will become permanent gains for the political system, making Brazilian democracy as such more effective over time, is a key but probably premature issue to raise. A word of caution may be useful at this point. Globalization and free market economics may be here to stay, but hardly as a worldwide, wholehearted consensus. Specifically with regard to the Brazilian case, support for stabilization and reform in the early 1990s, remarkable as it was, was perhaps more negative than positive—an immediate mandate to end inflation and a stock of good will would of course lose density and become contradictory as the whole range of structural reforms and their differentiated impact on various social groups unfolded. Powered by the clear understanding that chronic super-inflation had just about disorganized the economy and brought the country to the brink of serious social conflict, this "negative" consensus was more than enough to catapult Cardoso to the presidency in 1994. The fact that he over-took Lula a few weeks after the launching of the Real Plan and got the absolute majority of the vote already in the first round bear out this statement beyond any reasonable doubt. The reverse side of the coin was the formidable agenda that Cardoso faced, including the need to pass a string of important constitutional amendments. This complex task worked in his favor, giving him the time and the staff he needed to outmaneuver the other relevant political actors, including quite a few in his own congressional coalition.

As has been the case since he was appointed as a de facto prime minister in 1993, Cardoso has been drawing on the strength of the administration's reform program and on the inability of various branches of the left-wing opposition to unite and offer viable alternatives. This fact was clearly illustrated in 1999 by the behavior of the Workers' Party (PT) in the episode involving the Supreme Court ruling against a bill requiring retired and inactive civil servants to pay social security contributions. The PT initially tried to forbid state governors affiliated with the party from entering into political negotiations with the federal government in an effort to devise alternative legislative proposals. However, these same PT governors, directly in contact with the fiscal realities of their respective states, chose not to abide by the party's attempted veto. The national leadership of the PT was therefore forced to beat a retreat.

But the agenda for the 2002 presidential race and the remainder of the decade will of course be different in many ways. Currency stability, fiscal discipline, and public-sector modernization came to be highly valued in the public's mind, but law and order on the Right and redistributive policies on the Left will also loom large. The several important victories scored by the left-wing opposition in the local elections of 2000, local and international attempts to mobilize against globalization (vide the "anti-Davos" demonstrations staged in both Davos itself and Porto Alegre in early 2001), and other relevant media events suggest that, like the *oeuvre au noir* of ancient alchemy, the new agenda, no matter how diffuse, may well be something new in the making. It is premature to say whether the presidential succession of 2002 will again be a bipolar race between two "natural" candidates as Cardoso and Lula were in 1994 and again in 1998—battles almost entirely focused on inflation and the newly gained satisfaction with stability. Without inflation as an overriding issue and hence a "great elector," the 2002 presidential succession looks more open and uncertain.*

---

*In fact, Luiz Lula Da Silva of the Workers' Party (PT) handily defeated President Cardoso's chosen successor, José Serra. See Wendy Hunter's article in this chapter.

The issue now seems to be not so much the direction, but the scope and the pace of change. Assuming that Cardoso's economic reform program will stick and that the presidency will retain the strength gained under his leadership, it is quite plausible to argue that the party system will be simplified over the next decade or so—in practice, if not also in terms of nominal labels. As many of the parties currently represented in the Congress only voice personal ambitions or narrow regional or sectoral interests, they may sooner or later vanish as the bipolar competition between Cardoso's Center–Right coalition and the Left-to-Center one spearheaded by the PT takes hold of the electoral and governmental arenas. This trend is being reinforced by the concurrence of presidential and congressional elections since 1994, and should also be favored if the de facto single-member district pattern of electoral competition that already prevails in many regions becomes more widespread. By this logic, Brazil's party system may formally continue to display a relatively high effective number of parties, but with a simpler pattern of actual functioning, based on a few parties, perhaps even a two-bloc competition roughly like that of Chile or France.

7.3 A New Brazil?: The Changing Sociodemographic Context of Brazilian Democracy (2000)

TIMOTHY J. POWER AND J. TIMMONS ROBERTS

Understanding politics requires attention to social structure. As simple and intuitive as this observation may be, it has too often been overlooked in recent analyses of democratization. Single-country studies of political change . . . have an understandable tendency to become wrapped up in actors, institutions, and political processes and to disregard social and demographic factors altogether. This tendency appears premised on the assumption that one can always treat political factors as variables while holding social-structural factors constant. This assumption, more often than not, is erroneous—particularly so in the case of Brazil, a nation of extraordinary diversity and dynamism.

To appreciate this point, a brief comparison of political and social change is in order. Since World War II, Brazil has had three distinct political regimes: the democratic regime of 1946–1964, the military-authoritarian

Timothy J. Power and J. Timmons Roberts, "A New Brazil? The Changing Sociodemographic Content of Brazilian Democracy," *Democratic Brazil: Actions, Institutions and Processes,* edited by Peter R. Kingstone and Timothy J. Power, © 2000. Reprinted by permission of the University of Pittsburgh Press.

regime of 1964–1985, and the regime that is the subject of this [article], the democratic New Republic that began in 1985. Each has spawned a major literature, and studies of Brazilian politics are replete with comparisons, both explicit and implicit, among the three regimes. What these comparisons often fail to note is that these three political regimes existed in three fundamentally different social contexts. Table 1 documents these contexts with a broad brush, comparing 1955, 1975, and 1995. These dates were not chosen arbitrarily but, rather, represent convenient measurement points in recent political history. The years 1955 and 1975 represent the precise midpoints of the first democratic republic and the military regime, respectively. The year 1995 represents the tenth anniversary of the New Republic. Coincidentally, these dates also correspond rather closely to the rise to power of the dominant president in each of the three regimes: Juscelino Kubitschek (elected 1955), General Ernesto Geisel (inaugurated 1974), and Fernando Henrique Cardoso (inaugurated 1995).

Looking at the data in Table 1, a social scientist from Mars might reasonably wonder whether presidents Kubitschek, Geisel, and Cardoso governed the same country. Comparing only the two democratic regimes, one sees that the first, initiated in 1946, governed a nation that was predominantly rural, where a majority of workers labored in agriculture or mining, in which only a quarter of the citizens could vote, which depended on one product for more than half of its export earnings, and where television was accessible only to the wealthiest of families in large cities. The current democratic regime, initiated in 1985, operates in a country that is nearly 80 percent urbanized, where more than half of workers are in the service sector, in which three-fifths of the population is enfranchised, which has an extraordinarily diversified economy, and in which four-fifths of the households have television. The two democratic regimes were bridged by a military dictatorship that suspended political freedoms while presiding over revolutionary changes in the social and productive structures of Brazil.

The data in Table 1 provide only a rudimentary sketch of postwar social change, and we return to many of these same variables later in the chapter, but nevertheless, the data are sufficient to demonstrate that the three postwar political regimes existed in three different social contexts. It is evident that no analysis of the conditions for democratic sustainability in Brazil can be complete without an adequate exploration of the sociodemographic changes since 1985.

This [article] conducts such an exploration, for three primary reasons. First, while [others] analyze the "actors" in late twentieth-century Brazilian democracy, we must not neglect the "stage" on which politics is played out: social structure. A comprehensive appraisal of any regime requires attention to actors, institutions, processes, and structure. Second, we examine sociodemographic change to caution against inappropriate comparisons between the New Republic and the regimes that preceded it. When one is abstractly

Table 1

Selected Indicators of Social Change in Brazil, 1955, 1975, 1995

Indicator	1955	1975	1995
Population	61 million	105 million	155 million
Percent urban	41	62	79
Percent illiterate (>5 years old)	52	37	22
Life expectancy at birth (in years)	50	62	67
Voters as percentage of population	24	35	62
Workers in agriculture, mining (%)	56	37	26
Workers in services (%)	29	42	54
Coffee as percent of merchandise exports	55	17	6
Households with television (%)	1	40	81

Sources: Faria (1983, 120); IBGE (1993, 1995–1996, 1996); W. Santos, Monteiro, Caillaux (1990); Wood and Carvalho (1988, 87).

Note: Figures are approximations; 1955 and 1975 values are mostly linear interpolations from decennial censuses.

debating the social underpinnings of politics or the prospects for democratic consolidation in Brazil, it is reasonable to ask. Which Brazil? The Brazil of 1998 is very different from the one that witnessed the first steps toward liberalization and meaningful political competition at the end of the 1970s. Third, and most important, in sketching certain social and demographic features of contemporary Brazil, we propose to evaluate their positive or negative implications for the sustainability of political democracy.

It was not easy to choose which specific sociodemographic variables should be included in this democracy-centered review. Choosing only areas in which significant change has occurred might bias our results in a "positive" direction, portraying Brazil as increasingly hospitable to sustainable democracy. Likewise, choosing only areas in which little change has occurred (e.g., poverty and inequality) might promote the opposite bias, perhaps even veer into a sociological determinism that would predict a future democratic breakdown. Thus, we ultimately opted for a set of selection criteria that direct attention to both continuity and change and that have undisputed macropolitical significance.

The criteria led us to isolate seven core issue-areas for sociodemographic analysis, with some selected because of their novelty in the postauthoritarian era and some because they represent perennial problem areas for Brazil in which (relatively) little change has taken place since 1985. These core areas are the expansion of the electorate, the acceleration of urbanization, the rise of the informal labor market, the persistence of social inequality, the ongoing challenges of education and literacy, the rapidly increasing density of civil society, and the rise and oligopolization of television. Though the variables encompass both change and continuity, what links all of them together is that they have all impacted the kind of political system that has taken shape in Brazil since 1985. After reviewing these important sociode-mographic issue-areas, we conclude with some cautiously optimistic reflections on the possibilities for democratic sustainability in Brazil.

ELECTORAL DEMOGRAPHICS: POPULATION AND ENFRANCHISEMENT

Brazil has undergone tremendous demographic change since World War II. In the 1950s, high fertility boosted the population at a rate of nearly 3 percent a year, which meant the population was doubling every twenty-three years—with the urban population doubling at a rate of once every fourteen years through the 1970s. However, the situation has changed dramatically in the New Republic. Figures for 1996 from the Instituto Brasileiro de Geografia e Estatística (IBGE), the Brazilian census bureau, show that by that time, the overall population growth rate had plummeted to just 1.3 percent per year, a rate at which Brazil would double in size in fifty-four years. Brazil is now [as of 2001] therefore close to the U.S. population growth rate of 1.1 percent per year, and the Brazilian rate is expected to fall further in coming years.

[As of 2001] Brazil's population stands at slightly over 160 million, and the IBGE is projecting that the population will stabilize at around 230 million in the year 2030. The post-1980 drop-off in population growth occurred rapidly and somewhat unexpectedly. Therefore, in coming years, the nation will have relatively little time in which to shift its social policy priorities from those of a typical Third World country—in which the population is over-whelmingly young—to those of a First World nation, which must handle the twin challenges of an aging population and a shrinking labor force. These considerations are already finding their way into the public policy debate, particularly as they regard the solvency of the social security and pension systems.

Since 1945, Brazilians have tripled in number, but the electorate has multiplied by more than twelvefold. The most rapid and far-reaching changes in enfranchisement have taken place since the end of the military regime: the national electorate expanded by more than 40 percent in the 1980s alone. Only two months into the New Republic in 1985, the National Congress granted the suffrage to illiterates for the first time in the twentieth century. With the adoption of the constitution of 1988, the voting age was lowered to sixteen, which added 2 million potential voters. The tradition of compulsory voting has been maintained: voting is mandatory except for sixteen- and seventeen-year-olds, for citizens older than seventy, and for illiterates. In sum, the expansion of the electorate has been nothing short of revolutionary both in absolute and in proportional terms: while only 16 percent of the entire population had the right to vote in 1945, over 60 percent of Brazilians were enfranchised in the mid-1990s. The electorate is now over 100 million voters, making Brazil the world's third-largest democracy.

In terms of geographic distribution, Brazil's five distinct regions have experienced dramatically different population shifts since 1945. The drought-prone and still semifeudal Northeast region had tremendously high birthrates but during much of the period was the source of out-migration to the industrial cities of the Southeast and to the Center-West and Amazon regions. Although birthrates were significantly lower in the more developed South and Southeast regions, these regions are the most populous today. In 1994, the South and Southeast together had about 61 percent of the national electorate. Among the three less-developed regions, the Northeast had about 27 percent of the voters, and the North and Center-West about 6 percent each.

The skewing of the national population toward the South and Southeast is not reflected in the allocation of political power. The more modern regions of the country have an advantage in presidential elections, which are national and direct, but in the distribution of legislative power, the situation is quite different. Because of a constitutional cap on the number of elected deputies per state (currently seventy) as well as the gross overrepresentation of small states in Congress, the developed regions are deprived of the political power that would be theirs in a truly proportional system. São Paulo, which contains 22 percent of the national population and produces more than 35 percent of the GDP, is restricted to 12 percent of the seats in the National Congress. In contrast, the less developed North, Northeast, and Center-West regions, which together have 41 percent of the national population and only 38 percent of the electorate, control 53.4 percent of the seats in Congress. This malapportionment has actually worsened since the end of military rule, primarily because of the creation of new states in the North.

The explosion of electoral participation in the New Republic quickly revealed some of democracy's growing pains. In the 1986, 1990, and 1994 legislative elections, the percentage of blank and spoiled ballots averaged 40 percent of all votes cast. In previous research on this phenomenon, we found that the rapid extension of suffrage combined with the maintenance of compulsory-voting legislation and the open-list variant of proportional representation combined in ways that inhibited the effective incorporation of new voters and thus facilitated an increase in invalid votes.

The perception of growing voter alienation caused elite opinion to begin to swing against mandatory voting in the late 1990s. Its abolition would likely have immediate political consequences, as the effective electorate could potentially shrink by as much as a third and the new, reduced

electorate would afford greater relative influence to the more urban, educated, literate, and middle-class voters. With this in mind, the record of
opinion polling and election returns throughout the New Republic suggests
that voluntary voting would boost the performance of left and center-left
parties while reducing the electoral space of populist and clientelistic candidates. Thus, the question of compulsory voting has ethical implications for
future democratic development: maintaining mandatory voting is in many
ways dissatisfying but abolishing it would likely privilege in electoral terms
precisely those Brazilians who are already more privileged in economic and
social terms.

URBANIZATION AND "FAVELIZATION"

Brazil is now predominantly an urban nation, and it became so rapidly by
global standards: Brazil was nearly 70 percent rural in 1940 but is now
nearly 80 percent urban. From 1950 to 1980, the number of cities over 20,000
in population skyrocketed from 96 to 482, and in 1991, a quarter of the nation's people lived in their states' capitals. Urbanization is occurring in all
regions of Brazil, but the most dynamic industrial activities are being concentrated in the Southeast of the nation, especially the greater São Paulo
area, which has about 20 million residents and about one-third of the nation's economy.

The urban structure of Brazil is changing, and there is a flowering in all
regions of mid-sized cities with populations between 100,000 and 500,000
residents. The growth of these cities appears to be linked to the shift of
Brazil's economy from production for internal markets to a new emphasis
on exports as well as to cumulative improvements in the transportation infrastructure. Likewise, improvement of living conditions in Brazil has been
tied to the growth of these cities and the lessening of pressure on the older
megacities (São Paulo and Rio) and the state capitals.

A substantial proportion of residents in Brazil's cities live in favelas, or
squatter-settled self-constructed neighborhoods that are often on the margins or at the interstices of the cities. Living conditions in the favelas are
perilous. Recent figures indicate that there are over 3,500 favelas in Brazil
ranging in size from a few hundred residents to the Favela da Roçinha in
southern Rio de Janeiro, which has over 400,000 people. Favela conditions
can be identified in the 1991 census, which uncovered the facts that a quarter of all households in the nation still lack an inside water supply and 66
percent lack sewage treatment facilities. There were favelas in the large me-
tropolises and in the smaller interior cities in the 1980s, and it is now likely
that 3.3 million new houses and the upgrading of 3.1 million more are
needed to meet Brazil's housing and sanitation needs.

What does an overwhelmingly urban Brazil portend for democracy? Recent history offers some clues. In Brazil's first democratic experiment of 1946–1964, when the urban population was growing at the fantastic rate of 5 percent annually, urbanization had palpable political effects. The shift in population away from the interior meant a decline in traditional methods of political control, such as *coronelismo*, and the exposure of voters to new sources of political information and mobilization in the cities. In electoral terms, urbanization was associated with a secular trend away from traditional conservative parties and toward working-class movements.

The coup of 1964 only underlined the urban-rural cleavage. In the 1964–1985 period, urbanization was positively associated with resistance to the military government, and as the military recognized this fact it banned direct elections for mayor in the state capitals and in nearly 200 other "national security" cities. Likewise, in the New Republic, the "oppositionist" tendencies of the highly urbanized regions (especially the state capitals) are still visible—other things being equal, rural voters are more likely to support the national government while big-city voters are more likely to be critical.

Generalizing broadly, the larger urban centers are clearly the most politically pluralistic areas of Brazil, and they bring leftist and opposition parties, new social movements and NGOs, unions and professional associations, and diverse media outlets together into islands of vigorous debate. In this most abstract sense, urbanization is a positive democratic trend in the long term, as a more dynamic civil society, greater pluralism of political information sources, and heightened electoral competitiveness continue to make extensional gains throughout the national territory.

But moving from this abstract appraisal of urbanization to a more immediate assessment generates a very different picture. Inordinate pressures have mounted on the larger urban centers and state capitals, especially the twin megacities of São Paulo and Rio de Janeiro. Overcrowding, "favelization," pollution, transportation problems, spiraling crime rates, and a declining ability to deliver basic services have meant a downturn in the quality of life for many big-city residents. A declining quality of life in the larger, older, and predominantly coastal cities is not necessarily a threat to democracy, especially with the emergence of the economically dynamic and increasingly attractive mid-sized cities of the interior.

But it is the gradual loss of citizenship and "stateness" in the megacities that poses the most immediate challenge to democratic sustainability. The growth of the favelas and other "irregular" settlements means a decline in the ability of state authorities to deliver basic services to the population, thus depriving urban marginal residents of social, economic, and political citizenship. And where government agencies do not successfully penetrate, the "state" in the Weberian sense is often constituted by organized crime, particularly drug traffickers who control important favelas in Rio and São Paulo. These are important areas of urban Brazil that effectively escape state control, and in recent years, they have become battlegrounds pitting unaccountable state coercion, in the form of corrupt police forces, against equally unaccountable private coercion, in the form of heavily armed drug lords and their agents. . . . [T]hese conflicts impede the rule of law in democratic Brazil.

Arguments about the absence of "stateness" and the rule of law are also relevant to rural areas, but they are especially relevant in urban Brazil. First, in the absence of concerted state action, urbanization and "favelization" appear to be secular tendencies. Second, state authority and capacity are tested in precisely the areas that are political and administrative centers of Brazil. Third, the crime issue provides one of the easiest justifications for reactionary coercive elements to claim a breakdown in law and order under the democratic regime. Fourth, the large cities contain a significant portion of Brazil's middle class, whose support is crucial for democratic legitimation. And finally, urban marginals themselves are a constituency numbering in the millions whose basic needs have not yet been addressed by any regime, whether authoritarian or democratic. Only when they are convinced that the state can solve their problems, extending to them the true rights of citizenship, will they shift their loyalties from private to public authorities. Democratic sustainability is therefore intertwined with the resolution of Brazil's pressing urban problems.

ECONOMIC GROWTH, JOBS, AND THE RISE OF THE INFORMAL SECTOR

Although growing rapidly since 1945 (though sporadically after 1980), the Brazilian economy was broadly restructured in the course of five decades. In 1940, two-thirds of the economically active population (EAP) worked in the "primary" sector: in agriculture, mining, rubber tapping, Brazil nut extraction, and lumbering; in the mid-1990s the number stood at just above 20 percent. Moreover, agriculture went from 25 percent of the country's economic output to just 10 percent, and Brazil's historical export mainstay, coffee, was displaced by manufactured goods. Industry contributed over 35 percent of Brazil's gross national product (GNP) in 1990 while employing just 20 percent of its workers. Industrialization Brazil-style has therefore been described as unable to "absorb" significant portions of Brazil's labor force. Employment in industry doubled from 1950 to 1980 but has since decreased as a share of the workforce, supplanted by the boom in the service sector.

Employment in the service sector—a category of extraordinary diversity, ranging from hairdressers and street vendors to bankers, doctors, and real estate executives—now accounts for nearly half of the jobs in Brazil. Less discussed has been the growth of government employment in Brazil. The data on this are lacking, but when nurses, teachers, military, and state employees were considered in the 1990 count, the government sector accounted for more than 10 percent of all Brazilian workers. The growth of the Brazilian middle class, and especially women's career mobility, appear to have been closely linked to the expansion of public employment.

The recent boom in service sector employment was not matched by a commensurate increase in that sector's contribution to the country's GNP, which indicates the role that both urban and rural "informal" sector jobs played in absorbing the nation's unemployed during the economic crisis years of the 1980s and early 1990s. Informal-sector workers are usually defined as lacking a legal job contract, which in Brazil is popularly referred to as a *carteira assinada* ("signed work card"). Many of these "informals" work for themselves or for small firms, most are paid "under the table" in cash, and they have no legal recourse if they fall sick, are underpaid, mistreated, or laid off.

The size of Brazil's informal sector has been debated, but it is probably between half and two-thirds of the nation's workforce. Surveys in the early 1990s found over half of all Brazilian workers did not have a signed work card, and a 1995 household survey found that 57 percent did not contribute to the national social security system known as *previdência social*. There were substantial differences within these overall trends: three of every four northeasterners did not have employment that contributed to social security in 1995, and the same was true of four out of five domestic servants nationwide. Finally, despite frequent popular and journalistic assertions to the contrary, most informal workers were not in these jobs by choice—one of the IBGE surveys showed that a majority would have liked to switch to a job with a signed work card.

The implications of the informal sector are legion, but here we focus on those that are strictly political in nature. First, the expansion of the informal sector alters the traditional state-society relationship. From the perspective of the Brazilian state, the informal sector represents not only lost tax revenue but also an increasing portion of the economy and population outside the direct influence of policy. From the perspective of the informal workers, the social safety net does not normally encompass them, a fact that often renders meaningless both the discourses and the actions of politicians and state elites. For example, the worker protections innovated by the 1988 constitution, often described as *conquistas* by formal-sector labor activists, are devoid of meaning for half of the EAP. The arguments cited earlier about a decline in "stateness" and the lack of citizenship for nonelites are again relevant.

A second political implication of the informal sector is that a huge potential constituency of workers is lost to Brazil's labor unions, which not only weakens the ability of the unions to amass political clout through a majoritarian movement but also creates a gulf between formal and informal workers that politicians are all too willing to exploit. Kurt Weyland's elegant concept of "neopopulism" attaches theoretical significance to this phenomenon. According to him, there is a new wave of populists in Latin America who recognize that formal-sector workers are now less available for political mobilization, given that they were mostly incorporated in the earlier wave of "classical" populism and its promotion of import-substitution industrialization (ISI). But these same neopopulists also recognize that informal-sector workers are ripe for political mobilization, which is most easily achieved by pitting them against the entrenched "elites" who were the "winners" of the ISI era. For Weyland, neopopulists are also economic neoliberals. Thus, in the neopopulist vernacular, the term "elites" is also applied to established trade unions and their leaders, who are viewed as a "labor aristocracy" no less privileged and no less rent seeking than the middle class, the protected industrialists, the state bourgeoisie, and the other usual (ISI-bred) suspects that dominated from the 1930s to the 1970s.

Neopopulists, of whom the best Brazilian example is President Fernando Collor, mobilize informal workers against the "privileges" of organized labor, given that both neoliberal politicians and informal-sector workers have a common interest in the deregulation of the labor market. If Weyland's argument is correct and the politics of neoliberal adjustment works in this way to drive a wedge between formal-sector and informal-sector workers in Brazil and elsewhere, then the prospects for a broad, inclusive, and popular coalition building are bleak in the medium term.

This argument extends to macropolitical trends. Informal-sector workers appear easy to *mobilize* on a *temporary* basis (as voters) but difficult to *organize* on a *permanent* basis (into complex associations). Thus, these workers may contribute to the election of populist politicians but subsequently (in the absence of organizational clout and intermediating leaders) be unable to hold those same politicians accountable. This lack of any mediating structure is a key difference between classical populism and the current wave of neopopulism, and the problem is clearly rooted in the changing social structure of Brazil.

THE PERSISTENCE OF POVERTY AND SOCIAL INEQUALITY

Observers of Brazil are well aware that the tremendous postwar economic expansion did not bring benefits equally to the majority of Brazilians. Brazil's already skewed inequality of income worsened significantly after

1960, and by the end of the 1980s, Brazil was, as journalists pointed out, the "world champion of inequality." Bolivar Lamounier summed up the legacy of inequality that was bequeathed to the New Republic:

> [Income] concentration was still going on in the 1970s. The lowest 20% of the economically active population had gone from 3.9% of total income in 1960 to 3.4% in 1970, to 2.8% in 1980; the top 10% from 39.6% to 46.7%, to 50.9%. This means that the governmental policies practiced throughout this period, at best, did not counteract structural forces making for greater inequality; at worst they aggravated their effect. Combined with the massive character of absolute poverty that prevails in the Northeast and in the outskirts of all major cities, this degree of income concentration is undoubtedly one of the steepest challenges to democratic consolidation.

In 1990, five years into the democratic regime, the combined income of the richest 1 percent of Brazilians—about 1.5 million people—was two-thirds more than that of the poorest half of the country—about 75 million people. Another way to look at Brazilian inequality is that the richest 20 percent of the population earned thirty-two times more income than did the poorest 20 percent. Inequality in wealth (assets like property, vehicles, and stocks and bonds) and power are probably much greater but more difficult to measure and rarely discussed. Brazil's extremely high inequality is frequently cited as a prime cause of the country's phenomenal rates of violent crime, which are many times higher than those of similar nations.

Statistics, though important, do not express the devastating intensity of relative and absolute deprivation of the Brazilian poor. We do know that for three and a half decades, about 40 percent of the population was classified as "in poverty." The poverty line in Brazil is not consistently defined, but it often is directly or indirectly based on the basic food basket (*cesta básica*) needed to survive for a month, so families at or below the poverty line were often scarcely able to feed themselves, let alone clothe, house, and transport themselves to work. Many people were far below the poverty line. Though there is poverty in all regions of Brazil, the Northeast is still by far the poorest region, and the Southeast and South have the highest average incomes.

Inequality in Brazil cannot be understood without exploring its racial and ethnic dimensions. The nation was forged from the combination of Iberian colonists, indigenous peoples of the region, and slaves brought from Africa. Racial mixing occurred far more frequently than in most other nations, and recognition of skin color today represents more of a continuum than one of discrete categories. The legacy of miscegenation helped inspire the myth of a "racial democracy" of equal opportunity in Brazil, a thesis that has been thoroughly discredited by modern empirical research on race.

There was some change in the official statistics on the racial composition of Brazil over the period considered in this [article], but it appears to have been less the result of racial mixing than of a shift from categorical assignment by census takers (in the 1950, 1960, and 1970 censuses) to the option of re-spondent self-identification since 1980. The ranks of people calling them-selves mixed *(pardos)* have grown substantially from about 28 percent in the mid-1950s to around 40 percent since the 1980 census. These figures suggest that movements to create black pride and self-identification have not been entirely successful: the percentage identified by census takers as "black" in the 1950s was about 10 percent, twice the rate who identified themselves as such in 1995. Beliefs about the racial inferiority of blacks remain deeply en-trenched in Brazilians of all races. An influential 1995 book reported that black and *pardo* Brazilians were as likely as whites to agree with prejudicial survey statements about black Brazilians.

The myth of a "racial democracy" of a color-blind Brazil remains alive for many Brazilians, but there is substantial evidence that race continues to be a strong determinant of marginalization and poverty. Simply put, although not formally excluded from economic and political participation, Brazil's poor tend to be of darker skin than the wealthy and more powerful classes. In 1990, Afro-Brazilians were twice as likely as whites to live on less than one minimum monthly salary; *pardos* were far closer to blacks in this regard than to whites. At the other end of the spectrum, white privilege continues: whites were five times as likely as blacks and three and a half times as likely as *pardos* to earn ten or more minimum salaries a month. It has been widely noted that blacks are nearly completely absent from the top ranks of corpo-rate ownership and military and government bureaucracies. Racial inequal-ity in Brazil cannot be reduced to class: even controlling for education and other elements of "social capital," race continues to explain substantial por-tions of income and wealth inequality. Many of these observations about racial inequality are also true of gender inequality, which social change in Brazil has been slow to erase. There are also interaction effects of racial and gender discrimination: the combination of female and nonwhite status is a strong predictor of poverty.

The intense regional, racial, and income disparities in Brazil are well documented, but what do they imply for democracy? The political implica-tions of inequality have been exhaustively anticipated in the social science literature, and from Aristotle to Seymour Martin Lipset, social theorists have remarked that unequal societies constitute a daunting obstacle to de-mocratic governance. In his classic work on the conditions for democracy [*Polyarchy, Participation, and Opposition*], Robert Dahl noted that inequality tends to affect the chances for democratic consolidation in two major ways: in terms of the distribution of political skills among the population and in terms of the generation of social frustration that the regime is then hard-pressed to address. More recently, quantitative cross-national studies have tended to confirm an inverse relationship between inequality and democ-ratization.

The case of Brazil presents a stark test of these insights. If the persistence of poverty and inequality has not yet threatened the *survival* of Brazilian democracy, it has clear implications for the *quality* of democracy. Dahl's two intervening variables are clearly important here. First, the skewed distribution of economic power in Brazil clearly translates into inequality in the distribution of political skills and resources. It is true that this phenomenon has been partially offset by the astounding expansion of the franchise and by the proliferation of popular organizations, both of which are good news for democrats. But periodic voting does not come close to equalizing the entrenched power disparities caused by abysmal income distribution, nor does organized civil society yet encompass the majority of Brazil's poor and excluded. Second, social frustration may actually be aggravated by the combination of "inertial" inequality with democratic freedoms. For the vast majority of Brazilians, the only political resource is the vote. If, after repeated use, the vote has no apparent effect on the problems of poverty and inequality, the result is apathy, cynicism, and the delegitimation of parties and politicians. This phenomenon has been linked to the plebiscitarian voting patterns and to the weak legitimacy of democracy generally during the first decade of the New Republic.

With the brief exception of the Cruzado Plan in 1986, the persistence of inflation in the 1985–1994 period effectively prevented Brazil from making any headway on the twin issues of poverty and inequality. Inflation is an excellent though depressing example of how inequality often begets greater inequality. Prior to the onset of the inflationary spiral, the protective assets that afford a partial hedge against inflation were unevenly distributed among the population, being generally available only to the middle class and above. (Such assets include bank accounts, specialized financial instruments, access to dollars, ownership of real estate, and investment in consumer durables such as vehicles and telephone lines that hold value and are easily resold, not to mention the intellectual skills that are required to understand and cope with the economics of inflation.) When inflation hit, it effectively functioned as a punishing "tax" on the individuals who did not possess the protective assets. The poor were hit the hardest because their sole income was wages—which even with frequent adjustments could not keep pace with inflation—and because what little wealth they had was mostly held in cash. (Under hyperinflation, "cash kills.") The wealthy persevered.

The fact that inflation had a different impact on the rich and poor was no secret, and thus economists long suspected that the fastest-acting social policy in Brazil might simply be price stabilization. Initial data from President Cardoso's *Plano Real*, which began in July 1994, indicate it has indeed reduced the number of Brazilians living in poverty, initially by about a quarter. According to IBGE figures, the first year of the *Plano Real* markedly improved the Gini index of income inequality, from 0.600 in 1993 to 0.565 in 1995. When compared to cross-national data from the World Bank, the new Gini index would strip Brazil of the world championship in income inequality, moving it into sixth place behind Guatemala, South Africa, Kenya, Zimbabwe, and Panama. Still, comparisons such as these do little to comfort the majority of Brazilians: desperate poverty is widespread in Brazil, and the gap between the rich and poor is immense.

However salutary, Cardoso's inflation control was a necessary emergency measure, not a sufficient social policy. By 1998, the redistributive effects of the *Plano Real* had apparently run their course, and unemployment was at its highest point since 1984. The *Plano Real* needs to be supplemented by long-term and far-reaching social, educational, and employment policies, which amounts to a difficult balancing act, for although these social policies need to be implemented yesterday, their adoption must not adversely affect macroeconomic stability. We know that inflation punished the poor for the first ten years of democracy, and we know that if inflation returns it will do so again—thanks to entrenched inequalities that democracy has yet to solve.

EDUCATION AND ILLITERACY

Education is directly tied to Brazil's poverty and inequality, and officially reported rates of illiteracy dropped substantially, from around 60 percent of Brazilians over age fourteen in 1950 to about 20 percent in 1995. The official definitions have varied over the years, but usually respondents are considered illiterate only if they cannot sign their names. This definition has been harshly criticized, and estimates of "functional illiteracy" run as high as a third of adult Brazilians. These people cannot read newspapers or books, can barely do basic mathematics, and therefore tend to look for manual labor jobs. Half of Brazilian adults never completed more than four years of elementary school—six years is considered the minimum to participate in modern life in Latin America and to keep learning—and Brazil's rate of primary school completion is among the worst in Latin America.

Within Brazil, education and literacy—and the opportunities they bring—are unevenly distributed. Until 1980, females were less likely to be able to read and write than males, but that situation reversed slightly in the 1990s. Rural residents are nearly three times as likely as urban residents to be illiterate, and people with little or no income are nearly twenty times more likely to be illiterate as those with over two minimum salaries—27 percent versus 1.3 percent. Around 30 percent of black and mulatto Brazilians are illiterate, but only 12 percent of whites and 2 percent of Asian-Brazilians are. Finally, nearly a third of the people in the Northeast (32 percent) are officially classified as illiterate, nearly three times the rates in

Brazil's wealthier South and Southeast regions (11.6 percent and 12.4 percent, respectively).

Public universities in Brazil are free, and the federal institutions are the best in the country. But access to them is highly unequal: often, it is effectively only the upper-middle and wealthy classes that can afford the preparation in private secondary schools that is necessary for students to pass the competitive entrance exams, called the *vestibular*. Of the students in the federal universities, 44 percent come from the top 10 percent of the income distribution. The federal government spends over $5 billion a year on public universities, providing free tuition to many students who could afford to pay. Thus, at the university level, the children of wealthier families often receive a quality education at no cost while students from more humble backgrounds are forced to pay tuition at lower-quality, for-profit private institutions.

Meanwhile, primary schooling languishes. Public primary schools, especially in rural areas and small towns, are reported to be "so bad that students drop out. If they stay, they learn little or almost nothing." Somewhere between 3 million and 6 million Brazilian children between the ages of seven and fourteen are not attending school—the dropout rate can be inferred from the astonishing differential between the 1994 enrollments in primary school (31.1 million students) and secondary school (4.4 million students). In the same year, the number of students enrolled in institutions of higher education was about 1.7 million.

We draw attention to this disjuncture between university and basic education because it offers an additional insight into the maintenance of social inequality. Higher education policy has long directed resources disproportionately toward the relatively small number of students enrolled in the free federal universities (currently about 300,000, or one in six college students) rather than toward an alternative goal of boosting overall university enrollment rates, which would probably require charging tuition to those who can afford to pay. Thus, in 1989, Brazil's higher education enrollment rate, measured as the percentage of twenty–twenty-four-year-olds studying in all types of postsecondary institutions, was a meager 11 percent. This figure compared to about 16 percent in Thailand, 32 percent in Spain, and 38 percent in South Korea.

One might object that in spite of Brazil's comparatively low enrollments, the federal universities have served the country extremely well and that the goal of providing a free college education is a worthy one. We agree. But although the free federal university system may have been inspired by universalistic principles, in practice it tends to reinforce basic social inequalities via the erection of class-based barriers to university admission and the concentration of scarce budgetary resources in relatively few hands. Somewhat paradoxically, left-wing parties are the most vocal opponents of charging tuition for federal universities, despite persuasive evidence that free higher education serves to reproduce the national elite.

Turning to basic education, Brazil's shortcomings on this score have been magnified by recent changes in both local and global economic structures. In terms of the Brazilian economy, the immense dropout rate and the generally poor quality of primary education guarantee continued poverty and inequality, as well as hinder the increases in productivity that will be necessary to sustain economic vitality in the long term. In terms of the global economy, Brazil's educational system weakens its competitiveness vis-à-vis other industrializing nations. When the "Asian Tigers" burst onto the scene in the 1980s, for example, it was widely noted that countries such as Taiwan, South Korea, and Singapore had secondary education enrollment rates two to three times that of Brazil. Even taking into account the generally weaker commitment to education in Latin America, Brazil still fares poorly: of the cohort of Latin American children that began primary school in 1991, only 72 percent of Brazilian children reached grade five, compared to 84 percent of the children in Mexico and 95 percent of those in Chile and Uruguay.

Issues of education and literacy, then, affect Brazil in two fundamental ways: internally, in terms of income equality and social justice, and externally, in light of an increasingly globalized economy in which human capital is more important than ever before. Policymakers increasingly recognize these facts. In the 1990s, forward-looking local governments—particularly those of PT mayor Luiza Erundina in São Paulo, PT governor Cristovam Buarque in the Federal District, and PSDB governors Tasso Jereissati and Ciro Gomes in Ceará—have placed a renewed emphasis on primary education, especially teacher recruitment and student retention. To its credit, the Cardoso administration also emphasized basic-level education after 1995, with Education Minister Paulo Renato de Souza pushing to reverse the spending priorities that have favored elite universities for so long. These policies are necessary to ensure that Cardoso's economic reforms, which have stimulated renewed (albeit uneven) growth in the second half of the 1990s, do not aggravate poor income distribution owing to the very low educational baseline. Reviewing a decade of neoliberal reforms in Latin America, the Inter-American Development Bank warned in 1997:

> High inequality in education . . . has conditioned the impact of accumulation on income distribution. Greater inequality in education has brought with it greater income concentration. But there has also been an indirect effect. Educational inequity has limited the distributive effect of the accumulation of physical capital. In those countries with greater concentration of education, increased investment has *worsened* income distribution, possibly because it has increased the benefit of education, which is scarce, and reduced the need for unskilled labor. (Italics added)

These are sobering insights from an organization that has supported structural adjustment, and they point to some daunting challenges to future social development in a liberalized Brazil. Concentrations of education, income, and political power seem to go hand in hand, and Lamounier aptly characterized the Brazilian political economy as a case of "inequality against democracy." If Dahl is correct that inequalities in income and education translate directly into the distribution of political resources and skills, then persistent problems of illiteracy and inferior public education constitute a major challenge to democratic sustainability in Brazil.

CIVIC PARTICIPATION:
THE RISE OF CHURCHES,
SOCIAL MOVEMENTS, AND NGOS

Since 1985 Brazil has seen an explosion of participation in voluntary associations such as labor unions, professional groups, churches, environmental and women's social movements, and other nongovernmental organizations (NGOs). Because of the very dispersed and grassroots nature of these groups, their numbers are difficult to obtain or even estimate. However, trade union membership has increased by over tenfold since 1960, mostly since the political opening began to accelerate around 1980. Both rural and urban workers' unions reported memberships over 7.5 million each in 1992, and a 1995 household survey estimated that 11.3 million Brazilians were members of unions, equivalent to 16.2 percent of the labor force. Although fewer in number, professional white-collar workers have unionized at an even faster rate: only 40,491 were union members in 1960, but 549,680 were in 1992, a thirteenfold increase. Because salaries did not keep pace with inflation during military rule, unions of professionals were responsible for some of the most visible strikes during the democratic transition. Many of the newly unionized workers were government employees (*funcionários públicos*) in the direct or indirect federal administration.

Another important development in Brazilian labor is the growth of linkages between and among these various categories of workers. Many rural, urban manual, and professional workers in Brazil have been brought together in the first labor confederation to be truly independent of the Brazilian state, the Central Única dos Trabalhadores (CUT), which is closely tied to the Worker's Party (PT), both groups having had their origins in the labor unrest in greater São Paulo in the late 1970s. These two groups have attracted significant scholarly attention. But despite the considerable secondary literature on working-class militance in Brazilian politics, we still know surprisingly little about middle-class labor unions—especially the *funcionários públicos,* even though they occupy a central place in the battles over state reform. . . .

Religious groups have also become increasingly diverse and independent of the state . . . , and looking at religious identification, it is clear that the dominance of the Catholic Church has weakened considerably in recent decades. Historically, over 95 percent of the Brazilian population was Catholic, but the 122.4 million self-declared Catholics in the 1991 census would represent a considerable drop to around 83 percent, and most analysts believe that the true figure is now closer to 75 percent—possibly even lower. Whatever the correct percentage, these affiliation statistics often overstate religious commitment, because for many Catholics membership in the church is nominal at best.

Conversely, Protestant churches, which boast more cohesive and participatory congregations, are gaining considerable ground. From 1.7 million members in 1950, most of them in traditional, mainline denominations, the number of Brazilian Protestants rose to 13.2 million in the 1991 census, with almost all of the growth occurring in the burgeoning Pentecostal movement. A 1997 report estimated the figure at 16 million, which would mean that one in ten Brazilians is now a Protestant. Spiritualists and other religionists increased from 0.8 million and 0.4 million in the 1950 census to 2.3 million and 1.4 million in 1991, respectively.

Other civic groups grew rapidly during the period as well. The environmental movement exploded during the run-up to the Earth Summit in Rio de Janeiro in 1992 but has tapered off somewhat since then. Other NGOs are active in the areas of human rights, citizenship, racial justice, women's issues, and health, to name only a few, and many are becoming semigovernmental organs. . . . Their total memberships remain uncertain, but their political power is substantial as they control over $1.4 billion of resources, of which about $400 million is from abroad. Many of these groups grew with the support of the Christian-based communities of the progressive wing of the Catholic Church during the 1970s and 1980s. The Movimento dos Sem-Terra (Movement of the Landless) is just such a group. Exploding in the mid-1990s, it has flexed substantial political muscle by occupying ranches and sparking a national debate on the injustices of land tenure patterns in Brazil. Other groups, such as soccer clubs, neighborhood groups, and political and business interest groups, are more difficult to track, but many of them have increased substantially in number and membership.

This rapidly increasing density of Brazilian civil society is transforming the nation's politics, economy, and culture, and these transformations "from below" constitute what is arguably the most striking difference between the political landscape in the 1990s and that of the previous democratic experiment in 1946–1964. Today, a vibrant and diverse network of fully autonomous secondary associations provides a countervailing force against state power. . . .

As social theorists from Alexis de Tocqueville to Robert Putnam have argued, a vigorous civil society provides fertile ground for democratic government. An enormous amount of literature has suggested that as member-ship in secondary associations increases within a given society, then (one) "private" forms of political interaction, such as clientelism, are eroded; (two) "public" or "civic" styles of politics, based on republican notions of citizenship, are more likely to take root; (three) virtually all forms of politi-cal participation increase across the board; (four) values of equality and soli-darity tend to become more diffused; (five) norms of interpersonal trust—critical not only to political democracy but also to economic develop-ment—become more ingrained; (six) the ideal of self-government becomes more highly valued; and (seven) citizens are empowered in a way that al-lows them to hold their leaders more accountable.

Thus, it is not surprising that in Latin America, Eastern Europe, and else-where in recent years, the growth of civil society has weakened the long-term basis for authoritarian domination, facilitating transitions to democracy. Also, in their justly famous study of Italy, Robert Putnam and the others found that the growth of a civic community—or what the authors termed "social capital"—was causally linked to more effective government institu-tions at the local level. Although a longitudinal Putnam-like study has yet to be conducted in Brazil, impressionistic evidence indicates a similar pattern, with social movements and NGOs engendering innovative policies, greater accountability, and a gradual devolution of the policy debate to the level of ordinary people. These organizations are also a potent antidote to clien-telism and corruption. Although such practices will never be wiped out, the presence of civic associations deters them by promoting transparency and accountability. For all of these reasons and more, the new vibrancy of civil society and the popular organizations is likely to contribute positively to the quality of democracy in Brazil.

THE DIFFUSION AND CONTROL OF ELECTRONIC MEDIA

Because of Brazil's high levels of illiteracy and poverty, the electronic media cast a far wider shadow than any other source of information. Ra-dios spread earliest, reaching over half of Brazil's households by the late 1960s. The first television stations began to broadcast in Rio and São Paulo in 1950, and the medium began to spread slowly until its reach became nearly universal: while in 1970 just under one quarter of households had a television set, by 1995 some 81 percent did. Since 1980, the number of Brazilian households with a television set has been greater than the num-ber with a refrigerator, a pointed irony in a tropical country (74.8 percent in 1995. . .). The remote regions of Brazil's interior gained television trans-mitters just since the 1970s, and now in even the remotest Amazon there is access to national Brazilian television. Sales of television sets have again been skyrocketing since the *Plano Real* was introduced in 1994.

Statistics on the penetration of television are impressive, but they are meaningless without reference to the status of the other media. In 1994, there was one television set for every four Brazilians, a level similar to many neighboring countries, but only 1 newspaper for every 20 inhabitants, about one-third the level of developing nations overall. This disparity is best understood by comparing the circulation of print media in Brazil to that of neighboring countries at a similar level of economic development. In 1992, for example, the circulation of daily newspapers in Brazil was a paltry 55 per 1,000 inhabitants compared to 143 in Argentina, 147 in Chile, 205 in Venezuela, and 240 in Uruguay. Television dwarfs the print media, but within the television industry itself one player dominates. Despite the proliferation of cable and satellite dishes, many areas of Brazil still receive only the dominant Globo network, which regularly commands wide majorities of the viewership across the nation. It is only when one takes all factors into account—low literacy, the preeminence of television over newspapers, and a dominant player in network broadcasting—that one can truly appreciate the political salience of television's Globo network.

Far from being the result of a process of a natural "diffusion" of technology, the ownership, spread, and content of television stations in Brazil are the result of varied and widespread political manipulation. Two decades of policies by the military regime (1964–1985) subsidized television purchasing and infrastructure while helping TV Globo build a virtual monopoly in exchange for favorable coverage. Since then, positive coverage by Globo has proved a precious commodity for politicians.

In mid-1984, during the campaign for *Diretas Já!* ("Direct Elections Now!"), TV Globo abandoned its longtime military allies to support the opposition candidate, Tancredo Neves, for president. Tancredo then named to the Ministry of Communications a longtime Bahia governor, the indescribable Antônio Carlos Magalhães (known ubiquitously as ACM), owner of Globo affiliates in his home state and a close friend of Globo magnate Roberto Marinho. After Tancredo's death, Globo provided strong support for José Sarney, who maintained ACM at the ministry through the end of his term. In the 1989 elections, Globo provided none-too-subtle support for the campaign of Fernando Collor de Mello and backed him as president until the corruption scandals of 1992. Globo also gave favorable coverage to Fernando Henrique Cardoso in the campaign of 1994, once again illustrating the network's impressive impulse to support the government of the day. Although Globo's influence is often exaggerated in opposition discourse, there is no denying that presidents have cultivated Globo's support and vice versa.

Begun by the military regime, the politicization of media policy continues under the New Republic. Since 1985, licenses to operate television and radio stations ("concessions") have routinely been awarded to federal legislators in return for political support. Efforts to alter licensing policy in a more transparent direction have been thwarted by legislators and by the centralization of authority in the Ministry of Communications. Politicians who have won concessions from the ministry have developed media empires in their home states, which they then use to subtly or overtly influence their coverage on local television and radio news and in major newspapers they own or control. In some states, more than half of the local congressional delegation owns a television station, a radio station, or both. The electoral effect of this media manipulation is uncertain and much debated, but it is clear that Brazil's move to democracy has not been matched with a democratization (in this case, deconcentration of ownership and market share) of its most powerful communication medium, television.

Television has undoubtedly made some positive contributions to Brazilian democracy, notably by covering the mass mobilizations in favor of direct elections and Collor's impeachment. But the ongoing inequality in access to the electronic media weakens the quality of Brazilian democracy in several ways. First, the closed nature of the concessions-awarding process means that politicians grant most television and radio licenses to themselves, restricting entry to other actors and freezing the political elite in place. Second, oligopolization of television is an incentive to political personalism—this trend is actually most obvious, not at the federal level, but in subnational politics. Third, the political manipulation of the electronic media restricts the free flow of information and hampers true political pluralism. This factor is partially offset by the free television time that is awarded to all parties for sixty days prior to an election, but owner/politicians still have the upper hand when it comes to the day-to-day reporting of the news.

Two examples of political manipulation include the biased manner in which TV Globo reported on the final presidential debate in 1989, which is thought to have swayed some undecided voters away from Lula and toward Collor in the last days of the campaign, and the case of Lídice da Mata, a left-wing candidate who surprisingly won the mayoralty of Salvador da Bahia in 1992 and against whom the Magalhães clan used its local newspaper and Globo affiliate television station in a smear campaign that undermined her ability to govern. Of course, in a free market economy, owners of the means of communication are free to behave as they wish—but when public airwaves are consistently used for private ends, the quality of political debate suffers. Nonelite actors, especially popular organizations and progressive movements, find it difficult to express alternative viewpoints.

Historically, greater informational equality is a key requisite for successful democratization, and three reforms could alter the current Brazilian equation of inequality. Over time, improved literacy and education could reduce the dominance of electronic media over other forms of political information; the state could depoliticize communications policy by moving forward on current plans to create an independent regulatory agency, which would presumably remove licensing from the direct control of politicians; and various public interest groups, such as the National Forum for the Democratization of Communication, could succeed in forcing reforms that would grant greater media access to societal organizations. Until and unless such reforms are adopted, Brazilian democracy will enter the Age of Information with a decidedly unlevel playing field.

SUMMARY AND CONCLUSIONS

We began this [article] with an implicit question. In terms of conduciveness to democratic sustainability, how does the Brazil of the late 1990s compare to earlier time periods? The evidence indicates that, increasingly, this is a *new* Brazil: the shifting social context appears less and less like that of military rule and bears little resemblance to that which existed under the first democratic regime in 1946–1964. But as our analysis has shown, what is new is not necessarily positive for lasting democracy. For some of the "change" areas, the evidence seems quite unsettling. Unconstrained urbanization, for example, has contributed to crime, social exclusion, and a decline in stateness and governability in the largest cities. The rise of the informal sector fragments the working class, fosters "outsider" politics, weakens political accountability, and presents numerous challenges to public policy. And even though the Brazilian press is freer than ever before, the rise of television may have exacerbated informational inequality and contributed to a hitherto unimaginable form of machine politics—what Sylvio Costa and Jayme Brener, updating the classic 1948 work by Victor Nunes Leal, have termed *coronelismo eletrônico*.

The areas of "continuity" that we discussed—persistent poverty, inequality, and poor educational levels—constitute ongoing threats to democratic sustainability. Antedating 1985, 1964, and 1946, these are problems that seem impervious to political change in Brazil. However, long-term democratic legitimation (not to mention economic development and competitiveness) depends on the state's making some headway against these perennial problems. One of the most noteworthy aspects of Brazilian political discourse is that all parties and politicians, from left to right, give priority to these very same issues, offering "solutions" and pledging immediate redistribution should they be elected to power. But when real change is imperceptible at best, as it has been throughout the New Republic, the contrast between discourse and action is painfully obvious. In the 1990s, the addressing of social inequalities took a backseat first to inflation control and later to constitutional reform; this sequencing forces us to wonder whether the political willpower to bring about real change will materialize when neoliberal reforms are finally "complete," if they ever are.

But these problem areas should not distract our attention from some of the more positive trends we have identified. Rapid urbanization has created undeniable social problems, but the smaller proportion of Brazilians living in rural areas means that there is less space for traditional forms of political domination such as clientelism and *coronelismo*. At the midpoint of the previous democratic regime, 1955, only 41 percent of Brazilians lived in urban areas compared to 79 percent today. Moreover, basic literacy has increased from 48 percent in 1955 to about 78 percent today [in 2000] meaning that the country is much better prepared for a sustained investment in secondary education than it was during the first democratic experiment. The expansion of the suffrage has also made for a vastly more inclusive polity. It is difficult to imagine that in 1945, when Brazil's first democracy commenced, only 16 percent of Brazilians were voters; today, that figure stands at 62 percent. Finally, at the level of organized civil society, the Brazil of the turn of the millennium would have been utterly unrecognizable a generation ago. The explosion of interest groups, professional associations, churches, social movements, and NGOs since 1980 has changed the political landscape forever.

Given these extraordinary changes, we *suspect* that Brazilian civil society has now become too complex to govern by authoritarian means—although some actors would still be happy to test our hypothesis. Granted, the evidence for this assertion is suggestive, not conclusive, but in advancing it we draw attention to several factors. The first is that the twin concepts of suffrage and popular mobilization to make suffrage effective are now firmly inscribed in the repertoire of collective action in the New Republic. In 1984, the unprecedented *Diretas Já!* campaign helped bring about the transition to democracy; in 1989, the first presidential elections in twenty-nine years stimulated an impressive degree of mobilization within the electorate; and in 1992, the youthful *carapintadas* ("painted faces") spearheaded the popular campaign that helped drive Fernando Collor from office. These were three milestones of popular empowerment, and—thanks mostly to unforgettable television images—they are burned into the national consciousness. Mobilization is now always on the agenda. We note that an enfranchisement rate of more than 60 percent, and an electorate approaching 100 million, would presumably make it very difficult for a future authoritarian coalition to suspend direct elections or civil liberties, as the military did with relative ease in 1964.

The second factor, which we have briefly sketched . . . , is the phenomenal growth of civil society. The accumulation of nonstate organizational power in Brazil, when added to universal enfranchisement and to secular background changes such as urbanization and increasing literacy, would make it very difficult indeed to "turn back the clock" on Brazilian democratization at the end of the century. This is not to argue that democracy cannot be brought down, for it certainly could be. It is simply to suggest that any attempt to do so would have to reckon with an overwhelmingly urban nation, an empowered civil society, and the demonstration effect of periodic mass mobilization in Brazil since the early 1980s. Any one of these factors alone would be difficult enough for a coup to suppress, but taken together, they are quite formidable. We suspect that any authoritarian closure would likely be unsustainable and short-lived.

This points to our central, though still tentative, conclusion about the social context for democratic sustainability in Brazil. Sustainability refers both to survival and to the quality, i.e., the capacity for continuous self-improvement, of political democracy. As regards the quality of democracy, we have identified many problems that inhibit—and will inhibit well into the twenty-first century—the full inclusion of Brazilians into the polity, economy, and society. On many issues, especially poverty and inequality, prospects for the short and medium terms remain grim. But as regards the potential for *survival* of the post-1985 democracy, we have identified a number of trends that have solidified a social basis conducive to democracy, or perhaps to put it more accurately, *a social basis inimical to authoritarian retrogression.*

This tentative conclusion leads us to surmise that from a sociopolitical perspective, Brazil may now have entered a transitional phase of "low intensity democracy" that is likely to last for some time. With the polity having crossed the threshold into polyarchy, is it possible that sociodemographic factors now preclude a move backward into authoritarianism while simultaneously impeding the move forward into a regime of fully participatory, more egalitarian, higher-quality democracy? Is Brazil condemned to sociopolitical immobilism within a nominally democratic framework? Only time will tell whether democracy can be intensified, from above or from below.

We might conclude by saying that the glass is half empty, for in a cross-national, comparative perspective, the Brazilian social context for democracy remains relatively unattractive. But from our intranational, historical perspective, we prefer to see the glass as half full. Compared to the Brazil of a generation or two ago, the conditions for sustained democracy are better now than ever before.

SUGGESTIONS FOR FURTHER READING

Ames, Barry. *The Deadlock of Democracy in Brazil.* Ann Arbor: University of Michigan Press, 2000.

Evans, Peter. *Dependent Development: The Alliance of Multinational, State, and Local Capital in Brazil.* Princeton, N.J.: Princeton University Press, 1979.

Hunter, Wendy. *Eroding Military Influence in Brazil: Politicians Against Soldiers.* Durham: University of North Carolina Press, 1997.

Keck, Margaret. *The Workers' Party and Democratization in Brazil.* New Haven, Conn.: Yale University Press, 1992.

Kingstone, Peter, and Timothy Power. *Democratic Brazil: Actors, Institutions, and Processes.* Pittsburgh: University of Pittsburgh Press, 2000.

Lamounier, Bolívar. "Brazil: The Hyperactive Paralysis Syndrome," in *Constructing Democratic Governance: South America in the 1990s,* ed. Jorge I. Domínguez and Abraham F. Lowenthal. Baltimore: Johns Hopkins University Press, 1996, 166–187.

Lewin, Linda. *Politics and Parentela in Paraíba: A Case Study of Family-Based Oligarchy in Brazil.* Princeton, N.J.: Princeton University Press, 1987.

Pereira, Luiz Carlos Bresser. *Economic Crisis and State Reform in Brazil: Toward a New Interpretation of Latin America.* Boulder, Colo.: Lynne Rienner, 1996.

Power, Timothy J. *The Political Right in Postauthoritarian Brazil: Elites, Institutions, and Democratization.* University Park: Pennsylvania State University Press, 2000.

Stepan, Alfred, ed. *Authoritarian Brazil.* New York: Oxford University Press, 1973.

Stepan, Alfred, ed. *Democratizing Brazil: Problems of Transition and Consolidation.* New York: Oxford University Press, 1989.

Weyland, Kurt. *Democracy Without Equity: Failures of Reform in Brazil.* Pittsburgh: University of Pittsburgh Press, 1996.

USEFUL WEBSITES

Newspapers
O Estado de São Paulo
   www.estado.estadao.com.br

A Folha de São Paulo
   www.folha.uol.com.br

O Jornal do Brasil
   jbonline.terra.com.br

InfoBrazil (English language available)
   www.infobrazil.com

Government
Brazilian Finance Ministry (English language available)
   www.fazenda.gov.br

Chamber of Deputies
   www.camara.gov.br

Office of the President
   www.presidencia.gov.br

Senate
   www.senado.gov.br

General

Brazilian Studies Association
www.brasa.unm.edu

CIA World Fact Book: Resource for general information on Brazil.
www.odci.gov/cia/publications/factbook/geos/br.html

Latin American Network Information Center: Comprehensive website housed at the University of Texas with extensive Latin American links on a wide array of topics.
http://Lanic.utexas.edu

CHAPTER 8

Chile: A New Model for the Region?

READINGS IN THIS CHAPTER

*I*n October 1998, former Chilean dictator Augusto Pinochet made a trip to England for surgical work on his back. Pinochet, as well as virtually the entire Chilean office corps, benefited from an amnesty provision of the Chilean constitution that protected them from any kind of prosecution for their activities under military rule. Furthermore, Britain under former Prime Minister Margaret Thatcher had been a reliable ally of the general. As a result, Pinochet had reason to think he was safe from any kind of legal action. Great Britain, however, was a signatory to the European Convention on the Suppression of Terrorism, which exposed the former dictator to the risk of extradition to any country conducting a criminal investigation of Pinochet and his government. As it turned out, a Spanish judge, Baltasar Garzon, opened exactly such an investigation for the murder of Spanish citizens under Pinochet's notorious dictatorship from 1973 to 1989 and issued a request for the general's extradition to Spain on murder charges. Pinochet was arrested by British police as he came out of surgery. What followed was a period of weeks of tremendous tension and drama as the British government contemplated whether to honor their treaty obligations or whether to comply with the preferences of Chile's democratically elected government and send him home.

Ultimately, Pinochet was found medically unfit to stand trial and was sent home, but the weeks of tension had opened the issue of accountability of the military for the thousands of murdered, missing, jailed, and tortured Chileans under military rule. The issue of accountability and the understanding of the period of military rule itself made for deep divisions in Chilean society. For a large minority of Chileans, the sixteen years of military rule was justified by the efforts of Socialists to take over the country by illegitimate means. They believed the military did what it had to do to restore integrity and order to Chilean society. Yet, for a plurality, the military committed gross human rights violations and had escaped judgment, also through illegitimate means. The military itself hinted that it was not willing to permit a change to its status of impunity and that it was capable of preventing one. After ten years of stable and successful democratic rule, the Pinochet drama revealed that there were unexamined limits to Chilean democracy.

This division in Chilean society is tragic in some respects, not just because it is over a particularly harsh dictatorship, but also because Chilean society historically was much more successful at managing political conflicts through democratic means than virtually any Latin American country. By the early twentieth century, the Chilean political system had developed a tendency to form into three distinct political parties or clusters of parties on the right, on the left, and in the center ideologically. Chilean landed elites could mobilize the votes of peasants working their land in support of right-wing parties, and as a result felt that they were competitive in the electoral arena. This moderation among elites made it easier for all organized political groups to organize themselves through the political party system and to use the party system to broker deals and foster political moderation and compromise. This aspect of party politics was supported by an unusually strong commitment to legalism in Chilean society and even among the military. As a result, while democracy was under constant threat and subject to frequent failure in much of the region, Chile stood out as a model of democratic stability.

That situation changed in the 1950s and into the 1960s as the divisions in Chilean society grew deeper and deeper, ultimately undermining the more centrist and compromising elements in all three political groupings. The divisions intensified over economic policy and its social consequences, over the role of multinationals in Chile's crucial copper industry, and through the intense politicization of everyday life. In particular, Christian Democrats, supported by large amounts of U.S. money, campaigned to reform the Chilean economy and society through gradual, negotiated means and played on concerns about the connections between some left-wing parties and the Soviet Union. The left, led by the Socialist Party, focused on the increasingly obvious signs that Chile's economic policy was failing to address problems of urban and rural poverty and that the U.S. multinational corporations that operated Chile's copper mines were unwilling to reinvest their profits back into the country. The two parties competed intensely, with the Christian Democrats winning election in 1964 and the Socialists winning in 1970. Ultimately, neither party was able to solve the country's deepening economic problems while managing the sharp political divisions within the country.

The Socialist victory, under their leader Salvador Allende, was the beginning of the collapse of democratic rule in Chile. The breakdown stemmed from a variety of causes, although partisans of one view or another can and do limit their focus to a single or small number of factors. For example, many critics of the U.S. role in Latin America—whether in Latin America or in the United States—place much of the blame for the 1973 coup on overt and covert U.S. policy. The Nixon administration did restrict trade with Chile and cut off the Chilean government from U.S. financing and access to international financial institutions. On the covert side, the story of U.S. involvement is still not fully told, but there is no doubt that the Nixon administration supported the coup and at the very least provided intelligence information to coup leaders. Focusing exclusively on the U.S. role, however, diminishes the very considerable responsibility of many other actors and many other factors. For one, the strategy of the Allende government and its political allies greatly magnified the divisions already existing in society. The Socialist strategy pushed politics towards the extremes and frequently aimed more at outright defeat of the opposition than at the compromise and moderation that the Chilean system had encouraged for so long. Thus, the U.S. economic policy response was harsh, but it was a response to the Allende administration's decision to nationalize the copper industry (supported by most political parties), but to do so without any compensation (vigorously opposed by both the U.S.

and the Chilean opposition parties). Allende's government nationalized a large number of private Chilean firms and effected significant redistribution of land. While both moves were ostensibly legal—that is, they followed existing law—both stretched the law in dubious ways. Allende was a democratic president, but between 1970 and 1973, the behavior and decisions of Allende and his allies in smaller left-wing parties played a critical role in breaking democratic rule.

Similarly, the center Christian Democratic Party followed a strategy of brinkmanship making Allende's efforts to compromise much less likely to succeed and ultimately leading to the splintering of the party into the extremes on the left and right. Finally, the resistance of the elites on the right to compromise on issues crying for some kind of social justice and to rely on extreme tactics themselves made Allende's more extreme tactics likely as well. In short, the coup was made in Chile by Chileans with U.S. help and with plenty of blame to share all around.

Regardless of how one chooses to assign blame, there is no question that the 1973 coup led by Augusto Pinochet was one of the bloodiest episodes in Chilean history and one of the bloodiest coups in Latin American history. Roughly 3,000 people died as the military purged the country and its major institutions of leftists or suspected sympathizers. Land reform was reversed through brutally violent means. In place of Allende's socialist redistributive economic program, Pinochet's economic team introduced neoliberalism to Latin America. For sixteen years, Pinochet ruled through a combination of force and repression on one hand, and on the other hand through political support from elites and the middle class (as well as some of the poorest segments of society who obtained targeted social policy benefits especially in the 1980s). In economic terms, the Pinochet government oversaw a dramatic transformation of the economy from one with significant government involvement (as in most of Latin America) to one in which the market was the dominant organizing principle of the economy.

By the late 1980s, political opposition had begun to re-emerge in Chile, but Pinochet's economic policies had helped produce the most dynamic economy in Latin America. In that context, Pinochet permitted a referendum on whether to continue to rule or to permit elections. He lost both the 1988 referendum and the 1989 election, which brought to power an alliance of Socialists and Christian Democrats determined never to permit a breakdown of the political system such as occurred in 1973 again. Unfortunately for the new democracy and its newly elected government, the still very powerful military agreed to hand over power but wrote the terms of its own withdrawal from power. The legacy for Chile of this transition is the ongoing sharply divided evaluation of military rule as well as a number of authoritarian holdovers that limit the depth of Chilean democracy. These leftover elements from military rule are challenges to what is otherwise one of Latin America's most successful democracies. This chapter explores this theme.

In "Democratic Institutions and Civil-Military Relations," Gregory Weeks provides insight into the way the Chilean military operates since the restoration of democracy and the challenges it continues to pose to the new regime. Although the military wrote the constitution in effect in the new democracy and designed the institutions under which it was to operate, it has not been content with the functioning of the institutions. As a result, it has chosen to circumvent political institutions and express its preferences through other channels and to resist efforts to contain it through legal institutional means. Over time, two key institutions—the congress and the judiciary—have gained in strength and in their willingness to sanction officers who refuse to accept civilian authority. Nevertheless, Weeks observes that democratic governance requires military submission to civilian institutional controls and the continuation of military resistance to reliance on official institutional channels represents an important ongoing challenge to Chilean democracy.

Patrick Barrett explores the limits that Chile's transition to democracy established for the new regime. In "The Limits of Democracy: Socio-Political Compromise and Regime Change in Post-Pinochet Chile," Barrett warns that Chile's new democracy is built on a compromise that has limited the scope of economic policy. In brief, the political bargain exists between the country's powerful business elites and the leaders of the two main center-left parties that have ruled Chile continuously since the restoration of democracy in 1989. The breakdown of the democratic regime in the 1970s reflected the tension between the need to promote conditions for growth and the accumulation of capital on one hand, and the need to promote economic inclusion and redistribution on the other. The old democratic regime was not able to manage the tension. According to Barrett, the new regime has managed the tension by subordinating concerns about equity and socioeconomic justice to the need to promote capital accumulation and economic growth.

Judy Polumbaum, a scholar of journalism, illustrates another area in which Chile's democracy has settled into a quiet accommodation of the stalemate between different memories of the past. Polumbaum reviews the emergence of a daring and subversive press that challenged the dictatorship in Chile, often at great risk to journalists. But, in the new democracy, the same journalists have become part of a culture of "self-censorship" where elite pressure is subtle but pervasive and journalistic reporting has become passive rather than probing.

DATA TABLES

Table 8.1
Chile Fact and Data Sheet

Population (July 2003, estimated):	15,665,216
Ethnic Groups:	White and White-Amerindian 95%, Amerindian 3%, other 2%
Religions:	Roman Catholic 89%, Protestant 11%
Government Type:	Republic
Capital:	Santiago de Chile
Administrative Divisions:	13 regions
Date of Independence:	September 18, 1810
Constitution:	September 11, 1980, effective March 11, 1981, amended July 30, 1989, 1993, and 1997
Executive Branch:	President Ricardo Lagos Escobar, elected March 11, 2000; president and vice president elected on the same ticket by popular vote to a 6-year term.
Legislature:	Bicameral National Congress
	• Senate has 49 seats; 38 members are elected by popular vote to an 8-year term, 9 members are designated, and 2 members are former presidents who serve 6-year terms and are senators for life. Distribution of seats as of 2003: CPD, 20 seats (PDC 12, PS 5, PPD 3); APC, 16 seats (UDI 9, RN 7); independents, 2 seats.
	• Chamber of Deputies has 120 seats. Elected by popular vote to a 4-year term. Distribution of seats as of 2003: CPD, 62 seats (PDC 24, PPD 21, PS 11, PRSD 6); UDI, 35 seats; RN, 22 seats; independent, 1 seat.
Main Political Parties:	Alliance for Chile (Alianza) (APC)—including RN and UDI, Christian Democratic Party (PDC), Coalition of Parties for Democracy (Concertacion) (CPD)—including PDC, PS, PPD, PRSD, Communist Party (PC), Independent Democratic Union (UDI), National Renewal (RN), Party for Democracy (PPD), Radical Social Democratic Party (PRSD), Socialist Party (PS).
Military Spending (FY1999):	$2.5 billion
Military Spending, Percentage of GDP (FY1999):	3.1
GDP (2002, estimated):	PPP $156.1 billion
GDP Composition by Sector (2001, estimated):	Agriculture: 11% Industry: 34% Services: 56%

(cont.)

Table 8.1 (cont.)
Chile Fact and Data Sheet

Main Industries:	Copper, other minerals, foodstuffs, fish processing, iron and steel, wood and wood products, transport equipment, cement, textiles
Main Agricultural Products:	Wheat, corn, grapes, beans, sugar beets, potatoes, fruit, beef, poultry, wool, fish, timber
Export Partners (2002):	U.S., 19.1%; Japan, 10.5%; China, 6.7%; Mexico, 5%, Italy, 4.7%; UK, 4.4%
Import Partners (2001):	United States, 27.4%; Argentina, 13.5%; Germany, 8.9%; Japan, 5%
External Debt (2002):	$40.4 billion

Table 8.2
Presidents of Chile

Tenure	President
1876–1880	Aníbal Pinto
1881–1885	Domingo Santa María
1886–1890	José Manuel Balmaceda
1891–1895	Jorge Montt
1896–1900	Federico Errázuriz
1901–1904	Germán Riesco Errázuriz
1905	Rafael Rayas
1906–1910	Pedro Montt
1910	Elías Fernández Albano
1910	Emiliano Figueroa
1910–1915	Ramón Barros Luco
1915–1920	Juan Luis Sanfuentes
	Luis Barros Borgoño
1920–1924	Arturo Alessandri Palma
1924	Luis Altamirano
	Carlos Ibañez del Campo[1]
1925	Arturo Alessandri Palma[2]
	Luis Barros Borgoño
1925–1927	Emiliano Figueroa
1927–1931	Carlos Ibáñez del Campo[3]
1931	Pedro Opazo Letelier
1931	Juan Esteban Montero Rodríguez
1931	Manuel Trucco Franzani
	Juan Esteban Montero Rodríguez
1932	Arturo Puga
1932	Marmaduke Grove
1932	Carlos Dávila Espinoza

(*cont.*)

Table 8.2 (cont.)
Presidents of Chile

Tenure	President
1932	Bartolomé Blanche Espejo
1932	Abraham Oyanedel
1932–1937	Arturo Alessandri Palma
1938–1941	Pedro Aguirre Cerda[2]
1941	Gerónimo Méndez Arancibia
1942–1946	Juan Antonio Ríos Morales
1946	Alfredo Duhalde Vázquez
1946	Juan A. Irabarren
1946–1951	Gabriel González Videla
1952–1957	Carlos Ibañez del Campo
1958–1963	Jorge Alessandri Rodríguez
1964–1969	Eduardo Frei Montalva
1970–1973	Salvador Allende Gossens[3]
1973–1989	Augusto Pinochet Ugarte[1]
1990–1993	Patricio Aylwin
1994–1999	Eduardo Frei Ruiz-Tagle
2000–present	Ricardo Lagos Escobar

[1]Military.

[2]Resigned.

[3]Removed by coup.

8.1 Democratic Institutions and Civil-Military Relations: The Case of Chile (2001)

GREGORY WEEKS

INTRODUCTION

In December 1999, Chileans cast their votes in a presidential election, the third time they have done so since the end of the military government of General Augusto Pinochet (1973–1990). Pinochet himself retired in 1998 and has been harried by house arrest in England as a result of judicial proceedings against him in Spain. Given such major historical changes, we would expect that political institutions in Chile are becoming quite effective in channeling and dealing with military concerns. But how effective are they? This article analyzes the four main political institutions that mediate civil-military relations in Chile: the Defense Ministry, the National Security Council, Congress, and the Judiciary.

The construction and/or resuscitation of institutions has been a crucial part of building democratic political systems. The military regimes that once ruled Latin America are fading ever more into the past. In some cases, such as Ecuador, an entire generation has grown up not knowing military rule at all. Yet, interestingly, even though the military no longer governs Latin American countries, the scholarly debate over civil-military relations in the region has rarely been as nonconsensual. In particular, we face the question of whether or not civilian leaders have been successful in building and reinforcing political institutions, especially in a postauthoritarian context. Studies of different countries can examine the same situation and come to very different conclusions. Often, different studies appear simply to speak past one another.

The intent of this article is to speak directly to the central debate, namely the effectiveness of democratic institutions in the postauthoritarian era. Political institutions can have an independent impact on political outcomes, and therefore deserve further attention. Given the importance of institutions in determining policy, a useful strategy is to examine those formal institutions that mediate civil-military relations. By effective we mean whether the military accepts that formal institutions are the only appropriate avenues for expressing opinions, concerns, and/or suggestions with regard to military policy.

Gregory Weeks, "Democratic Institutions and Civil-Military Relations: The Case of Chile." *Journal of Third World Studies*, 2001, Vol. 18, no. 1, pp. 65–85. Reprinted by permission.

INSTITUTIONS AND POLITICAL ACTORS

In a commonly noted definition, March and Olsen characterize institutions as collections of interrelated rules and routines that define appropriate action in terms of relations between roles and situations. As such, institutions mediate between political actors. Rules govern these relationships. The scope of action of each actor is thus well-defined and fairly predictable in any given situation. If institutions are effective, then all involved in political decision-making know the roles of all other political participants and the manner in which those decisions will be reached and ultimately implemented.

These institutions are not often transitory. Considerable effort must be expended to construct them, which means they cannot be demolished easily. Consequently they become part of the political landscape. As they become entrenched, more and more they structure the ways in which different political actors behave. Over time, not only do they mediate but they can also help define political actors' goals.

The application of the new or historical institutionalism is novel for the study of civil-military relations. It represents an interesting avenue of inquiry, since civilian supremacy over the military depends so much on the ability of civilians to compel the military to accept decisions and to follow the rules that each institution carries with it. In the absence of effective rules, the military (as well as all other political actors) proceeds in an ad hoc manner to pursue its various interests, leaving civilians off balance and less able to respond effectively.

Pion-Berlin's institutional analysis of Argentina is therefore interesting. His thesis is provocative because it contradicts the many analysts who argue that continuity characterizes civil-military relations in Latin America and that the armed forces have retained significant political influence even after leaving power. Instead, he argues, those analyses fail to recognize the importance of democratic institutions. Those institutions were constructed precisely to limit the military's political influence to only those areas where such influence was widely considered legitimate. For example, few would expect U.S. military to miss the chance to flex its political muscles to lobby congress for weapons procurement or other issues related to professional development, and so, he argues, we should not expect differently from any other military establishment. In particular, high levels of institutional autonomy and concentration of authority lead to the strengthening of civilian policy makers.

Therefore, military behavior may be conditioned by institutions. As long as the armed forces follow institutional rules, then exerting pressure for or against certain policies will not necessarily be detrimental to civilian governance. Institutions thus stand between the military and its policy goals. Although the institutional process will be predictable, the outcome will not.

Political institutions can take on a life of their own, perhaps not even following the intentions of their creators. In this view, in the postauthoritarian context the military finds itself constrained by institutional rules even if it held a position of power at the time of transfer from military to civilian government. The transaction costs involved in manipulating them become too high even for the military, as they do for all other political actors as well. Not only are institutions difficult to destroy, but they also do not change easily. This does not mean that institutions are static or rigid, but rather that once created they can often resist major modifications.

According to the historical institutional argument, the military's range of options diminishes as a result of institutional roadblocks. Even if the military itself created the institutions, once constructed these same institutions will not necessarily always conform to military interests. The concerns of the military leadership become channeled through political institutions, which in turn increases the costs involved in defying institutional rules.

However, any emphasis on the institutional bases of civilian control over the military must take into account those instances where the military itself played an important role in formulating institutional rules. Even when military governments have given way to civilian rule, some institutions retain undemocratic features. Most Latin American constitutions, for example, include a number of military prerogatives. Indeed, some constitutions were written under the direction of military rulers. In sum, we must remain cognizant not only of whether civil-military relations take place primarily under the auspices of formal institutions, but also whether or not those same institutions are primarily democratic in nature. To what degree do military-created institutions correspond to the military's interests?

To determine the effectiveness of institutions, we must therefore make an assessment of how much they effectively limit the military's options. How much do institutional rules force the armed forces to accept decisions with which they expressly disagreed? If political institutions do not force the military to accept decisions with which it disagrees, then institutional strength cannot be deemed high.

Therefore, one critical issue that must be explored further is precisely the cost of circumventing institutions. As North argues, an essential part of the functioning of institutions is the costliness of ascertaining violations and the severity of punishment. In Latin America and elsewhere, political actors circumvent institutions at some point. With regard to the armed forces, in all countries the military will seek to exert pressure to achieve its goals through a variety of means that do not necessarily involve institutions. At the extreme, those efforts involve public defiance of stated civilian policy or even the use of force.

The idea that institutions are often circumvented is neither new nor controversial. A broad range of activities can take place outside the auspices of formal rules and procedures. In fact, it has been argued that activities such as avoidance, discretion, and overlooking can sometimes increase confidence in institutional structures. This is because they absorb uncertainty, thus contributing to a general aura of confidence within and outside the organization. In other words, if small deviations occur from those formal procedures, particularly in areas where the institution is less equipped to deal with a problem or issue, then the institution will benefit if the alarm is not sounded as to its lack of effectiveness.

Yet, with regard to civil-military relations this argument rings rather hollow, especially given how much is at stake, namely control over the state's coercive force. For civilian supremacy to hold, the institutional structures that mediate civil-military relations must be strong. If many deviations from the formal rules occur, then civilian supremacy will be eroded. We must assess empirically the degree to which the military follows formal institutional rules in addition to the ability of civilians to impose costs on the military for refusing to adhere to institutional dictates.

A number of authors assert that informal rules and practices play an integral role in determining political outcomes. Yet there has been little discussion about the manner in which less formal political interactions damage the credibility and effectiveness of formal institutions. This is particularly important in the context of civil-military relations. If the armed forces avoid formal institutions, civilian policy makers are left in a position of very high uncertainty. When the military ignores institutional structures, even the use of military force becomes a possibility. At the very least, civilians are left guessing.

CIVIL-MILITARY RELATIONS AND POLITICAL INSTITUTIONS IN CHILE

When President Patricio Aylwin took office in March 1990, Chilean political institutions in general were weak. Seventeen years of military government had undermined, temporarily erased them, or even created new ones. Soon after the coup d'état in 1973, the military regime made clear its intention to remake Chile's institutional structures. General Pinochet spoke of creating a new institutionality in Chile. Under his direction, a commission spent years working on a new constitution. A plebiscite ratified that document in 1980, thus replacing the 1925 constitution.

The military regime's goal in part involved fashioning a more prominent position for the armed forces in the country's political institutions. For example, as discussed below, Pinochet intended the National Security Council to be a vehicle for military influence over the political system. Given the military regime's emphasis on forging the new institutionality, the constitution grants them the role of the protectors of institutional order. In all, the military wanted to ensure that its voice would always be heard; if and when crises erupted, the military leadership would thus be an integral part of the process. Indeed, if a crisis reached the point where the commanders in chief believed that Chile's institutions were at risk, then the constitution codified the right to armed intervention.

The new administration thus faced the formidable challenge of reforming the more authoritarian institutions and reinforcing the democratic ones in order to assert civilian influence in the face of any military intransigence. The conception, creation, and implementation of policy, whether it be defense policy or not, had been the military's prerogative for nearly seventeen years. After 1990, the new civilian government sought to wrest back the policy process.

THE DEFENSE MINISTRY

The Defense Ministry is a political institution dedicated solely to military issues. As such, the ministry represents a critical link between civilian policy makers and the officer corps, an arena where issues related to the armed forces can be debated and/or negotiated. Importantly, the Defense Ministry is a forum for military concerns, but with the proviso that ultimately the President of the Republic will have the final word on all decisions. Although military opinions and suggestions will be taken into consideration, they need not be followed.

The administration of Patricio Aylwin, which took office in March 1990, inherited a largely powerless Defense Ministry. Created by decree in 1932, at the outset the ministry was an important contact point. Defense Minister Emilio Bello Codecido and army commander in chief General Oscar Novoa worked together to establish tranquil civil-military relations after the political upheavals of the 1920–1932 period. By the late 1930s, that goal had largely been accomplished. Thereafter the ministry's political relevance went on the decline, particularly since subsequent civilian governments began to show less interest in military issues.

During the military regime (1973–1990), Defense Ministers were all officers, and the ministry itself became regarded as a career graveyard. General Pinochet was simultaneously president of the Republic and army commander in chief. Defense policy was generated in his offices, not in the ministry. Despite the ministry's general lack of prestige as the new civilian government assumed power, the Aylwin administration attempted to compel the military leadership to accept the Defense Minister as a viable go-between.

First, Aylwin appointed a political veteran to the post. Christian Democrat Patricio Rojas had been Minister of the Interior under President Eduardo Frei Montalva (1964–1970) and more recently had been campaign manager for the successful senatorial candidacy of Andrés Zaldílvar. Second, Aylwin refused to follow the tradition of filling the subsecretary posts with officers.

In exchange, he granted the military veto power over the choices. The position of Subsecretary of the Army proved the most difficult, since Pinochet vetoed all of Aylwin's choices who had defense expertise, finally agreeing to Marcos Sanchez, a lawyer with no previous experience with either the army or defense issues.

Rojas confronted the extremely difficult task of persuading the military to utilize a hitherto ineffective political institution. Even before Aylwin took office, Pinochet declared that the Defense Ministry was a purely administrative body and that he planned to take all important matters directly to the president. Very quickly, enmity developed between Rojas and Pinochet that would be present during Aylwin's entire four year term.

In December 1990, Pinochet called for a quartering to barracks of every army soldier in the country, a measure traditionally associated with ensuring readiness for battle, but also often a precursor to military rebellion. Pinochet and his supporters blamed congress for making false accusations against him. Pinochet was also furious at Rojas for purportedly having demanded the general's resignation. The so-called ejercicio de enlace revolved around those two issues, as a congressional commission investigated whether or not Pinochet's son had been involved in illegal business deals during the military regime.

The crisis lasted several weeks, and Pinochet successfully bypassed the Defense Ministry as he negotiated a solution. Resolution of the conflict was reached in an ad hoc manner, outside the auspices of the Defense Ministry, excluding Defense Minister Rojas altogether. That strategy of going around Rojas would recur. Since Aylwin refused to bow to army pressure and fire Rojas, the Defense Ministry was not an important political player during his administration.

The second major political-military crisis for the new administration began in May 1993. During the so-called boinazo, soldiers we reposted outside the army's headquarters in downtown Santiago in response to an announcement in the press that the courts were about to reopen the aforementioned case against Pinochet's son. Yet the incident was further exacerbated by the failure of the Defense Ministry to process a number of army documents, including payments for promoted officers, which the army claimed were languishing in the office of Subsecretary of War Sanchez.

Pinochet believed that many within the government were intent on forcing him out and that, in particular, Defense Minister Rojas deliberately mistreated the army in order to foment discontent within the ranks against the commander in chief. In this view, the navy and air force did not receive similarly poor treatment, thus proving that there was a concerted effort to force Pinochet's removal. For these reasons, the general refused to allow crisis resolution to be channeled through the Defense Ministry. Instead, the army leadership dealt only with selected government officials.

When Eduardo Frei became president in March 1994, he used care in deciding upon a new Defense Minister. He chose Edmundo Pérez Yoma, a conservative Christian Democrat whose father had been assassinated by leftist terrorists in 1969. Immediately, Pérez Yoma announced that he would seek a much more professional as opposed to political relationship with the armed forces. Sending his own signals, Frei retained Jorge Burgos as Subsecretary of War. Burgos had worked well with the army after replacing Marcos Sanchez in the aftermath of the boinazo. The government's strategy was to emphasize technical defense issues within the Defense Ministry, an area in which the military had long believed civilians to be deficient. In addition, Pérez Yoma would not refer to military autonomy, but rather civilians' relative leadership.

Given Pérez Yoma's support for the military, relations improved considerably. During 1995, when the Chilean Supreme Court tried and convicted retired General Manuel Contreras for involvement in the murder of Orlando Letelier, the Defense Minister played an important role. The army negotiated largely with Pérez Yoma, extracting a variety of concessions before finally handing Contreras over. One impetus for the army came when Pérez Yoma threatened to resign as a result of his inability to end the crisis. A major drawback was that these discussions constituted a direct challenge to the court's authority. Although the Ministry of Defense's constitutional role is to mediate military-executive relations, it has no jurisdiction over the judicial system. The army's interest in the Defense Ministry, therefore, seemed limited to those times when a sympathetic minister held the position.

Interestingly, in January 1998, when the Chamber of Deputies began the process of launching a constitutional accusation against General Pinochet (see the discussion on congress), Pérez Yoma distanced himself and refused to act as mediator, stating that the accusation was a political, not military, matter and therefore was out of his sphere of authority. He still smarted from the President's decision in late 1997 to veto an army promotion that Pérez Yoma had initially approved. In fact, the Defense Minister resigned soon after. The army thus looked elsewhere to express its concerns.

The lack of ministerial leadership between January 1998 and July 1999 reinforces the notion that the military continued to adhere to the Defense Ministry only conditionally. During that time, Frei named two different ministers. The first was Raul Troncoso, an old political ally of Frei's who sought to reintegrate the ministry into the debate over the constitutional accusation. However, when the final vote failed to proclaim Pinochet guilty of the charges levied against him, the ministry had played only a limited role in influencing the outcome. The second minister was José Florencio Guzman, a close associate of Troncoso. The army in particular viewed him as weak and often continued contacting Troncoso even when he had moved from the Defense Ministry to Interior.

As the Pinochet crisis in England remained unresolved in mid-1999, Frei finally decided to bring back Pérez Yoma. The military simply refused to bring its concerns to the ministry unless the leadership trusted the Defense

Minister. Under the other Defense Ministers, less formal contact points were the rule, which undermined the formal institutions. For these reasons, the Defense Ministry cannot yet be considered an effective political institution for civil-military relations. When its institutional rules do not conform to military desires, the military circumvents the ministry, which becomes largely irrelevant.

If the ministry were an effective institution, we would expect the military leadership to contact the Defense Minister in order to express preoccupation with a given issue. Once that concern had been expressed, moreover, the military would accept the ultimate decision made by either the minister or the president, even if the outcome proved inimical to military interests. In Chile, that situation has yet to hold.

THE NATIONAL SECURITY COUNCIL

Created by the 1980 constitution, the Consejo de Seguridad Nacional (CSN) has represented a source of considerable leverage for the armed forces in Chile. Although a 1989 plebiscite limited its prerogatives, half of the council's eight members are commanders in chief, one each from the armed forces and the national police. The military regime intended the CSN to provide the armed forces with a mechanism for routine influence over the political system.

Many analysts argued that the CSN would have a very detrimental effect on civilian governments' ability to assert control over the armed forces. In practice, the CSN has had mixed results. Only sporadically has it been central to conflict resolution. In fact, neither civilians nor commanders in chief chose to convoke the CSN during the ejercicio de enlace and the boinazo. The primary reason was that the 1989 reform erased the military's advantage, thus making any vote a more risky proposition.

In 1993, the boinazo provoked a public discussion about whether a meeting of the National Security Council should be called. The army did not wish it to meet, because from the beginning of the boinazo army officers gave assurances that the troop movement was entirely normal. The army's goal had been to pressure the government while claiming that nothing was out of the ordinary. The Aylwin administration did not want the CSN to meet either. Calling its members together would represent an admission that national security had been at risk as a result of military disobedience, an admission the administration refused to make.

During the Frei administration, the Contreras affair did not lead to a meeting of the CSN and neither did the constitutional accusation levied against General Pinochet. However, it did meet after General Pinochet was placed under house arrest in England. Between October 1998 and July 1999, the CSN convened four times to discuss different aspects of the case, with the result of showing support for President Frei's initial attempts to secure Pinochet's release; proclaiming that Chile's sovereignty was being compromised; protesting the British government's decision to keep Pinochet in the country; and ultimately discussing the possibility of invoking humanitarian reasons to bring Pinochet back to Chile. As Pinochet's case progressed, the CSN had become a positive forum for civil-military dialogue.

Thus far, the military has not been able to use the CSN to put pressure on other civilian institutions, such as congress. Nonetheless, the power to convoke it grants the armed forces an important influence. The 1980 constitution allows two members to force a meeting. As a result, two commanders in chief can force the president to listen to their concerns and to bring issues to the table, even if the president wishes otherwise.

In addition, at different times both Aylwin and Frei felt obligated to call a meeting simply because commanders in chief were discussing the possibility of doing so first. The presidents convoked simply to avoid the appearance of having been forced to attend the meeting. As a consequence, the CSN's institutional rules continue to be detrimental to full civilian control over the policy process.

In terms of being an effective political institution, the CSN has shown mixed results. Since neither civilians nor officers can guarantee the outcome of a vote, they tend to seek other contact points when faced with political conflict. In this sense, the structural features of the CSN have made it a less relevant institution. Although the CSN has not proved the obstacle to democracy that many observers predicted, it does give the military the ability to force the president to hear the armed forces' opinions.

To be an effective institution, the CSN would represent a forum through which the commanders in chief could express opinions in time of crisis. The fact that even the armed forces have periodically chosen not to convene the council in the face of serious political conflict demonstrates its weaknesses. Finally, the military's ability to force a meeting means that the institution continues to be an obstacle to civilian supremacy over the armed forces because its own charter is not fully democratic.

CONGRESS

The Chilean Congress has worked to insert itself more forcefully into national debates on civil-military relations. Congressional investigations have brought certain controversies more into public view. For example, the ejercicio de enlace was sparked in part by the fact that a special congressional commission began investigating Pinochet's son. These first steps, however, proved tentative. Once the crisis erupted, the president of the Chamber of

Deputies agreed to bring the investigation to a hasty close. In addition, the congressional debate over the ejercicio de enlace highlighted the fact that the military had many supporters in congress.

Given the opposition's political power and its structural leverage in congress, the Aylwin administration faced serious obstacles as it attempted to pass substantive legislation on issues related to the armed forces. Even the congressional Defense Committees analyzed and debated only a few issues, such as intelligence reform and obligatory military service. Those commissions also generally lack expertise, and military officers were not commonly called to provide their opinions on defense matters. Congressional staff was minimal, and often lacked any background in the area of defense.

President Aylwin proposed a wide range of initiatives to congress, none of which successfully passed. Between 1990 and 1994, congress debated and rejected reforms related to officer retirement rules, intelligence gathering and budgets, moving the national police from the Defense Ministry to Interior, adding a civilian to the National Security Council, limiting the jurisdiction of military courts, and speeding up investigations of human rights abuses. For a variety of reasons, particularly the influence of military supporters, none of these measures passed. In particular, the constitution provides the military with four senate seats. One retired commander in chief from each branch as well as the national police becomes a designated senator. In addition, the electoral system ensures that the right (as well as any other major party coalition) remains a significant minority, disproportionate to its vote totals.

The Frei administration met with the same problems when attempting to enact reforms. With regard to military justice reform, for example, Defense Minister Pérez Yoma requested that a series of congressional proposals be shelved. He advocated a slow and incremental approach to military reforms, especially since Pinochet would soon be retiring. Both Frei and Pèrez Yoma wanted to ensure that the new commander in chief began his term with a favorable view of the government. Congressional debate over military policy would be potentially acrimonious and therefore undesirable. As a consequence, they believed the reforms were better postponed.

In some policy areas, Congress is legally blocked from becoming too influential. Since 1958, by law the military has received a share of the national copper earnings. During the military regime, this share expanded to become a guaranteed income, whereby the armed forces would share 10 percent of copper sales. Article 96 of the constitution also guarantees that the military budget cannot fall below 1989 spending levels, adjusted for inflation. Congress is thus prevented from making any major cuts to the military budget. Article 62 of the constitution states that Congress can only accept, reject, or decrease the budget proposal sent by the president, thus leading one defense expert to argue that its role in the budget process has been very limited, almost nil.

The strategy of civilian policy makers has been to make the budget floor into a ceiling. In other words, they would grant the military only what the law forced them to provide. Nonetheless, in 1996 the military budget reached just under $US2 billion, which represented 2.64 percent of GNP. The copper law itself represented 14 percent of the total, or $US285 million. In 1990, the percentage of GNP dedicated to the armed forces was 4.2, and that figure had gradually dropped each subsequent year. So while the share of national resources granted to the armed forces was indeed on the decline, the budget floors prevented any serious cuts from being made and since the Chilean economy continued to grow, the military budget did not suffer much as a result.

Despite congress' inability to pass substantive legislation related to the military and the constitutional-legal obstacles to cutting the military budget, the constitutional accusation against Pinochet, initiated by five Christian Democrats in January 1998, was a major initiative. The constitutional accusation constituted a way to make judgment on state officials for failing in their constitutional duties. Given the limitations imposed by the military regime, it was the sole manner by which Pinochet (or any general or admiral) could be judged. The constitution had been structured to prevent political judgments of officers, and offered only a narrow avenue through which politicians could exert authority. Article 48, part 2(d) grants congress the right to present an accusation against any general or admiral for having gravely compromised the honor or security of the Nation.

The accusation had limits. The most important was that Congress could not accuse Pinochet of any wrongdoing committed before March 11, 1990. The Constitutional Organic Law of Congress prohibited it. Promulgated on January 26, 1990, transitory article 3 states that constitutional accusations can be directed only at actions that took place after the end of the military regime. The accusation therefore focused only on Pinochet's comments and actions after he no longer was president.

Intense congressional debate ensued, and emotions ran very high on all sides. The conflict dragged on for four months, and ultimately was defeated by a vote of 62–55, with one abstention. Despite its rejection, the process of presenting the constitutional accusation represented a significant step forward. Congress asserted itself and the country engaged in an extended dialogue about the military regime and its abuses. The presentation of the constitutional accusation would have been inconceivable in the initial postauthoritarian period. Although the Frei administration opposed the measure given how it would rock the civil-military boat, administration officials did not fear outright military rebellion to the same extent as the 1990 and 1993 crises.

Congress' institutional effectiveness has thus been uneven. Its members have become increasingly bold with regard to making political judgments on General Pinochet. At the same time, over the long-term its ability to affect the military budget significantly will likely remain limited. Finally, without greater expertise the congressional committees will continue to have minimal influence over decisions related to more technical military matters. Moreover, when it sought to exert its investigative and oversight functions, overt military threats to civilian control resulted: the ejercicio de enlace and the boinazo.

At the same time, congress has become a much stronger institution since 1990. Although the constitutional accusation produced political tension, the situation did not match the high degree of uncertainty characterized by the ejercicio de enlace and the boinazo. In consequence, members of congress may become further emboldened to challenge hitherto untouched areas of the military's domain. If it were effective, congress would exert more oversight over technical military issues. Its members would also seek to judge military officers if they believed those officers had violated the law.

THE JUDICIARY

The Chilean judicial system entered the postauthoritarian period in a very debilitated position. Before leaving the presidency, General Pinochet ensured that the courts were full of judges favorable to the military regime. Even more importantly, the military government had decreed an amnesty in 1978. The amnesty covered the entire period following the coup. For what he termed humanitarian reasons, Pinochet also included some political prisoners and exiles. The effect was to virtually guarantee that the courts could not punish officers for their actions.

Chilean military courts also have broad jurisdiction, which at times extends to civilians. Article 276 of the Military Justice Code allows the armed forces to imprison civilians for saying virtually anything: Anyone who causes any disturbance or disorder, through speaking, written word, or any other medium, or causes anything to be known by the troops intended to cause them disgust or indifference to the service, or criticizes that service, will be punished with . . . military imprisonment . . . if cadet, soldier or non-military individual. In addition, if the Supreme Court hears a case that originated in an army court, the Auditor General of the army is integrated temporarily as a Supreme Court justice.

Given these constraints, the civilian judiciary was not a prominent institution in terms of civil-military relations in the first years after the military left power. Then in 1993 the Supreme Court found retired General Manuel Contreras guilty of being the intellectual author of the 1976 murder of Orlando Letelier in Washington, DC. In 1995, after nearly two years of appeals, the court sentenced Contreras to seven years in prison.

But for four months, with the support of both the army and the navy Contreras refused to go to prison. The military did not trust the Minister of Justice, Soledad Alvear, and therefore entered into negotiations with Defense Minister Pérez Yoma instead. Contreras did not surrender until the government made a number of concessions. These included an army pay raise, a declared end to the corruption scandal plaguing Pinochet, an agreement to provide mixed prison custody that would include the army, and the assurance that the government would not actively pursue more cases involving human rights violations. The fact that Contreras ultimately went to prison, however, demonstrated that the judicial system could function even in the face of military opposition.

In 1999, the Supreme Court made an even bolder decision. In June, the court denied application of the 1978 amnesty to five officers involved in the so-called caravan of death. The decision meant a reinterpretation of the amnesty, as the court declared that the amnesty would not cover any case where the victim's body had not been found. The armed forces and national police were unified in opposing this decision. They entered into negotiations with the government to find a way to overturn or at least alter the judgment.

Changes in the application of the amnesty will have a major impact on Chilean civil-military relations. The armed forces believe they deserve the amnesty, especially since, in their view, the country suffered a state of war during the 1970s. From that perspective, both sides committed lamentable excesses but that did not justify forcing officers to be judged or to stand as witnesses in civilian courts. Pinochet's replacement as army commander in chief, General Ricardo Izurieta, stated that any judgment of officers necessarily demands judgment of those who provoked the political crisis that caused the intervention. In the eyes of the military, that would include many civilians still prominent in politics. Given these very strong beliefs, the military will certainly be active in finding ways to avoid civilian judgment.

Like congress, the Chilean judiciary has come a long way since the end of the military government. The courts have long been criticized for being soft on human rights and too quick in its application of the amnesty. The Contreras case demonstrated that not even one of the most prominent architects of repression was immune from prosecution. The long-term effects of the reinterpretation of the amnesty remain to be seen, but at the very least the case revolving around the caravan of death shows that pursuing human rights in Chile is not a futile exercise. The judiciary, therefore, is stronger than ever although only more human rights cases will demonstrate whether or not the court's decision will continue to be applied. To be effective, judges would not feel constrained when examining cases involving military officers.

CONCLUSION

During the 1990s, the Chilean armed forces, most notably the army, have often circumvented political institutions in order to achieve their goals. Even though the military regime under General Pinochet constructed the institutional rules, the army has found that those institutions do not necessarily conform to its interests. However, instead of accepting that state of affairs, officers have found other channels to exert influence. As Pion-Berlin and Arceneaux note, a focus on institutions requires that soldiers not have the capacity or at least the desire to repeatedly disregard official channels by fulfilling their wants outside of them.

Time and again, the military in Chile did precisely that. In addition, civilians were unable to impose costs as punishment for utilizing less formal points of contact. In many cases, government officials accepted that state of affairs, if grudgingly, because they believed that some sort of dialogue was preferable to none.

Of the four institutions under examination, the Defense Ministry has clearly been the least effective. The military often refused to deal with the Defense Minister. Only one minister, Edmundo Pérez Yoma, ever established a rapport with the military leadership. But a strong political institution cannot be based on an individual. As yet, the military has not shown itself willing to accept the leadership and authority of the Defense Ministry as an institution.

The National Security Council has not consistently been an effective institution either. For their own reasons, both the military and civilian policy makers periodically found themselves reluctant to convoke the CSN even in the face of serious civil-military tension. At the same time, the CSN's very structure makes it an essentially undemocratic institution. As a result, following its institutional rules may very well not be beneficial to democracy until those rules are reformed.

Both the judiciary and congress, meanwhile, have slowly become stronger institutions. In the Contreras case, the armed forces defied judicial ruling and successfully held out for concessions. But the fact that Contreras was eventually imprisoned, combined with the more recent move toward reinterpretation of the 1978 amnesty signifies an important assertion of judicial power. There can be little doubt that the armed forces will seek to avoid sending its officers to civilian courts, yet time is required to judge how successful they will be in that endeavor over the long term. Furthermore, only reform of the military code of justice and the organic laws of the armed forces will alter the structure of military justice and its relation to the civilian courts.

Congress has increasingly flexed its political muscle. Much more meek during the Aylwin years, when it jettisoned a controversial investigation into illicit dealings in which General Pinochet's son was involved, in subsequent years its members gained the confidence necessary to face Pinochet squarely. The constitutional accusation against him was ultimately defeated, but the fact that congress (as well as the entire country) engaged in an open debate about the legacies of the military regime signified that progress was being made.

Given the very uneven performance of Chilean political institutions with regard to the relationship between civilian governments and the military, as yet the military's interests and goals are defined largely independently of those institutions. Effective institutions not only constrain political actors, but also begin to become part of the calculation of goals. If institutions can be avoided, then political actors need not take them into consideration at all times. Regardless of institutional rules, the Chilean military has become accustomed to striking a deal of some sort outside the auspices of formal channels when pursuing its interests. In such cases, neither an institution's autonomy nor its concentration of authority is very relevant. On the other hand, the military's threat of using force has become somewhat less credible; bargaining is an improvement over bayonets. Perhaps over time the institutional leverage that favors the armed forces in the bargaining structure may also be reformed. [As of 2004], however, there is at best a stalemate.

Constitutional and institutional changes in postauthoritarian Chile are not easy, requiring extraordinary majorities and offering certain actors special veto points, especially the armed forces. If civil-military relations are to be democratized and if civilian authority is to be enhanced then civilian governments must find ways to persuade the military leadership to utilize formal institutions. At the same time, they must also work on reforming undemocratic institutional legacies left by the military regime.

The fundamental issue at stake is whether the military will increasingly follow democratic institutional rules or if circumvention becomes the norm. Effective institutions represent part of the foundation of democracy. Making those institutions more effective by channeling civil-military relations through them will further strengthen that foundation. But in Chile this requires significant reforms in the basic constitutional and institutional framework. The institutional approach is a useful framework for civil-military relations, especially if the historical continuity and strength of institutions that frame civil-military relations are examined empirically.

8.2 The Limits of Democracy: Socio-Political Compromise and Regime Change in Post-Pinochet Chile (1999)

PATRICK S. BARRETT

INTRODUCTION

Since the early 1980s, Latin America (and the developing world more generally) has undergone a historically significant transition from military to civilian rule. Like the authoritarianism that preceded it, the number and co-incidence of these transitions have captured the interests of scholars, prompting a new inquiry into the causes of this most recent wave of regime changes and whether it represents a decisive movement toward democratic stability. Among the countries that have recently undergone the transition from authoritarian rule, Chile affords a particularly rich case study for addressing this question. Indeed, despite having suffered perhaps the most traumatic democratic collapse and undergone the most profound and far-reaching authoritarian transformation, its transition to civilian rule proved remarkably smooth and the regime that emerged from that process appears to be among the most stable of Latin America's new democracies. In fact, when a majority of Chilean electors voted for the presidential candidate of the center-left Concertacion de Partidos por la Democracia (CPPD) in December 1989, it was the first multiparty majority coalition to be elected in Chile since the early 1940s. Furthermore, the CPPD's subsequent victory in 1993 marked the first time that an incumbent government had been re-elected since 1946. For the first time in nearly half a century, moreover, there exists virtually no dispute over the country's development strategy, much less the system of capitalist development. And finally, perhaps the most noteworthy feature of Chile's newfound political stability is the unexpectedly harmonious relations between the CPPD and Chile's business community. In short, Chile is today enjoying a new socio-political compromise no less significant than the so-called estado de compromiso ("compromise state") of the 1930s and 1940s, the other moment in its history when it was regarded as the most stable and promising of Latin America's democracies.

This remarkable turn of events raises three intriguing questions. First, what are the causes of Chile's new socio-political compromise? Second, what are the substantive terms of this compromise; i.e., what tradeoffs underpin it and what tensions is it designed to resolve? Finally, what implications does this compromise have for the character and trajectory of the post-military order? Does it constitute the basis for continued democratic stability under post-military rule, or, like Chile's previous compromise, does it mask underlying political, social, and economic contradictions that bode ill for democratic stability?

Clearly, this Outcome has deep historical roots in Chile's prior experiences of socio-political compromise, democratic collapse, and authoritarian transformation. The focus of this article, however, is the 1990–1997 period, during which Chile's new compromise [was] consolidated. Its central argument is that this compromise can best be understood as a reflection of, and an attempt to contain, the historical and ongoing tension between the imperative of capital accumulation and the conflicts over socio-political inclusion and distribution. More concretely, the article examines struggles over three arenas of conflict that reflect that tension most clearly: development strategy; labor and social policy; and the structure of state decision-making. Central to those conflicts, moreover, was the evolving relationship between business, parties, and the state. Indeed, it is the limitations of that relationship, and more specifically the limitations on the state's capacity to discipline business, which constitute the limits of Chile's new socio-political compromise. The article concludes that this compromise can be characterized as a neo-liberal elite pact between big business and political party elites, which rather than reconciling accumulation and inclusion/distribution, has privileged the former over the latter.

The article consists of six sections. Section I presents the analytical framework. Section II briefly examines the period of authoritarian transformation from 1973 to 1989, which established many of the institutional and structural conditions that shaped and constrained the processes of transition and compromise. Sections III through V examine the CPPD administrations of Patricio Aylwin and Eduardo Frei (1990–1997), focusing on the three central pillars of Chile's new compromise. Finally, the conclusion briefly assesses the prospects for democratic stability in light of that compromise.

I. ANALYTICAL FRAMEWORK

The central theoretical argument of this article is that all capitalist societies are characterized by a permanent tension between the imperative of capital accumulation and the conflicts over socio-political inclusion and distribution. What distinguishes those societies, both from one another and over time, is the capacity to contain this tension. The degree of democracy and political stability attained by a given society can therefore be understood as the product of whether and how this tension is contained. More specifically, it is the product of whether and how state strategic capacity is generated:

i.e., the ability to adapt to changing domestic and international circumstances by making timely shifts in development strategy conducive to a process of sustained capital accumulation. Above all this means the capacity to discipline social classes, and private capital in particular. Indeed, it is whether and how that capacity is generated that determines the limits of democracy under capitalism.

By assigning a central role in the accumulation process to the state, this argument runs counter to much recent scholarship in the political economy of development. This is particularly true of the neo-orthodox perspective, which holds that rather than contributing to economic development, state intervention has been the principal cause of economic decline. This perspective, however, suffers from a number of analytical and historical shortcomings that have been amply discussed in the literature on development. A second, more compelling, line of argument holds not that the state is the cause of economic decline, but rather that because of the changing structural character of the international economy (specifically, the enormous increase in the international mobility of capital and the globalization of production and trade), the state's capacity for effective intervention has been greatly diminished. But while there is indeed evidence that these developments have constrained national policy-making autonomy (particularly in the area of macroeconomic policy), the state nonetheless remains central to economic development.

In the first place, as Robert Wade has recently argued, reports of the death of the national economy have been greatly exaggerated, as world production and investment remain very largely nationally owned and oriented. Moreover, the need to adapt to a changing international economy does not mean that all countries will adapt successfully or in the same way. States differ in their endogenous structural capacity for strategic action, in the extent to which their existing economic structures can adapt to international conditions, and in their vulnerability to international trends and pressures. Perhaps the most important implication of today's changing international economy, however, is not simply that it has made effective state intervention more difficult (which itself has increased the differences among states), but rather that it has made necessary a shift in the character of that intervention. More specifically, it has heightened the importance of supply-side, microeconomic forms of intervention, or a greater reliance on industrial and strategic trade policies. This has always been true of late developers, but it is particularly so in light of the changing structure of international trade (most importantly, the growing trade in high value-added or "elaborately transformed" manufactures), which has eroded comparative advantages based on natural resources and cheap labor, while greatly enhancing the importance of technology acquisition and development, product specialization, and skills training. International competitiveness has, in other words, come to depend increasingly on the ability to construct "competitive" advantage by actively identifying and selecting particular sectors in which to encourage investment, facilitate access to technology, promote R&D and skills training, and develop new infrastructure. Where catching-up is the priority, simply "getting prices right" is no guarantee of growth; instead, it is likely to attain static comparative advantage and allocative efficiency at the price of sacrificing dynamic comparative advantage and efficiency. Thus, rather than diminishing the importance of effective state action, the changing international economy has, if anything, increased it.

As stated above, the key to state strategic capacity resides above all in the ability to discipline social classes, but particularly the owners and corporate managers of capital, whose significance derives from their control over investment. In a capitalist economy, in other words, the satisfaction of business interests is a necessary condition for the satisfaction of all others. This means satisfying the conditions of profitability, which neither the state nor other social and political actors can undermine without risking losses in production, revenue, and employment and threatening the stability of the entire social and political order. But while profitability is a necessary condition for accumulation, it is not sufficient. Sustained accumulation also requires that private profit-seeking be disciplined by the state, for there is no guarantee that the discipline of the market alone will lead capitalists to invest at high levels and in activities that are both productive and domestic. Moreover, even market discipline depends on the existence of a state capable of enforcing it. Disciplining capital, however, is no easy achievement and indeed is fraught with tensions. This is particularly true of microeconomic forms of intervention, which constitute a potentially greater intrusion upon business autonomy and prerogatives and carry greater risks of the rent-seeking decried by neo-orthodox scholars. Crucial to disciplining capital, then, is the ability to influence private investment decisions without either opening the door to predatory rent-seeking or triggering a defensive reaction in the form of a decline in investment and/or efforts aimed at restricting the scope of state action. The state's ability to influence investment in this way, moreover, does not rest on a capacity to impose its policy objectives over the objections of an entire business class. The state may be able to do so temporarily, but certainly not in a sustained way and not without incurring serious economic problems.

The question then is under what conditions the generation of strategic capacity (and in particular, the discipline of capital) can be reconciled with democratization and under what conditions it cannot. In order to address this question, it is necessary to focus more closely on the tension between accumulation and inclusion/distribution and whether and how it can be contained. The latter half of this equation is most clearly reflected in labor and social policies and the structure of state decision-making.

The importance of labor and social policies resides in the fact that they constitute important instruments for correcting the distributional inequalities generated by capitalist development, and as such represent important indicators of democratization. According to the neo-orthodox perspective, however, efforts to achieve equity through such policies pose an inherent threat to accumulation and economic efficiency. In the first instance, this is because redistributive measures reduce the profit share of income and thereby lower investment and growth. Moreover, labor standards are seen as a major source of labor market rigidity. Indeed, it is only by restricting union power, deregulating labor markets, and allowing wages to respond flexibly to market signals that full employment, stable prices, and growth will be achieved. State-provided social protection, moreover, should be made available only to the certifiably destitute who are unable to participate in the labor market, while for those who are able to work, social protection should be provided by privately organized insurance, with entitlements and benefits reflecting contributions.

The impact of labor and social policies on accumulation and economic efficiency, however, is far more complex and varied than the neo-orthodox position suggests. In the first place, as Keynesians contend, wages are not only a cost of production, but also a source of demand and therefore a stimulus to profits and investment. Moreover, while it may be rational for labor to exercise wage restraint in order to generate the profits upon which future growth and employment depend, private control of investment makes this risky for labor, for it has no guarantee that the income it foregoes will be invested productively or that it will share in the resulting productivity gains. Furthermore, labor market flexibility is an insufficient basis for economic growth and may in fact be counterproductive, since enabling capital to continually squeeze labor can, on the demand side, limit the growth of the domestic market, and on the supply side, inhibit the switch to more productivity-enhancing business strategies. This is especially true in light of the changing structure of international trade, which has eroded comparative advantages based on cheap labor, while increasing the importance of technology acquisition and development, product specialization, and skills training.

At the same time, there is no guarantee that raising labor standards and incomes will lead capital to invest in a manner that generates increased productivity. It may instead lead more quickly to a fall in profitability, capital flight, and/or heightened distributional conflict. Again, the effort to raise productivity will depend in significant measure on the state's capacity to discipline private investment decisions. Moreover, the changes in the global economy have increased the importance of microeconomic forms of discipline. But this raises a fundamental problem: it is here that a workable compromise between capital and labor is most difficult to achieve. In other words, the state's ability to discipline capital on a microeconomic level through selective intervention may entail the exclusion of labor, for capital's reticence toward such discipline is likely to be considerably greater if labor has any say in it. This is especially true if labor is strong or there is already a considerable history of high labor-capital conflict.

This brings us to the relationship between state strategic capacity and inclusion. A central assertion of this article is that a primary (though not exclusive) motivation for engaging in political struggle is to affect how the state intervenes in socioeconomic conditions and relations (most importantly, the creation and distribution of wealth). But deciding how the state intervenes is not open to all social and political forces equally, because the state's forms of representation are typically structured in such a way as to privilege or "select" certain social and political actors over others. Similarly, the state's forms of intervention are also typically structured in a manner that privileges the policy preferences of certain actors over those of others. At the heart of the struggle over how the state intervenes, then, is the struggle over both the accessibility and the scope of state decision-making.

In the neo-orthodox view, a state decision-making apparatus that is broad in scope and accessible to the electorate poses a potentially serious threat to accumulation and sound economic policy-making. This is because it encourages voters and pressure groups to make unrestrained demands on politicians who are only too willing to satisfy them in order to attain and retain elective office, thus opening the door to uncontrolled rent-seeking and an ever expanding politicization of social and economic relations. The neo-orthodox solution to the problem, therefore, lies in restricting both the accessibility and the scope of state decision-making in order to insulate the economy and economic policy-making from the distorting effects of politics. However, the relationship between accumulation and inclusion, like that between accumulation and distribution, is more complex and varied than the stark choice painted by neo-orthodoxy. To be sure, a decision-making apparatus that is broad in scope and/or highly accessible may generate excessive politicization and rent-seeking. But the price for preventing such an outcome will be restrictions not only on democratic representation, but also on the state's capacity to foster accumulation. Hence, while a restricted decision-making apparatus may generate stability at time t, it may be the cause of instability at time t+1 because of the state's inability to accommodate rising demands for expanded popular representation and/or respond to changing economic conditions. Furthermore, a decision-making apparatus that is broad in scope or highly accessible is also clearly compatible with sound economic policy-making and sustained accumulation. The degree of compatibility depends not only on the particular combination of institutional factors, but also on the nature of the accumulation strategy. For example, a Keynesian-inspired strategy is compatible with an accessible decision-making arena, but the scope of that arena will likely be primarily limited to macroeconomic policies. Conversely, an industrial policy strategy will involve a broader scope of state decision-making (encompassing both macro- and microeconomic policies), but its accessibility will likely be considerably more restricted. Finally, a neo-liberal strategy will involve greater restrictions, not only on the scope of state decision-making, but very likely on its accessibility as well.

To summarize, the central theoretical contention of this article is that the principal driving force behind the historical process of regime change is the struggle to contain the tension between the imperative of sustained accumulation and the conflicts over socio-political inclusion and distribution. The degree of democracy and political stability attained by a given society can therefore be understood as a product of not only whether, but how, this tension is contained. More specifically, it is a product of whether and how the state succeeds in disciplining social classes, and private capital in particular, i.e., in a manner that reconciles accumulation and inclusion/distribution, privileges one over the other, or fails altogether. It is in this way that Chile's new socio-political compromise should be understood and it is to an analysis of that compromise that we now turn.

II. AUTHORITARIAN TRANSFORMATION AND TRANSITION: THE INSTITUTIONAL AND STRUCTURAL FOUNDATIONS OF COMPROMISE

In a remarkably striking way, the transformative project undertaken by the Chilean military regime in the mid-1970s reflected the fundamental tension between accumulation and inclusion/distribution that lay at the heart of democratic compromise, stalemate, and collapse between 1932 and 1973. The basic pillars of that project were: (1) a neo-liberal development strategy that transformed the Chilean economy from one built on state-led ISI to one founded on primary product exports, rapid integration into the world economy, and a drastically reduced role for the state; (2) labor and social policies that sacrificed distribution to accumulation and sought to depoliticize social relations by reorienting them on the basis of market principles; and (3) a highly restrictive constitution designed to prevent the type of politicization seen to have undermined the previous civilian regime and to institutionalize the regime's socio-economic model. Finally, the regime's transformative project came to be explicitly linked to the construction of a post-military (though not necessarily post-authoritarian) order, complete with elaborate transition mechanisms.

By 1981, the regime's transformative project appeared on its way to consolidation. The following year, however, the economic model collapsed, triggering the most severe economic crisis experienced by any of Latin America's authoritarian regimes. Yet, despite the explosion of mass protests and the reemergence of a political opposition, the regime was able to survive, owing to many of the same factors that made the implementation of its transformative project possible (most importantly, the concentration of institutional and coercive power in the hands of General Augusto Pinochet, the strong backing from big business, and the divisions among and within the parties of the opposition as well as the right). This in turn enabled the regime to maintain its transition timetable and to embark on a second, more solid phase of authoritarian transformation during the latter half of the 1980s. Indeed, within the relatively short span of five years, dramatic changes occurred, which not only made possible Latin America's most orderly and consensual transition to civilian rule, but more importantly laid the foundations for the construction of Chile's second socio-political compromise during this century.

What is particularly significant about this period is the way in which institutional and structural factors interacted in constraining and shaping the processes of transition and compromise. The most important institutional factors at play during this period were Pinochet's undiminished control over the state apparatus and the Armed Forces, the ongoing divisions among and within the parties of the opposition and the right, and the existence of a set of transition procedures and an institutional design for the future already in place to which the military had tied its own institutional interests. This combination of institutional factors gave the regime the strategic upper hand and frustrated the opposition's efforts to force an early transition to a more open and democratic regime. Yet, paradoxically, the regime's very strength and determination to defend the Constitution and its transition procedures eventually had the unintended effect of uniting the opposition. For by giving it no other choice but to participate in the October 1988 plebiscite over Pinochet's continuation as president, the regime enabled the opposition to submerge its substantive differences for the sake of the common goal of defeating Pinochet. The success of this strategy, moreover, opened the way to elections and gave the opposition sufficient bargaining power to negotiate a series of reforms to the 1980 Constitution, which while leaving the bulk of the latter's authoritarian features intact, provided the opposition greater room for political maneuver. At the same time, the continuing strength of the military regime and Pinochet's strong showing in the plebiscite maintained the urgency of preserving a united front and in fact enabled the opposition to perpetuate the plebiscite as the basis of political identification and struggle. The culmination of this process was Patricio Aylwin's victory in the 1989 presidential elections.

But while successful, this strategy had other consequences that augured less well for democratization. By participating in the plebiscite and obtaining only limited constitutional reforms, the CPPD helped to consolidate the 1980 Constitution and to restrict its own strategic options significantly. Moreover, despite its victory in the 1989 elections, it was unable to prevent the right from obtaining a majority in the Senate, a circumstance that was made possible by the regime's "binomial" electoral law and the existence of nine "designated" Senators. The CPPD's strategy also contributed to a de-mobilization and marginalization of popular sectors that had played a major role in opposing the military regime (most importantly the labor movement), and thereby weakened the social base for more far-reaching change. And perhaps even more significantly, by being forced to act in accordance with the regime's transition procedures and timetable, the opposition was unable to prevent the regime from carrying out a second phase of structural transformations, the most dramatic of which were the phenomenal growth of exports, a second wave of privatizations, the tremendous expansion of the privatized social security system as a source of investment capital, the emergence of a business community more structurally powerful and dynamic than ever before and firmly committed to the regime's economic model, and the greatly expanded presence of transnational capital within the domestic economy. These structural changes, combined with a series of laws designed to further institutionalize the economic model, in turn made the transition a rather smooth and stable affair. In other words, by the end of the 1980s, the structural constraints had become sufficiently strong that it was possible for the military regime to loosen certain institutional constraints and to tolerate the opposition's victories in the plebiscite and the 1989 elections.

This changing set of institutional and structural constraints thus exposed a major flaw in the opposition's strategy. The implicit premise of that strategy was that it was necessary to give priority to the task of increasing the opposition's politico-institutional space before pushing for changes of a more substantive, socio-economic character at a later stage of political struggle. But the elimination of politico-institutional constraints was sufficiently gradual and limited that it was more than offset by the emergence of new structural constraints, so that by the time of the CPPD's victory in the 1989 elections, both its capacity and its inclination to alter the regime's socio-economic model had been significantly diminished. In fact, the CPPD's very preferences and objectives had undergone a significant change, as it began to look increasingly favorably on the regime's economic model and the dynamic potential of Chilean business. The importance of the latter to sustained economic growth also led the CPPD to moderate its programmatic objectives considerably so as to overcome business' deep-seated distrust of the center-left and thereby avoid a destabilizing fall in investment.

The CPPD's positive assessment of the economic model contrasted with its critical attitude toward the profound social inequalities that had worsened over the course of the 1980s. It therefore called for increased wages and major reforms of the regime's repressive labor code. But this laid the basis for a potentially serious contradiction deriving from the central role that the flexible and extensive use of cheap labor played in the regime's accumulation strategy and business' determined opposition to strengthening the rights and organizational power of labor. The CPPD's endorsement of the economic model also contrasted with its determination to eliminate the constraints built into the politico-institutional order bequeathed by the military regime. But here too, it faced a potentially serious contradiction, given the latter's importance to preserving the socio-economic model. Finding a formula for containing the tension between accumulation and the pressures for redistribution and inclusion thus emerged as the principal challenge facing the CPPD. However, as the sections that follow will show, the structural and institutional constraints that restricted the CPPD's maneuverability during the 1980s, in some respects grew stronger during the 1990s. And just as had occurred during the previous decade, as a result of those constraints, the CPPD's very preferences and objectives continued to undergo a process of moderation. The result was the consolidation of a neo-liberal elite pact, which rather than reconciling accumulation and inclusion/distribution, has privileged the former over the latter.

III. DEVELOPMENT STRATEGY

Without a doubt, the most consensual element of Chile's new compromise, and that to which the other elements have to a large degree been subordinated, is in the area of development strategy. In a sharp departure from the more interventionist development strategy advocated by the center-left throughout most of the 1980s, upon coming to power the CPPD gave highest priority to the maintenance of macroeconomic stability (and in particular the control of inflation), which was considered critical to gaining the confidence of business and to creating a climate conducive to increased investment. In fact, under the CPPD, Chile distinguished itself from the rest of Latin America by demonstrating a greater capacity to reconcile the competing objectives of low inflation, a stable real exchange rate, and sustained economic growth. This was in large part the result of the set of heterodox policies it deployed in regulating Chile's exchange and capital markets: a crawling peg exchange rate policy accompanied by occasional reevaluations and sterilized intervention; and controls on the entry of short-term capital. The CPPD governments also demonstrated greater fiscal responsibility than other transition governments in Latin America. Indeed, the CPPD was determined to avoid the experience of Chile's neighbors, where policies of a more populist character unleashed inflationary pressures that subsequently undermined economic growth. With respect to trade policy, the most important non-traditional export promotion policies initiated during the latter half of the 1980s went unaltered. In fact, only two major policy changes were introduced after 1990: the reduction in the uniform tariff level from 15 percent to 11 percent; and the negotiation of a series of free trade agreements. Finally, in the area of financial policy, the CPPD governments placed controls on short-term capital inflows, but left the military regime's liberal regulations governing FDI unaltered, while enacting other policies designed to create greater investment opportunities both domestically and internationally (most importantly, in the area of pension funds).

The economic performance during 1990–1996 was perhaps the most impressive of any seven year period in modern Chilean history (see Table 1). GDP grew by an annual rate of 6.8 percent, inflation averaged 12.6 percent (falling to 6.6 percent in 1996), unemployment averaged 5.6 percent, the public sector registered an average surplus of 1.7 percent, and the rates of savings and fixed investment reached historic levels (averaging 26.8 percent and 25.2 percent, respectively). Exports also continued to expand at a fast annual pace, nearly doubling in value between 1990 and 1995. Nonetheless, it is dangerous to extrapolate from this impressive performance, not so much because of the brief period it represents, but more importantly because of the underlying characteristics of the accumulation model. Consider the structure of production, and in particular the share of manufacturing in GDP. The latter has declined steadily during the 1990s, falling from the already low level of 18.1 percent in 1989 to 16.2 percent in 1996, its lowest level since 1946. A somewhat similar pattern is evident in the composition of employment, with industry's share falling from 16.8 percent in 1990 to 16.0 percent in 1997 (Central Bank 1998). Clearly, with an annual growth rate of 5.2 percent during 1990–1996, industry has hardly stagnated; but it is also clear that it is not the driving force of the economy.

The character of Chile's accumulation model is further reflected in the composition of its exports. While some observers have claimed that Chile entered the so called "second export phase" during the 1990s, Central Bank data indicate that between 1989 and 1997, the percentage of natural resource-intensive exports fell only slightly, from 92.1 percent to 87.2 percent. Using a different classification scheme, Ffrench-Davis and Saez show that while manufactured exports grew from 5.4 percent in 1990 to 9.8 percent in 1993, only 0.8 percent were new industries with high technological content (up from 0.6 percent in 1990). Moreover, the component consisting of primary exports (i.e., unelaborated agricultural, forestry, and mining products) also increased from 27.8 percent to 31.8 percent. Meanwhile, semi-elaborated exports (e.g., refined copper, agroindustrial products, cellulose and paper, fishmeal), though falling from 65.4 percent to 56.5 percent, remained the largest component. Although these data extend only through 1993, those provided by the Central Bank suggest that if anything, the component consisting of manufactured products is likely to have diminished after that date.

Thus, the vast majority of Chile's exports continue to be concentrated in low value-added natural resource-intensive products, a pattern which contrasts sharply with the composition of trade worldwide and among East Asian countries in particular. Moreover, despite its considerable capacity in the area of macroeconomic policy-making, the CPPD governments were un-

Table 1

Key Macroeconomic Indicators, 1974–1996

	1	2	3	4	5	6	7	8	9
Year	Growth of GDP	Exports[1]	Imports[1]	Inflation	Public Sector Surplus/ Deficit	Gross Fixed Capital Formation	Total Savings	Unemployment	Real Exchange Rate 1990=100
Average 1974–1983	1.2	3039	3248	115.5	0.0	16.0	16.2	18.8	—
Average 1984–1989	6.5	5347	4108	20.4	-1.3	19.1	20.7	14.9	—
1990	3.3	8373	7037	27.3	0.8	$23.3^2 (23.1)^3$	25.8	6.0	100.0
1991	7.3	8942	7354	18.7	1.5	$20.9^2 (21.1)^3$	24.5	6.5	102.9
1992	11.0	10007	9237	12.7	2.2	$22.7^2 (23.9)^3$	26.8	4.9	108.8
1993	6.3	9199	10181	12.2	1.9	$25.6^2 (26.5)^3$	28.8	4.7	110.9
1994	4.2	11604	10879	8.9	1.7	$24.3^2 (26.3)^3$	26.3	6.0	113.2
1995	8.5	16137	14655	8.2	2.5	$23.2^2 (27.2)^3$	27.4	5.4	119.6
1996	7.2	15353	16500	6.6	2.2	$24.5^2 (28.3)^3$	27.7	na	123.8
Average 1990–1996	6.8	11374	10835	12.6	1.7	$23.5^2 (25.2)^3$	26.8	5.6^4	—

[1] Millions current dollars FOB
[2] Current pesos
[3] 1986 pesos
[4] Average 1990–1995

able to prevent a 23.8 percent appreciation of the exchange rate between 1990 and 1996, a mild version of "Dutch disease" which poses an important obstacle to exports that are not reliant upon comparative advantages in natural resources. Furthermore, the growth in manufactured exports has largely been concentrated in Latin America. This is undoubtedly the result of the economic recovery and greater exchange rate appreciation experienced by those countries, particularly Argentina and Brazil, which have accounted for roughly half of Chile's exports to the region. And although Latin America's share of Chilean exports grew rapidly from 12.5 percent in 1990 to 21 percent in 1994, it has declined since then. Asia's share, meanwhile, has grown steadily from 26.2 percent in 1990 to 34 percent in 1997. Its share of manufactured exports, however, declined from 6.2 percent in 1990 to 3.1 percent in 1993. Thus, the composition of Chile's export markets, while more diversified than in the past, nonetheless continues to pose obstacles to industrial exports and to leave the economy vulnerable to external shocks.

The foregoing would seem to point to the need for an industrial policy strategy aimed at accelerating the move to a more advanced stage of export-led growth, as was in fact originally proposed in the CPPD's 1989 program. As it is, much of the success that Chile has enjoyed to date is the result of substantial state intervention, not only the exchange rate policies and special incentives for non-traditional exports implemented during the military regime and the controls on short-term capital inflows instituted under the CPPD, but also the structural reforms and sectoral promotion policies in agriculture and mining undertaken prior to 1973. Accelerating the move to a more advanced stage of export-led growth would therefore involve increasing the state's capacity to channel savings and investment selectively into higher value-added products that are less intensive in natural resources. Throughout the 1990s, however, the CPPD has maintained a cautious, hands off approach to fostering the economy's productive transformation.

A clear illustration of this cautious approach was the government's program of support for small and medium-sized firms. According to Oscar Munoz, the old industrial policies based on sectoral priorities and selective state intervention do not fit into the new policy framework. The Aylwin administration therefore converted CORFO, the traditional industrial policy institution, into what it called a "third floor institution." This involved the allocation of subsidies "through the market and, in particular, through the commercial banks, subsidizing only the cost of access to financing when the latter poses entry barriers to small and medium-sized firms." The government soon discovered, however, that the credit program was ineffective. Consequently, in mid-1991, it launched a new program designed to foster associative networks of smaller firms, whose objective would be to improve the latter's access to new technologies, financing, training, marketing, etc. But while apparently somewhat more successful, the program has involved only a tiny minority of Chile's small and medium-sized firms and reflects the same reluctance to give the state a more active role in the economy's productive transformation.

Another indication of the CPPD's limited capacity, or willingness, to influence the allocation of investment is the pattern of foreign investment during the 1990s. As noted earlier, the CPPD introduced controls on the entry of short-term capital. This policy has helped to generate a larger proportion of FDI inflows than the rest of Latin America, which would appear to offer greater promise for the country's productive development than a heavy reliance on short-term capital, as evidenced by the Mexican foreign exchange crisis of December 1994. At the same time, however, reliance on regulating short-term capital alone is of limited usefulness. Unlike South Korea and Taiwan, which until recently carefully channeled FDI into selected industries and technological cooperation relationships with domestic firms, Chile has exercised little control over the direction of FDI. It is therefore not surprising that 42.9 percent of FDI via Decree Law 600 during 1990–1997 has been concentrated in mining and 28.4 percent in services (primarily banking, insurance, securities, pension funds, and leasing). Only 14.2 percent, meanwhile, has been in industry, which in fact represents a significant decline from the 22.4 percent registered under the military regime.

Finally, the CPPD has made no effort to strengthen the state's institutional capacity. The most powerful state institutions are the Ministry of Finance and the Central Bank, whose institutional bias favor a conservative approach to macroeconomic policy. By contrast, the Economy Ministry and CORFO, the traditional industrial policy agencies, have been greatly weakened by the military regime. In fact, as we saw earlier, CORFO's institutional mission was reduced even further by the Aylwin administration. Furthermore, during 1995–1996, CORFO's payroll was cut by 30 percent and in 1997, both its ministerial status and its role as the holding company for state enterprises came to an end. Moreover, although the CPPD had called in its 1989 program for the creation of a Ministry of Industry to replace the Economy Ministry as part of a proposed industrial policy strategy, this objective was never realized. The state's power is also restricted by the constitutional requirement that selective measures and state involvement in production gain the approval of Congress, where at least in the Senate, the rightist opposition has enjoyed a majority. In addition, both the Aylwin and Frei administrations have denied important policy-making positions to those who are critical of the prevailing economic model, particularly the left wing of the Socialist Party. Hence, even if the proponents of greater state intervention had a clear idea of the sort of intervention to engage in, they have lacked the institutional and political means to carry it out effectively.

In sum, the macroeconomic performance of the Chilean economy under the CPPD has been nothing short of impressive. To a large degree, that performance has been the result of a combination of heterodox state policies (i.e., controls on short-term capital inflows, a highly interventionist exchange rate policy, and selective incentives for non-traditional exports) and favorable circumstances (e.g., the rapid growth of the pension funds, the recovery of neighboring countries' economies, and an abundance of natural resources and unskilled labor). A close examination, however, reveals that this accumulation model contains important limitations. This is clearly indicated by the low and declining share of industry in overall production, the continued heavy reliance on natural resource-intensive exports, the sectoral allocation of foreign investment, the composition of Chile's export markets, and the declining profitability of the pension funds. Moreover, the growth in Chile's labor force is rapidly decelerating and there is a growing scarcity of skilled labor. Finally, the high rates of growth in recent years have come at the price of severe environmental degradation, a problem that the CPPD has been reluctant to address for fear of alienating the business community and slowing the process of accumulation. All of this suggests that without a more ambitious industrial policy strategy in which the state assumes a more active role in steering investment, and therefore a greater capacity to discipline capital, the current dynamism of Chile's accumulation model may prove unsustainable. Indeed, what Chile may experience in the not too distant future is an economic slowdown reminiscent of the exhaustion of the initial, "easy" phase of ISI in the late 1940s and early 1950s.

IV. LABOR AND SOCIAL POLICY

The second critical element of the CPPD's program, labor and social policy, was very much shaped by the priority given to development strategy. The CPPD's primary objective was to find a way of reconciling subordinate class demands for greater distributive equity with the maintenance of the accumulation model inherited from the military regime, an objective which was expressed in the slogan "Growth with Equity." However, as noted in section II, such an objective contained a potentially serious contradiction, given the functional importance of the military regime's labor and social policies to its accumulation model and business' strong opposition to strengthening the rights, organizational power, and income share of labor.

In its 1989 program, the CPPD proposed a series of "profound" changes in the labor code aimed at restoring the "fundamental rights of workers" and creating equality in labor-capital relations. Soon after its victory in the December 1989 elections, however, the Aylwin government began to view the military regime's Labor Plan more positively and even found that it contained many "modern" elements. It insisted that its goal was to reconcile worker protection with labor market flexibility, but while it attempted to stake out a middle position, in practice, it gave priority to the latter. Indeed, it argued incessantly that any reduction in flexibility would threaten the competitiveness of Chile's export economy. It also argued that changes in the labor code were not an effective means to strengthening the labor movement. If the latter sought to improve its bargaining position vis-a-vis business, it would have to achieve it by increasing its power as a social force rather than by relying on the state. Moreover, the set of legislative proposals it presented to the Congress were a considerably watered down version of the CPPD program. For many within the labor movement and the business community alike, it was also significant that the government introduced the first three of the four reform projects in the Senate, where it was in the minority. This effectively limited the range of debate and prevented the more open conflict that would have resulted had they been introduced in the Chamber of Deputies, where the CPPD enjoyed a majority.

The resulting reforms were a far cry from both the CPPD's own program and the aspirations of organized labor. Indeed, the overall thrust of the reforms was to preserve the fundamental features of the Labor Plan, introducing largely cosmetic changes that gave it the appearance of greater legitimacy. Nonetheless, the government hailed the new labor code as the first promulgated under a democratic regime in Chilean history. It also pointed to improvements in the material conditions of workers, the growth of unionization, and the absence of labor conflict as proof that its policies had succeeded in reconciling growth, stability, and equity. Upon closer examination, however, the experience of labor during this period does not warrant such a positive assessment.

Beginning with unemployment, it should be stressed that Chile's low unemployment rate (averaging 5.6 percent during 1990–1995) continues to mask the low quality and precarious character of employment experienced by the vast majority of Chilean workers, a trend which, in fact, has grown during the 1990s. Moreover, while the 3.2 percent annual growth in real wages and 5.6 percent growth in minimum wages during 1990–1995 signaled a major improvement over 1983–1989, the real wage level attained in 1995 was only 9.3 percent greater than it had been a quarter century earlier and the minimum wage level remained 11.2 percent below that attained in 1981. Without a doubt, the CPPD's most significant accomplishment has been the reduction in poverty from 38.6 percent in 1990 to 23.2 percent in 1996. But the rate of reduction has slowed considerably, and a large number of those who have left poverty (2 1/2 million or 18% of the population in 1994) remain precariously close to it. More importantly perhaps, the distribution of income has worsened slightly, with 56.7 percent of national income going to the top 20 percent and only 4.1 percent going to the bottom 20 percent, a ratio of 13.8/1 (compared to 56.9 percent, 4.4 percent, and 12.9/1, respectively, in 1990). In fact, Chile ranked as the sixth most unequal in a World Bank survey of sixty-four less developed countries, while its Gini Coefficient during the early 1990s (0.5469) far surpassed the average for Latin America and the Caribbean (0.4931), the most inequitable region in the world.

The Aylwin administration also argued that it had fostered a growth in unionization and peaceful labor-capital relations. In fact, the rate of unionization increased from 11.5 percent in 1989 to 15.4 percent in 1991, while strikes involved only 0.6 percent of the working population during 1990–1995. Despite the increase in unionization through 1991, however, it declined in the years that followed, falling to 12.7 percent in 1995 and registering a total growth of only 10.4 percent during the entire period (and starting from a very low level). Particularly striking is the decline in the absolute number of union members after 1992, which fell by 86,000, or 11.9 percent, between 1993 and 1995. Moreover, when taking into consideration only enterprise unions (still the only ones capable of bargaining collectively), the rate of unionization for 1995 falls to 8.3 percent, which in relation to 1989 represents an increase of only 5.1 percent (and starting from an even lower level). Meanwhile, the average size of unions fell from 71.3 workers in 1989 to 50 in 1995, a 29.9 percent decline. Finally, the number of strikes, striking workers, and days lost during 1990–1995 increased by 256 percent, 261 percent, and 258 percent, respectively, over 1983–1989. This apparently alarming growth in strike activity should not be regarded as significant, given the small percentage of the workforce involved and the short duration of strikes (an average of 12.8 days). But neither should the much more modest growth in unionization. Indeed, rather than evidence of peaceful capital-labor relations, the low level of strike activity can more accurately be interpreted as evidence of the fundamental power imbalance between capital and labor.

Government actions in the area of social policy provide an equally clear illustration of the limited priority given by the CPPD to distributive equity. Indeed, the most salient feature of social policy under the CPPD is its basic continuity with the policy orientation of the military regime, the main thrust of which was to reduce the state's role in the provision of social services, transferring it as much as possible to the private sector. Thus, with respect to social spending, the CPPD maintained the military regime's emphasis on targeting social spending toward the poorest social groups, combining it with more universal programs, particularly in education and health care. It also raised the level of social spending by 7 percent annually, or from 58.7 percent of total government spending during 1987–1989 to 62.6 percent during 1990–1995, the bulk of which was financed by the 1990 tax reform. It bears noting, however, that in 1993, the poorest 20 percent of the population received only 18.5 percent of social expenditure, while the richest 20 percent received 26.6 percent. If pension contributions, which constituted over 40 percent of social spending, are excluded, the share of the poorest quintile would increase to 28.3 percent and that of the upper quintile would decline to 12.7 percent; but the redistributive effect would still be quite small. An important component of the increased revenues generated by the tax reform, moreover, came from an increase in the Value Added Tax (VAT) from 16 percent to 18 percent, a regressive form of taxation which in recent years accounts for roughly 50 percent of total tax revenue. It is this tax, in fact, that the CPPD has been most determined to maintain. Furthermore, the problems in health and education remain severe, especially in the former, where inequalities are great. Finally, the CPPD abandoned its earlier calls for reforms of the military regime's privatized social security system designed to make it more "solidaristic" and increase worker participation in the administration of the pension funds. Instead, it focused its efforts on loosening the restrictions on fund investments as part of the capital market reforms passed in 1993. But many of the same trends that were a source of concern during the 1980s (with respect to coverage, administrative costs, and corporate control) continued, and even worsened, during the 1990s. And although the system continued to generate significant savings during the first half of the 1990s, in recent years the profitability of the funds has fallen dramatically.

While business was very pleased with the CPPD's labor and social policies, the labor movement was left profoundly disillusioned. Indeed, the Unitary Workers Central (CUT), Chile's principal labor central, strongly denounced the government's failure to fulfill its program and the "insensitivity" of the economic team, and made a series of threats directed at both the government and business. None of the threats were ever carried out, however, in large part because of the CUT's organizational weakness and its fear of undermining the still fragile process of transition. But this only served to deepen the internal divisions that had plagued the CUT throughout the 1980s, and rather than seeing its organizational and mobilizational capacity increase, the absence of tangible victories made the CUT appear weak and insignificant. The sense of disillusionment only deepened under the Frei administration. For while the CUT had been extremely disappointed by the Aylwin administration's policies, it had at least enjoyed strong personal ties with some of its principal policy makers. The same could not be said of the Frei administration, which was perceived as cold, distant, and even more importantly, strongly pro-business. The CUT's disillusionment was reinforced by the government's failure to offer a clear response to the set of labor reforms it had proposed soon after the new administration was inaugurated. As a result, the CUT quickly distanced itself from the government and pursued a more aggressive, mobilizational strategy. The government gave in to the pressure in January 1995, when it submitted a new package of labor reforms to the Congress. The CUT reacted favorably to the reforms and reestablished relations, but their rejection by the right and business, and the government's less than energetic efforts to see them passed, led the CUT to resume its confrontational approach. Furthermore, the rising tensions within the labor movement failed to abate, as evidenced by the declining support for the PDC and a surge in support for the Communists in a series of federation elections. The latter's resurgence only served to worsen relations between CPPD trade unionists, on the one hand, and their parties and the government, on the other. It also helped to set the stage for a dramatic CUT election in April 1996, in which the CUT's Socialist vice president brokered a deal with the Communists, thus marking the collapse of the CPPD alliance within the labor movement.

In sum, the foregoing provides strong evidence that the CPPD's stated goal of reconciling "growth with equity" can hardly be considered a success; indeed, it is increasingly being labeled a failure. Among the factors explaining this outcome are the precarious structure of employment, the extreme concentration of asset ownership, and the limited redistributive effect of the CPPD's tax and social policies. An equally important factor, however, has been organized labor's weak bargaining position vis-a-vis capital. Throughout this period, the CPPD governments have argued that the CUT's trouble has been its obsession with legislation that would afford it greater protection from the state, rather than focusing on the task of strengthening itself as a social force capable of bargaining with capital on an even footing. But while by its own admission, the CUT could have done more to build its organizational capacity, the overwhelming effect of the labor legislation enacted during these years was to create legal obstacles to strengthening the labor movement and putting it on an equal footing with business. Moreover, more than the labor movement being obsessed with its protection, the government has been obsessed with maintaining labor market flexibility and the confidence of business, the economic consequences of which have not been questioned. Most importantly, as argued in section I, by enabling business to place almost the entire burden of adjustment on labor, a flexible labor market can actually impede innovation. An equally, if not more justifiable objective, therefore, would be to impose greater flexibility (or discipline) on capital by protecting labor. Hence, the "stability" in labor-capital relations witnessed during this period has not been the product of a national "consensus," but rather the inability of a weak and marginalized labor movement to prevent an accommodation between the government, business, and the right. The growing turmoil in the labor movement suggests, however, that this stability may not endure.

V. STATE DECISION-MAKING

The third and final critical element of the CPPD's program concerned its proposals for politico-institutional reform. The principal target of those proposals was the 1980 Constitution and its supporting laws, which were no less central to the military regime's transformative project than its social and economic "accomplishments." Indeed, they were designed specifically to prevent the latter's unmaking, as well as to block the type of politicization that had undermined the previous civilian regime. More specifically, the Constitution established nearly total presidential domination over the Congress, while at the same time countering the president's powers by expanding the prerogatives and autonomy of several state agencies (most importantly, the Constitutional Tribunal, the Central Bank, the Comptroller General, the National Security Council, and the Armed Forces). The Constitution also sought to institutionalize the military regime's economic model by elevating its basic principles to constitutional rank. And it sought to prevent the politicization that had undermined the pre-1973 political system by imposing severe restrictions on the scope of popular representation (most notably, by limiting the powers of Congress, creating the autonomous state agencies mentioned above, requiring that a third of the Senate be non-elected and instituting a so-called "binomial" electoral system). In short, the politico-institutional structure embodied in the 1980 Constitution was designed to limit both the scope and the accessibility of state decision-making, thereby preserving a neo-liberal socio-economic order.

As noted in section II, in 1989 the CPPD succeeded in negotiating a series of modest constitutional reforms. No sooner had the reforms been approved, however, than the CPPD incorporated those that it failed to achieve as key features of its government program. Indeed, it was in this area that the CPPD advanced perhaps its clearest agenda of change. But this was also the area in which it saw its objectives most consistently frustrated. The only significant advances achieved during this entire period, in fact, were accords over the holding of municipal elections (the first since 1971) and the shortening of the presidential term from eight to six years. In all other respects, the CPPD confronted the permanent veto of the rightist majority in the Senate (see Table 2), which was itself a product of the military regime's institutional design (i.e., the designated senators and the binomial electoral system).

At the same time, the CPPD's actions in this area provide further evidence of the evolving character of its preferences, objectives, and internal relations of power. This was already evident, in fact, during the negotiation of the 1989 reforms. At the time of the Constitution's promulgation, the opposition strongly condemned the manner in which it institutionalized the military regime's economic model, arguing that the economic norms established in a constitution should be sufficiently broad and flexible to make possible the application of diverse economic schemes, including a mixed economy and democratic socialism. By 1989, however, this emphasis on the Constitution's link to the military regime's economic model had disappeared. The one exception was the CPPD's opposition to the new Central Bank law. But even here, it dropped its earlier criticism of the Bank's institutional autonomy in exchange for altering the composition of its board of directors. On this basis, it easily reached an accord with the military regime in August 1989.

The CPPD also came to look more favorably on other aspects of the politico-institutional order inherited from the military regime. With respect

Table 2
Congressional Elections (seats, % of seats, and % of votes), 1989–1997

Party	1989						1993						1997					
	Chamber of Deputies			Senate			Chamber of Deputies			Senate			Chamber of Deputies			Senate		
	A	B	C	A	B	C	A	B	C	A	B	C	A	B	C	A	B	C
PDC	39	32.5	26.7	13	28.3	na	37	30.8	27.1	13	28.3	10.2	39	32.5	23.0	14	29.2	29.2
PPD	16	13.3	13.5	4	8.7	na	16	13.3	11.8	2	4.3	14.7	16	13.3	12.6	2	4.2	4.3
PS	6	5.0	3.2	1	2.2	na	15	12.5	11.9	5	10.9	12.7	11	9.2	11.1	4	8.2	14.6
Others	11	9.2	9.8	4	8.7	na	2	1.7	4.5	1	2.2	7.8	4	3.3	3.9	0	0.0	1.8
Subtotal	72	60.0	53.2	22	47.9	na	70	58.3	55.3	21	45.7	55.5	70	58.3	50.6	20	41.6	49.9
RN	29	24.2	19.3	10	21.7	na	33	27.5	16.3	11	23.9	14.9	24	20.0	16.8	7	14.6	14.8
UDI	12	10.0	10.4	2	4.3	na	16	13.3	12.1	4	8.7	10.2	21	17.5	14.4	10	20.8	17.2
Others	7	5.8	5.5	4	8.7	na	0	0.0	5.5	1	2.2	9.8	4	3.3	5.0	0	0.0	4.6
Subtotal	48	40.0	35.2	16	34.7	na	49	40.8	33.5	16	34.8	34.8	49	40.8	36.2	16	35.4	36.6
PC[1]	0	0.0	na	0	0.0	na	0	0.0	6.4	0	0.0	4.3	0	0.0	7.5	0	0.0	8.6
Others	0	0.0	na	0	0.0	na	1	0.8	4.8	1	2.2	5.3	1	0.8	5.8	1	2.1	4.8
Desig.	—	—	—	8	17.4	0.0	—	—	—	8	17.4	0.0	—	—	—	9	18.8	0.0
Life[2]	—	—	—	—	—	—	—	—	—	—	—	—	—	—	—	1	2.1	0.0
Total	120	100.0	100.0	46	100.0	100.0	120	100.0	100.0	46	100.0	100.0	120	100.0	100.0	48	100.0	100.0

Source: A: Seats; B: % of seats; C: % of votes; PDC: Christian Democratic Party; PPD: Party for Democracy; PS: Socialist Party; RN: National Renovation; UDI: Independent Democratic Union; PC: Communist Party. 1. Includes independents. 2. In 1997, Pinochet was made Senator for Life.

to the electoral law, for example, the eagerness for reform among government officials was not always consistent with the government's public pronouncements. Indeed, the electoral system was most beneficial to the largest parties (especially the PDC; see Table 2), as well as the strongest candidates within each party. It also had the effect of fostering the emergence of two large electoral blocs—thus reinforcing the division between "authoritarians" and "democrats" generated by the 1988 plebiscite—and it helped to keep the government coalition together. Moreover, while important elements of the CPPD remained critical of the excessively presidentialist character of the 1980 Constitution, others, particularly those who occupied the Executive branch, came to view it much more positively. In fact, the key ministry in both CPPD administrations has been the Secretary General of the Presidency, a creation of the military regime which the Aylwin administration elevated to ministerial rank. It is also the case that the institutional constraints built into the Constitution have enabled the CPPD to make policy in a technocratic, anti-populist fashion. Indeed, according to one Finance Ministry official, the insulation and autonomy afforded to policy-makers by the current institutional environment is a major reason why "the period of conflictual politics, inefficient policymaking, and economic stagnation, which lasted for more than half a century, is finally coming to an end."

Finally, the fact that Constitutional reforms had little chance for approval allowed the CPPD to reap some important political dividends. Most importantly, their rejection enabled the CPPD to portray itself as the force for democratization and the right as its obstacle, thereby maintaining the political cleavage between "democrats" and "authoritarians" established in the plebiscite and strengthening its hold on power. In fact, during the Aylwin administration, the reform proposals were introduced into Congress with full knowledge that they would be rejected. This tactic had a significant effect on the right, particularly the moderate wing of the largest opposition party, National Renovation (RN), whose entire political strategy turned on shedding the authoritarian legacy of the military regime in order to put an end to the political division created by the plebiscite. Indeed, the issue nearly caused RN to splinter in April 1996, as seven of its senators voted against a constitutional reform package brokered by party president, Andres Allamand, and the Frei administration.

Thus, the CPPD's enthusiasm for politico-institutional reforms tended to wane over time, as some powerful elements of the coalition began to see certain advantages in the institutional order bequeathed by the military regime. But this evolution in the CPPD's position was not without negative consequences. First, it was cause for serious division within the coalition. This was most true during the Frei administration, which at the outset, placed little importance on politico-institutional reforms. Indeed, in a reversal of the strategy adopted by the CPPD in the late 1980s of seeking to expand its political space in order to realize greater socioeconomic change, the

Frei administration spoke of a separation between its socioeconomic and politico-institutional goals. Emphasis was to be placed on the former, while the latter was to be postponed until the end of Frei's term, at which point, apparently, they would be introduced largely for their electoral effects. This strategy triggered a major controversy and only intense pressure from within the coalition (particularly, the Socialists) forced the Frei administration to put the reforms back on the agenda. Even then, however, many perceived that the government did so only to get the issue out of the way, so as to concentrate on its socio-economic agenda.

Second, the institutional restrictions built into the Constitution not only severely limit the democratic character of the state, but also its repertoire of strategic options. As we saw in section III, the state does enjoy a degree of technocratic capacity in the area of macroeconomic policy. Moreover, the state's institutional features (e.g., the autonomy of the Central Bank, the Executive's control over the budget, and the constitutional restrictions on state intervention) have enabled it to resist the sort of rent-seeking that contributed to macroeconomic instability in the decades preceding military rule. However, not only is the state's maneuverability in this area limited by the heightened international mobility of capital, but domestically this is an essentially negative form of autonomy. In other words, the state can preserve its autonomy only by preserving its neutrality, for it is in no position to make the sort of selective interventions characteristic of East Asian industrial policy, without quickly succumbing to rent-seeking pressures. Most importantly, it lacks the means to discipline private capital and steer investment into productive activities, a defining feature of the East Asian model at the height of its success. Business, not surprisingly, has been strongly opposed to further Constitutional reforms, seeing in them a serious threat to Chile's new socioeconomic order. A growing imbalance has thus resulted, as the state's institutional capacity has not kept pace with either the growing power of capital or the demands of Chile's maturing export-oriented economy.

Finally, the state's capacity to make policy in a coherent, technocratic fashion has in significant measure been made possible by the nature of the government's relationship to the CPPD. This was best illustrated by the Aylwin administration, whose policy-making effectiveness was greatly enhanced by the autonomy granted to it by the CPPD. Because of their concern for ensuring the stability of the Aylwin administration, which they regarded as one of transition, the CPPD parties feared that a more active role on their part might generate some of the instability that plagued governments in the decade preceding military rule. Moreover, Aylwin proceeded to designate a cabinet, which while dominated by Christian Democrats, was composed of a group of moderate figures who had played key roles in the CPPD's formation and whose ties to each other and loyalty to his administration rivaled those to their respective parties. These characteristics, in fact, earned them the nickname Partido Transversal.

The Frei administration's relationship to the CPPD parties, by contrast, has been very different. Not only have those parties been determined to play a more active role (now that the transition is no longer perceived to be in jeopardy), but Frei, who himself was largely politically inactive during the 1980s, was not able to draw on a group like the Partido Transversal. Thus, after first putting together a cabinet composed of high-ranking party officials, he resorted to relying on a group of close personal friends. The result was a deterioration in the government's relationship with the CPPD and a great deal less policy coherence than that exhibited by the Aylwin administration. Moreover, there has been a growing competition both among and within the parties of the coalition. What is striking about that competition, however, is the degree to which it has focused on the distribution of political power, much more than substantive policy differences. Furthermore, the CPPD has paid a price for this growing preoccupation with power. This was evident in the string of Communist victories in student and union federation elections during the mid-1990s. Even more alarming was the outcome of the 1997 Congressional elections (see Table 2); while the CPPD lost only one Senate seat and maintained its share of seats in the Chamber of Deputies, it saw its total votes fall by over 1 million and its share of the vote fall to 50 percent. But more alarming still was the number of voters who turned in blank or defaced ballots (over 1.23 million or nearly 1 out of 5) and the similar number of young people who did not register to vote. Thus, while the CPPD remained the country's most important political grouping, there are growing signs that it is losing its popular support.

In sum, the decision-making apparatus inherited from the military regime has contributed to stability during the 1990s by limiting state action to a narrow range of strategic options and restricting popular representation. In this respect, it resembles the structure of state decision-making that prevailed during the 1930s and 1940s, the heyday of Chile's first compromise. However, if Chile's experience from 1952 to 1973 is any guide, that same institutional structure may subsequently become a major source of instability if the state is unable to respond to changing economic conditions by carrying out timely changes in the country's development strategy, if it is subjected to rising pressure for expanded popular participation, or if the governing coalition suffers a breakdown.

VI. CONCLUSION

The singularity of the Chilean experience has long been the fact that while it has undergone processes that have occurred elsewhere in Latin America, it took those processes further, such that their contradictions and consequences stood out in greater relief. This was true of its first socio-political compromise during the 1930s and 1940s, the instability and institutional collapse that was its legacy from the early 1950s to the early 1970s, and the process of authoritarian transformation following 1973. So too with Chile's new socio-political compromise; indeed, Chile is today [2003] widely regarded as the most promising of Latin America's new democracies. But as this article has demonstrated, it is also a great exemplar of how democracy can be severely hampered by institutional and structural constraints: among the former, an institutional apparatus that limits state action to a narrow range of strategic options, impedes popular access to state decision-making, and restricts the bargaining power of labor; and among the latter, an accumulation model that relies on the country's comparative advantages in natural resources and the flexible use of cheap labor, an extreme concentration of wealth and income, and a powerful domestic business class with strong links to international capital and determined to resist all but the most modest changes in the socio-economic status quo. In short, Chile's new compromise can be characterized as a neo-liberal elite pact that has privileged accumulation over both inclusion and distribution.

This outcome is no accident. Indeed, it has not departed significantly from the sort of post-military order envisioned by the authors of the military regime's transformative project. Moreover, the principal political opponents of military rule adopted a strategy that placed a high priority on stability and envisioned democratization as a gradual process, which has had the effect of privileging continuity over change. Thus, not unlike Chile's previous compromise, there are significant limitations built into its current one. Whether that compromise is capable of generating the strategic capacity that would enable the state to adapt to changing circumstances, and in a manner compatible with continued political stability and ongoing democratization, will depend on the nature of the relations between the party system, business, and the state. The key question is whether those relations are sufficiently resilient as to foster an evolving consensus capable of accommodating greater demands for social and political integration and changing patterns of state intervention, or, as in the case of Chile's previous compromise, are so narrow and contingent as to prevent such an evolving consensus.

With respect to political parties, the ability of the parties of the CPPD to forge a governing majority and implement a coherent policy program constitutes a significant historical accomplishment and distinguishes Chile from many other Latin American countries where weak and fragmented party systems have hampered the capacity of governments to resolve social and economic problems through democratic means. The existence of a center-left coalition, itself a major historical accomplishment, also places the Chilean government in a stronger negotiating position vis-à-vis business and its party allies, thereby increasing the prospects for the social and political integration of subordinate classes. At the same time, however, neither the integrity of the coalition, its ability to continue the current approach to policy-making, nor its capacity to bring about greater social and political integration can be taken for granted. In fact, there are serious tensions within the coalition, as well as between it and the executive. The suppression of those tensions has largely been facilitated by the perpetuation of the political cleavage created by the 1988 plebiscite and the resulting lack of political alternatives outside of the CPPD and the principal parties of the right. However, as soon as Chilean politics is no longer defined in terms of a referendum on Pinochet and the military regime, the ability of the coalition to maintain unity and make policy in a non-populist, supra-party, and technocratic fashion will diminish. Indeed, such a process has clearly begun under the Frei administration, though the rising levels of disillusionment remain without a clear, organized expression. Furthermore, much of the consensus that exists within the governing coalition over development strategy is more the result of inertia than of a clearly defined strategic choice. This suggests that should structural conditions change and economic growth become increasingly difficult, the current consensus may not be maintained and, more significantly, the CPPD may well be ill prepared to chart a coherent alternative course.

The CPPD demonstrates even greater short-comings with respect to the promotion of social and political integration. The current situation strongly resembles an elite pact, as there exist greater understanding and lines of communication between the parties in power and big business than between those parties and their popular constituencies among subordinate classes. Indeed, not unlike the Popular Front fifty years ago, the government is engaged in an accommodation with forces not part of its electoral coalition, pursuing policies far more in line with the latter's interests and demands than with those of their own supporters. This is a potentially risky formula, as Chile's experience in the 1940s demonstrates, but it can be sustained as long as the economy continues to grow, labor remains weak, and subordinate class actors perceive there is little alternative to the coalition in power. However, it bears repeating that once growth slows and/or the sense of limited alternatives fades, social conflicts are likely to intensify and the political pressure for meeting popular demands will likely increase, as the events of 1996–1997 would seem to indicate. This could lead to greater popular participation in state decision-making and the construction of a new consensus based on more equitably distributed sacrifices and benefits. Such a development, which approximates something of a transition from an elite pact toward a democratic class compromise, would in turn depend upon stronger ties with better organized subordinate class actors, particularly the labor movement. It would also depend upon the ability to confront potential opposition from business and the right. To the degree that those conditions fail to obtain, however, Chile's multiparty system could resume some of the populist, polarizing, and immobilizing tendencies it exhibited in the past.

Finally, Chilean business is far less defensive and enjoys a much more solid position within the political and economic order than at any time in the last seventy-five years. Moreover, as a result of this process, there exists a pragmatic element that has gained strength and has contributed to the forging of Chile's new socio-political compromise. This tendency may well continue, particularly if the sense of threat to capital diminishes even further. At the same time, however, the state's inability to discipline capital and steer investment into activities embodying higher levels of technological sophistication brings into question the long-term viability of the current accumulation model. Furthermore, one of the side effects of a more powerful business community is its greater determination to limit the participation of subordinate classes. Indeed, as was true during the 1932–1973 period, there are strong limits to the reformist inclinations of even the more pragmatic and conciliatory elements within Chile's economic elite.

It is altogether possible that, despite recent developments among social movements and at the polls, the civilian regime in place today in Chile can become consolidated and remain stable. Indeed, Chile may live up to its promoters' claim of being a model of the new Latin American democracy. But if that is the case, it will be a highly restricted model, a neo-liberal elite pact characterized by a very limited scope of social and political integration and an inequitable distribution of income. If it is not, it is possible that the regime will be unable to provide the institutional mechanism for reconciling the tension between the imperative of sustained accumulation in today's international economy and the conflicts over inclusion and distribution that until now have largely been held in check.

8.3 Free Society, Repressed Media: The Chilean Paradox (2002)

JUDY POLUMBAUM

Chile's a wonderful spot for tourists nowadays, a low-risk destination of advantageous exchange rates, ingratiating hospitality, abundant fresh fruit and vegetables, exquisite grilled meats, good and inexpensive wine. When it is summer in the northern hemisphere and winter in the south, you see them in Providencia, the tony sector of Santiago, with its glass-enclosed shopping malls and the usual suspects of the global fast-food industry, or in the Bellavista district, with its trendy night spots and upscale boutiques and mildly bohemian aura. Young people, groups from Europe or the United States, gathering for hotel breakfasts in their Gore-Tex and fleece before

Judy Polumbaum, "Free Society, Repressed Media: The Chilean Paradox." Reprinted with permission from *Current History*, February 2002. © 2002, Current History, Inc.

heading out to ski the Andes, or making the club scene after returning from a few days on the slopes.

The skiers are not the type to give street names a second thought, but one wonders whether Avenida 11 de Septiembre, which runs through Providencia, now gives even those untutored in contemporary history pause—for the wrong reason. The devastation of September 11, 2001 in New York City and Washington, D.C. may be emblazoned on the world's consciousness, but September 11 already marked Chile's tragic anniversary. Santiago's Avenue of September 11 proclaims the hubris of the Chilean generals who, on that date in 1973, turned on their own constitution and ruptured a long tradition of stable democracy. Nobody seems to mind that this boulevard lined with shops and restaurants continues to commemorate a dictatorship that technically ended with the restoration of elections in 1989.

Memories of that rupture are still raw in Chile. They have faded in the United States, despite shameful American complicity in the tragedy that befell this small nation of a mere 15 million or so nearly 30 years ago.

SEPTEMBER 11, 1973

In 1970 Salvador Allende—physician, Mason, Socialist, making his fourth try for the Chilean presidency as the candidate of the Popular Unity coalition of leftist parties—won an electoral plurality on a platform dedicated to dramatic social and economic reforms, including nationalization of major industries. United States–backed efforts to prevent Allende from winning failed, and a scheme to provoke a military rebellion to keep him from taking office resulted instead in the assassination of the head of the Chilean armed forces, a constitutional loyalist. Allende's inauguration went forth, as did a United States campaign of destabilization. The CIA funneled millions of dollars to opposition groups, conservative media, and bands of thugs to foment social unrest. Collaborating with multinational business and multilateral lending agencies, the United States also pursued a policy of economic aggression: blocking loans, squeezing credit, disrupting trade flows, terminating nonmilitary aid. This onslaught against a democratically elected government was authorized by President Richard Nixon and his national security adviser, Henry Kissinger. "Make the economy scream" was one of the instructions from the White House.

The relentless animosity from outside, compounding fierce political antagonisms within Chile, including divisions on the left and hostility from the middle classes, accomplished what policymakers in Washington had hoped. After three years the generals took matters into their own hands, although the United States military likely had advance knowledge of the coup. The Chilean air force bombed the presidential headquarters, Allende committed suicide, thousands of people were imprisoned and tortured for supporting him, and many were summarily executed—including a few North Americans who happened to be there. The unanticipated part was the military's refusal, once in power, to gracefully concede to the well-bred civilians of centrist and rightist parties supporting the coup. The Chilean junta, headed by General Augusto Pinochet, imposed a climate of terror that would last for nearly two decades. American military assistance and arms sales grew significantly during the years of greatest human rights abuses.

The Nixon-era contributions to subverting Allende make the story of Chile's September 11 a United States story as well. It is the sort of ugly involvement that makes taxpayers care about places they otherwise might ignore. Yet Chile has much else of beauty to command our attention, from great literature (two Nobel Prize–winning poets came from Chile) and scientific heritage (Chile was the site of much of Darwin's work) to rich mineral resources and spectacular geography.

If Chile's cultural and economic properties compel our attention in general terms, personal associations make Chile special to individuals. Mine go back nearly three decades when, as an obstinate girl avoiding college, I worked, saved, studied Spanish in Mexico for six weeks, then traveled further south on a trip of self-discovery. I reached Chile in the spring of 1972, halfway through Allende's tenure, joining my photographer father and artist mother, who were working on a book project on social change in shantytowns, factories, and farms. I ate the meat- and cheese-filled turnovers known as *empanadas* in a shack in an encampment on Santiago's fringes, where poor people were turning vacant lots into a community; sat in the boardroom of the Yarur textile factory, recently taken over by the state and being managed by the workers; and visited the legendary labor leader Clotario Blest, who shared his study with a dog and a cat and posters of religious figures and revolutionaries.

The coup took place as I was beginning my sophomore year of college in Montreal. I spent much of that year at meetings and rallies and helping Chileans get settled in Canada, which accepted hundreds of political refugees. Then, with Pinochet seemingly entrenched for the long haul, I left Latin America far behind. Today, although my Mandarin Chinese is quite good, my Spanish is pathetically rusty.

But Chile has been on my mind recently, and not only because of the horrible coincidence of September 11. Last summer [2001], for the first time, I returned for another look. As a media scholar, I was particularly curious about whether the passion for politics that had seemed so pronounced in 1972 still resounded, whether the boldness with which people across the political spectrum expressed themselves in those days had returned, whether any semblance of the riot of expression found on the newsstands back then was in evidence, whether the end to the dictatorship had opened the way for even greater expressive freedom.

THE RESIDUE OF REPRESSION

It is a weekday evening in July, midwinter in Santiago. The smoke-laden air at a café in the Bellavista district, the self-styled political salon named Off the Record, is abuzz as patrons take seats in an anteroom to listen to journalist Alejandra Matús talk about her return from involuntary exile. Matús is back from Florida for a visit more than two years after fleeing a lawsuit filed by the former head of the Chilean Supreme Court in response to her exposé *The Black Book of Chilean Justice,* documenting collaboration between the judiciary and the military. Recent passage of new press legislation that annulled the basis for the suit has enabled her to return home. Her book, barred from circulation but widely available in pirated editions, will be lawfully re-released in the near future. She thanks well-wishers for their support, makes wry comments about the warm welcome she has received from government officials, and observes that, despite her newfound freedom of movement, little has changed in the structures of power and influence in Chile.

The next night, Santiago's Museo de Bellas Artes is hosting an opening reception for an exhibition of Spanish paintings recently rediscovered in the museum basement. Hundreds of guests pause for speeches by the museum director and the Spanish ambassador to Chile, then resume mingling in the cavernous lobby. Attire identifies who's who: rakish, rumpled artists who lived in exile for years after the coup are conversing casually with business-suited curators and critics, while elegant patrons descend on the buffet tables. (Before leaving, they strip the tables of the floral arrangements.) Photographers capture the event for the society news that claims prodigious amounts of space in the first section of the country's dominant newspaper, *El Mercurio.*

Past midnight on a Saturday, as a concert by the Andean musical group Inti-Illimani winds down in Santiago's Teatro Oriente, audience members begin chanting *"El pueblo unido jamás será vencido!"*—"The people united will never be defeated!"— the mantra of the Popular Unity coalition that supported Allende's presidency. It's been an especially rousing and poignant occasion, for Inti's longtime musical director has announced he is leaving, and old friends have taken the stage for the sendoff. The ensemble, for whom a European tour turned into a 17-year sojourn after the coup, offers many old favorites, leavened by the jazz and world music picked up during those long years abroad. And then three encores. But the musicians have made it clear that they do not dwell in the past. Even nostalgia fails to elicit the politically charged song the crowd wants.

In postdictatorship Chile, the legacy of military rule persists as the usually unacknowledged back-drop to every public event, while the romanticism, contentiousness, and tragic fate of the Allende experiment still serve as touchstones of people's allegiances and convictions. Since a 1988 plebiscite in which voters rejected Pinochet's bid to continue in office, two moderate Christian Democratic presidencies and the year-old administration of Social-ist Ricardo Lagos, supported by a consortium of centrist and left parties, have ensued. Today, corpses no longer surface on the streets or in the Mapocho River, the deaths and disappearances of the 1970s and 1980s have been acknowledged in official reports, and some top military officers have been brought to justice. Yet in many ways the residue of repression has lasted far longer than seems logical for a country that, prior to 1973, had seen only one brief interruption to the electoral system in the entire twentieth century, a short military interregnum in the mid-1920s. A dozen years after the return of democratic elections, subtle tensions ripple beneath a veneer of civility, and politics remains polarized even as people purport to be getting along.

Pinochet himself has been back in the news, of course. Under legislation passed on his watch, he expected to remain an invincible senator-for-life, immune from prosecution—until British police detained him in a London medical clinic three years ago on a warrant from a Spanish court looking into the deaths of Spanish citizens during the coup. Then Chilean prosecu-tors sought his return on charges related to the infamous "trail of death" case in which scores of civilians were shot and buried in Chile's northern desert. He returned to Chile, where courts stripped him of his immunity but agreed with his defense: that he was too demented to stand trial. Other cases are pending against him, however, including one pursued by the rela-tives of murdered United States citizens.

During and since the dictatorship, Chilean journalists—among them a disproportionate number of women—have played a crucial role in exposing atrocities of the Pinochet regime, as well the military's continuing influence in business and affairs of state. The most important single example of Chilean reporting that has made a difference is Patricia Verdugo's *Los Zarpa-zos del Puma* [*The Claws of the Puma*], which formed the core of the prosecu-tion of Pinochet. Published in Chile in 1989, it became an immediate bestseller and is now available in an exacting English translation by Marcelo Montecino. The book describes in unflinching detail a spree of extrajudicial killings overseen by a team of military officers from the central command. Led by Pinochet special envoy General Sergio Arellano Stark and traveling in a Puma helicopter that touched down in five Chilean cities five weeks after the coup, the expedition left 75 summary executions in its wake.

This book became the most influential of a succession of books Verdugo wrote during the 1980s—the first published clandestinely—addressing human rights abuses under the dictatorship. Its extraordinary impact, as she explained when I visited her home in a wooded neighborhood of Santiago, hinged partly on its unusual perspective. In an earlier book she had recon-structed the same killing trail through the words of the victims' families. In this one she emphasized the experiences of local military commanders. "I had to tell the story in the voices of the military," Verdugo said. "It was a question of journalistic efficacy; only that would get the attention of the power of the courts. . . . Below a certain level, many members of the military were also victims, in being forced to carry out criminal orders. They were psychologically damaged."

Verdugo's awakening as a journalist of conscience began in the mid-1970s, when she was a writer for *Ercilla*, a Christian Democrat–backed magazine that was becoming a subtle voice of opposition to the dictatorship, and crystallized with the shock of her own father's abduction and murder in 1976. "We learned a cryptic language to communicate with dissenting readers," she recalls in her most recent book, the powerful memoir *Bucharest 187* [*187 Bucharest Lane*]. "We wrote between the lines, praying that the code would not be deciphered by the military. It is possible that our messages were not understood at their destination, but we were convinced that our work was serving some purpose." She had begun a series of interviews with political figures when her father, a mild-mannered man with no political ambitions who had become the head of a construction union when his predecessor resigned, disappeared. His family found his corpse in the city morgue. Although Verdugo does not like to speculate on the possibility, it is logical to suppose that her father's killing was meant as a warning to her. If it was, it backfired: her boldness and determination only grew.

Opposition to the dictatorship erupted into open protest beginning in 1983, and a newly critical journalism also emerged. It found expression in centrist magazines and newspapers that had continued to publish, and on the radio. An extraordinary concentration of experienced journalists came together at the new daily newspaper *La Época*, founded in 1986 by progressive Christian Democrats with support from the Catholic Church as well as from sympathetic trade unions and political parties in Western Europe and elsewhere. The highly respected paper lasted nine years, managing to avoid the label "left-wing" even though staff sympathies were largely in that direction, but finally falling victim to economic distress, partly because international donors had shifted their attentions to the emerging democracies of the former Soviet bloc.

THE CULTURE OF SELF-CENSORSHIP

Chilean journalists who supported the movement against the dictatorship retain a strange sort of nostalgia for those years of contention; now they see commercialism and complacency overwhelming the media, while space for critical and investigative journalism shrinks. Along with *La Época*, a number of other forums for serious reporting and writing closed during the 1990s. Pressures on the media these days are subtle, pervasive, and intractable. The Inter-American Press Association, at a meeting in Santiago last summer, issued a report noting the "culture of self-censorship" in the region; and Chilean journalists see it at work in their country. Not so long ago, when the consequences of offending the wrong people could be lethal, caution was entirely understandable as a matter of physical well-being. Today, deriving from passivity rather than self-defense, it is more a matter of economic, political, and social accommodation.

Concentration of media ownership is probably the most powerful constraint on expression of diverse opinions and ideas. Ninety percent of Chile's newspapers are controlled by two large publishing firms, the *El Mercurio* and *La Tercera* groups, both with extremely conservative owners. Surveys show that 80 percent of Chileans get most of their information from radio and television, and while radio allows for a greater spectrum of views, three of the four main television stations are conservative. One media analyst told me: "The press is an extension of power. In a democratic society, power is diluted. In a dictatorship or oligarchic society it is concentrated. Fifteen families [in Chile] own most of the country. The press is controlled by them via a fifth power, advertising."

Indeed, many Chilean journalists see their work as more restricted now than during the final years of military rule. Even state-owned media are subject to pressure from the Chilean elite. After Chile's national television station (TVN) broadcast a documentary about United States support for the coup, the station's board, dominated by conservatives, replaced both the station head and the news director. "Journalists are very sensitive to pressure," a TVN reporter told me. "They have very fine antennae." In his view, the personnel changes following that particular documentary sent a clear signal of disapproval for investigative journalism. In other cases, supervisors have made producers remove sensitive segments from programs, and the most troublesome reporters may find themselves kept away from subjects of any magnitude. "People who stick out their necks don't get good stories, don't get to travel, and so on," said this reporter, "so they don't do it."

Dissembling about the recent past, endemic in Chilean politics, also is evident with respect to journalism. I sensed this most clearly at a book party for the release of a volume profiling prominent Chilean journalists, where an incongruous cordiality seemed to mask historically incompatible positions. A conservative photographer whose good buddies in the air force gave him prime access to the bombed-out executive building, La Moneda, during the coup, was fêted along with reporters and editors who opposed military rule in the risky publications of the 1980s. A panel discussion organized for the event gingerly avoided any mention of the right-wing media's role in demonizing Allende and creating conditions for the military takeover. "There is more information now about human rights, the disappeared, and the responsibility of the military, judges, politicians, and so on," a Chilean media scholar who attended the gathering later told me, "but the responsibility of the press during the military regime is not going to be discussed. The press wasn't as valiant as it says."

Meanwhile, lacerations and dislocations endure in paradoxes and contradictions in Chile's newsrooms. It is not unusual to find that editors or reporters drawing paychecks from conservative newspapers are simultaneously working on projects documenting resistance to the dictatorship, state-sponsored terrorism, or corruption. Side by side with translations of North American self-help books and popular fiction, bookstores give prominent display to works of investigative journalism—notable recent examples include *La Conjura* [*The Plot*] by Mónica González, a meticulous history of Allende's overthrow and American involvement, and *El Saqueo* [*The Looting*] by María Olivia Monckeberg, revealing how the dictatorship enriched the military and elites. Yet the occupational lot of even the most acclaimed journalists on the left continues to be shaped by their political backgrounds. González, a tenacious woman who has prevailed in more than two dozen lawsuits filed against her investigative reporting, is a case in point. Returning from exile in Paris in 1978, she was unable to resume work as a journalist until 1983, and is said to be still shunned for top jobs in the field because of her affiliation with the once-strong Chilean Communist Party, which was decimated under the military.

An important landmark for journalism was reached last spring [2001], when both chambers of Chile's congress passed, and President Lagos signed, a new press law repealing some blatant restrictions on freedom of expression. Most significantly, legislators annulled what human rights monitors typically called the "notorious" or "infamous" Article 6b of the State Security Law (the provision hanging over Alejandra Matús), which effectively insulated high officials in government, the judiciary, and the military from public criticism. During the past decade, as state-sanctioned physical violence against critics receded, officials had continued to use this so-called *descato* or "disrespect" clause to seek bans on expression and threaten writers, editors, and publishers with jail terms, using military as well as civilian courts. The provision carried up to five years in prison for criticism of high government officials. It had been a main focus of a 1998 Human Rights Watch report finding that "freedom of expression and information is restricted in Chile to an extent possibly unmatched by any other democratic society in the Western hemisphere." Although most Latin American countries have similar insult laws on the books, only in Chile were they being regularly applied.

The new press law, which had taken eight years to wend its way toward passage, also repealed several other articles of the security law, including one authorizing suspension of publication and broadcasts and confiscation of publications deemed offensive, and another subjecting editors and printers of offending publications to criminal prosecution. The new legislation also prevents military courts from trying media cases; requires judges to show cause for sealing records; establishes a right to information; and grants journalists the right to protect sources. It does not eliminate all cause for worry, however. Journalists remain concerned about measures similar to the one repealed from the security law that still exist in Chile's criminal code. Others are dissatisfied with the new law's restrictive definition of "journalist," a designation reserved for individuals with college degrees from accredited journalism schools.

The rise of sensationalism and lowest-common-denominator journalism, with their emphasis on crime and celebrity, is another vexing issue. In a straight-laced Catholic country like Chile, where divorce as well as abortion is illegal (although church-sanctioned marital annulments have always been available for a price, and reforms in marriage and divorce law are under discussion), one might expect moral objections; but serious media practitioners are most troubled by the trivialization of news. The "news lite" trend has intensified over the last year or so, which has seen the appearance of free "subway" papers—*El Metro,* owned by a European company that specializes in putting out throwaway papers in large cities throughout the world, and a couple of local afternoon competitors.

NEW OUTLETS, NEW VOICES

Still, there are heartening countertrends. One is suggested by the subversive potential of new technology. Not only were pirated editions of the Matús book sold on the streets: the entire text appeared on the Internet. A two-year-old on-line daily, *El Mostrador,* has gained a reputation for independence and scoops. While the site itself is not widely accessible to the general public—Chile's Internet market is growing fast, but in absolute terms it is small, with an estimated 1.5 million users by the end of 2001—it has become a forum where disgruntled public figures can make their views known, as well as a major source for other news media, and thus has considerable influence beyond its direct readership.

Many agree, and not in jest, that the most viable alternative voice in Chile today is the twice-monthly satirical tabloid *The Clinic*—titled in English—that a group of friends in Santiago started on a lark when Pinochet was under detention at the medical clinic in London. The paper regularly showcases photos of toilets and naked butts, and its headlines blare insults and double entendres. Yet much of the content is sophisticated and profoundly serious. By the middle of 2001, circulation had reached 40,000, huge for Chile, with actual readership many times larger since issues are passed along. Perhaps the closest analogy is the United States weekly paper and web publication *The Onion*—except *The Clinic* is far raunchier on the outside, where it puts most of its humor, and also far more significant, since satire and criticism of the sort Americans have grown used to around the raucous margins of expression in the United States actually get noticed in Chile.

Most amazed of all at the paper's popularity are its editors. "We are the most-sold publication in Chile, which we think is hilarious," said founder and director Patricio Guzmán. I interviewed him in his makeshift office, part of a third-floor suite strewn with newspapers and permeated with the smell of cigarette smoke, on the eve of a move to presumably better quarters. A former art critic who studied art history in Italy, Guzmán also is surprised that his paper has not faced any lawsuits or suppression. "It's luck," he believes. "Also, we do things in a roundabout way. Anyway, self-censorship is a much more severe problem than censorship. Censorship exists, but it's less than people say."

The Clinic attempts to confront issues avoided in the conventional press, from political power to sex. "People want a press that will open windows," Guzmán said. "Right and left alike want that." His paper blares the tone from the newsstand; after Pinochet's defense won the argument that the former dictator was too demented to stand trial, the cover featured Pinochet's smiling face and the headlines *"Te salvaste viejo llorón"*—"You saved yourself, old crybaby," and *"Chile perdió el juicio,"* a play on words meaning both "Chile loses the judgment" and "Chile loses its mind."

Asked who the readers are, Guzmán quipped, "I'd like to meet them!" He surmises: "Young people, educated people, older people with open minds, people from the political world, probably more middle- and upper-middle-class people."

The spectrum may be even more diverse, if devotees I met are any indication: they ranged from a former shantytown resident who has returned from exile in Canada and now runs a snack bar, to an elegant cosmopolitan widow who disdained her class to support Allende and lived for a while in Argentina after the coup, to journalist Patricia Verdugo, who, along with other prominent writers, donates work to the paper. To her *The Clinic* is not merely an information alternative; it is a critical form of psychic affirmation. "We contribute articles to compartmentalize our pain and anger," she said. "We like seeing the front page. It's a kind of collective therapy."

SUGGESTIONS FOR FURTHER READING

Constable, Pamela, and Arturo Valenzuela. *A Nation of Enemies: Chile Under Pinochet.* New York: Norton, 1991.

Dandavati, Annie G. *The Women's Movement and the Transition to Democracy in Chile.* New York: Peter Lang, 1996.

Fleet, Michael. *The Rise and Fall of Christian Democracy.* Princeton, N.J.: Princeton University Press, 1985.

Loveman, Brian. *Chile: The Legacy of Hispanic Capitalism.* New York: Oxford University Press, 1988.

Munck, Gerardo L. "Authoritarianism, Modernization, and Democracy in Chile." *Latin American Research Review* 29(2) (1994): 188–211.

Oppenheim, Lois, ed. "Military Rule and the Struggle for Democracy in Chile." Issue 68, *Latin American Perspectives,* 18(1): Winter 1991.

Oxhorn, Philip. *Organizing Civil Society: The Popular Sector and the Struggle for Democracy in Chile.* University Park: Pennsylvania State University Press, 1995.

Report of the Chilean National Commission on Truth and Reconciliation, trans. Phillip E. Berryman. Notre Dame, Ind.: Center for Civil and Human Rights, Notre Dame Law School, 1993.

Schneider, Cathy Lisa. *Shantytown Protest in Pinochet's Chile.* Philadelphia: Temple University Press, 1995.

Sigmund, Paul. *The Overthrow of Allende and the Politics of Chile 1964–1976.* Pittsburgh, Pa.: University of Pittsburgh Press, 1977.

Valenzuela, Arturo. *The Breakdown of Democratic Regimes: Chile,* vol. 4, *The Breakdown of Democratic Regimes,* ed. Juan Linz and Alfred Stepan. Baltimore: Johns Hopkins University Press, 1978.

Valenzuela, Arturo, and J. Samuel Valenzuela, eds. *Military Rule in Chile.* Baltimore: Johns Hopkins University Press, 1986.

USEFUL WEBSITES

Newspapers
La Nación
   www.lanacion.cl

El Mercurio
   http://diario.elmercurio.com

El Diario
   www.eldiario.cl

Chip News: English language news website
   www.chip.cl

Government
Congress
   www.congreso.cl

Government of Chile, access to ministries
   www.gobiernodechile.cl

Office of the President
   www.presidencia.gov.cl

General
Georgetown University, Political Database of the Americas
   http://cfdev.georgetown.edu/pdba/Countries

CIA World Fact Book: Resource for general information on Chile.
   www.odci.gov/cia/publications/factbook/geos/ci.html

Latin American Network Information Center: Comprehensive website housed at the University of Texas with extensive Latin American links on a wide array of topics.
   http://Lanic.utexas.edu

CHAPTER 9

Colombia: The Collapse of the State

*I*n July 1991, a Constituent Assembly elected for the express purpose of writing a new constitution officially replaced Colombia's 1886 Constitution—the longest-standing in Latin America. It was rewritten to provide Colombia's leaders with the means to address deepening crises in the country over persistent rural violence and growing urban frustrations over unmet social demands. At the time, the perceived need to revise the country's constitution contrasted with the general perception that Colombia was a more stable democracy than most others in Latin America. From an outside perspective, the country had had stable, essentially competitive elections through much of the twentieth century with alternation of power between two well-institutionalized political parties. But, even the appearance of stability collapsed over the 1990s as Colombia instead became a case of virtual dissolution of the state in a context of narcotrafficking and intense rural and urban violence. How did one of Latin America's most stable democracies collapse so violently?

The answer lies in part in the fact that Colombia's relatively stable political arrangements have been accompanied by extraordinary political violence. This state of affairs dates back virtually all the way to Colombia's founding by the great Latin American liberator Simón Bolívar. The two leading figures in Colombia's war for independence, Bolívar and Francisco de Paula Santander, became the leading rivals for leadership of the new nation. Their rivalry, however, also split elites between competing visions of the organization of the new state. Bolívar's vision for Latin America generally and Colombia specifically was one based on strong central authority with a prominent role for the Catholic Church. By contrast, Santander championed a view of decentralized government authority and a more limited role for the Church (for example, secular authority over education and marriage). This split became the base for conflict between the two contending parties that have dominated Colombian politics since 1850: the Conservatives and the Liberals.

The two parties set the pattern for Colombian politics. On the one hand, the two competed in essentially fair elections and alternated in power on a regular basis. In fact, in contrast to much of the rest of Latin America, the Colombian presidential succession was interrupted by the military on only four occasions. Yet, while in power, the parties were also willing to press their advantage, which intensified political competition and raised the stakes of electoral competition. For example, in the late nineteenth century, first the Liberals then the Conservatives used their electoral victory to write constitutions that imposed their preferred organization of the state over the objections of their political rivals. The depth of the rivalry and the stakes of electoral competition led the parties to resort to violent means to advance their causes. The most striking instances of this use of violence came in the War of 1,000 Days in 1899 as Liberals launched a rebellion that left 100,000 dead and the country economically ravaged, and facilitated the secession of Panama and its establishment (with U.S. support) as an independent nation. An even more intense period of partisan violence, dubbed "the violence" (*la violencia*) broke out in the 1940s and lasted through the 1950s and claimed roughly 300,000 lives. The savagery of the fighting led to the only military coup in modern Colombian history as even the public supported the military's effort to contain the violence.

Ultimately, the violence was contained and democratic stability was restored as the two leading parties reached an accommodation with both positive and negative consequences. Beginning in 1958, the Conservatives and Liberals agreed to share power in what was called the National Front government. Under the terms of the agreement, the presidency alternated between the two parties during the sixteen-year duration, but all other positions—in the cabinet, in the municipalities and departments, in the bureaucracy, and even in the judiciary—were divided between the two parties. The agreement succeeded in restoring democratic rule to the country, but at a price that the country is still paying for today.

The price for democratic stability was a closing off of the political process to alternative views and an end to political debate over policy. The two parties closed off electoral competition to alternative parties and prevented the emergence of alternative mechanisms of representation. This might not have had serious consequences if the two parties genuinely competed for power by offering competing views of policy and attempting to build alternative, broad coalitions of voters. Instead, the two parties became patronage machines, drawing support by offering access to government resources and jobs. The system became a spoils system with party followers enjoying the fruits of government resources while outsiders were denied access as well as voice. By the end of the National Front experience in 1974, the mold had been set, and the parties continued operating as essentially corrupt, exclusionary patronage machines.

Perhaps it is no surprise, then, that larger and larger segments of Colombian society came to resent the political system. Such resentment and feelings of alienation and marginalization expressed themselves in the emergence of a number of guerrilla movements based in the countryside, most notably the National Liberation Army (ELN), the Revolutionary Armed Forces of Colombia (FARC), and the M-19. In the cities, the failure to provide adequate public services and infrastructure led to growing numbers of protests and mobilizations led by urban social movements seeking greater voice in Colombia's political process. Between 1974 and 1991, successive governments confronted the need to revise the constitution and increase the capacity of the president to address the country's problems. However, institutional limits on the president's power and the character of the political parties made reforms exceedingly difficult. Most important, factionalism within the two parties and their reliance on patronage and clientelism made them particularly resistant to change.

The 1991 constitutional reform was designed to address the problems in Colombian society, but many observers thought it exacerbated the weaknesses of the political system. In any event, the societal situation of the late 1980s and 1990s had deteriorated badly—perhaps too badly for any constitutional reform to resolve easily. Most important, narcotics production, trafficking, and related violence had grown substantially over the 1980s. Drug production had existed previously in Colombia, including traditional production of coca leaves by indigenous people as well as marijuana on the Caribbean coast in more modern times. But, a combination of the crackdown of U.S. enforcement on the Mexican border and the explosion of demand in the United States during the 1970s helped transform Colombia into the international leader of cocaine production. Cocaine production revealed the weaknesses of Colombia's state and political economy. Drug cartel leaders, such as the notorious Pablo Escobar Gavíria, were able to construct political followings by providing the same kind of clientelistic, patronage benefits that the political parties offered. With a strong state, the government provides these benefits and criminal figures lack the ability to build their own political bases. Colombia's failure to strengthen the state and its services made it possible for guerrilla movements and drug cartels to construct their own political worlds, including newspapers and other media. Drug cartel leaders also provided alternative sources of employment and income, which further undermined the legitimacy of the Colombian state. In fact, the growing power and violence of the drug cartels was part of the social pressure that resulted in the 1991 constitutional reform.

The drug situation got even worse through the 1990s, however, despite significant efforts to shut down the leading cartels based in the cities of Cáli and Medellín. Over the course of the decade, U.S. pressure and assistance helped weaken the drug cartels. Production, however, did not disappear as U.S. authorities hoped. Instead, the rural guerrilla movements, especially the FARC, were able to step into the vacuum and get into the drug trade themselves. Drug revenues increased the strength of the guerrilla forces. Over the decades of rural violence, the ELN and the FARC had remained relatively limited endeavors with limited capacity to threaten the Colombian government. By the 1990s, the two guerrilla movements had become capable of committing violent acts in dramatic fashion in both the cities and the countryside. Although the political system continued to operate with the two main parties retaining their dominant position, the state itself was in disarray and withdrew as a governing presence from large portions of the country. Basic government functions—most importantly that of providing public order—were no longer present in many rural communities. The failure of the government to provide an effective response to the guerrilla movements led to the formation of a right-wing militia movement, the AUC, which began a guerrilla-type war directed against the FARC and the ELN, but which also frequently abused rural communities. Together, the Colombian military, the FARC, the ELN, and the

AUC unleashed terrible violence and suffering on the populace without any indication that any party to the conflict was close to giving up. In effect, the violence had escalated to a civil war.

The political system suffered from a growing loss of legitimacy as a result of its failure to resolve the civil war and from a series of scandals and/or deeply unpopular decisions. The presidency of Ernesto Samper was badly compromised by revelations that Samper had received drug money for his presidential campaign. The episode led to sharp conflict with the United States amid charges that Colombia was not making a credible effort to thwart drug trafficking. Samper's successor, President Andres Pastrana, exhausted his credibility in a failed effort to reach a peace agreement. Under his effort, both the FARC and the ELN were granted very large areas of territory and permitted in effect to govern them free from harassment by Colombian government forces. The plan backfired as it became clear that both movements used the offering as an opportunity to strengthen themselves and their narcotrafficking activities. It ended when the FARC itself returned to violent attacks on Colombian citizens.

Recognizing the failure of the peace offering, Pastrana, working with U.S. President Bill Clinton, came up with an alternative plan called Plan Colombia. Plan Colombia represented a major initiative involving billions of dollars to re-establish order and the rule of law in Colombia. Much of the money was to be allocated to military assistance with the intent of strengthening the ability of the Colombian government to respond to the guerrillas militarily. But a portion was also set aside for assisting rural citizens economically to help them move from coca production to other forms of agricultural production. Other funds were to be allocated to state institution building measures to strengthen the presence of the state in the countryside in areas like public utilities (such as water, telecommunications) and in police.

The plan has been very controversial in Colombia, in the rest of Latin America, and in the United States. For many, the plan simply does not pay sufficient attention to the deep structural injustices in Colombia that underlie the conflict. Applying a military solution to a social, political, and economic crisis cannot solve the problem. For many Latin American governments, the concern is that efforts to limit coca production in Colombia will simply push the production into neighboring countries. In a related vein, many are concerned that the violence itself will spill over Colombia's borders into neighboring countries. For many in the United States, the concern is that the U.S. role is poorly conceived. For one, the U.S. role had been restricted to counternarcotics as opposed to counterinsurgency. Yet, the two are inextricably entwined in Colombia. For many, the concern is that the strong U.S. role in Plan Colombia implicates the United States either directly or indirectly in the terrible human rights abuses committed in Colombia. In 2002, a new president, Alvaro Uribe, was elected on a platform of a strong commitment to fighting the guerrilla movements and dismantling the right-wing militia groups. With the September 11, 2001, attack on the World Trade Center, the Bush administration shifted its emphasis in Colombia from counternarcotics to counterterrorism with the FARC, the ELN, and the AUC designated as terrorist groups. But, as of this writing in 2004, there was no indication that the war in Colombia or the deep involvement of the United States was over.

The articles in this chapter address different aspects of the crisis of governability that afflicted Colombia in the last decade of the twentieth century and continue to do so into the twenty-first century. Jeff Browitt, in "Capital Punishment: The Fragmentation of Colombia and the Crisis of the Nation-State," puts the country's troubles in long-term perspective. Browitt argues that Colombia's landed elites—its oligarchy—has failed over two-hundred years to create a nation-state that can successfully integrate most of its citizens, including its large, rural indigenous population. This is because the oligarchy is unwilling to contemplate any kind of polity that compromises its own political dominance. The 1991 Constitution represents an effort by the political elite to grant extraordinary powers to the president to deal with the extraordinary violence plaguing the country. Yet, Browitt points out that the neoliberal economic reforms promulgated through the 1990s have had disastrous economic consequences for the very citizenry that have been politically excluded. The exacerbation of the economic, political, and social justice problems has acted as a kind of capital punishment that has contributed to a further fragmentation of the nation.

Javier Guerrero Barón addresses the conflict and the prospects for its resolution in "Is the War Ending? Premises and Hypotheses with Which to View the Conflict in Colombia." Barón makes the important point that the conflict is not going to end until all major actors desire an end to it. He reviews the principal parties to the conflict and notes that unfortunately none of them have reached a point where ending the conflict is really their highest goal. As a result, Barón cautions against any optimism that the war will be ending soon.

Arlene Tickner, in "Colombia and the United States: From Counternarcotics to Counterterrorism," highlights another problem for resolution of the conflict that stems from the conduct of U.S. foreign policy. The United States has made important commitments, financially and militarily, to support the Colombian government. Tickner warns, however, that the United States tends to view the Colombian conflict through a narrow lens of narcotics and terrorism. This lens obscures the larger political, economic, and social considerations of the conflict and weakens U.S. policy as a result.

DATA TABLES

Table 9.1
Colombia Fact and Data Sheet

Population (July 2003, estimated):	41,662,073
Ethnic Groups:	Mestizo 58%, white 20%, mulatto 14%, black 4%, mixed black-Amerindian 3%, Amerindian 1%
Religions:	Roman Catholic 90%
Government Type:	Republic
Capital:	Bogotá
Administrative Divisions:	32 departments
Date of Independence:	July 20, 1810
Constitution:	July 5, 1991
Executive Branch:	President Alvaro Uribe Velez, elected August 7, 2002; president and vice president elected on the same ticket by popular election to a 4-year term.
Legislature:	Bicameral National Congress
	• Senate has 102 seats. Elected by direct vote to a 4-year term. Distribution of seats as of 2003: PL, 28 seats; PSC, 13 seats; independents and smaller parties (many aligned with conservatives), 61 seats.
	• Chamber of Deputies has 166 seats. Elected by direct vote to a 4-year term. Distribution of seats as of 2003: PT, 91 seats; PFL, 84 seats; PL, 54 seats; PSC, 21 seats; independents and other parties, 91 seats.
Main Political Parties:	Conservative Party (PSC), Liberal Party (PL), Colombian Communist Party (PCC), 19 of April Movement (M-19).
Military Spending (FY2001):	U.S. $3.3 billion
Military Spending, Percentage of GDP (FY2001):	3.4
GDP (2002, estimated):	PPP $251.6 billion
GDP Composition by Sector (2001, estimated):	Agriculture: 13% Industry: 30% Services: 57%
Main Industries:	Textiles, food processing, oil, clothing and footwear, beverages, chemicals, cement, gold, coal, emeralds
Main Agricultural Products:	Coffee, cut flowers, bananas, rice, tobacco, corn, sugarcane, cocoa beans, oilseed, vegetables, forest products, shrimp
Export Partners (2002):	United States, 44.8%; Venezuela, 9.4%; Ecuador, 6.8%
Import Partners (2002):	United States, 32.6%; Venezuela, 7%; Mexico, 5.3%; Japan, 5.3%; Brazil, 5.2%; Germany, 4.2%
External Debt (2002, estimated):	U.S. $38.4 billion

Table 9.2
Presidents of Colombia

Tenure	President
1898	Guillermo Qunitero Calderón
1898	José Manuel Marroquín
1898–1900	Manuel Antonio Sanclemente
1900–1904	José Manuel Marroquín
1904–1909	Rafael Reyes
1909	Jorge Holguín
1909–1910	Ramón González Valencia
1910–1914	Carlos Emilio Restrepo
1914–1918	José Vicente Concha
1918–1921	Marco Fidel Suárez
1921–1922	Jorge Holguín
1922–1926	Pedro Nel Ospina
1926–1930	Miguel Abadia Méndez
1930–1934	Enrique Olaya Herrera
1934–1938	Alfonso López Pumarejo
1938–1942	Eduardo Santos
1942–1945	Alfonso López Pumarejo
1945–1946	Alberto Lleras Camargo
1946–1950	Mariano Ospina Pérez
1950–1951	Laureano Gómez
1951–1953	Roberto Udarneta Arbelaez
1953–1957	Gustavo Rojas Pinilla
1957–1958	Military Junta
1958–1962	Alberto Lleras Camargo
1962–1966	Guillermo Leon Valencia
1966–1970	Carlos Lleras Restrepo
1970–1974	Misael Pastrana Borrero
1974–1978	Alfonso López Michelsen
1978–1982	Julio César Turbay Ayala
1982–1986	Belisario Betancur
1986–1990	Virgilio Barco Vargas
1990–1994	César Gaviria Trujillo
1994–1998	Ernesto Samper Pizano
1998–2002	Andrés Pastrana Arango
2002–present	Álvaro Uribe Vélez

9.1 Capital Punishment: The Fragmentation of Colombia and the Crisis of the Nation-State (2001)

JEFF BROWITT

In the [late 1990s], in Colombia there have been several major national strikes against the government's economic policies. Public sector and private sector labour unions have been agitating for a moratorium on the payment of foreign debt, a change from the dominant neoliberal economic model of the past 10 years and a rejection of IMF preconditions for loans. Suffering under the weight of its worst recession in 70 years, the Colombian economy is witnessing an unprecedented wave of bankruptcies and company failures: in the first half of 1999, over 70 major companies and 3,600 small businesses went to the wall. With very little growth in gross domestic product over the past three years and an official unemployment level over 20%, the signs are definitely not good. In addition, Colombia owes more than $17 billion to foreign creditors, and debt servicing alone (more than $2 billion annually) accounts for nearly 40% of the national budget. National economic statistics, however, very rarely indicate the regional and class variations of the full impact of the economic crisis. They throw little light on the living conditions and despair among poor Colombians (the majority), who have to deal on a day-to-day basis with chronic shortages of all the basic necessities, while their communities are shattered by generalised violence—whether guerilla warfare in the countryside, its paramilitary backlash, or the everyday street violence—all of which have left virtually no community untouched. Weber's idea of the nation as defined, in part, by the monopoly of violence held by the state no longer obtains in Colombia. In the first half of 2000, the National Police (*Dijín*) reported close to 13,000 killings throughout the nation, with Medellín and Cali continuing to be the most violent cities in the country. Included in these sad statistics are the regular massacres of indigenous and *campesino* peoples. It is also estimated that, in the past 15 years, two million people have become internal refugees fleeing from the violence, an exodus only eclipsed by the African continent taken as a whole. Colombians are leaving in record numbers to seek either refuge or a better way of life in other countries. Since 1999 alone, more than 50,000 have arrived in Spain. How did things get this bad?

Jeff Browitt, "Capital Punishment: The Fragmentation of Colombia and the Crisis of the Nation-State." *Third World Quarterly.* December 2001, Vol. 22, no. 6, pp. 1063–1078. Reprinted by permission of Taylor & Francis Ltd. http://www.tandf.co.uk/journals.

Just as many commentators misinterpret the recent emergence of democratic regimes in the previously militarised societies of the Southern Cone and Central America as a return to, or a restoration of, the ostensibly democratic national development projects of an earlier era, so too do they misinterpret the current institutional crisis in Colombia as driven primarily by drug cartels or revolutionary groups, the suppression of which will somehow usher in national stability and prosperity. They fail to see that the contemporary crisis in Colombia is but the latest manifestation of the historic inability of the Colombian oligarchy to forge national unity and stability ever since independence from Spain in the 1820s. Even if Colombia manages to emerge from the civil war presently tearing the country apart, it will find a world that has fundamentally changed. What we are now actually witnessing with the rise of the globalisation project is a withering away of nation-states based upon the notion of a "national social contract," under which citizens, in theory, identified with the constitutional order and national administrations designed and implemented nationally orientated social and economic development projects.

In the Colombian case state sovereignty and national identity are now challenged from without by multiple transnational links—global telecommunications and entertainment media, global capital flows, multinational financial institutions which shape economic investment and strategy—and from within by alternative or parallel power structures—local mafias, revolutionary groups and paramilitaries. The long-term crisis of the nation-state has created a vacuum of legitimacy into which have flowed military and paramilitary forces and the drug industry, especially over the past 15–20 years, all of which have virtually destroyed the successful functioning of electoral politics and the rule of law. It was in this climate that a new Colombian constitution, the first for over 100 years, was adopted in 1991. It was a constitution intended to address many of the above problems: the need to break the 150-year long "duopoly" of the Conservative and Liberal Parties; the need to institutionalise minority rights and devolve power to the regions; and the perceived need to arm the executive with constitutional powers strong enough to deal with unprecedented levels of civil strife. Globalisation, in its current but not necessarily permanent neoliberal variant, which got underway in the decade before the collapse of the Soviet Union, has exacerbated and deepened the crisis by depriving the national government (and that of most other Latin American countries) of the resources necessary to maintain the country in a state consistent with that of a manageable civil society. In fact the new Colombian constitution has written into it provisions which are explicitly aimed at facilitating neoliberal restructuring. Before turning to an examination of the impact of the new constitution, however, let us look briefly at the history of the Colombian national trajectory since independence.

THE ORIGINS OF THE COLOMBIAN
CRISIS 1886–1930

The fiction of an official nation was first established via the 1886 Constitution written after the 1885 coup by Rafael Núñez. Throughout the 19th century, whether in its initial expanded form as Gran Colombia—Colombia, Venezuela, Ecuador and Panama—or much later when it comprised what is now Colombia and Panama, the independent republic had been divided by an internecine struggle between centralists and federalists over questions of political power, national boundaries and protection of interests, a struggle reflected in the 15 constitutions drafted between 1811 and 1886. These years can be divided into four periods, each marked off by constitutional change, the re-drawing of national boundaries and the changing fortunes of particular fractions of the political elite. They are the war of independence (1810–19); Bolívar's alliance of *Gran Colombia* (1819–30); *Nueva Granada* (1830–58); and the period of liberal hegemony and radical reform (1858–86). The formation of the Colombian nation-state can thus be said to have passed through two key stages. First, the succession of civil wars and constitutional charters beginning in 1810 and extending to 1886, when an enduring constitution was finally settled upon. Second, the subsequent consolidation of the nation-state during the commodity-export boom of the final decades of the 19th century and the first three decades of the twentieth century. But according to Hernando Valencia Villa, the history of the Colombian constitutional charters and their various amendments, both before and after 1886, indeed the very framing of the new 1991 Constitution, must be regarded as stages in an ideological "battle," rather than some benign incremental evolution towards disinterested Enlightenment ideals of justice and civic harmony. The process displays certain broad similarities with the rest of Latin America, especially as regards the liberal–conservative struggles and the near-continental hegemony of liberalism in the latter half of the 19th century, although specific national histories often exhibit crucial distinguishing factors.

The 1886 Constitution marked the first major expression of political, military and administrative centralism, as well as the institutionalisation of Catholicism as the only officially recognised religion, and the introduction of a centralised education system. But this was a nationalism that was unaccompanied by popular enthusiasm or socialisation into national consciousness. Thus began the process of ignoring the sometimes quite different political, economic, cultural and social aspects of each region as *La Regeneración*, as the 1886 turning point became known, solidified into an overbearing centralism. While, at the time, the dominant language was Spanish and the dominant religion was Catholicism, this in no way encompassed the linguistic, social, cultural and religious heterogeneity covered by the "national" territory: "The presence of 81 indigenous peoples, with their languages, traditions, cultures and forms of political administration; the existence of Afro-Colombian communities; the frontier regions; all made the Westphalian concept of nationalities difficult to apply in our region."

The Conservatives dominated politics for 40 years after the *Regeneración*, their hegemony temporarily challenged by the Liberal uprising known as The War of a Thousand Days (1899–1902), which resulted in the historic Treaty of Neerlandia in 1902. The Treaty was a defining moment in national-bourgeois consolidation and a prelude to neocolonial penetration. The 40-year Conservative rule brought a period of relative peace and prosperity with the accelerated growth of coffee production and manufacturing industries and with textiles leading the way, but the same period also witnessed the expansion of the foreign-dominated areas of oil and bananas. The outward appearance of relative social and economic harmony was shattered, however, by the arrival of the Great Depression, the growth of more militant labour unions and the infamous massacre of banana workers by government troops in 1928 after a strike on a United Fruit plantation. The combined effect of economic slowdown and social unrest, Conservative complacency and a split in the Conservative Party itself all contributed to a Liberal victory at the polls and the beginning of the so-called Liberal Republic (1930–46). This period was dominated by the figure of the two-term president, Alfonso López Pumarejo (1934–38; 1942–44).

FROM THE GREAT DEPRESSION TO THE NATIONAL FRONT 1930–78

The centrepiece of Pumarejo's *La Revolución en Marcha,* a Colombian "New Deal" that paralleled Roosevelt's efforts in the USA and Lázaro Cárdenas's policies in Mexico, was an agrarian reform law which, like that of Cárdenas, sought to alleviate rural poverty and quell peasant unrest. Although the reforms were hardly radical, they did mark a new era for labour legislation and paved the way for the formation of major trade union organisations. In addition, the López Administration raised taxes on foreign companies and amended the national constitution in some key areas, including "spelling out . . . the doctrine that property rights must be limited by social rights and obligations." When he returned to the presidency in 1942, however, the climate had changed and reform was much more difficult within the context and economic problems of World War II. Indeed, many of López's policies now worked against the interests of peasants and labour generally. When an abortive military coup narrowly failed, López resigned in despair. The following elections saw victory go to the arch-conservative, Laureano Gómez, after a bitter split in the Liberal ranks brought on by the popularity of Jorge Eliécer Gaitán, a Liberal radical who sought to institute much more radical social and economic reforms than López. Gaitán's subsequent assassination in 1948 gave rise to the now infamous period in the late 1940s and 1950s known as *La Violencia*, when Liberals and Conservatives proceeded to murder each other throughout the country. The eventual death toll was 300,000. This period also saw the growth of rural self-defence units, the precursors to the current guerrilla organisations, which set up virtually autonomous regions, sometimes with their own currency and laws.

In 1953 Gómez was overthrown in a bloodless coup led by General Gustavo Rojas Pinilla. The coup seemed to have been welcomed by the majority of Colombians as the only way of halting the violence. But, when Rojas also proved unable to stop the bloodshed, a general strike, along with firm prodding from the military itself, forced Rojas into exile. In the wake of his resignation the Liberals and Conservatives decided on a historic pact, a power-sharing arrangement whereby both would take turns at ruling the country for the next 20 years (1958–78). The arrangement was primarily designed to diminish the 10-year long, widespread political violence, much of which was generated by inter-party hatred. Although the *Frente Nacional* (National Front), as the period of bipartisan rule came to be known, managed to curb the worst of the political violence, it also served to exclude third parties from government representation. In addition, it bred a self-contented and complacent political class and further entrenched clientelist politics and state corruption. Bipartisan rule in the 1960s was accompanied by policies of social and economic modernisation derived from the US-sponsored Alliance for Progress, designed to negate the support for the Cuban Revolution among many sectors of Latin American society that emerged in the 1960s. Another agrarian law reform was enacted in 1961 and a national agency, the *Instituto Colombiano de Reforma Agraria* (INCORA), was set up to appropriate idle land and redistribute it among the landless. Although 250,000 families benefited from the initiative over a 17-year period, the practical outcomes seemed to do little to alleviate overall poverty or change the basic structure of land tenure.

During the National Front period, import-substitution policies, which had their origins in the era of the Liberal republic (1930–46), were intensified and yielded significant results in the areas of car and steel production. By the 1970s Colombia had also begun to develop export industries, flowers being one of the most successful. During the late 1960s and into the 1970s, then, Colombia was able to achieve consistently high levels of growth in GDP. But spectacular macro-economic figures often obscured the more enduring statistics of underclass poverty (especially in rural areas) and huge disparities in income distribution. It was in this climate that a now hardened guerilla movement began to make its presence felt. The most significant grouping, the Fuerzas Armadas *Revolucionarias de Colombia* (FARC), the oldest guerrilla force in the Americas, grew out of the rural self-defence organisations formed by Liberals during *La Violencia*. During the 1960s the

FARC modulated into a well armed and well organised army, complete with a Marxist-Leninist discourse calling for a radical restructuring of the national economy and a halt to foreign exploitation of Colombia's natural resources. In the 1970s other guerrilla factions, such as the ELN and the M19, inspired by the Cuban Revolution, began to make their presence felt in daring urban guerrilla raids and kidnappings. It was also during the 1970s that the drug trade began to gather pace. Originally involved in the marijuana trade, the drug traffickers soon saw the enormous profits to be made from cocaine. They formed well oiled organisations, with Pablo Escobar's Medellín Cartel boasting a military wing used to kill off opponents, whether those of rival cartels, or politicians and government officials, especially left-orientated ones. From the early 1980s onwards there was a growing level of drug-related violence against public officials, including the assassination in 1984 of the Justice Minister and four presidential candidates in the run-up to the 1990 elections. The loss of these four major leaders was a severe blow for Colombian democracy, especially since they each represented different aspects of a substantial *apertura* (opening) in the electoral system and provided a real alternative to the establishment political parties. Their deaths left the political field to neoliberal technocrats.

THE NEOLIBERAL STRUCTURING OF THE COLOMBIAN ECONOMY

Throughout Latin America by the late 1980s and beginning of the 1990s, practically all governments had agreed to the stabilisation and structural adjustment programmes prescribed by the IMF and the World Bank. These programmes included the drastic reduction of tariff protections for local industries, a reduction of government spending and the privatisation of state-owned corporations. But the "modernisation of the state" has generally meant the selling of public utilities and other government corporations to foreign investors beholden only to their shareholders. Such neoliberal policies in Colombia have gone hand in hand with increasingly authoritarian state structures and the partial rollback of 100 years of hard-won social welfare protection for the average Colombian worker. Neoliberal policies were first introduced by the Barco Administration (1986–90), were subsequently consolidated and expanded under Cesar Gaviria (1990–94), and then deepened during the Administration of Ernesto Samper (1994–98). Economic policy development and implementation since the Gaviria Administration has become an affair restricted to presidents, their coteries of technocrat advisers and representatives of lending institutions like the IMF and the World Bank. The present government of Andrés Pastrana has continued in the same vein, although Pastrana himself has promised to address social problems in the last two years of his mandate.

During the first two years of the Gaviria government, import taxes were reduced from an average of 43.7% to 11.4% and the list of forbidden imports was abolished, exposing local industries to a flood of cheaply manufactured goods. The financial sector became the principal motor and beneficiary of the national index of economic growth in 1994–95 (5.7 in 1994; 5.28 in 1995), with agriculture and traditional industries such as textiles, clothing manufactures, leather goods and iron and steel being significantly weakened. Meanwhile, Colombian industries progressively lost national market share to the flood of foreign imports arriving under reduced tariff regimes: during the Gaviria administration, the textile sector lost between 30% and 40% of the national market and experienced 25% job losses because of imports and contraband. As a result, many Colombian companies are now reduced to assembling or distributing foreign products.

One of the most striking examples of the Gaviria administration's new policy direction was the restructuring of the *Caja Agraria* (a government-run agricultural development bank). Part of the *Caja Agraria*'s capital came from a 1948 law (Law 90) obliging the private banking sector to provide a certain amount of capital at low interest rates to the *Caja* for use in low-cost agricultural loans to stimulate agricultural expansion and growth. The Gaviria administration abolished the law, in effect scuttling a mechanism for social investment that still exists even in countries like the USA, one of the intellectual heartlands of neoliberalism. The Gaviria administration also transferred the underwriting arm of the *Caja* to private enterprise, thus jeopardising the ability of struggling farmers to weather the increasingly rapid fluctuations of global commodity markets. Finally, it sold off the 452 *agropuntos*, government entities that functioned as mediators between the market place and individual farmers for the sale of produce and for the regulation of prices. The administration also abolished a similar mechanism in the *Banco de la República*, which provided low-cost or interest-free loans. These mechanisms were *social* investments in the country's growth and thus not to be judged by the same criteria of efficiency and profitability that apply in open-market competition.

When the Samper Administration took over from Gaviria, its vision statement, *El Salto Social*, planned to maintain and strengthen the policies initiated by the previous administration by adopting a more aggressive strategy of internationalisation. It set out to finance the new policy by increasing taxes and by taking on more short-term foreign debt. It also undertook an aggressive round of privatisations of several state-owned entities: banks, housing-loan corporations, airports, electricity generating facilities, and the partial sale of some gas and mineral extraction industries. In order to redress the enduring social problems aggravated by the previous administration's neoliberal restructurings, it set up the *Red de Solidaridad Social* (Social Solidarity Network), which was meant to soften and alleviate the impact of the *Salto Social* on the poorest members of society. The *Red de Solidaridad*

Social, however, like so many other such palliative entities throughout recent Colombian history, became, in the words of Consuelo Ahumada, "an enormous clientelist apparatus, highly inefficient and fraudulent."

The Samper administration also established a development plan (*Pacto de Productividad, Precios y Salarios*), based around a tripartite socioeconomic agreement between government, business and labour unions, in which consumer prices, goods and services charges and wages would be indexed to inflation rates. But to add further insult to injury as far as the Colombian worker was concerned, the accord had so many exceptions for both the government, in relation to the freedom to increase certain key utility and fuel charges above inflation rates, and for business, in relation to products linked to the fluctuations of the international commodity markets, that the only party that was strictly pegged to inflation rates were Colombian wage earners, who saw their real buying power further eroded. In addition, the IMF pressured the Samper government into a sizeable reduction in public spending, which manifested itself, among other things, as drastic cuts to public works and social programmes. Instead of investing capital in productive areas within Colombia, thus stimulating employment growth, the government opted to leave a large portion of foreign reserves generated from the sales of oil and coffee in foreign banks for investment purposes and to hedge against inflation. This led to the absurd situation of the government spending upwards of 38% of GDP servicing foreign loans (especially from the IMF), while enacting welfare programmes to aid the same poor who would have benefited more appropriately from government investment in productive industries like agriculture and manufacturing.

OLIGARCHIC CAPITALISM AND THE MYTHS OF DEMOCRACY

One of the great myths of Colombian history is the frequent observation that Colombia ranks as the second-oldest (non-continuous) parliamentary democracy in the Americas, directly behind the oldest continuous democracy in the Americas, the USA. The statement conceals more than it reveals: since its initial period as a violent, wartime state immediately after the winning of independence, Colombia has been a republic based on authoritarian rule, controlled since the mid-19th century by a rigid two-party system dominated by Liberals and Conservatives, both representing the Colombian oligarchy. Whenever this situation has been threatened, democracy has gone out the window and assassinations and repression of civilians replaces the comforting image of a modern nation-state based on the rule of law and fair and open electoral politics. This has historically bred contempt for constitutional laws and human rights among the more ruthless and self-serving elements of Colombian society and has fostered a mentality according to which violence is the most effective way to win power and silence one's critics. It has also bred apathy, despair and abstentionism among the general populace, only too well aware that their political leaders, indeed practically the whole political class, speak with forked tongues and view public office as a chance to enrich themselves at all costs.

The push to write a new constitution, unsuccessfully attempted twice in the late 1970s, was revived in the late 1980s in the context of deep public distrust of the congress, which had come to be seen as a corrupt institution and long overdue for reform. The Gaviria administration set up an *Asamblea Constituyente* (a constitutional assembly) at a unique juncture in Colombian history. First, the Colombian state was under massive pressure from a generalised wave of violence, including attacks by guerrilla groups, the assassination of politicians, magistrates, police, union leaders and journalists by the cocaine Mafia, and a wave of mass kidnappings. Second, with the collapse of the Soviet Union and considerable revulsion towards the somewhat questionable tactics of guerrilla groups, which had contributed to the climate of fear and violence, the Left had lost credibility in Colombia and beyond as articulators of an alternative to oligarchic capitalism. The previous Barco administration had energetically lobbied for a new constitution as a cure for all the ills assailing the country—political violence, high-level corruption, institutional weakness, administrative inefficiency and so forth—but was blocked on three occasions by the Supreme Court as unconstitutional, the Court reconfirming that only the congress had the right to reform the constitution. Barco persisted, however, and, under the cover of special powers granted by a state of siege (the country was in a virtual civil war), forced through a referendum asking the Colombian people if they approved of the setting up of a body to write a new constitution. The referendum question was expressed in terms guaranteed to win the support of the majority of Colombians, including many on the disenchanted Left increasingly leaning towards forms of political action that focused on "civil society" and the "politics of difference." Under extreme pressure, the Supreme Court approved, by a narrow margin, the right of the president to set the terms of the constitutional debate.

The Constitutional Charter that emerged in 1991 marked a new era in Colombia, institutionalising for the first time minority political rights for women and indigenous Colombians, rights for the elderly and the young, and so forth. It also allowed for proportional representation and thus paved the way for minority political participation in the national congress. While admirable on the surface, the practical effect of these progressive measures, designed more than anything as a sop to indigenous groups and Leftists, was merely to serve as a smokescreen for the profound economic and political implications of the new constitution, which were not slow in manifesting themselves. What the new constitution did, in effect, was to weaken the social functions of both the congress and the myriad state enterprises, from social security agencies to public works to government credit and banking institutes, the latter being vital to low-cost credit for businesses and public housing. While this amounted to a frontal assault on the previously constitutionally guaranteed social functions of the state, it also invested the presidency with extraordinary powers to abolish or merge public enterprises, to change their juridical status, to change the structure of ministries without congressional consultation, and to exercise almost total control over the national budget. As far back as 1990, before the formation of the Constitutional Assembly, at least one commentator warned of the spectre of "presidential Caesarism as an institution and as a form of governmental practice."

The changes to the constitutional charter were tailor-made for enacting the new economic policies. Neoliberal restructuring of the economy was written into its very text: Article 336, for example, grants the state the right to liquidate what it considers to be monopolistic state enterprises and "grant to third parties [private industry] the development of such activities when said state enterprises do not meet the requirements of efficiency in accordance with the terms defined by the state." Furthermore, the new constitution also makes provision for zones of "free commerce" or industrial parks: "the law can establish in border zones, whether territorial or maritime, special legislation for economic or social initiatives which promote development" (Article 337). Twelve such zones already operate in Colombia and offer, among other things, tax concessions, customs streamlining, exchange-rate flexibility, and the possibility of repatriating profits with little or no red tape. Orientated towards the export market, they are often just offshore platforms for the cheap assembly of goods with cheap non-unionised labour, similar to the function of the *maquiladoras* in Mexico.

Other tactics used by the Gaviria government to enact these changes, now part of "world best practice," were the sale of part of the social security system to private companies, the abolition of retroactivity with regard to superannuation, and legislation on the right of an employer to operate a company 24 hours a day, seven days a week, without paying penalty rates for night shifts or weekend work. These measures were meant to free up capital and to create more jobs, and no doubt did so in many cases, but most of these positions were part-time or temporary. In addition, loopholes were written into the new labour reform programme: if a company establishes a new branch, subsidiary or production plant, 10 years must pass before the new entity can be considered an integral part of the main company (Article 32). This allows companies to take advantage of the new labour laws that came in to existence after 1991 by setting up phony subsidiaries ("new companies"), which come under the post-1991 guidelines and which can thus avoid offering appropriate wages and conditions.

The new economic restructuring has also affected government social security and health insurance systems. Both have been opened up to private enterprise via the mechanism of "free choice," meaning in practice that the majority of workers, rather than remaining with the government schemes, are attracted to the much larger private companies which seem to offer a better hedge against national economic uncertainty and inflationary pressures. The new arrangement for social security cover is not totally negative (a choice between private and state-run systems), but it invites the citizen to gamble on the, sometimes volatile, international financial markets. Thus enormous sums of money, which would otherwise have been available for investment in socially useful development projects internal to the country, are now available for private investment in global financial markets in which the primary beneficiaries are the shareholders of large private health insurance and social security companies. Like other neoliberal measures, such as the privatisation of state entities involved in banking, credit and housing finance, telecommunications, transport, public works and agriculture, this amounts to a massive transfer of public wealth into private hands (both nationally and internationally) by stealth.

Before neoliberal restructuring, Colombia could fairly boast one of the best performing economies in Latin America; today [2001] it has arguably the worst. According to José Amado, Colombia's insertion in the global economy over the past 10 years "didn't produce the modernisation of industry, nor an increase in our exports, but it did contribute to the deterioration of our balance of payments, to 5 per cent negative growth in GDP, to excessive growth of foreign debt and to the deindustrialisation of the country." The reduction of tariff barriers has predictably led to the surrender of the internal market to foreign-made products, severely contracting local industry and thus making it difficult to meet the export challenge: "Exports can't become the motor force of industrial policy because Colombia lacks the technology and capital to compete in a protectionist international economic environment against gigantic competitors. Its rachitic national industry must be strengthened in its internal market first." For Amado, the export-orientated model currently being promoted flew in the face of the national development model used by the most industrialised countries, in which the state was a central and active force in development: "Industrialised countries have constructed their capitalism on the basis of their internal markets. Even in the United States foreign commerce still accounts for barely 20 per cent of GDP." But Colombia is not the USA and industrial development models must function in a radically different global context. Amado's calls for the creation of more tariff barriers and for the country "to take sides with its own productive sector" (in effect, a return to a state-mediated import-substitution model), would be difficult, if not impossible, to achieve with global financial institutions controlling investment capital. For, whether one agrees or not with the neoliberal restructuring of the world's economies, the national is no longer the most important arena of political and economic activity.

THE NATIONAL OR THE GLOBAL?

In *El Modelo Neoliberal*, Consuelo Ahumada offers insightful analysis into the impact of neoliberalism on Colombia, from the Barco to the Samper administrations. She highlights the failures of successive development plans which have surrendered the Colombian economy to international financial speculators and which have created a crisis in the functioning of the welfare state much worse than that which preceded neoliberal restructuring. Her concluding remarks, nevertheless, are part of the problem: "an authentic development plan must respond to the national interest of those countries and not that of those who control the prevailing economic and political order in the world." But what exactly is the "national interest"? The national interest is never properly definable since the nation is only a whole in the imagination. Any effort to come to grips with an increasingly global market economy must adopt a more nuanced approach to the possibilities of engagement on a more localised or decentralised scale, since national approaches to economic (and social) development in Latin America have generally failed the underclasses.

From the very beginning, the formation of the Colombian nation-state did not obey in any sense the idea of a homogeneous social or natural geographical space, nor did it obey any linguistic, ethnic, popular or even official impulses towards an "imagined community." Successive administrations, especially conservative ones, have tried unsuccessfully via an overbearing centralised power structure to unite the regions (renamed *departamentos* in the 1886 Constitution), but have had only limited success. This centralism has contributed to the fact that the regions, instead of being semi-independent state actors, became quasi-feudal dominions of bipartisanship, controlled by state sinecures for the purpose of maintaining power. In this way Colombia's now famous bipartite political system was overlain by a centralising juridical and administrative discourse of the nation. This centralising national vision disregarded the regional diversity of cultural, popular, ethnic and linguistic nationalities, forsaking its real communities, the regions, in favour of an imaginary nation, removed from everyday reality. The survival of these regional loyalties and cultural and linguistic distinctions, however, may provide the only point of departure for engaging with global society in a way the dysfunctional nation-state cannot.

The energetic projection of the regions and regional cultures into the debate in the Constitutional Assembly in 1990–91 is reflected in the first article of the new constitution, which does not refer to the nation, but rather to a decentralised republic of law, a pluralistic and participatory democracy, one which explicitly recognises the rights of the regions to function juridically, politically and economically with a degree of autonomy never before officially sanctioned. This breaks with the previously rigid model whereby Bogotá, politically and economically, exercised massively centralised control over the rest of the country. It also means that, in the post-new-constitution era, the recognisable macro-regions of Colombia—the Eastern flood plains and the Amazon basin, the Caribbean coast, the Pacific coast and the Andean region—could in theory each adopt a more outward focus, while functioning according to their geographical, historical and economic orientation, and integrate into the international or global economic and social space on their own terms and with a much larger degree of autonomy.

One way forward would thus be to separate out the different needs, in terms of development assistance, administrative needs, social welfare provisions, and so forth, of the various sub-regions of current nation-states within globalisation and thus to tailor development projects to achievable outcomes and manageable checks and balances. This would replace the current dissipation of international aid via state clientelism, in which the massive bureaucratic apparatus and tortuous circuits of funding leave the system open to corruption. Less-developed regions like Vaupés, Vichada, Caquetá and Chocó, for instance, could be the prime beneficiaries of international development aid, responding to international organisations directly and thus bypassing national administrative bodies. Similarly, dynamic industrial and agricultural regions like Antioquia and Cundinamarca, for example, should be able, via devolution of taxation regimes and local engagement with global markets, to shape their development according to their own vision and their own economic traditions, free from having to answer to national directives or imperatives. Issues of political violence—drug trafficking, guerilla and paramilitary activity—could be broken down into smaller units of analysis, management and negotiation and tackled region by region, according to local conditions, needs and possibilities, instead of being funnelled through the perspective of a thoroughly discredited national government and its corrupt political class. Instead, the current Pastrana administration seems bent on solving the national crisis by recourse to a massive escalation of the conflict. In June 2000 the US Congress voted to grant Colombia a $1.3 billion package of mostly military assistance, ostensibly to fight drug traffickers. The money is part of the Plan Colombia, an ambitious attempt to inject into the country up to $3 billion-worth of international aid from Europe and North America designed to stimulate the economy, eradicate coca and heroin cultivation, and radically reduce the destabilising effect drug trafficking has on Colombian national life. But the aid can just as easily be channelled towards fighting the guerrilla forces and promises to send the situation spiralling further out of control, putting additional strains on regional ties and possibly dragging Colombia's neighbours into the conflict as guerrilla combatants and drug traffickers, not to mention another mass exodus of *campesinos,* try to take refuge from the conflict. Perhaps it is too early to say what the outcome will be, but the signs are not good.

Our contemporary global anxieties arise in large part from a crisis of the nation-state in its dual political and cultural dimensions: that of the "state" as the legal, administrative and military expression of the cultural "nation" as the body politic. When either enters into crisis—a crisis of identity for the body politic or of legitimacy for the state—it inevitably also draws the other into crisis as well. The globalisation of contemporary capitalism means that neither ordinary workers and their trade unions, who previously sought to secure their objectives primarily through compacts with national governments, nor their opponents, the shareholders and executives of global corporations, are meaningfully served by the nation-state in its traditional "modern" form. Voter apathy in the West reflects a loss of faith in these ways of doing politics, which no longer seem to have any organic link to the people themselves. Meanwhile, many prominent theorists of nationalism still maintain that national problems can only be solved by more nationalism. But surely only a global civic culture and global regulatory agencies working beyond a hamstrung United Nations can serve to protect the interests of low-income workers, still the vast majority of the world's population, against migratory global capital? Such global organisations would have to provide protection not only to existing national communities linked to a definite territory, but also to sub-national minorities persecuted by the likes of Pinochet or Milosevic. If required to choose between the UN conventions on national sovereignty and on cultural genocide, we should be educated to choose the latter. As John Gray sees it, "The real need of the postmodern age is for common institutions within which different cultures, communities and ways of life can coexist in peace." Nation-states have proven largely incapable of providing this without resort to some form of authoritarianism.

The second alternative is a radical popular nationalism, a postmodern Popular Front, of the kind suggested in Ernesto Laclau and Chantal Mouffe's theorisation of "new social movements." It is precisely the idea of the displacement of the nation-state as the locus of labour/capital relations under globalisation, the nation-state's loss of effective control of the economy, which may lead it to refunctionalisation as a radical popular nationalism. The reasoning behind this suggestion is that the nation-state still lends itself to political mobilisation, whereas capital and its global structures do not. Of course, any such "relegitimisation" of the nation-state would require a radical re-fashioning of its identity, in contradistinction to its traditional "homogenising" tendencies. It would thus mean the abandonment of previous attempts at integrative "populist" ideologies. It would seem that the global civil society alternative is therefore perhaps the more achievable alternative in the current climate. But it would need to be one that does not take the form of a global coterie of former "national" elites, merely seeking to perpetuate the existing relations of domination and exploitation under the guise of the new global civil society.

The push to decentralise and bypass failed national structures, however, is fraught with dangers. The current model pursued by the government of Colombia seems to be merely an exercise in cutting national public spending by pushing responsibility onto the regions and municipalities in areas where they can least cope, given the severe contraction in the national economy. Some sort of creative balance is needed between devolution and the ongoing role that the national government must play in a transitional period, between engaging creatively and flexibly with globalisation, while providing social welfare protections for those punished by the self-same global market forces. These ideas imply huge and difficult legal and constitutional questions, not forgetting the psychological barriers to be surmounted in the idea of radical autonomy. The new constitution, however, besides indirectly facilitating the implementation of neoliberal models of economic restructuring, has the capacity and flexibility to experiment with decentralisation. Given the history of 200 years of national failure as far as the inability of successive Colombian administrations and their development programmes to lift the underclasses out of poverty goes, not to mention the consequent violent destruction of the social fabric of a nation unable to reconcile its fragmented parts, the time for solutions linked to the global arena has come.

CONCLUSION: CAPITAL PUNISHMENT

This essay has attempted to trace the rise and fall of nationalist aspirations in Colombia since independence. It has charted this history with a focus on the oscillation between different faces of oligarchic capitalism (Liberal and Conservative) in Colombia. Through constitutional change, the state has attempted to manage the economy and population to provide the needed stability for capital accumulation and expansion. In the wake of a devastating civil war in the late 1940s and 1950s, the subsequent growth of narco-terrorism, and the neoliberal restructuring of the Colombian economy since the late 1980s, the Colombian nation-state is now on the verge of collapse. The drafting of a new constitution in 1991 has only hastened the insertion of Colombia into export-orientated global market systems, exposing the underclasses to the predations of an increasingly unfettered global capitalism. The future development of global civil institutions and engagement therewith, appear to hold out the only viable solution to the chronic economic, social and political crises in Colombia.

9.2 Is the War Ending? Premises and Hypotheses with Which to View the Conflict in Colombia (2001)

JAVIER GUERRERO BARÓN

Despite the hopes and the best efforts of many, it is possible—and, indeed, recent evidence suggests that it is likely—that rather than approaching a meaningful and effective peace process, Colombia is on the verge of a widespread civil war or at the very least of a significant deepening of the armed conflict. For the first time we have, simultaneously, crises in politics, in the economy, in the armed forces, and in our foreign relations, and it is hard not to imagine that these factors will together fuel the armed conflict and limit the chances of success in any peace negotiations.

I do not wish, with these words, to be the bearer of bad tidings or to pour cold water on the deeply felt hopes for peace that significant sectors of Colombian society and of the international community have been expressing of late. Nevertheless, an analysis of the dynamics of the conflict leads us to the conclusion that there is little hope of reversing the trend toward war if the search for peace continues to be based on good intentions rather than on the reality principle. However, there is no inexorable law at work here, and it may still be possible to modify the circumstances of the peace process, above all if the Colombian nation is able to reach agreement on certain fundamental points. And although I remain optimistic in the long term, I fear that in the short term Colombia has yet to pass through its worst moments if there is no change in the tendency toward chronic conflict that the country has suffered since 1948 and if the progressive degradation of the war continues, exacerbated by the recent rumors of foreign intervention. A critical review, in contraposition to naive common sense and the falsehoods and expediencies of conventional political discourse, would help us to understand this process.

It is urgent that we develop a national strategy to prevent the spread of the war. It is not easy, however, to think and act creatively in this domain, which has become a verbal battleground where words of peace become rhetorical weapons and where would-be actors on the political stage compete in the recycling of clichés and commonplaces.

We must recognize that there is an increasing call for peace in Colombian society, but what is still not clear is how much we are prepared to pay for that peace and whether the powerful sectors who are opposed to peace can continue to obstruct any meaningful negotiations. In this essay I hope to make explicit certain critical elements that might allow us to understand the tendencies at work in this particularly difficult situation. I outline ten premises that underpin two key hypotheses on the new conditions for a political solution to the state of civil war.

PREMISES

1. Concerning the content of the conflict, there is consensus that great social inequality and instability give rise to a dynamic that confers legitimacy on revolutionary projects and violent alternatives.

In general terms, the basic causes and issues of the Colombian conflict are rooted in the deep social inequality and instability that those who take up arms against the establishment propose to remedy through structural transformation. These are what have persistently been called the "objective causes of violence." If Colombian society does not accept this reality, peace will remain an impossibility. This means that the need for a profound transformation is socially legitimate. After all, this is a country in which it has not been possible to carry out agrarian reform or an urban reform to reduce the housing deficit and in which there is no effective antimonopoly legislation, let alone any mechanism for the redistribution of wealth or the redressing of inequalities in labor and economic relations. Fortunately, this is recognized even by the sectors that are most radical in their defense of order and the state. It should therefore be possible to reach consensus on this topic, something that would have been unlikely a few years ago. No one can really ignore the explosive conditions of poverty, unemployment, and marginalization in which large parts of the population live, granted that many of these conditions are themselves worsened by the war. In addition to these are the social effects of the structural adjustments brought about by the liberalization and globalization of trade, with its sequel of privatizations, the introduction of new technology, the replacement of stable employment by temporary contracts, the formation of large monopolistic consortia dominated by international financial capital, the unprecedented weakening of trade unions and the repositioning of the relation between labor and capital, and so on.

2. If there can be agreement over the "objective causes" of the crisis, efforts should be made to reach agreement on the solutions.

The protagonists of revolution justify their actions in terms of socioeconomic conditions (the poverty of the majority, the monopoly on wealth, etc.) and political conditions (lack of democracy, justice, political inequality, the oligopoly of power). In this last area we have made considerable advances in the legal structure of the political regime (in particular with the Constitution of 1991) and might equally consider approaches in the economic and social field (agrarian reform, employment legislation, antitrust laws, social investment, primary care for the vulnerable). Although such changes would directly affect the interests of capital, its representatives have realized the depth and extent of the national crisis and are prepared to negotiate. In private companies there is now a realization that "peace is good business" and that the level of the war is for the first time affecting macroeconomic indicators such as public expenditure and the capacity of the state to stabilize the economy, not to mention capital flow and investment.

It is time for the consensus to progress from the causes of the war to its solutions, which is where there are the greatest gulfs.

3. About the means of solving the conflict there is considerable disagreement: Colombia has not renounced violence.

The other component of the conflict is the means by which we will leave antagonism behind, and it is here that there is the greatest disagreement. Although it is obvious, sometimes we lose sight of the fact that Colombia is experiencing a clash between different visions of nationhood, different models of development, and different views of the nature and role of the state.

We can distinguish three principal currents in a society that has, since the middle of the eighteenth century—without being able to reach agreement on what is desirable or even possible—been trying to find a path to some form of modernity with which it can take its place in the concert of nations. First, there are the sectors that seek solutions through revolutionary change, that struggled then and struggle now for a fairer, more just, and more inclusive society—a route to modernity through major structural reforms imposed by revolutionary action following a political or political-military victory.

A second sector or, rather, range of views accepts the need for change but believes that the problems can be overcome by reforms and democratic procedures. It must be said that the stubbornly democratic are by no means the strongest participants in Colombian political life. Most have been satisfied with the construction of a formal, legalistic democracy without concerning themselves with the fit between forms and reality and without attempting to overcome the obstacles to the real exercise of a democratic modernity. Among them, too, are those who have used democracy as a tactic, not as a philosophy of government and political life but as a technique, an electoral ritual—those who have "combined the forms of struggle," sometimes democracy, sometimes authoritarianism, with violence not being ruled out as a means to an end. Historically, a project for a democratic modernity is very far from existing, as such, in Colombia.

Finally, there is an intransigent sector that believes that society can continue without any transformations in its social relations. It approves of modernity as technological progress that conserves the privileges of capital and property enshrined in statute, without any redistribution of wealth or transformation of political structures. These are the supporters of the two-party model, and they regard themselves as the country's natural leaders. Since the end of the 1970s, their power structure has in some cases competed and in others cooperated with the emerging local power of the drug industry, which resembles them in its authoritarianism and conservatism, and in many cases served their interests. They are in favor of the increased use of technology in production (reengineering and Taylorism in industry) but without any consultation with trade unions, mechanization of agriculture but as far as possible maintaining sharecropping arrangements, restricted participation and restricted democracy, and prohibition of social demands. In a sense they are the reflection of reactionary modernism or the selective modernism of the various right-wing sectors, some moderate and others radical, that have come into conflict on the world scene.

Nevertheless, in Colombia, in all three groups, to a greater or lesser extent there are important elements that have not renounced violence as a means of achieving their political objectives. As a whole, Colombian society has not explicitly renounced violence, in contrast, for example, to Spain, where, apart from a few activists completely out of touch with political reality, society has opted unequivocally in favor of the construction of a modern democracy, with all its implications. This ambivalence on the part of society and the state has led specialists to the view that violence is functional for Colombian democracy.

4. Although the protagonists of the violence do not represent the Colombian people, they do speak for them, and Colombian society allows them to do so.

This premise is closely linked to the preceding one. It is obvious that the violence does not represent the great majority of Colombians. The 15,000–20,000 guerillas, the 5,000 paramilitaries, the rogue elements within the state security agencies, and the organized criminal groups built up around the mafias of drugs, emeralds, and contraband do not represent the 37 million Colombians. But the 37 million Colombians have never given clear voice to a rejection of extrajudicial state violence and the systematic impunity of its perpetrators or of the protagonists of the conflict and their methods.

Just as an example, not even the ecological disaster caused by the millions of barrels of oil poured into rivers, streams, and lakes in more than 200 attacks on the oil pipeline has mobilized Colombian society or detracted from the legitimacy of the organization responsible for the attacks. Perhaps for this reason, the despairing state employees in charge of the problem have taken to accusing the organizers of the oil-workers' union, on the basis of suspiciously shaky evidence, of being behind the guerrilla attacks and to making use of the discredited legal structures as an antiunion weapon. Meanwhile, the bomb attacks continue, as does public unconcern not only with regard to the ecological disaster but also with regard to the misguided methods the state is using to deal with the problem.

Perhaps this is why each new massacre is more flagrant than the last and the leaders, the police authorities, and the spokespersons of an ever more powerful and independent military can give their rhetorical and almost insultingly formulaic response without having to answer to anyone—in the field of politics, that is.

But the violence cannot be reduced to politics. Much more widespread and more costly in terms of human lives is the violence of small-scale criminals and semiorganized groups of criminals, the violence of everyday life. The level of urban violence is astonishing, as is the level of violence associated with local economic bonanzas in some regions of the country. And those who kill are not only criminals or participants in the armed conflict; to these should be added the ordinary citizen who kills out of anger, revenge, jealousy, debts, honor, or drink, to give just a few examples.

In short, neither in political struggle nor in daily life have we been able to renounce violence, and violence reproduces itself in many areas. Anonymous threats, for example, are now used in the pursuit of the most varied goals: to further the aims of trade unions, to preempt collective action by popular organizations, even to influence the choice of the national soccer team.

To return to politics, there is nothing to indicate that the revolutionary forces believe that the conditions exist for a move toward democratic action. Although with some differences, they still believe that war is the quickest and surest route to their political goals. Although there is cautious discourse indicating the consideration of routes to a peaceful end to the conflict (and more in the Ejército de Liberación Nacional [National Liberation Army—ELN] than in the Fuerzas Armadas Revolucionarias de Colombia [Revolutionary Armed Forces of Colombia—FARC]), the actions of both groups force one to the view that their declarations of peace are largely rhetorical, and the tone and the level of their current demands effectively rule out this possibility; this is borne out by the experience of the new peace process initiated in 1999.

At the same time, just as in 1984, when the first cycle of agreements was initiated, the forces of intransigence both within and outside the state are interested only in a military solution to the conflict. Some sectors that could be described as democratic have clung blindly to the supposed legitimacy of the state and in its support have been prepared even to make use of instruments of warfare such as the Servicios Especiales de Vigilancia y Seguridad Privada (Special Services of Private Vigilantism and Security—CONVIVIR) or to give veiled support to armed groups of private justice. And large groupings in the rural sector justify the actions of the paramilitaries, thus demonstrating their willingness to continue on the path to war. The dynamics of the conflict have led certain sectors of society to adopt private mechanisms of defense of their own interests, weakening the legitimacy of the state. This is one of the paradoxes of the situation: the sectors of society that have opted for the most radical defense of the establishment have contributed most tellingly to its delegitimation.

All this shows that the large sectors that do call for peace have neither the audience, the power, nor the representation necessary to make themselves heard by the armed groups—besides which there is no national consensus on what should be aimed for in a negotiated political settlement.

To summarize, all of this is a clear sign that Colombian society has not reached a consensus on the renunciation of violence. Many sectors use violence for one reason or another or believe in it as a means of resolving conflict, and the rejection of violence does not have sufficient resonance to represent the national will. On the contrary, what predominates is indifference, and the protagonists of the war are able to assume, as in fact they have assumed, the representation of Colombian society.

5. Between the attitudes of the actors in the conflict there is an abyss: a peace process cannot be constructed using the gestures of war.

The attitude of the participants themselves is one of the main obstacles to the transformation of the conflict in Colombia. Merely by observing the language used to characterize the adversary, we see the extent to which it contributes to the deepening of the abyss separating the two sides. At a symbolic level there is no hint or gesture to indicate that any of the participants is looking for approaches that might lead to negotiations. Only the government makes frequent calls for peace, and this without offering anything, as if naively hoping for an unconditional surrender, while at the same time the military hardens its position. The use of symbols and gestures can affect the possibilities of negotiation, but ultimately it is by actions that the real possibilities of negotiation are determined.

The frequent violent attacks, the use of methods, such as kidnapping, that are in obvious violation of international humanitarian law, the widely publicized decision to view civil functionaries and electoral processes as military targets, the roadblocks that put the lives of travelers unnecessarily at risk, the use of antipersonnel mines and of car bombs and other forms of indiscriminate terror, the "execution" of civilians without due process, the impression that there are powers that decide the fate not only of those under their command but of ordinary citizens—all these mean that in their desire to involve the rest of the population in the conflict the armed protagonists, far from opening the way to a negotiated settlement, are closing it off.

The apparent path of the conflict and the complete absence of any conciliatory gestures suggest an attitude of "all-out war." We are led to conclude that inside the guerrilla organizations there is a belief that the crisis of the Colombian state and of its armed forces and the silence of society give legitimacy to their cause and that their victory is near, and not without reason. And no army that sees its triumph as imminent is prepared to sit down to negotiate with the enemy.

6. It is unclear how much are we prepared to pay for national reconstruction.

To unite the nation in a new national project entails bringing together the imagined futures of the different projects that are currently in conflict, establishing how much each side is prepared to sacrifice politically to bring about this rapprochement of futures and how much the owners of the establishment, the insurgent forces, and Colombian society as a whole are prepared to pay for peace. It is necessary to understand that peace pays, even though the initial cost of establishing it, especially for the defenders of the established order, will be very high. From the point of view of the revolutionary projects, there is little to lose. They have no great political capital to defend, except for a revolutionary tradition that now has several decades of struggle to take pride in and a military project whose control of territory is the result only of military conquest and whose political legitimacy has not been put to the test. It remains to be seen how much support will remain once the military domination of the guerrillas ceases; this is what would in effect be their political capital. From this perspective, one might imagine that for the guerrillas the military option is the most profitable, especially given the lack of success of demobilized excombatants in the field of politics.

For this reason, as in any transaction, getting an answer to the question of how much we are prepared to pay for peace is fundamental if we are to find out how near or how far we are from the possibility of real negotiation. And so far no one has asked this question with any seriousness. The president of the National Cattle-Raisers Federation, one of the most powerful agrarian associations in the country, recently said that they are prepared to concede 10 percent of their land—perhaps because many of them have been unable to return to their farms and some have lost 100 percent. He invited other sectors of the economy to offer similar concessions. However, a few days after making his offer, he withdrew it.

At a time of practically zero economic growth such as 1998, it is especially difficult to answer this question. What is clear is that any negotiation in Colombia will have to lead to profound transformations and not simply a surrender and the transfer of arms. One way or another, it will have to be a negotiated revolution; therein lies its difficulty.

7. There are "structurally intransigent" sectors with the capacity to obstruct a negotiated political solution.

The duration and intensity of the conflict have led to the formation on both sides of the conflict of groups that are "structurally intransigent" either because the war furthers their interests or because their radical attitudes are apparently too deeply rooted to change. These groups constitute the greatest obstacle to peace. All have the capacity to obstruct any eventual peace process, as they have done up to now, with complete success and absolute impunity. This is what the experts call the inertia of war. If these groups are not defeated politically or at the very least neutralized, it is unlikely that any political negotiations will prosper.

Nevertheless, these intransigent groups, some of them without doubt within the state security agencies, will continue to commit selective assassinations and carry out periodic campaigns of terror in order to impede any negotiation, at the same time as the guerrillas continue kidnapping, sabotaging elections, threatening mayors and civil functionaries, controlling territory, and carrying out military actions that demonstrate their strength and the weakness of the armed forces in order to strengthen their position in an eventual negotiation or, worse, in the belief that victory is near.

8. The weakness of the army is short-term; there is a strategic stalemate.

At the same time, everything indicates that the obvious tactical weakness of the army is of the moment; it is the result of 15 years of subcontracting the war, during which the initiative has passed into the hands of the private paramilitary groups. An examination of press reports makes plain that the army has carried out very few offensives during this period. No doubt soon, the emergency will be dealt with by means of "strategic changes": antiterrorist legislation, procedural upgrades, and military reoutfitting, meaning improved technology, satellite support, new equipment, reorganization of the intelligence agencies, and U.S. aid and advisers. In short, an increase in military expenditure and equipment will revitalize the armed forces and prolong the strategic stalemate—the vicious circle of death.

9. The tactical strength of the guerrillas diminishes the likelihood of negotiation.

In the meantime, the dream of winning the war will harden the position of the insurgent forces and reduce the likelihood of negotiation, so long as within them there is no leader or sector able to see that the military gains of the past few years have not led to any increase in the national legitimacy of the revolutionary project and that, despite the tactical offensives (and the opinion of the U.S. strategists), a military triumph is still a long way off. The large areas under guerrilla control, even though some of them, such as the oilfields, have strategic importance, are still relatively marginal for the great majority of the population and for the economy.

10. There are two possible scenarios: on the military side, containment or all-out war; on the political side, a realistic but unlikely solution, recognition of the unfinished Colombian revolution.

First, the military options, containment or all-out war: as things stand, the war could go on for many more years in one of two forms. In the first, the war continues to worsen the social situation of the country, further diffusing its violence throughout society, deepening poverty, eroding the quality of life, and provoking an ever more severe political crisis in which the legitimacy of the regime is more and more called into question. This is what has been going on for 50 years now; it is the classic model of containment, of a limited war. The second scenario is of an all-out war in which it is not clear what kind of revolutionary project would emerge from an eventual military triumph but we would see a steady reduction of the possibility of a negotiated settlement and the imposition of ever more authoritarian government, with special public order procedures—for example, with the armed forces taking on a role in the criminal justice system or the creation of special antiterrorist courts, as in Peru. For the sake of argument let us agree with the revolutionary forces—and with the Pentagon—that, the way things are going, in a few years they will triumph. This would leave us with a country devastated by war, like Laos or Cambodia, in which, as in Nicaragua, it would be impossible to sustain a political victory for more than a few years.

Second, a reasonable but unlikely solution: the recognition by society, the state, and the revolutionaries that in Colombia there has been, as in many other countries, an unfinished revolution that did not achieve military victory. Following Charles Tilly, we could recognize that what took place is what is known theoretically as a revolutionary situation without a revolutionary outcome. Nevertheless, from this unfinished revolution we could move toward a popular democracy in which many (though not all) of the transformations that were not achieved through a military victory could be brought about through political action, in the hands of a junta for national reconstruction, as if the war had ended. Let us imagine that someone has won, that the war has ended, that now we have to rebuild the country with a democratic program hammered out by the survivors, and that with the victors is a group that had split from the losers and that is in a position to impose some of its conditions on the program of national reconstruction. Why go on hoping for a military victory if we have known all along that this is the way wars end and that after their enormous human cost the survivors have to pool their strength and their ideas to rebuild? That is what happened in the Nicaraguan revolution, and that is how it has been and will be in the unfinished revolutions of Latin America and the rest of the Third World.

No doubt there are those in the revolutionary forces who believe that they could achieve more by these means than through a military victory but are prevented from expressing these views by the very structure of their organizations. Anyone who owned up to such a position on either side would immediately be denounced as a weak-willed defeatist; the extreme groups on both the left and the right would identify themselves through their intolerance of dissent, and there might be purges within the guerrillas, the paramilitary and the armed forces and in the secret high command of the extreme right that has been pulling the strings in the dirty war. Or perhaps there is sufficient maturity in the country to opt for this way of ending the war. To hope for this may be excessively optimistic in view of the preceding premises, although it is by no means impossible.

HYPOTHESES

On the basis of the above, two working hypotheses emerge as a means to understand the present moment. First, the Colombian civil war has become an international problem, and this will lead to the invocation of the concept of limited sovereignty on the way to a solution of the internal conflict. Second, Colombia is on the verge of losing the capacity to exercise its sovereignty over a negotiated solution to its internal conflict.

1. The Colombian civil war has become an international problem, and this will lead to the application of the concept of limited sovereignty to a solution of the internal conflict.

What is new is that the chronic state of war in Colombia, to which even the Colombians have been indifferent, is now becoming a growing international problem—the most acute problem in the region. There is less and less room for sovereignty. This is demonstrated by the following features of the international situation.

Colombia—and here it differs from the norm in Latin America—has not at any point in its recent history broken with the past on the road to the construction of a modern democracy that would earn it a place in the community of nations. It is a society that stores up its conflicts from the past without having the capacity to resolve them. In a Latin America that has seen the peace processes in Central America—without idealizing them and admitting their obvious difficulties—and the fall of the great dictatorships, the Colombian armed conflict is a disconcerting throwback to the days of the cold war. With symbols and language unchanged ten years after the fall of the Berlin Wall [in 1989], the parties persist in a war that most international observers describe as archaic.

There is consensus among analysts that for the first time our internal problem is being seen as a threat to the international order not only by the United States and the European powers but also by our neighbors and friends. In diplomatic circles Colombia has earned itself the sobriquets of the "Bosnia of South America" and "Latin America's open sore." The effects of the war are increasingly felt in the neighboring countries. In the case of Venezuela, the ELN has a deliberate policy of destabilizing its relations with Colombia, as well as causing serious ecological damage to the shared fluvial system by the spillage of crude oil resulting from its senselessly repeated attacks on the pipeline from Caño Limón to Coveñas. In addition to the arrival of refugees from the war, the Panamanian frontier suffers frequent incursions by paramilitary groups and the effects of the long-term traffic in arms and drugs, all of which cause serious problems for bilateral relations. Peru and Bolivia are trying to eradicate coca cultivation but know that the Colombian drug dealers are able to buy as much of the crop as can be produced, thus stimulating production and reversing the effects of their eradication programs. Faced with a crackdown in Colombia, drug mafia money has now found its way to Brazil, Argentina, Mexico, and, to a lesser extent, Chile and Central America. Adoption of the "Colombian model" of guerrilla finance through the narcotics trade could lead to the resurgence of armed groups in these countries, as now seems to be happening in Peru, and our neighbors now view us with mistrust, fearing that through our proximity the contagion could spread. And rather than showing solidarity, they prefer to exercise the "scalpel diplomacy" of the United States, which would like to "remove the cancer."

The problem of displaced persons is now not merely internal but is viewed with increasing alarm by the international community. The exile of people under threat and the emigration of whole families for economic or security reasons are becoming more and more common.

Even among friendly nations, Colombia is beginning to be seen as a country whose permanent structural violence makes it unviable as a modern nation and whose self-destructive momentum places it on the list of nations that are regressing from civilization to barbarism. It is one of the nations that have not succeeded in adapting to the changes brought by the end of the cold war and need a tutelary foreign intervention to place them back on the road to democracy in the new world order of "democratic security" designed and led by the United States.

The high level of violence in labor relations and the endemic murder of trade-union leaders are viewed by experts in the European Union as a kind of unfair trade practice in the sense that, while businessmen in the rest of the world have to negotiate with the unions, in Colombia trade-unionists are simply murdered with complete impunity. Besides being an outrageous human rights violation, this gives their products an unfair price advantage.

As a result of the Samper case and the thesis of the "narco-guerrillas," the antidrug policies of the United States have won the propaganda battle of presenting us as a "narco-democracy" dangerously close to becoming what the State Department calls a "bandit state"—one of those states that do not conform to internationally accepted norms (generally dictated by the United States as the world's only superpower) and against which the international community feels it is entitled to act to impose order in defense of its fundamental interests. With this strategy, the United States has convinced the diplomatic world that there is a new world enemy, namely, the drug trade, and, moreover, that this enemy is located in the producer nations, especially in Colombia.

The world powers have imposed the idea of "limited sovereignty" where the drug trade, human rights, and international humanitarian law are concerned. Colombia, critical on all three, is therefore a target for foreign intervention. Intervention is for the first time being profiled as a solution, and different hypotheses for intervention are already under discussion. Fear of a Vietnam-style containment suggests instead a multinational approach, as adopted in the former Yugoslavia.

Regional geopolitical tensions are on the rise with the approach of the transfer of the Panama Canal in fulfillment of the Torrijos-Carter treaty. No doubt the United States will exercise stricter control over the region in order to prevent any threat to its strategic interests and will argue that, so long as Colombia remains a focus for regional destabilization, the conditions for the transfer have not been met or insist on retaining a police or military presence in the Canal Zone.

There is now consensus both at home and abroad that intervention in Colombia is needed. There is still no consensus on how it should take place. The United States, in a gesture that suggests that for the first time it may be backing a negotiated solution, has announced that it is joining the group of countries that support the peace process. The question remains, what will happen if there is no peace process?

The peace process begun in 1999 is having difficulty in initiating conversations and even more in developing an agenda for negotiations. Meanwhile, the so-called Plan B of the armed forces, the Pentagon, and the neighboring armies is ever more openly showing its teeth. Infrared vision for nocturnal combat, helicopters, spy planes, satellite technology, smart missiles—these are the terms that are entering the language.

The fact that in 1999 Colombia was the world's third-largest recipient of U.S. military aid and that it will soon be receiving a level of aid similar to that dispatched to El Salvador in the last stages of the war there demonstrates that, like the Persian Gulf before it, it is on the way to becoming the testing ground for the latest arms technology.

This brings us to a second hypothesis concerning our internal war:

2. Colombia is on the verge of losing the capacity to exercise its sovereignty over a negotiated solution to its internal conflict.

Some years ago, Daniel Pécaut suggested that Colombia was at the point of no return. The financing of paramilitary groups by the drug dealers and the complicity of the state were becoming clear, and serious institutional problems could be glimpsed in the offing. At that time he wrote.

> Month after month, the situation in Colombia worsens. Cease-fire and dialogue have practically broken down. The terror carried out with complete impunity by obscure extreme right-wing forces and the stated intention of the guerrillas to step up their campaign for power are producing ever greater polarization. The authority of the government is too uncertain to halt this process. Colombia could easily become the scene of a large-scale social and political confrontation.

Today this prediction has been fulfilled. Never before have so many problems—political, economic, social, military, and in international relations—been in crisis at the same time. The experts of the International Monetary Fund speak insistently of the need for structural adjustment, with all that this has implied in countries such as Venezuela and Mexico. (Someone should convince them that public expenditure in a country on the verge of collapse and all-out war like Colombia cannot be treated in the same macroeconomic terms as in Costa Rica or Switzerland.) The social crisis alone is daunting: more than 16 percent of the workforce is in long-term unemployment, a larger and larger percentage of the population lives in absolute poverty, and a million and a half people have been displaced by the violence. All these factors combine to render the country increasingly ungovernable. Colombia risks the loss of its democratic stability and of its ability to exercise its enfeebled sovereignty through a negotiated political solution. With each month that passes the possibility of such a solution diminishes.

This narrowing of possibilities is demonstrated by the growing fragmentation of power, both of the state and of the guerrilla state-in-waiting, civil society and the insurgents. An all-out war, far from fusing in a revolution, can easily break up into "multipolar wars." Already various fronts of the ELN have categorized fronts of the Ejército Popular de Liberación (Popular Liberation Army—EPL) as military targets, and there have been armed confrontations between the ELN and the FARC in Arauca and Cubará over disagreements concerning the U'wa and Occidental Petroleum. This fragmentation of the war reduces the chance that any of the contending groups has of consolidating any kind of project and renders effectively impossible a negotiated settlement leading to a democratic reform. Thus we are left with neither reform nor revolution and instead the perpetuation of a barely legitimate status quo nevertheless able to limp along as it has for more than 50 years. In the new phase of globalization, the Colombian conflict is viewed as chronic and insoluble by the outside world and by Colombians themselves.

Never before has Colombian society accepted the possibility of intervention so willingly. A society that has systematically rejected any possibility of international mediation now not only accepts it but speaks openly of an international peacekeeping force. Either Colombians have not realized exactly what this means or they really are coming to a consensus in favor of international military intervention.

Although the military situation in Colombia has been described as a negative stalemate (that is, as a situation in which the Colombian state cannot defeat the guerrillas and the guerrillas cannot achieve any kind of revolutionary triumph), it could develop into a prolonged war with destructive effects for Colombia's territorial integrity. The continuation of the war might lead in the future to the dismemberment of the country into multiple sovereignties. The southern block of the FARC is proposing a strategy of "defense of its frontiers" that could lead to territorial separation, as in Arauca and Casanare. This "new independent republic" presents itself as the authority over a zone that "produces 80 percent of the world's cocaine" and is governed by "narco-guerrillas" against whom the Colombian state has been impotent and by whom "it will be defeated within five years."

The situation gives increasing legitimacy to a possible intervention. Each month that passes, the room for maneuver of society, of the government, and of the guerrillas is more and more limited in the face of an eventual negotiation. Perhaps foreign military intervention will bring the sides together in a cessation of hostilities, which might lead to a "Vietnamization" of Colombia or, less likely, to forced negotiations as in Kosovo.

If, however, against all predictions and in defiance of the negative tendencies of the present juncture, Colombia finds routes to a solution and begins serious negotiation soon, if it learns from the errors of the past and the experiences of other countries, it could find itself offered enormous support by the international community, including the United States, in terms of accompaniment in negotiations and mediation. If the insurgents and the forces of the establishment could finally understand the Gordian knot of the present situation, it would be, utopically, our second chance on earth. If not, we will certainly find ourselves on the road to intervention, with all that that entails.

POSTSCRIPT

Since I finished this essay many things have happened, but nothing that I have said has lost its validity. On the contrary, the tendencies highlighted previously have been confirmed. The negotiations begun in January of 1999 with the granting to the FARC of an extensive territory that covers five municipalities in the Caguan region, in the middle of the jungles of Orinoco, in the Amazon region, continue at the same pace. There have been some advances that have not signified any decline in the intensity of the war—the ELN has not been able to begin negotiations because of the strong opposition of the population, supported by the social forces underlying paramilitarism and by wide sectors of the community that are not prepared to submit to the political and military domination of the guerrillas, to the delivery to it of an area in the oil region of Magdalena Medio under similar conditions.

For its part, the FARC has launched a new Partido Bolivariano (Bolivarian party), clandestine in character, in pursuit of allies and a broad social base to legitimize its political project. Neither of the guerrilla groups has modified the rigid stance of an army that imagines itself as the victor.

But this is related to the weakness of the state and the mediocrity of Andrés Pastrana, who has presented to the departing Clinton administration a package in which military assistance dominates, supposedly for the "struggle against narcotraffic" but in fact merely a cautious method of counterinsurgency. However, Congress seems reluctant to approve the legislative package, as many of its members believe, with justification, that this would be entering a quagmire. It is clear that the situation of the Pastrana government is very precarious, and his domestic prestige has fallen to historical lows as his ability to govern declines with each passing day. The economic crisis is also historic, with unemployment figures over 21 percent and all economic indicators showing that the recession is far from being overcome.

A package of economic adjustment measures, negotiated with the World Bank and the International Monetary Fund, is in the making, and this has led to social protests, further frustrating the possibilities for a negotiated solution to the war. Meanwhile, endemic violence has worsened. Massacres continue daily, the paramilitary groups have not changed their pattern of death and threats, and selective assassinations now target not just unionists, popular leaders, and human rights defenders but also journalists, university professors, and officials at all levels. The crisis has overwhelmed the country's institutions.

Colombia is the result of a social, economic, and political model that attempted to enter modernity without rejecting violence, that is to say, performing the functions of *"orden y violencia,"* as Daniel Pécaut has lucidly put it. Therefore, every unsolved homicide from the massacre of the banana workers of United Fruit in 1928 through the two political genocides of the past 50 years—the first against Jorge Ellécer Gaitán and his party in 1948 and the second beginning in 1986 with the nearly 3,000 murders of the militants in the Unión Patriótica (Patriotic Union), the third party in the "oldest and most stable democracy in South America"—weighs more now than ever before.

All of this—the massacres, homicides, and disappearances that have accumulated over time—occurred as the result of a society trapped by a fatal disjunctive: Either Colombia is a corner of the world in which it is not worth investing US$1,600,000,000 (the value of one cargo of cocaine, according to President Pastrana) or, if this amount is invested, we will turn into the most formidable laboratory for war of the post–cold war era. Both alternatives would inevitably prolong the armed conflict indefinitely.

Colombia is a society in a labyrinth. If the military aid is not approved, the military balance will be broken, and the country will be subjected to the rise of military projects with incipient rural political programs that are far from being perceived as legitimate by the majority of the population, which is urban and little influenced by such alternatives. This means that it is not very clear that one of these disputed revolutionary projects will easily triumph, but there will definitely be some deterioration of the status quo. If the military aid is approved, it will still not guarantee the stabilization of the regime; instead it will deepen—in fact it is already happening—the greatest counterinsurgency experiment in the hemisphere. There remains a strategic link that is difficult to break in the short term.

Therefore, the only desirable alternative and the one that will avoid these two failed models is to intensify the pursuit of political negotiation and the reinstallation of the force of human rights and international humanitarian law, a process in which democratic forces from all around the world can play a role that is truly constructive and humanitarian. Colombia can and should avoid a state of total war with unpredictable costs and consequences for all of the countries of the region.

9.3 Colombia and the United States: From Counternarcotics to Counterterrorism (2003)

ARLENE B. TICKNER

During the past several years, United States foreign policy toward Colombia has undergone significant transformations. Long considered a faithful ally in the fight against drugs, as well as showcasing Washington's achievements in this camp, Colombia became widely identified as an international pariah in the mid-1990s during the administration of Ernesto Samper because of the scandal surrounding the president's electoral campaign, which was said to have been funded by drug money. Although the inauguration in 1998 of President Andrés Pastrana—a man untainted by drugs—marked the official return to friendly relations with the United States, Colombia came to be viewed as a problem nation in which the spillover effects of the country's guerrilla war threatened regional stability. The events of September 11, combined with the definitive rupture of the Colombian government's peace process with the rebels in February 2002, have converted this country into the primary theater of United States counterterrorist operations in the Western Hemisphere today.

THE PERVERSE EFFECTS OF THE "WAR ON DRUGS"

Any discussion of United States policy in Colombia must begin with drugs. Since the mid-1980s, when illicit narcotics were declared a lethal threat to America's national security, the drug issue has been central to relations with Colombia. Washington's counternarcotics policies have been based on repressive, prohibitionist, and hard-line language and on strategies that have changed little in the last few decades. The manner in which Colombia itself

Arlene B. Tickner, "Colombia and the United States: From Counternarcotics to Counterterrorism." Reprinted with permission from *Current History*, February 2003. © 2003, Current History, Inc.

has addressed the drug problem derives substantially from the United States approach, with most of Bogotá's measures to fight the drug trade the result of bilateral agreements or the unilateral imposition of specific strategies designed in Washington. These American-guided efforts to combat illegal drugs "at the source" have produced countless negative consequences for Colombia, aggravating the armed conflict that continues to consume the country and forcing urgent national problems such as the strengthening of democracy, the defense of human rights, the reduction of poverty, and the preservation of the environment to become secondary to countering the drug trade.

Perhaps the most perverse result of the United States–led "war on drugs" is that it has failed to reduce the production, trafficking, and consumption of illicit substances. Between 1996 and 2001, United States military aid to Colombia increased fifteenfold, from $67 million to $1 billion. During this same period, data from the United States State Department's annual *International Narcotics Drug Control Strategy* report show that coca cultivations in Colombia grew 150 percent, from 67,200 to 169,800 hectares (1 hectare = 2.471 acres). Clearly, the high levels of military assistance received by Colombia have had little effect on illicit crop cultivation in the country.

Efforts to eradicate coca cultivation, primarily through aerial spraying, have also increased progressively in Colombia. In 1998, for example, 50 percent more hectares were fumigated than in 1997; in 2001 the Colombian National Police fumigated nearly two times more coca than in 2000. In both instances, fumigation had no effect or even an inverse effect on the total number of hectares cultivated.

Intensive aerial fumigation—particularly in southern Colombia, where Plan Colombia efforts are concentrated—has created public health problems and led to the destruction of licit crops. According to exhaustive studies conducted by Colombia's national human rights ombudsman in 2001 and 2002, aerial spraying with glyphosate has not only killed the legal crops of many communities in southern Colombia but has also caused health problems associated with the inhalation of the pesticide and contact with human skin. On two separate occasions, the ombudsman called for a halt to aerial fumigation until its harmful effects could be mitigated. Echoing similar concerns, in late 2001 the United States Congress, as a precondition for disbursing the aerial-fumigation portion of the 2002 aid bill to the Andean region, requested the State Department to certify that drug-eradication strategies currently employed in Colombia do not pose significant public health risks. On September 4, 2002 the State Department issued its report, arguing that no adverse effects had been found. Members of the scientific community and environmental nongovernmental organizations in the United States and Europe criticized the report, primarily on methodological grounds.

Eradication efforts also have not affected the costs to users: in November 2001 the United States Office of National Drug Control Policy acknowledged that the price of cocaine in principal American cities has remained stable during the past several years. Yet Washington and Bogotá continue to insist that the war on drugs can be won simply by intensifying and expanding current strategies.

THE "WAR ON DRUGS" AND COUNTERINSURGENCY

The cold war's end saw drugs replace communism as the primary threat to United States national security in the Western Hemisphere. Military assistance to Latin America became concentrated in the "source" countries, particularly Colombia. At the same time, the definition of "low-intensity conflict"—the term used to describe the political situation in Central America during the 1980s—was expanded to include those countries in which drug-trafficking organizations threatened the stability of the state. And the strategies applied in the 1980s to confront low-intensity conflict in the region were subsequently adjusted in the 1990s to address the new regional threat: drugs.

In Colombia this view of the drug problem, and of the strategies needed to combat it, is especially troublesome, given that illegal armed actors, especially the leftist Revolutionary Armed Forces of Colombia (FARC) and the paramilitary United Self-Defense Force of Colombia (AUC), maintain complex linkages with the drug trade. At conceptual and practical levels, the United States war on drugs is nearly inseparable from counterinsurgency efforts in Colombia.

The conflation of low-intensity counterinsurgency tactics with counternarcotics strategies was facilitated initially through the "narcoguerrilla theory" (a term first made popular in the 1980s by former United States Ambassador to Colombia Lewis Tambs, who accused the FARC of sustaining direct links with drug traffickers). However, the fact that paramilitary organizations, most notably MAS (Muerte a Secuestradores, or Death to Kidnappers), were created in the early 1980s and financed by drug traffickers in retaliation for guerrilla kidnappings, seemed to belie the theory's validity. Yet by the mid-1990s, references to the "narcoguerrilla" slowly began to find their way into the official jargon of certain sectors of the United States and Colombian political and military establishment. Robert Gelbard, United States assistant secretary of state for international narcotics and law enforcement, referred to the FARC as Colombia's third-largest drug cartel in 1996. During his administration, President Ernesto Samper himself began to use the narcoguerrilla label domestically in an attempt to discredit the FARC, given the group's unwillingness to negotiate with a political figure that the guerrilla organization considered illegitimate.

Ironically, when the Colombian military during the Samper administration tried to convince Washington that the symbiosis between guerrillas and drug-trafficking organizations was real, and that counternarcotics strategies needed to take this relationship into consideration, the United States argued against the idea that the guerrillas were involved in the drug traffic. Indeed, although Tambs and others had made the accusation, the United States had never categorically associated Colombian guerrilla organizations with the latter stages of the drug-trafficking process. Only in November 2000 did the State Department accuse the FARC of maintaining relations with Mexico's Arellano-Félix Organization, one of the most powerful drug cartels in that country; it also argued that "since late 1999 the FARC has sought to establish a monopoly position over the commercialization of cocaine base across much of southern Colombia." One week later, United States Ambassador to Colombia Anne Patterson affirmed that both the FARC and the paramilitaries had "control of the entire export process and the routes for sending drugs abroad" and were operating as drug cartels in the country

In principle, the "narcoguerrilla theory," as employed in Colombia, argues that: 1) the FARC controls most aspects of the drug trade, given the demise of the major drug cartels in the mid-1990s; 2) the Colombian state is too weak to confront this threat, primarily due to the inefficacy of the country's armed forces; and 3) United States military support is warranted in wresting drug-producing regions from guerrilla control.

Although bearing a certain degree of truth, this description grossly oversimplifies the Colombian situation. For example, while a general consensus exists that the FARC derives a considerable portion of its income from the taxation of coca crops and coca paste and that members of this organization have participated in drugs for arms transactions, the involvement of the FARC in the transportation and distribution of narcotics internationally is still uncertain. (Contrary to the claims made by the United States State Department and its representative in Colombia, for example, the Drug Enforcement Agency has never directly accused the FARC of operating as an international drug cartel.)

The involvement of paramilitaries in drug-related activities clouds this picture even further. According to some sources, paramilitary expansion in southern Colombia during late 2000, in particular in the Putumayo region, was largely financed by drug-trafficking organizations in response to the FARC-imposed increases in the price and taxation of coca paste. This is not surprising, since the leader of the AUC, Carlos Castaño, has personally acknowledged since March 2000 that a large percentage of this organization's revenues, especially in the departments of Antioquia and Córdoba, are derived from participation in the drug trade.

Yet even with evidence that the "narcoguerrilla theory" is simpleminded, it seems to have informed many United States and Colombian political and military actors in the search for policy options in the country, while also lending credence to those who argue that counterinsurgency techniques used in other low-intensity conflicts can be applied successfully in Colombia.

SEPTEMBER 11 AND COUNTERTERRORISM

The events of September 11 and America's war on terrorism have introduced an additional ingredient to United States policy in Colombia: counterterrorism. On the day of the attacks, United States Secretary of State
Colin Powell was to have visited Bogotá on official business. Although
Washington's concern about the FARC's abuse of a swath of Colombia designated as a demilitarized zone created to facilitate peace talks was clear
(the FARC was accused of using the zone to cultivate coca, hold kidnapping
victims, and meet with members of the Irish Republican Army, allegedly to
receive training in urban military tactics), some members of the American
government were beginning to express reservations about the depth and nature of United States involvement in Colombia and the effectiveness of
counternarcotics strategies in the country. To a large degree, the incidents of
the day facilitated shifts in United States policy that had begun taking shape
much earlier.

In a congressional hearing held on October 10, 2001, Francis Taylor, the
State Department's coordinator for counterterrorism, stated that the "most
dangerous international terrorist group based in this hemisphere is the Revolutionary Armed Forces of Colombia." Both Secretary of State Colin Powell
and United States Ambassador to Colombia Patterson also began to refer to
Colombian armed actors, in particular the FARC, as terrorist organizations
that threaten regional stability. Given that the global war on terrorism has
targeted the links that exist among terrorism, arms, and drugs, a new term
was coined, "narcoterrorism," to describe actors such as the FARC and the
AUC that fund terrorist-related activities with drug money.

The Colombian government's termination of the peace process with the
FARC on February 20, 2002 placed Colombia squarely within Washington's
new counterterrorist efforts. Until that day, the government of President Andrés Pastrana had never publicly referred to the guerrillas as terrorists. In a
televised speech announcing his decision to call off the peace talks, however, Pastrana made this association explicit. Echoing this change, the presidential electoral battle of 2002 centered on the issues of counterterrorism
and war, and led to the election of hard-liner Álvaro Uribe on May 26.

Colombia's insertion into the global war on terrorism has been reflected
in concrete policy measures in the United States. In simple terms, Colombia
is now viewed through the lens of counterterrorism. Public officials from
both countries must frame Colombia's problems along antiterrorist lines to
assure continued United States support. This shift in terminology has led to
the complete erasure of differences between counternarcotics, counterinsurgency, and counterterrorist activities that formerly constituted the rhetorical
backbone of United States policy in Colombia. For many years, Washington
stressed the idea that its "war" in Colombia was against drug trafficking
and not against the armed insurgents. As was noted, some began to openly

advocate reconsideration of this policy as early as November 2000. Tellingly, United States Representative Benjamin Gilman (R., N.Y.), in a letter written that month to drug czar Barry McCaffrey that criticized the militarization of counternarcotics activities in Colombia, suggested the need for public debate concerning counterinsurgency aid to the country. A RAND report published in March 2001 also affirmed that Washington should reorient its strategy in Colombia toward counterinsurgency to help the local government regain control of the national territory.

On March 21, 2002 President George W. Bush presented a supplemental budgetary request to the United States Congress totaling $27 billion for the war on terrorism and the defense of national security. The request solicited additional funding for Colombia as well as authorization to use counternarcotics assistance already disbursed to the country. The antiterrorist package finally approved by Congress in July contains an additional $35 million for counterinsurgency activities in Colombia as well as authority to use United States military assistance for purposes other than counternarcotics—namely, counterinsurgency and counterterrorism.

In its 2003 budget proposal submitted to Congress on February 4, 2002, the Bush administration also requested, for the first time, funding for activities unrelated to the drug war in Colombia. The aid package, which totals over $500 million, includes a request for approximately $100 million to train and equip two new Colombian army brigades to protect the Caño Limón-Coveñas oil pipeline, in which the American firm Occidental Petroleum is a large shareholder.

MILITARIZATION AND HUMAN RIGHTS

One of the most severe challenges to United States policy derives from the human rights situation in Colombia. According to the United States State Department *Report on Human Rights* for 2001, political and extrajudicial actions involving government security forces, paramilitary groups, and members of the guerrilla forces resulted in the deaths of 3,700 civilians; paramilitary forces were responsible for approximately 70 percent of these. During the first 10 months of 2001, 161 massacres occurred in which an estimated 1,021 people were killed. Between 275,000 and 347,000 people were forced to leave their homes, while the total number of Colombians displaced by rural violence in the country during only the last five years grew to approximately 1 million. More than 25,000 homicides were committed, one of the highest global figures per capita, and approximately 3,041 civilians were kidnapped (a slight decline from the 3,700 abducted in 2000).

Although Colombian security forces were responsible for only 3 percent of human rights violations in 2001 (a notable improvement over the 54 percent share in 1993), the report notes that government security forces continued to commit abuses, including extrajudicial killings, and collaborated directly and indirectly with paramilitary forces. And although the government has worked to strengthen its human rights policy, the measures adopted to punish officials accused of committing violations and to prevent paramilitary attacks nationwide are considered insufficient. In the meantime, paramilitary forces have increased their social and political support among the civilian population in many parts of the country. Increasingly, Colombians sense that the paramilitaries constitute the only force capable of controlling the guerrillas' expansion. The AUC have also adopted parastate functions in those regions in which the government's presence is scarce or nonexistent.

Because of the questionable human rights record of the Colombian armed forces as well as Bogotá's unwillingness to denounce this publicly, United States military assistance to the country was severely limited during much of the 1990s. Nevertheless, the United States continued to provide the armed forces with military training, weapons, and materials. In 1994 the United States embassy in Colombia reported that counternarcotics aid had been provided in 1992 and 1993 to several units responsible for human rights violations in areas not considered to be priority drug-producing zones. As a result, beginning in 1994 the United States Congress anchored military aid in Colombia directly to antidrug activities. The Leahy Amendment of September 1996—introduced by Senator Patrick Leahy (D., Vt.)—sought to suspend military assistance to those units implicated in human rights violations that were receiving counternarcotics funding, unless the United States secretary of state certified that the government was taking measures to bring responsible military officers to trial.

The Colombian government itself began in 1994 to adopt a stronger stance on human rights and in January 1995 publicly claimed responsibility in what became known as the Trujillo massacres (committed between 1988 and 1991): more than 100 assassinations carried out by government security forces in collaboration with drug-trafficking organizations. Other measures directly sponsored by the Samper government in this area included the creation of a permanent regional office of the UN High Commissioner for Human Rights; the ratification of Protocol II of the Geneva Conventions; and the formalization of an agreement with the International Red Cross that enabled this organization to establish a presence in the country's conflict zones. Unfortunately, as the Colombian newsweekly *Semana* noted, "Little by little, the novel proposals made at the beginning of the Samper administration became relegated to a secondary status, given the government's need to maintain the support of the military in order to stay in power."

The moderate changes implemented by the Colombian government in its handling of human rights issues—combined with the intensification of the armed conflict and the military's need for greater firepower and better technology—facilitated the signing of an agreement in August 1997 in which the

Colombian armed forces accepted the conditionality imposed by the Leahy Amendment. In the past, the Colombian military had repeatedly refused United States military assistance on the grounds that such unilateral impositions "violated the dignity of the army." But the marked asymmetries between United States aid earmarked for the Colombian National Police (CNP), which immediately accepted human rights conditionalities, and assistance specifically designated for the Colombian army constituted a strong incentive for the military to finally accept the conditions attached by the United States. Until the late 1990s the CNP was Washington's principal ally in the war on drugs, receiving nearly 90 percent of United States military aid given to Colombia. The 2000–2001 Plan Colombia aid package, however, reversed this trend completely: while the Colombian army received $416.9 million, primarily for the training of several counternarcotics battalions, police assistance only totaled $115.6 million. In the 2002 and 2003 aid packages, the Colombian army continues to be the primary recipient of United States military assistance.

With the approval of the first Plan Colombia aid package in June 2000, the United States Congress specified that the president must certify that the Colombian armed forces are acting to suspend and prosecute those officers involved in human rights violations and to enforce civilian court jurisdiction over human rights crimes, and that concrete measures are being taken to break the links between the military and paramilitary groups. This legislation, however, gives the president the prerogative to waive this condition if it is deemed that vital United States national interests are at stake. On August 22, 2000 President Bill Clinton invoked the waiver. And although human rights organizations, the UN High Commissioner for Human Rights, and the State Department affirm that little or no improvements have been made in satisfying the human rights requirements set forth in the original legislation, President George W. Bush certified Colombia in 2002.

With the end of the peace process, human rights in Colombia have been further marginalized. (President Pastrana called off the process with the FARC on February 20, 2002, after continuous setbacks and halts in the peace talks, as well as late 2001 attempts on the part of the United Nations and several countries to serve as intermediaries and revive the process.) Several components of President Álvaro Uribe's national security strategy have caused alarm in human rights circles. Shortly after taking office on August 7, 2002, Uribe declared a state of interior commotion (*Estado de Conmoción Interio*), a constitutional mechanism that allows the executive to rule by decree. In addition to expanding the judicial powers of the police and military, plans to increase the size of the armed forces, create a network of government informants, and build peasant security forces are already under way. In a letter to the Colombian president on August 26, 2002, UN High Commissioner for Human Rights Mary Robinson expressed concern about Colombia's lack of human rights progress and suggested that some of the security measures adopted by the Uribe administration may be incompatible with international humanitarian law. In its November 2002 report on Colombia, Human Rights Watch also criticized the recent reversal of several investigations of military officers suspected of collaborating with paramilitaries.

WEAKENING THE STATE

Inherent to America's growing concern with Colombia is the perception that the state has become "weak" when it comes to confronting the domestic crisis and maintaining it within the country's national boundaries. (The new National Security Strategy of the United States, made public in September 2002, explicitly identifies weak states as a threat to global security because of their propensity to harbor terrorists.) Thus, in addition to combating drugs and terrorism and reducing human rights violations, another stated goal of United States policy is to enable the Colombian military to reestablish territorial control over the country as a necessary step toward state strengthening.

Although state weakness has been a permanent aspect of Colombian political history, during the 1990s the country's deterioration quickened—with the logic of United States "drug war" imperatives playing a direct role in this process. The expansion and consolidation of drug-trafficking organizations in Colombia during the 1980s were intimately related to increasing United States domestic consumption of illegal substances, as well as the repressive policies traditionally applied to counteract this problem. America's demand for drugs and Washington's prohibitionist strategies created permissive external conditions in which the drug business in Colombia could flourish. The appearance of these organizations coincided with unprecedented levels of corruption in the public sphere, growing violence, and decreasing levels of state monopoly over the use of force.

The dismantling in the mid-1990s of the Medellín and Cali drug cartels—the two main drug-trafficking organizations in the country—gave way to fundamentally different drug-trafficking organizations that combined greater horizontal dispersion, a low profile, and the use of a more sophisticated strategy that made them even more difficult to identify and eradicate. Part of the void created by the disappearance of these two cartels was filled by the FARC and the AUC, which became more directly involved in certain aspects of the drug business between 1994 and 1998. As a result, one might also conclude—correctly—that United States drug consumption and its counternarcotics strategies have also exacerbated the Colombian armed conflict, providing diverse armed actors with substantial sources of income without which their financial autonomy and territorial expansion might not have been as feasible.

The propensity of the United States to interpret the drug problem as a national security issue, in combination with the use of coercive diplomatic measures designed to effectively confront this threat, has forced the Colombian state to "securitize" its own antidrug strategy. One underlying assumption of this "war" is that the use of external pressure is a crucial tool by which to achieve foreign policy objectives in this area, and that United States power is an enabling condition for the success of coercive diplomacy. But realist-inspired counternarcotics efforts ignore that policy orientations in source countries must necessarily answer to domestic as well as international exigencies. If domestic pressures are ignored on a systematic basis, growing state illegitimacy and state weakness can result; in an already weak state, this strategy can accelerate processes of state collapse.

With the Samper administration, the United States drug decertifications of 1996 and 1997 and the continuous threat of economic sanctions combined with domestic pressures that originated in Samper's lack of internal legitimacy to force the government to collaborate vigorously with the United States. As noted, between 1994 and 1998 the Colombian government undertook an unprecedented fumigation campaign that, while returning impressive results in terms of total coca and poppy crop eradication, saw coca cultivation itself mushroom during the same period. More significantly, the fumigation campaign had tremendous repercussions in those parts of southern Colombia where it was applied. In addition to provoking massive social protests in the departments of Putumayo, Caquetá, Cauca, and (especially) Guaviare, guerrilla involvement with drugs heightened during this period, and the FARC strengthened its social base of support among those peasants involved in coca cultivation. The absence of the Colombian state in this part of the country largely facilitated the assumption of parastate functions (administration of justice and security, among others) by the guerrillas. Paramilitary activity also increased with the explicit goal of containing the guerrillas' expansion. The result was the strengthening of armed actors and the intensification of the conflict. Although the United States was clearly not directly responsible for creating this situation, the excessive pressure placed on the Samper government to achieve United States goals did make it worse.

At the same time, Samper, because of the taint of drug money, was ostracized by the United States; increasingly, Colombia became identified as a pariah state within the international community. The political costs of the country's reduced status globally were significant; during his term in office Samper received only two official state visits to Colombia, by neighboring countries Venezuela and Ecuador. On an official tour through Africa and the Middle East in May 1997, the Colombian president was greeted in South Africa by news that President Nelson Mandela had been unable to meet him. Equally considerable were the economic costs. Colombia was precluded from receiving loans from international financial institutions during the time in which the country was decertified by the United States, while United States foreign investment was dramatically reduced.

THE "RENARCOTIZATION" OF RELATIONS

Confronted with growing evidence that it had aggravated Colombia's domestic crisis, Washington became increasingly sensitive to the issue of state weakness and attempted to develop a more comprehensive strategy toward the country when Andrés Pastrana was elected president in 1998. This shift in policy partly explains the initial willingness of the United States to adopt a "wait-and-see" strategy regarding the peace process Pastrana initiated with the FARC in early November 1998. Moreover, because of the marked deterioration in the political sphere, it became difficult to ignore the calls of an increasingly strong civil movement for a negotiated solution to the country's armed conflict. Thus, during the first year of his government, Pastrana was able to effectively navigate between domestic pressures for peace and United States exigencies on the drug front. But less than a year later, the assassination in early March 1999 of three United States citizens at the hands of the FARC, along with growing difficulties in the peace process itself, led to a change in both the United States and the Colombian postures and facilitated the ascendance of the drug-war logic once again.

This "renarcotization" of the bilateral agenda saw the emergence of Plan Colombia in late 1999. At home the Colombian government was able to circumvent domestic pressures by manipulating information about its intentions. This was achieved mainly through the publication of distinct versions for public consumption (in both Colombia and Europe) of arguments in which peace (and not the drug war) were adeptly presented as the centerpiece of Plan Colombia's strategy. Public statements by the government downplaying the strong emphasis the United States version of the plan placed on the drug problem reinforced this idea. When the United States Congress approved the Colombian aid package in mid-2000, sustaining this argument became increasingly difficult, primarily due to the large military component (80 percent of the total) that was designated for the drug war. Instead, the Pastrana government attempted to highlight the approximately $200 million earmarked for initiatives related to alternative development, assistance to displaced persons, human rights, and democracy, while discouraging public debate concerning the significant weight attached to the military and counternarcotics aspects of the package.

Just as war-weary Colombians welcomed Andrés Pastrana's proposal for peace in 1998, a country tired of the failed peace process overwhelmingly elected Álvaro Uribe on a national security and war platform in 2002. Uribe's plans for reestablishing state control over the national territory and for crushing militarily those armed actors unwilling to negotiate on the

government's terms—goals widely supported by the Colombian population—rely heavily on United States military assistance. The use of that aid for
counterinsurgency and counterterrorism is conditioned on a series of measures with which the Colombian government must comply. In addition to
adopting explicit commitments in the "war on drugs," including fumigation
efforts that surpass those of previous administrations, the Uribe government
must implement budgetary and personnel reforms within the military and
apportion additional national funding for its own war on drugs and terrorism. Some of these monies will be accrued through the creation of new taxes
and reductions in the size of the state, but social spending is likely to be reduced as well. In early August 2002, Washington also requested a written
statement from Bogotá conferring immunity for United States military advisers in Colombia as a precondition for the continuation of military aid.

Although at first glance Colombia and the United States share a common
objective—winning the war against armed groups in the country—Colombia's insertion into the global antiterrorist dynamic leaves scant room for
autonomous decision-making by the new president. In the future, the
hands-on, take-charge attitude that has won Uribe a high public approval
rating could be blocked by decisions made in Washington. For example, the
September 2002 request for the extradition to the United States of a number
of paramilitary leaders and several members of the FARC on charges of
drug trafficking may work at cross-purposes with future peace talks. Although it is highly unlikely that negotiations with the FARC will resume
anytime soon, on December 1, 2002 a cease-fire was declared by the paramilitaries, who have said they would like to negotiate with the government.
The United States has been reluctant to state whether the extradition re-
quests, or its classification of Colombia's armed groups as terrorists, would
be revoked in the event of new peace negotiations.

THE WRONG PROFILE

United States policy in Colombia has worked at cross-purposes in terms of
reducing the availability of illegal substances, confronting human rights violations, and strengthening the state. In all these areas, United States actions
may actually have made an already grave situation worse. The world-view
that has molded Washington's twin wars on drugs and terrorism constitutes
an extremely narrow framework through which to address the complex
problems Colombia faces. National security, defined exclusively in military
terms, has taken precedence over equally significant political, economic,
and social considerations. Until this perspective undergoes significant
change, United States policy will continue to be ill equipped to assist
Colombia in addressing the root causes of its current crisis.

SUGGESTIONS FOR FURTHER READING

Angell, Alan, Pamela Lowden, and Rosemary Thorp. *Decentralizing Development: The Political Economy of Institutional Change in Colombia and Chile.* New York: Oxford University Press, 2001.

Bagley, Bruce Michael. "Colombian Politics: Crisis or Continuity." *Current History* 86(516) (January 1987): 21–24, 40–41.

Bagley, Bruce Michael, Francisco E. Thoumi, and Juan Gabriel Tokatlian, eds. *State and Society in Contemporary Colombia: Beyond the National Front.* Boulder, Colo.: Westview Press, 1986.

Berry, R. Albert, Ronald G. Hellman, and Mauricio Solaún, eds. *Politics of Compromise: Coalition Government in Colombia.* New Brunswick, N.J.: Transaction Books, 1980.

Dix, Robert H. *The Politics of Colombia.* Politics in Latin America: A Hoover Institution Series. New York: Praeger, 1987.

Dudley, Steven S. *Walking Ghosts: Murder and Guerrilla Politics in Colombia.* New York: Routledge, 2004.

Giraldo, Javier. *Colombia: The Genocidal Democracy.* Monroe, Maine: Common Courage Press, 1996.

Hartlyn, Jonathan, and John Dugas. "Colombia: The Politics of Violence and Democratic Transformation," in Larry Diamond, Jonathan Hartlyn, Juan J. Linz, and Seymour Martin Lipset, eds. *Democracy in Developing Countries: Latin America.* Boulder, Colo.: Lynne Rienner Publishers, 1999.

Kline, Harvey. *Colombia: Democracy Under Assault.* Boulder, Colo.: Westview Press, 1995.

Kline, Harvey. *State Building and Conflict Resolution in Colombia, 1986–1994.* Tuscaloosa: University of Alabama Press, 1999.

Marcella, Gabriel, and Donald Schulz. *Colombia's Three Wars: U.S. Strategy at the Crossroads.* Carlisle, Pa.: Strategic Studies Institute, U.S. Army War College, 1999.

Posada-Carbó, Eduardo. *Colombia: The Politics of Reforming the State.* New York: St. Martin's Press, 1998.

Richani, Nazih. *Systems of Violence: The Political Economy of War and Peace in Colombia.* Albany: State University of New York Press, 2002.

USEFUL WEBSITES

Newspapers
La Republica
   www.larepublica.com.co

El Tiempo
   http://eltiempo.terra.com.co

El Mundo
   www.elmundo.com

El Espectador
   www.elespectador.com

Colombia Journal: English language, peace-oriented reports
www.colombiajournal.org

Government
Office of the Government of Colombia
www.gobiernoenlinea.gov.co

Office of the President
www.presidencia.gov.co

National University Institute for Political and International Relations Studies (IEPRI)
www.unal.edu.co/iepri

General
Colombia Human Rights Network
http://colhrnet.igc.org

CIA World Fact Book: Resource for general information on Colombia.
www.odci.gov/cia/publications/factbook/geos/co.html

Latin American Network Information Center: Comprehensive website housed at the University of Texas with extensive Latin American links on a wide array of topics.
http://Lanic.utexas.edu

CHAPTER 10

Cuba: A Latin American Experiment in Socialism

READINGS IN THIS CHAPTER

*I*n 1959, Cuba's long-ruling strong man, Fulgencio Batista, correctly determined that he had lost the support of both Cuban society and his most important foreign backer—the United States. Faced with an intensifying guerrilla war, Batista chose to flee rather than continue to fight. His exit opened the door for Fidel Castro, the leader of the guerrilla movement, to enter Havana and assume control of the country. Over the next three years, Castro and U.S. presidents Eisenhower and then Kennedy all contributed to a rapid and total collapse of cooperative relations. Instead, Castro's Cuba became the Soviet Union's closest ally in the Western Hemisphere and arguably the most constant and consistent target of unwavering U.S. government hostility and opprobrium. For many critics of U.S. policy, both in the United States and outside of the country, the degree of opposition is anywhere from exaggerated to completely misguided. What makes Cuba such a subject of controversy?

Cuba's relationship with the United States began in 1898. Near the turn of the century, Cuba was one of the largest sugar producers in the world. It was, however, still a colony of Spain with a highly unequal social structure in which much of the population worked as seasonally employed rural labor. Despite its colonial status, Cuba's most important economic partner was the United States. As Cuban nationalist sentiment grew stronger and liberation efforts increased in intensity, the United States became involved as a champion of Cuban independence against Spain. The war was short-lived before Spain withdrew and Cuban independence was established. Unfortunately, it quickly became apparent that the United States was not championing an independent Cuba. Rather, the war became an opportunity for the United States to increase and consolidate its economic domination of the island's sugar industry. Between 1898 and 1959, the United States actively intervened in the island's affairs, including occupations from 1906–1909 and again in 1917, as well as through forcing the Cuban Congress to include a constitutional amendment authorizing U.S. supervision of the country (the Platt Amendment). These various interventions ensured the dominance of U.S. interests in the country. By 1950, roughly half the island's sugar production was owned by Americans.

Cuban nationalists did not give up their desire for independence. The focus of their efforts simply shifted from liberation from Spain to liberation from U.S. domination. Discontent, primarily expressed by the middle class and elites in Cuban society, continued throughout the early twentieth century, but successive U.S.-backed governments were able to suppress serious challenges to the regime through fraud and physical force.

One failed revolt, however, changed that. In 1956, a small group of middle-class rebels attempted to overthrow the government. Roughly eighty fighters followed a middle-class doctor named Fidel Castro, his brother Raul, and the Argentine revolutionary Ernesto "Che" Guevara. The Castro brothers had already served time in prison for an earlier failed revolt. This effort fared no better. The group failed miserably, with most of Castro's followers killed or captured. Castro, his brother, and Guevara avoided capture and ended up hiding in the countryside. Castro's exposure to the conditions of the rural working class opened his eyes to the depth of the social inequality plaguing the country and revealed to him the necessity of expanding his base beyond the educated, nationalist middle class. In this way, Castro's revolt ceased being solely a nationalist movement and instead acquired a revolutionary character. Castro cultivated support among the rural labor communities that allowed him to use his small force in a guerrilla campaign against the Batista regime. Batista responded with growing brutality to the Castro challenge, undermining his already limited legitimacy. Ultimately, Batista lost the support of both Cuban elites and the U.S. government and chose to flee Cuba rather than continue the fight. Batista's departure provoked joyous celebration.

In 1959, Castro entered Havana and assumed power without opposition, but without a broad, well-developed base of support either. That changed as Castro began implementing a redistributive agenda, nationalizing both foreign and domestically owned enterprises and sugar plantations and authorizing a sweeping land reform. In response, the United States imposed a trade embargo on Cuban sugar. Over the next three years, Cuba and the United States entered a pattern of tit-for-tat steps that increased the level of mistrust and antagonism. It culminated on the U.S. side with the unsuccessful 1961 Bay of Pigs invasion—a poorly executed, poorly conceived invasion of Cuban exiles with tacit moral support from the Kennedy administration, but ultimately no military support. It culminated on the Cuban side with the placing of Soviet intermediate-range ballistic missiles in Cuba in 1962—a decision that brought the world perilously close to nuclear war. By the end of the Cuban missile crisis, Cuba had become a solid ally of what was then the U.S.S.R. and the unwavering object of U.S. hostility.

Castro had successfully broken its economic dependence on the United States. In its place, however, Cuba had become economically dependent on the Soviet Union, selling the Soviets most of its sugar crop and relying on enormous quantities of foreign aid (estimated at close to $5 billion or 25 percent of the country's GNP) up to 1990. Cuba's passionate detractors point to this dependence on the Soviet Union as evidence of the failure of the revolution. In the decades since the revolution, Cuba has not been able to diversify its economy out of sugar production, and its repeated efforts to bolster sugar production, such as through so-called moral incentive schemes, have been unsuccessful as well. The economic failures left Cuba reliant on the U.S.S.R. for economic survival. The political concomitant of economic dependence was political alliance with the Soviets, even in contradiction of Castro's anti-colonial and anti-imperial rhetoric. Thus, in addition to supplying military forces to bolster Soviet sponsored regimes in places like Africa, Castro also sided with the Soviets against anti-Soviet domination movements such as the Solidarity Labor movement that proved instrumental in liberating Poland in the 1980s. Castro's regime provided plenty of its own questionable human rights practices to complement its supporting roles with the Soviet Union. For example, Castro has persecuted and jailed artists, intellectuals, journalists, and teachers among many others for offenses as small as criticizing the regime.

On the other hand, Castro's avid supporters point to a different array of indicators. While it may be true that Cuba has been unable to diversify and develop its economy, the United States bears no small measure of the blame. The United States has enforced an embargo on trade with Cuba since 1960 (and in fact deepened it in the 1990s through the Helms-Burton Act). For some, the embargo itself played a role in pushing Castro toward the Soviet Union as Castro was not a communist before the revolution. In any event, cutting off Cuba from international financial and trade markets left the country with no choice but to depend on the U.S.S.R. Moreover, the new dependence may have looked similar to the old dependence from the perspective of production and national wealth. But the Castro regime made very different choices about how to use its limited national wealth. The most fundamental difference is that the Castro regime chose to distribute wealth in ways that prevented sharp inequalities in income and in access to services. The results show up clearly when one looks at social indicators—health, housing, education, maternal and natal care, and so on. Cuba looks like a developed, democratic nation, not like the rest of Latin America. Thus, the Castro regime has done something that no other Latin American nation has done (and few have even tried): It has protected the poor.

The truth, of course, is that both detractors and defenders are correct. Castro's regime has not permitted elections and restricts basic freedoms—freedom of speech and freedom of assembly, for example—that we normally associate with democracy. But the flip side is that the Castro regime has addressed the basic needs of its population in a way that goes well beyond what its Latin American neighbors have achieved.

As of 1990, however, the situation changed for Cuba. The collapse of the Soviet Union led to the wholesale disintegration of the Soviet bloc and its related economic, military, and diplomatic alliances. This collapse was also the end of Cuba's economic base. By 1992, Cuba had lost all direct foreign aid from the U.S.S.R. and most of its market for trade. Castro and the Cuban Revolution were forced to turn to the West to increase its access to finances and trade. Although some predicted that the Cuban regime would collapse quickly (and the Helms-Burton Act was meant to help speed it along), Castro has defied all expectations. The flow of desperate Cubans taking to Florida in makeshift boats has increased—a reflection of the impoverishment of the island. But, overall, Cuba has managed the balance between protecting its revolutionary character while opening its economy to foreign investment and to the black market, primarily by trying to attract larger amounts of tourism money. Politically, Castro has not eased up on the restrictions on expressions of opposition, but he has faced little organized opposition nonetheless despite growing economic deprivation. In short, Cuba is in an undefined place today where many of the benefits of the past are withering away through economic stagnation and much speculation is focused on what comes after the seventy-seven-year-old dictator finally passes away.

The articles in this chapter give some sense of the complexity of the Cuban situation. As Jorge Domínguez observes, Castro's Cuba has enjoyed such longevity and survived what should have been a cataclysmic economic crisis precisely because it is more complex and fluid than the way it is often portrayed. Rather than a purely coercive dictatorship, Domínguez points out that the regime has delivered a considerable number of social benefits. Furthermore, the party has developed a significant number of good, credible leaders (despite the general antipathy to the Communist Party), and has allowed a fair number of outlets for expressions of frustration. Thus, even though the regime has cracked down on opponents and critics—at times brutally—it has left opportunities for citizens to express themselves. It has also allowed those who are least happy to leave. Finally, Domínguez notes that the implacable hostility of the United States has helped Castro stay alive by allowing him to scapegoat the United States and rally Cuban support on nationalist grounds.

Haroldo Dilla and Philip Oxhorn show another side of that complexity in their review of the "Virtues and Misfortunes of Civil Society in Cuba." Civil society, as the authors point out, is closely identified with democratic, market societies. Civil society is the realm of political and social organization that is separate and autonomous from the state. Typically, it is associated with markets because markets create the resources and the inequalities that both permit and promote political and social organization. Cuba, a communist dictatorship, is not a good candidate to find civil society, and in fact Dilla and Oxhorn demonstrate that civil society organizations in Cuba are often weak and face considerable obstacles. Yet, as the authors document, they are present and important in a variety of places in Cuban life.

Louis Perez confronts the external puzzle that has driven so much of Cuba's history in "Fear and Loathing of Fidel Castro: Sources of U.S. Policy Toward Cuba." The United States had more cooperative engagement with the U.S.S.R. at the height of the Cold War than it has ever had with Cuba. Why has Cuba been the target of the most unwavering hostility of the U.S. government so consistently since Castro came to power in 1959? The most common answer is either the political influence of Florida's Cuban community or anti-communism. But as Perez demonstrates persuasively, "the Cuban-American lobby and anti-communism alone do not explain adequately the steadfast commitment by the United States to a policy whose most remarkable feature has been its singular failure to achieve its intended objective." Instead, Perez reviews the history of U.S.–Cuba relations and situates them within the larger context of U.S. foreign policy and the perception the United States has of its own role in the world.

DATA TABLES

Table 10.1
Cuba Fact and Data Sheet

Population (July 2003, estimated):	11,263,429
Ethnic Groups:	Mulatto 51%, white 37%, black 11%, Chinese 1%
Religions:	Roman Catholic 85%
Government Type:	Communist
Capital:	Havana
Administrative Divisions:	14 provinces and 1 special municipality
Date of Independence:	May 20, 1902 (from Spain, December 10, 1898; administered by the U.S. from 1898 to 1902)
Constitution:	February 24, 1976, amended July 1992 and June 2002
Executive Branch:	President Fidel Castro Ruiz, since 1959 revolution
Legislature:	Unicameral National Assembly of Peoples' Power 609 seats. Elected directly from slates approved by special candidacy commissions; members serve 5-year terms. PCC holds 97.6% of the seats.
Main Political Parties:	Cuban Communist Party (PCC)
Military Spending:	NA
Military Spending, Percentage of GDP (FY1995, estimated):	Roughly 4%
GDP (2002, estimated):	PPP $30.69 billion
GDP Composition by Sector (2000, estimated):	Agriculture: 7.6% Industry: 34.5% Services: 57.9%
Main Agricultural Products:	Sugar, tobacco, citrus, coffee, rice, potatoes, beans, livestock.
Export Partners (2002):	Netherlands, 19.1%; Russia, 18.1%; Canada, 14.3%; Spain, 9.5%; China 7.3%
Import Partners (2002):	Spain, 17.2%; China, 12%; Italy, 9.1%; France, 7.6%; Mexico, 7.3%; Canada, 6.2%; U.S., 5.6%; Brazil, 4.7%
External Debt (2002):	U.S. $12.3 billion (convertible currency); another $15–$20 billion owed to Russia.

Table 10.2
Cuban Regime History

Tenure	President
1899–1902	John R. Brooke[1]
1902	Leonard Wood[1]
1902–1906	Tomás Estrada Palma
1906	William Howard Taft[1]
1906–1909	Charles Edward Magoon[1]
1909–1912	José Miguel Gómez
1913–1920	Mario García Menocal
1921–1924	Alfredo Rayas
1925–1933	Gerardo Machado Morales
1933	Carlos Manuel de Céspedes
1933	Council of 5
1933	Ramón Grau San Martín
1934	Manuel Márquez Sterling
1934	Carlos Mandieta Montefur
1935	José A. Barnet y Vinageras
1936	Miguel Mariano Gómez Arias
1936–1940	Federico Laredo Bru
1940–1944	Fulgencio Batista Zaldívar
1944–1948	Ramón Grau San Martín
1948–1952	Carlos Prío Socarrás
1952–1959	Fulgencio Batista Zaldívar[2]
1959–present	Fidel Castro Ruiz

[1]U.S. occupation.

[2]Removed by revolution.

10.1   The Secrets of Castro's Staying Power (1993)

JORGE I. DOMÍNGUEZ

HOW CUBAN COMMUNISM SURVIVES

Shortly after the fall of the Berlin Wall it became common in Washington and Miami to bet on the date that Fidel Castro would fall. Those bets were based on the premise that the Cuban regime could not survive without Soviet support. Gone was the Soviet economic subsidy worth no less than one-sixth of the island's total gross product; gone were the weapons transfers, free of charge. From 1989 to 1992 the Cuban economy contracted sharply, with imports shrinking from $8.1 billion to $2.2 billion. Yet the Cuban regime remains with Fidel Castro firmly at its helm. How has Cuban communism managed to survive?

Besides the fact that communism in Cuba was not guaranteed by Soviet tanks, Cuba is clearly different from the regimes of Eastern Europe. As early as the spring of 1990 the Cuban people understood that communism was reversible. Cubans had already witnessed its collapse elsewhere, and they were feeling the negative economic effects. A public opinion poll taken at that time showed that only one-fifth of respondents said that the food supply was good and only one-tenth could say the same of the quality of transportation. Such results make the poll credible, and therefore we ought also to believe that three-quarters of the respondents thought health services were good and that four-fifths believed the same about their schools. Cubans supported their regime because they made differentiated judgments about its performance. They understood its many failings but they could also identify its successes.

Equally important, Cubans felt free enough to tell a pollster their many criticisms of government policy. For many years the Cuban government has permitted, and even stimulated, forms of citizen complaint to expose corruption and mismanagement, allowing local governments to channel these grievances to the center. The pollsters tapped into this freedom to criticize specific, malperforming services. This modest but important political space has remained Havana's safety valve, and U.S. observers often err in their assessments of Cuba because they do not understand its full significance.

Research undertaken by Cuban scholars at the end of the 1980s shows also that Cubans do not accord much weight to the Communist Party as an institution but think highly of individuals who are Communist Party members. In elections to the municipal assembly in which at least two candidates had been nominated, fewer than one in ten voters reported choosing a candidate because he or she belonged to the party. Instead voters gave varied reasons: a good neighbor, a good worker, etc. It turned out, however, that many of these "good citizens" were in fact party members. Unlike their East European counterparts, these Cubans had not turned in their party cards. Although the regime was vulnerable because the party as an institution was not held in higher regard, it was nonetheless strengthened by the personal qualities of its members.

Criticism of or noncompliance with certain government policies has existed alongside significant tolerance by the regime. At the same time, the regime has earned vital public support for many of its programs and has honored important promises to its citizens. For example, when the regime vowed to rely on voluntary compliance in its efforts to promote membership in peasant cooperatives, it continued to do so even after participation slipped from its initially strong response.

Cubans have disagreed with some of their government's policies over the years; there is fertile ground in which to plant the seeds of opposition. But to understand why the Castro regime has endured it is important to focus on facts rarely reported outside Cuba: even among its critics, the regime may be considered inept on many but not all policies; it is not uniformly oppressive, and many of those who belong to the party are good folks.

LESSON FROM EASTERN EUROPE: DON'T REFORM

Cuban leaders have learned several lessons from the attempted reforms that eventually undermined other communist regimes. Lesson no. 1: undertake as few political reforms as possible. Lesson no. 2: get rid of deadwood in the party early on, before you are forced to do so. Lesson no. 3: deal harshly with potential or evident disloyalty. Lesson no. 4: do not allow a formal opposition to organize.

Following these rules, Cuba has averted the patterns that led to the demise of other communist regimes. One such pattern in Europe was the emergence of reformers within the party who ousted the old guard and then led in forming a political opening. In East Germany the makers of the transition wielded power only briefly before they themselves were swept out by elections. In Hungary the process of reform occurred over a period of years but, at the key opening, the reformers again lost out. Another pattern evident in Poland and Nicaragua (as well as in Pinochet's Chile and Marcos'

Philippines) might be called "spectacular leadership error": rulers confident that they had substantial public support called a national election, which they promptly lost.

Not surprisingly, Castro's own political reforms have been minimal. He has taken steps to eliminate discrimination against religious believers and to broaden the Communist Party's appeal, and a new electoral law authorizes direct elections for National Assembly deputies and Provincial Assembly delegates. But the number of candidates in these elections equals the number of posts, nominating procedures make it impossible for an opposition candidate or party to operate, and partisan electoral campaigning remains illegal.

Cuba's official media has flooded the country with the "bad news" from Europe's old communist regimes: the breakup of the Soviet Union, Yugoslavia and Czechoslovakia; the outbreak of civil wars; the increase in unemployment and inflation; the elimination of various consumer subsidies; and the increase of common crime. The message to ordinary Cubans is clear: the transition to capitalism is long and painful. Elites receive a more specific message: look at what happened to Mikhail Gorbachev and other reformers; the path of reformist concessions has no end—critics and opponents are never satisfied and will always demand more. For Cuban leaders, therefore, the images on the television screens tell them to close ranks and prevent reforms that might weaken the regime politically.

A related task has been to rejuvenate the leadership under President Castro and his brother Raúl, the armed forces minister. Until 1980 not one member of the party's Political Bureau was dismissed—this since its founding in 1965. In contrast, by the end of the Fourth Communist Party Congress in 1991 only five of those who were members in 1975 still remained. In the interim many of Cuba's most important officials were dismissed; some were disgraced.

Among those disgraced, three stand out. Humberto Pérez, the architect of Cuba's economic recovery in the 1970s, was dismissed in 1985 for excessive reliance on market mechanisms. Carlos Aldana, former party secretary for ideology and international relations and among the most pragmatic and open-minded of the senior leadership, was dismissed in 1991 for corruption and negligence of duty. Worse still was the fate of Division General Arnaldo Ochoa, a highly decorated war hero for his military campaigns in the Horn of Africa in 1977–78, who was executed before a firing squad in 1989 on corruption and drug-trafficking charges. Such trials—alongside the Nuremberg-style trials that Miami radio stations promise await them—leave Cuba's army officers loyal to the regime, grateful for their perks and unmotivated to revolt.

The government subsequently reversed its very modest political opening of the 1980s that had allowed the semi-legal formation of small human rights and opposition groups. Since 1991 many human rights and opposition activists have been arrested and sentenced to tough prison terms for their crimes of opinion and peaceful association, seeking to exercise their rights under Cuba's constitution. Since 1991 the Cuban interior ministry has authorized and organized "rapid reaction brigades" to harass and at times to beat up dissidents. These brigades are officially described as the spontaneous response of outraged citizens to those who defame the government, the Communist Party and their leaders. This officially sponsored violence is also intended to have a deterrent effect, intimidating those who might join the feeble opposition.

Cuba's opposition has been hit especially hard by the economy's catastrophic decline. For any individual to survive it takes longer to stand in line for breakfast; it takes longer to stand in line before dinner. Private automobile transportation has come to a virtual standstill. It takes much longer to walk or to bicycle to work. After such a "normal" day's travail, walking or bicycling to an evening political meeting becomes less thinkable. Economic hardship, which affects government officials far less, has further weakened Cuba's already enfeebled and always incohesive opposition groups.

In short, the Castro brothers have ruled over and dismantled an excessively stable oligarchy. Mid-level cadres most fear the "certainty" that reform communism in Cuba would in due course lead to their own personal demise. Harsh penalties are meted out to those elites and ordinary citizens who do not toe the official line. Although many abroad expected that economic hardship would increase support for opposition groups, the short-term effects of this hardship have weakened and disorganized them, making it easier for the regime to endure. These factors have enabled Cuba's regime to resist the fate of its erstwhile European allies. Cuba's would-be Boris Yeltsins have thus far been cowed. Its would-be Violeta Chamorros and Václav Havels are in prison or in Miami.

THE BLACK MARKET'S HELPING HAND

Castro has adjusted to the collapse of his communist partners by dramatically lowering Cuba's standard of living. Cuba's leadership seeks simply to persevere, proud but poor. The regime could survive for an indefinite period at this level of hardship. There is no serious prospect of economic improvement unless major changes are undertaken. But Castro is not so rigid and dogmatic that he will never change; backed into a corner, even now Cuba has already begun a transition toward freer markets.

This ability to adjust to circumstances helps explain the regime's durability. In the long run, the free-market transition will lay the foundation for Cuba's future, no matter who rules the nation or what form the government takes. Some of this transition has occurred within the framework of the formal economy. The regime has set aside a cornerstone: in the early 1960s it expropriated all foreign property; in the early 1990s it welcomes private foreign investment under attractive terms. Such investment is notable in the tourist sector, but it can also be found in agriculture, manufacturing assembly plants and risk contracts for petroleum exploration. Like their total value, the number of investment projects is small but rising.

This trend has occurred mainly in the export sector. But the government has also liberalized regulations to permit the private contracting of certain services. Some state enterprises that export goods and services have been semiprivatized—that is, they operate as private firms with the state as sole shareholder. It would be but a small additional step to permit their full privatization, leaving them in the hands of former government and party cadres. This move cleverly anticipates the do-it-yourself privatization underway in the former Soviet Union or the last-minute reward to the faithful undertaken by the Sandinistas in Nicaragua in 1990. But whatever the motivation, these changes extend the scope of Cuba's market economy.

The rise of the illegal market economy is more important in understanding how ordinary citizens have adjusted to economic adversity. The black market's present dimensions are difficult to gauge. Some illegal markets depend on theft, but many others represent markets at their best. For example, state agriculture has never developed an efficient food distribution system. Even today crops sometimes rot unharvested in the fields. Behaving illegally but efficiently, peasants and commercial intermediaries connect with urban consumers to bring supply and demand into balance.

These illegal markets have become the regime's "secret agent" in the adjustment process, although the official position is to denounce and repress them. Recurrence to illegal markets is commonplace, and the survival of ordinary Cuban families (and even the families of government officials and party members) has increasingly come to depend on them. It is difficult to live simply on what the regime's ration card allocates, and the black market enables ordinary Cubans to supplement their diets. It also makes food or other consumer riots less likely. As a result the regime's survival has come to rest on them as well, and these illegal markets are in fact tolerated.

Illegal markets are financed by the central bank, as the government's reliance on printing paper money to finance its own deficit creates considerable excess liquidity. As money in circulation increases, however, so does inflation. Because prices in the formal economy are repressed, inflation so far accelerates only in illegal markets. In this fashion, however, the state is losing effective control over both macroeconomic policy and the economic behavior of its citizens. The very process that has helped the regime to endure since 1989 may contribute to its weakening in the years ahead. But whether inflation in illegal markets eventually becomes a factor in bringing down the regime will depend on possible changes in Cuban domestic politics as well as in U.S. policies.

WASHINGTON'S UNWITTING SUPPORT

The Castro regime endures in part because its enemies unwittingly help it to survive. U.S. policies provide ample fodder for Cuban hardliners, help censor information Cuban-Americans could provide relatives on the island and prevent ordinary Cubans from learning about the outside world.

Examples abound of how Washington unintentionally bolsters the Castro regime. On a daily basis Miami radio stations, and occasionally the U.S. government's own Radio Martí, frighten Cuban citizens with the prospect of the return of exiles who will demand property restitution. Washington prevents A.T.&T. from activating a new telephone link to the island on a normal commercial basis and prohibits the export of communications equipment such as fax machines and electronic mail. In the late 1970s Castro's regime entered one of its most unstable episodes after opening Cuba's borders to international tourism; but in 1982 the Reagan administration helped Havana regain control of its borders by making it illegal for U.S. citizens to spend money in Cuba, thus stopping U.S. tourism cold. Continuing U.S. military maneuvers and overflights constantly remind Cubans of the possibility of a U.S. threat, making it easier for Castro to call for sacrifices to defend the homeland.

Most helpful to Cuba's hardliners has been the so-called Cuban Democracy Act, which Congress enacted in the fall of 1992 in the midst of partisan competition for Florida's electoral votes. The act's only significant measure has been to mandate penalties on U.S. firms whose third-country subsidiaries trade with Cuba. Since that trade was mostly in foodstuffs, Cuban leaders should now find it easier to blame food shortages on Washington. Prior to the Cuban Democracy Act Castro's regime had become internationally isolated. It has since been able to construct a large and heterogeneous coalition to defend itself. U.S. penalties on firms in third countries have provoked protests from nearly all the major U.S. allies and trading partners. In late 1992, for the first time since it began in 1960, the U.S. trade embargo was overwhelmingly condemned by the U.N. General Assembly, with the only U.S. support coming from Israel and Romania.

The Cuban Democracy Act's most likely result will simply be Cuban firms buying from non-U.S. subsidiaries. The act is politically counterproductive and economically ineffective. The United States has resurfaced as a credible international enemy, threatening Cuba once again, this time with starvation. What better gift could Cuban hardliners have received? . . .

CASTRO COULD WELL ENDURE

Why, then, has Fidel Castro survived so long in power? For the very reasons he may continue to do so for many more years, unless U.S. policies change to make opposition politics at long last possible in Cuba. Heir to an authentic social revolution, ordinary Cubans remain free enough to voice complaints while they distinguish carefully between what they do and do not like, and whom they do and do not respect. Cuba's civil society is no longer as weak as it once was, but opposition to the regime has been weakened disproportionately by economic duress and remains hampered by a lack of leadership and organization to capitalize on current social and economic hardships. The state remains strongly repressive but is now assisted by illegal markets that have enabled Cubans to adjust to economic decline.

Never before have so many Cubans expressed their disapproval of the communist system. Unofficial but reliable reports indicate that in the December 1992 municipal elections one-fifth to one-quarter of all votes cast—and up to a third in Havana—were blank or null ballots, a fivefold increase from previous elections. Such results may presage the beginning of a long-expected political transition in Cuba. Only by undertaking major political changes can Cuba's leaders hope to recapture the consent of the population. But those changes are nowhere in sight.

Those Cubans in the opposition must organize far more effectively than they ever have. As long as citizens express their dissidence through lawful channels, the regime will not tumble. But beyond repression and fear, an important barrier to the growth of organized opposition is that many opposing the regime do not wish to "commit treason" or to become "the party of the United States." To create the necessary political space for an organized opposition to grow—and perhaps eventually to triumph—Washington must moderate those policies that monopolize opposition to the regime and fuel the regime's hardliners.

Cuban leaders could stabilize their political system by undertaking careful changes of their own. They could legalize the black market to improve efficiency and production; they could decentralize power to energize those local political institutions that retain significant public support precisely because they are close and responsive to the needs of ordinary citizens. Such a strategy would not require political liberalization—Cuba would retain a one-party system. It would not return Cuba's economy to its pre-1989 circumstances; it would not reestablish the regime's full legitimacy. Such changes, however, could stem the economy's decline and even bring back some growth; they could make it more likely that ordinary citizens would remain allegiant enough for the regime to survive.

Castro may yet consolidate his style of socialism in Cuba. Even at this late hour, the regime remains in power because it retains the allegiance of enough of its people and the reluctant partnership of many U.S. allies. These circumstances prevail in part because Washington's rigid opposition continues to allow Castro to rally citizens to defend what many Cubans are able to recognize as the regime's legitimate successes. The United States has been a staunch enemy of Fidel Castro, but with an enemy like this one, he may not need friends.

10.2 The Virtues and Misfortunes of Civil Society in Cuba (2002)

HAROLDO DILLA AND PHILIP OXHORN

Civil society is one of the historical realities most subject to conceptual ambiguities, probably because the concept is often the subject of heated polemical debates over whether to define it in purely normative terms. A commonality among these definitions has been the delineation of a simple linear relationship between civil society and other concurrent historical facts such as the market, liberal values, political democracy, and the state. In an attempt to avoid these issues, we prefer to define civil society as "the social fabric formed by a multiplicity of self-constituted territorially—and functionally—based units which peacefully coexist and collectively *resist subordination* to the state, at the same time that they *demand inclusion* into national political structures." Civil society is thus seen as the communicative interaction of group actions that generate new power relations and either consolidate or erode existing ones. As such, it reflects a process that does not begin or end with the creation of the market and is not uniquely associated with any particular normative system. Civil society involves a continuous process through which different social segments organize themselves and interact with each other and with the state. This allows different groups (particularly those that are socially and/or politically disadvantaged) to acquire capacities for influencing political outcomes and contributes to the emergence of alternative development models.

From its first conceptualizations, the term "civil society" has been intimately linked to the development of capitalism, and the market has been understood as a necessary if not sufficient condition for its existence. Civil society implicitly, if not explicitly, became the inescapable end point in the teleology of economic development associated with the modernization theories of the 1960s. In a similar fashion, when civil society was rediscovered by social scientists in the 1980s, some analysts sought to interpret the growing opposition movement in Eastern Europe as a struggle for political and especially economic liberty.

Normative predispositions aside, one fact needs to be stressed: the strength of civil society is dependent upon, among other conditions, both its differentiation from the state and its modus operandi (the assignment of resources and values through the contestation of political authority) and the degree of dispersion of power—economic, coercive, political, ideological, and mobilizational—within it. This explains why, from a strictly theoretical point of view, it is not difficult to reduce civil society to the market. The market, by definition, generates new power resources that are independent of the state, and the unequal distribution of those resources provides a basis for the emergence of new actors that can counter the existing power relations. Historically, there has been a close relation between the development of the market and the appearance and development of civil society, particularly in the formation of North Atlantic societies. However, this does not mean that the market is the sole generator of civil society or that this linkage is so linear that we can establish a mutually reinforcing relationship between the two. On the contrary, over the course of its development, the market erodes civil society by undermining the associative principle with its intrinsic logic, the maximization of profits. The perception of civil society as a dependent variable tied to the market is not only too closely linked to an economistic understanding of social relations but also empirically inaccurate. This is a principal reason that earlier modernization theories proved incorrect.

Another important reference point is the link between civil society and liberal democracy. A strong democracy requires a strong civil society. Many democratizing processes have begun precisely with the social movements characteristic of civil society. In consolidated democracies, the autonomy of political and social actors is a key factor in preventing (or at least limiting) the elitist tendencies of politics and the marginalization, apathy, and anomic attitudes of those sectors that are organizationally disadvantaged. At the same time, only in a democratic regime can civil society find a propitious environment for its full development, one that includes civil and political liberties and rights, access to decision-making processes, and so on. Authoritarian and highly centralized regimes have historically demonstrated their institutional incompatibility with the development of civil society.

Nevertheless, such empirical observations are not devoid of contradictions. The most notable of these is the contradiction between the collective principles of civil society and the liberal matrix of existing democracies. Liberalism in its classical sense is a political doctrine based on the priority of individual rights in the social and political order, and this leads to notable distortions where the society is defined by asymmetry in the distribution of power. Contemporary liberalism has substantially reinterpreted the relationship between *the individual* and *the collective,* but even where it has led to consolidated democratic regimes, they still largely prioritize individual over collective rights. It is important to emphasize, however, that although civil society needs to be situated in a context that respects and guarantees the exercise of individual rights for its continued development, the essence of a powerful civil society lies in collective rights and collective action in pursuit of the goals of sociopolitical inclusion shared by its principal actors. Moreover, contrary to the opinion of many liberals that civil society is reducible to values or behavioral norms such as "civility" or "civil-spiritedness," what distinguishes it from other social formations is the protagonism of collective actors and what are in effect collective rights, as well as the specificity of their demands and objectives.

Lastly, as mentioned in the introduction, civil society is fundamentally distinguishable by its differentiation and autonomy vis-à-vis the state. However, none of these conditions imply isolation from or hostility toward the state. On the contrary, in an optimal situation the relationship between the organizations of civil society and the state should be fluid and mutually reinforcing, a synergistic relationship conducive to development and the expansion of democratic spaces. In a less propitious situation, as has been the case under authoritarian or exclusionary regimes, civil society organizations can be protagonists in legitimate struggles against the established order. In another sense, as with the market and the community, the state can build civil society. For example, a state that is concerned about the social welfare of the majority can contribute to building a social subject that is better educated and better able to confront public issues. Similarly, positive policies can be formulated that benefit the less-favored social sectors, increasing their capabilities in the public arena. Some of the corporatist experiments in Western Europe are palpable examples of this. Finally, the state can create specific spaces for popular-sector participation and inclusion, particularly at the local level around the areas of action of civil organizations, as has been the case in some Latin American countries such as Brazil and El Salvador.

All of these contradictions are present in the recent history and the present reality of Latin America. Civil societies have been weak and marked by a combination of structural marginalization and controlled inclusion. When the regulating institutions of controlled inclusion have proven ineffective in containing working-class demands, the dominant classes have resorted to regimes of exclusion under military control. Even today, among political democracies, neoliberal policies based on the myth of the "free market" have constrained the opportunities for the development of civil society. The emergent liberal democracies have been based on civil societies that are not very structured or that are fragmented by the opposition of different groups to specific policies that is observable in so many of the region's social movements and reduces their efficacy in achieving their desired goal of greater political inclusion. In those few cases where civil society has managed to achieve organizational strength and recognized areas of action, as in the Chilean case, its role in achieving a more equitable distribution of economic resources has been perceptible, particularly in comparison with other cases, such as El Salvador, where a very fragmented civil society has been incapable of limiting neoliberal depredations.

In light of the above, the idea of a civil society in Cuba would seem to be an oxymoron. Not only does Cuba have a closed political system in which political authority is extremely concentrated but also it possesses an economic system that for decades has excluded the market and today provides scattered openings that are far from creating what could be considered a "market economy." Nevertheless, the Cuban experience offers a unique case for understanding the nature and limits of an emerging civil society in a system clearly undergoing a controlled transition without signs of ungovernability.

The preceding discussion raises some questions for analyzing the Cuban experience. If, as in fact happens in Cuba, politics at the national level are characterized by only very limited democratic processes, is there sufficient room for people to organize and formulate demands? Is it possible that local political spaces, which exhibit more democratic processes and possess significant mechanisms for citizen participation, could play a significant role in the generation and protection of an emergent civil society? If this were the case, could one expect that a democratizing impetus capable of affecting the national level might emerge out of these local actions? In another sense, does this incipient dynamic of civil society represent a questioning of the one-party system, as has been the case in other parts of the world? From another perspective, how are the current market reforms affecting the emergence of civil society in Cuba? Are they strengthening it (as liberal theories of civil society would suggest) or eroding its capacities?

THE COORDINATES OF THE CUBAN SCENE

Until a few years ago, the term "civil society" (banished from Soviet Marxism) was used almost exclusively by a handful of Gramscian *criollos* who were mostly ignored. The situation changed greatly in the 1990s, when people from almost all theoretical vantage points began making references to the term. Many factors help explain the sudden diffusion of a term that had been repudiated for decades. One of them was the influence exerted by the debate that had been taking place at a global level, particularly in Latin America. There is no doubt, however, that the most relevant reason is strictly local: the reconstitution of civil society in Cuba.

In the Cuban academic world, the term "civil society" began to be used with notable frequency, albeit with a functional meaning that has undermined any basic theoretical conceptualization. For their part, nongovernmental organizations (NGOs), many of them only recently established, organized conferences and made declarations in which trade-union-type demands were more common than any clear vision of the world that they claimed to represent. Finally, at least until 1996, state officials and politicians have oscillated between a denial of the phenomenon itself and an acceptance of it as a "socialist civil society." This bureaucratic stance, as we will see, has had a significant practical impact.

What all of these positions share is an emphasis on civil society as a space for the rearticulation of consensus. Their preoccupation with expounding on the probable "uses" of civil society, however, highlights a factor that is central to our analysis: the reconstitution of Cuban civil society is taking place in the midst of a transition based on heterodox market-oriented economic reforms that is producing a noticeable shift in the power structure. The key question among academics, bureaucrats, politicians, and activists has been precisely this: what should be the place of the emergent civil society in the construction of the nation's future, uncertain as it is?

THE ANTECEDENTS

The Cuban Revolution represented a moment of radical societal change and consequently had a significant effect on civil society. A good number of the existing organizations disappeared, whether because they were declared illegal (when they had links with the preceding dictatorship or were involved in counterrevolutionary activities) or because their social bases had disappeared. Others, such as unions and some professional associations, experienced changes in their organizational forms, objectives, and relations with the new revolutionary power. At the same time, the intense popular mobilization headed by the emergent political class generated a series of mass social organizations such as the Federación de Mujeres Cubanas (Federation of Cuban Women—FMC), the Comités de Defensa de la Revolución (Committees for the Defense of the Revolution—CDR), and the Asociación Nacional de Agricultores Pequeños (National Association of Small Farmers—ANAP). The sociological literature from that period bears witness to this mobilization of the masses around a revolutionary program and the consolidation of a level of political consensus never before seen in the nation's history. In a way this represented the emergence of a civil society. One should note, however, that the ensuing revolutionary process, characterized by a centralizing tendency, slowly circumscribed these organizations' autonomy until they finally became "conveyor belts" between the new political class and the popular masses. Although this severe subordination did not lead to imminent contradictions—given the basic coincidence between the popular interest and the revolutionary program—it did reduce the vitality of public spaces and led to the consolidation of paternalistic, clientelist relations between the state and society.

THE REALITY AND POTENTIAL OF CUBAN CIVIL SOCIETY

The disintegration of the so-called East European socialist camp hit the Cuban economy hard and accelerated the bankruptcy of the state socialist economic-growth model. As a consequence, the whole system of vertical and centralized social regulation has been suffering erosion. This erosion has accelerated with the implementation of a program of economic reforms based on the market and deregulation. Although the state continues to play a significant part in economic and social planning, the crisis has led to some retrenchment and, perhaps more important, the emergence of contradictions associated with its role as an economic actor under the new conditions.

While the rearticulation of Cuban civil society cannot be understood independently of the fact that new areas of conflict have emerged and social heterogeneity has increased, other factors should be taken into account as well. Most important, civil society emerges from a social subject that is highly developed in terms of education, values, and political awareness because of income redistribution and social mobility, the participatory experience created by the revolutionary project, particularly at the municipal level, and the development of solidarity and associational values in what has been characterized as the molding of a new civility.

When public servants, leaders of associations, or scholars want to argue in favor of the vitality of Cuban civil society, they normally refer to the fact that there are 2,154 civil associations in the registry created for this purpose by the Ministry of Justice. That a significant number of these associations have been created since 1989 certainly points to a substantial associational vocation, but the meaning of such numbers is ambiguous. The following qualitative taxonomy of associations may help not only to show who the present actors are but also indicate the potential of the emergent civil society.

Fraternal, Cultural, and Sports Associations

The vast majority of the more than 2,000 registered associations are fraternal, cultural, and sports associations. It is likely that some of these, particularly the cultural ones, have significant visibility and are capable of establishing communication networks that affect public opinion. This seems particularly striking in the case of some theater groups, although a more comprehensive evaluation would require more sustained empirical research. Still, the very nature of many of these organizations (for example, Masonic lodges, associations of canary or pigeon lovers or stamp collectors, tango groups, Esperanto associations, etc.) makes one wonder about their actual public influence. For this reason, despite their meeting the taxonomic criteria for forming part of civil society, surely most are irrelevant for our analysis, although one cannot dismiss the possibility that some of them may assume more definite public roles in the future.

Mass Social Organizations

Mass social organizations are "conveyor belts" for the state in the classic, vertically centralized model of social organization. Some of them, particularly the Comités de Defensa de la Revolución, the Federación de Mujeres Cubanas, and the Central de Trabajadores de Cuba (Cuban Workers' Central—CTC), have millions of members. Others, such as the student associations and the small farmers' organization, have smaller memberships. Professional associations such as organizations of writers and artists, journalists, lawyers, and economists constitute an imprecise area between civil society and the state not because they have similar political objectives but because of the limited autonomy they have shown in their public activities. Nevertheless, in practice these organizations are capable of adopting their own positions in relation to specific problems that affect their sphere of action, and they regularly participate in the decision-making areas in which they are represented, whether in state institutions or in the party. At the same time they exhibit a certain autonomous dynamic at the grassroots level, especially where conditions are right for leadership and collective action. With the crisis, this tendency toward autonomy has increased, especially in the case of unions and professional associations involved in artistic and intellectual activities. One can presume that in the future official policies related to economic adjustment and reform will tend to affect the members of these organizations directly. Their ability to represent sectorial popular interests under these new conditions, even when this would involve substantial differences with some of the policies in place, remains to be seen.

Churches and Religious Congregations

Many churches and religious congregations have engaged in community actions that go beyond mere pastoral functions. This has been particularly the case since 1991, when the Fourth Congress of the Communist Party adopted a more flexible position vis-à-vis religion that was reflected in the constitutional changes of 1992. Pope John Paul Il's visit to Cuba in 1998 was also a significant moment in this opening. Consequently, there has been a substantial increase in the number of people publicly identifying themselves as religious and regularly observing the rituals of their congregations.

The majority of Cubans who practice religion follow Afro-Cuban cults. Normally these cults, given their characteristic atomization and extreme organizational fluidity, have no national or territorial centers. Nonetheless, they are capable of forming informal networks for communication and the socialization of values that are very effective at the level of the community. Recently it has been possible to identify in some neighborhoods a tendency toward the involvement of Afro-Cuban religious authorities in cultural promotion and other areas of local development. There is no doubt that these religious congregations have a considerable mobilizational potential that should increase in the future.

The situation of the Protestant and Catholic churches is different, given their higher degree of organization and the particular positions they have held in the political spectrum. Protestant churches are a minority in Cuba, but their membership has increased considerably in recent years. Some of them have become actively involved in community development projects, popular education, and theological reflection with great public impact. The Catholic Church has from the beginning been elitist and hostile to the revolutionary project. At the National Cuban Ecclesiastical Conference in 1986, the Catholic hierarchy seemed to reorient itself toward a more realistic and less hostile position, but this interregnum was broken in 1993 with the publication of the pastoral letter "El amor todo lo espera," which was viscerally conservative and regrettably close to the North American position toward Cuba. During this period a document elaborated by intellectuals linked to the Catholic hierarchy laid out the church's own vision of Cuban civil society, based on the "social doctrine of the church." According to the document's authors, there was no civil society in Cuba since there was a total lack of organizations with "their own ideas, initiatives to carry out, and the development of the human spirit." The organizations of the church were considered "the only space for communion and true participation." For this situation to change in a positive way, according to the authors, a radical change of the system would be necessary to allow for the appearance of "intermediary groups and organizations that were free and autonomous" in relation to a subsidiary state that guaranteed stability but was organized as a participatory and pluralistic democracy. In the economic realm, this system could only be conceived of as based on private property and the market, the areas for the development of individual initiatives par excellence. On a normative level, the new civil society would be founded on an ethics consecrated in the traditional values of the church, which would produce a transition from the "structures of sin toward more authentic forms of community."

Only recently, first after the meeting of the Cuban president with the pope in the Vatican and later with the papal visit to the island, a new period of détente has begun. As might be expected in an organization as hierarchical as the Catholic Church, each of these shifts has had an effect on the messages delivered from the pulpits. Although the mobilizational capacity of the Catholic Church in Cuba is limited, one might expect its public role to increase in the future.

Development Nongovernmental Organizations

According to the reports released by Cuban NGOs, Cuba has 50 development NGOs. In reality, however, the number is probably less than two dozen, some of which have very limited roles or are in fact appendages of state institutions with very little decision-making autonomy. Nonetheless, they have had a very significant qualitative impact on Cuban society and have been particularly favored by financial help from their European and Canadian counterparts, as well as by their contacts and exchanges of experiences with other Latin American development NGOs. Although the cooperation between European NGOs and Cuba started in 1982, the cooperation boom dates from 1993. Thus, in 1990–1992 cooperation through this channel did not exceed US$7 million, but in the next three years it reached US$42 million. By 1994 there were 108 registered development projects undertaken with 66 foreign NGOs. Approximately half of these projects were administered by Cuban development NGOs, but only three accounted for the majority of the projects and financing. These projects concentrated on six priority areas: alternative energy, community development, the environment, popular education, women, and institutional development.

In various meetings with their European counterparts that took place between 1993 and 1995, Cuban NGOs demonstrated remarkable aggressiveness with regard to the bureaucratic roadblocks and state political controls that hindered their activities. They spoke directly against restrictions on the creation of new NGOs and excessive state tutelage over their functioning and in favor of greater autonomy in the administration and coordination of projects. In addition, they expressed the need for greater coordination among themselves and with foreign NGOs and for increased technical skills. They were against any type of imposition of foreign projects that would contribute to U.S. policy against Cuba.

Academic Centers and Publications

Many social research centers have had a strong impact (particularly between 1990 and 1995) on the unfolding debates that have involved professionals from different areas, including public servants, community leaders, social activists, and other kinds of people with the capacity to influence national public opinion. Not all of these centers have legal NGO status, but in practice they have played a very important role in the articulation of emerging subjects in civil society and in the establishment of communication networks. Something similar could be said of some academic publications that have had an impact beyond the intellectual community.

Community Social Movements

Since the end of the 1980s, community movements have begun to appear that differ from traditional neighborhood associations at both the normative and the procedural level. Above all, these movements, essentially of only local significance, have no linkages with each other. This is not simply a question of some deficiency (for example, the scarcity of mechanisms for sharing information and coordination) but a defining characteristic that makes them unique and induces integral transformations of communities based on sociocultural considerations, practices of self-governance, and the promotion of "diffuse" exercises in leadership and activism that are distinct from the ordinary conception of leaders and members.

The origins of these movements are diverse, but almost all of them have at their base state initiatives implemented by technical agencies, municipal governments, popular councils, etc. Their evolution is normally expressed in a diversification of their agendas (local development, assistance for vulnerable sectors, environmental protection, cultural revival, etc.) and a tendency toward autonomy that often puts them in conflict with the local authorities. In some cases, these movements have managed to arrive at some sort of "pacted autonomy" that gives them some margin for action in consultation with local authorities. It should be emphasized that none of these movements has the juridical status of civil association and this limits their capacity for decision making and action.

"Dissident" Groups

Opposition groups seeking legal recognition are numerous but very small. They focus their pronouncements on various themes, with an emphasis on human rights, but lack systematic proposals. The inclusion of these groups in civil society is problematic. First, they have little or no influence on national life, even at the local level. Second, they are mostly made up of people who wish to emigrate to the United States, and this contributes to the instability of their organizations and membership. Third, their politics and proposals exhibit a remarkable degree of compatibility with U.S. policy toward Cuba, and this gives them an antinational character that limits their mobilizational capacity. The numbers involved do not exceed a few hundred, and their activities are tolerated only as long as they remain strictly private.

Cooperatives

With the creation in 1993 of the Unidades Básicas de Producción Cooperatives (Basic Units of Cooperative Production—UBPC), the agrarian social structure underwent a radical change. Although official statistics are lacking, it is estimated that close to 400,000 people have entered the cooperative agricultural sector and that this number could increase in the future. The creation of the UBPC and the implementation of policies to stimulate the traditional cooperative sector constitute the boldest socializing action taken by the Cuban Revolution in the past few years. In the same vein, the cooperatives represent embryonic opportunities for civil society. The establishment of the UBPC has, however, been characterized by a utilitarian productivism that exposes them to the danger of oligarchization, increasing inequality, and predatory relations with their social settings. Avoiding these effects will depend not on their economic success—although it is indispensable—but on the general political design into which the cooperatives are inserted.

There are no associations of cooperatives; their members have been urged to join existing unions. This is consistent with the bureaucratic nature of political control, but by any reckoning it is incompatible both with the aims of a union and with the profile of a member of a cooperative. This situation, coupled with the newness of these associations, has precluded an autonomous public presence except at the strictly local level.

New Economic Actors

With the advance of the economic reform, new actors have appeared that carry out their activities fundamentally in the market even when they have linkages with the state. The place of these actors in civil society is related not so much to their degree of organization (which for the moment is practically nonexistent) as to their notable capacity to influence political communication, ideological production, and the socialization of market values.

One group that stands out among them is the new technocratic-entrepreneurial sector and, in particular, foreign entrepreneurs (as internalized actors because of their involvement in activities that have an effect on domestic society) or their associated Cuban counterparts. These sectors do not yet have a distinguishable organizational structure except for an Association of Spanish Entrepreneurs that has had a very small public role. Nonetheless, the particular way in which these sectors fit into the social spectrum allows for rapid communication both among them and between them and their state interlocutors. In fact, this capacity for communication is gradually converting them into actors in civil society. Moreover, it is likely that professional associations will soon develop.

A second actor is constituted by the close to 200,000 self-employed workers that swell the emerging informal sector of the Cuban economy. This sector is not organized. For a while the possibility of the state's stimulating some sort of association among these workers, either as a corporatist organization independent of the mass social organizations or as a union linked to the CTC, was entertained. In the end, it was decided that each self-employed worker should join the union related to his or her activity, but the independent workers have declined to do so. Presumably, however, to the extent that this social sector matures and becomes consolidated, it will tend to find its own opportunities for collective action, particularly if we keep in mind that in some segments of the informal economy an intense process of accumulation has taken place.

It is not hard to distinguish some distinctive traits of the emerging Cuban civil society. In programmatic terms, it largely identifies itself with the achievements of the revolutionary process and a socialist political system. Antisystemic elements remain irrelevant. This does not, however, mean that it is indifferent to the ways in which this system and particularly the political regime function. In this sense, these associations and communication networks inevitably push for reforms and changes in traditional politics. For example, they do not propose an end to one-party rule but demand a new form of relationship between the party and society.

In institutional terms, the organizations suffer from a certain ambiguity in relation to spaces and roles. To a certain extent, this is because of their newness ([over the late 1990s] the majority of them have not had more than a decade of precarious existence) and their lack of experience in how to do things in a new context. Their communication networks (interorganizational and with the rest of society) are fragile and unstable, marking a kind of particularistic atomization even when their discourses express a desire to engage in universal issues. Except for the strong corporatist discourse put forward by the NGOs, at least until 1996, there is no clear sense of self-identification and of belonging to a distinct space.

CIVIL SOCIETY BETWEEN THE STATE AND THE MARKET

In the preceding pages we have described the Cuban state as a promoter of opportunities for the development of civil society, particularly through programs that have led to increasing mobilization and involvement of ordinary citizens in public activity. This encouragement has, however, been countered by policies that attempt to limit the opportunity for autonomous association and visibility. This has discouraged the development of Cuban civil society in that civil society cannot be the result of a simple aggregation of sociocultural conditions but requires a civic-political construction linked to a climate of freedoms and rights. Thus, the Cuban state faces a contradictory situation in which it is trying to restrict the opportunities for citizen action that it has itself made possible through its undeniable and commendable social commitment.

Until March 1996, the Cuban state had not presented an official definition of what it understood civil society to be, although many public servants and politicians had publicly talked about the issue, either in negative or positive terms but always with great care. In practical terms, this translated into a degree of tolerance for the activities of NGOs and civil associations and respect for an incipient public debate that was out of tune with the monolithic ambitions of Cuban politics. This situation started changing when the passage of the interventionist Helms-Burton Act was imminent and the Cuban economy was showing the first signs of a recovery. Already in July 1995 one could see an increase in the frequency of pronouncements by Cuban political leaders concerning the dangers of U.S. plans with regard to Cuba and the meaning of the initiation of academic exchanges. Within a few months, what could have been merely a politically pertinent alert was transformed into a virtual offensive against civil society headed by the most conservative sectors of the state and party apparatuses.

In January 1996, informed readers of the official newspaper *Granma* read an article titled "¿Sociedad civil o gato por liebre?" with concern. By means of weakly supported theory aimed at highlighting the distance between Marxism and the term "civil society," the article denounced civil society as a neoliberal appendage, and from this point on NGOs were depicted as an institutional mechanism aimed at "undermining socialist society from within." Civil society was turned into an instrument "for promoting the internal fragmentation of Third World countries and for resisting any progressive role the state may play in social development." In many ways, it was depicted as playing the role of a "fifth column" in line with U.S. interests and those who promoted them—a simple "impostor" working for either neoliberalism or social democracy.

This article would not have amounted to much more than an inelegant observation had it not served as a direct antecedent to an official statement on the issue made in late March by the Central Committee of the Communist Party. In this statement, the party lashed out at many NGOs, particularly the most important academic institution in the country, and against certain publications that had entertained critical debate. And, perhaps most important for our purposes, it presented a capricious utilitarian definition of a "socialist civil society" composed of associations compatible with the political goals of the system: the traditional social and mass organizations and the NGOs that were considered acceptable according to certain ill-defined rules.

These imprecisions were most likely taken into account by the organizers of a theoretical discussion under the auspices of the party's Superior School just a few months after the official statement. In an extensive and widely published document, the participants in that discussion recognized the existence of a civil society in Cuba (a "socialist" or "Cuban" civil society) and acknowledged it as a legitimate area of action. Although they did not offer their own definition of civil society, they declared themselves against the use of the term "in its bourgeois conception and with the destabilizing focus and intentions of the enemies of the Cuban Revolution." In its place was stressed the specific meaning of the term in Cuba because of the existence of workers' political power and "consequently of the sole leadership of the party" and the preeminence of "social and especially state property." In contrast to the documents already mentioned, this document did not reduce civil society to NGOs, although these were given a distinctive role as "legitimators of the Cuban state." It asserted the urgent necessity for "a greater concordance between the profiles and interests of Cuban NGOs and the administrative and government bodies of our revolutionary state power" and urged that discussion of the issue continue.

The results of this political offensive, although less serious than expected given the aggressiveness of the document released in March, were negative for the development of Cuban civil society. In the short term, it led to the virtual dismantling of the Center for Studies on the Americas, with a consequent warning to the whole intellectual community in the country, the doubling of controls over existing NGOs, the dissolution of some groups in the process of formation, and the refusal to give new organizations legal recognition. In the long term—and perhaps this is much more relevant—the official definition of "civil society" implied an attempt by the state to implement a kind of control over civil society and its dynamic.

The principal reason given for this offensive was geopolitical: the U.S. government's preparation of a series of interventionist policies that focused on the emergent civil society as a possible subversive antisystemic space that would ultimately allow it to become an internal actor in Cuban politics. One should not dismiss this argument out of hand. Since the 1980s, under the influence of Jeanne Kirkpatrick's thesis, various U.S. administrations have viewed Cuban civil society—together with other governmental actors—in terms of their political objectives. This view was made explicit in the 1992 Torricelli and 1996 Helms-Burton Acts and concretized in the approval of funding by the U.S. Agency for International Development to help stimulate the activities of small opposition groups on the island, coordinate the work of the U.S. foundations associated with the island, and finance extreme-right groups, among other actions.

From this point of view it is understandable that the Cuban state would establish political filters and "padlocks" to protect national independence and prevent U.S. intervention, even when that meant constraints on liberties and rights. However, it seems counterproductive for it to try to do so by imposing limitations and bureaucratic controls on organizations that engage in development programs to the benefit of the popular majority and that have always shown a complete alignment with the state position on national independence.

The government's reaction has been attributed to the existence in Cuba of a political class and a bureaucracy that are unwilling to allow competition over the distribution of resources, even when this competition complements their action and is animated by the same political goals as the official discourse. In addition, it is undeniable that, to the extent that civil society has occupied the spaces abandoned by the state or simply shared social action agendas, the state has tended to harden its position vis-à-vis the emerging associations and to extend its control over them. This, however, does not fully explain the situation. For example, the relaxation of bureaucratic controls that took place during the period of greatest tolerance toward the organizations of civil society was minuscule in relation to the concessions made to the market and its agents in the unfolding of what has been labeled pragmatic economic reform. The explanation of the official attitudes toward Cuban civil society probably has other referents in addition to the patriotic reaction of the political class or the traditional bureaucratic zeal for its quota of power. Possibly an increasingly relevant starting point is the extent to which Cuba continues to pursue a place in the world capitalist market and consequently will have to carry out large-scale socioeconomic restructuring in accordance with the exigencies of that market.

The process of economic reform has had multiple social effects. First, it has produced a notable fragmentation of the popular subject in production, distribution, and consumption processes that tends to weaken its capacity for public action. In the opposite direction, it has strengthened sectors linked to the market and to the dynamic sectors of the economy (foreign investors and their domestic agents, autonomous state entrepreneurs, technocrats, the incipient domestic private sector) that under the present circumstances have a high capacity for ideological-cultural production. The possibility of these sectors' becoming a hegemonic social bloc has led to a substantial reformulation of the framework of political power.

Hypothetically, one could argue that the official reaction to the popular organizations and the critical debate within civil society increasingly respond to the requirements of the economic reform and the rearticulation of the country with the world capitalist economy. In the end, we cannot forget that the economic reform requires a gradual restructuring of the traditional alliance between the revolutionary political class and the popular sectors (with the consequent "modernization" of its articulating principles) in favor of a new relationship with the technocratic-entrepreneurial bloc. This requires that the traditional bureaucracy maintain tight political control that guarantees social peace and a climate favorable to accumulation—a role that it would assume in exchange for the economic resources necessary to maintain its project of power. The retreating bureaucracy prefers to dilute its incapacities in the market and in individualism rather than in popular associations, to the detriment of the socialist project that animates its discourse, and by doing so, paradoxically, it encourages the emergence of actors in civil society whose programmatic options lead inexorably to a capitalist restoration. From a certain point of view, the bureaucratic limitations placed on civil society nicely fulfill the prophecy that Marx denounced as the inexorable tendency of nineteenth-century capitalism: the dissolution of community where money is not the community.

IS THERE A PLACE FOR CIVIL SOCIETY IN CUBA?

The process described above refers to a predominant tendency but not the only one. As a result, it is subject to contradictions and mishaps that may open up the possibility of the pursuit of alternatives within civil society itself. First of all, although the political alliance between the revolutionary leadership and the popular sectors is in the process of redefinition, it remains a basic component of the political consensus in a country that perceives itself as facing a real external danger: U.S. aggression. This has forced the political class to put a brake on the more predatory aspects of the economic reform, to search for ways to attenuate its effects (personal subsidies, policies to reduce unemployment, the maintenance of basic social services, etc.), and at the same time to open spaces for social mobilization.

Although such mobilization has more frequently been pursued to maintain governability than to contribute to the democratization of the political system, its effects have been positive in relation to the opening of potential spaces for the development of autonomous associational projects. The experience of the popular councils is illustrative of this. Created as a body below the level of the municipal governments for the control of services and the mobilization of resources in specific geographical areas, some councils have become incipient autonomous actors, with authentic leadership and participatory plans for community development. The development of such initiatives is certainly constrained by restrictive legislation and bureaucratic impasses, but it should be recognized that they represent an auspicious sign in relation to the development of civil society and particularly of its popular organizations.

Cuban society, including its political leadership, faces a challenge with respect to the future space for civil society. If the leadership that emerged from the revolution wants to extend the socialist political project of national liberation started in 1959, it will be very difficult to do so in the absence of a vigorous civil society. It is through such a civil society that its popular components will be capable of reversing the mercantile colonization of the areas of social action, confronting the external danger, rearticulating the political consensus on a more pluralistic basis in an increasingly complex environment, and achieving the unfinished process of democratic construction initiated in 1959.

10.3 Fear and Loathing of Fidel Castro: Sources of U.S. Policy Toward Cuba (2002)

LOUIS A. PEREZ JR.

In the State Department I find there is a professional reluctance to mention Castro by name; curious psychological quirk, that.
—David E. Lilienthal (January 19, 1962) (*The Journals of David E. Lilienthal: The Harvest Years, 1959–1963*) (1971)

Few issues are as emotionally charged in American foreign policy as those relating to Cuba.
—Under Secretary of State David Newsom (1987)

We should never forget that new small countries can afford the luxury of acting on their emotions; great powers usually only damage themselves by giving way to emotional impulses.
—Assistant Secretary of State Gerard C. Smith (1960)

There is a personal quality to this three-and-a-half decade conflict that has rarely been noted, but which nevertheless remains very much at the heart of the relationship.

—Strategic Studies Institute, U.S. Army War College (1993)

I

For more than forty years the United States has pursued a policy designed to remove Fidel Castro from power. The policy has passed from one presidential administration to another, through ten successive administrations—three generations of presidents—Republicans and Democrats, liberals and conservatives: with minimum public debate—and even less success.

Defenders of the U.S. embargo appear undaunted by four decades of failure. The historic rationale for sanctions ended the moment the United States proclaimed the Cold War won. But the policy has persisted unchanged. On the contrary, changes—such as they have occurred, most notably in the form of the Torricelli Law (1992) and the Helms-Burton Law (1996)—have been mostly more of the same, always accompanied by confident predictions that the application of more sanctions would deliver the desired results—but always with the same results as before.

U.S. policy presently stands at once as an anomaly and an anachronism. It has outlived its historical time and outlasted its political purpose. It is derived from assumptions that long ago ceased to have relevance to the post–Cold War environment, designed as a response to threats that are no longer present, against adversaries that no longer exist. The security imperatives that originally justified sanctions, based on the proposition that Cuba was an instrument of Soviet designs, to be contained on every occasion and countered at every opportunity, are no longer plausible.

This is not to suggest, of course, that sanctions against Cuba are without a constituency, possessed of an agenda and endowed with the capacity to allocate substantial financial resources through which to obtain political influence. The lobbying success of the Cuban-American National Foundation (CANF) is well-known. Nor are sanctions without support among those for whom communism and the attending curtailment of freedom of speech and press and violation of human rights are a genuine anathema, although it should be noted that many who deplore conditions in Cuba often appear to have fewer objections to cordial relations with other countries whose human rights record is less than exemplary.

But the Cuban-American lobby and anti-communism alone do not explain adequately the steadfast commitment by the United States to a policy whose most remarkable feature has been its singular failure to achieve its intended objective. The explanation must thus be sought elsewhere. That U.S. policy may have long ago lost its initial instrumental rationale does not mean, of course, that it is without an internal logic. The sources of sanctions can be located within the larger context of the narratives by which North Americans fashioned the terms of self-representation. We must examine the realms of policy where the premise of the propriety of the U.S. purpose assumed the appearance of being normal and universal, where the prerogative of power often passed for the pursuit of beneficence.

Much can be understood by returning to the beginning, to the point at which the interplay of complex historical circumstances and political conditions acted to give U.S. policy its enduring form and function. The context of U.S. policy offers insight into the content, from which to derive purpose as a source of persistence. This is to conceive policy as an artefact, a product of social circumstance, culturally derived and ideologically driven which, when turned in on itself, can be made to yield insight into the assumptions by which policy persists long after it has been shown to have failed and is without prospects of success.

The United States response to Cuba was very much conditioned by its deepening antipathy toward Fidel Castro. Policies that Washington perceived as inimical to U.S. interests and contrary to professed values came to be associated entirely with the person of the Cuban leader. That Castro embraced communism was sin sufficient to guarantee U.S. ire. That it happened in a country where the United States had historically imposed its will and got its way deepened the insult of the injury.

II

The die of U.S. policy was cast forty years ago, the product of the moment, assembled as a series of improvisations and impulses, in response to circumstances and events, sometimes as conditioned reflexes, other times as pragmatic expedients. Policy calculations were derived from cognitive categories often flawed by a mixture of misinformation and misinterpretation, sometimes driven by factors wholly extraneous to Cuba, a process in which the U.S. response as often as not contributed to the very Cuban outcomes it sought to prevent.

What happened in Cuba in 1959 must be viewed as one of the more improbable events in the most unlikely of places. North Americans viewed early developments in Cuba with a mixture of incomprehension and incredulity. Much had to do with the pace of events: everything moved so quickly, as events with portentous implications seemed to accelerate from one day to the next, in vertiginous succession. There was no frame of reference with which to take measure of developments in Cuba: no precedent, no counterpart, but most of all, there was no understanding of the larger historical circumstances from which the Cuban revolution had emerged. Senator Barry Goldwater was entirely correct when he described a U.S. public who "shook their heads in bewilderment" at developments in Cuba.

Much had to do with the nature of the Cuban revolution. Most immediate was what to do with/what to do about the sheer effrontery of the challenge presented by Fidel Castro: defiant, strident, at times virulent, denunciations hours at a time, day after day, stretching into weeks and then months: unrelenting condemnation of the United States for nearly sixty years of deeds and misdeeds in Cuba. "There has not been a single public speech by Castro since the triumph of the revolution," U.S. Charge d'Affaires Daniel Braddock complained from Havana as early as February 1959, "in which he has not shown some feeling against the United States, the American press or big business concerns in Cuba." U.S. Ambassador Philip Bonsai agreed, and on repeated occasions registered deepening concern with tenor of Castro's speeches. "Tone and attitude arrogant, insolent and provocative," Bonsai cabled Washington on one occasion. He would subsequently characterise speeches by Castro variously as "fulminations," "tirades" and "mendacious, repetitious, and comprehensively fraudulent anti-Americanism." Never before—certainly never before in Latin America—had a duly constituted and recognised government mounted so strident an attack on the past policies and practices of the United States. "We have never in our national history," Henry Ramsey of the State Department Policy Planning Staff commented ruefully in 1960, "experienced anything quite like it in magnitude of anti-U.S. venom."

The Cuban version of sixty years of Cuba–U.S. relations was, of course, wholly incomprehensible in the United States, and therefore easy to dismiss and even easier to attribute to persons who knew no better or were engaged in mischief, in this instance most likely communists. On the other hand, it was also possible that Fidel Castro was insane. Director of the Office of Intelligence and Research for the American Republics Carlos Hall described Castro as a "complete hysteric with a messianic complex, if not a manic-depressive," while Lloyd Free of the United States Information Service wrote of "Castro's psychotic anti-American campaign." By late 1959 Ambassador Bonsai had come to characterise Castro as a "highly emotional individual" who suffered "definite mental unbalance at times," adding that a speech delivered by Castro in October 1959 "was not that of [a] sane man," Secretary of State Christian Herter had also come to believe that Castro was "showing signs of increasing mental instability," and by early 1960 President Dwight Eisenhower had arrived at the conclusion that the Cuban leader was beginning "to look like a madman."

All the while, Fidel Castro proceeded with the nationalisation of U.S. property, beginning with the sugar corporations and cattle ranches and expanding to oil refineries, utilities, mines, railroads, and banks. And when it was all over, everything—absolutely everything—previously owned by U.S. citizens, all $1.5 billion of it, had been nationalised.

But the worst was yet to come. If it is difficult to underestimate the incomprehension with which Washington viewed Cuban domestic policies, it is nearly impossible to overstate the horror with which it reacted to Cuban foreign policy, specifically the expanding ties with the Soviet Union. Officials would later use the word "shock" to describe their reaction to developments in Cuba. There is no reason to doubt them. "Cuba's move toward communism," Secretary of State Dean Rusk later wrote, "had been a deep shock to the American people." Kenneth Skoug, the State Department Cuba Desk officer, commented in 1987 that the policies of the Castro government "came as a shock to the American people" as it "allied itself eagerly and wholeheartedly to the chief threat of the national security of the United States." "The Cuban problem," warned Under Secretary of State Livingston Merchant as early as January 1960, "[is] the most difficult and dangerous in all the history of our relations with Latin America, possibly in all our foreign relations."

How utterly implausible all this was, occurring in a country hardly thought about before 1959 as anything more than a place of tropical promiscuity, frequented by North American tourists in pursuit of illicit pleasures and risque amusements. Cuba was not a country to be taken seriously. It was exotic, a place for fun, adventure and abandon; it was a background for honeymoons, a playground for vacations, a brothel, a casino, a cabaret, a good liberty port—a place for flings, sprees and binges. Suddenly everything was different.

III

It is, hence, within the realm of trauma that an understanding of U.S. policy must begin. If the proposition of the Cuban revolution as shock in the United States is to be rendered plausible, its reach must be pursued deeply into the national narratives by which the moral and strategic terms of U.S. security had been assembled. The degree to which people in the USA invested their well-being in certain "truths"—incontrovertible and previously unchallengeable verities—was at the core of the calculus by which U.S. national security was defined and defended for nearly 150 years. Central to these formulations was the time-honoured notion of the United States insulated by two oceans and hence distant—that is, "safe"—from the potential perils of a hostile world. To be sure, the evidence suggests that this sense of invulnerability may have started to erode in the age of the Inter-Continental Ballistic Missile. The spectre of the ICBM notwithstanding, however, two-oceans still seemed to provide the United States with some measure of comfort.

The presence of Soviet missiles in Cuba shattered the terms around which the United States had fashioned a sense of its well-being since early in the nineteenth century. The missiles in 1962, and the subsequent deployment of Soviet combat troops, the establishment of intelligence-gathering facilities, and the maintenance of a Soviet submarine base on the south coast of Cuba challenged some of the central assumptions upon which U.S. strategic planning had rested. In a security culture so very much shaped by notions of "balance of power" and "spheres of influence," the presence of the Soviet Union at a distance of a mere ninety miles wrought havoc on some of the most fundamental premises of U.S. strategic thinking.

But the Cuban revolution upset more than balance of power arrangements. It also shattered the sense of equanimity by which the United States had fixed its geo-political place in the world. Dean Rusk later wrote of the missiles as having "a devastating psychological impact on the American people" and, indeed, what happened in Cuba was a nightmare come to pass. That Fidel Castro had provided the Soviet Union with entree into the "backyard" of the United States simultaneously stunned and sickened U.S. officials. Suddenly the United States seemed vulnerable. "Soviet missiles installed in Cuba," Rusk feared, "could destroy our Strategic Air Command bases with almost no advance warning; missiles coming from the Soviet Union at least gave fifteen to twenty minutes to get our planes airborne. Roger Hilsman, formerly Director of the State Department Bureau of Intelligence and Research, recalled the Soviet missiles and reflected on "what this sudden jump in the nuclear megatonnage the Soviets could deliver on the American heartland would portend for the balance of power in the world." Former Assistant Secretary of State Edwin Martin invoked "historical" reason as the source of U.S. indignation. "It was accepted as a fact of life. Americans had always rejoiced in the oceans that separated them from hostile powers . . . [N]o matter how great our military capacity might be, Cuba could be an enemy base for airplanes, submarines, and missiles which could penetrate our defense."

Related too was the matter of the Monroe Doctrine. Early in the nineteenth century the United States had proclaimed the primacy of U.S. interests in the Western Hemisphere, and in so doing claimed a sphere of influence on a grand scale from which the European presence was proscribed. These elements were central to U.S. strategic thinking, for they acted to expand the spatial buffers by which the United States sought to keep perils of the world at bay. No other formulation occupied a more cherished place in the canons of U.S. foreign policy than the Monroe Doctrine. It assumed fully the proportions of a national article of faith, possessed of time-honoured reverence and long regarded as the cornerstone of U.S. Hemispheric policy. That its value as a means of security was more illusory than real mattered less than its importance as a symbol by which to mobilise the political consensus necessary to protect and promote U.S. interests in the region.

The Cuban revolution had a devastating effect on assumptions of U.S. well-being. That Fidel Castro appeared to have lent himself to Soviet designs and allowed the use of Cuba as a base from which to threaten U.S. security produced deep disquiet in Washington. "Cuba has been handed over to the Soviet Union as an instrument with which to undermine our position in Latin America and the world," President Eisenhower feared. More than a decade after the triumph of the Cuban revolution, former Ambassador Spruille Braden continued to despair over the shift in the balance of power, noting: "We have permitted the Kremlin to establish a strongly fortified military and naval base only 90 miles from our shores, equipped with missile sites and underground submarines pens, imperilling the very survival of the United States and the independence of all the American republics."

Fidel Castro challenged the plausibility of the Monroe Doctrine. Previously the fundamental formulations upon which the United States had based its primacy in the western hemisphere, in the name of the defence of the New World, appeared to have passed into desuetude. A policy tenet of historic and sentimental value was no more. "The fears were in part military," presidential advisor Walt Rostow later recalled, "in part ideological, in part an ancestral sense that the Monroe Doctrine had been unacceptably violated." The Monroe Doctrine, former Under Secretary of State George Ball later reflected, "forbade European powers from intrusion into the Western Hemisphere, which we regarded—though we avoided stating it in those terms—as our exclusive sphere of interest and influence," and to the point. "Castro took over in Cuba, slowly strengthening his dependence on Moscow and thus confronting America with a patent violation of a revered item of our national credo." "This is the end of the Monroe Doctrine," presidential advisor Adolf Berle confided ruefully to his diary in June 1960. Almost twenty years later, former Ambassador Willard Beaulac continued to brood about Castro and the Monroe Doctrine. "Castro's success in communising Cuba and converting it into a satellite of the Soviet Union," Beaulac wrote, "had reduced the Monroe Doctrine to a faded scrap of paper."

U.S. officials were unanimous: the emergence of a communist government in Cuba hosting a Soviet presence in the Caribbean was inadmissible. The implications were apparent and appeared equally dire to everyone. "The United States faces in Soviet-supported Castro's Cuba an intolerable threat to its prestige and its security which has to be eliminated," warned U.S. Charge Daniel Braddock. The Cubans had "unacceptably violated" the Monroe Doctrine, Rostow insisted, adding. "As Cuba emerged under communist control, a visceral reaction developed in the government that this was an outcome with which the United States could not live." Richard Nixon was categorical, warning that "Castro is a dangerous threat to our peace and security—and we cannot tolerate the presence of a communist regime 90 miles from our shores." CIA Deputy Director Richard Bissell arrived at the same conclusion: "A Communist government in Cuba, ninety miles from the U.S. mainland, was unacceptable."

The principal discursive categories through which the United States responded to developments in Cuba set in relief some of the more anomalous circumstances of policy formulations. The U.S. response was fashioned within the realm of absolutes under circumstances in which U.S. power was relative. The problem of Cuba was that the traditional assumptions about U.S. hegemony in the region were valid more as a framework for narrative constructs than as a guide for action, a circumstance which officials seemed only to have dimly perceived—if at all—and certainly one with which they were unprepared—indeed, unwilling—to accommodate. Under Secretary of State Ball articulated the U.S. position clearly and succinctly in 1964: "Castro's political, economic, and military dependence upon the Soviets [is] not negotiable."

IV

The problem with pronouncements of this nature was that the United States could not act in defence of historic interests—not, at least, without the risk of far more serious international complications. Much of the U.S. angst over Cuba had to do with the degree to which available means were inadequate to desired ends. The deepening U.S.–Cuba dispute early insinuated itself in the East-West conflict. By terms of the negotiated settlement of the October 1962 missile crisis with the Soviet Union, the United States renounced the use of direct military force against Cuba, and thereby privately acquiesced to what it publicly had insisted was unacceptable.

These were important developments, for henceforth U.S. policy calculations involving Cuba were subject to larger international constraints. This was the meaning of the otherwise opaque statement made by Assistant Secretary of State Edwin Martin in September 1963:

> To those who urge "stronger action," I can only say . . . that while military action against Cuba sounds like a simple proposition of "going in and getting it over with," this involves awesome risks. . . . Neither should it be forgotten that what might ensue from a "tougher policy" against Cuba could not necessarily be limited to a clean-cut military operation in the Caribbean. The inter-relation of our global foreign policies practically insures that such an operation could not be delimited but rather could be expected to spill over into other areas, with unpredictable results.

The Central Intelligence Agency (CIA) expressed the same thought in much more explicit if classified language three months later. "There are only two courses which would eliminate the Castro regime at an early date: an invasion or a complete blockade. Both of these actions would result in a major crisis between the U.S. and the U.S.S.R. (in Cuba and/or Berlin) and would produce substantial strains in the fabric of U.S. relations with other countries—allied as well as neutral."

Other factors also acted to limit U.S. options. Considerable attention was given to the repercussions of unilateral action against Cuba in Latin America. Assistant Secretary of State Thomas Mann was not alone in his early opposition to unilateral U.S. efforts to remove Fidel Castro. "[I]f we were to go all out to get Castro," Mann cautioned, "it would obviously be what we would do. What would the effect be in the other Latin American countries? [W]e have to maintain a steady pressure and keep our motives well disguised in this business." Assistant Secretary of State R. Roy Rubottom warned that if the United States were to "proceed at this time with unilateral intervention it would turn the clock back 27 years . . . [and] cause incalculable loss in the hemisphere." The Cuban revolution exerted an alarming thrall over many in Latin America, with obvious implications. Fidel Castro had "gained great prestige in Latin America," President Eisenhower understood, which meant that "governments elsewhere cannot oppose him too strongly since they are shaky with respect to the potentials of action by the mobs within their own countries to whom Castro's brand of demagoguery appeals."

The United States was loath to undertake unilateral military action for one more reason. No one in Washington doubted that the Cubans would resist a U.S. invasion. The United States would prevail in the short run, to be sure, but only at great cost, many feared, and then to face the prospects of prolonged guerrilla warfare. "The Castro regime has made extensive preparations to resist a U.S. military intervention," the Board of National Estimates cautioned. "It apparently plans for a strong initial defense against invasion and protracted warfare in the interior . . . Substantial numbers [of Cuban troops] . . . would continue a guerrilla resistance. . . . The establishment of a representative and accepted Cuban government would be greatly hindered by the persistence of terroristic underground resistance in the cities, and by continuing guerrilla resistance in outlying areas."

The imagery was far too dire for many officials to contemplate with equanimity. A small country resisting an invasion by a larger country evoked memories of the Soviet invasion of Hungary. "[T]he result would help the U.S.S.R.," the National Security Council warned, "since American intervention in Cuba would be considered in many parts of the world as a counterpart of Soviet intervention in Hungary." One reason President John F. Kennedy refused to commit U.S. military forces at the Bay of Pigs was related precisely to the fear of another Hungary. "Under no circumstances," presidential advisor Richard Goodwin recalled Kennedy explaining. "The minute I land one marine, we're into this thing up to our necks. I can't get the United States into a war, and then lose it, no matter what it takes. I'm not going to risk an American Hungary. And that's what it could be, a fucking slaughter."

V

That the United States disavowed the use of direct military force against Cuba did not, of course, mean that Washington was reconciled to the continued presence of Fidel Castro. On the contrary, successive administrations never wavered on the desirability to remove the Cuban leader. Options had been reduced, however, and the few that remained risked consequences that went far beyond the realm of Cuba–U.S. relations. "The limits in which we must erect a Cuban policy," Under Secretary Ball acknowledged, "are . . . well defined and narrow."

Fidel Castro expanded into a brooding preoccupation in the United States. He cast a dark shadow over the country's sense of well-being, a bad dream that would not go away. His presence was unacceptable but his removal was unobtainable. President Kennedy seems to have developed an abiding fixation on Castro after the Bay of Pigs, driven by a determination to avenge what many in the administration characterised as Castro's "humiliation" of the United States. In early 1962, a White House task force proclaimed that "a solution to the Cuban problem today carries the top priority in the United States Government—all else is secondary—no time, money, effort, or manpower is to be spared."

Former policy officials later recalled the deepening personal preoccupation in the Kennedy administration with Castro. "The reactions . . . were emotional, almost savage." Under Secretary Chester Bowles described the mood of the administration after the Bay of Pigs in his memoirs. "The President and the U.S. Government had been humiliated." Something had to be done "to punish Castro for defeating our abortive invasion attempt," Bowles recalled, adding "that we were now running the danger of becoming so obsessed with Castro that it was increasingly difficult for us to think rationally of the area as a whole. Only days after the Bay of Pigs fiasco, the National Security Council committed the administration to continue "all kinds of harassment to punish Castro for the humiliation he has brought to our door." Richard Goodwin later remembered Kennedy being "furious at Castro, who had humiliated his fledgling administration," while former Deputy Undersecretary of State U. Alexis Johnson recalled that Kennedy was "greatly provoked" by Fidel Castro, whom he considered "an affront and wanted him out." Added Johnson:

> Having a Marxist regime seventy miles [sic] from American soil worried President Kennedy and offended him. Castro provided a base of operations for expanding Soviet influence in Latin America and made the United States look impotent and rather foolish . . . [T]he President felt personally humiliated by a communist Cuba, and toppling Castro became something of an obsession for him.

CIA Deputy Director Bissell later wrote of "the Kennedy administration's obsession with Cuba," adding: "From their perspective, Castro won the first round at the Bay of Pigs. He had defeated the Kennedy team: they were bitter and they could not tolerate his getting away with it. The president and his brother were ready to avenge their personal embarrassment by overthrowing their enemy at any cost." "We were hysterical about Castro at the time of the Bay of Pigs and thereafter," former Secretary of Defense Robert McNamara recalled years later, "and there was pressure from [President Kennedy and the Attorney General] to do something about Castro."

Notions of injured national pride, of humiliation and embarrassment, all attributed directly to the person of Fidel Castro, served to shape the context in which North American officials developed policy toward Cuba. Richard Nixon sustained an enduring preoccupation with Fidel Castro, one that dated back to his years as Vice President. "Cuba was a neuralgic problem for Nixon," Henry Kissinger recalled years later. On the matter of Fidel Castro, Nixon was adamant. "There'll be no change toward that bastard while I'm President," he vowed to an aide.

The casting of Castro as an "affront," of having "offended the United States," but most of all the proposition of Castro as a source of humiliation, insinuated itself deeply into U.S. sensibilities and early served to transform Castro into something of an enduring national obsession. The very presence of Castro seemed to diminish the prestige of the United States at home and abroad. He was an embarrassment. Communism in Cuba appeared to make a mockery of the U.S. claim to leadership of the Free World, for if the United States could not contain the expansion of communism 90 miles from its own shores, how could it be expected to resist communism in Europe, Asia, and Africa? An editorial from the *Battle Creek Enquirer and News* entered into the Congressional Record bristled with indignation:

> How much more of Fidel Castro can the United States swallow and still maintain—not its prestige and image abroad—but its own self-respect at home? Since the signing of the Declaration of Independence 185 years ago, this Nation has never submitted to such indignities as those heaped upon it in the last 2 years by the Cuban dictator . . . How can the United States talk of resisting Russia in Germany and elsewhere in the world when a little nation of about 6 million people tweaks the nose and pulls the beard of Uncle Sam as it please?

"We have become the laughing stock of the world," Representative Steven B. Derounian decried in Congress, adding:

> We have given the world high-sounding phrases, but have backed down recently whenever action has been required. The world has looked to America for leadership but has found only blundering retreat. Now it is in the open for all to see that a little twerp of a man, holding nary a high card in his hand, has managed to bluff the leaders of the most powerful Nation in the world and

forced them to cower in the corner . . . [W]e cannot let this situation continue any longer. Castro is making this powerful Nation appear ridiculous in the eyes of the world.

"Cuba," Congressman Mendel Rivers agreed indignantly, "stands as an insult to American prestige, a challenge to American dignity." Senator Barry Goldwater described the presence of Fidel Castro as "a disgrace and an affront which diminishes the world's respect for us in direct ratio to the length of time we permit the situation to go unchallenged." Decades later George Ball wrote with an ire reminiscent of the early 1960s. "Castro's Cuba formed an overhanging cloud of public shame and obsession. Many Americans felt outraged and vulnerable that a Communist outpost should exist so close to their country. Castro's Soviet ties seemed an affront to our history."

VI

Unable to topple Fidel Castro from without, the United States resorted to sanctions as a means to induce collapse from within. Many in Washington had initially viewed sanctions with misgivings, reluctant to adopt measures that punished the Cuban people for the sins of the Cuban government. But the realisation that Fidel Castro enjoyed widespread popular support acted early to diminish official reservations. Under Secretary of State Douglas Dillon was originally opposed to actions that "would have a serious effect on the Cuban people," but soon changed his mind. "[W]e need not be so careful about actions of this kind, since the Cuban people [are] responsible for the regime." It was thus permissible to punish the Cuban people. Explained Assistant Secretary of State Rubottom:

> We have gone as far as we can in trying to distinguish between the Cuban people and their present government, much as we sympathize with the plight of what we believe to be the great majority of Cubans. . . [T]he Cuban "people" have allowed themselves to be hoodwinked and out-maneuvered, assuming that some of them have been alert, by the communists.

Economic sanctions were designed in conjunction with covert action. Indeed, the pairing of sanctions with sabotage was designed to foster economic disarray, disrupt production systems, and increase domestic distress through shortages and scarcities as a way to generate popular discontent with Fidel Castro and thereby impair his ability to govern and undermine his capacity to manage the economy. Sanctions were designed to bestir the Cuban people to political action by subjecting the population to hardship as a way to erode popular support of the Castro government. The intent was to politicise hunger as a means of promoting popular disaffection, in the hope that driven by want and motivated by despair Cubans would rise up and oust Fidel Castro. President Eisenhower approved economic sanctions in the expectation that "if [the Cuban people] are hungry, they will throw Castro out." Eisenhower embarked on well-defined policy driven by the "primary objective . . . to establish conditions which will bring home to the Cuban people the cost of Castro's policies and of his Soviet orientation." The president continued:

> I anticipate that, as the situation unfolds, we shall be obliged to take further economic measures which will have the effect of impressing on the Cuban people the cost of this Communist orientation. We hope, naturally, that these measures will not be so drastic or irreversible that they will permanently impair the basic mutuality of interests of Cuba and this country.

"[A] change in the sentiment of the lower classes," CIA Director Allen Dulles similarly calculated, "would only occur over a long period of time, probably as a result of economic difficulties." Assistant Secretary of State Thomas Mann agreed, predicting that sanctions would "exert a serious pressure on the Cuban economy and contribute to the growing dissatisfaction and unrest in the country." President Kennedy was also confident that the embargo would hasten Fidel Castro's departure as a result of the "rising discomfort among hungry Cubans." General Edward Lansdale, charged with the coordination of covert action against Cuba, outlined U.S. objectives:

> Basically, the [covert] operation is to bring about the revolt of the Cuban people. The revolt will overthrow the Communist regime and institute a new government with which the United States can live in peace . . . The political actions will be assisted by economic warfare to induce failure of the Communist regime to supply Cuba's economic needs, [and] psychological operations to turn the people's resentment against the regime.

There was, moreover, always the possibility that economic difficulties might provoke a crisis within the Cuban government itself. "[E]conomic hardship in Cuba . . . ," CIA Director John McCone predicted, "supplemented by sabotage measures, would create a situation in Cuba in which it would be possible to subvert military leaders to the point of their acting to overthrow Castro."

The purpose of U.S. policy was set in place early, the cornerstone of which was sanctions against the Cuban people as a way to remove Fidel Castro from within. "The only foreseeable means of alienating internal support," concluded Deputy Assistant Secretary of State Lester Mallory, "is through disenchantment and disaffection based on economic dissatisfaction and hardship." Mallory recommended that "every possible means should be undertaken promptly to weaken the economic life of Cuba" as a means "to bring about hunger, desperation and [the] overthrow of the government." Assistant Secretary Rubottom similarly outlined the approach by which "the United States use judiciously elected economic pressures . . . in order to engender more public discomfort and discontent and thereby to expose to the Cuban masses Castro's responsibility for mishandling their affairs."

The latter point was essential to the U.S. purpose, for central to U.S. objectives was the need to maintain the appearance that the collapse of Fidel Castro was the result of conditions from within, by Cubans themselves, the product of government economic mismanagement, and thereby avoiding appearances of U.S. involvement. The United States sought to produce disarray in the Cuban economy but in such a fashion as to lay responsibility directly on Fidel Castro. The goal of the United States, Rubottom affirmed, was to make "Castro's downfall seem to be the result of his own mistakes." Ambassador Bonsai in Havana early stressed the importance of appearance: "It is important that the inevitable downfall of the present Government not be attributed to any important extent to economic sanctions from the United States as major factor." The United States, Bonsai wrote in 1970, sought "to make it clear that when Castro fell, his overthrow would be due to inside and not outside causes." This was the purport of a lengthy 1963 memorandum by George Denney, Director of State Department Bureau of Intelligence and Research. The idea was to eliminate Castro "without resort to invasion or attributable acts of violence and violations of international law," specifically by "creating the necessary preconditions for nationalist upheaval inside Cuba . . . as a result of internal stresses and in response to forces largely, if not wholly, unattributable to the U.S." Denney continued:

> If the Castro/Communist experiment will appear to have failed not on its own merits but as a result of obvious or inadequately disguised U.S. intervention, or as a consequence of the fraudulent invocation . . . of a unilateral and lopsided Monroe Doctrine, the validity of Castro's revolutionary course might remain unquestioned. This Castro/Communist experiment constitutes a genuine social revolution, albeit a perverted one. If it is interrupted by the force of the world's foremost "imperialist" and "capitalist" power in the absence of a major provocation, such action will discredit the U.S. and tend to validate the uncompleted experiment . . . Direct U.S. assistance should be avoided . . . Excessive U.S. or even foreign assistance or involvement will become known and thus tend to sap nationalist initiative, lessen revolutionary motivation and appeal, and allow Castro convincingly to blame the U.S.

Covert action played an important role in support of U.S. objectives, principally by laying siege to the Cuban economy and thereby making the island all the more susceptible to economic sanctions. For more than a decade, the United States engaged in acts that today would be understood as state-sponsored terrorism, including scores of assassination attempts against Fidel Castro, the infiltration of sabotage teams, and the disruption of Cuban agricultural and industrial production capacities. The CIA was specifically enjoined "to stress economic sabotage." Four key sectors of the Cuban economy were targeted: electric power facilities, including the destruction of electric generating plants; petroleum refineries, storage facilities, and tankers; railroad and transportation infrastructure, including bridges, railroad tracks, and rolling stock as well as port, shipping, and maritime facilities; and production and manufacturing sectors, including the industrial facilities, sugar cane fields and mills, and communication systems. The assault against the Cuban economy involved arson of cane fields, sabotage of machinery, and acts of chemical warfare, including the spreading of chemicals in sugar cane fields to sicken Cuban cane cutters. One operation was designed "to initiate and conduct aggressive psychological warfare operations including calling for work stoppages, slow-downs, sabotage, and other forms of military mass action and widespread overt resistance . . . conduct major sabotage operations targets against Cuban industry and public utilities, i.e., refineries, power plants, transportation, and communication." Another project undertook a "subtle sabotage program" that included "the contamination of fuels and lubricants [and] the introduction of foreign material into moving parts of machinery." Alexander Haig recalled the organisation of three or four "major operations against Cuba every month during the 1960s, noting: "The targets were always economic." The purpose of covert operations, former Deputy Secretary of Defense Roswell Gilpatric explained years later, was to "so undermine, so disrupt the Cuban system under Castro that it could not be effective."

The Department of Defense similarly designed projects to "accomplish the objective of economic harassment." One plan specifically enjoined "[f]uel and food supplies should be sabotaged," while another directive prescribed "major acts of sabotage on shipping destined for Cuba and on key installations in Cuba." Another project involved visible preparations for a feigned invasion of Cuba, including an augmented Marine presence at the Guantanamo Naval Station, increasing naval operations outside Cuban waters, and "heckler" flights in which high performance aircraft flew toward Cuba at high velocity and veered away just prior to penetrating Cuban air space, all planned to coincide with the sugar harvest. "[I]t is desirable," commented a Joint Chiefs of Staff report, "that the [Cover and Deception] plan be designed to cause a reaction of great enough magnitude to include a call-up of the militia or a complete disruption of the available labour force. Therefore, it must be capable of execution either at the beginning of the harvest period, or at least no later than a date when the harvest is in full swing." And to the point: "[R]esulting in the disruption of the available labor force during the latter portion of the harvest period."

Through much of the 1970s and 1980s the United States maintained unremitting pressure on Cuba. Relations between both countries improved slightly if only briefly under the administration of Jimmy Carter. However, the possibility of expanded ties was frustrated by U.S. efforts to demand "linkages," that is, imposing conditions as a requirement for normal relations that included Cuba distancing itself from the Soviet Union and the withdrawal of Cuban armed forces from Africa. Cuba rejected these demands outright.

The administration of Ronald Reagan adopted an increasingly hard line against Cuba, charging Castro with subversion and mischief in Central America. Reagan increased restrictions on travel from the U.S. to Cuba, suspending U.S. tourism as a way to deprive the island of a source of foreign exchange. In 1985, the United States government inaugurated Radio Marti.* In the following year Washington tightened still further the trade and financial embargo against Cuba. The Reagan administration also manoeuvred behind the scenes to make Cuban foreign debt negotiations as difficult as possible. New pressure was added on U.S. corporations operating in third countries to curtail trade with Cuba. New limits were placed on cash and gifts Cubans residing in the United States were able to send to family members on the island.

VII

Certainly the impact of U.S. sanctions and sabotage waned considerably after the 1960s, as Cuba was more fully integrated into the trade system of the socialist bloc. The embargo remained in place, to be sure, but its usefulness as an instrument through which to pursue the removal of Fidel Castro diminished substantially.

Conditions changed radically in the 1990s. These were years of retrenchment and reversal in Cuba, a time during which Cuban relations with the Soviet Union deteriorated, the electoral defeat of the Sandinistas in Nicaragua, the end of the insurgency in El Salvador, and a diminishing Cuban presence in Africa. These were years, too, of the disintegration of the socialist bloc in Eastern Europe and, of course, the collapse of the Soviet Union. By the end of 1992 Cuba had lost nearly 95 percent of the total value of its trade with the former socialist bloc.

For the second time in three decades Cuba's commercial relations with its principal trade partners collapsed, causing profound dislocation and disruption inside the island. Having lost Soviet patronage, Cuba found itself increasingly isolated and beleaguered, faced with dwindling aid, decreasing foreign exchange reserves, and diminishing resources, and confronting the need to ration scarce goods and reduce declining services.

The opportunity for the United States to settle old scores presented itself during the 1990s. At the precise moment that Cuba faced new and perhaps

*Radio Martí is a radio station owned by the U.S. government as part of the Voice of America network that broadcasts news and other programming into nations with restrictions on freedom of the press. Radio Martí targets Cuba specifically.

the most serious round of difficulties at home and reversals abroad, Washington acted to expand the scope and increase the severity of economic sanctions. The passage of the Torricelli Law (1992) and the Helms-Burton Law (1996) signalled the renewal of U.S. determination to oust Fidel Castro. Deteriorating conditions in Cuba encouraged the belief in the United States that the time was right to deliver the coup de grace to its enduring nemesis ninety miles away. The appeal of expanded sanctions was based on the perception that without Soviet aid Fidel Castro was vulnerable to increased U.S. pressure. "Castro is as weak as he has ever been," Senator Bob Graham argued during the debate surrounding the Torricelli Bill. Senator Joseph Lieberman defended the need to strengthen the embargo, insisting that "[t]his is no time to reduce the pressure on Castro," for renewed sanctions "would deal a significant blow to the Cuban economy." Representative Dan Burton agreed: "[T]his is the endgame for Fidel Castro. His time is up. Almost all of his dictator friends are dead, in jail, or disgraced." Representative Robert Torricelli was confident in his prediction: "The economic situation is already untenable. It is unlikely that with the tightening of the embargo Castro can be maintained for long."

The expansion of the embargo was designed to deepen Cuban economic distress as a means of political change, once more an effort to use hardship as a way to foment rebellion among the Cuban people. The Torricelli and Helms-Burton laws were particularly harsh, both in timing and in kind, for they sought to visit upon the Cuban people unrelieved punishment, to make daily life in Cuba as difficult and grim as possible, to increase Cuban suffering in measured but sustained increments, at every turn, at every opportunity at a time when Cubans were already reeling from scarcities in goods and the disruptions of services in the wake of the Soviet collapse. Cubans faced a new round of shortages, increased rationing, declining services, and growing scarcities, where the needs of everyday life in their most ordinary and commonplace form were met often only by Herculean efforts. Representative Torricelli proclaimed his intention succinctly: "My objective is to wreak havoc in Cuba . . . My task is to bring down Fidel Castro."

VIII

Sanctions did indeed contribute to exacerbating Cuban economic hardship and, from time to time, even produced the internal opposition desired by the United States. But the larger failure of the embargo—from the outset—was due principally to the contradictions of U.S. policy. So fully determined to topple Castro, Washington employed a variety of contradictory strategies, seemingly oblivious to the ways that these policies tended to counteract and neutralise each other. The embargo initially inflicted the greatest hardship on those social groups with the greatest ideological affinity with the United States, including large sectors of the Cuban middle class, which is to say those social groups most fully assimilated into U.S. normative systems. Sanctions took their toll first on middle class Cubans, adding—as anticipated—to their discontent, and increasing their dissatisfaction. The suspension of U.S. exports, for example, including consumer commodities, durable goods and spare parts, likewise played havoc with retail merchants, manufacturers and industrialists, many of whom found it impossible to continue in business and increasingly difficult to remain in Cuba long before their properties were nationalised. Richard Cushing of the Bureau of Inter-American Affairs travelled to Havana in early 1960 and took note of the early effects of scarcity. "There are increasing shortages of certain luxury food items such as butter and imported canned goods," Cushing observed, "but, from all indications, the poor still are eating fairly well because of ceiling prices on the basic popular food items . . . Shortages of import items such as spare machine parts, pharmaceutical supplies, and electrical appliances are beginning to plague the upper and middle classes." Six months later, President Eisenhower wrote with a pleased if misplaced sense of achievement of "the great majority of the liberal middle-class elements in Cuba, which were primarily responsible for Castro's accession to power, have now withdrawn their support and many have fled the country to engage in open opposition." The first casualties were those social classes historically aligned with the United States, who shared U.S. values and identified with U.S. ways, and who in defence of their own interests could simultaneously have been relied upon to defend U.S. interests.

The United States also encouraged Cuban immigration as a means of propaganda against Castro. "We should speak of difficulties in Cuba as though they were a natural catastrophe warranting the sympathy of all free countries for the Cuban people," Assistant Secretary of State Gerard Smith explained U.S. immigration strategies. "Our propaganda line should be in favor of the 'poor Cubans'." Smith continued:

> We should organize to receive refugees from Cuba as the Americans did in the case of Hungary. If necessary, we should arrange to house and feed Cubans in special camps in Florida. As the Austrians did, we should revise our immigration laws to favor refugees and urge other members of the OAS to do the same. We should use such a program to demonstrate the rule that when given a chance people generally flee toward freedom and away from communism. Our case would be improved if Castro took military steps to block the flow of refugees. A few pictures of Castro's men shooting refugees attempting to escape would do more to hurt Castro than a host of economic sanctions.

It was the hope of U.S. officials, moreover, that the flight of the middle class and the ensuing "brain drain" would contribute further to Cuban economic difficulties. "Cuba has become far more exposed and vulnerable to economic pressure," Under Secretary Ball insisted in 1964, "because Castro's internal policies have driven into exile several hundred thousand Cubans—the managerial and professional elite. There is now a great shortage of skills."

The concept of sanctions, from the early 1960s up to the 1990s, was deeply flawed. The pressures created by four decades of sanctions—and these pressures were at times real and substantial—were in large part relieved by Cuban emigration. Even as the United States tightened economic pressure on Cuba, it also and at the same time loosened immigration restrictions for Cubans, thereby providing relief from the very distress it succeeded in creating.

Measures designed to produce economic distress thus resulted less in organised opposition than in sustained emigration. For sanctions to have had the desired political effects, it would have been necessary to have discouraged or otherwise deterred the departure of hundreds of thousands of Cubans, whose very discontent was the objective of US policy. The logic of the policy required containing Cuban discontent inside Cuba.

Immigration policies, and especially the Cuban Adjustment Act (1966), whereby all Cubans who reached U.S. shores were guaranteed political asylum in the United States, served to facilitate the departure of the very Cubans whose discontent was the goal of sanctions, and actually contributed to the consolidation of the Castro government. Confronting daily increasing hardships and deteriorating living conditions, vast numbers of Cubans sought relief through emigration rather than risk even greater difficulties by engaging in political opposition—a wholly reasonable and eminently rational decision, made all the more compelling by the presence in Florida of a community of friends and families and the promise of public assistance. That more than one million Cubans were in the end sufficiently discontented with conditions on the island to abandon their homes, friends and family, often under difficult and hazardous circumstances, provides powerful testimony to the depth of popular discontent and, in fact, in some measure corroborates the effectiveness of U.S. policy. Sanctions did indeed add to economic distress and contribute to hardships for countless hundreds of thousands of Cubans, for many of whom the better part of valour was to seek relief through migration abroad rather than risk protest at home. As long as the United States was prepared to provide Cubans with relief through immigration, the policy of sanctions was transformed into an ill-conceived means to an improbable end. As long as the United States persisted both in applying sanctions and permitting unrestricted emigration, the principal effect of the embargo was to exacerbate Cuban economic difficulties and increase pressure on Cubans to emigrate.

IX

Dispassionate policy discourse on Cuba under Fidel Castro was impossible. Castro was transformed simultaneously into an anathema and phantasm, unscrupulous and perhaps unbalanced, possessed by demons and given to evil doings, a wicked man with whom honourable men could not treat. "He is a thug," thundered Senator Connie Mack in 1992. "He is a murderer. There is no question about that. You cannot enter into some kind of normal relations with an individual like this." Georgie Ann Geyer's 1991 biography of Fidel Castro gave vivid voice to some of the more excessive forms of anti-Castro sentiment. According to Geyer, Fidel Castro was partly responsible for the Central American immigration to the United States, the hostages in Iran, and the Persian Gulf realignment; he was implicated in the assassination of President Kennedy. Without Fidel Castro there would have been no Sandinistas, no Grenada, no guerrillas in Latin America, no Marxists in Africa, no terrorists in the Middle East. Fidel Castro was "wholly without human principle," "always a destroyer," and with "dreams of world conquest." He "invented, or perfected, or expanded the uses of every single one of the techniques of guerrilla warfare and of terrorism." In sum, Geyer pronounced, Fidel Castro was "an alchemist of the law, the century's doctor of disintegration and its vicar of breakdown."

The issue of U.S. relations with Cuba under Fidel Castro early ceased to be a matter of rational policy calculation and passed into the realm of pathology. "As a nation," observed former Secretary of State Cyrus Vance, "we seemed unable to maintain a sense of perspective about Cuba." A report from the Strategic Studies Institute of the U.S. Army War College in 1993 cautioned against the "innate emotional appeal" driving U.S. policy, adding:

> To many, Castro is not merely an adversary, but an enemy—an embodiment of evil who must be punished for his defiance of the United States as well as for other reprehensible deeds. In this sense, U.S. policy has sought more than a simple solution or containment of Cuba. There is a desire to hurt the enemy that is mirrored in the malevolence that Castro has exhibited towards us. If Fidel suffers from a "nemesis complex," so most assuredly do we.

X

The policy bears the traces of the trauma by which purpose was fixed more than forty years ago and derives sustenance in the umbrage that Fidel Castro visited upon the United States. Castro deeply offended U.S. sensibilities. For more than four decades he has haunted the United States: a breathing, living reminder of the limits of U.S. power. He challenged long-cherished notions about national well-being and upset prevailing notions of the rightful order of things. This is exorcism in the guise of policy, an effort to purge Fidel Castro as an evil spirit who has tormented U.S. equanimity for more than four decades. Cultures cope with the demons that torment them in different ways and indeed the practice of exorcism assumes many forms. Castro occupies a place of almost singular distinction in that nether world to which the United States banishes its demons. Fidel Castro is the man the U.S. public loves to hate: political conflict personified, loaded with Manichaen insinuations, the frustration of decades of unsuccessful attempts to force Cuba to bend to the U.S. will vented on one man. U.S. policy possesses a punitive aspect to its purpose, a determination to punish Castro, a way to avenge past wrongs, which in this instance means vanquishing Fidel Castro once and for all. *New York Times* foreign affairs editor Thomas Friedman was entirely correct in suggesting that the U.S. position on Cuba is "not really a policy. It's an attitude—a blind hunger for revenge against Mr. Castro." That Fidel Castro has endured at all, that he has survived countless U.S.-sponsored assassination attempts, one armed invasion, and four decades of economic sanctions and diplomatic isolation, has resulted in no small amount of confoundment and consternation in Washington. Only the total and unconditional vanquishing of Fidel Castro can vindicate the policy to which the United States has so fully committed itself. By the end of the 1990s U.S. policy assumed a life of its own. Its very longevity serves as the principal rationale for its continuance.

The United States refuses to deal with Fidel Castro in any mode other than a repentant one. Indeed, reconciliation with an unrepentant Castro is almost inconceivable. Fidel Castro has thus far been unwilling to submit to the demand that President Ronald Reagan made to the sandinistas: to say "Uncle." When asked in 1982 under what conditions the United States would consider normalisation of relations with Cuba, Reagan responded: "What it would take is Fidel Castro, recognising that he made the wrong choice quite a while ago, and that he sincerely and honestly wants to rejoin the family of American nations and become a part of the Western Hemisphere." President George [H.W.] Bush similarly encouraged Castro "to lighten up," vowing: "Unless Fidel Castro is willing to change his policies and behaviour, we will maintain our present policy toward Cuba." Kenneth Skoug, former chief of the Cuba desk at the State Department, made the same point. Fidel Castro "has never been prepared to change his principles or his politics." Skoug affirmed, adding: "While Castro holds power, genuine rapprochement between the United States and Cuba is difficult to contemplate . . . Cuba is no longer a danger to the United States, but it will not be turned around. After the Castro era, rapprochement is all but inevitable." Representative Torricelli made the same point in 1992: "The United States has an interest in ending the Castro regime's tyranny over Cuba. That is a simple fact. We have endured decades of Cuban subversion in this hemisphere and at trouble spots across the globe. We were brought to the brink of nuclear war by Castro's maniacal hatred of the United States. Clearly, this is a regime with which we can reach no accommodation."

More than forty years after the triumph of the Cuban revolution, the United States shows no disposition to arrive at an understanding with Fidel Castro: a time longer than the U.S. refusal to recognise the Soviet Union, longer than the refusal to normalise relations with China, longer than it took to reconcile with post-war Vietnam. To put it another way, Cuba has been under U.S. economic sanctions for almost half its existence as an independent republic. The Cuba policy of the United States has entangled itself in multiple layers of contradictions and inconsistencies, for which there is no resolution except the passing of Fidel Castro. The Helms-Burton Act made the issue explicit: there can be no normalisation of relations with Cuba as long as Fidel Castro remains in power.

At the heart of the difficulty with Cuba [as of 2003] is that the United States is in conflict with the consequences of past policy. What may appear to U.S. eyes as Cuban intransigence is, in part, a manifestation of Cuban refusal to submit to the United States, borne by a people still convinced that they have a right of self-determination and national sovereignty. Not for the first time in the twentieth century, the larger moral seems to have gone quite unheeded. Small, obstinately independent peoples, imbued with exalted if perhaps romantic notions of nation, can be crushed but never conquered, not even by superpowers, and as soon as the big power weakens or turns its attention elsewhere, they will be back. It is precisely with such people that a mutually satisfactory reconciliation must be negotiated if long-term accommodation has any prospect of success.

Sanctions have been less a source of a solution than a cause of the problem. The Cuban condition is in varying degrees historically a function of its relations with the United States. It could be not be otherwise. For forty years the United States has pursued unabashedly a policy designed to destroy the Cuban government. It should not come as a surprise, hence, that internal security has developed into an obsession in Cuba. It is the height of cynicism for the United States to condemn Cuba for the absence of civil liberties and political freedoms, on one hand, and, on the other, to have pursued policies variously employing assassination, subversion, sabotage and threatened invasions as means to topple the government of Fidel Castro. U.S. policy does nothing to contribute to an environment in which civil liberties and political freedoms can flourish. So too with the failures of the Cuban economy. The embargo must be factored as a source of Cuban economic woes—indeed, that has been its overriding objective. The degree to which deteriorating economic conditions have been the result of internal factors, on one hand, and the effect of external pressures, on the other, may never be knowable but neither is the relationship disputable.

The only certainty in an otherwise wholly unpredictable relationship is that relations between both countries will resume, some day: perhaps sooner, but certainly later. The logic of geography and history simply provides for no other alternative. Cuba and the United States cannot escape each other.

The important questions, hence, are driven not by "if" but by "when"— and under what circumstances and with what enduring legacies—will relations resume, for when relations do become "normal" again, the people of each country will carry memories of the last four decades for years to come. How these memories will shape the future can be considered only in the realm of conjecture, of course, but it requires no gift of prophecy to understand that the deeper the wounds the more difficult the healing. Cubans and the U.S. population will long be affected by these years of "non-relations." It is in the nature of long-standing close ties between both nations, in those realms of shared vulnerabilties, that fallings-out tend to be particularly acrimonious, and that the negotiation of reconciliation and the renewal of trust must be considered among the most difficult transactions to complete.

SUGGESTIONS FOR FURTHER READING

Anderson, Jon. *Che Guevara: A Revolutionary Life.* New York: Grove Press, 1997.

Chaffee, Wilber, and Gary Prevost, eds. *Cuba—A Different America.* Savage, Md.: Rowman and Littlefield, 1992.

Centeno, Miguel A., and Mauricio Font, eds. *Toward a New Cuba.* Boulder, Colo.: Lynne Rienner, 1997.

del Águila, Juan M. "Development, Revolution, and Decay in Cuba," in *Latin American Politics and Development,* 4th ed., ed. Howard J. Wiarda, and Harvey F. Kline. Boulder, Colo.: Westview Press, 1996.

Franklin, Jane. *The Cuban Revolution and the United States: A Chronological History.* Melbourne, Australia: Ocean Press, 1997.

Kirk, John. *Between God and Party: Religion and Politics in Revolutionary Cuba.* New York: Pathfinder Press, 1989.

León, Francisco "Socialism and Sociolism," in *Toward a New Cuba,* ed. Miguel A. Centeno and Mauricio Font. Boulder, Colo.: Lynne Rienner, 1997, 39–51.

Lutjens, Sheryl. *The State, Bureaucracy and Cuban Schools: Power and Participation.* Boulder, Colo.: Westview Press, 1996.

Pérez, Louis A. *Cuba: Between Reform and Revolution.* New York: Oxford University Press, 1995.

Roman, Peter. *Cuba's Experiment with Representative Government.* Boulder, Colo.: Westview Press, 1999.

Smith, Wayne S. *The Closest of Enemies: A Personal and Diplomatic Account of U.S.–Cuba Relations Since 1957.* New York: Norton, 1987.

Smith, Lois M., and Alfred Padula. *Sex and Revolution: Women in Socialist Cuba.* New York: Oxford University Press, 1996.

USEFUL WEBSITES

Newspapers

CubaNet: Opposition paper (in English and Spanish)
www.cubanet.org

CubaDebate: pro-Castro paper
www.cubadebate.cu

Granma International: Cuban paper (in English and Spanish)
www.granma.cu

Government
Office of the Government of Cuba
www.cubagob.cu

Communist Party of Cuba
www.cuba.cu/politica/webpcc

Cuban Interests Section, Washington, D.C.
www.geocities.com/Paris/Library/2958

General
The Cuba Project, Queen's College, CUNY
www.soc.qc.edu/procuba/index.html

CIA World Fact Book: Resource for general information on Cuba.
www.odci.gov/cia/publications/factbook/geos/cu.html

Latin American Network Information Center: Comprehensive website housed at the
University of Texas with extensive Latin American links on a wide array of topics.
http://Lanic.utexas.edu

CHAPTER 11

Mexico: The Emergence of Democracy?

*I*n 2000, Vicente Fox, candidate of the National Action Party, won the Mexican presidential elections despite both expectations at the time and Mexico's history. Fox, a former executive for Coca-Cola, had a number of factors weighing against him. He was a newcomer to politics, emerging as the leader of his party from the ranks of the corporate world rather than from a long career in politics. His relative political inexperience made him something of an outsider in the world of politics, with even some members of his own party questioning him. Moreover, he was openly Catholic, overtly relying on and promoting Catholic symbols during and after his campaign in a country where the Church had long been relegated to the sidelines of political life. Perhaps most surprisingly, however, was that his victory was the first defeat of the incumbent's political party, the Institutional Revolutionary Party (PRI), in over seventy years.

How did Vicente Fox win, and what did the election mean? The answer to that question lies in the history of the long-ruling PRI and the reasons for its downfall. In turn, the story of the PRI lies in the Mexican Revolution (1910–1917) and the containment of the conflicts that produced the revolution and continued to fester even after it officially ended. The Mexican Revolution was a social explosion in which the weak glue holding Mexican society together came apart. Mexico attained independence in 1821, but for roughly fifty years afterward was unable to achieve any kind of political, economic, or social stability. Mexico went through multiple regime changes, wrote and rewrote multiple constitutions, and fought several foreign wars, including one in which ultimately it lost roughly half its territory to the United States.

The country stabilized only in 1876 with the rise to power of Porfirio Diaz. Diaz promoted economic development by opening Mexico to foreign investment and by supporting large landowners' efforts to consolidate their land holdings at the expense of small landowners and communal holdings. Supported by a group of technically trained bureaucrats (*científicos*), Diaz integrated Mexico into the global economy in ways that greatly favored foreign (mostly U.S.) interests over virtually all Mexicans—including landowning elites. By the turn of the century, Mexico had grown significantly with huge increases in mining and investments in infrastructure, but at high social and political costs. Mexican peasants, small landowners, and communal landowners (*ejidos*) were being pushed off the land by wealthy landed elites seeking to consolidate their holdings. Workers, especially in foreign-owned mining operations, were increasingly organized and radicalized by their experiences in harsh working conditions. The middle classes were dissatisfied with their exclusion from the political system by Diaz and his *científicos.* Even wealthy landowners were frustrated as the influx of foreign capital undermined their economic status and security. By the early 1900s, Mexico's social fabric was badly frayed and needed only a crisis to break Diaz's grip on power.

Diaz himself proved the ultimate catalyst for the crisis by wavering on the possibility of holding presidential elections and on whether he would be a candidate for reelection. His indecision and interference helped provoke the first calls for violent resistance. The opening of the conflict in 1910, however, set in motion a much larger process as multiple armies representing different regions and different socioeconomic interests mobilized. The war was intensely destructive with as many as 2 million Mexicans dying in the conflict. It culminated in 1917 in a constitutional convention held by the winning forces. The 1917 Constitution was a triumph of revolutionary, nationalist forces and it articulated a wide array of rights for peasants, communal landowners, and workers, and established the primacy of Mexican sovereignty over the nation's resources. But, the victors were not a unified group, and the constitution did not reflect all victorious parties' views, nor did it define mechanisms to settle ongoing political differences. Thus, it is no surprise that political violence continued in Mexico into the 1920s.

The PRI (initially called the PNR and then renamed the PRM) was the institution designed by the revolution's leaders to contain conflict within Mexican society. The PRI did this in a number of ways. First, the party organized all key sectors in society and in turn the organizations themselves were formally linked into the party. For example, industrial workers and peasants joined separate organizations formally linked to the PRI, and those organizations enjoyed monopoly rights to represent the interests of their respective constituencies. This ensured that the party was the main channel for representing interests, for communicating preferences, for making demands, and for addressing them. In short, the PRI tried to contain all social conflict within itself. Second, the party used a mix of carrots and sticks to maintain control over the diverse social groups linked into the party. Since the party was the main vehicle for expressing demands and for addressing them, party leaders could reward cooperative behavior and punish uncooperative behavior. Party leaders used the same tactics with social groups or independent labor unions that formed outside the party. Leaders of new groups could gain if they allowed themselves to be coopted by the PRI and brought under the confines of the party. Failure to comply could and did lead to coercive responses, the most famous of which was the massacre of student protestors in Tlatelolco Plaza in 1968. The final mechanism the PRI used to maintain social control was to contain electoral conflict and competition within itself. Although opposition parties existed, the real electoral struggle played out in the PRI between more left-wing and more conservative factions within the party. One characteristic of this struggle is that for several decades, the pendulum in the party leadership shifted back and forth between left and right wings of the party in response to changing social conditions. Thus, when the party had gone too far to contain and control conflict and political expression, the subsequent president would allow greater openness, and vice-versa. In all these ways, the PRI proved a supple and dynamic organization that successfully contained political conflict with a minimum of physical coercion and which was run by an entirely civilian dictatorship.

The economic crises of the 1980s and 1990s, however, created problems that could not be contained. Mexico's first profound economic crisis began in 1982 as the Mexican government defaulted on its external debt. Large oil reserves had been discovered in Mexico in the 1970s and President López Portillo borrowed heavily on the promise of future oil revenues. But by 1982, the price of oil had fallen very sharply from its high in 1979—the year of the second OPEC oil shock. As a result, Mexico was saddled with very high foreign debts and insufficient oil revenues such that they would not even cover the annual interest on the loans. The Mexican default triggered a brutal recession domestically as well as triggering the much larger Latin American debt crisis that affected the whole region.

The debt crisis also broke the pattern of the PRI shifting from left to right and back through the various presidential administrations. Instead, the neoliberalism-oriented right of the party gained control in the aftermath of the debt crisis and launched Mexico down a gradual path of neoliberal economic reform. The economic pain of recession and difficult economic adjustment, however, created political pressures for change both within and without the PRI. Outside of the PRI, the party found it harder to contain demands from groups independent of the party and indeed found it harder to control opposition parties on both the right and the left. Within the party, left-wing members angered over the loss of influence threatened to leave and in some instances actually did leave the party. The most important defection was of Cuauthemoc Cárdenas, the son of former President Lázaro Cárdenas (1935–1940), the country's most beloved post-revolution hero. Cárdenas ended up heading up a coalition of left-wing opposition parties in the 1988 election. By all accounts, the election was sullied by corruption and fraud, and by many accounts the PRI outright stole it from Cárdenas. In any event, Mexico had had its most competitive election ever and arguably the country was locked into a process of inevitable political liberalization.

The process of political liberalization was assisted by yet another economic crisis in 1994. What came to be known as the Peso Crisis (and the resulting Tequila Effect that spilled over onto the rest of Latin America) was the first financial crisis of the new, liberal, open economic order that was emerging in the 1990s. In brief, the Mexican government found itself at the end of 1994 with debt obligations that exceeded the country's capacity to pay. The developing payments problem led to a panicked capital flight as both Mexicans and foreigners worried that the government would devalue the peso. Investors wanted to convert their pesos into dollars before the government devalued the currency. But, the resulting rapid flight from pesos turned a difficult payments problem into a crisis of huge proportions. By early 1995, Mexico was plunged again into a brutal recession. The PRI government of Ernesto Zedillo, elected in 1994 before the crisis unfolded, committed itself to a strict adherence to neoliberal economic policy. As part of the political negotiation to follow strict neoliberal policies, Zedillo also committed the PRI to a much broader and faster political liberalization. Economic growth returned, but with it also came the birth of truly competitive elections in Mexico as the PRI first lost its majority in the Congress in 1998 and then the presidential elections of 2000 to Vicente Fox of the National Action Party. In 2001, President Zedillo turned over the government to President Fox in the first democratic presidential transition in the history of the country.

Alejandro Moreno and Patricia Méndez examine the character of support for democracy in Mexico before and after the decisive elections of 2000 that brought Mexico to its democratic transition. In the article, Moreno and Méndez show the consequences of long-term authoritarian rule and of sharp inequality in access to education. In brief, the authors show that the 2000 elections were helpful in increasing support for democracy and in the belief that democracy had come to Mexico. But the data also show that Mexican support for democracy is relatively weak—even compared to other Latin American nations—and the critical aspects of democratic rule (such as tolerance for others and interpersonal trust) are also weak. Thus, democratic elections and governance may have come to Mexico, but Mexican political culture remains less democratic.

The articles in this chapter review the emergence of democracy in Mexico and consider some of the challenges facing the new regime. Chris Gilbreth and Gerardo Otero review the special role the Zapatista rebellion played in promoting the emergence of democracy. The Zapatistas—*Ejército Zapatista de Liberación Nacional,* Zapatista National Liberation Army (EZLN)—rebellion began at the start of 1994, at least nominally in response to the formation of the North American Free Trade Agreement (NAFTA) and the firm acceptance of the neoliberal economic model it signified. The EZLN and its charismatic leader, Sub-Comandante Marcos, quickly became popular symbols in Mexico and around the world of resistance to neoliberalism. The Zapatistas did not commit any of the brutalities associated with some other Latin American guerrilla movements, such as in Colombia or Peru, and the eloquent and even poetic Marcos made an attractive symbol around which to organize. In turn, the brutality of the Mexican government response triggered social mobilization in Mexico that deepened civil society and allowed Mexicans to organize around a set of social and economic issues that had been removed from the agenda. As a result, the authors argue that the EZLN uprising played a key role in pushing Mexico toward democracy.

The limits to democratic culture make the performance of the newly elected leader, Vicente Fox of the National Action Party, even more important. But, as Pamela Starr shows, in "Fox's Mexico: Same as It Ever Was?" the Fox administration faces serious challenges to good governance. In addition to the potential splintering of the main parties, Starr also shows how Fox's corporate background and outsider status within his own party have limited his understanding of how to govern effectively. In addition, Starr notes that normal democratic politics in which the executive does not dominate the legislature is something new for Mexico and, as of 2002, something which Mexico's parties have not easily adjusted to. As a consequence, both President Fox and Mexico's legislature have performed relatively poorly.

DATA TABLES

Table 11.1
Mexico Fact and Data Sheet

Population (July 2003, estimated):	104,907,991
Ethnic Groups:	Mestizo (Amerindian-Spanish) 60%, Amerindian or predominantly Amerindian 30%, white 9%, other 1%
Religions:	Roman Catholic 89%
Government Type:	Federal Republic
Capital:	Mexico (Distrito Federal)
Administrative Divisions:	31 states and 1 federal district
Date of Independence:	September 16, 1810
Constitution:	February 5, 1917
Executive Branch:	President Vicente Fox Quesada, elected December 1, 2000; president and vice president elected on the same ticket by popular election to a 6-year term.
Legislature:	Bicameral National Congress
	• Senate has 128 seats; 96 members are elected by popular vote to a 6-year term; 32 members are allocated on the basis of each party's popular vote. Distribution of seats as of 2003: PRI, 60; PAN, 46; PRD, 15; PVEM, 5; PT, 1; CD, 1.
	• Chamber of Deputies has 500 seats; 300 members are directly elected by popular vote to a three-year term; 200 members are allocated on the basis of each party's popular vote, to a three-year term. Distribution of seats as of 2003: PRI, 224; PAN, 153; PRD, 95; other, 28.
Main Political Parties:	Convergence for Democracy (CD), Institutional Revolutionary Party (PRI), Mexican Green Ecological Party (PVEM), National Action Party (PAN), Party of the Democratic Revolution (PRD), Party of the Nationalist Society (PSN), Social Alliance Party (PAS), Workers Party (PT).
Military Spending (FY1999):	U.S. $4 billion
Military Spending, Percentage of GDP (FY1999):	1
GDP (2002, estimated):	PPP $924.4 billion
GDP Composition by Sector (2001, estimated):	Agriculture: 5%
	Industry: 26%
	Services: 69%
Main Industries:	Food and beverages, tobacco, chemicals, iron and steel, petroleum, mining, textiles, clothing, motor vehicles, consumer durables, tourism

(cont.)

Table 11.1 (cont.)
Mexico Fact and Data Sheet

Main Agricultural Products:	Corn, wheat, soybeans, rice, beans, cotton, coffee, fruit, tomatoes, beef, poultry, dairy products, wood products
Export Partners (2002):	U.S., 82.7%; Canada, 5.4%; Japan, 1.1%
Import Partners (2002):	U.S., 70.6%; Germany, 3.5%; Japan, 2.7%
External Debt (2000, estimated):	$150 billion

Table 11.2
Presidents of Mexico

Tenure	President
1876–1880	Porfirio Diaz
1880–1884	Manuel González
1884–1910	Porfirio Diaz
1911	Francisco León de la Barra
1911–1913	Francisco Madero
1913	Victoriano Huerta
1914–1920	Venustiano Carranza
1920	Adolfo de la Huerta
1920–1924	Álvaro Obregón
1924–1928	Plutarco Elías Calles
1928–1930	Emilio Portes Gil
1930–1932	Pascual Ortiz Rubio
1932–1934	Abelardo Rodríguez
1935–1940	Lázaro Cárdenas
1941–1946	Manuel Ávila Camacho
1947–1952	Miguel Alemán
1953–1958	Adolfo Ruiz Cortines
1959–1964	Adolfo López Mateos
1965–1970	Gustavo Díaz Ordaz
1971–1976	Luis Echeverría Alvarez
1977–1982	José López Portillo
1983–1988	Miguel de la Madrid Hurtado
1989–1994	Carlos Salinas de Gortari
1995–2000	Ernesto Zedillo Ponce de León
2001–present	Vicente Fox Quesada

11.1 Attitudes Toward Democracy: Mexico in Comparative Perspective (2002)

ALEJANDRO MORENO AND PATRICIA MÉNDEZ

INTRODUCTION

Mexico's gradual democratization came to a critical point in 2000, when the presidential election brought about political alternation in that country. After remaining in power for 71 years, the Institutional Revolutionary Party (PRI) was defeated at the polls. Vicente Fox, the National Action Party (PAN) candidate, became the first President from a party other than the PRI in Mexico's modern history. Three years earlier, the PRI had lost its majority in Congress, and the 1990s witnessed how opposition parties defeated the PRI in local and state-level elections, gradually ousting the PRI from office in every level of government. After all of these significant transformations, how democratic are Mexicans nowadays and how do they value democracy? This question derives from the early studies on political culture which stated that democracy requires a compatible value system that helps it endure.

Our task in this article is to assess how Mexicans value democracy and to what extent they possess the elements of a democratic political culture. We do this by comparing Mexican democratic values with those of other regions of the world, and also by observing how Mexicans' democratic attitudes have changed in the last few years. We also look at the differences among Mexicans, focusing on education as an important predictor of democratic values.

Academic efforts to measure democratic values and support for democracy in Mexico are not new, but the 1990s brought a new wave of quantitative studies that used increasingly reliable and sophisticated opinion surveys based on national representative samples. These studies, as well as the surveys that provided the empirical evidence, reflect a period of profound political transformation. Moreover, Mexico included regularly national representative samples in international surveys that monitor, among other things, citizen support for democracy and the spread of democratic values. Both the World Values Survey, which serves as evidence to this article, and the Latinobarómetro surveys are good examples.

The literature on support for democracy in Third Wave democracies has recently raised interesting paradoxes. Let us mention three of them. First,

Alejandro Moreno and Patricia Méndez, "Attitudes Toward Democracy: Mexico in Comparative Sociology," *International Journal of Comparative Sociology,* December 2002, Vol. 43, no. 3, pp. 350–367. Reprinted by permission.

democracy has nowadays a widespread legitimacy in the world, but trust in democratic institutions has declined. Moreover, political participation has also lost the enthusiasm of the democratic honeymoon in third wave democracies.

The second paradox is that, although open support for democracy is almost universal today, its measurement is not a precise indicator of how rooted democracy is in society. A very illustrative indicator is that democracy is highly valued in Islamic societies, but very few Islamic societies have functioning democratic regimes. Given the little difference in democratic principles and ideals between Islamic societies and the West, there is hardly a "clash of civilizations" in those terms.

A third paradox is that today, when survey researchers measure support for democracy, they are measuring support for a socially desirable concept, and measurement validity only reflects overt support. The fact is that measures of overt support for democracy do not tell us how democratic societies are, or how tolerant. On the contrary, measuring tolerance may tell us how democratic a society is.

Support for democracy may erode, especially when the economic context may raise doubts about the functioning of democratic institutions. References to the Weimar Republic often illustrate this syndrome. Support for democracy was not enough to allow democracy to endure in a profound economic crisis. Precisely, many third wave democracies have faced the challenge of economic transformation and recovery, and a decade ago some observers identified economic performance as one of the main obstacles to democratic consolidation. Moreover, corruption and political scandals might bring disillusionment with democracy in newly democratic societies. In any case, good measurements of a democratic political culture are not limited to support for democratic rule—particularly when, today, survey responses on the issue are strongly subject to social desirability bias. Instead, such measurements should allow us to know something more than overt support for democracy: they should tell us something about tolerance, trust, and rejection of non-democratic forms of governance, for example.

DEMOCRACY AND POLITICAL CULTURE IN MEXICO

Mexico's democratization was significantly achieved through electoral reforms and a gradual increase in political competition. The 1988 presidential election witnessed the first major electoral challenge to the Institutional Revolutionary Party, PRI, which was made possible thanks to a party split in 1987. Mexican opposition parties started to win elections earlier, especially at the municipal level. The first state governor from a party other than the PRI, in this case the National Action Party (PAN), was elected in Baja California, in 1989. The 1990s witnessed a more rapid increase in political competition thanks to further electoral reforms and both 1997 and 2000 were critical years in electoral terms. In 1997, the PRI lost its majority in Congress, obtaining only 39 percent of the national vote. The PAN and the PRD (Party of Democratic Revolution) obtained 27 and 26 percent of the national vote, respectively. In 2000, the PRI lost the presidency, obtaining 38 percent of the vote, whereas Vicente Fox, a candidate of the Alliance for Change (a coalition of PAN and the Greens) obtained about 43 percent. During the 1990s, the issue of democracy was the main determinant of party support and party competition. Those who favored a democratic transformation were more likely to support the PAN, whereas those who sought to keep the PRI in power expressed more authoritarian attitudes and values.

Recent surveys conducted in Mexico by government institutions have shown that a great majority of Mexicans support and value democracy. The results have been published with enthusiasm and optimism, speaking in favor of the strength of democratic values in that country. The simple fact that government institutions have polled Mexicans on this matter and published the results of their study shows an important change in Mexican political culture. Why would political elites do so under authoritarian rule? However, as a society, Mexico is far from having a very strong value system that is compatible with democracy. Comparatively, Mexicans show lower levels of tolerance and trust, and higher deference for authority and support for non-democratic rule than societies in other countries of the world. For example, Mexico's average score on a composite index of support for democracy is well under the average of 48 societies included in the 1995–1997 World Values Survey. This does not mean that democracy is not likely to endure in Mexico. It means that Mexicans are just starting to know democracy, both its virtues and its problems, and developing a real sense of it.

Our task in this article is to empirically answer the following questions: How does Mexican democratic culture compare to democratic culture in other regions of the world? How have Mexican democratic values evolved in recent years? How diverse is democratic culture within Mexico? In a more rhetorical, less empirical sense: What implications are there for the consolidation of democracy in Mexico? By democratic culture we mean a set of values and attitudes that are compatible with democratic principles and practices, such as tolerance, interpersonal trust, emphasis on civil liberties and rights, political participation, support for democracy, and rejection of non-democratic forms of government. We are aware that our answers to these questions may not be definitive, but we hope that their empirical basis serves as a portrait of the Mexican political culture at the end of the twentieth and beginning of the twenty-first centuries.

DATA DESCRIPTION

This article is based on data from the 1995–1997 and 2000–2001 World Values Survey (WVS), the third and fourth waves of the project, respectively. Our analysis of the WVS is mostly descriptive and, for illustration purposes, we decided to compare Mexico with regions of the world rather than with particular countries. The countries included in each region are the following: *Latin America and the Caribbean:* Argentina 1995 and 2000, Brazil 1995, Chile 1995 and 2000, Peru 1995, Puerto Rico 1995, Dominican Republic 1995, Uruguay 1995, and Venezuela 1995 and 2000. *Africa:* Ghana 1995, Nigeria 1995 and 2000, South Africa 1995 and 2000, Uganda 2000, Zimbabwe 2000. *East Asia:* China 1995 and 2000, South Korea 1995 and 2000, Japan 1995 and 2000, and Taiwan 1995. *South Asia:* Bangladesh 2000, Philippines 1995 and 2000, India 1995, Turkey 1995 and 2000, and Vietnam 2000. *Advanced Democracies:* West Germany 1995, Australia 1995, Canada 2000, Spain 1995 and 2000, United States 1995 and 2000, Finland 1995, Israel 2000, Norway 1995, Switzerland 1995, Sweden 1995 and 2000. *Post-Communist Societies:* East Germany 1995, Armenia 1995, Azerbaijan 1995, Belarus 1995, Croatia 1995, Slovenia 1995, Estonia 1995, Georgia 1995, Latvia 1995, Lithuania 1995, Moldavia 1995, Montenegro 1995 and 2000, Poland 1995, Russia 1995, Serbia 1995 and 2000, Tambov 1995, and Ukraine 1995. Mexico was analyzed separately from Latin America. The dataset with these countries has 97,643 respondents.

In this article we also use the National Survey of Political Culture and Citizen Practices, a national representative sample of 4,183 adult Mexicans sponsored by the Interior Ministry of Mexico (SEGOB), and conducted by the National Institute of Statistics, Geography, and Information (INEGI). Fieldwork took place from November 4 to December 7, 2001. Our use of the ENCUP here is more analytical. We use multinomial logistic regression analysis and show the predicted probabilities from the models. The models based on the ENCUP are rather weak, but the differences by education show that there is a significant variation among Mexicans, as shown elsewhere. Also, by looking at individual differences we recognize the problems of just reporting societal averages, as if each society was homogeneous. We are well aware that this is not the case.

COMPARING MEXICO'S DEMOCRATIC CULTURE

Comparisons always bring conceptual and empirical problems: what aspects should be compared and how valid are the measurements in different national and regional contexts? Trying to respond to the first part of the question, we identify some of the main qualities considered as crucial factors in the flourishing of democracy. Such factors are tolerance, trust, emphasis on civil rights and political participation, and a general sense of subjective well-being. Subjective well-being reflects the level of economic development in society, which, according to several studies, is the basis of democratic development. Rather than focusing on economic development and the sense of well-being, we focus on tolerance and authority as elements of political socialization, on trust and the openness to understand others' preferences, on support for democracy and rejection of non-democratic rule, and on citizen evaluations of democratic performance and respect for human rights.

Tolerance and Obedience

A great deal of the literature on political culture follows the idea that political values are learned during the years of individual formation and socialization. Without being a study of socialization, this article shows some of the priorities that Mexican adults consider important in children's education, and how they compare to other regions of the world. The first and second columns of Table 1 show the percent of respondents in different regions of the world that say that tolerance and obedience, respectively, are "very important" to encourage among children. This combination of tolerance and obedience responds to the fact that tolerance is a favorable attitude towards democracy, while obedience reflects deference towards authority, not necessarily democratic. It is still common in Mexico to hear that children should be obedient, and that a "good" child is the one who obeys his or her parents without questioning them. The obvious translation into politics is that obedience reflects some subjection to political authority, and little questioning.

According to the third and fourth waves of the World Values Survey, tolerance is considered a very important aspect to encourage among children in advanced industrial democracies, where an average 81 percent of respondents believe so. In contrast, post-Communist societies and East Asian countries express the lower average levels of support for tolerance as a value that should be taught to children. Comparatively, Mexico is slightly under the overall regional average: 65 percent of Mexicans consider tolerance important for children, vis-à-vis 67 percent expressed in all countries included in the analysis. On average, Latin American and Caribbean societies appear as more tolerant than Mexicans. Nonetheless, emphasis on tolerance in Mexico increased from 57 to 72 percent from 1997 to 2000. The 1997 survey was taken a few months before the PRI lost its majority in Congress in the mid-term 1997 elections. Perhaps the new political reality after 1997 contributed to the increase of the percent of Mexicans who consider tolerance important. Also, the Federal Elections Institute permanent media campaign of political values has placed an emphasis on political tolerance as well.

Mexicans are, on average, less interested in encouraging tolerance among children than other countries of different regions of the world, including

Table 1

Measures of Democratic Attitudes: Tolerance, Obedience, Trust,
and Interpersonal Relations

	Tolerance a	Obedience b	Trust c	Interpersonal Relations d
	%	%	%	%
Advanced Democracies	81	29	41	64
Africa	67	62	16	61
East Asia	59	16	41	75
Latin America and the Caribbean	69	47	14	46
Mexico	65	54	24	41
Post-Communist Societies	62	30	23	59
South Asia	67	57	19	49
Mexico 1997	57	50	26	40
Mexico 2000	72	59	21	43

Source: 1995–2002 World Values Survey.

Notes: (a) The encouragement of tolerance in children is "very important"; (b) the encouragement of obedience in children is "very important"; (c) "most people can be trusted"; (d) "understanding others' preferences is more important than expressing one's own preferences in order to have successful human relations."

Latin America. At the same time, they are more interested in promoting obedience. Only African societies consider obedience more important than in Mexico: 64 percent of the African publics surveyed emphasize obedience, vis-à-vis 54 percent of Mexicans. However, emphasis on obedience has increased in Mexico in recent years. In contrast, less than one-third (29 percent) of the publics in advanced industrial democracies, and about 16 percent of the East Asian publics emphasize obedience as an attribute that children should learn. In sum, Mexicans are more oriented towards promoting obedience and less towards expanding tolerance, in comparison to other regions of the world. The importance of tolerance increased in the last few years, but so did the importance of obedience.

Trust and Interpersonal Relations

Trust is a fundamental aspect in the functioning of democracy. The combination of trust and tolerance reflects a will to understand others' preferences and aim at successful social relationships. Table 1 shows the percent of respondents who express trust in people and who prioritize an understanding of others' preferences before the clear manifestation of one's own preferences.

In comparison to the levels of trust expressed in advanced democracies (41 percent, a similar percent to East Asia's), only 24 percent of Mexicans express trust in most people. The Latin American average level of trust is even lower, 14 percent, a lower level than the one registered in post-Communist societies, where the average trust is about 23 percent. Still, Mexico's level of trust is relatively low, in comparison to the one expressed in advanced democracies, and it decreased from 26 percent in 1997 to 21 percent in 2000.

Mexicans are, on average, less open to understand others' preferences. Only 41 percent place emphasis on the understanding of others' preferences in order to have successful human relations. This percentage is slightly lower than the Latin American average of 46 percent, and significantly lower than the percentage expressed in advanced democracies (64 percent) and in East Asia (75 percent). From 1997 to 2000, the percentage of respondents in Mexico who agree with the importance of understanding others' preferences was stable, only moving from 40 to 43 percent.

Comparatively, Mexican political culture is characterized by low levels of trust (or high levels of distrust, if preferable), and by low interest in other people's ideas and preferences. If these are parts of the social capital that make democracy work more efficiently, Mexicans lack a great deal of the lubricating factor for democracy: they seem to have a deficit of trust and are relatively closed to coexistence. Nonetheless, trust is not a trait of the majority, even in advanced democracies, where the overall average of trust is about 41 percent.

Support for Authoritarian Rule

The consolidation of new democracies requires that there are no real possibilities of an authoritarian regression, and that there is mass rejection to such possibilities. In Mexico, unlike other regions of the world, there is significant support for authoritarian forms of government, and even for military rule, which most living Mexicans have not experienced in their lifetime. Table 2 shows the percentage of respondents who say that having a strong leader who does not have to bother with Congress/Parliament and elections is good or very good, and the percentage of respondents who consider having the military rule as good or very good.

In Mexico, 41 percent of respondents support having a strong leader who does not bother with Congress and elections. This percentage is only outweighed by the one registered in South Asia, composed with countries such as India, Bangladesh, Turkey, Vietnam, and the Philippines. In that region, 52 percent of respondents say that this autocratic form of government is good. In contrast, 22 percent of the publics surveyed in advanced democracies support the idea of a strong leader. This is the lowest regional percent, but it is still a significant proportion: about one-fifth of those who live in stable industrial democracies are willing, at least in word, to accept a strong leader who does not bother with Congress and elections. The Latin American average of support for a strong leader is about 35 percent, similar to that of Africa (34 percent) and the post-Communist world (37 percent). Support

Table 2

Support for Democratic and Non-Democratic Government

	Strong Leader	Military Government	Support for Democracy	Democracies Are Indecisive
	a	b	c	d
	%	%	%	%
Advanced Democracies	22	6	86	47
Africa	34	22	72	41
East Asia	27	9	77	36
Latin America and the Caribbean	35	20	84	57
Mexico	41	25	65	46
Post-Communist Societies	37	10	70	48
South Asia	52	26	78	44
Mexico 1997	39	23	65	44
Mexico 2000	44	27	65	48

Source: 1995–2002 World Values Survey.

Notes: (a) Having a strong leader who does not have to bother with parliament and elections is "good" or "very good"; (b) having a military government is "good" or "very good"; (c) "Democracy is the best system," percent "agree"; (d) "Democracies are indecisive and have too much quibbling," percent "agree."

for a strong leader grew in Mexico in the last few years from 39 percent in 1997, right before the first plural Congress came about, to 44 percent in 2000, right before Vicente Fox defeated the PRI candidate, Francisco Labastida, in the presidential election.

Most living Mexicans have not experienced military rule. In fact, the last president who had a military background after the Mexican Revolution, Manuel Ávila Camacho, ended his term in 1940, but his government cannot be characterized as a military rule. Despite this lack of military governments, today one out of four Mexicans thinks that having military rule is good. In South Asian societies, 26 percent of respondents support military rule, as well as 22 percent of the African publics. About 20 percent of Latin Americans say that military rule is something good, while only 6 percent of the publics in advanced democracies share that view. In sum, support for military government in Mexico is relatively higher than in other countries and regions, and it has increased in the last few years from 23 percent in 1997 to 27 percent in 2000.

SUPPORT FOR DEMOCRATIC GOVERNANCE

Today, overt support for democracy is high in most countries of the world, which means that having a simple majority or two-thirds of the public supporting democracy may be seen as a rather low score. Most Mexicans believe that democracy is the best system, but the percent in agreement with democracy is comparatively lower than the averages observed in most regions of the world. Moreover, overt support for democracy has not increased in Mexico in the last few years.

Table 2 shows the percent of respondents who agree that democracy is the best system, and the percent of respondents who agree that democracies are indecisive and have too much quibbling. About 86 percent of the publics in advanced democracies are convinced that democracy is the best system. Latin Americans (Mexico not included) are close to that level, with 84 percent; South Asia and East Asia have averages of 78 and 77 percent; African publics have an average 72 percent: and post-Communist societies 70 percent. Below all these averages of democratic support is Mexico, with about 65 percent. The same proportion was observed in 1997 and in 2000. This means that only two-thirds of Mexicans believe that democracy is the best system, and that proportion has not changed in the last few years. One-third of Mexicans are not convinced (or lack the information to say) that democracy is the best system.

Mexicans just started to live in a democracy and most of them just began to see their political system as such. According to a series of national polls conducted by *Reforma* newspaper in Mexico, fewer than half of Mexicans thought of their country as a democracy before the presidential elections of 2000. However, more than six out of ten Mexicans were convinced that Mexico was a democracy right after the presidential election.

Newly democratic experiences have brought different political dynamics to Mexicans' attention. After the 1997 mid-term elections, a plural Congress changed the balance of power in Mexico by changing the Executive-Legislative relations. Mexicans could watch on television or read in newspapers that democracy is an arrangement where disorder and lack of deference could be part of Mexico's institutional life without risking political stability. After the 2000 presidential election, Vicente Fox changed the style of the Mexican presidency in many ways, but perhaps the most significant change was not one of style, but of substance. The Mexican presidency has become more open and less effective. It is difficult for public policy and prospective legislation to move from a presidential initiative or good will to an actual government action or instituted law. The Indigenous Law in 2001, the Tax Reform in 2002, and the cancellation of a new airport construction in Mexico City in 2002, show how the new Mexican president has been unable to achieve his original goals.

Admitting that democracy may be slow and inefficient is not a signal of anti-democratic attitudes. Democracy implies that political outcomes are uncertain within institutional certainty. Table 2 shows that most societies are divided along the idea that democracy is indecisive and has too much quibbling. About 57 percent of the Latin American societies share that view. In Mexico, that percentage is about 46 percent, similar to that of advanced democracies (47 percent) and post-Communist societies (48 percent).

Believing that a democracy is indecisive and troublesome is not an indicator of anti-democratic views. On the contrary, what is democracy if not an institutional arrangement that opens the possibility for different and generally opposing views and interests to be expressed, advanced, and negotiated? Tolerance of homogeneity is a contradiction in terms. Tolerance has to do with diversity and coexistence. Tolerance is tested precisely when political conflicts can be processed through institutions with no need of violence. In Mexico, the belief that democracy is indecisive and has too much quibbling increased from 44 to 48 percent from 1997 to 2000. Rather than being an increase in anti-democratic attitudes, this may be seen as a greater acknowledgement of some of democracy's features. Unfortunately, this particular question has so much ambivalence that a stronger conclusion cannot be reached.

Satisfaction with Democracy and Respect for Human Rights

Satisfaction with democracy and perceptions of how such a system guarantees respect for human rights are important pillars in the way societies value democratic governance. Many of the new democracies had to build democratic institutions and develop mechanisms that changed the very fundamental relations between government and citizenry. Some new democracies opened their past in search of violations of basic human rights. What are the current perceptions of the way democracy is developing and the way human rights are respected?

Table 3 shows the percentage of respondents who said they are "very" or "somewhat" satisfied with the development of democracy in their country. Comparatively speaking, the level of satisfaction is about 70 percent in South Asia, 63 percent in advanced democracies, 53 percent in Latin America and the Caribbean, and 50 percent in Africa. In East Asia, which includes China, the percentage of satisfaction with the development of democracy is about 45 percent. In Mexico, only 37 percent say they are satisfied with the way democracy is developing in the country. This level is just above the percentage expressed in post-Communist societies. It is clear that, before political alternation in 2000, Mexican society was not very satisfied with the development of democracy in their country. The fourth wave of the WVS in Mexico was conducted in February 2000, four and a half months before the presidential elections.

Table 3 also shows the percentage of respondents who believe that there is a great deal or some respect for human rights in their country. About 74 percent of the publics in advanced democracies think that there is respect for human rights in their respective country. The average in East Asia is about 59 percent, in Mexico it is 45 percent, in the post-Communist world 43 percent, and in Latin America 41 percent. There are important episodes of violations to human rights in Mexico, such as the student massacre in 1968, and the "Dirty War" in the early 1970s, just to mention two of the most important ones; and perceptions of respect for human rights among the Mexican public are very similar to those in Latin America and post-Communist

Table 3

Satisfaction with Democracy and Perceptions of Respect for Human Rights

	Satisfaction with Democracy	Respect for Human Rights
	a	b
	%	%
Advanced Democracies	63	74
Africa	50	54
East Asia	45	59
Latin America and the Caribbean	53	41
Mexico	37	45
Post-Communist Societies	35	43
South Asia	70	53

Source: 2000–2002 World Values Survey.

Notes: (a) "Very" or "somewhat satisfied" with the way democracy is developing in the country; (b) there is "a lot" or "some" respect for human rights in the country.

societies. One should expect that an indicator of how the public perceives respect for human rights not only reflects the authoritarian past, but also the way newly democratic governments have dealt with the issue. The more respect for human rights, the higher the quality of democracy.

The data shown in Table 3 suggest that Mexicans were comparatively unsatisfied with democratic development before political alternation, something that changed after the presidential elections. According to Moreno (2002), an index of satisfaction with democracy in Mexico, based on national representative samples shows that, on a weighted scale from 0 to 100, where 100 means very satisfied and 0 not at all satisfied, the average score obtained in October 1999 was 39. By August 2000, one month after the presidential election, the score increased to 60, and remained in the same level by November 2000. By November 2001, the average score was down to 50. Mexicans also share the lower positions in perceptions of respect for human rights.

With this descriptive account of democratic attitudes we conclude the first part of the article, which addressed the questions of how democratic Mexican political culture is, comparatively speaking, and how it has evolved in the last few years. The next part addresses a third question: how different are Mexicans among themselves, in terms of their democratic political culture? Before we move onto the second part, let us summarize our findings so far:

In comparison to the regional averages in the world, Mexicans encourage tolerance relatively less and obedience relatively more than most societies. In the last few years, emphasis on tolerance has increased in Mexico, but so has emphasis on obedience.

Mexicans are characterized by little interpersonal trust, which has in fact declined in the last few years. They are also relatively less open to understanding others' preferences in their human relations, an attitude that may hinder social and political coexistence in a heterogeneous society.

Mexicans show larger levels of acceptance of non-democratic forms of governance, such as autocracy and military rule, than in most regions of the world. Such acceptance has increased in the last few years.

Mexicans are comparatively less convinced that democracy is the best system. However, they are, as most societies, divided in the way they perceive democracy. Perceptions that such a system is indecisive and that it has too much quibbling are not indicators of anti-democratic attitudes, but an acknowledgment of those characteristics.

Mexicans were unsatisfied with the development of democracy until the 2000 elections. Fewer than half also considered that human rights are respected in that country. Both indicators show how perceptions about the quality of democracy in Mexico were at the end of the twentieth and beginning of the twenty-first centuries.

INTERNAL DIVERSITY: FINDINGS FROM THE NATIONAL SURVEY OF POLITICAL CULTURE

Which Mexicans are more likely to hold democratic values and attitudes? In this section we analyze the individual differences in support for democracy and tolerance among Mexicans. The analysis is based on multinomial logistic regression, and focuses on the predicted probabilities of holding one attitude or another with respect to democracy by levels of education. This variable has proved to be an important predictor of democratic attitudes.

According to the National Survey of Political Culture, conducted for the Interior Ministry, 62 percent of respondents consider a democratic system preferable to any other form of government. This figure is consistent with the 65 percent of Mexican respondents of the 2000 World Values Survey that think democracy is the best system. In contrast, 9 percent of Mexicans polled by the ENCUP think that, under some circumstances, an authoritarian government is better than a democratic one.

As mentioned in the preceding section, the majority of Mexicans think democracy is the best system, but such a majority (62 to 65 percent, depending on the survey) represents a relatively low percentage in comparison to other regions of the world. Moreover, this majority is reduced to a plurality when respondents face some particular questions. What is more preferable: living under economic pressure without sacrificing civil liberties, or sacrificing civil liberties if that means not having economic pressures? About 47 percent of Mexicans would rather live under economic pressures without sacrificing civil liberties, whereas 32 percent think that civil liberties should be sacrificed in exchange for economic security. The distribution of responses to this question reveals that about one-third of Mexicans are willing, at least in word, to support suppression of civil liberties under economic pressures. Moreover, in terms of political tolerance, 52 percent of Mexicans disagree that television shows people with ideas politically different to their own, and about 35 percent agree.

Who is more likely to hold democratic attitudes? Who is more tolerant? Who is more likely to accept non-democratic forms of governance? Education and socioeconomic status are important predictors of pro-democratic attitudes in society, cross-nationally speaking. In order to show the impact of education and income, among other variables, we ran multinomial logistic regression models with different attitudes as dependent variables. The values taken by the dependent variables represented a pro-democratic position, a pro-authoritarian position, and an indifferent position. We used 6 different dependent variables with this coding. The model used gender, education, income, and region as independent variables. Additionally, we included economic retrospective evaluations, assuming that the most disaffected Mexicans would be more likely to reject democratic rule. The model is not an exhaustive one and has a relatively poor goodness of fit. The ENCUP survey did not offer any other independent variables (such as partisan orientations or left/right self-placement) that we think might improve the model. The only option we had was to include other attitudinal questions as independent variables, but this would have led us to a problem of endogeneity, so we decided not to include them. The analyses done in this section are unweighted. Let us now turn to the results.

Democracy and Political Effectiveness

Table 4 shows the predicted probabilities derived from the multinomial regression model by education using dependent variables that represent support for democracy and attitudes toward political effectiveness. As stated earlier, education has a positive and significant impact on pro-democratic attitudes. The higher the respondent's education level, the more likely he or she will hold favorable attitudes toward democracy.

Generally, most Mexicans prefer democracy to authoritarianism, but such preference varies significantly by education. Eighty percent of the most educated Mexicans are likely to prefer democracy, whereas slightly over 40 percent of the least educated are likely to prefer democracy. Nonetheless, preferences for authoritarianism are not clearly related to education: the highly educated are as likely to prefer authoritarian governance under some circumstances as the least educated. This means that the lower the respondent's education, the more likely it is that he or she does not have a position towards either democracy or authoritarianism.

It has been demonstrated that Mexicans, as other Latin Americans, hold different concepts of democracy, and that education and the level of political sophistication make a difference on how democracy is perceived. The lower

Table 4

Democratic Attitudes in Mexico by Education, 2001

	Citizen Preferences					
	(a) Democracy	Authoritarian Government	(b) Heeding Government	Effective Government	(c) Civil Liberties	No Economic Pressures
Education Level						
High	0.78	0.10	0.48	0.37	0.59	0.33
	0.72	0.10	0.43	0.40	0.54	0.35
	0.64	0.10	0.39	0.40	0.49	0.35
	0.56	0.10	0.34	0.40	0.43	0.34
Low	0.46	0.09	0.31	0.38	0.37	0.32

	(d) Democracy	Dictatorship	(e) Different Values	Same Values	(f) Tolerance	Intolerance
Education Level						
High	0.79	0.10	0.81	0.16	0.55	0.42
	0.70	0.13	0.76	0.19	0.44	0.49
	0.60	0.14	0.70	0.22	0.34	0.56
	0.48	0.15	0.62	0.25	0.25	0.59
Low	0.37	0.14	0.54	0.26	0.18	0.60

Source: *National Survey of Political Culture* (ENCUP), 2001. Author's calculations. Entries are predicted probabilities from multinomial logit model described in text.

Notes: (a) Democracy over any other form of government vs. an authoritarian government under some circumstances; (b) A government that takes citizens into account even if it doesn't act when needed vs. a government that achieves its tasks but imposes its decisions; (c) living under economic pressure without sacrificing civil liberties vs. sacrifice civil liberties if that means living without economic pressures; (d) Democracy even if it doesn't ensure economic security vs. a dictatorship that guarantees economic security; (e) people with different values and ideas vs. people with the same values and ideas; (f) tolerance towards a person with different ideas to one's own in TV.

the level of education, the more likely it is that democracy is conceptualized in terms of elements that are not exclusively characteristic of democratic rule, such as fighting crime or maintaining order. Variables that represent levels of information and media consumption are even stronger predictors of the conceptualization of democracy than typical cultural variables, such as trust. Thus, political sophistication is positively related to support for democratic governance in Mexico.

However, education is a weaker determinant of the following attitude: what is better, a government that consults and takes citizen preferences into account even if it does not act when needed; or a government that acts effectively even if it imposes its decisions. Mexicans are clearly divided on this issue: fewer than half support the first position, and a similar proportion supports the second position. Table 4 shows that, as education increases, preferences for a government that consults citizens slightly increases. The differences, however, are not very significant. Even the most educated Mexicans are less than 50 percent likely to prefer a government that consults citizens to a government that imposes its decisions. The fact that the former option implies an ineffective government and the latter an effective one is causing this ambivalence. Citizens like to see government results.

Democracy and Economic Performance

The syndrome of the Weimar Republic represents the abandonment of democratic ideals and principles because of economic depression. How vulnerable are Mexican democratic values to economic adversities? Table 4 also shows that there are more Mexicans willing to live under economic pressure but without sacrificing civil liberties, than Mexicans who think the other way around. Moreover, as education increases, the desire to keep civil liberties, even in economically adverse times, also increases.

What about democracy vis-à-vis economic security? Table 4 shows that more Mexicans prefer democracy even if it does not ensure economic advancement to a dictatorship that guarantees economic security. Again, well-educated citizens express a higher preference for democratic rule. It is very noticeable, however, that one in ten Mexicans prefer a dictatorship that guarantees economic security. The question is hypothetical, since dictatorship does not necessarily "guarantee" economic security. Perhaps the "Asian Tigers" approach something similar to this situation, in which economic growth was significant under authoritarian rule. The current economic crisis in Argentina will show how rooted democratic values and attitudes are in that country.

Diversity and Tolerance

Table 4 shows that most Mexicans prefer that people have different ideas and values, but a considerable proportion prefers that people hold the same ideas and values. Support for diversity increases as education increases.

Paradoxically, tolerance is not as widely shared as the taste for diversity, as shown in the same table. Although the majority of Mexicans prefers that people have different values and ideas, only a minority of them agree with television showing people with different and opposing ideas to their own. Even the most highly educated Mexicans seem clearly divided on this issue.

In sum, the data shown in this section indicate that Mexicans prefer democracy to authoritarianism, but are divided on the issue of effectiveness, suggesting that a government that imposes its decisions would be sometimes better than one who consults citizens but does not act when needed. There is a significant proportion of Mexicans who would be willing to sacrifice civil liberties if that means not living under economic pressures. Finally, most Mexicans prefer cultural diversity to homogeneity, but tolerance in practice is much more limited than such a preference for diversity would suggest. As noted earlier, tolerance of the homogeneous is a contradiction of terms. There is no ground for tolerance without diversity.

CONCLUSION

The presidential election of July 2, 2000, confirmed the completion of Mexico's transition to democracy. The question addressed here is how supportive Mexican political culture is of democracy. About two-thirds of Mexicans believe that democracy is the best system, but this is a comparatively small proportion if we take regional averages from other countries of the world. A good assessment of democratic values should not be limited to measuring overt support for democracy, because democracy has become a concept affected by social desirability bias. Even non-democratic societies express relatively high levels of support for democratic principles. Good measurements of democratic values should also include the elements that effectively contribute to make democratic life possible.

Focusing on Mexico from a comparative perspective, in this article we asked three central questions. How different are democratic attitudes in Mexico with those held in other societies? How have Mexican democratic attitudes changed in the last few years? How different are Mexicans amongst themselves in terms of their democratic attitudes? Data from the World Values Survey and the National Survey of Political Culture serve as the empirical evidence to provide some answers.

These data show that most Mexicans are convinced that democracy is the best system, but such a majority is, on average, a smaller proportion than in most regions of the world. Mexico's newly democratic experience is developing both different views of democracy and elements of judgment about it. Mexicans received democracy enthusiastically, according to opinion polls. Alternation in 2000 changed many of the citizen's disenchantment with the previous regime and increased trust in political institutions. Nonetheless,

Mexican democracy and political culture are in a process of development, redefinition, and consolidation.

From a comparative perspective, tolerance and interpersonal trust in Mexico are more limited than in other regions of the world. Moreover, a significant proportion of Mexicans would be willing to sacrifice civil liberties in exchange for economic security. The proportion that thinks well of an autocratic government or a kind of military rule that has not even been witnessed by most living Mexicans is larger than in many other countries. Also, most Mexicans doubt that there is a widespread respect for human rights in their country. Such doubts obviously reduce favorable perceptions about the quality of democracy in Mexico.

Individual differences in the Mexican political value system are significantly explained by education. Less educated Mexicans are less likely to support non-democratic forms of governance or to be indifferent to democracy. The more educated Mexicans are, other things being equal, the more likely they are to hold democratic values and support democracy. Nonetheless, authoritarian and intolerant attitudes are observed among highly educated and non-educated Mexicans alike.

Asking whether Mexican political culture is compatible with democracy is an old question. [Gabriel] Almond and [Sidney] Verba addressed it in the late 1950s, when they wrote *The Civic Culture.* Mexican political reality was different than it is today. However, these authors' statement that Mexicans were aspirational may have another meaning now. Mexicans may aspire not just to live in a democracy, as it was the case for a long time, but to live in a better, high-quality democracy. As they learn about it, we should expect changes in democratic values and attitudes in the future.

11.2 Democratization in Mexico: The Zapatista Uprising and Civil Society (2001)

CHRIS GILBRETH AND GERARDO OTERO

January 1, 1994, will enter the history books as a date that marks a notable paradox in contemporary Mexico. Just when the country was being inaugurated into the "First World" by joining its northern neighbors in an economic association represented by the North American Free Trade Agreement (NAFTA), an armed rebellion broke out in the southeastern state of Chiapas. In the wake of a cease-fire following 12 days of fighting, a new social movement emerged that contested the direction of the nation's future as envisioned by the state and its ruling electoral machine, the Partido Revolucionario Institucional (Institutional Revolutionary Party—PRI). The adherents of the new movement are primarily Mayan peasants, both members and sympathizers of the Ejército Zapatista de Liberación Nacional (Zapatista National Liberation Army—EZLN), and their national and international supporters.

By focusing on the Zapatista uprising and its emergence as a social movement, we examine the relationship between civil society activity and political democratization. We argue that the social movement set in motion by the Zapatista uprising has been a driving force in Mexico's democratization, even more significant than opposition parties, which have historically been undermined or drawn into an alliance with the ruling PRI only to push for changes that left the authoritarian nature of the political system virtually intact. In contrast, the social movement generated by the EZLN has encouraged higher levels of political activity and inspired a deepening of the democratic debate. The key difference is that political parties have focused their efforts on reforming political society from within while the EZLN has interpellated civil society to push for democratization from the bottom up.

The Zapatista uprising placed Mexico's political system at a crossroads, and a merely procedural democracy is not likely to address the concerns of an invigorated civil society. As one of us had anticipated elsewhere, one possible outcome in 2000 was that the PRI would continue to harden its policies of social control; yet this direction was hardly compatible with the image Mexico had been promoting as a member of NAFTA. It was argued instead that the historically most likely scenario for the electoral process of 2000 was a liberal-democratic outcome in which the Partido Acción Nacional (National Action Party—PAN) would win the presidential elections. This would come about as the result of combining the continuation of a market-led economic model with an electoral democratization from below. On July 2, 2000, this prediction turned out to be accurate: a clear majority of Mexicans elected Vicente Fox of the PAN, thus ousting the PRI after 71 years of continuous rule. In this article we argue that continued citizen activity and popular mobilization have been able to redirect Mexico's political transition toward a more inclusive democracy in which the government must respond to a broad range of societal interests. In the first section we describe some of the post-1994 reforms that accelerated Mexico's process of democratization. In the second section we outline the range of ways in which civil society responded to the uprising. The third section addresses the state's response to the uprising and the repressive practices used to disable the Zapatista movement. The fourth describes the EZLN's efforts to mobilize the groups and individuals that rose in support of its demands and the strategy it employed to build new ties of solidarity. The concluding section discusses the Zapatista movement's contribution to Mexico's democratization in the context of the challenges that remain.

DEMOCRATIZATION AND THE ZAPATISTA UPRISING

The EZLN's declaration of war represented a break from traditional strategies associated with guerrilla movements in Latin America. After the uprising, the EZLN advocated bottom-up democratization rather than the seizing of state power and nonviolence rather than guerrilla warfare. It emphasized the potential of "civil society" (in EZLN usage, the subordinate individuals and organizations independent of the state's corporatist structures) for bringing about democratic change. The Zapatistas' vision sharply contrasted with the PRI's policy of a managed transition to electoral democracy including radical free-market reforms that had a negative impact on peasant life. Rather than making war to take power and impose its vision from above, the EZLN sought to open political spaces in which new actors in civil society could press for democracy and social justice from below. This view was consistent with that of the new Latin American left, which conceptualized power as a practice situated both within and beyond the state and exercised through what Gramsci referred to as "hegemony," the dissemination of beliefs and values that systematically favored the ruling class. In expressing this view the EZLN established a cultural strategy that called into question the PRI's hegemony by reinterpreting national symbols and discourses in favor of an alternative transformative project.

Throughout the PRI's 71-year rule, presidential candidates were handpicked by the incumbent president and ensured victory by use of electoral fraud when necessary. The presidency dominated the judicial and legislative branches, while civil society was co-opted by mass organizations controlled by the state. Opposition parties were rather insignificant until 1978, when there were only four legally recognized political parties. Of these, two had proposed the same presidential candidate as the PRI in various previous elections; they were seen as minor appendages of the ruling party. Only the right-of-center PAN represented a serious opposition, and in 1976 it had undergone an internal crisis that prevented it from naming a presidential candidate. This had led the state to initiate an electoral reform to prevent a crisis of legitimacy, allowing for the legal registration of several other political parties. The most relevant of these newly legalized parties was the Partido Comunista Mexicano (Mexican Communist Party—PCM). After a series of fusions with other parties, the PCM's heirs eventually formed the Partido de la Revolución Democrática (Party of the Democratic Revolution—PRD) by joining a nationalist faction of the PRI and other leftist political parties in 1989.

Before the 1994 uprising, the party system had not been able to provide incentives for a major reform of the state. It was only when the EZLN appeared as an external challenge to the system of political representation that political parties were prompted to cooperate among themselves and effect some meaningful changes. Immediately after the uprising, the interior minister and former governor of Chiapas, Patrocinio González, was forced to resign, and electoral reforms were announced that permitted international and civic observers to monitor the August 1994 presidential elections. Moreover, by 1996 the Instituto Federal Electoral (Federal Electoral Institute—IFE) was transformed into an independent body run by nonpartisan citizens rather than the government. In addition, the government appointed a peace commissioner, Manuel Camacho Solís, to initiate negotiations with the EZLN within a month of the 1994 uprising. This represented one of the quickest transitions from guerrilla uprising to peace process in Latin American history. During the 1997 mid-term elections, the opposition gained control of the Lower House of Congress for the first time in history, and Cuauhtémoc Cárdenas, a member of the left-of-center PRD, became Mexico City's first elected mayor. In 1999, the PRI held primary elections to choose its presidential candidate, breaking with the tradition by which the outgoing president chose his successor. Although critics have questioned the true competitiveness of the primary election, it represented a considerable contribution to Mexico's protracted process of democratization.

Until July 2000, though, significant obstacles remained on the path to democracy. Mexico continued to be described as a semidemocratic political system, since electoral fraud was still practiced. Moreover, the political system had not passed the test of alternation of power, the PRI having monopolized executive office for over 70 years. Democracy had also been threatened by the state's dismal record on respecting human rights and the rule of law. Security forces had routinely employed authoritarian practices, including threats, torture, intimidation, and repression against opposition movements. The state's link to the massacre of 45 indigenous people in Acteal, Chiapas, on December 22, 1997, was emblematic of the repressive conditions that challenged the basic requisites of liberal democracy: respect for civil and political rights, competitive elections, and a significant degree of political participation.

The 1994 uprising and ensuing social movement sparked a wave of commentary from Mexican intellectuals. Roger Bartra, a sociologist, remarked: "The war in Chiapas has provoked the strongest political and cultural shakeup that the Mexican system has suffered in the last quarter century." He argued that even though the violence used by the rebels ought to be considered antidemocratic, it had produced the unexpected result of reviving Mexico's prospects for democracy: "We are faced with the paradox that the EZLN has opened a road toward democracy." Antonio García de León, a historian, wrote: "The EZLN's contribution to the transition, or the constellation of small transitions, toward democracy is now an undeniable historic fact." Finally, Mexico's celebrated cultural critic and analyst of social movements, Carlos Monsiváis, similarly agreed that the EZLN had brought an impulse to the democratic project. If the EZLN has had an impact on Mexico's democratization, it can be seen in this awakening of civil society.

THE CIVIL-SOCIETY RESPONSE TO THE ZAPATISTA UPRISING

The Zapatista uprising inspired a flourishing of organization and support at the national and international levels. Civil society responded in many forms: protesting for the government to stop the war; organizing human rights security lines to encircle the dialogue site when peace talks were in session; bringing supplies to jungle communities surrounded by federal army units; establishing "peace camps" and observing human rights conditions in communities threatened by the military presence; organizing health, education, and alternative production projects; forming nongovernmental organizations (NGOs) to monitor respect for human rights; building civilian-based Zapatista support groups; and participating in forums and encounters convoked by the EZLN to discuss democracy and indigenous rights. A great deal of mobilization has taken place outside traditional political channels, motivated by the EZLN's call for democracy.

The first movement by civil society was a spontaneous reaction as thousands of protestors rallied against the government for ordering the Mexican air force to strafe and rocket the retreating rebels and for its summary execution of rebels captured by federal soldiers (verified in human rights reports). President Carlos Salinas found himself in the midst of a crisis as the Mexican stock exchange dropped 6.32 percent—the largest fall since 1987. He initially denounced the Zapatista insurgents as "professionals of violence" and "transgressors of the law," yet by January 12, because of sustained protest, he had ordered the resignation of his interior minister and called for a ceasefire and negotiations.

EZLN communiqués made it clear that the rebels opposed not only the lack of democracy but also the neoliberal free-market reforms that had opened Mexico's economy and people to the forces of global capitalism. Speaking to reporters in San Cristóbal's plaza on January 1, Subcomandante Marcos said: "Today is the beginning of NAFTA, which is nothing more than a death sentence for the indigenous ethnicities of Mexico, which are perfectly dispensable in the modernization program of Salinas de Gortari." A graffito left in San Cristóbal after the uprising read "We don't want free trade. We want Freedom!" One analyst noted, "Chiapas is the first armed battle against the Global Market and simultaneously . . . for Democracy."

The uprising undid the PRI's work to restore the public's confidence after fraudulent elections in 1988 had brought Carlos Salinas to power. The Salinas administration promised to bring Mexico into the First World and undertook profound reforms to lay the groundwork for NAFTA, reversing decades of statist and nationalistic policies in just a few years. The privatization of 252 state-run companies, including national banks and Telmex (Mexican Telephone Company), netted about U.S.$23 billion in state reserves and massively reduced government subsidies to hundreds of money-losing firms. One journalist wrote: "Salinas has worked hard to convert Mexico's socialist, nationalist economy into a capitalist, pro-American economy open to international trade." *Forbes* magazine remarked: "You can't any longer think of Mexico as the Third World."

The signing of NAFTA was meant to provide the PRI with renewed support for the 1994 elections. After the uprising, however, a harsh reinterpretation of Mexico's socioeconomic reality began. One Mexican writer remarked: "Just when we were telling the world and ourselves that we were looking like the U.S., we turn out to be Guatemala." Heberto Castillo, a left-nationalist politician, declared: "Those who applauded our growing economy . . . olympically ignored that while the rich got richer, the nation got even poorer."

On the local level, the Zapatista uprising represented the culmination of more than 20 years of independent peasant struggle, the manifestation of a long history of regional indigenous resistance, and an open demonstration of a guerrilla struggle that had operated in Chiapas since the early 1970s. One of the fundamental issues for EZLN fighters was the government's modification of Article 27 of the Federal Constitution, which had ended land reform, meaning that new petitions and outstanding claims would no longer be administered. The threat to land and the prospect of importing cheaper corn from the United States through NAFTA posed a serious threat to Mayan farmers' traditional way of life and their capacity to maintain subsistence production.

The uprising was carried out by actors whose collective identity was constructed around the Mayans' historical experience of racism and socioeconomic subordination. Even after the end of Spanish colonial rule in the early nineteenth century, indigenous people continued to suffer exploitation through slavery and debt peonage. Into the twentieth century, Mayans continued to serve as maids, farm hands, and laborers for the local ladino (non-indigenous) population of Chiapas. The slogan of the uprising was "Enough Is Enough." When asked why she had joined the EZLN, Comandante Hortencia, a Tzotzil woman, declared: "I became a Zapatista to struggle for my people, so that one day there will be justice and peace in Mexico." Zapatista members expressed the strong conviction that their historical condition would change only through their own efforts.

For some of the ladinos in Chiapas, the uprising embodied their fear of the *"indiada,"* the rebellion of the "savage Indians" who would come to rob, rape, and pillage. San Cristóbal, Ocosingo, Altamirano, and Las Margaritas are ladino-controlled towns in the midst of rural communities of Mayan subsistence farmers. Throughout history, a discourse has persisted that views the ladino population as naturally superior to the Indians. One government representative, a ladino woman from San Cristóbal, told an international delegation: "Before the uprising, there was a harmonious relationship between the indigenous people and the Ladinos. They worked in our homes, and we treated them as we would our children." Comandante Susana, a highland Tzotzil-speaker and EZLN spokesperson, said: "When we go into big cities they see us as nothing more than *indios* . . . they curse us for being indigenous people as if we were animals . . . we are not seen as equal to the mestizo women."

The uprising also raised the issue of socioeconomic disparities, particularly with regard to land distribution. In much of the conflict zone (the eastern municipalities of Ocosingo, Altamirano, and Las Margaritas), Mayan peasants had taken over and occupied land after 1994, seeking to improve their living conditions. A land reform movement had been in motion since the 1970s, but the uprising further politicized Mayan farmers and increased their militancy. In many cases, landlords abandoned their property during the uprising, fearing for their personal security. A great deal of this land remained unoccupied for several years, having been stripped of its livestock and work implements. In other cases, land was taken over, or "recovered," and new communities were formed. A representative from the New Population Moisés-Gandhi, Ocosingo, explained why community members came to occupy the land.

> This property belonged to our grandparents, who spoke Tzeltal but could not communicate in Spanish. Because of this, they were cheated out of their land. Their fields of corn were converted into a large cattle ranch, and our grandfathers were made to work as peons. Eventually they were forced to a small piece of land in the hills to work as their own. When our fathers were born, there was not enough land. And many families were forced to seek work as peons on other fincas. We had to live in other communities. Therefore we did not steal this land; when the owners left after the uprising, we recovered it as our own.

The Zapatista uprising and subsequent land takeovers inflamed ethnic relations. Ladinos expressed resistance to the idea of indigenous people's declaring their right to be equal members of Mexican society. A cattle rancher who had abandoned his land deep in Zapatista territory said: "The Indians do not want to work because they are lazy. Zapata was right when he said, 'Land for those who work it,' but he forgot to add 'for those who want to work it' and 'for those who know how to work it productively.'" This disregard for a culture rooted in subsistence farming was a reflection of the attitude that the Zapatistas wished to transform.

The uprising initiated a new emphasis on indigenous cultural empowerment. As the image of the rebel indigenous figure swept across Mexico. San Cristóbal's Tzotzil artisans reacted by sewing ski masks on their folk dolls and carving small wooden rifles to place in their hands. The new Zapatista dolls were an instant commercial success. Indigenous vendors proudly explained which EZLN commander was represented by each doll as they fashioned them to replicate the photos on the front pages of local newspapers showing Zapatista women and men negotiating with government officials. Seeing fellow indigenous people in their traditional clothing being shown respect was a source of pride and amazement for many Mayans who learned about the Zapatista uprising only after it took place. The impact of this new empowerment contributed to the growth of the movement after 1994 as communities in the highlands and the northern zone began to support the Zapatista project openly.

The impact of the uprising transformed Chiapas's social and political landscape. Indigenous people achieved a space for developing their demands and making themselves heard despite resistance by the local ladino population. Yet, the conflict also exacerbated tensions in indigenous communities, with members unsure of where they stood as government (PRI) or Zapatista supporters. The government's response to the uprising failed to contribute significantly to the overall process of conflict resolution but succeeded in reducing the EZLN's capacity to interact with national and international civil society to seek peaceful means for social transformation.

THE STATE RESPONSE TO THE ZAPATISTA UPRISING

Soon after the uprising, the Mexican government appeared to advocate peace by establishing a cease-fire and agreeing to negotiate with the EZLN. The government appointed a peace commissioner, and just three months after the uprising EZLN representatives and government officials were meeting face-to-face in San Cristòbal. The first round of negotiations broke down in June 1994 as national elections approached, but the process was reestablished in spring 1995 in response to a military action by Ernesto Zedillo's government aimed at arresting the EZLN leadership. The 1995–1996 negotiations in San Anlrés Larráinzar established a framework for discussion and a process for achieving signed accords.

The restart of negotiations took place as part of an agreement that required the government to limit the number of troops in the eastern lowlands as a measure of security for civilian communities threatened by their presence. Despite the agreement, soldiers continued to pour into regions with known support for the EZLN as the peace talks continued through 1996. The policy of pursuing peace on one hand and using repression on the other was interpreted by human rights organizations as a form of low-intensity warfare, with parallels to counterinsurgency strategies used during the wars in Vietnam and Central America. In low-intensity warfare, the army uses public relations to favor civilians who align themselves with the government, rewarding them with material aid, health services, or work on road projects, while communities in resistance face harassment and intimidation. Attacks by the public security police and federal army on "autonomous communities" (so declared by EZLN forces) demonstrate that in Chiapas low-intensity tactics have been combined with direct coercive practices by the state.

The February 1995 military offensive in eastern Chiapas resulted in the establishment of dozens of new camps. The bases served to reestablish the state's presence in the region and reduced the degree to which these isolated communities could carry out peaceful oppositional activities. Numerous trips into this zone between 1995 and 1998 provided us with firsthand experience of the extent to which daily life had been transformed by the presence of soldiers. There were regular ground and air patrols. It was common for locals and outsiders alike to be questioned at military roadblocks or startled by military fly-bys and circling helicopters or to become the subject of surveillance. Under these conditions, freedom of political expression was substantially reduced. Federal soldiers and paramilitaries sometimes considered even local opposition activity subversive.

Parish workers testified to the military presence's negative impact on daily life. The cost of living increased because of a rise in demand for basic products such as soap, sugar, salt, and oil. Local price inflation was accompanied by declining food production, as farmers no longer felt safe working on their distant cultivated lands. In addition, soldiers reportedly abused alcohol and drugs and had established a network of prostitution. In communities suffering extreme poverty, there were reports of indigenous girls being forced into prostitution to provide food for their families.

The government offered short-term material support to civilians but would not reduce the presence of its troops. Aid was in some cases distributed by local PRI authorities who made it clear that the assistance was for families who supported the government. These policies and the presence of soldiers slowed the Zapatistas' momentum, polarized communities with divided loyalties, and eventually erupted into violence as government supporters, emboldened by local PRI authorities, were encouraged to form paramilitary groups to attack EZLN sympathizers, particularly in regions outside the eastern-lowland conflict zone. In some cases, the violence was government-supported, while in others it was officially tolerated and allowed to persist through institutionalized impunity. The Portuguese Nobel laureate José Saramago criticized Zedillo's assertion that "there was no war in Chiapas": "There are wars that are wars and there are 'no-wars' that are the same as wars." Mary Robinson, the head of the United Nations High Commission for Human Rights, was critical of the level of violations and impunity in Chiapas during her 1999 visit.

Paramilitary violence first appeared in the Chol-speaking municipalities of Tila, Salto de Agua, Yajalón, Sabanilla, and Chilón (the northern zone) in 1995. In the beginning it was not evident whether the localized violence was part of the broader pattern of conflict, but subsequent popular mobilizations demonstrated that support for the EZLN's demands had indeed spread to the northern zone. The 1996 construction of a fifth EZLN "New Aguas-calientes" site in Roberto Barrios, Palenque, involved hundreds of Chol-speaking activists from the northern zone. They expressed their grievances and demonstrated their support for the EZLN on banners hung at the site that denounced the government's lack of will to resolve the violence in Tila. Sympathy for the EZLN was also demonstrated by the indigenous activists who took over the municipal hall in Sabanilla and by the thousands who participated in a march for peace when the opposition politician Cuauhté-moc Cárdenas visited Tila in 1996. Consequently, the violence against popular mobilization in the northern zone was interpreted as a direct coun-termeasure to the growing regional support for the EZLN.

During a human rights mission in 1996 to investigate the relationship be-tween the growing violence and the government's militarization of the re-gion, testimony was provided linking PRI politicians and members of the public security police in the northern zone to the clandestine supply of weapons and training to civilians who would violently oppose the EZLN. The most notorious example was the transformation of a rural development organization, Paz y Justicia, into a front for paramilitary violence supported by the PRI state government. Paz y Justicia's violent actions resulted in the displacement of thousands of non-PRI-supporting families from their homes and a string of confrontations and assassinations by both sides in the conflict. At one point it was impossible for human rights observers to enter the northern zone after two shooting incidents by Paz y Justicia militiamen, targeting a human rights observer mission and a material-aid caravan.

By 1997, the same pattern of violence began to appear in Chiapas's cen-tral highlands as a rash of local skirmishes between government and EZLN supporters resulted in several deaths and the displacement of hundreds of families. The situation culminated in the massacre of 45 indigenous women, children, and men while they were praying in a small chapel in the hamlet of Acteal, Chenalhó, on December 22, 1997. The subsequent investigation exposed direct links between the paramilitary militia responsible for the killing and the municipal PRI government and state public security forces.

The government had agreed not to increase its troops in the conflict zone as part of the 1995 Law for Peace and Reconciliation under which the peace process was regulated. In addition, Article 129 of the Mexican Constitution prohibited soldiers from patrolling outside their bases in times of peace. Yet, the military justified its roadblocks, patrols, and new encampments as part of a mission to combat drug trafficking and control the flow of arms. More-over, the military claimed that its growing presence, following outbreaks of violence in the highlands and northern zone, was required to maintain security, even though opposition groups complained that the military presence repressed their right to political expression and their capacity to seek political change through peaceful means. Given these conditions, it would be easy to infer that political activity throughout Chiapas had been constrained. On the contrary, however, a remarkable groundswell of civil society mobilization has taken place in response to the uprising, and this activity has contributed significantly to Mexico's difficult process of democratization.

THE ZAPATISTA APPEAL TO CIVIL SOCIETY

From the moment that the Zapatistas' first communiqué was faxed to the national press, the indigenous rebels entered history, becoming cultural icons in Mexico. Subcomandante Marcos's writings in the name of the Comité Clandestino Revolucionario Indígena-Comandancia General (Clandestine Revolutionary Indigenous Committee-General Command—CCRI-CG) were published worldwide, along with personal letters, poetry, and short stories. Marcos took full advantage of the media coverage, giving dozens of interviews that contributed to his transformation from masked rebel to freedom fighter. Reproductions of his image were embossed on calendars, ashtrays, key chains, T-shirts, stickers, lighters, and pens sold throughout Mexico. Marcos was called the "poet rebel" in *Vanity Fair*, and CBS's *60 Minutes* sent a crew to interview him in English for U.S. audiences. Even Mexico's conservative Nobel Prize–winning writer Octavio Paz, who initially came out against the EZLN, later referred to one of Marcos's communiqués as "eloquent" and said that it had truly moved him. The European press widely covered the EZLN's initial actions, and high-profile Latin American intellectuals and European public figures, including the Uruguayan writer Eduardo Galeano and the former first lady of France, Danielle Mitterrand, took an active role in defending the Zapatista cause.

The uprising was seen as a bold statement by an oppressed minority against an encroaching global capitalism that threatened the small Mayan farmer and, by extension, any subordinate group unable to shoulder the weight of global competition. It also set in motion a technological novelty. For the first time observers around the world could follow the development of the movement from their computer screens as EZLN communiqués and subsequent debates and discussions went whirling through cyberspace (http://www.ezln.org). Reflections from various disciplinary perspectives on cultural politics on the Internet were also inspired by the Zapatista struggle.

Many people felt that Marcos's communiqués revealed the truth about the disgraceful conditions under which a large portion of the population lived at a time when national and international leaders were promoting Mexico's new partnership in NAFTA. The communiqués resonated with other popular movements, attracting a network of supporters inspired by the Zapatistas' ideals of democracy, justice, and freedom. In 1995, Marcos was on the list of nominees for the Premio Chiapas in recognition of his contribution to the promotion of culture in the state. His literary pieces included a popular series of conversations with a beetle named Durito and narratives describing the teachings of Antonio the elder, a Tzeltal Indian portrayed as a wise man who had taught Marcos how to live in the jungle and understand the Mayan people. His political writings were popular and praised by political analysts. The following communiqué was issued on January 18, 1994, in response to President Salinas's initial offer to "pardon" Zapatista rebels who accepted the cease-fire:

> For what must we ask pardon? For what will they "pardon" us? For not dying of hunger? For not accepting our misery in silence? For not humbly accepting the huge historic burden of disdain and abandonment? For having risen up in arms when we found all other paths closed? For not heeding Chiapas's penal code, the most absurd and repressive in history? For having shown the country and the whole world that human dignity still exists and is in the hearts of the most impoverished inhabitants? For what must we ask pardon, and who can grant it?

These communiqués, representing the CCRI-CG, were published in national newspapers, translated and posted on the Internet, and debated in electronic mail, helping to build an international network to support the Zapatistas' right to use peaceful means to attain their political goals. When the army unleashed an offensive in Zapatista-held territory in February 1995, international solidarity groups and human rights activists from around the globe protested at Mexican consulates and embassies. NGOs and human rights organizations sent representatives to Chiapas to accompany the return of hundreds of families displaced by the military's violence. Citizen lobbies of national parliaments and congresses in Canada, the United States, Denmark, Italy, Spain, and Germany resulted in formal petitions encouraging the Mexican government to comply with the 1996 San Andrés Accords on Indigenous Rights and Culture.

After just 12 days of fighting, the EZLN sought to advance its agenda in various arenas, from negotiations with the government to the establishment of a relationship with the public. In this way, the Zapatista movement was able to challenge both state power and what it perceived to be the sociocultural embeddedness of power in everyday life. Its use of counterdiscursive framing to reinterpret national symbols furthered support for its alternative transformative project. It sought to build a movement based on a shared understanding of the obstacles it confronted (an authoritarian regime and an increasingly unaccountable market) and a collective will to seek alternatives. In Gramsci's terms, the EZLN changed its strategy from a "war of movements" challenging state power through the force of arms to a "war of positions" contesting the moral and intellectual leadership of Mexico's ruling class.

The first negotiation session took place in the San Cristóbal Cathedral in March 1994. The presence of the media placed the movement in the national spotlight. Radio transmissions brought the indigenous voices of Zapatista representatives into villages across Chiapas. The EZLN took advantage of the media attention to present its discourse of inclusion as Comandante David introduced himself to government negotiators as "David, Tzotzil, one-hundred percent Chiapanecan, one-hundred percent Mexican." The point was further emphasized when Zapatista delegates unrolled and displayed the Mexican flag. The government commissioner, Manuel Camacho Solís, felt obliged to join them by holding up a corner. The Zapatistas conveyed to the public that their fight was not against the nation but for a new form of nationhood in which Mexico's diverse cultures would be recognized equally.

The Zapatistas have made political use of culture to communicate with civil society. For example, they have restored the symbolism of Aguascalientes, the city where the original followers of Emiliano Zapata and other revolutionaries convened in 1914 for a constitutional assembly ("La Convención") to define the future of the Mexican revolution. The first new Aguascalientes was constructed in Guadalupe Tepeyac in 1994. Following failed peace talks in June, the EZLN issued a Second Declaration from the Lacandón Jungle, calling on civil society to participate in a national democratic convention, based on the 1914 assembly, to take place just weeks before the August 1994 presidential elections. The construction of Aguascalientes was a large-scale collective undertaking, involving the labor of hundreds of local indigenous Zapatista supporters who carved an amphitheater and lodgings from the jungle to host more than 6,000 participants from throughout Mexico. The meeting served to establish new citizen networks and resulted in the creation of a permanent forum for discussion of a democratic transition.

The convention represented a significant advance for the EZLN. In less than a year the Zapatistas had progressed from being "professionals of violence" and "transgressors of the law" to a new social movement capable of calling upon some of the nation's most important progressive intellectuals and grassroots leaders. The fact that the government saw the symbolism of Aguascalientes as a threat was made clear when, after the February 9, 1995, government offensive, the soldiers demolished it. This aggression forced the abandonment of Guadalupe Tepeyac and the displacement of thousands of indigenous families. A large military base was established there, closing the local population's access to the best medical structure in the region.

The cultural significance attached by the EZLN to its Aguascalientes site was made evident during restarted peace talks in San Andrés Larráinzar. As discussions took place about the possible withdrawal of federal troops, the government let it be understood that the removal of troops from Guadalupe Tepeyac was not negotiable. Comandante Tacho responded by declaring that the government could keep its Aguascalientes because the EZLN had plans to build many more. Several months later, shortly before the second anniversary of the uprising, national and international civil society was invited to attend celebrations on January 1, 1996, at one of four New Aguascalientes sites—three in eastern jungle communities and one in the highlands, just a 40-minute drive from San Cristóbal. A fifth Aguascalientes was inaugurated in Roberto Barrios, near Palenque, in May 1996.

The building of the New Aguascalientes symbolized a rebirth for the EZLN. Under heavy security, hundreds of Zapatista supporters worked around the clock constructing the new sites. At Oventic in the central highlands, convoys of federal soldiers, including 40 wheel-based armored tanks, passed through the perimeter of the site in an attempt at intimidation. In the jungle, airplanes and helicopters menaced workers, taking photos and pointing guns. The Zapatistas nevertheless persisted in their task, and the four New Aguascalientes were inaugurated on New Year's Day 1996 with cultural festivities organized by an artistic caravan from Mexico City under the rallying cry, "We are not making a call to take up arms, instead we are going to sing to the ones who have dared to shout, Enough is Enough!" At the highland Aguascalientes site in Oventic, Comandante Moisés stated: "The government has threatened us while building this site, but we, the indigenous people of Chiapas, do not have to ask permission to use our land any way we want to. The construction of this site proves that if the government takes away a part of us, it will come back and multiply."

Zapatista negotiators also used the peace talks at San Andrés Larráinzar in 1995 as a forum to assert their cultural identity as Mayan people. EZLN communiqués referred to the town as "San Andrés Sacamch'en de los Pobres" in recognition of sacred caves in the region and rejection of the colonial legacy inherent in the municipality's official name (the Larráinzar family had controlled most of the land in the region). Such displays of cultural pride proved popular in the region, where there had not been a significant presence of ladinos since the 1970s. The emphasis on indigenous identity was also highlighted by Marcos's notable absence from the peace talks. The EZLN negotiating team was made up of nine Mayan representatives from different regions of the highlands and eastern lowlands. Several EZLN delegates wore traditional highland ceremonial clothing, consisting of large hats with ribbons, cotton tunics, wool capes, woven belts, and leather sandals. The ski masks covering their individual identities were meant to highlight the collectivist nature of the struggle.

In addition to the peace talks, the EZLN pushed forward its agenda through organizing national and international meetings with civil society. In January 1996, it convoked the National Indigenous Forum, in which representatives from 35 indigenous ethnic groups from across Mexico took part. These encounters followed the EZLN principle of "rule by obeying," calling for Zapatista delegates to derive their position at the negotiating table democratically from the concerns expressed by representatives of civil society. The document produced by the National Indigenous Forum provided the basis for the San Andrés Accords on Indigenous Rights and Culture, signed by the government and the EZLN in February 1996.

The National Indigenous Forum was in many ways a watershed moment for Mexico's indigenous cultures. The historian Jan de Vos described it as follows:

> This is the first national forum of its type for indigenous people in Mexico. It has been an important way to demonstrate to the government that the indigenous people in Chiapas are not just making local demands. Their demands are being echoed here by a large number of indigenous cultures and organizations from across the country. . . . The forum will demonstrate the national character of indigenous demands.

The second forum, on the reform of the Mexican state, was convoked by the EZLN six months later, in July 1996. It again took place in San Cristóbal, this time bringing together intellectuals from across Mexico to discuss the themes of political democracy, social democracy, national sovereignty and democracy, citizen participation, human rights, justice reform, and communication media. Manuel López Obrador, leader of the opposition PRD, met with Marcos to discuss the possibility of a strategic alliance for the 1997 national congressional elections. The forum was meant to provide the basis for the signing of a second accord between the EZLN and government. Instead, the peace process broke down a month later because of the EZLN's frustration with the lack of progress on the implementation of the San Andrés Accords. On September 2, 1996, the negotiations were suspended, and a wave of repression aimed at human rights activists in Chiapas followed.

Since the breakdown of the peace process, political debate has revolved around the implementation of the San Andrés Accords, particularly on the issue of autonomy. When President Zedillo rejected a proposal put forth by a multiparty commission of legislators (Comisión para la Concordia y la Pacificación—COCOPA) to translate the accord into law, indigenous communities saw this as government betrayal and initiated a movement to enact the accord in practice by establishing new autonomous municipalities and parallel governments throughout Chiapas. It is no coincidence that one of Vicente Fox's first acts as president was to appoint Luis H. Alvarez, a former governor of Chihuahua and former PAN senator, to head a negotiating team to reestablish talks with the EZLN. As a senator, Alvarez had been part of the commission that turned the San Andrés Accords into a legislative proposal. (The newly elected governor of Chiapas in 2000, Pablo Salazar Mendiguchía, elected with the backing of a coalition of seven opposition parties, had also been a COCOPA member.) Fox also ordered the withdrawal of most troops from Chiapas, with the sole exception of those that might have been there before the uprising. From all evidence, then, it seems that the conditions are now in place for a peaceful solution to the EZLN uprising with justice and dignity. Accomplishing this would be an additional boost to Fox's legitimacy as a democrat.

CONCLUSIONS

An examination of the Zapatista movement and democracy in Mexico raises a number of questions: Is Mexico's transition to democracy responding to the concerns raised by the Zapatista movement? What has been the movement's contribution to the transition, and how can it continue to influence the process? What priorities should be established for advancing Mexico's democratization beyond the electoral sphere? Before reflecting on these questions, we examine some recent theorizing on democracy that helps highlight the issues raised by the Zapatista uprising.

Ellen Meiksins Wood argues that confining democracy to the realm of politics allows market forces to operate without democratic accountability in fundamental spheres of life, calling into question the degree to which democracy in its original conception as "power by the people" can be achieved under capitalism. Alain Touraine makes a similar argument: "To some extent, the market economy is democracy's antithesis, as the market attempts to prevent political institutions from intervening in its activity, whereas democratic politics attempts to promote intervention so as to protect the weak from the domination of the strong." John Dryzek also conceives of capitalism as an obstacle to democracy, but he argues for civil society's potential to advance democracy. For him the prospects for democracy under global capitalism "are better in civil society than in the formal institutions of government, across rather than within national boundaries, and in realms of life not always recognized as political." Finally, Takis Fotopoulos proposes a new model of inclusive democracy that expands democratic practices beyond the formal domain of politics to include the sphere of everyday life and social control over the market. The common thread among these theories of democracy is that each judges the political realm, if confined to political society or the state, incapable of offering citizens sufficient access to democratic power over critical decisions that affect their everyday lives.

The Zapatista uprising contributed to an expansion of democracy in the domain of political society but also beyond it—into civil society and the cultural sphere. In addition, it has sought to expand democratization to the economic realm in order to address the social costs of neoliberal market reforms. Perhaps the most notable paradox has been that the EZLN became the first guerrilla organization to propose resolving its grievances through peaceful means. After the uprising, it sought to encourage civil society to change the correlation of forces between the state and civil society and to defeat the ruling PRI. While the PRI won the elections in 1994, the uprising inspired civil society to call into question the PRI's monopoly on power, which, in turn, accelerated the pace of political reform. The significant results it produced included the establishment of international and civic electoral observation, a reformed and independent IFE, a Lower House of Congress controlled by the opposition, and elections for Mexico City mayor. For the first time, in 2000 the PRI held primary elections to select its candidate for the presidential elections. Finally, PAN's Vicente Fox's electoral triumph in 2000 set the stage for a major overhaul of Mexico's political system.

Because of the Zapatista movement, new spaces for political participation have been opened within civil society. Through popular consultations with civic groups ranging from indigenous supporters to members of international civil society and through direct encounters with civil-society organizations, the EZLN has encouraged democratic discussion and debate. Networks of NGOs began to emerge in Mexico in the 1980s, but the Zapatista uprising inspired a tremendous proliferation of NGOs that spread both to stop the war in Chiapas and to struggle for a host of issues under the broad agenda of democratization. Some NGOs restricted their activity and linkages to the realm of civil society and were able to retain their autonomy, while others became "political associations" or established links with the state, following the path previously taken by political parties. Acción Cívica (Civic Association), for instance, received funds from the state, and the resulting commitments diminished its autonomy. Ilán Semo has pointed out that as members of NGOs join political parties, compromises are made in terms of their organizations' identity and ability to operate autonomously. For this reason, the Zapatista movement, perceiving the PRI political regime as exclusionary and authoritarian, focused on the realm of civil society.

In the sociocultural sphere, the Zapatista movement challenged racist practices in Mexico by establishing a new awareness of indigenous rights. This is perhaps one of the most direct contributions that the EZLN has made to democratization. As Monsiváis noted: "Mexican racism has been exposed for the first time at a national level. . . . Since the 1994 Chiapas revolt . . . more books on the Indian question have been published than in the rest of the century." Indeed, the San Andrés Accords outline a significant program of reform that, if implemented, would go a long way toward redressing the historical grievances of Mexico's indigenous population. The debate around autonomy and Mexico as a pluricultural nation has included several alternative proposals for decentralization and strengthening local democracy.

The Zapatista movement has sought to expand democratization in the economic sphere by taking issue with neoliberalism (the trend toward free markets and globalized trade) as an economic model. The exacerbation of socio-economic disparities following free-market reforms provoked the EZLN to question the relationship between economic marginalization and political exclusion and the extent to which this hampers democracy. The Zapatista movement has criticized the diminishing ability of the nation-state to shape the domestic economy as it becomes increasingly integrated into global capitalism. It has joined the concerns of a transnational movement advocating a reconceptualization of how market forces can be made accountable to principles of social justice to address the harsher effects of neoliberal globalism.

As an external challenge to the political system, the Zapatista movement has accelerated Mexico's democratization. It has called into question the PRI's 71-year monopoly of power and strengthened civil society's capacity to articulate its grievances. In this way, it has contributed to redressing the historical imbalance of an overbearing state in state-society relations. The sad irony, however, is that the gains achieved by the Zapatista movement have eluded its immediate constituency, namely, the indigenous support-base communities in Chiapas. In fact, some could argue that this constituency is considerably worse off in terms of physical and economic security. One may hope that this tragedy will be reversed under the new administration.

In the long run, many questions about Mexico's transition to democracy will need to be addressed. One thing that is clear about Vicente Fox's administration is that it will continue on the path of neoliberalism. The question is to what extent it will be responsive to pressure from below to address some of neoliberalism's worse social consequences. Can the social movement supporting the Zapatistas' demands achieve its vision of social transformation through a democratization of the Mexican state with pressure from below? Even if democracy deepens to include the concerns of Mexico's majority, how will an empowered civil society ultimately confront the extension of the neoliberal economic model? More centrally for Mexico's long-term political development, can the state be transformed enough to incorporate the demand for autonomy and the control of land resources that the emboldened indigenous movement is demanding? Today's conflicting agendas with regard to Mexico's path to democracy will be the basis for future debates. The strong networks and alliances developed by the Zapatistas among Mexico's indigenous ethnic groups and more broadly within Mexican civil society, as well as dialogue and the cross-border citizen alliances that they have created, will prove central to their resolution.

11.3 Fox's Mexico: Same as It Ever Was? (2002)

PAMELA K. STARR

Vicente Fox's inauguration as president on December 1, 2000 brought with it great expectations for Mexico's future. Fox's electoral victory over the Institutional Revolutionary Party (PRI) the previous July had broken over 70 years of continuous PRI control of an authoritarian presidency and hence of the country. It thus promised to usher in a new era of expanded democracy, increased individual rights, and a significant positive change in the country's political and economic course.

Fox's victory undoubtedly has deepened democracy in Mexico, created a new image for the country in the world, and established a new style of governance. And no one honestly expected significant policy advances would come quickly and easily. The new government lacked experience and faced enormous challenges. Errors in strategy and tactics were virtually inevitable as the first opposition administration in living memory took the reins of power, and efforts to change a highly institutionalized and deeply ingrained political order would inevitably be painfully slow. Further, the enormously high expectations produced by the first post-PRI government guaranteed that Fox's advances would be seen as insufficient by a country desperate for change. Yet even considering these caveats, the performance of the Fox administration during its first year in office has been disappointing.

Since the arrival of Vicente Fox to the presidency, Mexico has been stuck in neutral. The executive has been characterized by confusion, indecision, and repeated policy mistakes. Mexican political parties have shown a striking inability to adjust their behavior to the new democratic political environment. And Mexicans of all stripes remain steeped in an authoritarian culture that has prevented them from embracing the political opportunities offered by Mexico's new democratic setting. The consequence has been a year dominated by political bickering and legislative inaction on reforms essential to the long-term health of the Mexican economy and of Mexico's democratic experiment.

If nothing changes in Mexico during 2002, the country can look forward to a future characterized by a lack of robust economic growth and increased vulnerability to international economic shocks, and a growing likelihood that an only moderately reformed PRI will retake full control of the national legislature in 2003 and of the presidency in 2006.

CONFUSION AND INCONSISTENCIES REIGN

During its first year in office, the Fox administration has shown a striking inability to get things done. It did manage to get two austere budget laws through Congress and win the approval of important elements of a much-needed financial reform. But there is little else legislatively to crow about. The Fox administration managed to ensure the approval of a new law on indigenous people, its top legislative priority. But after extensive revisions imposed by Congress, the law was unable to achieve its true objective of convincing the Zapatista rebels in Chiapas to initiate peace negotiations with the federal government. Meanwhile, fiscal, energy, and labor reform, improved security, reforms designed to increase democracy and efficiency in the Mexican state, and increased investment in human capital and infrastructure development all made little headway during 2001, and a desperately needed judicial reform never found its way onto the agenda. Behind this failure to deliver is the administration's inability to pursue an established policy course and send a clear policy message to the nation, and its failure to work effectively with the legislature. Although blame for this circumstance does not lie entirely with the Fox administration, much of it reflects a marked lack of consistency and coordination within the executive branch.

One of the most striking features of the Fox government's first year in office has been its tendency to contradict itself, creating the perception that the government does not know what it is doing or where it is going. For example, throughout the presidential campaign Fox insisted that he would transform the national oil company, PEMEX, into an autonomous firm managed on the basis of market principles. In this vein, soon after taking office he announced the appointment of four prominent businessmen to the administrative board of PEMEX. Not surprisingly, this move produced a great deal of consternation within the political opposition. The opposition's deep mistrust of Fox's ultimate aims for PEMEX led it to conclude that the inclusion of private-sector interests on the board was a first step toward the privatization of the firm. The president of the PRI, Dulce Maria Sauri, referred to this move as the "silent privatization" of the firm and vowed to block it. Also unsurprising was the opposition of PEMEX's union, which feared the move signaled future job cuts. What was surprising was Fox's decision to back down. Within weeks Fox caved in to opposition pressure, apparently fearing that the issue could obstruct other, more important administration objectives.

In much the same way, after insisting for months that a new 15 percent value-added tax on food, medicines, and books was completely nonnegotiable, Fox suddenly changed his mind. At an event with Carlos Fuentes during August in which the most famous of Mexican novelists criticized the tax on books, Fox unexpectedly reversed course and announced the elimination of the tax from his proposal. Backtracking from an established position is an obvious and commonly used negotiating tactic. But in these two instances the Fox administration gave without receiving anything in return from its opponents. This produced a growing perception on the part of the opposition that the administration was weak and could be bullied into abandoning its policies. The result was a more aggressive and obstructionist opposition.

Inconsistencies and contradictions have also emerged regularly from within the Fox cabinet. The debate on fiscal reform was punctuated throughout the spring and early summer by conflicting statements from seemingly every corner of the president's cabinet. And following the September 11 attacks on the World Trade Center and the Pentagon, Mexican foreign policy was a perfect muddle. Foreign Minister Jorge Castañeda immediately announced Mexico's full backing for the United States and any response it might deem appropriate. This statement of unconditional support for the United States produced a nationalist backlash in the Mexican political class and unease throughout the country. Sensing a political opportunity, Interior Minister Santiago Creel took over the leadership of this opposition. An open dispute between the two ministers persisted for over two weeks before President Fox finally ended it by coming down on the side of Castañeda. In the meantime, confusion reigned. What was the government's policy? Why didn't Fox end the debate sooner? Was he incapable of making a decision or was he incapable of controlling his own cabinet? Whatever the answers to these questions, the incident raised doubts about Fox's ability to lead the nation.

THE MONTESSORI CABINET

The continuing cacophony of disparate policy opinions emerging from within Fox's cabinet has earned it an unwanted nickname: the Montessori cabinet. Each minister seems to be following his or her own script with little or no policy coordination and without anyone willing or able to impose order. This dynamic has three drivers: the institutional structure of the administration, the political inexperience of the cabinet, and Fox's governing style.

The institutional structure of the executive branch under Vicente Fox is more complex than that of his predecessors. In addition to 19 cabinet secretaries it includes a new innovation: 7 coordinators with the responsibility of easing communication and increasing policy management within the cabinet. To this end the executive branch has been organized into three groups—quality growth, order and respect, and social development—with a coordinator to oversee each group. These chiefs of staff for the ministries under their purview were expected to increase the operational efficiency of the executive branch. Quite the opposite occurred. Rather than increasing cooperation and communication, they have deepened confusion and inconsistency within the administration.

Created out of nothing, the coordinators lacked the funds and institutional base that would have given them the legitimacy and power needed to coordinate the activities of cabinet ministries jealous of their autonomy. Nor did the cabinet secretaries adapt easily to someone other than the president giving them policy direction. They thus often limited communication and cooperation with their coordinator and thereby directly and intentionally undermined the capacity of the coordinators to do their job. The coordinators thus became another layer of government designing their own policy proposals independent of the offices they were supposed to coordinate. Since these proposals often differed from those of the ministries, increased policy conflict and confusion rather than greater coordination and efficiency ensued.

Policy confusion and inefficiency also have reflected the inexperience of most of the Fox cabinet. Although Fox made a point of choosing people highly qualified to head each ministry, in most cases he neglected to include political experience in the mix of qualifications. The result has been a cabinet with strong personalities and extensive experience in the private sector but with very little understanding of the subtleties of politics. Fox's cabinet secretaries have thus regularly ruffled congressional feathers and publicly aired contradictory and often polemical points of view.

The costs of a cabinet lacking government experience have been deepened by Fox's governing style. Fox runs Mexico much as one would manage a firm: he sets out policy goals and allows his cabinet to design and implement the means to achieve them. Although a delegative managerial style can be a very efficient strategy of governing under appropriate conditions, it does not work well under a flawed organizational structure and with ministers who are very self-assured yet politically inexperienced.

AN UNSUPPORTIVE GOVERNING PARTY . . .

The inability of the Fox administration to make legislative advances during its first year in government is not solely the consequence of policy confusion and inconsistencies in the executive branch. It also reflects the limited ability of Mexican political parties to adjust their operations to the demands of Mexico's new democratic political environment. The National Action Party (PAN) has not yet figured out what it means to be the party in government. The Democratic Revolutionary Party (PRD) continues to believe that the opposition's only job is to oppose. And the PRI has been politically paralyzed by an internal leadership struggle and the search for an identity as the opposition. The result has been a legislature both unwilling and unable to take the political risks associated with the passage of essential but controversial legislation.

The relationship between Vicente Fox and the party under whose emblem he was elected to the presidency, the PAN, has never been an easy one. Fox has not gotten along with the leader of the PAN's dominant traditionalist faction, Diego Fernandez de Cevallos, since 1991, when Fernandez de Cevallos sacrificed Fox on the altar of political expediency. (As candidate for governor of Guanajuato state, Fox was declared the loser in a clearly fraudulent election. Fernandez de Cevallos negotiated a compromise with then-President Carlos Salinas under which both Fox and his PRI opponent would step aside in favor of another PAN politician.)

When Fox decided to make a run for the presidency, he correctly recognized that a party structure controlled by Fernandez de Cevallos would not be overly friendly to his candidacy. So Fox made an end run around the party hierarchy. He established a campaign structure independent of the party, appealed directly to the voters, and forced the party to accept his candidacy as a fait accompli. He succeeded, but at the price of further angering the traditionalist wing of the party. Given this history, it was not surprising when President Fox named a cabinet virtually devoid of traditional PAN politicians and when he made little effort to involve the party in the process of governing. It was equally unsurprising when this sort of treatment generated resentment within the party even among Fox's supporters.

While Vicente Fox was doing little to make the PAN feel like the party in government, the party itself was suffering an identity crisis that undermined its ability to support President Fox. The PAN feared that Fox's election would transform it into what it had criticized for over 60 years. It was petrified of becoming a new PRI—a party controlled from the presidency, indistinguishable from the government, and devoid of an independent identity. In its zeal not to become the new party of state, the PAN has been hesitant to give its full support to President Fox and his legislative proposals.

This combination of factors—a traditionalist wing of the party led by Fernandez de Cevallos, who also controls the party leadership and its legislative leadership, Fox's disdainful treatment of the PAN, and the PAN's fear of becoming a new PRI—culminated in a party that operated as if it were the opposition during the first months of the Fox presidency. The most visible example of this relationship was the PAN's opposition to the new Indigenous Law, the first legislative initiative sent to Congress by President Fox.

The PAN had long opposed the proposal to increase the autonomy of indigenous communities on which Fox based his legislative measure. This opposition and the party's lukewarm support for President Fox led the PAN to work actively in Congress to modify this proposal. The real showdown between the PAN and Vicente Fox, however, came over the Zapatista rebels' request that their representative be permitted to speak before Congress in favor of the Fox proposal. Fox strongly supported this request while the PAN delegation in both houses of Congress unanimously opposed it. The leader of the PAN in the Chamber of Deputies insisted that neither Subcommander Marcos (the leader of the Zapatistas) nor Fox would dictate to the legislature. The PAN leader in the Senate, Fernandez de Cevallos, received an ovation at a party assembly when he argued that Fox "is the promoter, he is the representative and the publicist of Marcos." The lower house of Congress ultimately authorized a Zapatista appearance, but not a single PAN deputy voted in favor. In late April the Indigenous Law passed the legislature, but it was the PAN's highly modified version of the Fox proposal. Given that the Zapatistas had demanded the measure's approval without any modifications, the legislation was insufficient to convince the rebels to initiate peace talks. The PAN thus delivered a clear defeat to Vicente Fox on his very first legislative initiative as president, and it did so in a manner highly critical of the president.

This political disaster chastened both sides in the dispute. In the ensuing weeks, Fernandez de Cevallos lowered his tone significantly, the party leadership made a concerted effort to develop a working relationship with its president, and Fox and his cabinet ministers began to communicate more effectively with PAN legislators. But this entente came only after a great deal of political damage had been done. Further, even after its change of heart, the PAN remained hesitant to support Fox unconditionally.

. . . AN IMPOTENT OPPOSITION . . .

The opposition of the PRD to Fox's legislative agenda has been unrelenting throughout the president's first year in office, and it seems unlikely that this posture will change. For the PRD, the transition from the PRI to the PAN has brought few real changes in the policy direction of the nation, and the party remains a minority in the legislature and thus has limited incentives to collaborate with the government.

The PRD strongly opposes the market-based economic strategy former President Ernesto Zedillo initiated and Fox continued. From the party's perspective, the market is not sufficiently efficient to provide economic well-being for the majority of Mexicans. Given this bias in economic policy, the party finds very little of value in the administration's economic strategy. On questions such as the reform of the state—changing the structure of the Mexican state to make it more democratic and more efficient—there is more room for cooperation. But even here a deep-seated mistrust of the ultimate objectives of the Fox administration will obstruct cooperation.

The PRD also lacks institutional incentives to modify its behavior in Congress. As a minority party whose votes are not sufficient to build a majority even when combined with those of the PAN, the PRD is a minor player whose legislative cooperation is not essential. The PRD can therefore oppose the government without actually obstructing the legislative process—not unlike its position during the era of PRI governments. This institutional reality will not likely change any time soon. The PRD lacks national appeal and shows no sign of reversing this trend. To the contrary, the nourishment the party had traditionally received from defecting PRI politicians fell off sharply in 2001 as the revival of the PRI got under way.

The appeal of the party at the ballot box is also not improving. Even the party's great victory of 2001, the election of Lázaro Cárdenas Batel (the son of former Mexico City Mayor Cuauhtémoc Cárdenas and grandson of the legendary former President Lázaro Cárdenas) as governor of Michoacán state was actually a near defeat. Even with the historical name of Cárdenas in the family's home state, a charismatic personality, a divided PRI, and a 20-point lead at the start of the campaign, Cárdenas Batel edged the PRI by only 5 points. This does not bode well for the PRD's future electoral prospects.

. . . AND A HYDRA-HEADED BEHEMOTH

With a majority in the Senate, the largest plurality of seats in the Chamber of Deputies, and holding more than half the nation's governorships, the PRI is undoubtedly the dominant opposition force in Mexico. Little legislatively can be achieved without its support. But the PRI has not been highly cooperative during the first year of the Fox administration. In part, this stems from honest policy differences, but, more important, it reflects the party's extreme difficulty in adapting to its new role as the opposition.

From its inception the PRI has existed to serve the interests of the national president, was led by that president, and hence never developed any autonomous identity. When the PRI lost the presidency in July 2000, it lost more than the leadership of the country. It lost its bearings. Who would lead the party? What would the party stand for? How would the party proceed? The first year of the Fox presidency was, therefore, blighted by an essential opposition force trying to find its way in a totally new political world.

In the absence of a national president, the PRI developed three competing centers of power: the PRI governors, the party leadership, and the legislative leadership. Each attempted to lead the party in a somewhat different policy direction. Despite efforts to coordinate their positions, the result was a confused compilation of competing positions emanating from within a single party. With which element of this hydra-headed behemoth should the government negotiate?

Worse still, while each PRI power center made demands of the government, internal party politics prevented them from making any significant sacrifices in return. Throughout 2001 the party leadership was dominated by supporters of the vanquished presidential candidate, Francisco Labastida, yet it faced a continuing challenge from the supporters of Roberto Madrazo, a former governor of Tabasco state and determined adversary of Ernesto Zedillo and his heir apparent, Labastida. As the PRI struggled to find a means to resolve this leadership battle without dividing the party, there was no room for the party leadership or its allies in the congressional leadership to stick out their necks and support any controversial policy positions.

The PRI's eighteenth national assembly held in late November took important strides toward establishing a legitimate and powerful party leadership. It called for the direct election of the new party president and effectively concentrated political power in the hands of the party president and his/her National Executive Council. But it left the resolution of the factional battle for control of the party to the February election for party president. Until the new party president takes power on March 4, 2002, PRI internal politics will continue to prevent the party from taking any controversial positions.

THE CASE OF FISCAL REFORM

Vicente Fox's proposal to reform Mexico's fiscal policy failed to win legislative approval during 2001, the victim of a misguided legislative strategy combined with confusion in the executive branch and maladjusted political parties. For the first six months of his presidency, Vicente Fox followed a legislative strategy built on the logic of presidentialism even though the political setting in which he operated was characterized by a tangible separation of powers. The executive thus did not countenance any negotiations with the opposition on the content of its reform proposal for months. When the government finally reversed course, Fox's honeymoon was over and the PRI had become increasingly distracted by the demands of internal party politics. Negotiations continued in earnest throughout the remainder of the year but to little effect. Rather than the thoroughgoing fiscal reform Mexico very much needs, the outcome was a compilation of isolated tax increases incorporated into the 2002 budget.

From the moment word began to leak out in early December 2000 that the new fiscal reform would include a value-added tax of 15 percent on food, medicine, books, and school fees, objections were strong. The PRD immediately announced its total opposition, the PRI expressed opposition but couched in terms that suggested that there might be room for negotiation, and the PAN raised strong concerns about the political costs of such a measure. Despite this evident discomfort in the legislature with its proposed tax changes (opposition to a reduction in the income tax was also quite strong), the executive made no effort to negotiate either with the opposition or with its own party. It did not attempt to work out a consensus proposal prior to presenting the legislation to Congress in the first days of April. Instead it designed the proposal in splendid isolation from the political process in the best tradition of the old PRI system.

The government apparently believed it could convince the PAN to support the project and would be able to win the support of a sufficient number of PRI members of Congress by wooing the governors who were believed to control their votes (the initial proposal included a carrot directed specifically at the governors—40 billion pesos [$4.2 billion] of the increased tax collection would be directed to states and municipalities). The problem with this strategy was threefold. First, the PAN was not willing to support the president unconditionally on the issue. To the contrary, half the PAN deputies either openly opposed the initiative or were undecided. And in the midst of the party's revolt against its president on the issue of the Indigenous Law, there was no guarantee that the PAN would back the president on fiscal reform. In fact, PAN legislators preempted the president by presenting their own fiscal reform proposal in early March.

The second problem with the initial Fox legislative strategy is that the governors were not the only center of power within the PRI, making their hold over party legislators much less than absolute. The legislative leadership and the party leadership also mattered, and their support for the fiscal reform was undermined by three other factors: the lack of PAN support for the initiative, the absence of public support, and history. It should not be surprising that the PRI was unwilling to go out on a limb for President Fox if he was not even able to guarantee the support of his own party. This sentiment was deepened by polls showing that the vast majority of the Mexican populace opposed the centerpiece of the Fox fiscal reform proposal. The weight of history also came into play. In 1995 the PRI supported the initiative of President Ernesto Zedillo to increase the value-added tax from 10 percent to 15 percent. To this day the PRI is convinced that this decision was a determining factor in its electoral losses of 1997 and 2000. The PRI thus withheld its support.

The third shortcoming of the government's legislative strategy was its assumption that the Indigenous Law and hence the start of peace negotiations would be quick and easy. With this victory in hand, it was believed that Fox would enjoy the increased political capital needed to push the fiscal reform through Congress. This supposition was patently wrong, yet even after this became evident the government failed to modify its legislative strategy. Instead, the fiscal reform was introduced in the midst of the debate on the Indigenous Law. Given that 44 percent of legislators gave greater priority to passing the Indigenous Law in the spring congressional session while only 29 percent prioritized the fiscal reform, the fiscal reform took a back seat. On April 17 Congress decided to postpone consideration of the fiscal reform until a special session of Congress could be arranged, or until the next regular congressional session began in September.

Following this congressional decision, the executive modified its legislative strategy on the margins. Still unwilling to negotiate the contents of the proposal, it began to apply pressure on the legislature to approve the president's proposal as soon as possible. Fox's coordinator for public policy, Eduardo Sojo, referred to the congressional decision to postpone consideration of the reform as "irresponsible" and the president himself called on all political forces to put aside their differences and to come together in the national interest to approve the fiscal reform. In late May a newly cooperative PAN aired a series of television spots that took a more hard-line approach. They argued that in the past, tax increases were absorbed by corrupt politicians rather than applied to productive investments. In the new post-PRI democratic reality, however, this would no longer occur.

Not surprisingly, the PRI reacted badly to this new strategy. More troubling was the strategy's total failure to generate pressure on the PRI and thereby force it to cooperate. The strategy was based on the belief that a popular president could go over the heads of the politicians and appeal directly to the people. Popular support for the president would pressure legislators to cooperate out of fear of the electoral consequences associated with defying public opinion. This strategy failed for two reasons. It incorrectly assumed that Mexican legislators are susceptible to public pressure. In a political system that prohibits reelection, the political future of politicians is determined by the party rather than by voters. As such, politicians are not accountable to the electorate and hence largely immune to public opinion. Further, the Mexican public never supported Vicente Fox's proposal to tax food and medicines. The likelihood that they would pressure legislators to approve this measure, even if they had the power to do so, was far-fetched at best.

Only following the failure of this "revised" legislative strategy did the Fox administration begin to negotiate with the legislature in search of a consensus proposal. Unfortunately, the negotiations quickly stalled over the value-added tax. Without progress through June and July, President Fox began to lobby personally for his initiative in meetings with business leaders, union leaders, and the national governors, but still without success.

Throughout the fall the fiscal reform remained hostage to PRI party politics, a total lack of public support for the initiative, and more strategic errors. As the November date of the PRI's national assembly approached, there was little hope that any competing power bases within the PRI would be willing to risk approving a massively unpopular tax reform. Driving this point home was the decision by the party leadership to prohibit PRI legislators from voting for any fiscal reform that included a value-added tax on food and medicine. Meanwhile, the failure of the Fox government to convince the public of the wisdom of its proposed reform guaranteed that the electoral costs during the 2003 legislative and the 2006 presidential elections associated with this obstinacy would be few.

Elements of the government's political strategy also did little to advance the fiscal reform. With the fiscal reform stalled in Congress, the executive began to blame the legislature for the lack of progress on the initiative. Not only was this argument disingenuous, it backfired. In a political order where the legislature recently won its independence after decades of subjection to the executive, any attack on the legislature by the executive will inevitably be seen as an effort to reduce Congress's newfound autonomy. The unsurprising reaction of the Mexican Congress in this circumstance was a jealous protection of its autonomy against "unwarranted attacks" and an associated reduction in its willingness to cooperate with the government.

As the end of the legislative session approached and with no significant progress on the tax issue being made, the government's strategy seemed to shift once more. The government now seemed willing to consider any and all recommendations to modify its value-added tax proposal. The flurry of proposals that emerged from government circles in early December created the impression of an administration desperate for reform. This image of desperation only deepened the PRI's conviction that it could block all the core elements of the government's reform proposal and benefit from it politically. In the end Mexico was left with some tax increases incorporated in the 2002 budget instead of a comprehensive fiscal reform.

WHAT LIES AHEAD FOR MEXICO?

The first year of the Fox administration produced much less legislatively than even the worst prognostications anticipated. This poor legislative performance owes much to the difficulties encountered by all Mexican political actors in their effort to adapt to Mexico's post-PRI political environment. The Fox administration has found governing much more difficult than campaigning for the presidency. As the candidate capable of successfully challenging the PRI, popular opinion tended to discount Fox's inconsistencies. In the presidency this characteristic has made the administration appear weak and rudderless. As president of Coca-Cola, a delegative managerial strategy worked very well but in a presidency populated by powerful personalities with overlapping responsibilities and very limited experience in government, it has proved problematic at best. Emerging from a sociopolitical culture shaped by over 70 years of authoritarian rule, the Fox government initially adopted a legislative strategy steeped in presidentialism but without the presidentialist structures to make it operate. And in its effort to fine-tune its legislative strategy, the Fox administration drew heavily on tactics designed in the advanced democracies but ineffective in a fledgling democratic order.

Mexican political parties have also shown a limited aptitude for adjustment during 2001. The process within the PAN of adapting its behavior to the reality of being the party in government has been difficult and remains incomplete. The PAN's resulting early opposition to the Fox government followed by somewhat tepid support created a strong disincentive for opposition cooperation with the administration and thereby helped torpedo Fox's legislative initiatives during 2001. For the PRD, the small size of its legislative faction continues to create a powerful disincentive to adapt its legislative strategy to Mexico's more democratic political environment. Obstructionism remains the rule of the day. And the internal PRI struggle throughout 2001 to determine how the party would be governed in the absence of presidential leadership prevented it from working constructively with the Fox government.

There is great hope in Mexico that the country's political actors will learn from their mistakes in 2001, adapt tolerably to democratic politics, and finally begin to get things done in 2002. Some positive signs point in this direction. The PAN ceased to operate as an opposition force and by the end of the year the party's legislative leadership was leading the charge for the administration in the search for a consensus on fiscal reform. The PRI will have a strong and legitimate president as of March 4, 2002, which should finally give the party a unified leadership structure with the capacity to take political risks. And the executive has clearly learned that it must negotiate with Congress and that it must establish a much more unified and coherent image as government.

But many signs also suggest that Mexico is likely to remain in neutral during 2002. Although the PAN is cooperating more with the government, it is still extremely jealous of its autonomy and continues to search for a means to avoid damaging party interests while supporting its president. The PRI may have an effective leadership beginning in March, but it remains a party dedicated almost exclusively to the mission of retaking political power. If working with Fox will further this aim, the PRI will cooperate. But if the party perceives weakness on the part of the executive or sees political opportunity to be had by opposing its initiatives (especially in the run-up to the 2003 legislative elections), the PRI will be obstructionist. And there is much to suggest that the Fox administration will not perform significantly better in 2002 than in 2001. Although there were rumors in late 2001 of a significant restructuring of the executive branch, it seems likely that whatever changes are implemented will not be sufficient to alter the essential structural characteristics of the Fox government. The administration will remain one composed of strong personalities with limited political sensibilities, overlapping missions, and without strong guidance from the top.

Mexico during 2002 is therefore likely to continue muddling along. It will make few positive advances toward the implementation of essential structural reforms, but neither will it descend into ungovernability and economic crisis. Mexico is on a trajectory toward economic growth constrained significantly by unresolved structural problems such as rising fiscal liabilities, insufficient energy production, and an inefficient judicial system. Slow growth and the resultant increase in the country's economic vulnerability will inevitably undermine the popularity of the Fox government and generate opportunities for the opposition. Although the PRI is still seen by most Mexicans in a negative light, this image could easily change should public disappointment with the Fox government deepen. Mexico thus faces the real prospect of a return to power by a largely unreconstructed PRI in the near future.

SUGGESTIONS FOR FURTHER READING

Bethel, Leslie, ed. *Mexico Since Independence.* Cambridge: Cambridge University Press, 1991.

Camp, Roderic A. *Politics in Mexico: The Decline of Authoritarianism.* New York: Oxford University Press, 1999.

Centeno, Miguel Angel. *Democracy Within Reason: Technocratic Revolution in Mexico.* University Park: Pennsylvania State University Press, 1997.

Collier, Ruth Berins. *The Contradictory Alliance: State-Labor Relations and Regime Change in Mexico.* Berkeley: International and Area Studies, University of California, 1992.

Cook, Maria Lorena, Kevin J. Middlebrook, and Juan Molinar Horcasitas, eds. *The Politics of Economic Restructuring: State-Society Relations and Regime Change in Mexico.* La Jolla: Center for U.S.-Mexican Studies, University of California, San Diego, 1994.

Cornelius, Wayne. *Mexican Politics in Transition: The Breakdown of a One-Party-Dominant Regime.* San Diego: Center for U.S.-Mexican Studies, University of California, 1996.

Cornelius, Wayne, Ann L. Craig, and Jonathan Fox. "Mexico's National Solidarity Program: An Overview," in *Transforming State-Society Relations in Mexico: The National Solidarity Strategy.* La Jolla: Center for U.S.-Mexican Studies, University of California, San Diego, 1994, 3–26.

Foweraker, Joe, and Ann Craig, eds. *Popular Movements and Political Change in Mexico.* Boulder, Colo.: Lynne Rienner, 1991.

Gibson, Edward. "The Populist Road to Market Reform: Policy and Electoral Coalition in Mexico and Argentina." *World Politics* 49 (April 1997): 339–370.

Nash, June. "The Reassertion of Indigenous Identity: Mayan Responses to State Intervention in Chiapas." *Latin American Research Review* 30(3) (1995): 7–42.

Oppenheimer, Andres. *Bordering on Chaos: Mexico's Roller-Coaster Journey Toward Prosperity.* New York: Back Bay Books, 1998.

Rodriguez, Victoria E., ed. *Women's Participation in Mexican Political Life.* Boulder, Colo.: Westview Press, 1998.

Schedler, Andreas. "Mexico's Victory: The Democratic Revelation." *Journal of Democracy* 11(4) (2000): 5–19.

Smith, Peter H. "Drug Trafficking in Mexico," in *Coming Together? Mexico–United States Relations,* ed. Barry Bosworth, Susan M. Collins, and Norm C. Lustig. Washington, D.C.: Brookings Institution Press, 1997, 125–47.

Teichman, Judith A. *Privatization and Political Change in Mexico.* Pittsburgh: University of Pittsburgh Press, 1995.

Wise, Carol. *The Post-NAFTA Political Economy: Mexico and the Western Hemisphere.* University Park: Pennsylvania State University Press, 1998.

USEFUL WEBSITES

Newspapers
Reforma
   www.reforma.com

La Jornada
   www.jornada.unam.mx

La Crónica
   www.cronica.com.mx

El Informador
   www.informador.com.mx

El Milenio
   www.milenio.com/monterrey

Government
Senate
   www.senado.gob.mx

Chamber of Deputies
   www.cddhcu.gov.mx

Office of the President
   www.presidencia.gov.mx

Federal Electoral Institute
   www.ife.org.mx

General
Texas A&M International University Western Hemispheric Trade Information Center (NAFTA)
   http://freetrade.tamiu.edu/ic

CIA World Fact Book: Resource for general information on Mexico.
   www.odci.gov/cia/publications/factbook/geos/mx.html

Latin American Network Information Center: Comprehensive website housed at the University of Texas with extensive Latin American links on a wide array of topics.
   http://Lanic.utexas.edu

INDEX